Israeli National Security

Israeli National Security

A New Strategy for an Era of Change

CHARLES D. FREILICH

OXFORD
UNIVERSITY PRESS

OXFORD
UNIVERSITY PRESS

Oxford University Press is a department of the University of Oxford. It furthers
the University's objective of excellence in research, scholarship, and education
by publishing worldwide. Oxford is a registered trade mark of Oxford University
Press in the UK and certain other countries.

Published in the United States of America by Oxford University Press
198 Madison Avenue, New York, NY 10016, United States of America.

© Oxford University Press 2018

CIP data is on file at the Library of Congress
ISBN 978–0–19–060293–2

1 3 5 7 9 8 6 4 2

Printed by Sheridan Books, Inc., United States of America

*To Idit
and always
Lior and Tal*

The most dangerous enemy of Israel's security is the conceptual inertia of those responsible for its security.

—David Ben-Gurion,
Israel's founding prime minister

CONTENTS

LIST OF MAPS, TABLES, AND FIGURES

Maps

Tables

Figures

PREFACE

Israel's national security has always been a personal and professional passion, starting with my childhood in New York, when I observed the Six Day War from afar, and ever since moving to Israel in my teens, as a soldier, defense official, and now scholar. Those who share a visceral memory of the Jewish people's long exile, the Holocaust, and Israel's dramatic rebirth understand the depth of sentiment. A lifelong commitment to Zionism and a love of Israel, with a deep concern for its future, animate this book.

Only a truly dispassionate analysis, however, as this work purports to be, best serves the needs of Israel's national security. Israel has come a long way, from the embattled state of the early decades, fighting for its life, to the stable, prosperous, and essentially secure one that it is today. Israel still faces daunting threats, and potentially existential ones may re-emerge, possibly even in the not-distant future. Nevertheless, Israel has never been more secure, its existence is no longer truly in doubt, and it has a window of opportunity both to prevent the ominous scenarios from emerging and, no less importantly, to make fundamental choices about its future course as a state.

ACKNOWLEDGMENTS

I wish to warmly thank a number of people for their invaluable support for this book. First and foremost, I am grateful to Dan Meridor, former cabinet minister and one of the foremost experts in Israel on national security affairs, for his boundless willingness to be of help. In five lengthy interviews, Dan shared his vast experience, many penetrating insights, and general wisdom with me, greatly enriching the book in the process. Many others, some very senior, also graciously agreed to interviews; their names appear in a separate list, and I am indebted to all.

Coincidence, or good fortune, is always important in life. Ms. Saskia Becaud, at the time a brilliant young graduate student at Sciences Po, one of France's foremost universities, whom I did not previously know, reached out to me and rapidly became an esteemed collaborator on various projects. Saskia conducted much of the research and wrote the first draft of chapter 5, on issues related to Israeli society and national security. With her truly tireless efforts, it rapidly evolved from what had initially been conceived of as a secondary chapter, to one of the most important and best of the entire book. Saskia also helped with the extensive and often frustrating research necessary for the section on the demographic challenges Israel faces (in chapter 4). I look forward both to her many future accomplishments and to further work together.

I am similarly grateful to Mr. Matthew Cohen, a former graduate student of mine at Harvard, who has since become a coauthor of many shared projects. The sections on the cyber-threat (in chapter 3) and on the diplomatic and delegitimization campaigns underway against Israel (in chapter 4) draw on previously published joint work. Matthew is now doing his doctorate at Northeastern University, and I look forward to soon calling him Dr. Cohen and to future work together. We are already in advanced stages of a book on Israel and the cyber-threat.

A number of my former students at Harvard and Columbia also very graciously and generously offered their time and help. Brit Helena Felsen-Parsons assisted with research on the regional arms race and US-Israeli relations. Charlotte
Partow and Andrew Lobel also did research on US-Israeli relations and helped
make order out of the voluminous notes in this book. Wright Smith did extensive research on both Israel's and the Arab countries' military capabilities. Yoav
Shaked researched UN votes pertaining to Israel and helped put together my research notes for chapter 9, on Israel's foreign policy. Maya Kornberg and Matan
Hoberman also contributed.

I am deeply appreciative of the comments I received on various chapters. Edo
Hecht and Eitan Shamir commented on the issues of military decision and the
changing nature of warfare, Stuart Cohen and Reuven Gal on the long and particularly complicated chapter dealing with Israeli society and national security
affairs, Sergio Della Pergola on demography, Martin Malin on Israel's nuclear
and regional arms control policy, and Marvin Feuer and Eran Lerman on US-
Israeli relations. Daniel Sobelman generously commented on a few chapters.
Yoram Hemo, Shlomo Brom, and Assaf Orian commented on the conclusions.
Bruce Heiman's insightful comments on the recommendations chapter ended
up requiring an extensive rewrite and vastly improved it.

I am especially grateful to Professors Graham Allison, long-time Director of
the Belfer Center for Science and International Affairs at the Harvard Kennedy
School, and Steven Miller, Director of the Center's International Studies
Program, for providing me with the opportunity to spend many years at the
Center as a senior fellow. Under their leadership, the Belfer Center continues to
be a place of endless intellectual stimulation and a joy to be part of. My thanks to
them also for their insightful comments on the book, as well as to Joe Nye and
others from the Center who participated in an early presentation of the primary
conclusions and recommendations.

Thanks also to General Amos Yadlin, Director of the Institute for National
Security Studies (INSS) and Professor Efraim Inbar, former Director of the
Begin-Sadat Center for Strategic Studies (BESA), for giving me the opportunities
to present the findings to their senior fellows. Both sessions produced important
additions to the analysis presented.

My warm thanks to the two unknown reviewers who graciously reviewed
the book on behalf of Oxford University Press, (wisely) recommended that it
be published, and suggested important improvements. Special thanks to David
McBride, the editor-in-chief for social sciences, for recognizing the book's merits
from the initial proposal stage and shepherding it, along Anne Dellinger, Katie
Weaver, and all of the people at Oxford University Press, through a lengthy ges-
tation. I am also indebted to Paul Tompsett and Richard Isomaki for the excellent help at the copyediting and production stage.

Particular thanks to Sidney Topol and Hillel Bachrach, whose friendship made the Hebrew version of the book possible. Both are serial doers of good deeds, and their friendship and support for numerous worthy causes are deeply appreciated. Finally, my appreciation to the Memorial Foundation for Jewish Culture for a research grant.

Hod Hasharon, November 2016

LIST OF ABBREVIATIONS

APC's	Armored Personnel Carriers
BDS	Boycotts, Divestment and Sanctions movement
BESA	Begin-Sadat Center for Strategic Studies
BWC	Biological Weapons Convention
CoS	chief of staff
CT	Counterterrorism
CTBT	Comprehensive Test Ban Treaty
CW	chemical warfare
CWC	Chemical Weapons Convention
EU	European Union
FMCT	Fissile Missile Cutoff Treaty
IAEA	International Atomic Energy Agency
IAF	Israel Air Force
ICC	International Criminal Court
ICJ	International Court of Justice
IDF	Israel Defense Forces
ISA	Israel Security Agency (also known as "Shin Bet," "Shabak")
ISIS	Islamic State in Iraq and Syria
JPMG	Joint Politico-Military Group
LIC	low intensity conflict
MABAM	*haMaaracha Bein haMaarachot* (campaign between the campaigns)
MAD	mutually assured destruction
MCoD	Ministerial Committee on Defense
MENWFZ	Middle East Nuclear Weapons Free Zone
MFA	Ministry of Foreign Affairs
MoD	Ministry of Defense
MoU	memorandum of understanding

MTCR	Missile Technology Control Regime
NGO	nongovernmental organization
NPT	Non-Proliferation Treaty
NSG	Nuclear Suppliers Group
NSS	National Security Staff (previously Council)
NWFZ	Nuclear Weapons Free Zone
OECD	Organization for Economic Development
PA	Palestinian Authority
PIJ	Palestinian Islamic Jihad
PLO	Palestine Liberation Organization
QME	Qualitative Military Edge
RMA	Revolution in Military Affairs
UAV	unmanned aerial vehicle (drone)
UNHCR	UN High Commissioner for Refugees
UNIFIL	UN Interim Force in Lebanon
UNRWA	UN Relief and Works Agency
WMD	weapons of mass destruction

LIST OF MAJOR WARS
AND MILITARY OPERATIONS

War of Independence, 1948–1949
Sinai Campaign, 1956
Six Day War, 1967
War of Attrition, 1969–1971
Yom Kippur War, 1973
Litani Operation, 1978
Attack on Iraqi nuclear reactor, 1981
First Lebanon War, 1982
First intifada, 1987–1990
Operation Accountability, 1993
Operation Grapes of Wrath, 1996
Second intifada, 2000–2004
Second Lebanon War, 2006
Attack (reported) on Syrian reactor, 2007
Operation Cast Lead (*Oferet Yetzuka*), 2008
Operation Defensive Pillar (*Amud Anan*), 2012
Operation Protective Edge (*Tzuk Eitan*), 2014

PART ONE

CONFRONTING A STRATEGIC NIGHTMARE

Introduction

Israel has long confronted a uniquely hostile and harsh strategic environment, which bears little comparison to that of any other state in modern history. The threats it has faced have included not just the prospect of politicide, destruction of the state, a danger encountered by numerous countries throughout history, but even of genocide and national extinction. The Arab states long threatened Israel's destruction. Iran, an extremist theocracy, seeks Israel's demise and will pose a potentially existential threat should it ultimately succeed in acquiring nuclear weapons. Saudi Arabia, a similarly radical theocracy, and other regional actors may also acquire nuclear weapons. Syria still has some chemical weapons. Hezbollah's mammoth rocket arsenal is truly frightening, and Hamas's rockets pose an ongoing threat. Heinous terrorism continues to take a toll of Israeli lives, and the cyber-realm poses a new and largely uncharted challenge. The stability of both Egypt and Jordan is far from guaranteed, and the region as a whole is embroiled in deep turmoil, some of which may be turned against Israel.

In addition to these and other military challenges, some of the greatest dangers Israel faces today stem from nonmilitary sources, such as diplomatic isolation and international delegitimization, as well as demographic processes. No state can afford to live alone today, certainly not one as deeply immersed in the processes of globalization as Israel. Israel lost the support of much of the public in Europe and beyond long ago, and disturbing trends have begun emerging in the United States as well. Whereas the loss of European support had important ramifications for Israel, a mere modulation of American support would be critical, a loss thereof possibly existential. The demographic threat to Israel's future as the democratic nation-state of the Jewish people, stemming from the de facto annexation of the West Bank and growing emergence of a one-state reality, is existential.

This well-known and even dire depiction of Israel's strategic circumstances, the theme of most studies of Israeli national security, still holds true today. It is, however, only part of the picture. Israel no longer faces a conventional threat of consequence from the Arab states, which are now either engulfed in domestic upheaval or at peace with Israel, or from any combination of them, the ultimate nightmare of the past. Iran's military nuclear ambitions have been postponed, at the least for the meantime, and it is unclear whether it will renew them in the future. The other threats Israel has faced from weapons of mass destruction (WMD) have been nearly eliminated. Israel has largely neutralized the Hamas rocket threat, though it remains disruptive of civilian life, and in time a solution will be found as well to the far graver one posed by Hezbollah. Terrorism is painful, but Israel has succeeded in keeping it at a level its society can tolerate.

Israel has diplomatic relations today with more states than ever before, and close commercial and military ties with many. In addition to the unique relationship with the United States, it has close ties with Germany, Russia, China, Canada, Poland, and India, to mention just a few. It has enjoyed stable peace with Egypt and Jordan for decades, and there have been encouraging signs of late that shared interests, first and foremost, a fear of Iranian hegemony, are driving additional Arab states toward greater openness and cooperation with Israel.

In reality, Israel has become a regional power and is more militarily secure today than ever before. The difficult constraints of a very tough regional "neighborhood" notwithstanding, Israel's positions have greater influence over its affairs than ever before,[1] and it has never been better able to chart its course as a nation. Indeed, Israel's national security strategy has been a resounding success. It has not only ensured Israel's existence, a significant achievement in and of itself, which was not a foregone conclusion during the early decades, but has enabled it to thrive and prosper.

As Israel enters its eighth decade, the paradox of its existence is that it has both very much to be proud of, along with some deeply worrying trends for the future. For many in Israel and its supporters abroad, the picture presented above, of military strength and diplomatic vulnerability, will be controversial and will undoubtedly elicit emotionally charged responses. Only a hard and dispassionate analysis of Israel's overall strategic circumstances, however, best serves its true interests.

A national security strategy is a function of a state's strategic circumstances, including the threats, constraints, and opportunities it faces, the diplomatic and military capabilities it develops in response, and the exigencies of its unique socioeconomic and national character. When any of these elements undergoes significant change, a revision of the national security strategy is called for. It is the contention of this book that, in Israel's case, significant change has taken place in all of these elements.

There is broad agreement among many strategic thinkers in Israel today that the nation's strategic environment has been transformed and mostly for the better, though decidedly not entirely so.[2] The nature of the military threats Israel faces has also changed drastically, from primarily conventional state-based ones, to asymmetric threats from substate actors—and Iran. Israeli society, too, has changed significantly over the years. These changes, and their ramifications for Israel's national security strategy, are the theme of this book. To put matters in social science terms, the hypothesis posited is that changes in three independent variables (Israel's external environment, the nature of the military threats it faces, and Israeli society) require change in its national security strategy, the dependent variable.

For decades, Israel has been a "laboratory" and bellwether for changes in defense affairs, studied by national security experts and agencies around the world. Its changing national security circumstances, and especially the lessons and conclusions derived from its experience, are thus of great interest not just to those who specialize in its affairs, or the Middle East generally, but far more broadly, as a testing ground for changes that other states, too, are likely to face.

To illustrate, during the period following the 1967 Six Day War, at a time when the United States had only limited access to Soviet weaponry and military doctrine, Israel provided it with captured weapons and shared its battlefield experience. Israel's dire encounter with Egypt's and Syria's innovative application of Soviet military doctrine in the 1973 Yom Kippur War, in which they made unprecedented offensive use of surface-to-air (SAM) and antitank missiles to devastate Israel's air and ground forces, served as a harbinger of the changes the United States and Western allies would later face. Israel's development of an effective response to the SAM threat, so dramatically displayed in the 1982 Lebanon war, served as a further turning point studied closely by the American and other militaries in the world.

Both the United States and Israel were world leaders in the "revolution in military affairs" of the late 1980s and 1990s, in which the innovative use of information warfare and precision weapons provided an effective response to the saturated battlefield of the day. Arab impotence in the face of Israel's conventional military superiority led substate actors, such as Hezbollah and Hamas, to adopt new asymmetric responses, in a hybrid combination of terrorist, guerilla, and even state-like forms of warfare, which the United States and its allies later encountered in Afghanistan, Iraq, and Syria.

Israel's attacks on the Iraqi and, reportedly, Syrian nuclear reactors, in 1981 and 2007 respectively, are the sole examples to date of direct military counterproliferation operations. The innovative tactics Israel is said to have applied in the latter case were undoubtedly studied closely around the world. Israel's own policy of nuclear ambiguity is a unique model that may be emulated in the future by such unlikely followers as Iran and Saudi Arabia. Israel is also considered a global leader in the use of cyber-warfare, both for defensive and offensive purposes,[3] and in missile and rocket defense.

Following 9/11, virtually every agency of the United States and of other friendly governments engaged in counterterrorism flocked to Israel to learn from its greater experience in this area. It was Israel that made initial use of drones for military purposes, an innovation subsequently expanded upon greatly by the United States. The highly honed interdiction methodology Israel developed during the second intifada, the "closed circle," which reduced to just minutes the time between an impending terrorist attack, or one that had just occurred, and the deployment of an operational unit on the ground capable of dealing with it, was a model later emulated by others. Following the operation in Gaza in 2014, the United States again studied Israel's counterterrorism tactics closely. A distinguished panel of senior former defense officials and military experts from around the world claimed that the tactics Israel used in the operation set a new bar for casualty avoidance.[4]

Israel has also been studied as a test case of how democratic states cope with the political stresses of long-term military confrontations. The resilience of its society, in the face of these ongoing stresses, has also been the subject of much study. In short, there are many reasons for the Israeli case to be of broad importance, far beyond an interest in Israel itself.

Surprisingly, perhaps, Israel does not have a formal national security strategy, or defense doctrine, to this day, despite its overwhelming preoccupation with such affairs. Israel has not issued the equivalent of American Presidential Policy Directives, National Security Strategies, Quadrennial Defense Reviews, British-style White Papers, or other overall strategic statements, whether classified or unclassified. The one partial exception to this rule, the landmark "IDF Strategy" published in 2015, was a narrowly focused military document nonetheless. This does not mean that extensive strategic thinking does not take place within the national security establishment, or that numerous policy papers are not generated, but they are overwhelmingly issue-specific and ad hoc, rather than being couched in a broad strategic construct.

Founding premier David Ben-Gurion was Israel's only sitting leader to conceptualize an overall national security strategy. Formulated in the 1950s, the "Ben-Gurion doctrine" remains the closest thing Israel has to date to a national security strategy, but even it was never fully elucidated or officially adopted. In the decades hence, a number of attempts have been made to update the doctrine and adapt it to the dramatic changes that have taken place in Israel's strategic circumstances. All either failed to reach fruition or were not adopted. The lone near-exception, a major strategic review chaired in 2006 by Dan Meridor, a former minister and highly regarded expert on national security affairs, was widely hailed for its quality and thoroughness, but was never considered by the cabinet, let alone formally adopted. The 2015 IDF Strategy, important though it was, explicitly recognized the need for the higher-level strategic statements embodied in a defense and national security strategy.

Why Israel has not formulated a national security strategy is an important issue in its own right and a reflection of its overall approach to national security policymaking (see Freilich 2012). In essence, Israel's political leaders have refrained from doing so, and from systematic policymaking processes generally, because the very process itself conflicts with their political needs. In a highly politicized coalition system, premiers, as well as defense and foreign ministers, do not wish to be bound by processes that require that they present the cabinet with a systematic analysis of Israel's objectives and the optimal means of achieving them. Strategic clarity encourages divisions and puts political futures at risk. Ambiguity, conversely, can be constructive and is crucial to premiers' abilities to hold shaky coalitions together. As a result, Israel's premiers have manifested a long-standing predilection to either avoid systematic policymaking processes or to limit them to narrowly focused issues.

In recent years, a dramatically transformed Middle East, the difficulties Israel has encountered in the pursuit of its military endeavors, and a growing sense among both practitioners and scholars alike, that Israel has lost sight of its strategic objectives and course as a nation, have led to renewed interest in the conduct of basic strategic thinking. This has been best evinced by the Israel Defense Forces itself, whose strategic statement in 2015 was actually just one of a number of important internal review processes it has conducted since the early 2000s, especially following the inconclusive 2006 war in Lebanon. We have already mentioned the 2006 Meridor Report. The National Security Staff, the equivalent of the American National Security Council, has also conducted basic policy reviews in recent years of Israel's military and counterterrorism strategies and has completed, at least in draft form, a review of its entire national security strategy. This has been further manifested by the increased attention devoted to the subject by some Israeli think tanks and scholars.[5]

For a country as preoccupied with national security as Israel, it is remarkable just how little academic study there has been, of a comprehensive nature, of its national security and defense strategies. This is not to say that a vast literature does not exist on Israeli foreign and defense affairs and relevant areas of its socioeconomic policy, indeed, virtually every dimension, subdimension, and often even subcomponent thereof, has been addressed, often with considerable thoroughness. The literature, however, has been almost entirely in the form of journal articles, think tank studies, edited volumes, and various case studies, almost all addressing specific issues. None of the works published in recent decades have taken an overall view of the principles and concepts underlying Israel's national security thinking, assessed the changes that have taken place in its military, diplomatic, and domestic environments, and proposed an overall new national security strategy based on a systematic analysis of their ramifications.

There have been a few partial exceptions. Arad et al. (2017) present a broad-stroke, grand strategy for Israel, focusing largely on societal, economic, and technological issues. Dekel and Einav (2017) provide a very interesting, but unfortunately brief, proposal for a new national security concept. Shelah (2015) is in many ways an excellent account of the defense and military challenges Israel faces today, primarily regarding Hezbollah and Hamas, but is narrowly focused on those areas, does not deal with foreign affairs, and some of the important recommendations made are not sufficiently substantiated. Ben-Israel (2013) merely presents the elements of the classic national security strategy, without an attempt to update it or to assess its relevance to current needs. Maoz (2006) and Rodman (2005) are important works that set out many of the changes that have taken place in Israel's strategic environment and address some of the major issues in Israeli policy, but do not take a truly comprehensive approach. Inbar (2008) is also an important work, but primarily retrospective. Shelah (2003) proposes changes in the IDF but is a rather simplistic journalistic account. Heller (2001) provides an excellent overview of continuity and change in Israeli defense policy but is now largely dated. Tal (1996), an important attempt to propose a broad strategy, is still focused primarily on the military side and, in any event, is the product of a different strategic era.

Some books have addressed important aspects of Israeli national security strategy, such as its purported nuclear capability (Cohen 2000 and 2010), experience in fighting asymmetric wars (Kober 2009), or counterterrorism strategy (Byman 2011). Unfortunately, no books have been written in recent decades on the principles of Israeli foreign policy (the last were by Brecher in 1977 and Klieman in 1990), though Dror (2011) addresses Israeli statecraft and some of the threats Israel faces. Cohen (2008) focused solely on problems faced by the IDF, not foreign policy.

The present book seeks to close the gap in the literature and provide an overall assessment of Israeli national security strategy, focusing primarily on the period from the 1990s to the present. It makes extensive use of academic materials but, to be as current as possible, is based largely on press reporting. Interviews with numerous officials in the national security area were also invaluable. The book is somewhat unusual for an academic work, in that the desire to be as current as possible has necessitated constant rewriting and updating, up to the manuscript's completion in late 2016, even a few factual updates in the year and a half between then and the book's final publication.

A few words about the terminology used in this book. "Conventional warfare" takes place between the "regular" militaries of state actors and typically refers to battle between infantry, tanks, artillery, aircraft, and naval vessels. There are also two types of "asymmetric warfare." The first and most extreme, unconventional warfare, refers to nuclear, biological, and chemical weapons, known collectively as weapons of mass destruction (WMD), whose destructive power has accorded them a class of their own. The second type of asymmetric warfare is somewhat harder to define and has thus come to be known by a variety of terms, such as terrorism, irregular warfare, low-intensity conflict (LIC), wars of attrition, persistent warfare, protracted guerrilla campaigns, and subconventional warfare. At times, conventional and irregular forces can switch tactics, for example, regular forces using irregular tactics or vice versa.

The term "effective response," used repeatedly in regard to various military threats, should be understood to refer to a state's ability to achieve its politico-military objectives at a price it finds acceptable. "Military decision" refers to the ability to force an end to warfare either by breaking an enemy's ability or will to continue the fighting.

A national security strategy, according to prominent American strategists Art and Posen, refers to the ways in which states choose to link their politico-military objectives with the capabilities at their disposal, in order to promote their security. To this end, states must identify and prioritize the threats that are most likely to pose the greatest dangers to them and devise the best political, military, and economic means of remedying them, given finite resources.[6] A broader definition of national security adds all of the other components of state power, including economic and societal strength, educational achievement, health, sense of identity, national consensus, and more, to the traditional dimensions of foreign and defense policy.[7]

In Israel, political and military leaders, as well as academic experts, have used a few different terms, at times interchangeably. Most have spoken either of the defense concept (*tfisat habitachon*), which might be better translated as defense strategy, or of the defense doctrine (*torat habitachon*). The former, at least according to one scholar, refers to strategic thinking at the level of the senior national decision-makers, whereas the latter refers to defense and military leaders.[8] Others have defined these terms as overall intellectual constructs that express both a nation's values and the relatively permanent conclusions it derives from its strategic circumstances, which guide its action in the areas of foreign, defense, social, and economic policy.[9]

Still another scholar, as well as former deputy chief of staff Israel Tal, differentiate between the terms "defense strategy and doctrine" and "defense policy." The latter, they believe, derives from the former, guides its day-to-day implementation, and changes in accordance with the policies of the government in office, beliefs of senior defense officials, and circumstances. The defense strategy, or doctrine, in this view, defines the threats to national security that the state must defend against, the instruments it will use to this end, including the circumstances in which it will use military force and even go to war, and how force will be applied.[10]

The theoretical debate in the literature regarding the concept of national security is extensive, and the above is designed merely to give a brief impression of some of the differing views. For our purposes, national security strategy will be understood to focus primarily on foreign and defense affairs, but also on those dimensions of socioeconomic policy that have a direct bearing on Israel's ability to achieve its goals in these areas. The downside to this more expansive approach is that it can ultimately come to encompass almost all areas of policy, and a term that encompasses everything ends up losing its conceptual clarity and unique meaning.[11] Bearing this in mind, the book will adopt the broader construct, but attribute only a narrow definition to those areas of socioeconomic policy that are held to be relevant to national security strategy.

In reality, no state acts precisely according to its national security strategy, nor should one expect it to. Circumstances, people, a host of factors affect states' day-to-day conduct. National security strategies are not designed to provide a detailed blueprint for daily conduct, but to leverage the intellectual rigor that goes into their formulation to improve the quality of ongoing decision-making and produce greater common understanding among decision-makers in regard to what they wish to achieve and the primary options available to them for doing so. As the famous Chinese expression states, if one does not know where one wishes to go, all roads are equally good. Or in the words of Henry Kissinger, "In the absence of a [national security] doctrine clearly understood by all, we will act randomly; conflicting proposals will compete with each other without any significant basis for achieving a decision. Every problem that arises will appear new and we will use up our energy analyzing their character, rather than truly looking for solutions."[12]

Throughout this book the greatest effort has been made to divorce the analysis presented from the author's personal beliefs and preferences and to ensure a dispassionate and "objective" academic approach. In the two final chapters, the primary conclusions and the policy recommendations derived from them, particular care was given to the attempt to demonstrate that they stem from a strategic analysis of Israel's strategic circumstances and objectives, not personal belief. National security, however, is certainly not an exact science, and personal beliefs inevitably color one's conclusions. Reviewers and readers will judge the author's success in maintaining objective distance and in advocating policies that are truly vital to Israel's future. It is hoped that they will not find him wanting.

Three disclaimers are in order. First, the above claims to professional objectivity notwithstanding, the author is an ardent lifelong Zionist, deeply committed to Israel's security and well-being. This deep love of Israel and the belief that

Israel has been floundering in recent decades and faces severe challenges in the future were the motivations for this book.

Second, as a former defense official, the author was required by Israeli law to submit the book for a security review or, to use a less generous term, censorship, prior to publication. This is entirely as it should be and is the common practice in the United States and other democracies, as well. Indeed, the author would have asked that the book be reviewed even had he not been bound to do so by law. In seeking to analyze and enrich Israel's national security thinking, the author has no desire to present particulars that might undermine it. Self-censorship was thus also applied in isolated cases.

The reader may, however, rest assured. Israel is an extraordinarily open society, and the publicly available literature is vast. Reliable details regarding Israel's military capabilities in terms of quantities of weapons and forces, as well as operational plans, are understandably hard to find, but much of the rest is available, and the broad strokes of its policies are usually plain to see. With the partial exception of chapter 8, on Israel's nuclear policy, the limitations, both legal and self-imposed, applied to little more than a few lines throughout the book and had no bearing on the overall information, analysis, conclusions, and recommendations presented.

Third, lest the book fail to meet some readers' expectations, this is the place to stress that it is not about the peace process and the settlements issue, but Israel's national security strategy. Peace is, of course, both a fundamental means and objective thereof, and the peace process is thus addressed in a number of contexts, although not in any historical depth. Settlements, conversely, are barely mentioned, other than in terms of their impact on Israel's international standing. Some may be surprised, but it is the author's contention that settlements, which had an important role in Israel's defense strategy in the early years, have little if anything to do today with Israel's national security strategy, everything to do with its domestic politics.

A discussion of a national security strategy begins with a definition of a state's national objectives. Israel's national objectives are the subject of considerable debate. For our purposes, they will be defined as the following:

- Constituting the democratic nation-state of the Jewish people and a home and spiritual center for them
- Ensuring Israel's existence, territorial integrity (including the West Bank and Golan Heights, pending resolution of their final status), the security of Israel's citizens, and the effective functioning of its core governmental system and critical infrastructure (civilian and military)
- Achieving peace with Israel's neighbors, or at least coexistence
- Promoting the socioeconomic well-being of Israeli society

In addition, Israel has a variety of lesser, though still highly important, national objectives, some relatively permanent, others that change with circumstance. Current examples, at the time of this writing, include issues such as preventing Iran from acquiring nuclear weapons, preventing Hezbollah and Hamas rocket attacks and other forms of terrorism, maintaining close strategic dialogue and cooperation with the United States, defeating international delegitimization efforts, expanding new opportunities for cooperation with Sunni states, and much more.

A national security strategy is, of course, bound by time and strategic circumstance and must adapt itself accordingly. It is a living and dynamic strategic statement, not a hard-and-fast set of rules. In a Middle East undergoing historic flux, it would be foolhardy to aspire to a strategy relevant, at least in some areas, to much more than 10 years, and even that may be ambitious. Conversely, a proposed national security strategy appropriate to a significantly shorter period could hardly be considered a strategic blueprint for national action. The national security strategy presented in this book thus strives to relevancy for some 10 to 20 years, longer in some areas, but recommends mid-course assessments and recalibrations every five years.

Readers should bear in mind that the manuscript was completed in late 2016 and terms such as "today," "recent decades," "for now," and more refer to that date as their baseline. Moreover, in a dramatically changing Middle Eastern and international environment, much will have changed by the time of the book's actual publication in early 2018. Russia's growing influence in the Middle East, Iran's expanding influence in Syria and across the region, and a diminishing American role, all noted in chapter 2, would have received far greater emphasis were the book to actually have been written closer to the time of its publication.

The book is structured around four parts. Part I comprises of this introduction and chapter 1, which presents Israel's classic defense strategy as formulated by Ben-Gurion. The chapter describes the nature of the external environment and security threats that gave rise to the strategy and its primary principles, and is designed to provide a baseline for Israeli strategic thinking ever since.

Part II examines the changes in Israel's external and domestic environments in recent decades. Chapter 2 begins with the dramatic changes that have taken place in Israel's strategic setting since the classic strategy was formulated, including such fundamental strategic constraints as the qualitative and quantitative asymmetry with the Arab states and the desirability of territorial acquisition. Chapter 3 describes the changing nature of the military threats Israel faces today, from existential, state-based threats from Arab armies, to various forms of asymmetric warfare, including terrorism and rocket fire, ballistic missiles, WMD and cyber-warfare, primarily from substate actors. Chapter 4 presents the two primary nonmilitary threats Israel faces today, neither of which was envisaged by the classic strategy and which may prove as dangerous to its long-term future as the military ones, including its diplomatic isolation and growing delegitimization as a state, and the demographic challenges it faces. Chapter 5 examines the primary changes that have taken place in Israeli society and their effects on its national security, inter alia, the motivation to serve, casualty aversion, the national consensus and societal resilience.

Part III presents Israel's strategic response to its contemporary military and diplomatic challenges. It begins, in chapter 6, by assessing the continued relevance of the primary military and strategic responses envisaged by the classic strategy to the threats Israel faces today, along with a brief overview of the various attempts to update its military and strategic doctrine over the years. Chapter 7 presents a critical analysis of Israel's military responses to the major threats it faces today, and the degree of success it has met in so doing. Chapter 8 presents the essentials of Israel's nuclear and regional arms control policy, as an essential component of its overall military response. Chapter 9 sets out the principles of Israeli foreign policy, which have been addressed only rarely in previous works, such as self-reliance, superpower alliances, the Jewish factor, the search for allies, and peace as a security strategy. Chapter 10 surveys the military and strategic dimensions of the "special relationship" with the United States and raises three troubling questions: whether Israel could even survive today without the United States, whether it has largely lost its independence to it, and future directions in the bilateral relationship.

Part IV is the heart and purpose of this book, a proposal for a new Israeli national security strategy. Chapter 11 presents the primary conclusions derived from the information and analysis in the preceding background chapters, as the basis for the proposed strategy that appears in chapter 12. All 10 background chapters, with the exception of chapter 1, conclude with a section entitled "primary observations," the most important conclusions derived from the information and analysis presented.

Israel's Classic Defense Doctrine

700,000 vanquished 30 million and this occurred because in the prevailing conditions, the 700,000 Jews possessed greater willpower than
the 30 million Arabs.
—David Ben-Gurion, on Israel's War of Independence

In the 1950s founding prime minister David Ben-Gurion formulated the primary components of what has since come to be considered Israel's classic
defense doctrine. The "Ben-Gurion doctrine" had a major impact on Israel's strategic thinking until the 1980s and continues to inform it to a significant extent to
this day. In reality, it was far broader than just a defense doctrine, encompassing
significant elements of both foreign and socioeconomic policy, and should
thus rightly be considered Israel's classic national security doctrine. Most of
the attention to the doctrine over the decades, however, has been devoted to its
military dimensions, not the foreign and socioeconomic ones; indeed, few in
Israel are even aware of the latter today. The term "defense doctrine" has become
deeply entrenched in Israeli discourse when referring to Ben-Gurion's formulation, and this is the term used in this regard throughout the book.

Although only partly elucidated in writing, there is broad agreement among
both practitioners and scholars regarding the components of the Ben-Gurion
doctrine. The doctrine was an outgrowth of the strategic environment Israel
faced in its early years, including the threats and constraints it posed, as well
as Israel's economic circumstances at the time, and led to a number of fundamental assumptions and consequent strategic responses. The classic doctrine, as
presented below, is a composite picture both of Ben-Gurion's initial concept and
of some additions that developed in Israel's early decades.

The Strategic Setting

A Uniquely Long and Bitter Conflict. The Arab-Israeli conflict is unique,
at least among modern conflicts, for its century-long duration and, arguably,

bitterness. The conflict has been all-encompassing: diplomatic, military, ter-ritorial, economic, ideological, national, and religious. For decades, the Arab countries refused to recognize Israel's existence and to have any contact with it whatsoever, pursuing a policy of total negation. Many continue to do so.

From the beginning Israel's leaders believed that the conflict would last for decades, or even centuries.[1] Ben-Gurion viewed the various wars with the Arab states as mere stages in one long one. Yigal Allon, another founding father, shared this view, believing that the early wars were just the first rounds in a conflict that would last 100–200 years.[2] This view has persisted into more modern times. Former chief of staff (hereinafter CoS) Raphael Eitan considered the 1982 inva-sion of Lebanon a direct continuation of Israel's War of Independence and "part of the battle for the Land of Israel that has already lasted 100 years."[3] One of his successors, Moshe Yaalon, who later became defense minister, similarly argued that the first intifada (1987–1990) should be seen as a resumption of the War of Independence.[4]

Six wars, numerous major confrontations, and ongoing violence, from low-level terrorism to large-scale rocket attacks, as well as WMD threats, have been basic features of Israel's external environment. Facing multiple threats at any one time, Israel has long perceived its external environment as one of perpetual low-level tension, punctuated by brief outbreaks of larger-scale and major hostilities, necessitating a need for constant vigilance. Consequently, a sense of nearly unre-mitting Arab enmity prevails, of a conflict of unlimited hostility and objectives. In recent decades, there have also been all-too-brief periods of diplomatic prog-ress and hope, partially mitigating the perception of a monolithic wall of Arab enmity.

Arab hostility was considered so fundamental that merely thwarting efforts to destroy Israel would not suffice to achieve deterrence. The tremendous disparity in size and resources would sustain Arab hopes of future success, and both intra- and inter-Arab politics would perpetuate the conflict. A state of semidormant warfare, with recurring eruptions of active conflict, would be the status quo.[5]

An Existential Conflict. Israel's strategic thinking has long been predicated on the fundamental assumption that the Arab countries—and today Iran and nonstate actors such as Hamas and Hezbollah—seek its destruction. Numerous states throughout history have faced a threat of politicide (destruction of the state); Israel is again unique in that both its leaders and the public have always shared the belief that it also faces a realistic threat of genocide, annihilation of the people, and national extinction. The dangers posed by Israel's external en-vironment were thus viewed as bearing little substantive comparison to other countries, in either magnitude or persistence.[6]

Defense Minister Dayan's infamous warning, during the bleak early days of the Yom Kippur War, regarding the possible "end of the Third Temple" (i.e.,

Israel's destruction), is one of the more extreme expressions of this primal fear, but it has been manifested often, even when the dangers were far more circumscribed. Indeed, much of Israel's national security decision-making and public discourse are deeply colored by this existential fear, often referred to as Israel's "Masada Complex" or "Holocaust Syndrome." "Our fate in the land of Israel," former prime minister Begin stated, "is that we have no choice but to fight with selfless dedication. The alternative is Auschwitz."[7] Prime Minister Netanyahu has warned, in regard to Iran's nuclear program, that "it is 1938 and Iran is Germany. And Iran is racing to arm itself with atomic bombs."[8] Holocaust Remembrance Day, commemorated just one week before Memorial Day for Fallen Soldiers, are both poignant annual reminders of the dangers the nation continues to face. Countless offices are decorated with a famous picture of Israeli F-15s flying over Auschwitz, a truly remarkable and incomparable visual portrayal of the dramatic transformation in the fortunes of the Jewish people in just a few decades. Each year, on Passover, virtually all of Israel's Jewish population recites the warning that "in every generation they have risen-up against us to annihilate us." A centuries-old ritual it may be, but it strongly resonates for much of Israel with modern-day realities.[9]

Experience has further demonstrated that national security decisions contain the potential to fundamentally transform the nation's course, even when they do not threaten its destruction. The Six Day War, for example, had far-reaching ramifications for Israel's future, indeed, the state's very character. The Oslo Accords similarly had a fundamental impact on the conflict ever since. Decision-making in Israel is thus uniquely critical and fateful.[10]

Wars of "No Choice." In these circumstances, it was believed, Israel's actions could only affect the Arabs' cost-benefit calculus, not their fundamental enmity, and that Israel was destined to live under a prolonged existential threat. Israel could not afford to lose a single battle, let alone a war; each was a matter of survival, and there would never be a "second chance." If defeated once, Israel would not survive to fight another day. The Arabs, conversely, could permit themselves a series of military defeats. As a consequence, Israel faced "wars of no choice," leading to a broad national consensus regarding the dangers the nation faced and to a high level of national motivation.[11]

A Conventional Military Threat. In Israel's early decades, until the 1980s, the primary military threat it faced was of a major conventional attack(s) from the "first tier" (the bordering Arab countries), or a coalition of neighboring countries, with some limited support from those in the "second tier," such as Iraq and Saudi Arabia. Iraq, for example, sent forces in support of Jordan in 1948 and 1967 and of Syria in 1973, as did Saudi Arabia in 1948 and 1973.[12] The defense doctrine took into account a worst-case scenario, termed the "complete case," in which the Arab countries would succeed in banding together and surprising

Israel in a joint attack. During the early decades the threat of a major conventional attack was manifested repeatedly, on average every eight years. Although Israel also faced ongoing Palestinian terrorism throughout this period, assisted and abetted by the Arab states, the dangers of "current security," as it was called at the time, were not given high priority.[13]

"A Nation Dwelling Alone." From the beginning, Israel recognized that it would be highly dependent on the outside world, economically and militarily. The lesson to be learned, however, from both Jewish and Israeli history, was that the international community was not a reliable ally and that Israel could only depend on itself for its security.[14] This fear was realized in practice with the French arms embargo of 1967, which was viewed as an ultimate betrayal, but also by various other events. The United States and other Western nations imposed an arms embargo on the Middle East in 1948, but since the Arab countries could procure weapons from the Soviet bloc, the only practical impact was on Israel. The United States forced Israel to withdraw from Sinai in 1949 and 1956 and then failed to live up to its commitment to open the Red Sea straits to shipping in 1967. Most Third World countries severed relations with Israel after the Six Day War, a war viewed by Israel as one of survival.

Strategic Constraints

Geography as a Strategic Nightmare

Surrounded by hostile Arab states on all sides, Israel saw itself as a state under siege until 1967 and its geography as a strategic nightmare.[15] Indeed, the borders were considered indefensible and, by their very nature, an invitation to Arab attack.[16]

As seen in Map 1.1, Israel is tiny, slightly over 7,700 square miles (20,000 km^2) in its 1967 borders, approximately the size of New Jersey or Slovenia, and approximately 9,600 square miles (25,000 km^2) with the West Bank and Golan Heights. Moreover, its borders are highly elongated and narrow. From north to south Israel measures just under 300 miles. The width varies, just 80 miles at the widest, in the Beersheba region, with three particularly narrow points; the so-called "finger of the Galilee" in the north, where it is approximately 5 miles wide, the "narrow waist" at Netanya, just 20 miles north of Tel Aviv, the very heart of the country, where it is 8.7 miles wide, and especially at the southern tip, below Eilat, where the V-shape ends in a narrow point.

Israel's geography was held to have the following strategic ramifications:

A Vulnerable Frontier State. The disproportion between the country's length and width turned all of Israel into a frontier.[17] Moreover, virtually everything that makes Israel a viable state is concentrated in the narrow coastal plain,

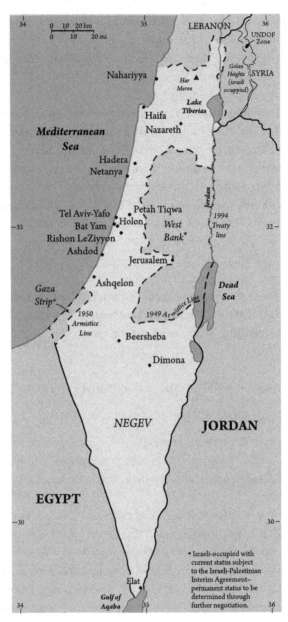

Map 1.1 Israel (1967 Borders with West Bank and Golan Heights)

primarily in the area between Haifa and Ashkelon (the one significant exception, Beersheba, is an isolated enclave in the south), in all a strip about 100 miles
long and 10–15 miles wide in most areas. Most of the population and economic
base (today approximately 70% and 80% respectively)[18] are located in this area,
as are most governmental institutions, the international airport, airbases and

most other strategic targets, national infrastructure, academia, and the arts. All are within easy artillery, let alone rocket, range from the West Bank and other borders. Armored forces deployed in the West Bank would literally abut Jerusalem and be just minutes from Tel Aviv, and flying time for combat aircraft based in any of the neighboring countries would also be a matter of minutes. The entire country was vulnerable.[19]

Absence of Natural Borders. The frontier character was further exacerbated by the absence of natural obstacles on any of the borders and by the generally difficult topography. The Syrians, sitting atop the Golan Heights, had a commanding military presence dominating all of northern Israel. The border with Jordan was the longest and most difficult to defend; the West Bank constituted a deep salient extending into the very center of Israel, near Tel Aviv, and the hilly ridge running its length provided a commanding presence overlooking all of central Israel. Jerusalem was surrounded on three sides. The border with Egypt was a long and largely barren desert, while the northern section, the Gaza Strip, constituted a deep wedge reaching just 30 miles from the outskirts of Tel Aviv.

Indefensible Borders. Israel's elongated geography raised the fear that the country could be overrun and split into a number of parts; by Syria in the north, Jordan in the center, and Egypt in the south. It also rendered Israel particularly vulnerable to surprise attack and to strategies of attrition.[20] Former foreign minister Abba Eban spoke of the pre-1967 lines as "Auschwitz borders."[21]

Fundamental Asymmetries

The balance of power between Israel and the Arab countries was held to be characterized by a series of fundamental asymmetries, in terms of geography, population, economic resources, political backing, and war aims.[22] Some of these asymmetries are immutable; some, as will be seen in the following chapters, have changed dramatically over time.

Territorial Size. One has merely to look at Map 1.2 to understand the fundamental territorial asymmetry between Israel and the Arab countries, whether one includes the entire Arab world, or just what were once called the "confrontation states" (Egypt, Jordan, and Syria). Egypt is 50 times Israel's size, Jordan almost five times its size, Syria nine times. Saudi Arabia is the size of all of Western Europe, while the other Arab countries are of various sizes, but most far larger than Israel. Israel could never conquer the Arab countries, but the opposite was not the case.

Absence of Strategic Depth. More fundamentally, Israel's minute territorial dimensions meant that it lacked strategic depth and that most of its population was within easy artillery range, in many cases even small arms, whereas

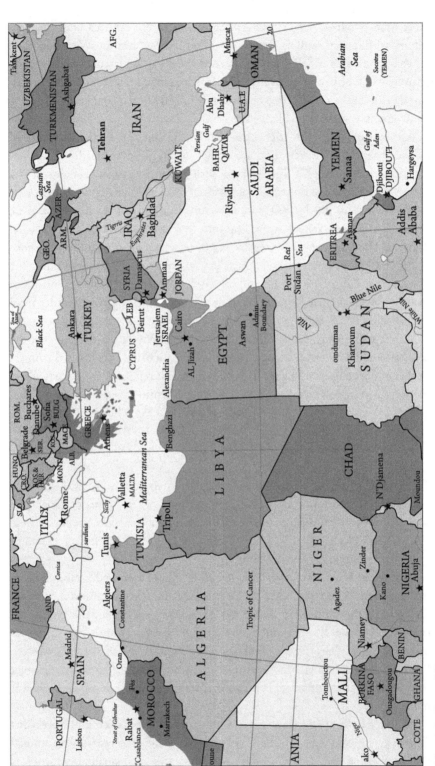

Map 1.2 The Middle East

most of the Arab population was far from the border with Israel. In reality, the problem was even more severe; Israel not only lacked strategic depth, but tactical, as well. Given both its geographic limitations and the fear that the population in any territory conquered by the Arabs, even temporarily, would be annihilated, Israel could not conduct a tactical withdrawal, let alone a strategic one. Moreover, the Arabs had large standing armies with considerable mobility and firepower, whereas Israel's standing army was quite small and relied on the mobilization of reserves. Hence the particular Israeli sensitivity to the danger of surprise attack.[23]

Population Size. In 1948 Israel's Jewish population numbered only 630,000, compared to an Arab world of some 30 million (the comparable figures today are about 6.5 million Jews in Israel, versus 300 million Arabs, in both cases a ratio of roughly 50 to 1). For Israel, the population disparity had two primary consequences: the Arabs would have infinitely greater reserves of manpower to draw upon, and their tolerance for pain, ability to suffer losses, and consequent staying power would be greater.[24]

Economic Resources. From the beginning the Arab side was able to draw on much larger economic resources than Israel, a critical component of national power, which provided the Arab countries with a far greater capability to purchase weapons and sustain large militaries and with economic staying power. The explosion in Arab oil income, starting in the early 1970s, further magnified this asymmetry.

Staying Power. As a result of the above asymmetries, Israel would never have the staying power required for a protracted confrontation, could not sustain a large standing army, and could not even afford to mobilize its reserve forces for long, because this would shut down the economy and lead to socioeconomic paralysis.[25] Add to this Israel's sensitivity to casualties, and a serious problem of staying power was thought to exist.

Military Objectives. Given the overall asymmetry between the sides, the defense doctrine was predicated on the assumption that Israel would never be able to terminate the conflict through military means, compel the Arabs to accept its existence, or even make meaningful and enduring political gains. Moreover, Israel would not be able to translate its military capabilities into political objectives and so had no political justification for initiating a war, nor clearly defined war aims. The most it could realistically hope for would be a temporary respite between ongoing rounds of warfare. Israel's war objectives were thus defined mostly in military terms and were essentially defensive in nature, maintaining the status quo by building an impregnable iron wall and thwarting Arab attempts to destroy it.[26] Conversely, the Arabs could continue fighting indefinitely and had the ability to achieve a final and complete military victory, by realizing their objective of "driving the Jews into the sea." Indeed, they would only accept Israel's existence if they were ultimately forced to conclude that there was no realistic prospect of destroying it militarily.[27]

Overall Military Power and Number of Fronts. Given the far greater size of their populations and economic resources, the Arabs would be able to field far larger armies, equipped with more advanced weapons. Israel, it was thought, would always be at a major disadvantage in terms of the size of the military forces it could deploy and the quality of its weapons. Moreover, Israel had to take into account the danger that it would have to fight an Arab coalition and divide its military efforts between different fronts simultaneously. The Arabs could focus their efforts entirely on Israel.[28]

Diplomatic Asymmetry. The Arab side would begin every dispute with Israel with the relatively unanimous support of the entire Arab and Muslim world, a large starting coalition. This basic disadvantage was further augmented by strong support from many Third World countries, which came to be known in Israel derisively as the "automatic" pro-Arab majority in the UN and other international forums, and often from Western countries, as well. Israel would have only one permanent ally, the Jewish people, though it received vital assistance from friendly powers, initially France, later the United States.[29]

Great Power Intervention

The great powers were believed to pose a major constraint on Israel's defense doctrine from the early years. The United States forced Israel to withdraw from Sinai in 1949 and once again in 1956. The United States pressed Israel not to launch a pre-emptive strike in 1967 and 1973 and together with the Soviet Union prevented clear victories in the War of Attrition in 1970 and Yom Kippur War in 1973. The great powers might also intervene directly on behalf of the Arabs, as the Soviet Union threatened to do in 1973, and the United States might impose sanctions or suspend aid. Furthermore, intervention in the fighting might come before Israel had succeeded in achieving its objectives, or worse, after the Arabs had achieved some of theirs, freezing the situation on the ground and making them permanent. Israel could win the wars, but the great powers might deprive it of victory, and it would lose the diplomatic battle.

Israel, therefore, had to prevent the Arabs from gaining even temporary territorial gains and to achieve its own objectives rapidly, before the great powers intervened. Even rapid military action might prove insufficient. This gave rise to a possibly unique Israeli concept of "political time," the period it would have to conduct military operations before external intervention forced a ceasefire. "Political time" was a primary consideration in every war and major operation Israel fought until 2006.[30]

The Classic Response

Faced with the above strategic setting and constraints, Israel's classic defense doctrine was based on the following primary components.

"The Three Pillars": Deterrence, Early Warning, and Military Decision

Deterrence. The best war, of course, is one that never actually breaks out, and, in any event, the classic defense doctrine was predicated on the assumption that Israel could not achieve its political objectives through the use of military force. Deterrence thus became the centerpiece of the classic doctrine, the organizing concept that defined situations, objectives, achievements, and failures.[31]

To prevent, or resurrect, a perceived deterioration in its deterrence, Israel went to war in 1956, launched numerous reprisals during the 1950s and 1960s, went to war again in 1967, escalated the War of Attrition during 1969–1970, seized additional parts of the Golan Heights and of Egyptian territory in the latter stages of the 1973 war, attacked the Iraqi nuclear reactor in 1981, and went to war against the PLO in Lebanon in 1982.[32] There were many more examples at the time and ever since.

Israel's deterrent posture was designed to convince the Arab states that their efforts to destroy it were futile, that they would be defeated every time they sought to achieve their objectives through military means, and to thereby diminish their motivation to even try. Only through a cumulative process would the Arabs ultimately despair of destroying Israel and come to accept it. Deterrence was to be achieved both through full-scale wars and ongoing limited military confrontations, such as retaliation raids and special operations.[33]

Israel's deterrence was based primarily on denial, rather than punishment, that is, thwarting Arab military efforts, destroying the attacking forces, and conquering territory, not punishing the population or destroying the economic infrastructure. There were, however, some exceptions, such as the retaliation raids in the 1950s, the deep penetration raids in Egypt during the War of Attrition, or those in Syria during the 1973 war, which were designed to destroy its energy production capabilities.[34]

Early Warning. A number of factors, such as Israel's lack of strategic depth, the Arab ability to shift rapidly from defensive to offensive operations, given their large standing forces, and Israel's inability to maintain frequent and extended mobilizations of its primarily reservist military, all imbued the concept of early warning with a place of special importance in its defense doctrine. If the first pillar, deterrence, failed, the second one, timely and precise early warning, was expected to alert Israel to impending hostilities and provide sufficient time to mobilize and deploy the reserves, while the small standing force would blunt the initial enemy attack. "Sufficient" warning time was normally defined as 48 hours.[35]

Over the years, Israel sought to define a clear set of indicators that would provide it with early warning of Arab intentions to initiate hostilities, or of casus belli, which would necessitate preventive or pre-emptive action. The indicators and casus belli adopted included, inter alia, an Egyptian attempt to block freedom of navigation through the straits in the Red Sea, deployments of foreign forces in Jordan, arms buildups that threatened the military balance, concentrations of large forces along Israel's borders, geographical "red lines," such as Syrian deployments of ground forces or surface-to-air missiles in southern Lebanon, violations of the military annex of the peace treaty with Egypt, and Arab nuclear weapons programs.[36]

Military Decision refers to the ability to prevent the enemy from continuing the fighting, whether by destroying its military capabilities or undermining its psychological will to do so. The need to achieve military decision reflected the classic defense doctrine's presumption that Arab hostility was so deep that Israeli deterrence would fail every few years and wars would break out. Military decision was thus designed to restore failed deterrence and prolong the lulls between wars, not to end the conflict. It was, however, also designed to end each round with a clear victory, because nothing else would provide for the cumulative deterrent effect Israel sought, that is, to convince the Arabs that their efforts to destroy it were futile and ultimately lead them to accept the need to end the conflict. The two concepts had a synergistic effect; decision would restore deterrence, deterrence would limit the need for decision. Since military decision was the only mechanism for resolving hostilities once they had broken out, it was the most crucial of the three pillars.[37]

"The Few against the Many," or Quality over Quantity

Israel, the classic doctrine stressed, could not compete with the Arabs in terms of population size, economic resources, size of military forces, and other categories of national power. It could, however, better marshal the limited resources it did have and compete qualitatively, to counter the qualitative imbalance.[38] On the military level, this meant better training, command and control, resourcefulness, and especially air superiority. Israel's more advanced operational and technological capabilities would make it possible for the same number of aircraft to fly more sorties, for tanks to achieve a higher percentage of hits, and for Israel's ground forces to conduct wars of greater mobility. Motivation was believed to be the most important qualitative component, based on a sense of a shared fate and a consequent "unity of purpose" in the face of existential threats.

The concept of "the few against the many," or quality over quantity, also had clear implications for Israel's socioeconomic policy, addressed below in the section on nation-building. The qualitative emphasis notwithstanding, Israel's leadership sought to build the greatest military capability possible and (at least in the early years) to ensure that the quantitative imbalance did not exceed a ratio of three to one.[39]

"A Nation in Arms"

To ensure national survival in the face of Arab hostility and to overcome the fundamental asymmetries with its enemies, Israel had to be prepared to mobilize all of the human and material resources at its disposal, indeed, to become the most highly mobilized democracy in the world.[40] The transition from peace to war might be very rapid, and Israel had to be able to mobilize quickly and fully. Maximal national mobilization meant making use of all parts of the population, not just certain classes or sectors, through nearly universal military conscription, including women. At the same time, Israel would also have to provide its people with a standard of living, freedoms, and basic rights similar to those of any advanced democratic society.[41]

Israel's quantitative inferiority and budgetary constraints led it to devise a multitiered military structure based on a core of a limited number of professional soldiers, with an overall force comprised primarily of conscripts and reservists. By so doing, Israel was able to maintain one of the world's largest militaries relative to its population size and even to achieve rough parity with the Arabs in terms of total manpower, without paralyzing its economy. Indeed, fledgling Israel in 1948, with a total population of 630,000, was able to field an army similar in size to that of the Arab countries combined, with a total population of about 30 million, approximately 100,000 on each side.[42]

Professionals. Professionals are the backbone of the IDF, designed to provide it with those capabilities that the conscript and reserve forces lack: military expertise, especially in areas requiring high degrees of specialization, continuity of military thought, and the formulation of military strategy. The professionals were to focus on building the overall force structure and training the conscript and reserve forces, and constitute the skeleton of the command structure. Due to the need for sophisticated skills, the air force, navy, and Intelligence Corps have always been largely professional, while the ground forces consisted primarily of conscripts and reservists.[43]

Conscripts. Together with the professional forces, conscripts would be responsible for current security and for defending the mobilization process and "holding the line," until the reserves could be mobilized.[44]

Reserves. Unlike the Arab states, Israel could not afford to maintain a large standing army, and the reserves were thus to be the largest component of the IDF, ready to be mobilized and deployed within days. Moreover, the reserves would bear the primary responsibility for achieving military decision.[45]

Status Quo

Israel's leaders accepted the territorial status quo at the end of the fighting in 1949 and eschewed further territorial ambitions. At the same time, the Arab refusal to accept the 1949 armistice lines as Israel's final borders enabled its leaders to contemplate future changes, should circumstances permit, designed to improve Israel's strategic posture.[46] Israel did not intend to expand its territory in 1967, but did so when a perceived war of survival provided the necessary context. In the post-1967 era, Israel's maximum military ambitions have been maintaining control of the territory within the 1967 lines and, depending on the individual's political views, the West Bank and Golan Heights. For the Arabs, the latter territories remained their minimum, all of Israel their maximum.

"Defensive Strategy, Executed Offensively"

Israel's classic defense doctrine was fundamentally defensive strategically, to ensure the survival of the state, but offensive operationally, to impose repeated defeats on its Arab adversaries and improve Israel's strategic circumstances every time hostilities broke out. In the early decades, the objective of attaining a clear victory in every war was translated into the belief that the fighting must end with the IDF in control of more territory than it held at the beginning of the confrontation.[47]

The primary components of this offensively executed defensive strategy, were as follows:

Offensive and Mobile Maneuver Warfare. A broad consensus existed among virtually all Israeli strategists, from the earliest days, in favor of an offensive strategy, and it became the hallmark of Israeli military thinking. Offense was viewed as the only means of compensating for Israel's lack of strategic depth and quantitative inferiority and of achieving a victory sufficiently decisive to compel the Arabs to cease hostilities. Offense would allow Israel to determine the timing, tempo, location, and overall course of the battle, transfer the battle to enemy territory, bring Israel's qualitative advantage to bear, and facilitate rapid military achievements of the sort that might create new diplomatic openings. Israel would thus launch major ground operations at the very onset of hostilities and seek to rapidly conquer vital areas deep in enemy territory. Defensive warfare, in contrast, was viewed as war by attrition, with higher losses, and would require that Israel split its forces in different places, whereas the attacker would be able to concentrate its forces. Until 1967 defense was thus viewed as no more than a brief and unavoidable phase prior to attack. Whenever possible Israel would take the offensive, whether on the ground through rapid and deep armored thrusts or in the air.[48]

Transferring the Battle to Enemy Territory. Given Israel's lack of strategic depth and the presumption that even a tactical retreat would lead to the annihilation of the local population, Israel could not afford to wage a war, or even to sustain significant low-intensity hostilities, on its own territory. Defensive warfare, in which one trades space for time, was precluded as an option, and it was deemed imperative that the fighting be transferred to enemy territory as rapidly as possible, an approach that also suited the IDF's superiority in high-tempo battles of maneuver and that reduced casualties by shortening the fighting.[49]

Pre-emption. The absence of strategic depth and of staying power required that Israel mobilize its reserves as soon as a threat was identified and that it aspire to pre-empt the enemy in order to prevent it from using predetermined battle plans, disrupt the mobilization and concentration of its forces, and neutralize its quantitative advantages. Preemption would also reduce the chances that additional Arab countries, or the superpowers, could intervene. Preemption was never a binding or automatic principle, but an option dependent on the strategic circumstances.[50]

Inflexible Defense. The lack of strategic depth and fear of the annihilation of the population in any areas conquered by the Arabs led to the principle of inflexible defense, the need to defend every inch of territory and, consequently, to the concept of "regional defense" (*Hagana Merhavit*). Regional defense was based on rural communities (villages and kibbutzim) located near the borders, which were given partial responsibility for their own self-defense, and on forward deployment of IDF forces. It was designed to maintain a permanent forward defensive deployment in the field, to force the enemy to devote forces to overcoming it during the early stages of the attack, and to delay and disrupt enemy maneuver. Long before the establishment of the state it was believed that Israel's borders would be determined largely by the demographic dispersal of the people residing in a given area. During the War of Independence the rural communities truly played a central role in their own self-defense and in so doing in determining the state's ultimate borders.[51]

Short Wars. Wars with the Arabs threatened regional stability, raised the specter of a US-Soviet confrontation and intervention, endangered Western access to oil, risked the involvement of Arab expeditionary forces, and increased the danger that Israel would have to fight on more than one front simultaneously. Moreover, full mobilization would bring Israel's economy to a halt, whereas short wars would cause less economic disruption and minimize casualties. With a limited military-industrial base, budgetary resources, and overall staying power, Israel would also have to fight its wars from existing stocks of munitions and supplies, and a short-war strategy would allow it to end the conflict without having to petition a foreign patron for emergency resupply.[52] For all of these reasons, the classic doctrine placed a premium on short and fast wars.

Defensible Borders

The territories acquired in 1967 provided Israel, for the first time, with some strategic depth and with what were then believed to be comparatively defensible borders, with such natural barriers as the Suez Canal, Jordan River, and West Bank mountain ridge. The new strategic depth was particularly pronounced on the Egyptian front, where the Sinai Peninsula, three times the size of Israel, constituted a seemingly vast buffer zone. Crucially, the new territories were perceived to provide Israel with a margin of safety in terms of time and space, in case of a surprise attack, or following initial setbacks, and consequently with the ability to absorb an attack without the need for pre-emption.[53] In 1973 Israel could thus afford to refrain from last-minute pre-emption, even when the imminence of the Arab attack became known.

Great Power Alliances

Israel's fundamental sense of insecurity and isolation led to an ongoing preoccupation with the need to secure at least one patron from among the major international powers. Such alliances were considered essential in order to ensure diplomatic and economic support and, above all, to maintain ongoing access to weapons, and were deemed particularly important before Israel undertook large-scale military action. An alignment with a major power would further improve Israel's strategic posture both through external balancing and by providing some measure of extended deterrence.[54] In 1956 Israel went to war only after coordination with France and Britain; in 1967, 1973, and 1982, with the United States. Indeed, Ben-Gurion repeatedly sought to establish formal alliances with a great power during the 1950s and early 1960s,[55] an option that arose again at various times later on.

Strategic Autonomy and Self-Reliance

The overriding importance of a close alliance with great powers notwithstanding, the defense doctrine also stressed the need to maintain strategic autonomy, in other words, the will and capacity for independent action, even in the face of opposition from outside powers. In the final analysis, Israel was a "nation dwelling alone" and could only rely on itself for its defense. Allies could be relied on to help maintain the balance of power and deterrence between the wars, but not for direct participation in them, and, in any event, alliances were believed to be temporary and fleeting. Even under optimal conditions, self-reliance was essential, as days might pass before external military support arrived, by which time it might very well be too late.[56]

Israel alone would be responsible for its defense, and it would not ask foreign patrons for troops or other direct assistance,[57] just weapons with which to wage its own battles. Although Israel would become highly dependent on foreign sources for weapons, France until the 1960s and the United States ever since, the principle of self-reliance also meant that Israel would do its utmost to develop an indigenous capability to manufacture weapons.

Israel maintained a domestic arms industry from the prestate days, but its primary growth only came after France imposed an arms embargo in 1967, a deeply traumatic experience, and after the 1973 Yom Kippur War. At that time, Israel initially sought to achieve self-sufficiency in all primary areas, including tanks, aircraft, and naval craft, but economic constraints in the 1980s forced it to forgo production of the latter two. Nevertheless, Israel continues to manufacture tanks and armored fighting vehicles, missiles, air defense systems, precision-guided munitions, unmanned aerial vehicles, various electronic systems, and more.[58]

Pursuing Peace

The overarching strategic objective of Israel's defense doctrine was to achieve peace with its Arab neighbors and gain acceptance as a Jewish state in the region, or at a minimum, end active hostilities. Peace was considered a distant dream, given the Arabs' fundamental and unremitting hostility during the early decades, and was accorded a place of importance in the classic defense doctrine, but little concrete conceptualization.

Nation Building and Socioeconomic Policy

Given the focus of this book on the "hard" dimensions of national security strategy, defense, and foreign policy, no more than a brief mention will be given to the great importance the classic defense doctrine attached to the processes of nation-building and socioeconomic policy. Focused as Ben-Gurion was on ensuring the survival of the state, both from external enemies and domestically, he believed that Israel's achievements in the areas of education, science, and technology, as well as its industrial, agricultural, and economic development, were no less important dimensions of national security than military power. Encouraging population growth and absorbing immigrants were central socioeconomic challenges, especially in the early decades, but also had clear ramifications for Israel's security; Ben-Gurion famously believed that if Israel were to reach a Jewish population of five million, its existence would be assured. Population dispersal, including in outlying areas, again served both socioeconomic and defense purposes, as did promotion of a new Israeli identity and social cohesion among the highly diverse immigrant population.

Chapter 1 has presented Israel's classic defense doctrine, as initially formulated in the 1950s and further developed during the early decades. The doctrine guided virtually all Israeli strategic thinking well into the 1980s and continues to inform it to a significant extent to this day. The next chapter will explore the significant changes that have evolved in Israel's strategic environment in the decades since the classic doctrine was formulated.

PART TWO

A STRATEGIC ENVIRONMENT TRANSFORMED

2

Israel's New Strategic Setting

The Zionist regime is a true cancerous tumor on this region that should
be cut off and it definitely will be cut off.
—Ali Khamenai, Supreme Leader of Iran

Chapter 2 has three primary parts. The first two analyze the primary changes
that have taken place in recent decades in the nature of Israel's strategic environment and the strategic constraints it faces. The third part presents an
overview of Israel's strategic environment today. All three are broad-stroke
analyses, and we will return to many of the issues raised in greater detail in
later chapters.

We begin with a brief recap of Israel's strategic setting in the early decades,
which the classic defense doctrine was designed to address, before turning to
an analysis of the changes that have taken place. This setting, as presented in
chapter 1, was characterized by the following:

- A uniquely long and bitter conflict, stemming from such fundamental Arab
  enmity that even repeated Israeli victories would not suffice to deter further
  attempts to destroy it
- An existential conflict in which Israel faced not just a threat of politicide, but
  of genocide
- Wars of "no choice," in which Israel had no alternative but to fight for its existence and win each round decisively
- Conventional military threats from bordering Arab countries, or a coalition
  thereof, with some limited support from states in the second tier
- "A nation dwelling alone," or such fundamental national isolation that Israel
  could only rely on itself for its security

Changes in the Strategic Environment

The Uniquely Long and Bitter Conflict Is No Longer as Extreme and Existential

The 1967 Six Day War was the first in a series of dramatic developments that have transformed Israel's strategic circumstances beyond recognition, in ways that the classic defense doctrine neither anticipated nor was equipped to handle. Until the Six Day War, the Arab world maintained a virtually monolithic commitment to Israel's destruction. Israel's victories in 1948 and 1956 were attributed by the Arab world to various exogenous factors, such as foreign intervention, or written off as some sort of inexplicable historic error, a fluke, that would ultimately be rectified through its destruction. Denial, conspiracy theories, and control of the media by authoritarian regimes, all contributed to this. The magnitude of the defeat in 1967, however, was so crushing that it could not be explained away, and the Arab masses no longer bought into the regimes' propaganda, nor could the regimes themselves truly deny reality.

This rude awakening began a process of growing Arab acceptance of the reality of Israel's existence. It did not entail recognition of Israel's legitimacy, reconciliation to the idea of its existence, or a willingness to live alongside it in peace. It did, however, begin a process of acknowledgment that Israel would probably remain a long-term fixture of the region, with which the Arabs would have no choice but to live. Accordingly, the outcome of the war began to transform the conflict from one focused on Israel's very existence to one centered primarily on attempts to regain the territories lost in 1967, with the fundamental desire to "rectify" the defeat of 1948–1949 put off to some undefined future.

This process certainly did not take place evenly among the different Arab countries nor within them, and many in the Arab world refuse to accept Israel's existence to this day. It was, however, the beginning of a fundamental transformation that further gelled after the 1973 Yom Kippur War.[1] The fact that Israel ultimately succeeded in turning the tide during the war and achieved military (though not strategic) victory, despite the devastating surprise attack that had initially placed its very existence in some jeopardy, had a decisive impact on many of those who still harbored lingering doubts regarding Israel's long-term viability. Israel, it was now abundantly clear, was here for the duration, and the emphasis on regaining the 1967 territories truly became the focus of the conflict, even if many continued to harbor long-term aspirations of a far more aggressive nature.

Egypt's peace treaty with Israel less than six years later, in 1979, was a reflection of the broader changes underway. Rather than true peace and reconciliation with Israel, Egypt sought to regain its territory, the Sinai, end the bloodletting that had cost it so dearly in lives and resources, and promote a rapprochement with the United States. In so doing Egypt also sought to refocus its national energies from the conflict to domestic affairs and economic growth. Regardless of Egypt's motivations, the peace treaty had a dramatic effect on Israel's strategic posture. The most powerful Arab state, the only one that had participated in all of the wars up to that time, had now renounced military conflict, vastly decreasing the threat Israel faced and allowing it to focus its resources on other threats, cut its defense spending significantly, and, most importantly, devote far greater resources to domestic issues.[2]

Moreover, once Egypt had made peace, it rapidly transpired that the other Arab states no longer had an independent capability to wage conventional war against Israel; if they could not win with Egypt, they certainly could not do so without it. Syria, heretofore the most vociferously anti-Israel Arab state, was probably the first in the region to understand the full magnitude of the change that had taken place, long before many in Israel did. In so doing, Syria abandoned its ambitions to confront Israel on its own and instead sought other, indirect, means of continuing the conflict. Jordan, which for all practical purposes had already ceased hostilities by the early 1970s, maintaining a de facto peace and good security cooperation with Israel, formalized this in a peace treaty in 1994. In effect, the dangers of an attack by an individual Arab state or, Israel's ultimate nightmare, of an attack by a coalition of Arab states, had now decreased dramatically and even come to an end. So, too, had the interstate military dimension of the Arab-Israeli conflict and with it the conventional existential threat as well.

Israel has now enjoyed nearly 40 years of peace with Egypt, over 20 with Jordan. The relationship with both is cold and devoid of virtually any bilateral normalization. Nevertheless, both countries' commitment to peace has successfully withstood a number of significant challenges, including controversial events that some feared might lead to its collapse, leadership changes in both, and even the year long rule by the virulently anti-Israeli Muslim Brotherhood in Egypt (2011–2012).[3] A cold peace is infinitely better than a hot war, and peace with Egypt and Jordan has transformed Israel's strategic circumstances.

The collapse of the Soviet Union in 1991, in essence an enemy state and active participant in the confrontation with Israel, without which Syria and other Arab players had no conventional military option to begin with, further undermined their military capabilities and any possibility of a renewed attempt to conduct conventional military warfare against Israel. Syria was now truly on its own; having already "lost" Egypt, it no longer had a superpower ally to rely on either, one that had provided it with vast military assistance, including rapid replacement of weapons lost during previous wars, unconditional diplomatic support, major economic assistance, and strategic backing. With the exception of a few select areas, notably missiles (surface-to-surface, antiaircraft, and antitank), Syria did not have the economic wherewithal to modernize its forces following the collapse of the Soviet Union, leaving it with a massive and out-dated military, unlike the IDF, which modernized rapidly. Nevertheless, Syria did not abandon all hope and found in Hezbollah a useful tool for maintaining pressure on Israel and making it bleed, even if this could not rectify the funda-mental power imbalance.

The United States was now the sole superpower and a close ally of both Israel and Egypt, a further transformation of the strategic landscape. The "American era" in the Middle East, including the emergence of an almost unprecedented alliance with Israel, which had begun in the early 1970s, fully took hold by the early 1980s. From that time on, one cannot understand the region generally, and Israeli national security policy specifically, without taking the American role into account. Among its many other effects, intensive US involvement has helped mitigate the Arab-Israeli conflict, or at least reduce the chances of active warfare, promoted a peace process that was successful in some cases and contributed to managing the conflict in others, contained and deterred regional aggressors and WMD programs, and more. Moreover, Israel came to enjoy a de facto American security guarantee during this period that further contributed to its security, even if it did not eliminate the threats it faced.

In the early 1990s an intensive peace process with Syria and the Palestinians also got underway, along with attempts at reconciliation with the broader Arab world, including the establishment of low-level relations with Morocco, Tunisia, Oman, and Qatar. Although the negotiations with Syria and the Palestinians ul-timately failed, in the latter case even leading to a bloody terrorist war in the early 2000s (the second intifada), they indicated for many in Israel that the con-flict was not irreconcilable and that a diplomatic alternative to military force did exist. For years in the 1990s it even appeared that the long conflict might be nearing an end and that diplomacy and economic ties might finally come to re-place warfare in Israel's relations with the Arab world.

The "Arab Peace Initiative" of 2002, renewed on a number of occasions since then, was a further manifestation of the evolving Arab position. Some of the initiative's elements are highly problematic for Israel, even nonstarters, and it is plain that not all members of the Arab League are truly committed to it. Nevertheless, it does reflect the long-term Arab process of coming to terms with Israel's existence.

Saddam's final defeat in 2003 eliminated the danger of an "eastern front," Israel's longtime nightmare scenario of a combined Syrian-Iraqi operation against it, with or without Jordan and possibly even Saudi involvement. The threat of an eastern front had already diminished greatly following Saddam's de-feat in 1991, but his final demise in 2003 allayed any residual fears.[4] The strategic environment had now been truly transformed beyond recognition.

In recent decades, however, new asymmetric threats have emerged, in the form of terrorism by nonstate actors, including the unprecedented rocket threat Israel now faces from Hezbollah and Hamas and WMD capabilities, first and foremost Iran's nuclear program. We will return to these threats in chapter 3, but let it suffice to say here that Israel does not yet appear to have a fully effective response to the new and disruptive threats posed by Hezbollah and Hamas and there is no effective response to nuclear threats other than deterrence.

The dramatic changes in Israel's strategic circumstances notwithstanding, its existential fears remain deeply ingrained. During the 2006 Second Lebanon War, for example, really more of a large operation, Mossad director Dagan went so far as to warn that "if we do not win this war, the hour glass of our existence will start running (out)."[5] A nuclear Iran is widely thought in Israel to pose an existential threat, and Prime Minister Netanyahu has repeatedly spoken of it in terms evocative of 1938, the eve of the Holocaust, when the world failed to take action, thereby invoking the specter of genocide. Existential fears were similarly evoked by Saddam's launching of missiles against Israel during the first Gulf War in 1991 and even by the bloodshed during the second intifada in the early 2000s. Syria and other Arab countries, as well as Hezbollah and Hamas, are also widely presumed to seek Israel's destruction, capability permitting.[6]

At a 2005 conference entitled "A World Without Zionism," Iranian president Ahmadinejad called Israel a "disgraceful blot" that "must be wiped off the map."[7] In 2013 Iran's Supreme Leader, Ayatollah Khamenei, called Israel a country "doomed to failure and annihilation," "an illegitimate regime" led by "untouchable rabid dogs," whose leaders "cannot be called human beings, they are like animals," arguably an improvement over his previous characterization of Israel as a "cancerous tumor." In 2014 he outlined a nine-point plan for Israel's elimination.[8] Hamas's charter states that "Israel will exist and continue to exist until Islam obliterates it, just as it obliterated others before it." The charter blames Jews generally, not just Israelis, for many of the world's ills, including the two world wars. Hezbollah repeatedly calls for Israel's destruction, as does al-Qaeda, whose leader Osama bin Laden said that "the creation of Israel is a crime that must be erased" and that Muslims have a religious obligation to fight Jews in Israel and wherever they live.[9]

If the existential dangers are real, they have certainly come to be overblown at times and to be a reflexive prism that greatly colors Israel's threat perception, even when its existence has not been in danger, as in the 1991 Gulf War, or during the second intifada. In practice, Israel has not truly faced an existential threat since Egypt made peace in 1979, and some would argue earlier. Although Israel continues to face significant threats, it is unlikely to face existential ones again, unless Iran or some other country acquires nuclear weapons. There is a world of difference between significant threats and existential ones.

No Longer Just "Wars of No Choice"

As the decades passed and the peace process unfolded, more and more people in Israel came to recognize that Israel's own policies and deeds had an important impact on the conflict, that it was not just a matter of an Arab desire to destroy Israel, and that they, too, felt threatened and victimized. As a result, doubts grew regarding the previously almost sacrosanct assumption that Israel's wars were all ones of "no choice," especially after Prime Minister Begin explicitly invoked the right to wage war "by choice" as a justification for the 1982 invasion of Lebanon. For many, the repeated operations in Lebanon and Gaza were not existential wars, but ones of choice, some of debatable necessity.[10]

The peace talks with Syria and the Palestinians also had a deep effect on the nature of political discourse in Israel. As domestic controversy over the peace process grew, especially over the West Bank settlements, public confidence was further shaken by doubts regarding a second fundamental assumption, that Arab hostility was truly implacable and that their very willingness to make peace was the issue, rather than the terms thereof. These twin developments had a significant impact on the long-standing national consensus on defense affairs and eroded confidence in policymakers' decision-making capabilities.[11] Today, following the second intifada and the two unilateral withdrawals, from Lebanon and Gaza, the public has once again come to view the operations conducted in both areas ever since 2006 as "wars of no choice."

The Primary Threats Are No Longer Conventional Military Attack

Israel fought four wars with the Arab states during its first 25 years (five if one includes the 1969–1971 War of Attrition). In the almost 45 years since then, however, Israel has not fought a single war against an Arab state.[12] Moreover, the very character of the threats Israel faces has changed fundamentally, from the primarily conventional military challenges posed by the Arab militaries to a range of asymmetric threats. For the foreseeable future and maybe beyond, the likelihood of major conflicts between Israel and the armies of the Arab states is low.[13]

No Longer Quite a "Nation Dwelling Alone"

Israel is singled out for international opprobrium as no other nation and the subject of grossly distorted efforts to delegitimize everything about it, including its right to exist. Votes on Israel at the UN and other international forums are not just lopsided but grotesque, and its policies on the West Bank issues are almost universally criticized. Conversely, it has not received appropriate international support on numerous issues and occasions, even when clearly warranted. Israel is not a member of any international bloc, alliance, or coalition.

Nevertheless, for all of the focus in recent years on Israel's growing international isolation, it is decidedly not a "nation that dwells alone." Israel has extensive diplomatic, military, and economic ties today with nations around the world, special relations with a variety of countries, including Germany, Canada, India, and Poland, to name just a few, and a truly unique relationship with the United States. It has, at times, enjoyed a modicum of support, at least from the West, when faced with direct aggression, for example, during the second intifada and 2006 Lebanon war, and the international community's efforts to deal with Iran's nuclear program were partly motivated by the threat to Israel.

Israel does continue to face a broad range of threats as do few, if any other, countries, and it can ultimately rely only on itself. Accordingly, it remains a "nation dwelling alone."[14] To a significant degree, however, this is true of all countries in the anarchic international system, and Israel both has built a unique defensive capability to ensure its existence and also appears to enjoy a de facto American security guarantee. Indeed, the relationship with the United States is so broad that it largely counterbalances Israel's overall diplomatic difficulties. Moreover, although not formally a part of any international bloc, alliance, or coalition, it is in practice a part of the American camp, a status unlikely to change for the long term, and to some extent of the broader Western camp.

As the preceding section demonstrates, the strategic setting envisaged by the classic defense doctrine has changed greatly in the decades since it was formulated. The conflict is no longer as bitter and all-encompassing as it was in the early decades; Egypt and Jordan have made peace. Only Iran, among the states in the region, as well as nonstate actors such as Hezbollah and Hamas, still actively seeks Israel's demise. Israel no longer faces conventional military threats of consequence and is no longer a "nation dwelling alone." As a consequence, not all of the military challenges it has faced in the last few decades have been wars of "no choice." Nevertheless, the Middle East today remains a dangerous and tumultuous region, which continues to pose numerous threats to Israel's security, as explained below.

Changing Strategic Constraints

The following section sets out the changes that have taken place in recent decades in the strategic constraints envisioned by the classic defense doctrine. To briefly recap, they included

- Israel's geography, which was considered a strategic nightmare, turning it into a vulnerable frontier state, lacking in strategic depth and defensible borders, as a result of which Israel believed that transferring the fighting to enemy territory was necessary to ensure its security
- Fundamental asymmetries with the Arab states, which provided them with important advantages in the conflict with Israel, including territorial and population size, economic resources, military power, and strategic objectives
- Superpower intervention, which had forced Israel at various times to withdraw from territory, prevented it from pre-empting possible enemy attacks and achieving victory, and limited the "political time" available for military operations.

The Changing Importance of Geography and Territory

The Six Day War had a dramatic impact on Israel's territorial circumstances. Still tiny even with the new territories, Israel believed that it had now acquired a modicum of strategic depth and far more defensible borders. Indeed, the new borders were thought to shield Israel from catastrophic failure, by allowing it to absorb an Arab attack without having to pre-empt, as in fact happened in 1973, or to wage a war for survival right on its borders and major population centers. The new borders thus provided Israeli decision-makers with greater freedom of maneuver.[15] Even more importantly, they enabled the fundamental transformation in the conflict's nature mentioned in the previous section, from one focused on Israel's very existence to a more limited one centered on the newly acquired territories.

The strategic depth and defensible character of the new borders was relative, of course, but the West Bank now gave Israel over 50 additional kilometers of depth in areas where it had previously been only 15 to a few dozens of kilometers wide, and placed its border with Jordan along a more natural line, the Jordan River. The Golan Heights, just some 12–26 kilometers wide, largely placed Israel's northern towns beyond the range of Syrian artillery (though not modern rockets, missiles, and even long-range artillery), and Damascus was now within striking distance, just 60 kilometers from the border.[16] Whereas Tel Aviv and Jerusalem, Israel's two primary cities, had been in artillery range before 1967, in Jerusalem's case even small-arms fire, they were now far less vulnerable. The Sinai Peninsula created a buffer 220 kilometers wide, even after being returned to Egypt, when it was demilitarized and placed under international monitoring.

Conversely, the new "defensible borders" did not prevent the outbreak of the 1967-1969 War of Attrition, the 1973 Yom Kippur War, the Iraqi missile attacks during the first Gulf War in 1991, the spillover into Israel proper of the first and second intifadas, in the 1990s and 2000s respectively, and the violence in 2015, nor the numerous terrorist and rocket attacks from Lebanon and Gaza in recent decades. Moreover, Israel's conquest of the 1967 territories increased the Arab countries' motivation to go to war, for unlike the war in 1948–1949, they had now lost territory of their own.[17]

Israel's long-standing assumption that the conquest of territory would serve as an incentive to bring the Arab countries to the negotiating table and as a negotiating card ("land for peace") has proven fully correct only in regard to Egypt. Israel's willingness to withdraw from the Golan Heights in the negotiations during the 1990s, culminating in the Geneva Summit of 2000, did not prove sufficient to entice the Syrians into making a deal. Similarly, Israel's willingness, on at least three occasions, to withdraw from all of Gaza and virtually all of the West Bank (Camp David Summit 2000, Clinton Parameters 2000, and Olmert proposal of 2008) was also insufficient to close a deal with the Palestinians. In these circumstances, there was certainly no point in trying to acquire additional territory for negotiating purposes.[18]

These conclusions were part of a broader Israeli disenchantment with the advantages of territorial acquisition as a decisive factor in wars with the Arab countries. Unlike the Sinai, whose population in 1967 was small, southern Lebanon, the West Bank, and Gaza have large and hostile populations, and Israel has found the attempt to control them to be a heavy and growing burden, militarily, politically, socially, and maybe most importantly, in the case of the West Bank, demographically. This disillusionment with the advantages of territorial acquisition led to the unilateral withdrawals from Lebanon in 2000 and Gaza in 2005, to increasing domestic controversy over the wisdom of the ongoing control of the West Bank, and to Prime Minister Barak's and Prime Minister Olmert's dramatic peace proposals in 2000 and 2008, respectively. It is also incontrovertible today that the ongoing occupation of territory plays into Arab hands diplomatically, whatever the justification, and has deeply undermined Israel's international standing.[19]

All of the major military operations in the post-1973 era have taken place in heavily populated areas (southern Lebanon, West Bank, and Gaza), and any future warfare is likely to do so as well, whether in these areas, Syria, or even the Sinai, parts of which now have a sizable population. To illustrate, approximately four million people lived very close to Israel's borders in 2007; by 2027 this number is expected to nearly double, with 20 million at a distance of up to 50 kilometers.[20] Indeed, for reasons to be discussed, Israel has become extremely wary, even loath, to conquer additional territory, to the extent that the Winograd Commission (the special commission established to investigate the failings of the 2006 Lebanon war) even cited the "IDF's mystical fear of conquering additional territory" as a primary reason for the resulting failings.[21]

The desire to avoid acquisition of additional territory poses a fundamental dilemma for Israel's defense doctrine. Although still overwhelmingly offensive at heart, Israel has found it increasingly difficult in recent decades to transfer the ground battle to enemy territory.[22] As a result, it has preferred to conduct limited defensive operations, designed to gain time, temporarily alleviate the threats along its borders, and restore deterrence, rather than the former emphasis on territorial conquest to achieve rapid military decision. In all of Israel's military operations in Lebanon from 1982 to 2006, as well as those in Gaza since 2008, Israel either refrained from conquering territory or did so for only brief periods.

The establishment of Israeli settlements deep in the West Bank and Golan Heights further undermined the strategic depth and defensible nature of the borders that Israel had acquired in 1967. During the 1973 war the IDF had to evacuate civilians from the settlements before it could fully turn its attention to the Syrian onslaught,[23] thereby raising questions about the validity of the former assumption that settlements played a vital role in the nation's defense. Palestinian violence in the West Bank and Gaza starting in 1987, and continuing to this day, has forced the IDF to devote significant resources to the defense of the settlements, which have increasingly come to be seen as a military burden rather than an asset. The West Bank and Golan Heights still provide Israel with strategic depth in the face of external state-based threats, but these threats have become less probable. Moreover, the de facto annexation of the West Bank has incorporated Palestinian violence into Israel itself, thereby undermining the advantages of strategic depth and defensible borders.[24]

Strategic depth is largely irrelevant to wars against the "second tier" countries (Iraq and Libya) and the "third tier" (Iran).[25] The argument can also be made that the value of territory has decreased in an era of rockets and missiles. To an extent, this is undoubtedly true: rockets and missiles can be fired from great distances and eliminate the need to cross borders and confront a military force. Conversely, most of Israel's territory and population are within easy range of Hezbollah and Hamas rockets, and Israel has only limited territory to disperse its population, infrastructure sites, and military forces and installations. We will return to this theme at far greater length, but the conquest and control of territory remain the only way to ensure that rockets and missiles, as well as mortars, cannot be fired at Israel. Most importantly, wars are still won on the ground, and thus geography, topography, and strategic depth remain vital.[26]

Changing Asymmetries

Some of the fundamental asymmetries envisaged by the classic defense doctrine have proven immutable, others have changed considerably, as follows.

Territorial Size. Even with the added territory afforded by the West Bank and the Golan Heights, Israel remains a tiny country (25,000 square kilometers, instead of 20,000) and the fundamental territorial asymmetry, whether compared to the Arab world as a whole, or even many of the Arab countries individually, is immutable. Israel can never compete on a territorial level or gain true depth, though it has been argued that the sea and space can provide a form of "virtual depth" today.

Population Size. Israel's Jewish population has grown dramatically since independence, by a factor of 10, from 630,000 in 1948 to some 6.5 million today, plus a non-Jewish population of two million (see Table 2.1). Israel will always be at a drastic numerical disadvantage compared to the Arab countries, but the latter have never truly succeeded in acting in concert, and so a more realistic basis for comparison is with individual Arab states or partial coalitions thereof. Even so, Syria's pre-civil war population alone was approximately three times that of Israel's, Egypt's well over 10 times, Iran's some nine times. In some ways, however, the Arab countries' large, but poorly educated and impoverished populations, have proven more of a strategic burden than an advantage, and if one compares just the more educated segments of the population, those particularly suited to the requirements of modern economies and militaries, the asymmetry is far more limited.

Staying Power. This has long been held to be Israel's Achilles heel. In fact, however, Israel's staying power and resilience have proven to be far greater than either it or its adversaries ever believed.

Political Staying Power. Despite its vast oil wealth, the Arab world has experienced decades of political, social, and economic stagnation, leading to the convulsions of the "Arab Spring" and subsequent regional turmoil, and to threats to the future stability, unity, and even existence of many Arab states. Some have already disintegrated or become failed states, and the rise of radical Islamism and the Sunni-Shia rift present a growing risk to their future.

Table 2.1 **Populations of Israel, Arab Countries, and Iran, 2015 (millions)**

Israel	Egypt	Jordan	Syria	West Bank and Gaza	Lebanon	Iraq	Iran	Saudi Arabia	Arab League (22 states)
8.4 (6.3 Jews)[61]	91.5	7.6	18.5 (22–23 before civil war)	4.4	5.8	36.4	79.1	31.5	369

Source: www.data.worldbank.org.

Israel, in contrast, has maintained a vibrant democracy for seven decades and, the myriad faults of its political system notwithstanding, has been a remarkable national success story. Not only has Israel survived, in itself a major achievement given Arab enmity, but it has grown rapidly and thrived. Many of the threats Israel faces today no longer stem from the strength of the Arab countries, but from the potential spillover of their internecine conflicts into Israel. Indeed, Israel is widely recognized today as a leading regional power and is one of the few countries in the Middle East, arguably even the only one, in which the survival of its governmental system is not in any doubt.

Economic Staying Power. In recent decades Israel has undergone an economic transformation, from a statist, semisocialist economy to a highly competitive and export-based market economy. Between 1973 and 2015 Israel's GDP grew over fivefold, and it achieved a mid-European standard of living ($33,700 in PPP terms in 2015),[27] becoming a global leader in high tech. In 2014, for example, Israel registered 13,437 patents, whereas Egypt registered 883, Jordan 83, and Saudi Arabia 4,123 (Iran, however, registered 13,768).[28] In terms of investment in R&D as a percentage of GDP, Israel spent 4.21% in 2013, whereas Egypt, Jordan, Iraq, Saudi Arabia, and Iran all spent well under 1%.[29]

More importantly, Israel's GDP in 2015, as seen in Table 2.2, was almost as big as the combined GDPs of Syria, Jordan, Lebanon, Iraq, and the Palestinian Authority, or as Egypt's, which has a population 10 times larger.[30] In 2015 Israel's economy allowed it to spend more on defense (without US aid) than the group of states that formed the basis for its traditional threat assessment and force buildup plans (Egypt, Syria, Jordan, and one-third of the Iraqi army). With US aid, it has been able to spend nearly as much on defense as all of these countries plus Iran and has thus been able to modernize its armed forces far more than the Arab countries (with the exception of Saudi Arabia).[31] Table 2.3 provides the comparative data.

Table 2.2 **GDP of Israel, Arab Countries, and Iran, 2015 (billions of current US dollars)**

Israel	Egypt	Jordan	Syria	West Bank and Gaza	Lebanon	Iraq	Iran	Saudi Arabia	Arab League (22 states)
296	330.8	37.5	40.4 (107.6 in 2011)	12.7	47.1	168.6	425.3	646	2.5 trillion

Source: www.databank.worldbank.org.

Table 2.3 **Military Budgets of Israel, Arab Countries, and Iran, 2015**

	Israel	Egypt	Jordan	Syria (2010)	Iraq	Iran	Saudi Arabia
Billions of Constant USD	17.5	5.4	1.6	1.8	12.8	9.9	85.3
Percentage of GDP	5.4	1.7	4.2	4.1	9.1	2.5	13.7

Source: www.portal.sipri.org/publications/pages/expenditures/country-search.

Conversely, Israel continues to face a problem in terms of its ability to maintain an ongoing mobilization of reserve forces during times of crisis, without causing unacceptable damage to individual employers and the economy as a whole. The classic example of the impact of a prolonged large-scale reserve mobilization was the infamous three-week "waiting period" on the eve of the Six Day War, when the national economy was largely paralyzed and strong public pressure was exerted on the government to either go to war or discharge the reservists. More contemporary examples are the government's great reluctance to mobilize the reserves even for shorter periods during the 2006 war in Lebanon and operations against Hamas in Gaza between 2008 and 2014.

Societal Staying Power. Israel faces a number of important challenges to its societal staying power and resilience that will be addressed in detail in chapter 5. Nevertheless, what stands out in even greater relief, after nearly a century of conflict, is the Israeli public's high overall level of commitment, ongoing willingness to serve in the IDF, strong societal resilience in the face of decades of terrorism and ongoing hostilities, and, in most areas of national security affairs, strong national consensus. Palestinian hopes that the second intifada would break Israeli society and force Israel to accede to far-reaching concessions, Hezbollah's belief that Israeli society was just a "cobweb," and Hezbollah's and Hamas's shared hope that massive rocket fire on the home front would have a significant impact on Israeli policy have all proven illusory. Israeli society's great sensitivity to casualties notwithstanding, the public has been firmly supportive of all of the operations in Lebanon, the West Bank, and Gaza in recent decades. In truth, Israel's society has proven to be an area of national strength.

Military Staying Power. Israel continues to face a problem of military staying power in terms of the size of the stores of weapons and munitions it can afford to maintain, which can be depleted rapidly by the intensity of modern combat. During the 2006 war in Lebanon, for example, Israel had to turn to the United States for urgent resupply of bunker busters, and for air-to-ground missiles during the 2014 conflict. Nevertheless, Israel enjoys a virtual guarantee today that the United States will replenish lost stocks of both weapons and munitions.

This is not the case of the Arab countries. Neither Russia nor Iran can replace the role the Soviet Union played on behalf of Syria. Egypt, Jordan, and, to a lesser extent, Saudi Arabia would face a possible decrease and even cutoff of US assistance were they to take measures directly at odds with American policy.

In terms of long-term military staying power, the dramatic increase in the size of Israel's economy in recent decades has enabled it, together with US assistance, to sustain a large and increasingly sophisticated military. The Arab countries, with the exception of the oil-rich ones, have been increasingly hard-pressed to do so, and the collapse of oil prices has affected their ability to continue spending on defense as well.

Politico-Military Objectives. The traditional asymmetry in politico-military objectives largely persists to this day. The minimum Arab military objective continues to be the territories occupied by Israel in 1967, but for many, certainly Hezbollah and Hamas, as well as Iran, the maximum remains all of Israel. Israel, conversely, has no territorial ambitions beyond its current borders and has withdrawn from territory on a number of occasions (Sinai, southern Lebanon, Gaza), and a majority of the public recognizes the need for compromise on the West Bank.

Beyond this, Israel's politico-military objectives remain fundamentally defensive, limited primarily to thwarting enemy ambitions. In the pursuit of these objectives, however, Israel has at times sought to achieve more far-reaching goals and even fundamental change. This was certainly the case in the 1982 invasion of Lebanon, when Israel sought to install a friendly Lebanese regime that would sign a peace treaty with it and to expel PLO and Syrian forces, and even toyed with the idea that the PLO would return to Jordan, topple the monarchy, and create a Palestinian state in its stead.[32] In the 2006 war in Lebanon, Israel sought a fundamental transformation in the strategic situation prevailing at the time and has long sought to drive a wedge between Syria, Iran, and Hezbollah. On a number of occasions it has sought to overthrow, decapitate, or simply affect a change in enemy leaderships, such as Iraqi president Saddam Hussein following the first Gulf War, Palestinian leader Yasser Arafat at the height of the intifada and on additional occasions, or Hezbollah leader Hassan Nasrallah during the 2006 war in Lebanon and possibly ever since.

Today, however, Israel is a fundamentally status quo actor, especially given its disenchantment with the benefits of territorial acquisition and the failure of past attempts to influence Arab politics. Since the 1980s and 1990s Israel's operational objectives have also become increasingly defensive. This has stemmed from a variety of factors, including changes in the nature of warfare and the threats Israel faces, growing constraints imposed by Israel's international isolation, decreasing international legitimacy for military operations, the desire to achieve progress in the peace process and more.[33]

Number of Adversaries and Fronts. The Arab world's deep political and military disarray has long been a strategic boon to Israel. Of the three wars in which Israel confronted Arab coalitions, the Arabs failed to form a joint military command in 1948 and 1973, while the coalition formed in 1967 was of little practical value. Moreover, Syrian and Jordanian involvement in the fighting in 1967 was initially limited, as was Egyptian-Syrian cooperation during the 1973 war.[34]

In fact, the Arabs' perennial inability to act in concert has been of crucial importance for Israel, providing it with the great advantage of only having to fight on one front at any given time. Even during the War of Independence, Arab disarray was such that Israel was largely able to focus its military efforts on the different fronts sequentially.[35] Given the balance of forces at the time, Israel could not have won the war otherwise. In the lone exception, when Israel was forced to fight a coordinated Egyptian and Syrian surprise attack, during the 1973 war, it found itself in great difficulty. In a similar vein, even though the Palestinian cause has been one of the few consensual issues in the Arab world and has served as a rallying point for much of it, the resources it has devoted to the issue have not been commensurate with the ostensible sense of commitment and the degree of difficulty that Israel could have faced.[36]

Overall Military Power. During the War of Independence, with a tiny population of 630,000, Israel succeeded in fielding a staggering military force, relative to the size of its population, of some 100,000, which actually exceeded the size of the combined forces of its five primary Arab adversaries, with a population of 30 million. Over the years, it has succeeded in maintaining a similar mobilization rate. In 2015 total IDF personnel (professional, conscript, and reservist) was 649,500,[37] out of a Jewish population of over six million. This high level of mobilization, far higher than the Arab rate, has enabled Israel to maintain a tolerable military balance.

Popular perceptions to the contrary, Israel has not always faced quantitative inferiority even on the battlefield. In 1948 there was rough parity, in 1956 Israel enjoyed slight superiority, and in the asymmetric operations of more recent decades, from the 1982 invasion of Lebanon to the present, it has enjoyed overwhelming superiority. Only in 1967 and 1973 did Israel suffer from clear numerical inferiority, although this was partially offset in the former by its ability to operate sequentially on the different fronts.[38] On a qualitative level, Israel enjoys a margin of superiority in areas like software, munitions, and avionics, some basic weapons platforms, tactical excellence, training, and social cohesion.[39]

Diplomatic Asymmetry. The fundamental diplomatic asymmetry in the UN and other international forums, in which Israel begins virtually all issues facing a coalition of 22 Arab countries, further augmented by a majority of Muslim and Third World countries, will continue for the foreseeable future. Moreover, since the 1980s, many Western countries have also adopted positions, on the West Bank, peace process, and other major issues, that have been highly critical of Israel, and its overall standing in the international community has plummeted. Conversely, numerous countries established diplomatic relations with Israel in the 1990s, following the Madrid Peace Conference and Oslo Accords (Russia, China, India, and Turkey, to name just a few), and since then. It is also clear that many more would like to do so, including Arab and Muslim states, subject to progress with the Palestinians. Moreover, Arab political disarray has hampered their ability to turn their numbers into concrete diplomatic action.

Changing Nature of Superpower Intervention

The United States played an absolutely decisive role in the region from the 1970s until recent years, and Israel's unique relationship with it has become a primary source of its national security. Indeed, it is hard to imagine how Israel could survive today without American support; there is no doubt that it would be immeasurably harder and would require major changes in the allocation of resources between the social and military spheres. The United States is also the primary constraint on Israeli national security policy, and Israel makes few decisions without first consulting—to a large extent really clearing them—with the United States. Indeed, Israel has become so overwhelmingly dependent on the United States that it has lost much of its freedom of independent action. We will return to this issue in chapter 10.

Russia has come to play an increasingly important role in the region in recent years, much of it highly injurious to Israeli interests. Nevertheless, the Russian constraint on Israeli policy remains much more limited than that of the Soviet Union in the past or the United States today. Russia has become a friendly state and has shown at least some willingness, on more than one occasion, to take Israeli interests into account (e.g., the delay in the sale of advanced antiaircraft systems to Iran, or establishment of a joint air deconfliction mechanism following the Russian air deployment to Syria in 2015). The EU as a whole, and some of the primary European powers separately, also play an important role for Israel, but their regional influence and the actual constraints they impose on Israeli policy are ultimately limited.

"Political time," the period available to Israel to achieve its military objectives during hostilities before international intervention either forces a ceasefire or an Israeli withdrawal, has long been a major constraint on its wartime decision-making. In the 2006 war in Lebanon, however, for the first time ever, political time was not a significant factor; the United States provided Israel with diplomatic cover, and international pressure as a whole was comparatively muted.

Political time was once again not a significant factor during the 2014 operation in Gaza. Conversely, it played a crucial role in Israel's choice of the timing for the 2008 operation in Gaza. Deeply concerned that President Obama would be less supportive of military action than his predecessors, Israel launched the operation just weeks before he took office. Political time will in all likelihood remain a major constraint in most confrontations in the future, as well.

To conclude this section: Israel's expanded post-1967 borders provided it with some strategic depth and the ability to absorb a first strike, but did not prevent the outbreak of wars and lower-level hostilities. Territory did serve as a decisive incentive for Egypt to make peace, but not for Syria or the Palestinians. Moreover, acquisition of additional territory has become a liability to be avoided, and Israel has even sought, under some governments, to withdraw from most of the 1967 territories. The disadvantages of conquering further territory, with large and hostile populations, make it increasingly difficult to transfer the ground battle to enemy territory, which is usually essential to achieve military decision.

Israel's population has grown dramatically since independence, and though it will always be at a severe quantitative disadvantage compared to the Arabs, it benefits from an important qualitative advantage. Given Arab disarray, Israel has even managed to achieve military parity and at times even quantitative superiority. Israel has maintained a thriving democracy, while the Arab countries are today in a state of crisis or collapse, and its growing economy and better mobilization of its national resources have enabled it to compete successfully. A fundamental asymmetry persists in military objectives and diplomatic clout, while superpower involvement in the region remains a major constraint on Israeli policy, if not quite as critically as in the past. Overall, however, most of the strategic constraints on Israeli defense policy have diminished over the years.

Israel's Strategic Environment Today

A small nation, a virtual city-state by international standards, Israel faces numerous and complex national security "environments," diplomatic, military, economic, and technological. Although this is true to varying extents of all states, Israel is affected by changes in a far broader external environment than most and to a far greater degree. If in the past, Israel was focused primarily on the "first-tier countries" (neighboring states) and to some extent the "second tier" (Iraq, Libya), by the 1990s Israel's national security environment had come to extend far beyond its "natural" interests and immediate neighbors, indeed, to span much of the globe.[40] To illustrate:

- Ties with the United States grew even deeper, requiring new areas of expertise and ways of thinking. From a comparatively simple patron-client relationship, bilateral ties now came to include cooperation in advanced weapons development, counterterrorism and counterproliferation programs, and strategic planning regarding issues such as Iraq and Iran. Israel even became a "major strategic partner."

- The European Union's regional role grew, and EU-Israeli relations took on a whole new range of issues, following a significant upgrade of the relationship. The possibility of Israeli membership in the EU was mooted, in the context of a final peace agreement, and significant ties were established with the North Atlantic Treaty Organization (NATO). Relations with individual European states also expanded, including military and strategic ties, even while diplomatic tensions grew.

- The collapse of the USSR led to the establishment of friendly relations with Russia, the arrival of a million immigrants in Israel, which has had a dramatic effect on Israeli society, and to a change in Russia's role in the region.

- The Far East and Indian subcontinent became areas of considerable Israeli interest as a result of North Korean and Pakistani WMD proliferation, the establishment of relations with China, with whom economic ties grew rapidly, expanding ties with Japan and a growing strategic relationship with India.

- The bombings of the Israeli embassy and Jewish community center in Buenos Aires in the early 1990s brought South America into Israel's areas of interest, particularly as it subsequently became aware that there is a large Shiite population in the region, in which Hezbollah is active. In recent years Africa too has become a focus of renewed Israeli interest, as countries such as Kenya, Uganda, Ethiopia, and more have either renewed relations or significantly strengthened existing ones.

- For both economic and military reasons, Israel found it necessary to compete at the forefront of military technology and high tech generally. As Israel's economy advanced, its interest also grew in international economic trends and organizations, such as the World Trade Organization and the Organization for Economic Cooperation and Development.

Israel is no longer just a minor player in the international drama, swept along by forces beyond its control, and its policies can have an impact on important global developments. To illustrate, Israeli intervention could have endangered American efforts to build regional and international coalitions against Iraq during the two Gulf wars. Israel's arms sales to China in the early 2000s were viewed by the United States, whether appropriately or overly dramatically, as a threat to its global security and caused a crisis in bilateral relations until Israel was forced to back down (see chapter 10). International efforts to deal with the Iranian nuclear program were motivated by fear of the potential consequences of a unilateral Israeli strike as much as by the ramifications of an Iranian nuclear capability.

The great advantages of the peace treaties with Egypt and Jordan notwithstanding, they have also somewhat reduced Israel's freedom of military maneuver,[41] as has the emergence of a positive relationship with Russia following the collapse of the USSR and a partially cooperative one with the Palestinian Authority from the mid-2000s. As long as Israel had purely adversarial relationships with these and other actors, it could act on the basis of entirely unilateral considerations, but once they had become at least partly cooperative, it had to take their interests into account as well. Recent examples of this change are Israel's limited military objectives in the operations against Hamas in 2008 and 2012, in which preservation of relations with Egypt was a primary constraining factor; the careful manner in which Israel has handled disagreements with Moscow over its policies toward Iran, Syria, and the Ukrainian crisis in 2014; and in the relationship with the Palestinian Authority, in which Israel has refrained from fully exercising its military might.

The regional turmoil that began with the "Arab Spring" has transformed the Middle Eastern strategic landscape, weakening many of the military threats Israel faces, at least in the medium term, while posing new dangers of its own. An Arab world preoccupied with severe domestic crises is less able to mount credible challenges to Israel, individually and collectively. Indeed, Israel now faces weak and even failed states on all of its borders.

The civil war that broke out in Syria in 2011 and the rise of ISIS in 2014 threatened not just the future of the regime, but Syria's very existence as a state. Syria has become a devastated failed state, unified in name only, and its internal weaknesses and dislocations will continue to be a source of potential instability for years to come.

The Syrian military, already suffering from a poorly trained and badly outdated Soviet-era force structure, has been weakened dramatically by the civil war, and it will be many years, at the very least, before it can once again pose a significant military threat to Israel. The growing role of Hezbollah and Iran in Syria, including a growing presence along the Golan Heights border with Israel, means that the likelihood of hostilities may grow, even if at a lower level.[42] As of this writing, a number of limited military incidents have already taken place, with the potential for further escalation. Moreover, Syria retains a residual chemical warfare capability, despite the regime's commitment to destroy its chemical arsenal in 2013, some of which fell into the hands of ISIS,[43] and which may still fall into the hands of Hezbollah or some other radical group. The heinous character of the Assad regime and the rigidity and extremism of its foreign policy notwithstanding, the painful lessons it learned in 1967 and 1973 had the great benefit of making it extraordinarily risk averse and cautious in its dealings with Israel.

For Israel, virtually any resolution of the civil war is likely to have significantly adverse consequences. Should the Assad regime, or at least an Allawite one, ultimately remain in power, it will be largely due to the extensive assistance provided by Iran, Hezbollah, and Russia. Syria, long a close ally of Iran and Hezbollah, is likely to come under far greater, possibly decisive, Iranian influence. Accordingly, it stands to become a forward base for Iran, whose enmity toward Israel constitutes the greatest military threat it faces today, as well as a greatly expanded operating space and source of weapons for Hezbollah. In effect, Syria and Lebanon would become one extended northern front, causing a severe deterioration in Israel's posture in the area. This has already begun happening.

Russia's renewed role in Syria has also already had significant effects for Israel. Not only did Russia play a decisive role in saving the Assad regime, which may have been on the ropes despite the Iranian-Hezbollah intervention, but its deployment of advanced antiaircraft systems in Syria, with ranges that cover much of Israeli territory, pose a potentially severe constraint on the IAF's freedom of maneuver.[44] In practice, Russia's interests are different from Iran's and Hezbollah's, may partially counterbalance their future domination of Syria, and prove to be a stabilizing force.

Conversely, should parts of Syria ultimately be taken over by various other opposition groups, which largely comprise extremist Islamic forces, an increasingly unlikely eventuality at this point, they may behave in radical and reckless ways, leading to increasing hostilities. Whichever eventuality ultimately plays out, Syria will be far weaker, but also a source of great instability and a variety of new threats. After over 40 years of quiet, the Golan Heights has once again become an active and particularly combustible front.

Iraq, too, at the time of this writing, is no longer a truly unified state. The Kurdish autonomous region is just shy of full independence, and Shiite Iraq is increasingly subject to Iranian influence. Accordingly, Iraq constitutes a growing threat to the stability of Jordan and Saudi Arabia, two of Israel's neighbors whose external behavior has long been moderate, and thus an indirect threat to Israeli security. One can also not discount the danger of Iraq once again becoming a direct danger to Israel in the future. The creation of an Iranian-dominated arc, from Iran through Iraq and into Syria and Lebanon, presents a significant change for the worse in the regional balance of power, with potentially severe ramifications for Israel. Since Iran is the only state in the region that still aspires to a nuclear capability in the foreseeable future, the nuclear agreement in 2015 notwithstanding, an Iranian-dominated Syria would appear to be the worst outcome for Israel.

For all practical purposes, Lebanon has been a failed state ever since the early 1970s. Its ongoing internecine conflicts and inability to control the terrorist organizations operating from its territory, especially the Palestine Liberation Organization (PLO) from the late 1960s to the early 1980s and Hezbollah ever since, has repeatedly forced Israel to intervene, beginning with the Litani Operation in 1978 and numerous operations ever since, and culminating in the 2006 war. At present, Lebanon's internal dislocations continue, exacerbated by events in neighboring Syria, and a renewed Lebanese civil war is an ever-present danger. Hezbollah, by far the most powerful actor in Lebanon today, remains committed to Israel's long-term destruction, and renewed hostilities are possible at any time. Although there have now been more than 10 unprecedented years of quiet on the Lebanese border, due partly to the deterrent effect Israel achieved during the 2006 war and partly Hezbollah's involvement in the fighting in Syria, it is unclear how long this calm will continue. At some point, renewed hostilities with Hezbollah appear almost inevitable. Given Hezbollah's vast rocket and missile arsenal, the next round will be highly painful for both sides.

The domestic convulsions in Egypt, following the overthrow of President Mubarak, further exacerbated its loss of control over Sinai, which had already become largely lawless during his later years. The breakdown in law and order in Sinai has led to a number of terrorist attacks against Israel and ended over 30 years of virtually complete quiet on the Egyptian-Israeli border. It has also caused bilateral tensions, and, at least during the brief reign of Muslim Brotherhood president Morsi, even posed some danger to the peace treaty. By 2015–2016, conversely, rising ISIS activity in Sinai had become the basis for unprecedented bilateral security cooperation.[45] Egyptian-US relations, long a mainstay of the peace with Israel, have taken a marked turn for the worse since the fall of the Mubarak regime, at the same time that Egypt has improved its ties with Russia.

Even if current Egyptian president al-Sissi succeeds in stabilizing Egypt politically and it avoids becoming a failed state in the near term, Egypt's dire poverty and burgeoning population mean that the long-term danger to its stability, and consequently to the peace with Israel, is significant. Furthermore, a domestically unstable Egypt will be unable to play a moderating role in the Arab world. As it is, Egypt has been unable to regain the regional leadership it lost many years ago. For Israel, for whom the peace treaty with Egypt has become a fundamental pillar of its national security, Egypt's future course is of vital importance.

So far, Jordan has weathered the regional turmoil of recent years comparatively well. Nevertheless, unrest continues, and Jordan's fundamental challenges, especially its poverty and the ongoing tensions between the "East Bankers" and growing Palestinian majority, further exacerbated by the huge influx of refugees from Syria and Iraq, currently some 20% of the population, continue to pose threats to its long-term stability and viability. In recent decades, Jordan's location as a buffer between Israel and more radical Arab states turned the ongoing viability of the Jordanian regime into a foremost Israeli interest.

Gaza and the West Bank are under rival Palestinian governments, neither of which has a monopoly over force and full control of its territory. In recent years, the Palestinian Authority (PA) in the West Bank has somewhat strengthened its governing institutions and, in partial cooperation with Israel, its security control as well. Nevertheless, the PA's long-term future as a governing entity is unclear, whether because of internal Palestinian divisions or as a result of frustrations over the failure of the peace process. The process of succession following President Abbas, presumably the last of the leaders of Fatah's founding era, may also prove destabilizing and could even lead to the collapse of the PA. Hamas remains in control of Gaza, which has become a radical, impoverished, and theocratic ministate. Gaza's demographic explosion and social tensions will further contribute to the "exporting" of its domestic troubles to Israel in the form of rocket fire and other types of violence. The already bleak prospects for peace and the establishment of a Palestinian state are further reduced by Palestinian divisions.

Saudi Arabia is in the midst of both unprecedented domestic change and an energy crisis, stemming from the collapse of oil prices starting in the mid-2010s, as well as a growing rivalry with Iran. The succession process, including the rise of a dynamic, but brash new leader, may threaten the stability of the regime, as some of the grandsons of the founder, Ibn Aziz, and others feel passed over. Unless Saudi Arabia succeeds in dramatically diversifying its energy resources, as called for by the 15-year economic plan unveiled in 2016, it is, remarkably, expected to become a net importer of oil by around 2030,[46] with grave implications for its future.

Regime change in Saudi Arabia, should it happen, is likely to be in the form of an even harsher Islamist state. Already one of the world's most radical states domestically, Saudi Arabia has been relatively moderate in its external behavior and has not posed a significant threat to date to Israel's security, but this could change rapidly in the event of regime instability or change. A combination of the Saudis' financial resources and petro-influence, large arsenal of the most sophisticated American weapons, and ability to procure virtually any weapons they wish, possibly including nuclear ones, could present new and severe threats to Israel. At the time of this writing, however, there have been some as yet limited, but tantalizing signs, that a shared fear of Iran's expanding influence in the region, may be leading to an initial thaw in Saudi attitudes toward Israel.[47] The Saudis, in any event, are increasingly coming to fill the void in Arab leadership stemming from the loss of Egypt's regional position.

Further afield, ongoing instability in the Arab world could lead to the rise of a number of additional failed states. Libya, Sudan, and Yemen already are failed states. Advanced weapons from Libya's former military forces have made their way to Gaza, and not all of its chemical arsenal has been secured or accounted for. Tunisia and Morocco, the Arab states most amenable to a relationship with Israel in the past, both face significant problems of domestic stability, as does Bahrain.

Failed states present a further threat to Israel's security because of the heightened opportunities they afford for external involvement, both by state and by nonstate actors. Syria, Iran, and Saudi Arabia have been deeply involved in Lebanon. Iran, Saudi Arabia, Qatar, Hezbollah, ISIS, Russia, and the United States have all been deeply involved in the Syrian civil war. Iran is deeply involved in Iraq, as are the United States and Hezbollah. Failed states also provide fertile ground for terrorist organizations, as a refuge and source of activists. Syria and Iraq have become focal points for al-Qaeda, ISIS, and other jihadists from around the world. In Lebanon, Hezbollah and other terrorist organizations have taken over where the state is absent, as have jihadi organizations in the Sinai. Sudan and Yemen have become way stations for organizations such as al-Qaeda and for sponsors of terrorism such as Iran. Yemen has exported jihadi activists to Gaza and, together with Sudan, become a transit point for Iranian arms shipments to Gaza. Most dangerously, failed states may be unable to ensure effective control over their WMD capabilities.[48]

Many years after it began, the root causes of the Arab Spring continue to exist, even more so, including a huge demographic explosion, large numbers of impoverished people with limited prospects, especially among the young, an absence of political freedoms and effective governance, and great income disparities. The failure of the Arab Spring to address these fundamental problems, indeed, the grave further deterioration that has taken place in most of the region, indicates that the pressures for change will continue to build and that the Middle East will remain highly combustible for years, if not decades, to come. The ramifications for Israel's security are manifold and potentially severe.

In these circumstances, one of the greatest threats Israel faces today is no longer from the strength of its Arab neighbors, but their weakness, and the danger that domestic instability, when combined with weak and failing governments, will lead to renewed hostilities. Each individual actor may be weaker than the more centralized Arab states of the past, but overall the Middle East may be characterized by a growing number of radical actors willing to use force, including nonstate actors.[49] A particular danger is that a local incident with one of the nonstate actors, which the weak state-actors are unable to prevent, may escalate, lead to a significant attack on Israel's home front, and even deteriorate into a confrontation with the host country. Tactical events risk escalations of strategic importance.[50]

Iran has become one of the primary actors in the region, arguably the driving force, and the most sophisticated adversary Israel has ever faced. It poses the greatest threat to Israel's national security today, not just because of its nuclear program, massive support for Hezbollah and in the past Hamas, and active efforts to derail the peace process, but also due to its carefully calculated approach to its long-term objective of weakening and ultimately destroying Israel. The 2006 war in Lebanon has been dubbed the first Iranian-Israeli war,[51] and events in Syria, should they further deteriorate, could be the basis for the second. Despite the 2015 nuclear deal Iran has probably not given up its long-term nuclear aspirations and may be biding its time instead until more propitious circumstances arise.[52] The nuclear threat will thus still be with us for quite some time, and the overall confrontation with Iran will continue to be one of the primary issues Israel faces for the foreseeable future.

The Sunni states harbor similar fears of Iran's hegemonic ambitions in the region and are at least as wary of the nuclear deal the United States concluded with it as Israel. While there are no immediate indications of a decision by any of the Sunni states to begin military nuclear programs in response, a number have begun civil programs in recent years, for energy purposes, but which can be used as the technological basis for later attempts to develop military ones. Down the line there is a danger of a multinuclear Middle East, a daunting prospect given the nature of the regimes, their instability, and tense relations with each other.

The entire region is undergoing a dramatic period of change, whose ultimate outcome, once the dust settles, is far from clear. It is, however, likely to result in change to at least part of the colonial division of the Middle East into separate nation-states. Some states may fragment, resulting in new states, cross-border entities, and lawless areas. Increasingly, people throughout the region are turning, or returning, to their fundamental identities, Sunni, Shiite, or tribal, rather than their national ones.[53] Transnational organizations such as al-Qaeda, and those who aspire to such a role, for example, the Muslim Brotherhood and Hezbollah, may play an increasingly important role.

The region today is divided between four contending camps, one Shiite and three Sunni. The Shiite camp, led by Iran, includes Hezbollah, Assad's Syria, much of Iraq, and the Palestinian Islamic Jihad. The Sunni side includes the so-called pragmatic camp, led today by Saudi Arabia, together with Egypt, Jordan, and the smaller Gulf states; the Salafi-Jihadi camp, such as al-Qaeda, ISIS, and various other organizations; and the political Islamists, with Turkey at the center, the Muslim Brotherhood, and Qatar. All of the camps are deeply hostile to Israel, but their enmity toward each other, at least in the short term, is as great or even greater.

Rising Islamism and with it the growing clash between the Sunni and Shia worlds have been among the central trends in the Middle East in recent decades and are likely to continue to be so, with important ramifications for Israel. Indeed, the Middle East has come to be defined today largely by Iran's pursuit of regional hegemony and the countervailing spread of radical Sunni ideologies and forces. The result, as Robert Satloff has pointed out, is a vast area in which Israel is not only unwelcome, but in which it finds itself increasingly compelled to build fences along its borders, both physical and psychological, to isolate itself from the cataclysmic battles taking place all around.[54]

In most parts of the region, such as Syria, Iraq, and Bahrain, the two forces are locked in a battle for primacy, but the Arab-Israeli arena has provided a unique opportunity to join forces against a common enemy and is likely to do again in the future. Shiite Iran, for example, has provided weapons to Sunni Hamas, while Sunni Qatar, Tunisia, Turkey, and Egypt (under the brief tenure of President Morsi) provided Hamas with diplomatic and financial support. Predominantly Sunni Syria has long had an extraordinarily close relationship with Iran, directed against Israel, and provided considerable military and other assistance to its Shiite proxy, Hezbollah.[55] Conversely, the Sunni fear of Iran has led to some initial signs of willingness to open up to Israel and cooperate, albeit to a very limited extent.

The rise of Islamism, or religiosity generally, in Israel too, has the effect of changing the region's conflicts from national conflicts to religious ones,[56] making them even more intractable, indeed, potentially unresolvable. The conflict was already extraordinarily bitter and resistant to resolution during the decades when it was primarily a territorial battle between conflicting national movements. The absolutist nature of religious fundamentalism—what former Israeli cabinet minister and leading strategic thinker Dan Meridor has called "the return of God"—further diminishes the possibility of compromise and reconciliation. It also makes it harder for major powers, such as the United States, to exercise a moderating influence on regional players.[57] In effect, Israel is now surrounded by nonstate Islamist actors on almost all sides: Hezbollah and numerous other groups on the northern border, Hamas in Gaza, and ISIS and others in the Sinai.

The primary power centers in the region no longer border Israel and have moved toward the Gulf, with Iran and Saudi Arabia the primary contending poles, and possibly Turkey, too. The Arab-Israeli conflict, the Palestinian issue in particular, have been shunted aside, as the Arab world has become preoccupied with its greater internal divides and increasingly weary of the issue. Identification with the Palestinians remains a primary source of consensus and identification in the Arab world, nevertheless.

The United States is still a primary player in the Middle East, indeed, the one almost all actors in the region look to either as a source of their security or a threat to it. Nevertheless, its regional stature is at a decades-long nadir and long-term trends in the region will pose ongoing challenges to its restoration, possibly partly counterbalanced by the decrease in American dependence on Middle Eastern oil. Changes in American policy, as well as international and regional developments, could reverse the decline, but restoring US stature will not be easy and will take time. For Israel, whose strategic and military posture is intimately linked to American global and regional influence, the ramifications are significant. The United States is an ultimate guarantor of Israeli security, only the United States can lead international efforts to confront such major threats as the Iranian nuclear program, and only the United States, to date, has successfully brokered peace agreements between Israel and its neighbors. With Egypt weakened as well, two of the mainstays of regional stability can no longer play their long-standing moderating roles.

As US influence in the region has waned, Russia's stature has grown, especially after President Putin's apparent decision to make the Middle East a primary arena of renewed US-Russian competition. On a variety of important issues, such as the Iranian nuclear program, Syrian civil war and chemical weapons, peace process, arms sales, and more, Israel and Russia have found themselves on opposing sides. Nevertheless, Russia is no longer an adversarial state; indeed, the bilateral relationship is quite strong. Moscow's policies on these issues are not directed against Israel, detrimental to its security though they often are, and both sides do strive to take each other's interests into account. For its own reasons, however, Russia is likely to play an increasingly problematic role for Israel in coming years.

Europe, both the EU as a collective body and leading European powers individually, has been an increasingly important actor for Israel. Europe played a major role in the Iranian nuclear issue in recent years and its long-standing opposition to Israel's policies on the Palestinian issue has been a source of both growing bilateral friction and of the deterioration in Israel's overall international standing. Europe, as a whole, is Israel's primary trading partner, and there are extensive political, socioeconomic, and, increasingly, military ties with a variety of European countries. Accordingly, Europe will continue to grow in importance for Israel, particularly if US influence in the region continues to decline, but relations are likely to become even tenser, with growing pressures for sanctions and other measures against Israel.

China, for the most part, has stayed out of regional diplomatic and security issues and has thus yet to become a major player in the Middle East or significant factor in Israel's strategic (but not economic) calculus. Nevertheless, as a permanent member of the Security Council, where it generally opposes sanctions and other forms of direct intervention, China has taken positions on a number of regional issues that have been highly problematic for Israel, for example, the Iranian nuclear issue, Syria, and the peace process. To date, China's primary involvement in the region has focused on the purchase of large and rapidly growing quantities of oil, a trend that may lead to growing interest in greater diplomatic and military influence as well.

One of the greatest problems Israel faces today is from changing international norms and its growing international isolation. Partly, of course, this is simply a result of the controversial policies it has pursued for decades, first and foremost in regard to the West Bank. It is, however, also very much a result of the concerted campaign of diplomatic warfare and delegitimization that the Arab states have conducted against it for decades, increasingly joined in recent years by pro-Palestinian activists and NGOs around the world.

One of the primary changes in international norms is the growing illegitimacy of territorial conquest and, increasingly, of the use of force at all, certainly the disproportionate force usually needed to achieve military decision.[58] International norms such as this, along with the growing role of the international media, serve to decrease Israel's ability to make effective use of military force, whereas non-state actors and even some state actors, such as Iran and Syria, are not bound by the same strictures. In the crucial battle for legitimacy and international opinion, the more Israel uses military force and the greater the number of casualties caused, the more it loses. Indeed, Israel is increasingly encountering the limits of military power, which can often become counterproductive. Although Israel enjoys clear conventional superiority, some of its state and nonstate adversaries are pursuing "asymmetric strategic parity," or even mutually assured destruction (MAD), through the asymmetric capabilities they have developed in response.[59]

Today, nonmilitary power, such as economic clout, moral suasion, and "soft power," are both increasingly accepted and of growing effectiveness.[60] Palestinian leader Abbas, for example, came to the conclusion that terrorism had become counterproductive to Palestinian interests, spoke out publicly against it—though on pragmatic, not moral grounds—and in so doing improved the Palestinians' international standing. Today, the Palestinians are waging an effective campaign to internationalize the conflict with Israel, delegitimize it, and position themselves as the "moral David" to Israel's Goliath. The Turkish government's support for an international flotilla designed to break the blockade of Gaza in 2010 caused Israel severe diplomatic harm without the need for military force. The international community was able to coalesce around the need for economic sanctions on Iran, not military action, and it was the sanctions that ultimately led Iran to the negotiating table and to the final nuclear deal. NGOs, human rights organizations, and even major corporations have come to play an even greater role in international affairs.

To conclude this section: Israel's military victories convinced most of the Arab states to forgo their efforts to destroy it. Egypt and Jordan made peace, Syria has been greatly weakened, and the prospects of renewed warfare with any Arab state are minimal. Israel has not faced an existential threat for decades, and the active conflict with Arab actors is now limited to painful irregular warfare with nonstate players and terrorism. Israel faces growing international delegitimization but has relations with more countries than ever, a number of special relationships, and a unique one with the United States.

Conversely, Israel has not gained acceptance by the Arab world. Even Egypt and Jordan really only terminated belligerence, rather than making peace, and Israel's military victories have not yielded extended respites from hostilities. New threats have replaced those that have diminished, and Iran is an adversary of unprecedented sophistication, which may pose an existential threat if it acquires nuclear weapons. Although Israel's overall strategic circumstances have improved considerably, it continues to face a daunting array of threats.

Many in Israel believe that the primary reason for the conflict's perpetuation is a fundamental Arab and broader Muslim refusal to accept its right to exist as a Jewish state, not the 1967 issues (territories, settlements, Jerusalem). Some Arab actors may have acceded to Israel's existence as a temporary expedient, but the Arabs as a whole, and Iran, are believed to be unalterably committed to its demise. Others perceive far greater room for accommodation.

The jury is still out. Iran, Hezbollah, Hamas, and many others explicitly seek Israel's destruction as a concrete, if long-term, objective. At a minimum, the "moderates" remain committed to a restoration of the 1967 lines and establishment of a Palestinian state; the as yet open question is whether they have truly abandoned the battle over Israel's existence. The failures of the dramatic attempts to reach peace in 2000 and 2008, as well as the negotiations in 2014, make it unlikely that significant progress will be achieved for the foreseeable future, and the Palestinian issue will remain the primary strategic challenge Israel faces.

Primary Observations

- Israel's strategic environment has been transformed, mostly for the better. The Arab world is in a crisis, and the primary threat it poses to Israel today stems from its weakness, not strength. Israel no longer faces existential threats, or even major conventional ones, but nonstate actors have become significant threats, and Iran may still become an existential one if it acquires nuclear weapons.
- The prospects for peace with the Palestinians are meager, at least for the foreseeable future, regardless of Israel's policies. It is an open question whether the conflict with them is over the 1967 issues or over Israel's very existence. In the case of Iran, Hezbollah, and Hamas, there is no question. Nevertheless, Israel's policies have a decisive impact on the prospects for a future agreement and its international standing.
- Superpower involvement in the region remains a major constraint on Israeli policy, but less than in the past. The decrease in US stature adversely affects Israel, whose strategic posture is heavily dependent on it. Russia has become increasingly influential.

- Israel's post-1967 borders provide some strategic depth and the ability to absorb a first strike but have not prevented the outbreak of wars and lower-level hostilities. Moreover, settlements largely negate the strategic depth acquired, and the de facto annexation of the West Bank incorporates Palestinian terrorism into Israel itself.
- Acquisition of additional populated territory has become a liability that Israel seeks to avoid, and, on a few occasions, it has even sought to withdraw from most of the 1967 territories. Without territorial acquisition, it is difficult to transfer the ground battle to enemy territory and achieve military decision.
- Israel continues to suffer from fundamental asymmetries with the Arabs, but its qualitative advantage, growing economy, better mobilization of its resources, and US assistance have enabled it to compete quantitatively as well. Given Arab disarray, Israel has managed to achieve quantitative parity and even superiority.
- Israel's classic defense doctrine was a dramatic success. Israel not only survived but flourished. The overall military threat and strategic constraints Israel faces have eased considerably, and Israel is more powerful, relative to its adversaries, than ever. The situation is not static, however, and Israel must be prepared for the worst.

3

The Changing Military Threat

The wars today are conducted in the rear. The rear is the battlefield.
—General Sammy Tourgeman, commander of
the southern front, May 2015

The primary threats envisioned by Israel's classic defense doctrine stemmed from conventional military attacks by neighboring Arab countries (the "first tier"), possibly acting in concert, with some assistance from countries in the "second tier" (Libya, Iraq) and others. Today, the nature of warfare has changed dramatically and, consequently, the military threats Israel faces. The threat of a large-scale conventional war with an Arab state, or even a limited one, is the least likely contingency, there is little prospect of Israeli territory being conquered, and the danger of an Arab war coalition is now almost nonexistent.[1]

The primary dangers Israel faces today stem from various forms of irregular and asymmetric warfare, including terrorism and rocket fire, cyber-warfare, and ballistic missiles. In the future, WMD, especially nuclear weapons, may once again become the dominant threat. With the important exception of Iran, the threat today is from nonstate actors, motivated by radical Islamist ideologies, not states.

In 2013 IDF CoS Gantz offered the following sobering assessment of how a future confrontation might begin. One scenario envisioned a multifront confrontation triggered by an Israeli response to an antitank missile fired at an IDF patrol along the Syrian border, with Islamist organizations trying to penetrate the Golan Heights, Hezbollah firing rockets on virtually all of Israel, rocket fire on Eilat from jihadis in Sinai, and hundreds of Hamas activists storming an Israeli checkpoint on the Gaza border. Alternatively, according to Ganz, a future conflict might begin with a missile hitting the General Staff headquarters in Tel Aviv, a cyber-attack paralyzing public services, from traffic lights to banks, or a Hamas attack on a nursery school.[2]

Technology, today, partly offsets distance, and the Middle East has become part of an extended, if not yet quite global battlefield. Far-off countries, such as

Iraq and Libya, in the 1990s and early 2000s, and Iran, today, can pose greater dangers to Israel than its neighbors, as can truly distant ones like Pakistan and North Korea. Although not directly involved in the Arab-Israeli conflict, their nuclear and missile assistance to Iran, Syria, and other states in the region has had an important effect on Israel's national security. Palestinian terrorism was mostly local; al-Qaeda and ISIS are global phenomena. Nuclear and missile proliferation networks span the world. Cyber-attacks can be launched from virtually anywhere on earth.

Modern satellites and GPS systems enable militaries to track both their own and enemy forces around the globe. Territory and strategic depth remain of great importance even in an era of rockets, missiles, and unmanned aerial vehicles,[3] but borders and topography are of little relevance to them. Precision weapons have greatly undermined the utility of conventional military forces, especially armor, and allow an attacker to target not just major sites, such as airbases, but even specific aircraft shelters. Weapons today have far greater capabilities, with one aircraft, for example, capable of doing the work of a number in the past.

Modern warfare has become nearly continuous, especially with nonstate actors, without clearly identifiable beginnings and ends. The civilian home front and military rear, not the borders or front lines, are often the primary arena of modern warfare, which often becomes a matter of mutual damage and deterrence. Moreover, new technologies have led to the empowerment of nonstate actors and even individuals, who can make use of them to achieve destruction of a magnitude previously reserved for state actors, whether through terrorism, cyber-warfare, rockets, or WMD. The new superempowered nonstate actor can also operate "under the radar" far more easily, creating a problem of identifying and locating the enemy, or the absence of a "return address," which is vital for deterrence.[4]

The following chapter sets out the primary changes that have taken place in the nature of the military threats Israel faces. It begins with the conventional threats, then turns to the irregular and asymmetric ones, the primary threats today, including rocket and missile arsenals and cyber-warfare, and finally to the threats posed by unconventional weapons. The chapter concludes with a few words regarding the military ramifications of potential peace agreements with the Palestinians and Syria.

Conventional Military Threats

The Arab states never actually realized their potential capability to hit Israel's home front during the early decades, and WMD threats were not yet a primary concern. Israel has faced terrorism ever since its establishment, actually long

before, but it was considered a secondary threat until the late 1980s, and counterterrorism operations, known at the time as "current security," were relegated
to a place of lesser importance. In these circumstances, the IDF's force structure
and operational concepts, indeed, virtually all Israeli strategic thinking, were
concentrated on the one overwhelming preoccupation of a conventional battle
with the Arab armies on the borders or military front.

In reality, the threat of conventional warfare had already diminished greatly
after the peace treaty with Egypt in 1979, the weakening of the "eastern front"
following the Iran-Iraq war in the 1980s and two Gulf Wars in 1991 and 2003,
and the disappearance of the Soviet Union as Syria's and Iraq's superpower patron. Indeed, it has been well over four decades since the last major conventional
confrontation, during the Yom Kippur War, and this type of warfare is unlikely
to recur for the foreseeable future, if at all.[5]

During the 1980s and 1990s Israel continued to fear a limited Syrian
conventional attack designed to retake part of the Golan Heights, possibly
augmented by an Iraqi expeditionary force. Under this scenario, essentially
a limited variant on the Yom Kippur War, Syria would seek to exploit its significant advantage in standing forces in order to achieve surprise and grab
almost any piece of territory, no matter how small, on the assumption that
the narrow and densely defended Golan front would provide only limited
opportunity for maneuver and thereby neutralize Israel's military superiority.[6] The presumed objective was not to defeat Israel, but to improve Syria's
negotiating posture in postwar talks and freeze its gains in place before the
IDF had time to mobilize and the international community could impose a
ceasefire. The scenario never materialized in practice, and the great disparity
in capabilities made it increasingly unlikely by the mid-1990s, almost unthinkable ever since.

The dramatic advances in warfare beginning in the 1990s, commonly called
the Revolution in Military Affairs (RMA), decisively shifted the military balance
from one based on quantity to quality, and thus in Israel's favor. For Syria, the
problem was further exacerbated by its inability to modernize its forces following
the collapse of the Soviet Union, as a result of which they fell decades behind
modern standards. Even Syria's advanced air defense system did not keep up
with improvements made by the IAF. Israel, in contrast, with US assistance, was
able to modernize its forces to a far greater degree. It was also an international
front runner in the RMA, which provided it with a far greater capability to destroy armored and other targets both from the air and from the ground. In so
doing, it further diminished the already limited prospects of a Syrian attempt
to regain territory through military action. Israeli and foreign observers are in
agreement that the overall gap in Israel's favor had increased, in most areas,[7] long
before the Syrian civil war broke out.

Nevertheless, Syria remained the only confrontation state among Israel's immediate neighbors and wielded a sizable and potent conventional military capability until the civil war devastated it. If few had doubted the final outcome of a confrontation with Syria, it would have been very costly for Israel, nevertheless. Moreover, Syria was pursuing a military nuclear capability until an air strike, thought to be Israeli, destroyed its nuclear reactor in 2007. Syria also had a very large chemical weapons arsenal, possibly the third largest in the world, and retains a residual capability today, even after it was forced to dismantle most of the arsenal under international pressure in 2014. It may also still have some biological weapons. Accordingly, Syria was the primary basis for Israeli force planning during the decades following the peace treaty with Egypt.[8]

Cognizant of its military weakness, Syria sought to use the limited resources at its disposal, in the years prior to the civil war, to develop a number of specific capabilities designed to offset key elements of Israel's military superiority. Drawing on lessons learned from Hezbollah's successes in the war in 2006, and with Iran's guidance and financial support, Syria partly restructured its forces and conducted an arms buildup that was unprecedented in magnitude in recent decades, though limited to a few areas. The Syrian army, heretofore heavily armored and mechanized, greatly improved its infantry and commando capabilities, supported by advanced antitank missiles and an arsenal of some 100,000 missiles and rockets capable of reaching any target in Israel. Syria also invested heavily in naval missiles, a limited number of advanced combat aircraft, and, as mentioned, chemical weapons.[9]

Adopting Iran's and Hezbollah's approach, Syria no longer sought to defeat Israel in one or more major rounds, but to wage an ongoing war of attrition designed to erode its military superiority in the long term. A future war might still have included armored battles, but the Syrians would presumably have focused primarily on use of their massive missile and rocket arsenals, in order to hit Israel's cities and infrastructure, and more selective use of the limited number of precise missiles they had to attack IDF targets, such as airbases, staging areas, and command-and-control sites. As part of the growing focus on attrition, the Syrians also built many villages along the border to force the IDF into difficult urban warfare, and dug numerous antitank obstacles.[10] As it is, Syria's defenses on the Golan Heights were long considered to be among the densest in the world.

The civil war has left Syria's military in a shambles. Syria also used most of its rocket and missile arsenal during the fighting, and the forced dismantlement of most of its chemical weapons has left it without a strategic deterrent.[11] It will be many years before Syria again constitutes a major threat to Israel. Conversely, as noted in chapter 2, Iran's and Hezbollah's presence in Syria and the consequent emergence of one united northern front, extending from Lebanon into Syria, as well as Russia's new role there, have created new dangers for Israel.

Despite decades of US military assistance, approximately one-third of the Egyptian army is still based on obsolete Soviet weapons. Moreover, it has been decades since the Egyptian army last participated in combat, and its operational capabilities have been further degraded by the domestic turmoil of recent years. Nevertheless, the Egyptian army remains the largest Arab military, the one without which other Arab countries do not have a viable conventional option against Israel, and most of its forces today are equipped with advanced American weaponry. It thus still constitutes a potentially formidable foe, certainly given time to prepare, and Egypt's future course may hold the key to the Arab-Israeli conventional balance.[12]

The Saudi army, though smaller than Egypt's, is still sizable and is equipped with large quantities of the absolutely latest in American weaponry. As demonstrated by its intervention in Yemen in 2015, however, its actual ability to conduct offensive operations is uneven, primarily due to manpower problems. Saudi Arabia never participated in large numbers in any of the Arab-Israeli wars (it did send a brigade to Syria during the Yom Kippur War), but the potential exists and must be taken into account, especially given the challenges to its future stability. A Saudi Arabia led by an actively hostile regime, with the resources to procure vast quantities of advanced weapons from virtually all potential sources, could pose a serious threat.

With expanded US assistance, Jordan has been relatively successful in modernizing its forces in recent years, both ground and air. They remain well trained, though of comparatively small size.[13]

Iraq does not present a military threat to Israel for the foreseeable future, and its future as a state is still in doubt. It may, however, become a threat in the longer term, especially given its oil revenues, and a resurgent Iraq might have strategic reasons for once again pursuing WMD capabilities. For the meantime, it is Iraq's weakness, which essentially allowed Iran to incorporate it into its sphere of influence and provided for the rise of ISIS, that is the danger.

In stark contrast with these generally positive trends, a huge conventional military buildup is currently underway in the Middle East. As seen in Tables 3.1–3.2, most of this buildup was by the Gulf States, primarily Saudi Arabia, whose military expenditures between 2000–2014 exceeded Iran's by a factor of almost four and accounted for roughly half of the Gulf States' whopping $1.1 trillion in total military expenditures. In terms of weapons purchases alone (i.e., without manpower and infrastructure costs), the Gulf States spent $53.9 billion between 2007 and 2014, of which the Saudis again accounted for about half. The impact of the international sanctions on Iran and of low oil prices account for the comparatively paltry $0.6 billion it spent on weapons purchases. Egypt, Jordan, and Syria, in contrast, continued significant purchases, though on a very different order of magnitude from the Saudis.

Table 3.1 **Total Military Expenditures, Gulf States (2014 current billion USD)**

	2000	*2005*	*2010*	*2012*	*2014*	*Total 2000–2014*
All Gulf States	46.7	49.7	89.5	120.8	150.2	1,129.9
Saudi Arabia	19.9	20.1	45.2	56.7	80.7	567.0
Iran	12.4	7.2	9.4	18.1	15.7	149.0

Source: International Institute for Strategic Studies, as adapted from Cordesman 2015, p. 10.

Table 3.2 **Arms Deliveries to Select Middle Eastern States (2014 current billion USD)**

	2007–2010	*2011–2014*	*Total*
All Gulf States	**18.4**	**35.5**	**53.9**
Saudi Arabia	10.9	16	26.9
Iran	0.5	0.1	0.6
Egypt	4.9	6.1	11.0
Jordan	1.4	1.6	3.0
Syria	2.2	2.4	4.6
Total	26.9	45.6	72.5

Source: US government data, as adapted from Theohary 2015, pp. 49–50.

The weapons procured include the latest in military technology, including aircraft, missiles, antiaircraft systems, tanks, and more. The overwhelming majority of the arms sales were American, though in recent years there has also been a worrying uptick in Russians sales, especially to Iran. Given the uncertain future stability of most of the recipients, including Saudi Arabia, Egypt, and Jordan, the military buildup is a source of considerable concern in Israel.

Table 3.1 provides a picture of the total military expenditures of the Gulf States as a whole and of Saudi Arabia and Iran separately. Table 3.2 shows actual arms deliveries to the primary Middle Eastern states between 2007 and 2014.

Table 3.3 provides a quantitative picture of the regional military balance today.

Irregular and Asymmetric Threats

By the 1990s Israel's conventional superiority was such that its adversaries concluded that they no longer had an option to wage large-scale conventional warfare against it. As has always happened throughout military history, however,

Table 3.3 **The IDF Compared to Primary Arab Militaries and Iran, 2015**

	IDF	Egypt	Jordan	Syria (2012)	Iraq	Saudi Arabia	Iran
Personnel (active, reserve)	649,500	917,500	180,500	492,000	209,000	251,500	873,000
Tanks	1,260	2,710	752	4,800	270	730	1,663
Combat aircraft	440	584	75	262	16	325	334
APCs / armored vehicles	1,300	4,060	1,014	4,540	2,502	1,573	640
Artillery	960	4,468	1,429	3,620	1,061	831	8,798

Source: International Institute for Strategic Studies: The Military Balance 2016 (except Syria, 2013 IISS Military Balance), www-tandfonline-com.ezp-prod1.hul.harvard.edu/toc/tmib20/116/1.

when one side has gained overwhelming superiority, the other has sought to develop a new and different response to redress the imbalance. In the case of asymmetric responses, the strategy is based on the attempt to turn the scale against the militarily stronger side, both by exploiting its weak points and, conversely, by utilizing the weaker side's strengths. The latter, for example, may attach greater importance to the conflict, be more determined and resolved, and thus willing to accept greater risks and casualties. For Israel's adversaries, its weak points are its vulnerable home front and military rear, and sensitivity both to military and to civilian casualties. The responses they developed are thus all aimed at targeting Israel's home front and military rear.[14]

As long as the threats Israel faced stemmed primarily from Arab militaries deployed along its borders, and from cross-border Palestinian terrorist attacks, the IDF focused on "perimeter defense." The Palestinian intifadas in the 1980s and 2000s, however, gave rise to new "intrafrontier" threats, from Gaza and the West Bank, at the same time that an additional "interfrontier" threat was evolving—Hezbollah's and Hamas's rocket arsenals. Furthermore, the Iraqi and later the Iranian missile programs, coupled with unconventional warheads, created potentially existential threats from distant countries.[15]

The first major sign of the changing nature of the military threats Israel faces began with the massive PLO bombardment of the north in July 1981, the first time the home front had been heavily hit since the War of Independence and the precursor to the Lebanon war the following year. All together, the PLO shelled Israel from Lebanon more than 1,000 times prior to the 1982 war.[16] The 39 ballistic missiles that Saddam Hussein fired at Israel a decade later, during the 1991 Gulf War, were a further and particularly rude awakening, as the home front now became vulnerable to attacks from distant countries that did not even share a border with Israel. In both cases, massive and traumatic flights of civilians took place. Repeated rocket attacks by Hezbollah and Hamas during the 1990s and 2000s, along with Iraq's and Iran's missile and nuclear programs, turned the danger of asymmetric warfare into the primary threat Israel faces and the home front and military rear, not the front lines, into the primary theaters of battle.[17]

In irregular warfare, nonstate actors such as Hezbollah and Hamas and, as noted, even state actors such as Syria and Iran, do not seek to achieve decisive military victory in the near or mid term, which they know to be beyond their capabilities, but "victory by not losing,"[18] as part of a long-term strategy of "attrition until destruction." To this end, they merely seek to withstand Israel's military superiority and deny it victory, survive, and rebuild for the next round, one of many. Moreover, by repeatedly targeting Israel's civilian and military rears over a protracted period, through rocket and other terrorist attacks, they seek to cause demoralization, psychological exhaustion, and a general sense of failure and hopelessness, and to erode Israel's societal resilience. The combined long-term objective is to convince Israel that the threat they pose cannot be re-solved militarily and ultimately lead to Israel's collapse.[19] From their perspective, and not just theirs, Israel's unilateral withdrawals from Lebanon in 2000 and Gaza in 2005 were successful examples of the strategy at work.

Inflicting casualties has always been part of warfare, but Hezbollah and Hamas do so not to weaken Israel militarily, but to play on its sensitivity to casualties and on changing international norms. In so doing, they seek to promote do-mestic and international pressures to end the fighting before Israel has achieved its military objectives and to further undermine its staying power. To a degree, the threat is more of socioeconomic disruption, including heavy damage to buildings and infrastructure, than of the relatively limited number of casualties likely. During the 2014 operation in Gaza, for example, Hamas's rocket attacks did not cause many casualties, but did severely disrupt the economy and the daily life of 60% of Israel's population, which was in rocket range. The magnitude of a future conflict with Hezbollah will be many times greater.[20]

Imbued with radical fundamentalist fervor, these nonstate and state actors believe that time is on their side and knowingly pursue a policy of cumulative attrition that may take decades to achieve its ultimate goal of Israel's demise. Since the struggle is long term and Israel enjoys clear military superiority in the meantime, they seek to ensure the survivability of their forces and to minimize losses by avoiding head-on military confrontations, as well as through a variety of irregular tactics, such as concealment, deception, dispersal of forces, tunneling, and extensive use of "low signature" weapons and forces (rockets, missiles, com-mando units, guerrilla fighters, suicide bombers). In recent years, however, they have also been equipped with advanced weapons, including antitank and antiair-craft missiles, as well as ballistic missiles, and have gained improved intelligence, surveillance, and command-and-control capabilities.[21]

The military doctrines and capabilities that Hezbollah and Hamas have developed, much like the irregular and guerrilla groups that other "regular" militaries have often faced in the past, enable them to at least partially neu-tralize Israel's technological superiority, including its air and ground maneuver capabilities, and thereby avoid military defeat. They effectively blend into the civilian populations and "disappear from the battlefield," making the process of locating and destroying their forces very difficult,[22] especially the many tens of thousands of short-range rockets, which are quite small and easily hidden in pri-vate homes. Indeed, during the 2006 war in Lebanon, IDF soldiers were often no more than yards away from deeply camouflaged Hezbollah rockets, at times literally standing on top of them. Gaza's densely populated rabbit warren layout presents a similarly difficult problem.

Moreover, Hezbollah and Hamas deliberately seek to increase the number of civilian casualties, both Israel's and their own, in the former case by targeting

Israel's civilian population, and in the latter by placing weapons in or near schools, mosques, hospitals, and homes. By leaving Israel with no choice but to cause civilian casualties when it attacks these targets, they seek to undermine the legitimacy of its operations and of Israel itself, and create further international pressure to end the fighting before Israel is able to achieve its objectives. Finally, they seek to use the threat of large-scale military and civilian casualties to deter Israel from escalating to a full-scale conflict, in which they are clearly the weaker side.[23]

Hezbollah and Hamas further presume that an Israeli invasion will be limited in time and probably extent and will, in any event, most likely end with an Israeli withdrawal. They thus do not believe it important to prevent the IDF from temporarily occupying their territory and may even seek to draw it in, since a ground invasion provides far more targets for guerrilla attacks, both against the invading force and against its logistical "tail."[24]

Hezbollah poses the primary military threat to Israel for the foreseeable future.[25] Its daunting rocket arsenal remains, by far, the biggest danger, but Hezbollah is also in the process of becoming more of a regular military force. As early as 2013 Hezbollah reportedly began operating tanks and conducting operations at the company level and above, and its involvement in the Syrian civil war has provided it with important experience in large-scale urban warfare.[26] It has presumably also gained considerable experience working alongside or with the Russian forces now deployed in Syria. The buildup of its mammoth rocket arsenal continues unabated.

Iran is the most sophisticated adversary Israel has ever faced and arguably the most powerful. Setting aside Iran's ongoing nuclear program, discussed below, the reality is more mixed. Iran is far away from Israel, and its conventional capabilities, including the air force, which would be crucial to any attack against Israel at these distances, are limited. Its ability to transfer large-scale ground forces to the area, in any timely fashion, is also limited and would be highly vulnerable to Israeli attack. Conversely, Iran has embarked on a military modernization program following the 2015 nuclear deal, including advanced Russian aircraft and antiaircraft systems, and its involvement in Syria provides it with new possibilities for positioning forces near the Golan border. Indeed, as of late 2017, it had already built a military base near Damascus and is reportedly interested in deploying ground forces to Syria, building air and naval bases, and building missile factories in both Syria and Lebanon, thereby complicating Israel's interdiction efforts. These developments are a source of considerable concern for Israel. Iran is also believed to have an arsenal of approximately 400 ballistic missiles with the necessary range to hit Israel.[27] As long as the missiles are armed with conventional warheads, however, the actual threat they pose is limited. One need only recall the minimal loss of life caused by the 39 missiles

Saddam fired at Israel in 1991 to gain some perspective; just one person killed by a direct hit and 10 others due to various indirect reasons (e.g., heart attacks, choking on gas masks). Iran's arsenal is far larger, but it will presumably wish to retain a significant percentage in strategic reserve, and, unlike 1991, Israel now has the Arrow antimissile defensive system.

If, for example, Iran were to launch half of its arsenal and Arrow to achieve a successful interception rate of 80% (the Iron Dome antirocket system, admittedly a different technology, achieved a rate of mid-90%), the number of missiles that would hit Israel would be very similar to 1991. Iran is undoubtedly trying to develop various means of penetrating the defensive system and increasing warhead size, but—as long as the warheads are conventional—the actual threat is more a matter of the potential disruption to daily life and the economy, and the psychological toll, than the numbers of casualties and physical destruction. Conversely, as Iran improves the missiles' accuracy, they may also become an effective means of striking Israel's military capabilities and infrastructure sites.

Iran has conducted terrorist attacks against Israeli and Israeli-affiliated targets in the past, such as the bombings of the Israeli embassy and Jewish community center in Buenos Aires in the early 1990s. The primary threat it poses to Israel, however, is overwhelmingly indirect and covert, through Hezbollah, Hamas (in the past and maybe again in the future), and its alliance with Syria.

Hezbollah is an Iranian proxy, founded and largely armed, trained, and financed by it. Hezbollah generally also takes its strategic and operational guidance from Tehran. For the meantime, the magnitude of the threat posed by Iran's missiles pales in comparison with Hezbollah's rocket arsenal, which remains Iran's primary means of creating mutual deterrence with Israel. It was also the primary means, in the past, by which Iran sought to deter Israel from attacking its nuclear program.[28]

Iran established a close strategic alliance with Syria back in the 1980s, originally based on a shared desire to defeat Israel, and the two concluded a defense agreement in 2006 whose precise content is unknown but is reported to include the manufacture of missiles and possible Iranian security guarantees for Syria in the event of a conflict with Israel. A further defense agreement was signed in 2017.[29] In recent years, following the outbreak of the Syrian civil war, it was Iran and Hezbollah that stepped in and saved the regime from collapse. In fact, most of Hezbollah's fighting force has been actively engaged in the civil war for the last few years, and Iran itself sent some 3,000 Islamic Guard fighters to Syria at the height of its involvement in 2015, as well as Shiite militiamen.[30]

As noted in chapter 2, if Iran and Hezbollah ultimately succeed in keeping the regime in power, Syria is likely to become an Iranian-dominated entity, thereby providing both Iran and Hezbollah with a second base of operations, in addition to Lebanon, from which to attack Israel. It would also create one largely contiguous Iranian-dominated territory, through Iraq and Syria to the Golan border, from which Iran would be better able to supply weapons to Hezbollah and its own troops.

The Iran-Hezbollah-Syria axis has deepened greatly as a result of their shared involvement in the civil war, and they now constitute, for all practical purposes, one joint front under Tehran's leadership. Consequently, a significant Israeli clash with any one of the three is increasingly likely to lead to one with the others as well.[31] The escalatory dangers are further compounded by the growing presence of Hezbollah, and other radical organizations, near the Golan border. For Israel, as already noted, an Iranian-dominated Syria would be the worst of all the bad potential outcomes of the civil war.

The Rocket and Missile Threats

Until the 2006 war, Hezbollah rockets had a range covering the northern third of Israel, approximately up to Hadera, a northern Tel Aviv exurb. Today its rockets not only cover Tel Aviv and the entire center of the country, but almost all of the south, including the nuclear reactor in Dimona. During the operation in Gaza in 2014 Hamas rockets reached Tel Aviv, Jerusalem, Haifa, and Dimona.[32] Both organizations are constantly at work to extend their rocket ranges, payloads, and precision.

The overwhelming majority of Hezbollah's and Hamas's rockets are highly inaccurate, meaning that they could only target towns and cities, not specific sites, and that the threat they pose is a "statistical" one, that is, the probability of inaccurate fire hitting a population center. Today, Hezbollah is in the process of enlarging its arsenal of precision missiles that can be targeted against specific civilian and military sites.[33]

The new precision missiles present a possible game changer. For the first time, one of Israel's enemies now has a concrete ability to disrupt the mobilization of the IDF's reserves and conduct of offensive operations, as well as the national decision-making process, at both the political and the military levels. This heretofore unprecedented capability can be achieved by using the new precision missiles to attack, inter alia, mobilization centers and weapons storehouses, airbases, air-control centers, and ground staging areas, as well as command-and-control facilities, such as the Ministry of Defense, General Staff Headquarters, and prime minister's office. They can also now attack highly sensitive national infrastructure sites, such as power plants, oil refineries, communication nodes, and the international airport, with severe consequences for Israel's economy. A major attack on the power plant in Hadera, for example, could leave Israel with reduced electric power for months.[34]

Furthermore, and maybe most importantly, the fear of the potentially massive destruction that Hezbollah and Hamas can wreak on the home front has had a significant impact on Israeli decision-making and strategy, forcing Israel, for the first time, to choose between investment in offense and defense, and creating a form of mutual deterrence.[35] The latter contributed, among other factors, to Israel's hesitation to attack Hezbollah's rapidly growing rocket arsenal during the six-year period between the unilateral withdrawal from Lebanon in 2000 and the war in 2006, and ever since, and to a lesser extent, to attack Hamas's rocket arsenal, during the lulls between the repeated rounds since 2008. A similar situation prevailed in the past in regard to Syria's rocket and missile arsenal.[36]

The rocket and missile threat Israel faces today is as follows:

- **Syria** was thought to have had an arsenal of approximately 100,000 missiles and rockets on the eve of the civil war in 2011, but has expended most during the fighting.[37] Most of the arsenal consisted of short-range rockets, with a few hundred long-range missiles capable of carrying relatively heavy payloads of 750 kilograms.[38]
- **Iran**, as noted, has approximately 400 missiles with a range capable of reaching Israel.[39]
- **Hezbollah** had approximately 12,000–14,000 rockets on the eve of the war in 2006.[40] It is now thought to have 130,000–150,000 rockets, including thousands of intermediate-range ones, capable of reaching Ashdod (a southern Tel Aviv exurb) and hundreds of long-range ones capable of covering most of Israel.[41] Much of this mammoth arsenal is located in private homes and apartment buildings in some 240 villages, towns, and cities throughout southern Lebanon.[42]
- **Hamas** had an arsenal of approximately 10,000–12,000 rockets prior to the Gaza operation in 2014, including thousands with a range of up to 40 kilometers and hundreds with a range of 80 kilometers.[43] At the end of the fighting it was left with some 3,500 rockets, the rest having been used or destroyed. Today, it is thought to have fully replenished the arsenal, but with rockets of shorter ranges and poorer quality.[44] All told, Hamas fired over 17,300 rockets at Israel between 2001 and 2014, of which more than 12,500 were after the unilateral withdrawal from Gaza in 2005.[45]

The IDF estimates that Hezbollah may fire 1,000–1,500 rockets at Israel each day in a future war, of which 95% will be short range, that is, up to 45 kilometers, and with a small warhead of 10 kilograms.[46] Other informed sources estimate that Hezbollah may be able to maintain this rate of fire for some 30 days, a whopping 30,000–45,000 rockets, with the danger of an additional front with Gaza and possibly Syria and Egypt (Sinai) as well.[47] The IDF estimates that thousands of rockets will hit built-up areas, dozens of them in Tel Aviv, but that because of Iron Dome and other factors, only 10 buildings will suffer direct hits each day.[48]

Hundreds of thousands may be forced to leave their homes for safer areas, of whom 70% will be able to take care of themselves, but 30% will require shelter and assistance in public places, such as underground parking lots, IDF bases, and even nature preserves.[49] In a two-front war, with Hamas as well, up to 750,000 may be forced to leave their homes,[50] even though no part of the country will be out of rocket range and truly safe. The overall number of Israelis killed in a round of this magnitude with Hezbollah may be in the range of 300–500, with thousands wounded.[51]

In the next round, Hezbollah reportedly intends to try to overrun an Israeli town, or even a part of the Galilee, take numerous hostages and block major crossroads.[52] Even if successful for no more than hours, the psychological impact on Israel will be enormous. In addition to rockets, the Hezbollah threat consists of offensive UAVs, advanced shore-to-sea missiles, and air-defense systems.[53] Altogether, Hezbollah is estimated to have some 45,000 fighters, of whom 21,000 are full time, the rest reserves, with somewhere between 5,000 and 8,000 involved in the fighting in Syria.[54]

A number of reports suggest a possible change in Hezbollah's operational approach, from one based on the attempt to prolong each round, to a brief but massive few days of rocket fire at the outset of a conflict. The change, which is said to stem from Israel's ability to bomb targets throughout Lebanon on a massive scale and to cause large-scale infrastructure damage, is designed to bring about an early end to the fighting by eliciting rapid international intervention.[55] An alternative explanation holds that the reported change reflects Hezbollah's greatly improved ability to hit targets with precision and in a short period of time, and consequent desire to end the fighting before Israel has the time to bring its technological capabilities to bear.[56] In either case, if these reports are correct, the changing Hezbollah approach is a further manifestation of the threat of mutual destruction that has evolved between the sides.

The West Bank overlooks Israel narrow coastal strip, in which some 70% of the population, 80% of the commercial and industrial base, and most government institutions, strategic sites, and civil and military infrastructure are located. Political considerations aside, the possible introduction of mortars and short-range rockets into the West Bank would present an unacceptable danger. Surprisingly, perhaps, long-range rockets, such as those Hezbollah has in Lebanon, are more easily dealt with than the short-range ones that could be deployed in the West Bank, should Israel cede control over the area. The long-range rockets require comparatively large launching pads or vehicles that are much easier to find and destroy.[57]

Contrary to the popular impression, irregular and asymmetric warfare are actually not new phenomena at all, but have been the primary form of warfare ever since antiquity.[58] Some research has even established that approximately

80% of the conflicts during the Cold War were of this nature, as were 95% of those between 1989 and 1996.[59] Modern irregular warfare has its roots in the conflicts in China, Cuba, Algeria, and especially Vietnam during the 1950s and 1960s. It is not new for Israel either. Palestinian terrorism, then known as the fedayeen attacks, began in the 1950s, or even as early as 1920 if one refers to the prestate days, and the PLO began firing artillery and rockets at Israel from southern Lebanon in 1969 and massive barrages in 1981. The Hezbollah and Hamas threats started in the 1980s.[60] Israel, itself, practiced irregular tactics in the prestate era.

Nevertheless, a number of changes have taken place. The magnitude and range of the capabilities in the hands of Israel's irregular adversaries now enable them to hit virtually all of Israel, including all of its primary population centers, from the other side of the border, without ever having to penetrate Israeli territory. Moreover, they have come to believe that Israel's civilian home front and military rear are its Achilles heel and are so vulnerable that they offset its military superiority. This has led to their consequent decision to adopt an overall strategy of long-term attrition in which the home front, not the military front-lines and battlefields, has become the primary theater of fighting.[61]

Various state and nonstate actors had the ability to strike Israel's home front in the past, and did on occasion, but the threat was limited to a certain area, usually along the border, and no single player could threaten virtually the entire nation. Today, all of Israel truly has become one "home front." No longer a secondary threat, irregular warfare and asymmetric warfare have become the primary threats that Israel faces today.[62]

The advent of long-range missiles has also enabled distant countries to strike Israel with relative impunity and without the need to obtain the agreement of bordering states, or the expense and time required to send expeditionary forces. Like the nonstate actors, their efforts are focused on Israel's home front. With the dismantlement of Iraq's and Libya's missile programs, this threat is limited today primarily to Iran and whatever residual capability Syria retains.

Hezbollah and Hamas have four attributes that distinguish them from most terrorist organizations of the past. First, they no longer have to struggle to obtain state sanctuary and sponsorship, traditionally one of the foremost challenges and constraints faced by terrorist organizations. Hamas *is* the state in Gaza, Hezbollah is the most powerful political and military force in Lebanon, and they both essentially provide themselves with state sanctuary and sponsorship.[63]

Second, the Lebanese government and to some extent even Hamas have achieved partial immunity from Israeli retaliation.[64] The Lebanese government is too weak to exert control over Hezbollah or other terrorist organizations operating from its territory, and so Israel has been unable to hold it accountable for their actions—the very basis for its counterterrorism policy toward other state sponsors of terrorism in the past. Moreover, the international community has often considered Israeli operations in Lebanon, both preventative and retaliatory, to be illegitimate attacks against an ostensibly defenseless player. Israel has thus been forced to focus its military efforts on Hezbollah itself, even though it is extremely difficult to defeat a terrorist organization when one cannot attack its state sponsor.[65] The Hamas government in Gaza, unlike the Lebanese government, is mostly in control of its territory. Like Hezbollah, however, it intentionally embeds weapons and forces among the civilian population to deter Israel from attacking or to gain a PR and diplomatic advantage when it does. The civilian casualties caused lead to international condemnation and force Israel to at least partially limit the nature and extent of its responses.

Third, Hezbollah and Hamas are not just terrorist organizations as in the past, but "hybrid" organizations, or "terrorilla armies,"[66] which combine the characteristics, structures. and methods of terrorist organizations, guerilla groups. and even state militaries. They are also major providers of social services to their respective populations and are the primary political, or governmental, factors in their territory as well.

Fourth, while Hezbollah and Hamas are comparatively small organizations and no match for the IDF's overall power, they have built up very large capabilities in a few important areas designed to neutralize Israel's superiority, first and foremost rockets, but also antitank and antiship missiles and more. Indeed, virtually no conventional military in the world has as many rockets as Hezbollah. Hamas's arsenal is much smaller, but still potent.

Achieving victory in conventional warfare may be difficult, but defining it in terms of concrete military objectives is comparatively straightforward. One of two states of affairs usually prevails, peace or war, and a war's beginning and end are clearly discernible. Recognized governmental actors have the authority to make the relevant decisions, including how and when to end the conflict, and they can be held accountable for their actions. With Hezbollah and Hamas, in contrast, and to a lesser extent the PA, the conflict is ongoing, with an interminable series of starts and stops, there is no one who can be held accountable, and the formulation of political and military objectives becomes far more difficult.[67] Achieving military decision against irregular actors is thus particularly problematic, as are detection and deterrence of the threats they pose. We will return to this in detail in chapter 7.

The governmental division of authority required for irregular warfare is very different from that needed for conventional conflicts. In the past, the division between the IDF and Israel Police, for example, was clear; the former fought the Arab armies on Israel's borders and the latter were responsible for dealing with domestic criminal activities. During wartime, most policemen were mobilized for military service. Today, the police play a major role in preventing and responding to terrorism within Israel and preserving order following rocket attacks, and can no longer be mobilized for reserve duty during crises. Indeed, the overlap between military and police missions has been estimated to reach 30%.[68] Moreover, an entirely new range of organizations, needed to provide assistance to the civilian population, has come to be of great importance, such as municipalities and emergency services (firefighters, ambulances), and even governmental real estate assessors to assess damage and compensation.

A further example of blurring organizational lines of authority is the relationship between the intelligence agencies, which used to be relatively straightforward: Military Intelligence was responsible for all external threats on Israel's borders, the Israel Security Agency ("Shin Bet") for all internal threats, including terrorism from the West Bank and Gaza, and the Mossad for threats from beyond Israel's borders. Today, a terrorist attack may be planned, armed, and equipped in Europe, with Hezbollah and Iranian assistance, the perpetrators may travel to Gaza via Egypt, and only then enter Israeli territory, raising questions of responsibility between the different agencies and the need for heightened levels of interagency coordination.[69]

In conventional warfare much of the necessary intelligence is physical, for example, the location of command-and-control facilities, airbases, or armored forces, and the "shelf time" of targets is relatively long. In the irregular conflicts with Hezbollah and Hamas, conversely, many targets simply consist of small numbers of personnel or isolated weapons, and real-time intelligence is measured in hours, minutes, and even seconds.[70]

The repeated rounds with Hezbollah, Hamas, and the Palestinians in the West Bank present new technological and operational challenges that are very different from those of the conventional warfare of the past. In conventional warfare, for example, the greater the explosive capability and destruction caused by a weapon, the better. In irregular conflicts, in contrast, especially in densely built-up areas, a loss of civilian lives can cause international opprobrium and pressure that outweighs the operational benefits. As a result, the IDF has been forced to develop and use weapons with lower yields and to limit its operations.[71]

Hezbollah and Hamas, unlike Palestinian terrorists in the PA, operate from territory that is not under Israeli control.[72] This forces Israel to pursue different means of gathering intelligence and conducting day-to-day counterterrorism operations, imposing certain constraints on its ability to thwart possible attacks and prevent the establishment of the organizational and operational infrastructure they require. It also imposes limitations on Israel's diplomatic freedom of maneuver vis-à-vis the international community, as well as Egypt and Jordan, with whom Israel's ability to respond to threats emanating from their territory is inhibited by the overarching strategic importance it attributes to the preservation of the peace treaties with them. In 2012, for example, when

Egypt was under the rule of Muslim Brotherhood president Morsi, Israel launched the operation in Gaza but greatly limited it, so as not to put the peace agreement at risk.[73]

Finally, Israel's overwhelming military superiority, compared to nonstate actors such as Hezbollah and Hamas, creates gaps between public, media, and political expectations regarding the anticipated outcomes of confrontations, and the IDF's ability to deliver in irregular warfare. The gaps exist on four levels: the length of the operation, which is expected to be short; Israeli military and civilian losses, which are expected to be minimal; enemy civilian losses, which are also expected to be low; and the ability to achieve decisive victory.[74] These gaps generate frustration and unhappiness with the results achieved, as happened following the 2006 war in Lebanon and 2014 operation in Gaza.

Terrorism

The terrorist threats Israel faces[75] range from stabbings, drive-by shootings, kidnappings, and bombings to the far more difficult-to-prevent suicide bombings; rocket attacks; cyber, chemical, and biological terrorism; and ultimately the truly nightmare scenario of nuclear terrorism.[76] Having already addressed the rocket and missile threat, the following section focuses primarily on the "traditional" forms of terrorism, especially bombings and suicide bombings.

The primary sources of terrorism Israel has faced have been the Palestine Liberation Organization (PLO) in the past and Hezbollah and Hamas today, though numerous additional organizations, Palestinian and otherwise, have been involved to varying degrees. In recent years ISIS, al-Qaeda, and other jihadi organizations have become increasingly active in Sinai, Gaza, Lebanon, and especially Syria, with some indications of an initial presence in the West Bank. Like Hezbollah and Hamas, these organizations seek to use their territorial proximity to hit Israel's civilian home front, undermine the peace treaties with Egypt and Jordan,[77] and provoke broader confrontations between Israel and its neighbors. Egypt's loss of control in the Sinai in recent years, and Syria's in areas bordering the Golan border, have raised concerns that terrorist attacks by Islamist elements operating from these areas may also lead to interstate conflicts.[78]

In reality, terrorism has been an integral part of the Arab-Israeli conflict from the earliest days, indeed, long before Israel was established. Some readers may find the data in the next four paragraphs to be too detailed and can skip ahead to Figure 3.1; others will find it worth the effort.

During the 18-month-long riots of 1920–1921, in many ways the "first intifada," 47 Jews were killed and 140 wounded; during the 1929 riots 33 were killed and 230 wounded. In 1950, two years after Israel's establishment, 50 civilians were killed in cross-border infiltrations, 97 in 1951, 182 in 1952, and 146 during

May–November 1953 alone. Altogether, more than 400 Israelis were killed between 1951 and 1956 in more than 6,000 cross-border attacks, an average of about three attacks a day, greatly contributing to Israel's decision to launch the Sinai Campaign in 1956. The first terrorist attack by Fatah, the primary component of the PLO, occurred in December 1964, shortly after it was founded.[79] So much for the claim that Palestinian terrorism is a reaction to the post-1967 occupation.

Between the 1967 and 1973 wars 269 Israelis died in terrorist attacks. The peak year was 1968, with 1,480 attempted cross-border attacks, 1,373 in 1969, and 1,280 in 1970. Between December 1987 and February 1989, the height of the first intifada, 12 Israelis were killed and 1,280 injured in terrorist attacks.[80]

The second intifada, which began in September 2000 and petered out by the mid-2000s, was the worst period of terrorism Israel has ever faced. Between 2000 and 2004, the height of the intifada, nearly as many Israelis died from terrorism as in the entire period from independence in 1948 until 2000. In 2001, the first full year of the intifada, 207 Israelis were killed, and 452 in 2002, the worst year of all. By 2003, however, the number had decreased to 208 and has decreased dramatically ever since, 15 in 2009, 10 in 2012. Altogether, by 2009, the intifada had claimed the lives of 1,178 Israelis in some 15,000 terrorist attacks; of these, 516 were killed in 146 suicide attacks, over 850 within the Green Line, not the West Bank, and approximately two-thirds were civilians. More than 5,000 attacks took place from Gaza.[81]

From the 1982 invasion of Lebanon until the unilateral withdrawal in 2000, more than 1,500 Israelis soldiers died in the battle against the PLO and later Hezbollah; 670 were killed during the invasion itself, and over 250 were killed and 840 seriously wounded between 1985 and the withdrawal in 2000.[82] In the five years before the withdrawal, Hezbollah conducted almost 5,000 attacks, eroding public support for Israel's presence in the security zone in Lebanon.[83] In the 2006 war, 119 soldiers were killed.[84] Figures 3.1 and 3.2 provide data regarding Israel's fatalities and wounded due to Palestinian terrorism from the second intifada through 2014.

Terrorism has never posed an existential threat for Israel, though at times, during the first and especially the second intifadas, it was perceived as such by some senior officials, while others believed that it might become existential if Israel failed to suppress it.[85] The costs in civilian and military casualties have, however, been heavy; indeed, the percentage of the Israeli population killed by terrorism is higher than in any other democracy[86] and few other countries have ever confronted the ravages of a greater terrorist threat than the second intifada. Threats do not have to be existential, however, to be severe, and terrorism has come to constitute a "strategic threat" for Israel, a term first used by Premier Rabin in 1995 and by many others ever since.

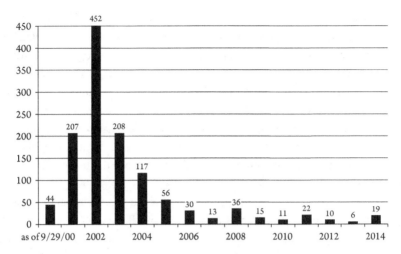

Figure 3.1 Fatalities Due to Palestinian Terrorism, Second Intifada through 2014
Source: adapted from www.shabak.gov.il/publications/study/Pages/ReportY2014.aspx. https://www.shabak.gov.il/publications/Pages/study/ReportY2014.aspx Note: An additional 73 people, including six civilians, were killed in 2014 during the operation in Gaza.

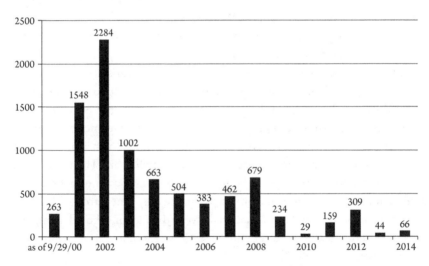

Figure 3.2 Wounded by Palestinian Terrorism, Second Intifada through 2014
Source: adapted from www.shabak.gov.il/publications/study/Pages/ReportY2014.aspx https://www.shabak.gov.il/publications/Pages/study/ReportY2014.aspx Note: 312 people were wounded in 2014 during the operation in Gaza.

The strategic threat posed by terrorism is far greater than the simple numbers of killed and wounded and even than the societal impact. Terrorism was a primary factor—in a number of cases even the decisive one—in all of the elections during the last two decades, except 2012 and 2015. In 1996, for example, the polls indicated a severe defeat for the Likud, but the result was the opposite, primarily due to the massive wave of suicide terrorism that preceded the elections. The second intifada, which began at a time when the peace process at its height, led to Labor's defeat and to the rise of a right-wing Likud government in 2001. Overall, terrorism caused a significant hardening of public opinion toward possible compromise with the Palestinians, served as the basis for the powerful right-wing slogan "This peace is killing us," and decimated the Israeli peace camp. Rather than forcing Israel to make concessions under fire, terrorism has had the opposite effect, hardening the positions of both the leadership and the public as a whole.[87]

Terrorism has also had a major, at times even decisive, impact on Israel's negotiating positions.[88] Premiers Rabin, Peres, and Barak, in particular, sought to isolate the peace process from terrorism and proceeded at times with negotiations despite ongoing attacks. Terrorism, however, repeatedly forced them to go slow, back away from possible concessions, and ultimately, as indicated above, led to their electoral defeat. Ongoing Hamas rocket fire following the unilateral withdrawal from Gaza in 2005, together with the Hezbollah attack that provoked the 2006 Lebanon war, led to the demise of Premier Olmert's plan for a unilateral withdrawal from the West Bank as well.

For the most part, terrorism has not had a significant impact on Israel's economy, though there have been some exceptions, mostly short term. Israel's tourist industry has been repeatedly disrupted by terrorism, but has usually recovered rapidly. Major military operations, such as the 2006 war in Lebanon and 2014 operation in Gaza, had a temporary effect on the economy, but it rebounded immediately in both cases, and overall economic performance was not materially affected.[89] The economies of certain areas, such as the northern towns and those near Gaza, long subjected to Hezbollah and Hamas terrorism respectively, were deeply affected, but the impact was local, not national. The second intifada was the lone major exception, the only time terrorism had a significant economic impact at the national level, when it contributed, along with the global economic downturn at the time, to Israel's first year of negative economic growth since 1953.[90]

Terrorism has caused ongoing disruptions of civilian life and undermined the public's sense of security, especially in the last two decades, during the second intifada and as Hezbollah and Hamas developed their rocket arsenals. For much of the country, the Hezbollah, Hamas, or Palestinian terrorist threats are ever present, with an ongoing psychological cost for Israeli society. Indeed, a 2007 study found that over 25% of adults and 72%–94% of children living in the border town of Sderot, which has long borne the brunt of Hamas's rocket attacks, suffered from post-traumatic stress disorder.[91] During the second intifada, all of Israel became a part of the terrorist war, at least psychologically, with an impact that has not fully dissipated to this day. Beginning with the PLO bombardment of the northern towns in 1981, there have been repeated cases of civilian flight during periods of heightened rocket fire, both in the north, especially during the 2006 war in Lebanon, and in the south, in communities near Gaza. Overall, however, the disruption of life has been temporary and the public, as seen in chapter 5, has demonstrated admirable societal resilience.

For all of the attention and vast resources devoted today to the rocket threat, suicide terrorism, a cheap and comparatively simple threat to carry out, has proven far more lethal to Israel. There were 260 suicide bombings in the period between 2000 and 2006 that killed some 550 Israelis, whereas approximately 20,000 rockets and mortars fired between 2001 and 2015 killed a few dozen.[92]

Unconventional Threats

Iran's ongoing nuclear program remains the greatest threat to Israel's security and, subject to the ultimate outcome of the 2015 nuclear agreement, the only potentially existential one. The dangers posed by a nuclear Iran include the possibility of actual use of nuclear weapons, devastating for any country, but certainly tiny Israel, whose population is concentrated in a small area and which, as former Iranian president Rafsanjani once infamously stated, could be destroyed by one bomb.[93] More plausibly, Iran might just threaten to use nuclear weapons, whether explicitly or implicitly, with dire ramifications for Israel's strategic calculus and freedom of maneuver. The threat could be made in the course of a direct confrontation with Israel or as a means of bolstering regional allies, such as Syria and Hezbollah, and of dictating outcomes favorable to them. A nuclear capability might also provide the basis for a generally more aggressive Iranian foreign and defense posture and a greater capacity to influence (or coerce) other regional actors.[94]

Furthermore, the danger of nuclear proliferation from Iran to radical states or terrorist organizations cannot be discounted, low though the probability may be.[95] There is also a danger of the nuclear capability falling into the hands of an even more extremist Iranian regime, if the current one falls, or of a loss of control over it in a scenario of regime change and internal disarray. If Iran succeeds in acquiring nuclear weapons, especially after the major effort the international community made to prevent it from doing so, international nonproliferation norms and regimes, especially the Nuclear Nonproliferation Treaty (NPT), will have been dealt a severe and even terminal blow, with critical ramifications for future cases of proliferation in the region.[96] Moreover, a nuclear Iran may be a catalyst for a regional nuclear arms race. Over a dozen regional countries (including Egypt, Saudi Arabia, Syria, Jordan, Turkey, the UAE, and Algeria) have already responded to Iran's nuclear quest with a growing interest in civil nuclear programs of their own. A number of "civil" nuclear programs in the Middle East have turned into military ones in the past.[97]

The possibility of a multinuclear Middle East is a nightmare scenario that makes the complexity of the US-Soviet nuclear rivalry pale in comparison, though not in destructive capacity. The relations between the likely potential proliferators in the region, their relations with both Iran and Israel, and, of course, Iranian-Israeli relations, are tenuous at best. Unlike the United States and Soviet Union, some do not even have diplomatic ties or any bilateral channels of communication at all, and none have good relations. To illustrate, Iran refuses to have any contact whatsoever with Israel, its relations with Saudi Arabia are tense, and it has no diplomatic relations with Egypt. Saudi Arabia does not have relations or direct channels of communication with Israel, and Saudi-Egyptian relations have ups and downs. Egypt, Saudi Arabia, Iran, and Israel all have tense relationships with Turkey. Managing a nuclear crisis in these circumstances would be acutely difficult and fraught with risk.

A nuclear Middle East would differ from the US-Soviet rivalry in two other important ways. First, Iran and Saudi Arabia are extremist theocracies, and even though both are probably "rational actors," rationality may be different when God plays such a central role in decision-making. Religion plays an important role in national security decision-making in Turkey and Egypt as well. Second, whereas the United States and Soviet Union sought to defeat each other's economic and political systems, but not to annihilate each other, indeed, went to great lengths to avoid this, Iran explicitly and actively seeks Israel's destruction, and the Arab states would welcome it.

The question of rationality is at the crux of the debate in Israel regarding the threat posed by Iran's nuclear program. For analytical purposes, we can speak of two schools of thought in Israel regarding the ramifications of a nuclear Iran. The first views a nuclear Iran as an absolutely existential threat to Israel, in the narrowest sense of the word; if Iran acquires a bomb, it will eventually use it. The logical strategic conclusion from this approach is that Israel must do *everything possible* to prevent Iran from going nuclear, including military attack, because the consequences of a nuclear Iran would be far worse than any other option.

The second school of thought does not dismiss the existential danger, but thinks that Iran is highly unlikely to ever use nuclear weapons against Israel and that the true danger lies in the influence it would gain in a variety of lesser scenarios, a dire (but not existential) threat in its own right. The logical conclusion from this approach is that Israel must do *everything within reason* to prevent Iran from going nuclear, but not everything possible, thereby providing it with somewhat greater decision-making leeway. The differences between the approaches may be narrow in conceptualization, but are highly significant for Israel's response.[98]

One can debate the prospects of the above scenarios ever evolving in practice, especially the likelihood of Iran actually using nuclear weapons against Israel. What is not in dispute, however, is that nuclear capabilities do fundamentally change the nature of a conflict, raising an existential specter, and thus have a profound impact on a country's national security decision-making processes and strategy. For Israel, a nuclear Iran would risk turning virtually every significant conflict in the region in the future into a potentially existential one. In a future round with Syria or Hezbollah, for example, Israel would fear that Iran might place its nuclear forces on alert to deter Israel from acting, or even possibly try to coerce it into various otherwise unacceptable courses of action.[99]

In the past, Syria, Libya, and Iraq also had nuclear and chemical weapons programs. Egypt ceased its nuclear weapons research under US pressure but has continued with chemical and biological weapons research and may have small stockpiles.[100] In 2015 it signed a deal with Russia for the supply of its first nuclear power reactors. Iran has declared that it has chemical weapons but has not specified the types and quantities or where they are located. Its efforts to develop biological weapons are unknown, but Iran has the necessary technology.[101] Syria is thought to still be hiding some residual chemical capabilities, has made use of nonbanned chemical weapons, and may have biological weapons as well. ISIS has used chemical weapons.[102]

A possible Saudi decision to acquire nuclear weapons is a source of deep concern. According to various reports, the Saudis may have engaged in nuclear cooperation with Pakistan and even received Pakistani nuclear guarantees, whether in the form of a promise to provide a bomb or a nuclear umbrella. Leading Saudis have openly called for a nuclear capability in the event that Iran acquires nuclear weapons, and the Saudis have the financial clout to develop a nuclear program or even purchase a turnkey capability.[103]

The ultimate threat Israel faces is of nuclear terrorism. Although it does not appear to be a likely threat for the next few years, due to technological and operational challenges, it may materialize in the future, as may other forms of WMD terrorism. The elusive nature of terrorist organizations, that is, the absence of a clear "return address" for purposes of retaliation or to defeat the threat, makes it particularly hard to counter. Organizations such as Hezbollah and Hamas have important interests that they wish to preserve, beginning with their roles in Lebanon and Gaza respectively, and have thus proven to be at least partially deterrable to date, but nuclear capabilities could change this. ISIS, al-Qaeda, and other nihilistic organizations, in contrast, may prove to be far more difficult, even impossible to deter, increasing the actual dangers of nuclear terrorism.[104]

The Cyber-threat

As a nation that relies heavily on cyber-technology,[105] Israel is particularly vulnerable to cyber-attacks and has been a primary target thereof. Indeed, Israel faces a nearly constant barrage of cyber-attacks, roughly 1,000 every minute in 2012, or over one million cyber-attacks every day during the 2014 operation against Hamas in Gaza.[106]

Foreign nations, sophisticated hacker groups, and cyber-activists have attacked numerous Israeli websites, including hospitals, the Tel Aviv Stock Exchange, and Bank of Israel. During the 2009 operation against Hamas in Gaza, four waves of progressively stronger cyber-attacks were directed against Israel from over half a million computers, with roughly 15 million junk-mail deliveries every second at the height. Israel suspected the attacks were paid for by Hamas or Hezbollah and conducted by an unknown organization in the former USSR. Among the public websites taken offline were the Israel Security Agency ("Shin Bet") and the Home Front Command.[107]

In 2011–2012 a group linked to China's People's Liberation Army reportedly hacked three Israeli defense firms, apparently to steal blueprints of Israel's rocket and missile defense systems. During the 2012 operation against Hamas Israel faced a sophisticated cyber-operation aimed primarily at government websites, including the prime minister's office and the foreign and defense ministries. A total of over 100 million cyber-attacks were launched during the operation, major commercial and governmental sites were disrupted, and TV broadcasts on Israel's two commercial channels were briefly replaced with Hamas propaganda films. On the eve of Holocaust Remembrance Day, in 2012, hacker groups coordinated a series of cyber-attacks to make financial, business, educational, nonprofit, and news sites inaccessible. During the 2014 operation in Gaza the Home Front Command website was again temporarily taken offline, as were some public IDF websites. The Syrian Electronic Army was able to hack the IDF blog and Twitter account and post its own images. In 2015 Anonymous threatened Israel with an "Electronic Holocaust" in which it would "erase" Israel from cyber-space.[108]

Iran has been steadily improving both its own cyber-capabilities and those of Hezbollah and Hamas. In 2014 Israel uncovered Iran's "Newscaster" cyber-attack, which was launched in 2011 against the United States and other Western nations, too, and which was designed to gather intelligence by creating a series of false virtual identities with ties to government officials and reporters. The attack compromised over 2,000 computers. Iran has reportedly been able to penetrate defenses in several Israeli government agencies and to successfully access restricted information. In 2013 Iran, Hamas, and Hezbollah conducted a series of large-scale attacks against Israeli water, power, and banking sites. During the

2014 Gaza campaign Iran's attacks exceeded all of its previous ones together, including civilian infrastructure, financial networks, and government security systems.[109]

The IDF is concerned that enemies will be able to penetrate, disrupt, and take control of military communications networks and even use them against it, especially during hostilities. Every major weapons system in the IDF, as in other advanced militaries, including submarines, missiles, aircraft, and radar, have electronic components that are vulnerable to attack. One report spoke of an attempt to seize control of Israeli drones during the 2014 Gaza operation.[110]

In addition to Iran, Hezbollah, and Hamas, Israel has faced cyber-attacks from around the world, including Turkey, North Africa, and the Palestinians. The danger from nonstate actors and "cyber-activism" by individuals and groups is also growing. Such operations can already interfere with the government's ability to communicate instructions to the public in times of emergency, such as when the Home Front Command's site was taken down during the operations in Gaza in 2009 and 2014.[111]

Cyber-attacks on Israel also raise interesting questions regarding the attackers' political motivations. Many of these attacks are conducted without any specific demands in mind and are instead offshoots of wider campaigns aimed at undermining Israel's international standing or weakening it physically. While a limited number of cyber-attacks are unlikely to force Israel to change its policies, the constant barrage is designed to force it to do so by disrupting daily life and governmental functions. In effect, it is warfare by other means.[112]

To date, the actual impact of cyber-attacks has been limited. Nevertheless, the cyber-realm has quickly come to occupy a significant place in Israeli security thinking. Prime Minister Netanyahu declared that cyber-attacks are "one of the four main threats to Israel." Former premier and defense minister Ehud Barak warned that "cyber warfare has taken asymmetric warfare to a new height, allowing a lone hacker to cause major damage."[113]

Future Peace Agreements: Some Security Dimensions

The emergence of an independent Palestinian state will have major ramifications for Israel's long-term security, even on the assumption that stringent security arrangements are a precondition for its establishment. Security arrangements have been raised repeatedly in past negotiations, most recently and extensively during Secretary of State Kerry's efforts to broker a peace deal in 2014. A comprehensive discussion of the security concerns and possible solutions is beyond the scope of this book, but a few highlights are appropriate.

The potential efficacy of the putative security arrangements is, unsurprisingly, a source of considerable debate in Israel, and to downplay the dangers would be foolhardy, to say the least. Nothing in this section should be misconstrued, however, as detracting from the vital importance of a peace agreement with the Palestinians for Israel's long-term national security; indeed, little would be of greater benefit for it. A Palestinian state may prove more stable and peaceful than that portrayed in what follows, indeed, should have important reasons for being so, but the purpose of this section is to highlight the dangers.

An independent Palestinian state may rapidly become an irredentist one, actively seeking to regain control of territory believed to have been lost in 1948 or ceded as part of a peace agreement. Should the central government lose control over parts of its territory and even collapse, as already happened with Hamas in Gaza, there is a danger of a "Lebanonization" of Palestine, with various factions refusing to submit to its control and continuing the conflict against Israel. Moreover, Hamas, or some other extremist entity, may well gain control over the entire Palestinian state.

A Palestinian state might also conduct a conventional arms buildup, in violation of the likely demilitarization clauses of a peace treaty. It may certainly become a platform for ongoing terrorist and rocket attacks. This would pose a particularly severe danger for Israel, given that the West Bank commands the high ground overlooking the coastal plain, where the overwhelming majority of Israel's population and economic base are located. There is also a danger that a Palestinian state might assert growing influence over Israel's Arab minority and encourage it to demand cultural autonomy and even political independence. The emergence of a radical, Hamas-led terrorist entity in Gaza, which has fired thousands of rockets at Israel, is the living embodiment of every Israeli nightmare regarding a future Palestinian state in the West Bank as well.

The establishment of a Palestinian state might present a clear danger to the future stability and security of Jordan, which deeply fears this, and thus threaten a fundamental Israeli strategic interest. A Palestinian state could also become a springboard for a renewed "eastern front" against Israel, with possible Iranian involvement, and with the West Bank serving as a staging area. The danger of a renewed "eastern front" has diminished greatly in recent years with the demise of the Syrian and Iraqi armies, but Iran's expanding influence in both countries is a source of growing concern.

In this regard, it is worth reiterating the territorial dimensions of Israel's security concerns in a peace agreement with the Palestinians. The entire width of Israel and the West Bank together averages about 40 miles, of which the Jordan Valley comprises 6 to 9. The valley is roughly 1,300 feet below sea level and is also adjacent to the steep eastern slopes of the West Bank mountain ridge, which reach 3,300 feet above sea level. Moreover, there are only five east-west passes through which an attacking army can move, each of which can be defended with relative ease. The valley thus constitutes a natural military barrier. In these circumstances, the IDF has been able to make do in recent decades with only a very small force in the area, at the brigade level.[114]

The IDF is primarily a reserve army and needs at least 48 hours to fully mobilize and reach the battlefield. Territorial depth is what provides the IDF with the necessary time to mobilize, withstand an attack until mobilized, and conduct a defensive battle.[115]

For these reasons, the Jordan Valley has long been a critical component in Israeli thinking regarding the security arrangements needed in the West Bank in a final peace agreement. During past negotiations with the Palestinians, Israel sought to preserve a limited military presence in the valley, which would serve as a tripwire for full mobilization, along with the right to deploy additional forces in times of emergency. Early warning stations alone were not considered a fully reliable substitute for a forward presence in the valley, as demonstrated by the catastrophic intelligence failure of 1973.[116]

Needless to say, some argue that Israel can find sufficient substitutes for a presence in the valley, such as an international force or reliance on air power to block an advancing army. This may be the case. On the other hand, in future conflicts the IAF may have to focus first on suppression of enemy air-defenses and rocket and missile fire, before it is able to provide close air-support to the ground forces. Be that at it may, Israel simply cannot afford to allow the West Bank to become a launching pad for rockets, as happened in Gaza. To prevent that from happening requires at least some form of control over the access points to the West Bank and security arrangements inside it.[117]

Territorial considerations are paramount in regard to the future of the Golan Heights, as well, in some ways even more so. The entire Golan "Heights" is only about 35 miles long and 7.5–16 miles wide. Its unique terrain, however, provides Israel with invaluable defensive advantages. The slope at the western edge drops 1,700 feet to the Sea of Galilee below. The hills on the eastern edge force enemy armor into narrow areas under IDF control and provide fire and observation control over an area extending tens of miles into Syria. The Golan's unique topography, including Mount Hermon, the highest peak in the region, also provides Israel with vital advantages in terms of electronic intelligence gathering. As long as wars are ultimately decided by ground forces, considerations of terrain will remain critical in the Golan.[118]

To conclude this chapter: Israel no longer faces major conventional threats, at least for the foreseeable future and probably beyond. With the dismantlement of most of Syria's chemical weapons, end of the Libyan and Iraqi WMD programs, and at least temporary postponement of the Iranian nuclear issue, the WMD threats have also been drastically reduced. Terrorism remains an ever-present and significant problem but has been decreased drastically, brought down to levels that Israeli society can generally tolerate. Cyber-warfare is a new and potentially severe threat, which could lead to widespread disruption. The primary military dangers Israel faces today are from Hezbollah's and Hamas's rocket arsenals, severe but not existential threats, the possible emergence of new radical regional players, and above all, Iran's ongoing nuclear aspirations.

No country can base its national security on a static snapshot of the strategic situation, certainly not Israel, which confronts one of the world's most volatile and hostile regional environments. An endlessly changing Middle East, now engulfed in a state of unprecedented upheaval, can lead to the emergence of new threats or resurgence of old ones, almost without warning. Given the risks, Israel must continue to plan for severe scenarios, even if the likelihood of their actually materializing has decreased drastically and Israel's security margins are broader than ever.

Primary Observations

- Attacks by Arab states, the primary threat envisioned by the classic defense doctrine, are now the least likely contingency. It will be many years, if ever, before Syria again constitutes a major threat.
- Israel's conventional superiority led its adversaries to adopt irregular and asymmetric responses. They no longer seek short-term victory, but decades-long attrition to neutralize Israel's superiority, undermine its society, and ultimately lead to its collapse. The home front is now the primary battlefield and wars a matter of mutual deterrence and destruction.
- Iran is the most sophisticated adversary Israel has ever faced and its ongoing nuclear program the greatest threat. The danger is not primarily of use, but of the influence Iran would gain and of the emergence of a multinuclear Middle East, a nightmare scenario. Nuclear weapons would turn almost every regional conflict into a potentially existential one.
- Hezbollah's rocket arsenal is the greatest immediate threat Israel faces. Its precision rockets are a potential game changer, allowing it to disrupt reserve mobilization, offensive operations, and national decision-making processes.
- Iran, Hezbollah, and Syria now constitute one joint northern front. They and Hamas believe that the home front is Israel's Achilles heel, which allows them to offset its military superiority. Hezbollah and Hamas are hybrid mixes of terrorist and guerrilla organizations, with some state-like attributes and military capabilities.
- Terrorism is a strategic threat to Israel. It has had a decisive effect on electoral outcomes and negotiating processes, caused a significant hardening in public

attitudes, and disrupted daily life, but has generally not had a significant effect on the economy.

- The emergence of a radical terrorist entity in Gaza is the living embodiment of Israel's fears of a future Palestinian state in the West Bank as well. The efficacy of the potential security arrangements is a subject of debate.
- A large conventional buildup is underway in the region, primarily by Saudi Arabia, whose future stability in unclear. Most of the weapons sales are American, with an increase in Russian sales, especially to Iran.
- Israel has been a primary subject of cyber-attacks. Heavily reliant on cyber-technology, Israel is particularly at risk and views cyber-warfare as one of the greatest threats it faces.
- The overall threat to Israel has diminished for the foreseeable future but remains daunting. The potential negative trends require great vigilance.

4

Nonmilitary Threats

Diplomatic Warfare, Delegitimization, and Demography

> If Algeria introduced a resolution (in the UN) declaring that the earth
> was flat and that Israel had flattened it, it would pass by a vote of 164 to
> 13 with 26 abstentions.
>
> —Abba Eban, former Israeli foreign minister

The previous chapter set out the primary military threats Israel faces today, but
Israel also faces foreign policy and demographic challenges that may prove to
be almost as dangerous to its long-term future as the military threats, in some
ways maybe more so. The foreign policy challenges stem from the growing delegitimization of Israel as a state, of its very right to exist, along with ongoing
diplomatic warfare and isolation. Few countries can afford long-term isolation,
certainly not Israel, which is deeply tied into the international system diplomatically, economically, militarily, and culturally. The demographic challenge
stems from the threat to Israel's character as both a Jewish and democratic
state,* posed by its ongoing control of the sizable Palestinian population in the
West Bank.

No issue has undermined Israel's international standing and played into
the hands of its adversaries more than the settlement policy in the West Bank,
which the international community simply does not understand, let alone
accept. Settlement activity by repeated Israeli governments, at times even
at the height of various diplomatic initiatives, has been viewed not only as
gratuitously provocative, but counterproductive to Israel's own interests,
assuming it wishes to achieve peace and security and preserve its Jewish and
democratic character. As seen in chapter 5, the issue is highly controversial
in Israel itself.

---

* Israel defines itself as the "nation-state of the Jewish people," but the "Jewish state" has become
a common shorthand.

The settlements and other West Bank issues are at the core of international opprobrium toward Israel, but there is more to it. Arab countries, certainly Iran, Hezbollah, and Hamas, broad parts of their publics, and many NGOs in the Arab and Muslim worlds and beyond are still not reconciled to Israel's existence and seek its ultimate destruction. Many around the world still question the fundamental legitimacy of the very concept of a "Jewish state," that is, one ostensibly based on religion. They fail to recognize that the Jews are a unique people, at least in the West, in that they constitute both a religious and a national group and that, as such, their right to national self-determination was recognized long ago both by the League of Nations and by the United Nations. Be that as it may, Israel's definition as the Jewish state is out of sync with the prevalent mood in much of the Western world and Far East today, especially among young people.

Moreover, the seemingly never-ending conflicts in which Israel is embroiled are almost totally foreign to the experiences of much of the international community today. In a "postmodern" world, in which most countries have not faced military threats of significance for many years and in which the processes of globalization and economic competition have largely supplanted the military confrontations of the past, at least for now, most people today have little experience of military affairs and even encounter difficulty thinking in such terms. Israel simply appears, once again, to be out of sync with much of the world. Moreover, with the passing of time and effective Arab propaganda, fewer and fewer are aware that Israel has actually made or accepted a number of dramatic proposals for peace, including the Oslo Agreement in 1993 and its follow-on agreements, the Camp David Summit in 2000, Clinton Parameters later that year, and the Olmert proposals in 2008.

Israel has long faced a semiorchestrated and nearly all-encompassing campaign of diplomatic warfare and delegitimization, designed to isolate it. In this sense, Israel truly is what the classic defense doctrine called a "nation dwelling alone." The chapter begins with a description of some of the particularly salient examples of the diplomatic warfare underway against Israel, the general campaign of delegitimization, and the attempts to impose boycotts and sanctions. It then turns to the second set of nonmilitary threats, the demographic issue, providing detailed data regarding the future population trends.

Diplomatic Warfare, Delegitimization, Boycotts, and Sanctions

For decades the Arab countries maintained a formal boycott on relations of any sort with Israel, diplomatic, economic, and social, indeed refused to have any contact with Israel whatsoever and even imposed sanctions on foreign companies that conducted business with it.[1] Long before the Six Day War and the beginning of the "occupation," in reality ever since its establishment, Israel has been subject to an ongoing campaign of diplomatic isolation and delegitimization, in which it has been portrayed as an illegitimate, brutal, and racist state. Positive Israeli attributes and actions have long been denied or dismissed, failures and weaknesses greatly magnified. In recent decades the delegitimization campaign has intentionally compared Israel to apartheid South Africa and remarkably even Nazi Germany, and Israel's actions are regularly depicted as war crimes and genocide. The absurdity of these allegations notwithstanding, terms applied repeatedly take on a momentum of their own and stick in the minds of many. The diplomatic and delegitimization campaign has gained growing momentum and taken on new forms in recent years, including so-called lawfare, all greatly amplified by the impact of the mass and social media.

The diplomatic and delegitimization campaign has two primary objectives. One, short term, is to create overwhelming international pressure on Israel to change its policies, circumscribe its military and diplomatic freedom of maneuver, and curtail its ability to even respond in the face of terrorist attacks and other provocations. The second, long term, is to weaken and ultimately defeat Israel by eroding its international standing, isolating it, and undermining the credibility of its positions in future negotiations and military confrontations.[2] Both objectives fully complement the PA's diplomatic strategy against Israel, as well as the military attrition doctrine pursued by Iran, Hezbollah, and Hamas.

The diplomatic and delegitimization campaign, originally begun by Arab countries, was later joined by Iran and various Third World countries and has expanded to a variety of international actors, including NGOs, media groups, academics, and more, with growing inroads into mainstream attitudes toward Israel. Much of the campaign has been waged in the UN, other international forums, the media, and in recent years through increased use of international legal forums.

There are no precise measures for assessing the strength of a country's diplomatic standing and acceptance, or conversely, its isolation and delegitimization. A state may have tense relations with virtually all countries in the world, for example, or excellent relations with just a few. Whether one emphasizes the breadth of relations or their depth, which is far harder to assess, is at least partially a judgment call. It is also difficult to assess the lost opportunity costs, that is, how a country might have been benefited from better relations had they not been adversely affected by the sources of disagreement. In Israel's case, the picture is further muddied by conflicting positive and negative trends, making it hard to reach any unequivocal conclusions.

Diplomatic Warfare and Isolation

If one looks just at the numbers, Israel is certainly not isolated. Israel had formal diplomatic relations with 158 countries in 2016, more than ever before, up from 98 in 1967.[3] Israel also enjoys extensive economic and military ties with countries around the world, which have expanded greatly over the years.

It is not just the number of relations, but in many ways their quality, too. In addition to the United States, Israel has particularly strong ties with Canada, Australia, Germany, Poland, Italy, Russia, and India, to name just a few, and a booming economic relationship with China. Germany established a strategic dialogue with Israel with the express purpose of institutionalizing the bilateral relationship and making it impervious to political developments and changes in leadership. Various other countries also hold strategic dialogues with Israel, such as Russia, India, Britain, and France, with whom relations have improved greatly in recent years. Israel also holds military exercises with more countries than ever before.

Egypt and Jordan have been at peace with Israel for decades. There is growing cooperation with them, and there are even potential signs, at the time of this writing, of a thaw in the diplomatic relationship with Cairo. Unprecedented public contacts have taken place in the last two years with former Saudi officials, and numerous press reports speak of growing covert Israeli ties with Riyadh and other Gulf states, possibly heralding overt relations in the future. The Arab League, which adopted the Arab Peace Initiative in 2002, has repeatedly reaffirmed it ever since and even made some changes to accommodate Israeli concerns. As imperfect as the initiative remains, since some clauses are clear nonstarters for Israel, it is a welcome change in mindset and is obviously far better than some of the League's previous resolutions, such as the infamous "three no's" of the 1967 conference in Khartoum. A number of African and Latin American countries have also begun warming their relations with Israel, after decades of alienation.

For all of the tensions in Israel's relations with Europe, it enjoys an advanced Association Agreement with the EU, which was further upgraded in both 2008 and 2012. Possible Israeli membership in both the EU and NATO was even mooted in the early 2000s, at the height of the peace process, as inducements for Israel to make some of the concessions necessary to reach an agreement with the Palestinians. Times have changed, but Europe may proffer important inducements such as these once again, in the context of a renewed push for a final settlement. As it is, Israel already has closer ties with NATO than any other nonmember state. Israel no longer has to go to great lengths, as it did in the past, to defeat annual Arab attempts to unseat it in the UN and generally to persuade countries not to submit to Arab blandishments and threats to sever ties.

In 2017 the Globalization Index ranked Israel 38th out of 207 countries in terms of its overall integration into the processes of globalization, in other words, in the top 20%. The Index further ranked Israel 40th in economic and 34th in social integration, both still in the top 20%. Only in terms of political integration, such as membership in international organizations, ratification of international treaties, participation in UN national security missions, and number of embassies, was Israel well below this, in 116th place.[4]

Above all, Israel has a truly unique relationship with the United States, which in many ways counterbalances any sources of isolation and delegitimization. If a country was to be relegated to a close relationship with only one other—which is not Israel's case—and that country was the United States, it would be doing something right. By definition, an important US ally can never truly be isolated. Given a long-term perspective, Israel has thus made important strides toward fulfilling its objective of becoming an accepted part of both the international arena and the region.

So much for the half-full part of the diplomatic glass. The UN has been the central venue for the diplomatic and delegitimization campaigns against Israel, in the General Assembly, Security Council, various councils and commissions, the specialized agencies, indeed, virtually every UN forum. With an automatic Arab, Muslim, and Third World majority against it, Israel has been largely helpless to confront the hostile onslaught.

UN resolutions on Israel are ludicrously biased. In most years, four or five countries are the target of one General Assembly resolution regarding violations of human rights. Israel, which cannot be considered a major violator of human rights by any objective comparative standard, is the focus of numerous resolutions each year. In 2006 the General Assembly passed 22 such resolutions against Israel, 19 in 2007. In 2012 it passed a total of 26 human rights resolutions, 22 of which were against Israel, and 21 out of 25 in 2013. Terrorism against Israel has been condemned in just one resolution.[5]

As seen in the Figure 4.1, the attention devoted to Israel by the General Assembly, compared to a list of leading international rogue states and violators of human rights, is simply astounding.[6]

The disproportionate focus on Israel is not limited, however, to the General Assembly. About one-third of all Security Council activity is also related Israel,[7] as seen in Figure 4.2.

The UN has also created four special administrative units to deal with the Palestinian issue, whose very names indicate their biased character: the Committee on the Inalienable Rights of the Palestinian People, the Special Committee to Investigate Israeli Practices Affecting Human Rights of the Palestinian People, the Special Political and Decolonization Committee, and the UN Relief and Works Agency (UNRWA). The latter was established

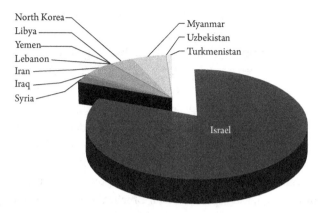

Figure 4.1 General Assembly Resolutions, Select Countries, 2000–2014
Note: Number of votes: Israel 196; Iraq 3; Iran 13; Myanmar 14; North Korea 9; Uzbekistan 1; Syria 5; Libya 1; Turkmenistan 3. See appendix for the list of votes.

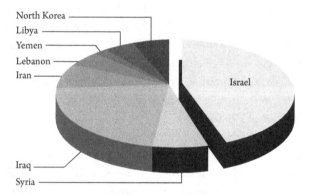

Figure 4.2 Security Council Resolutions, Select Countries, 2000–2014
Note: See appendix for explanation of votes.

to provide social services solely to Palestinian refugees, whereas all other refugees, the world over, are handled by the UN High Commissioner for Refugees (UNHCR). UNRWA is the only UN body ever created to help a specific group of people displaced by war. It is also the only refugee organization that defines refugees as not just those actually displaced, but all of their descendants. In so doing, UNRWA has vastly inflated the number of Palestinian refugees, from the 700,000–750,000 estimated to have been displaced by the fighting in 1948–1949, most of whom have obviously passed away in the interim, to some five million today. Designed to bolster the Palestinian position and place a unique moral and diplomatic burden on Israel, this unique definition also makes resolving the Palestinian refugee issue that much harder to achieve.[8]

The UN Human Rights Council was established to make a "contribution to the promotion and protection of human rights," but its members have included such known human rights abusers as Saudi Arabia, Angola, Uganda, Qatar, Cuba, and China and it has even been chaired by Libya and Sudan. Approximately one-third of the Council's resolutions have focused on Israel, including a permanent agenda item devoted solely to supposed Israeli human rights violations. Between 2006 and 2013 the Council adopted 43 resolutions and held 19 emergency sessions related to Israel, compared with 103 resolutions against all other states. In 2011 it adopted 20 resolutions criticizing Israel, only seven against all of the other 193 member states. The Council never adopted a single resolution critical of Syria (until the civil war), Saudi Arabia, China, and Zimbabwe, nor did it ever hold a special emergency session on the genocides in Rwanda and Darfur, the ethnic cleansing in Yugoslavia, or the massacres in East Timor.[9] Human Rights Council resolutions on Israel and select countries appear in Figure 4.3.

There have been some positive developments in the UN over the years. In 2010 Israel became a member of the Western European and Others Group, the first time it was ever a member of any of the UN's regional groupings (Arab opposition kept it out of its natural membership in the Asian or Middle Eastern groups). In 2016 Israel was elected, for the first time, to chair a permanent UN committee, the Sixth Committee, which deals with legal issues. Chairs are usually approved by consensus, in this case a vote was held, with Israel gaining the approval of 109 out of 175 votes.[10]

It is not just in the UN and other international forums that Israel faces diplomatic warfare and deep isolation. Israel's relations with virtually all countries would be better were a peace agreement to be reached with the Palestinians, or even just significant progress made. To illustrate, 34 countries established ties

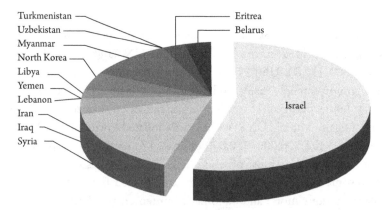

Figure 4.3 Human Rights Council Resolutions, Select Countries, 2006–2014
Note: See appendix for explanation of votes.

with Israel following the 1991 Madrid Conference and 1993 Oslo Agreement. Many more, including Arab, Muslim, and Third World countries, would clearly like to establish relations today or upgrade existing ties, subject to progress with the Palestinians. Some countries have separated their bilateral relationships with Israel from their differences with it over the Palestinian and other issues, for example, the United States, Canada, Russia, China, and India, but they are the exceptions.

Relations with Egypt, Jordan, Turkey, and Europe, in particular, have been adversely affected by the Palestinian issues. Various European countries have at times imposed partial or complete arms embargoes on Israel, including Britain and France, even without formal EU decisions to this effect. Israel is often presented with highly critical diplomatic demarches by the EU and individual European states,[11] in addition to critical public statements. European anger and frustration, which have been brewing for decades at both the public and governmental levels, have finally begun manifesting themselves in recent years in concrete, if still limited, measures.

In 2013 the EU decided, over strenuous Israeli objections, that cooperation agreements with Israel would no longer apply to institutions based in the West Bank.[12] In 2014 the parliaments in Britain, France, Spain, Ireland, and Sweden all adopted resolutions calling for the establishment of a Palestinian state and expressing what was clearly growing impatience and antipathy toward Israel. In 2015, in a highly demonstrative act, the EU announced that it would start labeling products made in the West Bank as such, not as made in Israel.[13] In 2015–2016, over strong Israeli opposition, France began promoting the idea of an international peace conference, based on a possible Security Council resolution. A significant increase in measures such as these, and European pressure on Israel generally, is likely if renewed diplomatic progress is not achieved by the Trump administration. Even in the United States, as discussed in chapter 10, alienation is growing among important parts of the public.

The Delegitimization and Boycott Campaign

Arab and other states have sought to delegitimize Israel from the early years of the conflict. At its heart, the delegitimization campaign has been based on a long-standing denial of the right of the Jewish people to a nation state of their own in the Land of Israel. It was not the size of the state, or its borders, but its very existence, that has been the issue.[14]

A turning point in the contemporary delegitimization efforts came in 2001, with the convening of the UN Conference against Racism, Racial Discrimination, Xenophobia and Related Intolerance in Durban. The new "Durban Strategy," led by Arab, Muslim, and Third World countries, along with various anti-Israeli

NGOs, was based on the model applied against South Africa, including the language of human rights, humanitarian relief, and international law, coupled with a media campaign. Coming shortly after the collapse of the Oslo peace talks and the beginning of the second intifada, the new strategy used the violent uprisings to criticize Israel, equated Zionism with racism, and referred to Israel as an apartheid state. It further charged Israel with "racist crimes against humanity, including ethnic cleansing (and) acts of genocide" and called for its complete isolation, the imposition of mandatory sanctions, and the end of all diplomatic links with Israel.[15]

The one-sided nature of the outcome was clear from the start. Israel was excluded from preparatory conferences, including one in Tehran where a draft document preposterously claimed that Israel was anti-Semitic, and the final document failed to even mention Palestinian terrorism.[16] The Durbin Strategy set the tone for subsequent attempts to summon Israeli officials before foreign courts and helped launch the Boycott, Divestment and Sanctions movement (BDS), formally established by Palestinian activists in 2005.

The stated goals of the BDS movement are to force Israel, through nonviolent means, to behave justly toward the Palestinians and pay a price for the crimes it commits against them, expose the nature of Israel's occupation and apartheid regime, and demonstrate that support for Israel means oppression of Palestinians.[17] In so doing, and by creating legal, political, and normative obstacles to Israel's use of military force, the BDS movement seeks to delegitimize it generally and constrain its ability to defend itself.[18] BDS does not take a formal official position on the "one-state solution," in essence, Israel's demise as a Jewish (and probably democratic) state, but supporters of this approach are identified with the movement and have begun calling for BDS tactics to be used until Israel accepts it.[19]

BDS seeks to undermine Israel's economic, cultural, and technological ties with other countries by promoting a campaign of boycotts, divestments, and sanctions, including, most controversially, an academic one. The movement has been most active in Europe, notably Britain, but in 2013 the Association for Asian American Studies and the American Studies Association passed resolutions endorsing an academic boycott of Israel, as did the Modern Language Association in 2014 and the American Anthropological Association in 2015.[20]

The movement also promotes an annual "Israel Apartheid Week" on college campuses, as part of a broader campaign to convince Western publics that Israel pursues repressive policies that violate human rights and Western values. To this end, it has worked with churches, student organizations, trade unions, municipal authorities, and social movements to spread the BDS message, including comparisons of Israel to the Nazis.[21] Talks and lectures by Israeli academics and speakers generally are commonly heckled today on campuses and various other

venues around the world, and Israeli musicians, artists, and other cultural figures often have their appearances disrupted and even canceled. A few musicians
and other celebrities have also canceled appearances in Israel.[22] The anti-Israel
atmosphere, often blatantly anti-Semitic, is palpable on many college campuses,
and pro-Israel, or just Jewish students, often feel under attack.[23]

The BDS campaign has made inroads in various Christian denominations,
including Quaker groups in both America and England. The Church of
Sweden has endorsed boycotts and sanctions against companies and products
from Israeli settlements in the West Bank.[24] The United Church of Canada
similarly adopted a campaign to convince people to boycott products from
Israeli settlements.[25] The United Methodist Church, the largest Protestant
denomination in America, voted to support a boycott on products made
in settlements, but against divesting from Israeli companies generally, or
companies that make equipment for the IDF.[26] The Presbyterian Church in
the United States decided in 2014 to divest from three companies that supply
Israel with products used in the West Bank. Although it stated that this was not
an endorsement of the BDS movement, or a call to divest from Israel, the decision makes the church, with 1.76 million members, the largest religious group
to adopt such measures. It also passed a measure calling for an investigation
into the two-state solution, accusing Israel of responsibility for "an increasing
loss of their [Palestinian] human rights, freedom, livelihoods, property, and
even their lives."[27]

A particular focus of the delegitimization campaign has been the attempt
to create a situation in which any Israeli use of force, even clearly defensive, is
considered illegitimate almost by definition. Facing a massive wave of terrorism
during the second intifada, Israel began construction of a security fence designed
to impede the infiltration of terrorists from the West Bank. Portrayed by the
BDS movement as a heinous "apartheid wall," it is almost entirely a simple security fence, such as Israel has long had on its Lebanese and Gazan borders (the
"wall" parts, approximately 5% of the total, are only in built-up areas, where a
fence would not have been effective). The result, significantly but not solely due
to the fence, was a dramatic decrease in the number of attacks.

Palestinian groups and NGOs tried to challenge the fence's legality before the
International Court of Justice (ICJ) and Israel's Supreme Court, on the grounds
that parts of it ran though West Bank territory.[28] The ICJ issued a nonbinding
advisory opinion in 2004, which found that construction of the fence, in and
of itself, was not a violation of international law, but that doing so in parts of
the West Bank, rather than along the 1967 border, was.[29] The advisory opinion
received a great deal of international coverage and was a heavy diplomatic blow
for Israel. The General Assembly overwhelmingly adopted the ICJ ruling and
called upon UN members "to comply with their legal obligations as mentioned

in the Advisory Opinion."[30] The resolution also led to calls for UN sanctions and boycotts against Israel.

In 2002, at the height of the second intifada and in response to a horrific terrorist attack in which 29 people were killed and 160 wounded at a Passover Seder, the IDF launched an operation designed to suppress Palestinian terrorism. Anti-Israel groups claimed that 500 people were killed in the Jenin refugee camp alone, accused Israel of a "massacre," summary executions, and genocide, and pushed the UN to appoint a fact-finding team to investigate alleged Israeli war crimes. A report written by the secretary-general ultimately found that 52 people had been killed, of whom half were combatants. According to IDF figures all but five were combatants.[31]

The pattern established in the Jenin investigations was repeated during the following years, whenever Israel responded to terrorist attacks. Various NGOs would condemn Israel and demand "independent investigations," usually under the purview of the UN Human Rights Council. The members of such investigative teams typically held strong anti-Israel beliefs, and reports were issued based on questionable legal views and dubious eyewitness accounts.[32]

Further attempts to constrain Israel's ability to use force, through delegitimization efforts, took place during the 2006 Lebanon war. At the very outset of the fighting many NGOs immediately issued condemnations of both sides, but most of the criticism was directed at Israel, including accusations of war crimes. Human Rights Watch, for example, issued patently false accusations against the IDF, such as deliberately targeting relief convoys and attacking civilians.[33]

Later in 2006, Israel was accused of the intentional deaths of 19 civilians by shelling in the Gaza town of Beit Hanoun. Israel expressed regret over the incident, stated that it was an accident, the result of a malfunction in a guidance system, and offered to provide humanitarian aid to the wounded. It also argued, however, that Hamas bore ultimate responsibility, because it had provoked Israel's response by firing rockets into Israel and intentionally embedding its own forces among civilians. The UN Human Rights Council issued a report claiming that Israel had violated human rights and humanitarian law and that it had imposed collective punishment on Gaza.[34] The timing of the report, coming prior to the operation in Gaza in 2008, was particularly damaging to Israel, harming its image even before the fighting had begun.[35]

During the 2008 operation, anti-Israel NGOs initiated even more strident delegitimization efforts than in the past. Ostensibly basing the campaign on international law, they accused Israel of indiscriminately killing civilians and other war crimes, and called for a UN investigation while hostilities were still underway. The accusations were widely echoed by the international media.[36] The UN Human Rights Council issued a statement at the start of the conflict, contrary to the requirement that the General Assembly authorize it to do so, demanding that Israel withdraw its military forces, stop the "targeting of civilians and medical facilities and staff, and the systematic destruction of the cultural heritage of the Palestinian people," and calling for an investigative team to be allowed to investigate the damage.[37] In conjunction with the Arab League, PA, and various NGOs, the Council also sent a formal request to the ICC to investigate Israeli war crimes.[38]

The UN report on the 2008 conflict (the "Goldstone Report", issued in 2009) accused Israel of deliberately targeting civilians and of war crimes during the operation. It further charged Israel with a "deliberately disproportionate attack designed to punish, humiliate and terrorize a civilian population," and of a campaign of "massive and deliberate destruction."[39]

A major focus of anti-Israel groups at the time was the attempt to delegitimize Israel's heretofore highly regarded judicial system.[40] The Goldstone Report thus rejected Israel's ability to investigate war crimes objectively, called upon the Security Council to establish an independent committee to monitor its investigations, and suggested new mechanisms for ensuring that Israel comply with international law. In accordance with standard international practice, Israel should have been given the chance to conduct an investigation of its own, but the UN Human Rights Council issued a report before it had a chance to do so, and the Goldstone Report recommended that it be submitted to the Security Council and then to the International Criminal Court (ICC).[41]

In 2011 Goldstone partially retracted the report's findings, saying that Israel had not deliberately targeted civilians. Goldstone also reconsidered his criticism of the Israeli judicial system and praised IDF investigations into wrongdoing, noting that Israel had conducted over 400 investigations, Hamas not one.[42] The Goldstone Report badly hurt Israel's image, nevertheless, and immediately became a central piece in the delegitimization campaign. Many NGOs continued to make use of the report, claiming that Goldstone had recanted due to ulterior motives (he is Jewish).[43]

For decades, the "two-state solution" has been the internationally accepted basis for a resolution of the Israeli-Palestinian conflict, to which Israel, the PA, and the Arab League are also all officially committed. The failure of diplomatic efforts to reach an agreement, however, has led to heightened interest in recent years in a "one-state solution," or a binational state (i.e., a unified Jewish and Arab state, democratic or otherwise, in place of Israel). The growing support appears to stem from three different sources, although there is presumably considerable overlap between them.

One group of supporters simply appears to have despaired of the prospects of achieving a two-state solution and seeks, in desperation, almost any alternative to the impasse. A second group is attracted, rather naively, to the idea of Israelis and Palestinians living together harmoniously in one unified democratic state.

A third group seeks to use the one-state paradigm as part of the delegitimization campaign, by stressing Israel's opposition to what appears, to those unfamiliar with the history of the conflict, or unaware of what has happened to other binational states (e.g., Syria and Iraq), to be the ultimate democratic solution to the conflict.

Most of the increased attention to the one-state binational solution has been on the Palestinian side and among academic and anti-Israel groups around the world. For Israel, except an insignificant fringe, it is a complete nonstarter, which would guarantee an end to Israel's Jewish character. In reality, the one-state paradigm has been the preferred Arab position since the earliest days of the conflict and there is nothing new about it. Unrealistic though it may be, it has become a further tool in the delegitimization campaign, one that "sounds good."

A relatively new component in the delegitimization campaign is the concept of "lawfare," defined as a "strategy of using—or misusing—law as a substitute for traditional military means to achieve an operational objective."[44] Others have expanded on this definition, arguing that lawfare includes the manipulation of international law by nonstate actors as a means of countering stronger military adversaries, the intentional violation of international law by one side in order to gain advantage over another that does attempt to adhere to it,[45] and the use of universal jurisdiction statutes in lawsuits in Western courts in the attempt to criminalize a nation via its governmental and military officials.[46]

Hezbollah and Hamas conduct lawfare by intentionally violating international law, in the knowledge that Israel, in contrast, does try to observe it and is thus at a disadvantage. Such actions include storing munitions in mosques, hospitals, and schools and intentionally firing rockets and fighting from residential areas.[47] When Israel attacks these targets for lack of choice and civilian casualties occur, it is excoriated in the international media and diplomatic forums.

The first attempt to bring Israeli officials before foreign courts was in Belgium in 2001, when the principle of universal jurisdiction was used to file civil charges against then-prime minister Sharon, for his role in the "Sabra and Shatila massacres" in 1982, during the First Lebanon War.[48] Since Sharon now had immunity as prime minister, the case was dismissed and Belgium amended its laws to avoid having its courts used again for such purposes.[49] The damage to Israel's image, however, was done.

In 2005 three cases were filed against Israel in the United States by a group called the Center for Constitutional Rights (CCR). In one, Moshe Yaalon, then the IDF chief of staff, was charged with "war crimes, crimes against humanity, extrajudicial killing, and cruel, inhuman or degrading treatment or punishment," due to an accidental bombing of a UN compound during a 1996 operation against Hezbollah. CCR also brought charges against the Caterpillar Corporation over its alleged responsibility for the death of a US activist crushed by a bulldozer during a protest in the West Bank. The third case was filed jointly by the CCR and the Palestinian Center for Human Rights, on behalf of the relatives of Palestinians killed in an air strike against Israel's most wanted terrorist. The suit charged the former director of the Israel Security Agency, Avi Dichter, with essentially the same misdeeds as Yaalon. All three cases were dismissed on the grounds of immunity or of the political question doctrine.[50]

After their failure in the United States, anti-Israel NGOs pressed the case in Europe. In 2009 a Spanish judge announced that he would investigate the incident as a possible crime against humanity, but Israel appealed to the Spanish Foreign Ministry and the case was shelved.[51] The PA repeatedly attempted to bring Israeli officers and leaders before the ICC on charges related to the 2010 Gaza flotilla incident (discussed subsequently) and the Goldstone Report, but the ICC declared that it could not investigate because the PA was not a state.[52]

The threat of prosecution, by pro-Palestinian activists, has forced numerous Israeli officials to cancel trips to London for fear of arrest, and some have faced charges, or even been briefly detained, including then-defense minister Barak and Foreign Minister Livni. In 2015 former defense minister Mofaz and a retired IDF officer, who had fought in the Gaza operation the previous year, were also nearly arrested.[53] Under British law, based on the principle of universal jurisdiction, anyone can apply to the courts for an arrest warrant against those they deem to have committed war crimes anywhere in the world.[54] Israel placed pressure on Britain to change its universal jurisdiction laws, and the British government has attempted to do so, but the legal changes have not yet eliminated the possibility of arrest.[55]

In 2010 nine Turkish activists were killed in the course of a forcible attempt to break Israel's naval blockade of Gaza. Israel was severely criticized in the international media for its handling of the incident, and pro-Palestinian activists and NGOs presented a number of legal arguments, including the charge that the blockade was illegal. In this case, however, the secretary-general's panel of inquiry (the "Palmer Report") proved a major blow to the lawfare efforts against Israel, concluding that the blockade was legal under international law, even if excessive force had been used.[56]

Boycotts, sanctions, and divestments of Israeli products and firms are another form of delegitimization and isolation. Campaigns to this end have been conducted around the world, primarily in Europe and other Western countries, in which societal norms are increasingly driving economic behavior and governmental policy, and in which public opinion is increasingly hostile toward Israel. Trade relations with European countries have been affected by developments with the Palestinians more than with any other countries to date, and the EU has explicitly tied further upgrades in its relations with Israel to the peace process.

Public and civil society pressure for boycotts of Israel, especially by unions and student groups, has been particularly prevalent in Europe.[57] We also cannot know how many firms have simply chosen not to do business with Israel, or how many consumers prefer not to buy Israeli products. The numbers still appear to be relatively small, but growing. Trade with the United States and Far East is far less sensitive to political considerations.[58]

The pressure for boycotts and divestment from Israel has led to a significant backlash in the United States and, to a lesser extent, elsewhere. A growing number of US states, 12 as of August 2016, ranging from New York and California to South Carolina and Alabama, have passed legislation denouncing BDS efforts and generally blocking the state from investing in or contracting with companies that support the movement, in some cases also providing for divestment from them.[59] At the federal level, Congress passed anti-BDS legislation, which is also designed to put pressure on European governments to refrain from participation in boycotts or sanctions against Israel. The Canadian parliament, too, passed legislation condemning the BDS movement. In Britain the government has taken measures to bar public institutions from cooperating with boycott and sanctions measures.

The Media Campaign

Virtually all events today are reported immediately in the international and social media, with profound effects on public opinion. By exposing the horrors immanent to warfare, including the operational blunders that are a tragic but unavoidable part thereof, media coverage can easily undermine a combatant's domestic and international legitimacy. Public legitimacy is affected by the perception of reality no less than reality itself, and the images generated by television and the social media often present an only limited and even distorted picture.[60] The "media arena" has become an essential component today not just of diplomacy, but of military operations, as well.

Gaining legitimacy in the irregular confrontations with Hezbollah, Hamas, and the PA is particularly difficult. The causes of the hostilities are often blurred by the conflicting claims of the different sides, abetted by propaganda campaigns and by the seemingly endless cycles of tit-for-tat. The almost inevitable loss of innocent lives caused by Hezbollah's and Hamas's intentional use of their civilian populations as defensive shields leads to a blurring of moral judgment and to an inversion of power.[61] The often misleading appearance of disproportionate use of force by Israel in the battle against such nonstate adversaries further exacerbates the problem. Israel, the stronger side, with an organized military, comes to appear oppressive and evil, while its irregular adversaries appear to be underdogs worthy of sympathy and support. Moreover, Hezbollah and Hamas intentionally exaggerate the damage and casualties they suffer, in order to shape coverage in a manner designed to undermine the legitimacy of Israel's military operations, lead to pressure on it to curtail or cease them, erode its societal resilience, and shore up their own domestic public opinion.

As a result, Israel is increasingly constrained in its ability to wield military power effectively, and the irregular adversaries often gain the upper hand. The United States encountered similar problems fighting insurgencies in Iraq and Afghanistan. In these circumstances, the international media have increasingly joined with international norms and laws as sources of significant impact on modern warfare and international relations.[62]

The international media have played a primary role in the delegitimization campaign. Many highly critical reports of Israel are readily accepted, regardless of their validity and without questioning or verifying the facts. For instance, the media readily accepted the Palestinian claims of an Israeli "massacre" in Jenin in 2002, even though the actual number of casualties was a fraction of those claimed.[63] In June 2006 seven Palestinian civilians were killed at a Gaza beach by a Hamas mine, not the IDF, as falsely alleged, and at around the same time television footage was faked of Israeli naval vessels supposedly shelling Gaza. During the 2008 and 2012 operations against Hamas in Gaza, which had fired thousands of rockets at Israeli civilians, the media again readily accepted reports of excessive use of force by Israel and unconfirmed claims of Palestinian civilian casualties.[64]

Controversial Israeli policies, especially the settlements, play into the hands of Israel's detractors and lend a veneer of legitimacy to their efforts. Added to this are the nature of media coverage, which inherently favors pictures of demonstrators, children, and lightly armed guerrillas over the tanks of an organized military; Palestinian intimidation of foreign reporters; and even mundane economic considerations, such as the frequent employment of Palestinian "stringers" whose commitment to professionalism is often overridden by nationalism. Further complicating the picture is that Israel is an open society that projects numerous conflicting views to the media, often highly self-critical, and has always been ruled by coalition governments that are beset by infighting. In contrast, the PA and Hamas are autocratic in nature and generally project far clearer, simpler, and unified messages.[65]

Israel has been pilloried in the international media for decades. Much of the criticism may certainly have been justified, but much has also been blatantly one-sided, disproportionate, and simply incorrect. If to the media onslaught one adds the delegitimization campaign, including the intensive efforts on college campuses, a global generation has grown up with a highly negative view of Israel. This generation has already begun filling positions of importance in their respective countries, in the media, academia, arts, and, most importantly, government and will increasingly do so in the coming years. Unlike previous generations of Israeli interlocutors, who grew up knowing Israel of the post-Holocaust and early heroic era, or the Six Day War, those who have come of age since then have internalized an entirely different narrative. This long-term change in international perceptions has had a highly deleterious impact on Israel's international standing and, as recognized by senior government officials, Israel has come to be viewed by international opinion as a pariah state.[66] Most worrisomely, trends such as these are now apparent in the United States, as well.

A 2013 poll of citizens in 25 nations found Israel to be the fourth most unpopular in the world. Only 21% of all respondents had a favorable image of Israel, 52% a negative one. Remarkably, only Iran, Pakistan, and North Korea had more unfavorable ratings.[67]

The United States was the only Western country polled in which a majority (51%) had favorable views of Israel, though 32% had negative ones. In Canada 57% had negative views, and 69% in Australia. The EU as a whole had strongly negative views of Israel, ranging from a high of 72% in Britain to a low of 44% in Poland. In Germany 67% had negative views, only a devastating 8% positive ones, and in France 63% held negative views. In Russia and China views were somewhat more balanced; 32% in Russia had negative views, 23% positive ones, while in China 33% had negative views, 32% positive ones. In other parts of the Far East matters were worse. In Japan 54% had negative views, a mere 3% positive ones. In South Korea 56% had negative views, 23% positive. Surprisingly, perhaps, in Nigeria, Kenya, and Ghana views were considerably more positive.[68]

To conclude this part of the chapter: the overall diplomatic and delegitimization campaigns have met with mixed success to date. Israel has diplomatic relations with more states than ever before, including a number of particularly deep relationships, none more so than with the United States, and its economic and military ties have expanded greatly. Ties are also growing with a number of African and Latin American countries and even with some Arab states, with whom Israel has had little or no contact to date. In terms of the number and extent of its ties, Israel is far from isolated.

The scandalously biased nature of UN resolutions related to Israel, in willful disregard of human rights violations and war crimes that make even the worst of Israel's alleged misdeeds pale in comparison, is not new. This, however, does not detract from the severity of Israel's isolation in the UN and international forums. More importantly, perhaps, the quality of Israel's bilateral relationships, even with its closest friends, has been adversely impacted by differences over the Palestinian and other issues, and the problem is growing worse. This is especially true of European and other Western countries, with which a crisis point, or at least significant deterioration, may be reached in the coming years.

The campaign to impose economic sanctions and boycotts on Israel has achieved little to date, even generated a partial backlash, and most attempts at lawfare have simply failed. Nevertheless, the cumulative impact of decades of diplomatic warfare and delegitimization efforts has been a severe deterioration in Israel's international image; it is now widely perceived as a pariah. This status is beginning to have a concrete effect on government policies. The greatest problem today is in Europe, but it is steadily spreading around the world and has even begun to make inroads in the American public, which is the basis for US support of Israel and much of its national security.

The impact of increasingly hostile European public opinion has been mitigated in recent years by the chance election of a number of friendly leaders, such as Merkel in Germany, Sarkozy and Hollande in France, and Cameron and May in Britain, a highly fortuitous electoral constellation that is unlikely to continue for long. An entire generation of officials and leaders around the world, who have grown up with a narrative that is highly hostile to Israel, have now reached positions of influence, including in the United States. The campaigns of diplomatic isolation and delegitimization are likely to be among the more severe challenges Israel faces in the coming years.

Demography: A Nonlethal Existential Threat

Demography has become a primary consideration in Israeli national security thinking, at least since the 1990s. In a short period of a few years, numerous leaders of the right, including Dan Meridor, Ehud Olmert, Tzipi Livni, Roni Milo, and even Ariel Sharon, changed their approach toward this issue, and consequently the peace process as a whole, warning of the demographic threat and embracing the need for a two-state solution to save Israel from the dangers to its Jewish and democratic character.

Prime Minister Rabin explained his concessions under the Oslo Agreement by saying that "we prefer a Jewish state to a binational state." Sharon spoke of the "demographic reality that has been created on the ground" and of the need to ensure Israel's future as a Jewish and democratic state, as a means of justifying the unilateral withdrawal from Gaza in 2005.[69] Olmert went even further, stating that "Israel is finished" if a two-state solution is not achieved.[70] The public impact of the demographic issue has receded somewhat in recent years, or been overshadowed by the de facto failure of the peace process. It still informs the thinking of various leaders, however, including Netanyahu, who has expressed concern over demographic trends and the possibility of a binational state and called for a two-state solution.[71]

Demography has also had an effect on Israel's military strategy. As noted in chapter 6, the IDF no longer seeks to conquer territory in battle, largely in order to avoid having to assume control of additional hostile populations and further undermine Israel's demographic balance. Territorial conquest has long been, and remains, the primary means of achieving military decision, and in its absence the IDF has encountered severe difficulties in achieving its objectives in all of the past rounds.

In talking about demography, a word of caution is in order. Whereas the data for Israel are derived from the Israel Central Bureau of Statistics (CBS), a highly regarded source, other sources were needed for the West Bank, Gaza, and East Jerusalem, some of which are less reliable and which use different projection methods, or work from different databases. Even the CBS provides three projections, high, medium, and low, to account for different analytical assumptions. For the West Bank and Gaza, only high and low projections were available, not a medium one, and for East Jerusalem, just one. Israel counts the Arab residents of East Jerusalem in its population projections, as do the Palestinians and international sources, therefore creating a small double count (factored out in Table 4.2). The different sources also make projections for different years, making it hard to compare data. Moreover, projections of the future are, of course, just that.

In short, addressing the demographic issue poses serious analytical challenges, and the various projections for both sides, between the high and low estimates, differ sometimes by millions. Definitive conclusions are thus hard to reach. What makes it possible for us to draw a number of important conclusions with confidence, nonetheless, is that all of the projections, disparate as they are, tell the same overall story. To be conservative the CBS's medium projection has been chosen, where possible, for the following discussion.

Table 4.1 demonstrates the dramatic growth expected in Israel's population over the next decades, as well as that of the West Bank, Gaza, and East Jerusalem. Israel's total Jewish population of 6.47 million in 2015 is expected to reach 10.42 million by 2050 (low projection 8.43; high 12.63 million) and its Arab population to grow from 1.71 million in 2015 to 3.16 million in 2050 (low 2.64; high 3.73 million). The West Bank population is expected to grow from 2.64–2.89 million in 2015 to 4.21–4.72 million by 2050 and Gaza's population from 1.71–1.85 to 3.05–4.79 million. The numbers are worrisome, if only in terms of population density, urban planning, and quality-of-life issues, a whopping 6–13 million more people in a very small area. The numbers are also worrisome because of their ramifications for Israel's future character as a state and for the future of the conflict between Israel and the Palestinians generally.

Table 4.1 **Demographic Projections, Israel, West Bank, Gaza, and East Jerusalem (millions)**

	Projection	*~2015*	*~2025*	*~2030*	*~2050*	*~2060*
Israel total[a]	High	8.30	10.02	10.99	16.36	20.38
	Medium	8.18	9.52	10.23	13.58	15.60
	Low	8.06	9.04	9.50	11.07	11.61
Jews and others	High	6.57	7.82	8.52	12.63	15.84
	Medium	6.47	7.42	7.92	10.42	12.00
	Low	6.37	7.04	7.34	8.43	8.82
Arab Israelis (including East Jerusalem)	High	1.73	2.20	2.47	3.73	4.54
	Medium	1.71	2.10	2.31	3.16	3.60
	Low	1.69	2.00	2.16	2.64	2.79
Jews (% of Israel total)	High	79	78	77	77	77
	Medium	79	77	77	76	76
	Low	79	77	77	76	76
West Bank (including East Jerusalem)	High	2.89	3.52	3.76	4.72	—
	Low	2.64	3.15	—	4.21	—
East Jerusalem (Palestinians)	—		0.26	0.31	0.33	0.42	—
Gaza	High	1.85	2.65	3.13	4.79	—
	Low	1.71	2.12	—	3.05	—

Source: Israel Central Bureau of Statistics for Israeli figures, http://www.cbs.gov.il/publications/tec27.pdf; other sources as indicated: for West Bank high projection, Palestine 2030 Demographic Changes: Opportunities for Development, Full Report, 2016, p. 143, http://palestine.unfpa.org/sites/default/files/pub-pdf/Palestine%202030%20Full%20Report%20English.pdf; for West Bank low projection, US Census International Data Base, drawing on data from Palestinian Central Bureau of Statistics, https://www.census.gov/population/international/data/idb/region.php?N=%20Results%20&T=13&A=separate&RT=0&Y=2050&R=-1&C=WE; for East Jerusalem, Palestine 2030 Demographic Change: Opportunities for Development, Full Report, 2016, p. 151; for Gaza high projection, Palestine 2030 Demographic Changes: Opportunities for Development, Full Report, 2016, p. 143; for Gaza low projection, US Census International Data Base, drawing from data from Palestinian Central Bureau of Statistics, https://www.census.gov/population/international/data/idb/region.php?N=%20Results%20&T=13&A=separate&RT=0&Y=2050&R=-1&C=GZ.

Note: Israeli figures are for years 2014, 2024, 2049, 2059, Palestinian as shown.

[a] Including Israel's pre-1967 Borders, the Golan Heights, and East Jerusalem.

Table 4.2 **Demographic Projections, Jewish Population as Percentage of Total**

	Projection	*~2015*	*~2025*	*~2050*
% of Israel total and West Bank	High	60	59	61
	Low	61	59	56
% of Israel total, West Bank, and Gaza	High	51	49	49
	Low	52	50	47

Note: Israeli figures are for years 2014, 2024, 2049, Palestinian as shown. The double Jerusalem count is discounted.

Table 4.1 further shows that Jews already constitute just 79% of Israel's total population today. Due to rapidly declining Israeli Arab birth rates, and comparatively high Jewish ones, this figure remains relatively stable over time, declining somewhat to 76%–77% in 2050. The flip side of these numbers is that 21% of Israel's population is not Jewish already today, a figure that will increase by a few more percent over the next decades, reaching nearly a quarter. The very size of Israel's Arab population at that time may further fuel demands for cultural and national autonomy and increase possible security concerns. In any event, it will constitute a very large minority with unique characteristics and needs that must be addressed.

Table 4.2 brings in the Palestinian populations of the West Bank and Gaza, factoring out the double count of East Jerusalem, to assess the share of the Jewish population out of the overall total. When the West Bank Palestinian population is added to Israeli Arabs, Jews constituted just 60–61% of the total population under Israeli control in 2015; in other words, 39%–40% of the population were not Jewish. Had Israel not withdrawn from Gaza, just 51%–52% of the total population (Israel, West Bank, and Gaza) would have been Jewish in 2015, a bare majority that will become a minority by 2025.

In 2050, according to the high projection, Jews will constitute 61% of the entire population of Israel and the West Bank, not substantially different from 2015. If the low projection is more accurate, the proportion of Jews decreases from 61% to just 56%. The important point is that regardless of the projection, approximately 40% of the combined populations of Israel and the West Bank are not Jewish today, and will not be in 2050. If we bring Gaza into the picture, a minority of just 47–49% of the population are Jewish in 2050.

An additional UN study,[72] which was not used more extensively for this chapter, because it does not break down the Palestinian population by the West Bank and Gaza, projects a total population of 6.73 million in 2030 and 9.70 in 2050. This then leads to a Jewish population of 48% of the total in 2030 or 47%–49% in 2050, essentially the same picture we already have.

Figure 4.4 shows population trends from 1947, on the eve of Israel's establishment, to 2060, based on a medium projection. The impact of the West Bank on Israel's demographic character is apparent once again.

According to Table 4.1, demographic parity between Jews and non-Jews in Israel, the West Bank, and Gaza will be reached somewhere between 2025 and 2030. Other respected sources maintain that parity had already been reached prior to 2015. It has been further argued that to maintain the present balance, Israel would have to sustain a net annual immigration rate of 80,000 Jews; current rates are far lower, and there are no realistic scenarios in which rates at this higher level are sustained over time. Declining Palestinian birth rates also do not change the overall picture. The demographic momentum created by the young age of the Palestinian population means that it will continue to grow at a significantly higher rate than the Jewish population, despite declining fertility.[73]

One controversial study maintains that there has been a large overcount of the Palestinian population in the West Bank and Gaza, motivated mostly by political considerations, but also due to errors and differences in demographic methodologies.[74] According to this study, the total overcount in 2004 was 1.34 million people, of whom just over a million were from the West Bank. The study has been flatly rejected by highly respected Israeli demographers,[75] but is noted here, nevertheless, both in the interests of comprehensiveness and because in seeking to disprove the demographic challenge Israel faces, it actually strengthens it.

Let us assume, for analytical purposes, that the study's fundamental argument is accurate, in essence if not necessarily precise numbers, and that the size of the West Bank population has been substantially overestimated. Let us also assume, in the absence of better projections, that the West Bank population was smaller by 1.5 million in 2015 and either 2 million or 3 million in 2050. Table 4.3 presents the figures for the three scenarios.

A calculation of the Jewish population in the areas under Israel's control (i.e., Israel and the West Bank) under these scenarios yields 70%–71% in 2015, assuming a West Bank overcount of 1.5 million, 65%–67% in 2050, assuming an overcount of 2 million, and 71% in 2050 assuming an overcount of 3 million. In other words, approximately 30%–35% of Israel would still not be Jewish even under these hypothetical scenarios. This is considerably less than the approximately 40% of non-Jews according to the accepted demographic estimates above, but it does not fundamentally alter the picture and the ramifications for Israel's future character as a state.

The steady growth in the settler population in the West Bank is the primary source of concern regarding the impact of demographic trends on Israel's future character. It has also led to growing doubts in recent years regarding Israel's ability to actually carry out a withdrawal of the magnitude that would be required

Table 4.3 **Percentage of Jews, Assuming Reduced West Bank Population: Three Scenarios**

	Projection	2015 (less 1.5 million)	2050 (less 2 million)	2050 (less 3 million)
West Bank[a]	High	1.04	2.30	1.3
	Low	0.88	1.79	0.79
Israel total	High	8.30	16.36	16.36
	Low	8.06	11.07	11.07
Total	High	9.34	18.66	17.66
	Low	8.94	12.86	11.86
Israeli Jews	High	6.57	12.63	12.63
	Low	6.37	8.43	8.43
% Jews Israel & West Bank	High	0.70	0.67	0.71
	Low	0.71	0.65	0.71

[a] Less East Jerusalem.

to achieve a two-state solution and consequently regarding the future viability of this paradigm. The sheer size of the potential population to be resettled (approximately 20% of all settlers, by most estimates, 80,000–100,000 people, not including East Jerusalem), and even more importantly the pro-settlement public's political clout, does, indeed, warrant some skepticism. Some believe Israel is already nearing a point of no return; former Mossad director Tamir Pardo fears we may have already crossed it.[76] Nevertheless, the following data may at least partly ease some of the concerns.

There has been a drastic drop in internal migration from Israel to the West Bank during the last 20 years, from 6,000 in 1996 to less than 2,000 in 2016. Consequently, 90% of the growth in the settler population between 2010 and 2015 was from natural growth (15,523 people in 2015). In 2015, 40% of all natural growth was among the Haredi (ultraorthodox) population, of which almost all was in just two settlements right on the border (Modiin Illit and Beitar Illit). Both are located in the settlement blocs that will presumably remain on the Israeli side of the border, as part of the land swaps expected in any realistic future peace agreement. Significantly, 75% of the total growth in the settler population in the West Bank in the last 40 years has been in the settlement blocs, which constitute just 4%–5% of the total land area, thereby easing the prospects for an agreement.[77]

There is no agreed definition in Israel regarding the percentage of the population that must be Jewish for it to retain its Jewish character and constitute

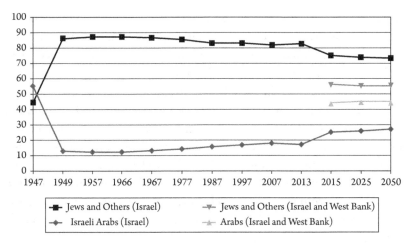

Figure 4.4 Percentage Jews and Arabs, 1947–2060, Medium Projection
Source: Israel Central Bureau of Statistics.

a Jewish state. The current situation, in which approximately 80% of the population are Jews, can already be considered problematic and call into question Israel's Jewish character, as some Israeli Arabs indeed have. Many in Israel simply consider an overwhelming Jewish majority to be a sufficient criterion and have become used to the approximately 80% majority that has existed throughout most of Israel's existence (see Figure 4.4), even if this has meant a large Arab minority and is not entirely consistent with the Zionist dream. An Israel which is only about 60% Jewish, however, hardly constitutes a Jewish state by any definition. It is a binational one.

Different experts may challenge some of the numbers presented above, possibly easing the picture by a few years. Nevertheless, the overall ramifications are clear and inescapable; Israel cannot retain its overwhelming Jewish majority and character if it remains in full control of the West Bank. Demography thus poses an existential threat to Israel's future, not in the physical sense, but in terms of its fundamental character as a nation. There is no known solution to the challenge other than a separation of the two peoples, presumably on the basis of the "two-state" paradigm.

Primary Observations

- The overall effort to isolate and delegitimize Israel has met with mixed success. Israel has broader diplomatic and other ties than ever before and a number of particularly deep relationships. Sanctions and boycott efforts have achieved little, and most attempts at lawfare have failed.

- Decades of diplomatic warfare and delegitimization have led to a severe deterioration in Israel's international standing. Its isolation in international forums is extreme, and its bilateral relationships are increasingly affected, too. Efforts to constrain Israel's military freedom of maneuver have not prevented it from acting, but have affected the nature of operations and their outcomes.
- No issue has undermined Israel's international standing and played into its adversaries' hands more than the settlements. To the international community it is a gratuitously provocative policy, rendered inexplicable because it appears incompatible with Israel's character as a Jewish and democratic state.
- Diplomatic warfare and delegitimization are likely to pose major challenges to Israel in the coming years, and relations with European and other Western countries are increasingly affected, adversely, by Israel's West Bank policies. Delegitimization has made inroads in the United States.
- Demographic trends stemming from the control of the West Bank pose a severe threat to Israel's future as a Jewish and democratic state. Demography is also a major reason for Israel's reluctance to conduct ground maneuver, which has undermined its ability to achieve military decision.
- Already today only 60% of the population of Israel and the West Bank is Jewish. Declining Palestinian fertility rates and increased Jewish fertility and immigration cannot reverse the inexorable demographic reality. There is no known solution other than separation, presumably based on the "two-state" paradigm.
- The growth in settlers has been primarily in the "settlement blocs," which constitute only 5% of the total area and will likely be part of a land swap, easing a future peace agreement. The overall numbers, however, raise growing doubts about the political viability of the two-state solution. The point of no return is nearing.

Israeli Society and National Security

The internal threats should concern the country more than the external ones. If a state goes beyond a certain degree of division, one can reach such phenomena as a civil war. I am afraid that we are heading in that direction. There is more that divides Israel today than unites it.
—Tamir Pardo, former head of Mossad, August 2016

A nation's perceptions of the national security challenges it faces, and its responses to them, are profoundly linked to the nature of its society, which is the source of the resources from which it draws its national strength.* These resources are both tangible, such as budgets and manpower, and, no less important, intangible, such as motivation, tolerance for casualties, and societal resilience. In recent decades, as Israel's strategic landscape has been transformed, its society, too, has undergone significant change, with important ramifications for its national security strategy. Precisely because Israel is now engaged primarily in nonexistential conflicts, these intangible societal resources are brought into sharper relief.

Israel, today, is a mixed society. Much of Israel is deeply immersed in global trends, at the forefront of science, technology, and innovation, and has adopted many of the values and norms of its contemporaries abroad. This Israel has developed a highly competitive export and technology-driven economy, dubbed informally, if with some hyperbole, the "start-up nation," and has led to Israel's overall emergence as a prosperous country with what is, statistically, a mid-European standard of living. The other Israel, comprised largely of the ultra-orthodox and Israeli Arabs, have either largely opted out of these processes, in the case of the former, or participate at significantly lower levels, in the latter case. The deep disparities that result in socioeconomic achievement and income mean that these population groups do not share proportionally in the wealth

---

* This chapter was written together with Ms. Saskia Becaud.

and often live below the poverty line, even as they have gained greater weight in national life.

National security affairs and the IDF, in particular, continue to play an unusually important role in Israeli life, unlike that in any other democracy today. Nevertheless, some signs of tension have emerged in recent decades between IDF needs and societal norms, further aggravated by a partial erosion of the national consensus regarding national security affairs. Moreover, the IDF must now operate in an environment in which numerous domestic actors, many nongovernmental, demand a growing voice in the formulation of national security policies and play an important role in determining societal attitudes toward them.[1]

Israel's national security strategy is therefore increasingly constrained today, not just by the exigencies of its external environment, but by domestic societal factors, as well. This reality was explicitly recognized by the 2015 "IDF Strategy," which states that "changes in the national order of priorities are leading to a decrease in investment in defense, in favor of socioeconomic development," even while the public continues to expect the IDF to achieve rapid victory and to provide an effective defense against all threats.[2]

The following chapter sets out the primary societal changes that have taken place in Israel in recent decades and their ramifications for its national security strategy. These changes include the rise of an affluent Western society and liberal culture, based on a market economy, in which the individual, not the collective, is now at the center, along with the rise of social groups that do not participate in the national security burden, and in which ethnicity and religiosity remain major determinants of national security attitudes. The changes have taken place in the context of a substantially transformed strategic landscape and affect Israeli society's willingness to continue bearing the defense burden, as measured by such variables as the motivation to serve, casualty aversion, willingness to pay for defense expenditures, national consensus, emigration, and societal resilience. These factors have important consequences for Israel's national security strategy, including its fundamental identity as a "nation in arms," the IDF's force structure and operational concepts, and national security decision-making processes, as presented in Table 5.1.

A chapter focusing on societal developments and attitudes cannot but mention, if only briefly, some of the political changes in Israel in recent decades. Somewhat greater attention is afforded to changes in public attitudes toward the primary national security issues Israel faces. In some cases the data presented refer to Israel's entire population, in others, where noted, just to attitudes among the Jewish population.

It is important to stress the point noted in passing above, that this conceptual model takes place within the context of a substantially transformed overall

Table 5.1 **Israel's Changing Society and National Security Ramifications**

Independent variables (causal factors)	Intervening variables	Dependent variables (outcomes)
Societal changes: • Affluent market economy • Liberal culture • Civil society involvement • Ethnicity and religiosity	Societal willingness to bear defense burden: • Motivation to serve • Casualty aversion • Willingness to pay for defense expenditures • National consensus • Emigration • Societal resilience	National security strategy: • Identity as "nation in arms" • IDF force structure • IDF operations National security decision-making processes

strategic setting and is not independent thereof. The independent variables, such as the rise of an affluent market economy and liberal culture, are themselves at least partly the result of Israel's more relaxed strategic environment in recent decades, which also affects such factors as casualty aversion and the willingness to pay for defense expenditures. These changes have already been set out in detail in the previous chapters, enabling us to focus here more narrowly on the societal changes.

Israel's Changing Society

Rise of an Affluent Market Economy

Israel has undergone a major transformation in recent decades, from a largely statist economy controlled by trade unions (*Histadrut*) to a dynamic and competitive, export-driven, market economy. It has become deeply integrated into the processes of globalization, with ever-closer economic and commercial ties to the international economy, and has also become a leading international center of high tech. Between 1980 and 2015 Israel's per capita GDP rose in PPP terms[†] from $17,000 to $33,700, placing Israel at a mid-European level.[3] Overall Israeli foreign trade increased from approximately $35 billion in 1995 to $105 billion in 2014.[4] In the 15-year period between 1991 and 2006 alone, Israeli high-tech exports grew nearly tenfold, from $3 billion to $29 billion.[5]

[†] Purchasing power parity, a method used to calculate the comparative purchasing power of currencies in different countries.

A Liberal Culture for an Affluent Society

Globalization is a process that leads to a standardization of cultures and lifestyles across nations and to growing interlinkages between economies, legal systems, and cultures. Globalization has a particularly strong impact on young people, who "inhabit the global space," increasingly embracing a global culture and, in so doing, can diminish the traditional sense of belonging to a more narrow national community, identity, and border. The most obvious result of globalization is adoption of a liberal culture, which emphasizes such values as conflict avoidance, diplomacy, and the individual, not the state, as the focus of society's concerns. It further attaches greater importance to market-related objectives, such as consumption and leisure, and to individual aspirations than to the traditional collective ethos of the national effort.[6]

In Israel's case, the rise of a more affluent society and liberal culture have had a number of effects, including the following:

Heightened Importance of Economic Considerations. Surveys of the Jewish population demonstrate the rising importance it attaches to socioeconomic issues. In 2003, for example, 43% believed that defense was the most important issue, while 38% gave priority to economic issues and 11% to social ones; in 2012 just 15% gave priority to defense, whereas 39% viewed education and 17% health as their number one priorities.[7]

Clearly, there are many polls, and public sentiment reflects the changing military and strategic circumstances prevailing at any given time. What is not in doubt is that the public accords far greater importance today to socioeconomic and quality-of-life issues than in the past. The shift toward a market economy has also greatly increased the relative attractiveness of the private sector, compared to public service, including the IDF. In a society in which material consumption and personal fulfillment have come to be highly valued, the IDF is no longer necessarily the preferred route to social advancement, and military service is no longer the primary factor determining social mobility, future professional careers, and political leadership.[8]

A New "Economic Logic." The growing importance that Israeli society attaches to economic considerations imposes a logic of its own, of maximized profitability and efficiency, with significant ramifications for national security policy. An early and prominent example of the new emphasis on economic efficiency came in 1985, with the decision to shift the cost of compensation for reserve duty from the National Security Administration[§] to the defense budget.[9] For the first time, reserve duty now carried a price tag for the IDF, forcing it to take budgetary factors into account when mobilizing reservists.[10] The effect was immediate. Before the new law was passed reservists served a total of 10 million

---

[§] Israel's equivalent of the American Social Security Administration.

days a year; by 2006 the number had decreased dramatically to 3 million and to just 1.85 million in 2015.[11]

Popular demands in the early 2000s to provide reservists with financial compensation and other rewards for their service, especially those in combat units, an unheard-of concept in the past, greatly further increased the cost of calling up reservists. As a result, the IDF has increasingly been forced to rely on the conscript and professional force,[12] in other words, to make a major change in how it operates.

Israeli society generally, and the IDF in particular, long committed to the egalitarian ethos of the "nation in arms" and "people's army," traditionally viewed all military service as being of equal intrinsic value and motivation, and deserving of no more than symbolic compensation, essentially pocket change. The very idea of compensation for conscripts, small as it may be, and especially of differential rewards, was alien to the IDF, but by the late 1990s societal pressures had forced it to begin doing so. In 2015–2016 conscript compensation was increased by a full 75%, and compensation for combat soldiers, though still largely symbolic (1,600 shekels a month, about $420), is much greater than in the past and double that of support troops. Ever since 2000 combat soldiers have also received larger grants upon completion of their service than those in noncombat positions.[13]

Both the public and government cost-cutters have also increasingly begun to question some of the special benefits that IDF professionals have long enjoyed. Designed to attract quality personnel and to keep IDF ranks young, these benefits include above average pay scales and early pensions after just 20 or so years of service. Many argue today, however, that most of the staff officers and soldiers who fill noncombat positions, often in the comfort of major population centers, such as Tel Aviv, do not provide a service fundamentally different from other public employees and should be compensated accordingly, with special benefits limited to those in combat units or those who have truly unique skills in great demand in the private sector. The IDF has objected strenuously, but has been forced to accept a number of important changes, including on the crucial issue of pensions. In an atmosphere in which the public is demanding greater emphasis on social welfare spending, the IDF is fighting an increasingly uphill battle.[14]

Popular Longing for Normalcy. Heightened public expectations of a more peaceful existence, growth, and prosperity, of "normalcy," have partly replaced the long-standing societal norms of a mobilized society, which placed a premium on defense affairs. The electoral campaigns of 2013 and 2015 were cases in point, the first in Israel's history to focus primarily on domestic issues, such as employment, social inequality, the cost of living, housing, and education, rather than national security issues, even though they took place shortly after the 2012 and 2014 operations in Gaza, respectively. As such, they were an indication that Israel, despite decades of conflict, has become both increasingly "normal" and that the public is deeply desirous of this. Moreover, a broad public sense that a significant change for the better in Israel's external environment is not likely for the foreseeable future, especially the feeling that negotiations with the Palestinians are unlikely to yield a peace agreement for a long time to come, further contributes to the focus on domestic issues. In a situation in which the public believes that there is little Israel can do about its national security challenges in any event, it has shifted its attention toward problems perceived to be more readily solvable.[15]

Greater Individualism and Decrease in the Importance of the Collective. The rise of an affluent, globalized society in Israel has been accompanied by societal and cultural processes of "Americanization" or "Westernization," fueled by the impact of the mass media and Internet. Part of this is an increasingly individualistic lifestyle, in which material desires and comfort have become a core element[16] and in which far greater attention is focused on the individual and the individual's immediate circle of family and friends. In 1981 64% of Israelis thought that the national interest was more important than the individual's; by 2007 only 27% thought so, and 85% believed in 2009 that people were "concerned mainly with themselves."[17] With the emphasis now on the individual and on economic achievement, Israel's strong sense of collective solidarity, at its height during the early decades and long embodied by the IDF, is now less intense and uniform than in the past. As a result, participation in collective duties, such as military service, has ceased to be the primary component of Israeli identity, and it has become far broader in nature. The trend toward globalization and individualism is particularly pronounced among the secular middle and upper classes, but is not limited to them.[18]

Heightened Civil Society Activism and Scrutiny. The relative decision-making autonomy and freedom of action traditionally granted to the IDF has given way to an era of heightened involvement by civil society organizations, interest groups, protest movements, and more in national security affairs. Empowered by the information revolution and generally less deferential to authority, they have gained a far more influential role in Israeli public life generally, and affect the formulation and implementation of national security policy in ways that occurred only rarely in the past, including the objectives of military operations, their necessity, and especially conduct and effectiveness.[19] The change began with the shock of the Yom Kippur War and the 1982 war in Lebanon, but was accelerated by the two intifadas and the "wars of choice" against Hamas and Hezbollah.

Part of the change has also been reflected in the role of the media and of some governmental institutions. The State Comptroller, a highly respected governmental watch-dog agency, has greatly expanded its scrutiny of IDF affairs, conducting inquiries into almost all of its operations. The Knesset, too, has made some initial attempts to increase its highly limited oversight role. In 2004, for the first time in its history, it conducted an inquiry into the failings of the Israeli intelligence community during the first Gulf War, and in 2006 it conducted public hearings to verify charges of military failings leveled by some IDF soldiers and reservists.[20]

The Supreme Court has also played a growing role in national security affairs, as evinced, inter alia, by the issue of the West Bank security fence. The Court was successfully petitioned several times—by Palestinians—to modify the route of the fence, and in the end it was the Court, not the IDF nor the government, that determined its final delineation. The Court has also demanded that the IDF show greater care for Palestinian rights and humanitarian law. Regulations governing operational activities in populated Palestinian areas have been determined by the Court, including rulings strictly forbidding the IDF from endangering innocent bystanders when apprehending terrorists and in regard to "targeted killings."[21]

The "Israeli Difference." The liberal values that go hand in hand with globalization are in conflict, at least in part, with the deep role that the IDF and military preparedness continue to play in Israeli life. Indeed, Israeli society remains unusual among Western democracies in its continuing degree of mobilization, commitment, and involvement in national security affairs, and Israel remains one of the two most patriotic states among Western democracies.[22] The seeming contradiction reflects the unusual threats that Israel continues to face, unmatched in the West, which lead to comparatively strong national cohesion. The 9/11 attacks in the United States in 2001 and the terrorist attacks in Paris in 2015 produced similar responses, even if not quite to the same extent or for such a protracted period.[23]

Ethnicity and Religiosity: A Domestic Demographic Crisis in the Making

Israelis' attitudes toward national security affairs continue to be deeply affected by religiosity and to a lesser extent ethnicity. Significant differences in voting patterns are long established; the secular middle and upper classes, largely composed of Jews of Ashkenazi (European) origins, tend be more centrist and leftist in their political views, whereas the lower classes and those of Mizrachi (Middle Eastern) descent are more supportive of the Right. Some argue that ethnicity and socioeconomic status have lost much of their impact on political positions, and there have always been important exceptions to these generalizations; immigrants from the former Soviet Union (mostly of Ashkenazi background) tend to vote for the Right, while socioeconomic status has become the primary determinant of voting patterns among the nonreligious population today, regardless of ethnic background. In the case of the "national religious" and ultra-orthodox populations, at least, voting patterns are clear: they tend to vote for the Right and for religious parties, regardless of their socioeconomic status.[24]

The Haredim (ultra-orthodox Jews; singular Haredi). In 2015 the Haredi population in Israel numbered between 893,000 and 910,500, 11% of the entire population, or approximately 14% of the Jewish population. Haredi population growth is extraordinarily high, about 5% a year, meaning that it doubles every 14 years. Given current demographic trends, the Haredim will comprise over 24% of the Jewish population in 2029. Looking further ahead, to 2060, whereas the non-Haredi Jewish population is expected to grow by 1.07- to 1.65-fold and the Israeli Arab population by 1.51- to 2.3-fold, the Haredi population is expected to do so by a whopping 2.6- to 5.11-fold! Due to their size, low participation in the job market, and lack of employment skills, 50% of Haredi households live beneath the poverty line.[25] Table 5.2 provides data for the anticipated growth rates among the Haredi and non-Haredi Jewish populations and Israeli Arabs between 2014 and 2059.

In chapter 4 we noted the growing demographic challenges Israel faces from the de facto absorption of the West Bank Palestinian population. As Table 5.2 demonstrates, however, Israel also faces a major domestic demographic challenge in the form of the burgeoning Haredi population. If the non-Haredi

Table 5.2 **Demographic Trends in Israel, Medium Projection (millions)**

	~2015	~2025	~2050	~2060
Non-Haredi Jews and "others"	5.56	6.09	7.34	7.85
Haredim	0.91	1.32	3.07	4.15
Israeli Arabs	1.71	2.10	3.16	3.60
Non-Haredi Jews and others out of Jewish population	86%	82%	70%	65%
Non-Haredi Jews and others out of total population	68%	64%	54%	50%

Source: Israel Central Bureau of Statistics, http://www.cbs.gov.il/publications/tec27.pdf.

Note: "Others" (included in the figure for non-Haredi Jews) were estimated at 500,000 for both 2050 and 2060. The original years in the CBS projection were for 2014, 2024, 2049 and 2059, rounded off here for simplicity.

Jews (i.e., secular and "national religious" Jews) now constitute some 86% of the Jewish population and 68% of the total, this number is expected to decrease precipitously to 65% and 50% respectively by 2060. Both less and more severe projections are presented in Table 5.3, but even in the "medium" projection, over a third of all Israeli Jews would be Haredim by 2060.

The low rate of Haredi participation in the workforce, although increasing, means that their rising numbers will have profound ramifications for Israel's fundamental nature as a society and potentially severe consequences for its economy. Only 36% of Haredi men worked in 2002 (the rest were yeshiva students or unemployed), although this number had risen substantially to 48% by 2011. The level of employment among Haredi women, conversely, is now close to the national average, rising significantly from 41% in 1979 to 71% in 2015.[26]

The Haredim have enjoyed preferential treatment from Israel's earliest years, when Ben-Gurion agreed, largely for reasons of political expediency, to exempt a few hundred yeshiva students from military service each year. The number of exemptions has grown rapidly and now constitutes approximately half of all of the exempted draft-age males. In 2012 only 6% of Haredim actually served, and they constituted about two-thirds of those who received psychological discharges.[27]

In 2014, rising anger among the secular population led to the passage of legislation aimed at increasing both Haredi service in the IDF and participation in the labor market. It was highly controversial from the start, both for the secular

Table 5.3 **Demographic Trends for Jewish Population, Low and High Projections (millions)**

	Projection	~ 2015	~ 2025	~ 2050	~ 2060
Non-Haredi Jews and others	Low	5.48	5.80	6.14	6.08
	High	5.63	6.38	8.67	9.95
Haredim	Low	0.89	1.22	2.29	2.73
	High	0.93	1.42	3.96	5.89
Non-Haredi Jews and others out of Jewish total	Low	86%	82%	72%	69%
	High	85%	81%	68%	62%

Source: Israel Central Bureau of Statistics. http://www.cbs.gov.il/publications/tec27.pdf.

Note: The original years in the CBS projection were for 2019, 2029, 2049, and 2059, rounded off here for simplicity.

population, many of whom believed that the legislation did not go far enough and was a further sellout, and for the Haredim, who perceived it as an attack on their way of life and special benefits and reacted strongly, including large protests. In 2015, with the election of a new governing coalition, heavily dependent on the Haredim for its survival, even the limited changes in military service mandated by the new law were rolled back, a change subsequently struck down by the Supreme Court in 2017.[28] Further back-and-forth changes are likely in coming years, as the growing frustration and resentment of the majority secular public confronts the increasing numbers and political clout of the Haredim.

The social and political tensions between the Haredi and non-Haredi publics notwithstanding, a growing number of the former have chosen in recent years to serve in the IDF and to participate in the labor market. Many do not wish to devote their lives to religious studies in yeshivas and instead seek the skills necessary for participation in the labor market. A steadily increasing number have thus begun to join the special units and service tracks that the IDF has established to facilitate Haredi service. Despite intensive efforts by the Haredi community to prevent this emerging trend, military service has, de facto, become a viable option for many. In 2010 2,100 Haredim enlisted, in 2014 2,203, and in 2015 2,475, over 25% of the age cohort, compared to only 288 in 2007.[29] The previously mentioned rollback in 2015 of the changes to military service and restoration of all preferential transfer payments to the Haredi population will likely slow this trend significantly, but not reverse it completely.[30]

Israeli Arabs. The Israeli Arab population numbered approximately 1.7 million people in 2015,** 21% of the total. The Arab population is very young (over 50% are under the age of 20) and is projected to increase to 2.1 million in 2025 and 3.6 million in 2060. Overwhelmingly desirous of integration into Israeli society, the Arab population shares a deep sense of discrimination and divided identity as both Israelis and Palestinians. The government is aware of the need to improve socioeconomic conditions in the Arab sector, and significant efforts have begun, including a special five-year spending program begun in 2015.[31]

The picture is decidedly mixed. The Arab population, currently 18% of the working-age population, constitutes just 13% of the overall civilian workforce.[32] The low Arab employment rate is at least partly a result of early retirement by Arab men, many of whom work in physically demanding labor, and of the low participation of Arab women in the labor market. In the past, the proportion of Arab men aged 25–64 in the labor market was higher than that of Jewish men, by as much as 5% in 1980, but has decreased ever since, and was 9% lower in 2014.

** Including 300,000 people in East Jerusalem, who are permanent residents, not citizens.

Unemployment among Israeli Arabs aged 25–64 was approximately double that of the Jewish population, corresponding, inter alia, to a decreased demand for unskilled manpower, primarily among men. Employment rates among Israeli Arab women, conversely, have improved greatly, from a mere 11% in 1980 to 30% in 2014, but are still very low in comparison with Jewish women, 78% of whom worked in 2014.[33] The low overall Arab rate of employment is translated into high poverty rates; in 2014 52.6% of all poor families in Israel in 2014 were Arab.[34]

Fertility rates among Israeli Muslim women (the vast majority of the Arab population) have decreased precipitously from an average of 9.2 in 1960 to 4.6 in 2000 and just 3.4 in 2013, still high, but similar to the average among Jewish Israeli women, who gave birth to an average of 3.4 children in 1960, 2.7 in 2000, and 3.1 in 2013.[35] The level of university education in the Arab sector has improved significantly; from approximately 22,000 in absolute numbers in 2006 to 40,000 in 2014, or from 9.1% of Arab men in 2001 to 12% in 2013 and from 5.2% of Arab women in 2001 to 13% in 2013[36] The increase in educational levels among Arab women is likely to have an impact on the role of women in the Arab sector generally and has already been translated into the increase in employment rates.

The Arab population is increasingly integrated into Israel's broader society and economy, but the gap between reality and expectations is large. Unless Israel devotes far greater attention and resources to the Arab sector, its sense of alienation from the state will grow, along with already existing sectarian, even separatist, trends. Accordingly, the challenge Israel will face may go from being a primarily socioeconomic one to a growing national security threat.

Due to the low employment rates of both Haredim and Israeli Arabs, about 20% of men in Israel between the ages of 35 and 54 do not work, 60% higher than the OECD average. In 2010 the educational achievements of about half of the children in Israeli primary schools (28% of Israeli Arabs and 20% of Haredim) were lower than in a number of Third World countries. Arab Israelis and Haredim simply do not have the skills necessary to work in Israel's modern economy. Indeed, over 50% of Haredi men today have less than an eighth-grade education. By 2040, at current trends, Israeli Arab and Haredi children will account for about 78% of primary school children. The lack of education is a direct cause of unemployment and poverty within these populations and has led to an increase in the number of families who live below the official poverty line (18.8% in 2014,[37] a very high figure compared to other OECD countries, when after-tax revenue is considered).

In reality, Israel has become the story of two countries, a highly advanced one, at the forefront of international technology and science, and a second one, comprising largely, but not solely, the Haredi and Arab populations, which lags way behind, suffers from low productivity, and has become an insupportable burden on the whole. If current trends continue, Israel will face a severe economic crisis, and its innovative high-tech sector, heretofore the primary engine of growth, will be insufficient to counterbalance the combined effects of low employment rates and poor educational achievement.[38]

Societal Willingness to Bear the Defense Burden

The following section explores the ways in which the changes in Israeli society have affected its willingness to continue bearing the overall defense burden. The factors studied include the motivation to serve, casualty aversion, willingness to pay for defense expenditures, national consensus, emigration, and societal resilience.

The Motivation to Serve

Israeli society's willingness to continue shouldering the burden both of compulsory military service (conscription) and reserve duty is critical to its national security; indeed, it is the fundamental pillar on which Israel's three-tiered concept of a "nation in arms" is based: a small professional military, backed by a larger conscript force and mass mobilization of reserves (see chapter 1). Crucially, the "nation in arms" concept has enabled Israel to mobilize for war in far greater numbers than would have otherwise been possible.[39] Moreover, in a nation of diverse immigrants, military service, both compulsory and reservist, has traditionally constituted the heart of Israel's collective identity.

Political and even some military leaders have warned in recent years of a "motivation crisis," due to the low percentage of draft-age youth who actually serve in the IDF, despite Israel's ostensible policy of universal conscription: by 2020 just 40% of all draft-age Israelis. In fact, reports of a "motivation crisis" are largely an illusion and originate more in the nature of Israeli politics and the dramatic demographic changes underway in Israel than in a drop in motivation.[40] The motivation levels of conscripts, reservists, and the professional military will each be addressed separately.

Conscripts

"Universal" conscription in Israel has never truly been universal: two groups, the Haredim and Israeli Arabs, have been exempted from military service ever since Israel's establishment. The Haredim constituted approximately 11% of Israel's overall population in 2015, Israeli Arabs 21%. 32% of Israel's total population is thus exempt from military service to begin with, but if one takes into account the young average age of these two groups, their relative share is even higher. The overall cohort of draft-age Haredi males is approximately 8,000, but a total of some 60,000 have been exempted from service over the years, sufficient for a few IDF divisions. The vast majority of those who serve remain secular Jews, but the numbers of "national religious" Jews are rising rapidly.[41] Minority groups, such as the Druze and Bedouins, also serve.

Secular Motivation to Serve Remains High, Including Combat Duty. Among those of draft age, 25% of Jewish males and 42% of Jewish females were not drafted in 2012.[42] At first glance, these figures do, indeed, appear highly worrisome, and they have been used for demagogic purposes on all sides of the debate. When looked at in detail, however, it turns out that the motivation to serve is not the problem.

In fact, nearly half of the males who avoided conscription in 2012 were Haredim and thus exempt from service (11% out of the 25% who do not serve). The remaining 14% consisted of those with a criminal record (3%), living abroad (4%), and the physically incapacitated or prematurely dead (2%). The final 5%—the problematic group—included those exempted for reasons of psychological incompatibility and plain draft evasion. This last category has grown slightly since 1980. When all is said and done, however, the number of nonorthodox who actually dodge the draft is no more than 1%–2% of all potential recruits.[43]

Despite some fluctuations, the willingness to serve in combat units has also remained high and stable. The IDF estimates that about 75% of conscripts were willing to serve in combat positions in 2015, the same figure as in 1990, compared to 67% in 2008, 79% in 2010, and 70%–72% between 2011–2013. The number of volunteers for the most difficult and dangerous combat units continues to greatly exceed requirements and, as the former head of the IDF Manpower Branch has stressed, "Someone is educating them to do this."[44] Fluctuations in the willingness to serve in combat positions appear to be closely related to the ongoing security situation. Thus, the figure for 2010, one of the highest rates recorded in recent years, was apparently in direct response to the 2008–2009 Cast Lead operation in Gaza. At the same time, there is also a built-in tension between the need for highly qualified recruits for the elite technological units and the no less important, even greater need to preserve the fighting spirit of the IDF and willingness to volunteer for combat units.[45]

The numbers, therefore, do not bear out the idea of a "motivation crisis." Indeed, if one discounts the Haredi population, as well as those who have criminal records, live abroad, or are physically incapacitated, virtually all non-Haredi male Jews (secular and national religious) continue to serve in the IDF, and the number of those willing to do so in combat positions has remained stable.

Among male conscripts there is actually a surplus of manpower, primarily due to the large immigration from the former Soviet Union. The IDF itself would greatly prefer a more selective draft,[46] which would preserve the principle of the "nation in arms" and universal conscription, to which it remains deeply committed ideologically, but authorize it to decide which potential draftees it actually needs.

While recruitment rates remain high, the IDF faces other personnel problems. A lack of motivation does not necessarily translate into a refusal to serve; it can take other forms, such as avoiding service in combat units, pressure to serve close to home, or failure to complete a full three-year period of service. In 2015 approximately 17% of male recruits did not serve a full three years, compared with 13.5% six years earlier[47] (some of the increase apparently reflects an IDF decision to discharge unneeded conscripts).

Many conscripts today, especially from the secular middle and upper classes, serve in technologically advanced IDF units in which they can not only bring existing skills to bear, but often gain extremely valuable experience for their future careers. For the most part, service in these units simply reflects IDF personnel and operational needs, but the choice to serve in such "risk free" positions can also be considered to be a more legitimate means of quasi-evasion of combat duty, or "gray" draft dodging.[48]

The recruitment problems among potential female conscripts are greater than males. In 2013 fully 42.6% of draft-age women did not serve. Among them, 36% were exempted on religious grounds, although the IDF estimates that at least 25% were not truly religious.[49] Women have been successfully integrated into pilot and naval commanders' school, as well as artillery, air defense, and other units. Following a successful experience with the first mixed male-female light infantry battalion (70% female, 30% male), which has been deployed along the Egyptian border and involved in skirmishes with terrorists, two mixed-gender battalions are to be deployed along the Jordanian border, and a fourth is being established. Nevertheless, 20 years after the Supreme Court directed the IDF to open combat positions to women (only 8% of all positions remain closed to them, primarily those requiring extreme physical stress), a mere 7% served in combat positions in 2016, up from 3% in 2012, and just 20% serve in the technologically advanced units, such as intelligence unit 8200, cyber-warfare and UAVs. Conversely, only 13% serve today in clerical positions, compared to twice that proportion 15 years earlier. The ratio of female officers is double that of men.[50]

Interestingly, a significant change has begun among women from the national-religious community, many of whom are actively discouraged from serving by their schools, rabbis, and families. Between 2010 and 2014 the number of national-religious women choosing to serve doubled, from 935 to 1,830, approximately one-quarter of the cohort. Between 2013–2015 the number of such women serving in combat units increased by 71% and the number of officers by 30%. The IDF invests considerable efforts in encouraging them, as a highly motivated group, to serve, and top IDF units compete for them.[51]

A Sociological Shift. The largely Ashkenazi secular middle and upper classes were greatly overrepresented in the past, both in Israel's political and economic elites and in the IDF's highest ranks and combat units. Some today argue that there has been a drop in their motivation to serve, sacrifice, and generally engage in military activity.[52] Others strongly dispute this, and, indeed, most of the publicly available information supports the view that the secular middle and upper classes' motivation to serve remains high.[53]

On a more mundane level, the secular middle and upper classes' higher levels of educational achievement and technological proficiency, as well as their geographic proximity to the technologically advanced bases generally located in Israel's center, make service in these units a more practical option for them than it is for other population groups. Moreover, some noncombat or semicombat units, such as Iron Dome rocket defense batteries and cyberwarfare and intelligence units, have gained a stature today once reserved for those engaged in combat. Conversely, the perceived desirability and prestige associated with some combat units, such as the armored corps and combat engineers, has diminished compared to others, for example, the various special forces (*sayarot*).[54]

The level of motivation among the national-religious population, which constituted only a small proportion of the IDF in the past, is very high today. In the early 1990s national-religious males accounted for just 2.5% of the graduates of infantry officer training courses; today they account for more than 25% and make up as much as 50% of new officers in some combat units—roughly quadruple their share of Israel's population. This upward trend has had a major impact on the composition and character of some IDF units.[55]

To the extent that a sociological shift has taken place, it has occurred primarily because of the rise of other groups in Israeli society generally and in the IDF in particular. The secular middle and upper classes are not serving less, but their numbers have been diluted and they no longer constitute the near monopoly in the elite combat units that they were in the past. For the lower-class population, still largely of Mizrachi extraction, as well as the national-religious community and immigrants from the former Soviet Union and Ethiopia, service in the IDF remains an important means of social mobility, and many choose to serve in combat positions. With the exception of those from the former Soviet Union, these groups tend to be more religious. All tend to identify with a narrower national ethos.

From Ideological to Personal Motivation. The true change in the motivation to serve today is not in the overall levels, which remain high, but in its nature. In Israel's early years the motivation to serve was based both on its military fragility and on a strong ideological commitment to the pioneering spirit of Zionism. The IDF played a central role in building the state and ensuring its survival, and military service was perceived to be the essence of Israeli identity. The IDF's prestige was such that the simple act of service was a sufficient symbolic reward in itself.[56]

As Israel has become more secure and the siege perception has eased, the sense of belonging to a collective effort has diminished, and military service no longer appears quite as crucial as in the past. Conscript military service has also become routinized, something that virtually everyone does, and is no longer a novelty or special expression of personal commitment. Most of all, the nature of the motivation to serve has become less uniform today and stems from different sources. For most conscripts, including the secular middle and upper classes (and a limited but growing number of Haredi recruits), individual motivations and self-fulfillment have now increasingly come to supplant the old ideological ones. They thus seek service that meets their personal preferences and long-term career prospects, rather than the way they can best serve the IDF and contribute to the national interest. For many, including the most highly motivated, it is often a matter of being placed in the challenging and self-actualizing positions they seek, or of doing the easiest service possible. Among the national-religious conscripts, conversely, ideological motivations continue to be far more prominent.[57]

With the prolongation of the military control of the West Bank and growing Palestinian resistance, including the intifadas, a large share of IDF activities have come to consist of policing operations or occupation measures, whichever terminology the individual soldier chooses, which many find distasteful and at times even objectionable. The perceived effectiveness of IDF operations has also diminished, as it has proven unable to defeat small substate actors and prevent ongoing attacks, compared to the old heroic image of the IDF advancing into enemy territory and defeating large Arab armies. All that notwithstanding, what may be surprising, after a century-long conflict, is how strong the motivation to serve remains among the secular and national-religious majority.

Reservists

The motivation to serve among reservists presents a more mixed picture. Most reservists today are called-up far less than in the past and for far shorter periods, or not at all. In 2013 a typical reservist served 14 days,[58] compared with 36 days for soldiers and 42 days for officers in the past.[59] Over the years large numbers of reservists have been discharged entirely, and in 2015, responding to both societal and budgetary pressures, the IDF announced the discharge of a further

100,000, approximately 20% of the entire reserve force at the time, some of which had existed largely on paper.[60]

In practice, reserve duty, the epitome of Israeli identity in the past, has become the exception today and is almost entirely voluntary. Whereas just 20% of reservists in 1974 said that, if given the choice, they would not have served the full annual number of days required, in the early 2000s a large majority said they would not have served at all. Attempts to avoid reserve duty have become widespread and for many the motivation to serve has dropped precipitously. Among those who do choose to serve, conversely, motivation remains high.[61]

In 2004, in response to various protest movements and lobbying efforts by reservists and their families, the government imposed new limits on the length and frequency of reserve service and lowered the discharge age. These and other measures were then included in a formal Reserve Law in 2008, which further stipulated that reservists would no longer be used for current security missions, such as policing in the West Bank and border patrols (not including operations against Hezbollah and Hamas), but for training and actual combat. The new law also provided, for the first time, financial compensation for reservists (beyond the previous coverage of the cost of the reservist's absence from work), a special tax credit, life insurance, and beneficial terms for university students who serve in the reserves.[62] In some ways these measures constituted initial steps toward a professional reserves model.

The change in the motivation to serve in the reserves is a function of many factors, of which four will be mentioned. In the past, when most of Israel's economy consisted of state or trade union-owned companies, an employee's absence for reserve duty did not have as great an effect on either the employer or the reservist's career prospects. Today, in Israel's competitive market economy, reserve duty has become highly problematic, both for the company, which loses a needed employee, and for the individual,[63] who often fears the possible impact on prospects for professional advancement and—legal protections notwithstanding—even the loss of a job. Family concerns also affect the willingness to serve, along with aspirations for individual freedom and leisure.[64]

Second, the knowledge that fewer people serve at all, and even fewer in combat positions, created a sense of injustice and resentment over the inequitable reserve burden. Indeed, in the early 2000s about one-third of all reservists bore some 80% of the burden, and only 10% did annual service in excess of 10 days.[65] The sense of resentment was further exacerbated by the high frequency of mobilization in recent times, during the second intifada and the successive operations in Lebanon and Gaza between 2006 and 2014.

Third, the nature of reserve duty in recent decades has also had a deleterious effect on reservists' willingness to serve. Rather than training and border security operations, the reserves' classic function, they have been used extensively for counterterrorism operations in the West Bank (and in the past Gaza), in an atmosphere of tense confrontation with a deeply hostile civilian population. The task is difficult, thankless, and seemingly never ending, and married workingmen, preoccupied with families and jobs, are less eager to do reserve duty of this nature.

Fourth, the IDF demands that reservists be prepared for a variety of difficult missions but has not provided commensurate resources and rewards. Due to budgetary constraints the reserves have been accorded far lower priority in recent decades than the regular forces, in terms of weapons, equipment, and training.[66] As result, the reserves' level of readiness has deteriorated, and questions have been raised regarding their ability to carry out their missions. The lack of sufficient training also put reservists at risk and sent a message that they were not as important as in the past and no longer enjoyed the same prestige.

By far the biggest reason for the decrease in reserve service, however, as opposed to the motivation to serve in the reserves, stems from the aforementioned law, which shifted the budgetary cost of reserve duty to the IDF. As a result of this change, and in order to better utilize its budgetary resources, the IDF has drastically reduced the use of reservists ever since, including those whose skills are not needed or who do not wish to serve.[67] With reserve duty limited today mostly to those who do wish to serve, and the other changes instituted, the tensions surrounding reserve duty in the 1990s and early 2000s have largely dissipated. When called up for emergency duty, such as the rounds in Lebanon and Gaza between 2006 and 2014, the number of those reporting for duty was overwhelming, exceeding requirements.

Professional Military (Keva)

The professional military is under greater stress than in the past, as career officers and soldiers—and their spouses—weigh the relative benefits of military and civilian career paths. Many refuse to extend their periods of service or seek early discharge. For those with advanced skills, high-tech and otherwise, the temptations in the private sector are particularly great, whether in terms of financial remuneration or lifestyle. Maybe most importantly, military professionals no longer enjoy the great societal prestige they did in the past, instead often encountering a lack of understanding and even disregard for their professional path.[68] Budgetary cuts and doctrinal changes in 2014–2015 led to the adoption of a new five-year work plan ("Gideon"), which provided for a cut in the size of the IDF's professional force, thereby easing the overall retention problem, but not that of those with highly specialized skills.

Casualty Aversion

Israeli society has always manifested great sensitivity to casualties,[69] both civilian and military. This is true to varying degrees, of course, of all societies, but Israel has long been held—and has certainly perceived itself—to be particularly sensitive. Explanations for this are numerous, including the harsh circumstances of Israel's rebirth, shortly after the cataclysm of the Holocaust; the long era of Jewish persecution and powerlessness that preceded it; the overwhelming enmity of Israel's Arab neighbors and consequent fragility of its existence during the early decades; the ongoing hostilities ever since; and Israel's relatively small numbers, a tiny Jewish community of 630,000 at the time of its establishment, still just about 6.5 million today, no more than a midsized city by international standards.

The following section addresses two questions: whether a significant change has taken place in recent decades, first, in the nature of Israeli casualty aversion and, second, in its magnitude. The answer to both appears to be in the affirmative, certainly in the case of the former, more cautiously in the latter. What is not in doubt is that its adversaries believe this to be the case and view it as Israel's national Achilles heel.[70] Nonstate actors, such as Hezbollah and Hamas, have been emboldened by the belief that this fundamental weakness provides them with the ability to counter Israel's otherwise overwhelming military superiority and that they can achieve their objectives through massive rocket fire against its home front. State actors, too, such as Syria and Iran, have similarly focused their strategies for military confrontation with Israel on the vulnerability of its home front. Paradoxically, this is a rare case where Israel's leaders appear to share their adversaries' assessments.

The Changing Nature of Casualty Aversion

A number of factors illustrate the apparent change in the nature of casualty aversion in Israel.

An "Inverted Death Hierarchy." Israeli society, many believe, has come to attribute even greater importance today to the loss of soldiers' lives than of civilians, thus upending the very nature of the IDF's role as the nation's protector.[71] Within this "death hierarchy," the groups to which both Israeli society and the IDF are held to attach the greatest importance are reservists, followed by civilians from "privileged social groups" and conscripts from the middle class, that is, those groups that are most likely and best positioned to engage in political protest against the government. Reservists, in particular, tend to be well represented among the privileged groups and, as fathers of children, their concerns and possible loss engender especially strong public emotions.

Conversely, it has been argued, conscripts from the lower social classes, the "periphery" (areas more distant from the major economic and political centers), and the religious occupy a lower rung in the hierarchy. They are also typically more supportive of military initiatives and thus less likely to be a source of opposition to government policy.[72]

One can certainly take exception to the nature of this posited hierarchy and to the relative importance attached to the different groups. The sensitivity to soldiers' lives, however, is striking and does indicate an at least partial inversion of the traditional approach to civilian and military losses.

From Stoicism to "Everyone's Children." Military losses were announced in the past in impersonal formal statements and presented as a matter of valiant national sacrifice. Today, the emphasis is personal, not national, focusing on the conscript's young age and lost potential, or on the loss suffered by a reservist's wife and children. The IDF is thus no longer a heroic monolithic entity in the public's eyes, but a multitude of young faces, full of unfulfilled dreams.

The massive media coverage given to fallen soldiers has been growing for decades, with lengthy, dramatic, and even lurid descriptions of the soldier's life and death, but has reached new levels of intensity. During the 2014 operation in Gaza, for example, the daily coverage of casualties included full-page spreads in the press, lengthy TV and radio reports, extensive discussions in the social media, and interviews with emotional family members and friends. The all-pervasive coverage strengthens the shared sense that the soldiers are "everyone's children" and that their death is a tragedy for the entire nation. Public tolerance for casualties, traditionally an accepted consequence of the need to defend the nation, cannot but be affected.

Far greater light is also shed today on the reality of the hardships that soldiers experience during both training and wartime, thereby eroding the ideal and noble image that military service enjoyed in the past. Discussion of the physical and psychological traumas soldiers experience, a partial societal taboo in the past, is commonplace today, both in the media and in Israeli literature, theater, and cinema. Soldiers are no longer uniformly depicted as heroes, but often as victims, suffering harmful physical and psychological effects, and it has become accepted today for soldiers to openly display emotion, whether weeping at a comrade's funeral or acknowledging despair and fatigue during wartime.[73]

The growing price Israel has been willing to pay in prisoner exchanges is a further illustration of casualty aversion. No case better exemplified this than that of Gilad Shalit, who truly became "everyone's child." Whereas Israel had been willing to exchange 10 Palestinian prisoners for each Israeli soldier in the 1970s,[74] this ratio ballooned to over 1,000 to 1 in 2011 in Shalit's case. His parents, acting out of understandable self-interest, orchestrated a remarkable PR campaign designed to play on societal compassion for their son's plight and ultimately to force the hands of decision-makers. Other families have acted similarly, if not quite on the same scale or as successfully. The willingness to pay such a vastly disproportionate price plays into the hands of Israel's enemies, who have turned the abduction of soldiers into a primary objective.

Bereavement: From Statist to Confrontational. Bereavement ceremonies for fallen soldiers were used in the past, both by the political leadership and by the IDF, to strengthen national cohesion, the war effort, and IDF prestige. Today, the nature of bereavement ceremonies is often tied to the family's perception of the circumstances of their loss. The greater the sense that it was for legitimate reasons, the more likely the family is to conduct bereavement ceremonies in accordance with state practice and in a manner that blends personal loss into the national ethos. Conversely, many families today blame the IDF and the state for their loss, and some have even chosen to hold private ceremonies, away from military cemeteries and state institutions.[75] The refusal to participate in state ceremonies is a significant break with what was previously the IDF's unquestioned societal role.

In many cases bereaved parents have gone far beyond rejection of state ceremonies, explicitly criticizing the IDF's conduct of operations and engaging in overt political protest. Cognizant of the impact of media attention, they choose to display their anger and frustration in public, rather than the past emphasis on stoicism in support of the national effort. Moreover, criticism is often clearly linked today to the specific family's political beliefs, which tend to be reinforced by their loss and which they now feel empowered to express publicly. Left-leaning families commonly blame the government and the IDF for having engaged in an operation that put soldiers' lives at unnecessary risk. Right-leaning families typically stress that an earlier and more forceful response could have prevented casualties to begin with.

Some families have even turned to the judicial system in cases both of accidental and of operational deaths. In one case, a training accident, the parents charged that their son's death was due to a superior's failure to adhere to safety precautions and sought to have his later promotion to a prestigious position in the IDF blocked by the Supreme Court. A number of bereaved parents worked to block the nomination of a former IDF brigadier general as chief of police in 2015, even though he had been largely cleared of any wrongdoing. A number of parents decided to conduct independent investigations of IDF operations during the 2006 war, despite the establishment of a formal commission of inquiry, and released their own findings to the media, including allegations of operational failures.[76]

Parents involved in these changing forms of bereavement are still a small percentage of the overall number of bereaved families. Their numbers are not insignificant, however, and it is the very fact that they exist at all, and that cases of this nature are growing, that is significant.

The Success-Sacrifice Trade-off. The military and political stakes involved in an operation, and especially the public's perception of its likely outcome, have a significant impact on casualty aversion and societal resilience. Indeed, the likelihood of substantial military and political gains has been found to significantly increase societal tolerance for casualties, whereas operations whose prospects of success are viewed less favorably engender greater reluctance to engage in combat and absorb losses. In short, nothing increases public support as much as success.[77]

The buffer zone established in Lebanon in the aftermath of the 1982 war was a case in point. Its effectiveness in providing for the security of northern residents, as perceived by the public, decreased significantly from 77% to 64% between 1995 and 1998. By 2000 fully 86% believed that ongoing control of the buffer zone was simply not worth the cost in soldiers' lives.[78] Although the number of IDF casualties was actually decreasing at the time, the fact that the public perceived IDF efforts in the buffer zone to be both ineffective and dangerous made the relatively small number unacceptable.

The Four Mothers Movement (FMM), one of the protest movements with the greatest impact on civil-military relations in Israeli history, clearly illustrated the effect of the success-sacrifice trade-off on casualty aversion. Founded in 1997 by the mothers of four combat soldiers serving in Lebanon, the FMM argued that the security zone was not essential for Israel's security and that the ongoing casualties could be avoided if Israel withdrew to the border. The concept of unilateral withdrawal had been both political and strategic anathema in Israel until that time, but highly effective use of the media and grass-roots mobilization by the FMM had a great, possibly decisive impact on the ultimate decision to do so anyway in 2000.[79]

The Israeli public was overwhelmingly supportive of the four operations in Lebanon and Gaza between 2006 and 2014, and whatever criticism did exist was restricted largely to the operations' conduct and outcomes, not the decision to launch them or the price in lives. In 2006 public support for the operation was very high during the early weeks, indeed strengthened the cabinet's resolve to extend the fighting. Two weeks after the conflict began, a whopping 90% supported continuation until Hezbollah had been pushed back from the border; 71% supported the operation's expansion following a month of massive rocket fire, during which the residents of the north had been largely confined to shelters and 300,000 people fled their homes; and the public remained more than willing to give the government additional time to prosecute the war until the very end, provided that it did so effectively. The public mood did turn at the end, and ultimately soured so severely that the government was forced to establish a commission of inquiry into the failings of both the political and the military echelons. The focus of the criticism, however, was the cabinet's willingness to terminate the fighting without having achieved Israel's goals, when only 20% thought Israel "had won the war" and 43% that no one had won,[80] not the decision to launch or extend the operation.

Strong support was manifested during the 2014 operation in Gaza, as well: 90% of the public supported the decision to launch the operation, a full 85% supported continuation three weeks later, and support remained strong even after the more controversial decision to send in ground forces, waning only toward the end when just 27% still believed that Israel had won. The previous rounds in Gaza, in 2008 and 2012, enjoyed similarly high levels of support.[81]

The Changing Magnitude of Casualty Aversion

One has only to look at Western countries to understand that heightened casualty aversion is not limited to Israel but is a far broader international phenomenon, linked to the rise of a liberal global culture. The United States, one of the few Western countries still willing to send troops in harm's way in recent decades, has become far less willing to do so in the aftermath of the two Gulf wars and Afghanistan. A global colossus, with the greatest military might known to mankind, has become averse to military options that may endanger the lives of just a handful of soldiers.

Initial signs of change in Israeli casualty aversion surfaced in the aftermath of the Yom Kippur War, in which the very high number of casualties and widespread sense that it had been the first of Israel's wars to end in failure had a deep effect on public morale and trust in the IDF.[82] The impact on the IDF's conduct of war was both prompt and long lasting. During the 1978 Litani Operation the IDF demonstrated far greater hesitance to use ground forces and risk soldiers' lives than it had previously, but the 1982 Lebanon war was the true watershed. The 1990s were characterized by a growing reluctance to commit ground troops and to enter deep into Lebanese territory, and consequently IDF operations were limited in scale. During the 2002 operation designed to suppress the second intifada, then at its height, the IDF refrained from entering Gazan cities out of concern that casualties in urban warfare would be prohibitive.[83] The same was true, to varying extents, of all of the operations in Gaza since then.

The frequency of such low-intensity conflicts in recent decades, in which Israel has faced serious, but not existential, threats, and which have thus been, at least to some extent, "wars of choice," appears to have had a significant impact on public tolerance for casualties. Moreover, in situations in which the primary objective has simply been to gain a limited amount of time until the next round, public reluctance to suffer losses has increased. Israel's operational and technological superiority in precision firepower, as well as its advanced intelligence capabilities, also led the public to believe that a policy of near-zero casualties was feasible. Both of these developments were conducive to the rise of "postheroic" warfare, that is, an aversion to the casualties that are the very essence of warfare and a consequent concern both for one's own losses, civilian and military, as well as for enemy civilians, at the expense of operational effectiveness.[84]

The Winograd Commission of Investigation found that "disproportionate" casualty aversion compromised Israel's chances of operational success during the 2006 Lebanon war.[85] The government was especially reluctant to mobilize the reserves, doing so only very belatedly, due to concern that a loss of reservist lives would undercut public support for the operation even more than conscript losses. A total of 156 Israelis were killed in the fighting, of whom 117 were soldiers. Although not a large number, it was sufficient to create a public sense of failure,[86] lead to a severe increase in public criticism of the IDF, ultimately force the resignations of the defense minister and CoS, and contribute to the pressures that led to the premier's resignation as well.

To conclude this section: casualty aversion fluctuates in accordance with public perception of an operation's perceived necessity and legitimacy, and especially its probable outcome. It is hard to quantify casualty aversion in comparative terms, but it does appear to be even greater today than in the past. However, it is unclear to what extent this truly reflects a deep societal change or is a logical adaptation to a strategic change; in a situation in which military conflicts are no longer perceived to be existential battles, but mere "rounds" in a seemingly never-ending succession of limited clashes, the willingness to tolerate casualties understandably diminishes.

The Israeli public has also become far more wary and skeptical, less inclined to give decision-makers a blank check and more demanding of a convincing explanation and accountability. The strong public support for the operations in Lebanon and Gaza and the very high rates of reservist turnout, followed by greater numbers of conscripts volunteering for combat units, suggest that when the public feels that the cause is justified, its tolerance for casualties is commensurate. What appears to be incontestable, however, is that the government and IDF believe public casualty aversion to be greater and that this has had a significant influence on their decision-making processes in all of the rounds in recent decades.

Willingness to Pay for Defense Expenditures

Israel's deep and growing income disparity, among the highest today in the OECD, the rising cost of living, but also rising expectations, and the fact that nearly a quarter of the population lives below the official poverty line have fed popular discontent and led to growing demands in recent years to cut defense expenditures in favor of social services.[87] The mass protests of the summer 2011 were a case in point and had a clear, if temporary, effect on the national agenda.

Rising public discontent over the defense burden is particularly significant since it is based on a widespread belief, which only partially corresponds with reality, that defense expenditures are growing. In absolute numbers, the perception is accurate: the defense budget has increased steadily, but Israel's GDP has grown even more rapidly and the relative share of defense, out of the overall budget, decreased to an unprecedented low of 5.2% in 2014[88] (compared to 17.7% in 1988 and 8% in 2000).

With the public focused on economic achievement and budgetary efficiency, its willingness to devote resources to defense is no longer something decision-makers can take for granted. In 2007 only 29% of the public were willing to pay higher defense taxes, whereas 48% had been willing to do so in 1986.[89] In 2015 strong public opposition to defense expenditures forced the IDF to make changes to its personnel practices, including the heretofore sacrosanct issue of early retirement benefits for career personnel. Moreover, there has been mounting public pressure, fed by the sense that Israel has become more secure, to transfer funds from defense to domestic social needs.[90]

This is not to argue that a fundamental change has taken place in the public's willingness to shoulder the economic cost of the defense burden—it has not, and the public remains committed to the need for heavy defense expenditures. Israeli society is, however, increasingly focused today on a socioeconomic agenda, rather than defense, and the competition for resources has become harder.[91] As a result, the IDF and government have to make a stronger case than in the past to justify new expenditures and to assuage the public's discontent when it believes certain expenditures to be excessive.

The National Consensus

Given the tenuous nature of Israel's existence during the early decades, the public rallied around a strong defense posture with little dissent, and Israel enjoyed an unusually broad consensus on national security affairs. Ever since the Six Day War, however, it has become commonplace to say that the historic consensus has unraveled and that the absence thereof has come to pose a challenge to Israel's national security. Israelis might be surprised to hear it, but in reality they continue to share a broad consensus on many important matters of national security.

The following section makes the case for the accepted wisdom first, that Israel's national consensus has unraveled, before turning to the counterargument, that it actually remains quite strong. Some of the issues overlap, and we will return to them when making the case for the counterargument.

The Accepted Wisdom: A National Consensus Undone

Changing Views of Zionism and of Israel's National Character. Zionism, the national movement of the Jewish people, remains an important value for most of Israel's Jewish population, including the young.[92] The main objectives of the Zionist movement, however, as envisioned in the early years (establishment of a state for the Jewish people, its preservation and well-being), have long been achieved, leaving the contemporary definition of Zionism unclear and Israel with the need to formulate new and agreed national objectives. In the absence thereof, Zionism, as a core structuring element of Israeli society, has become less of a unifying concept and instead a focus of competing visions.

The Zionist movement never clearly defined its territorial aspirations, and Israel's territory has thus always been a function of military success and circumstance rather than design. Today, the future of the West Bank has become the primary battleground over the meaning of Zionism, between those for whom Zionism's territorial context takes precedence, and who thus seek to rebuild the national home on the entire historic Land of Israel, and those for whom Israel's character as a Jewish and democratic society is the determining factor. Over the years, the West Bank issue has become increasingly associated with the claims of a highly motivated and politically organized religious and nationalist minority, which is committed to the ongoing control of Judea and Samaria as the historic heart of the Jewish people.[93]

Once a largely secular ideology, Zionism has become more pluralistic, increasingly embraced by the national-religious segments of Israeli society. Usually estimated at about 10% of Israel's population, some polls show that 21% of Israeli Jews identify today with a national-religious ethos, and another 23% identify with it "somewhat." These growing numbers also reflect the political divide in Israel; 47% of the national-religious population place themselves firmly in the right wing, 31% in the "moderate" right.[94]

The relative importance the public attributes to Israel's Jewish and democratic characters has also changed in recent years. Between 2010 and 2014 alone, the number of those who attributed equal importance to them diminished by half, with an increase in the number who gave precedence to the Jewish character. The Jewish character was the top priority for 59% of those affiliated with the Right, whereas 72% of those who voted for the Left gave preference to the democratic character.[95]

Different political, social, and cultural groups in Israel embrace highly divergent visions of Zionism today, and the Right and Left are engaged in a competitive process to represent the "most legitimate" and "true" version. During the 2015 national elections, for example, the "Zionist Union" (a new merger of the Labor and Hatnua Parties) attempted to revive Zionism as a left-wing cause.[96] The Likud and the Jewish Home Party, the long-standing "national camp," conversely, repeatedly challenged the Left's Zionism, purporting to be the true standard bearers.

The Wedge Issue: The Future of the West Bank. Until 1967 Israel's national objectives were relatively clear, simple, and agreed. The Arab threat was extreme and there was a virtually wall-to-wall consensus on the need to defend Israel's borders and existence against imminent attack. The Six Day War, however, caused a fundamental transformation in Israel's national security situation, providing it for the first time with some of the strategic depth it had previously lacked. Most of Israel's public viewed the territories won in 1967 as "negotiating cards" to be held in exchange for peace, but a large minority came to view them as part of Israel's national birthright, and as areas even more important than its pre-1967 borders. Over time the domestic debate ceased to be purely strategic and instead began including elements of mysticism and millenarianism, as some came to think in terms of a "Greater Israel." For them, the dramatic improvement in Israel's strategic circumstances and its renewed control of the ancient heartland of the Jewish people could only be explained by divine intervention, a belief that came to be the ideological basis for the establishment and growth of the settlement movement.[97] It also marked the beginning of the breakdown of the prior consensus on Israel's national security objectives.

Deep differences divide the public regarding the future of the West Bank, or Judea and Samaria, one that is reflected in the very choice of terminology and has been *the* wedge issue in Israel since the Six Day War.[98] Few remember today that the cabinet formally adopted a decision in favor of a withdrawal from Sinai and the Golan Heights, in exchange for peace and security guarantees, just days after the war ended, but made no mention of the West Bank.[99] This was not a chance omission, but a reflection of the fundamental ideological fissure that already existed within the cabinet at the time.

Partisans of territorial compromise and the creation of a Palestinian state view religious and historic ties to the West Bank as an impediment to a peace agreement, while those who view Judea and Samaria as a biblical patrimony reject most territorial concessions. Opponents of virtually any territorial concessions are a minority of the Israeli electorate, just under a third,[100] but constitute a highly motivated and mobilized one, in effect, a single-issue constituency, which is capable of generating great political pressure on behalf of its cause.

The public, including those supportive of compromise, is also deeply divided over the terms of peace. Nothing better illustrates this than public differences over what has often been considered to be the "realistic" contours of a final agreement:[‡] in 2012 46% were in favor, 34% opposed, and 20% undecided. A similar poll in 2014 showed 51% in favor, 24% opposed, and the rest undecided.[101]

The future of the settlements is a source of particular discord. Whereas some 60% of the public supports withdrawal from part or all of the settlements in the West Bank, between 34% and 40% are completely opposed to this. Support for withdrawal from settlements also varies widely by area. According to a 2012 poll, the parts of the West Bank from which Israelis are most willing to withdraw are the "isolated settlements on the mountain ridge of eastern Samaria" and the "Arab neighborhoods of Jerusalem," 58% and 47% respectively, whereas only 20%–34% favor withdrawal from Hebron, the Jordan Valley, western Samaria, and the Etzion Bloc. The public is almost split in its willingness to cede Arab neighborhoods of Jerusalem (47% in favor).[102]

A word of caution is appropriate regarding these polls. In the absence of any realistic prospects of a peace agreement with the Palestinians, at least for the foreseeable future, positions have hardened and the polls reflect attitudes toward what many respondents presumably viewed as essentially hypothetical questions. A significant change in responses is likely in a situation in which an agreement is viewed as feasible, presumably strengthening those in favor of compromise. Conversely, long-term demographic trends in Israel favor the Right.

Deep Domestic Divides. A variety of important domestic issues divide Israelis today. Many are the sort that would exist in any democracy, such as rising income disparities, which have created a well-to-do Israel alongside one that still lives an austere life. Some, however, are more unique to Israel and are of such consequence that they affect the fundamental national consensus, thus making them a source of concern from a national security perspective. It is, of course, difficult to draw a clear line between the two categories, but issues that clearly fall in the category of challenges to Israel's national security include the status of its Arab population, Jewish-Arab relations, and secular-religious relations, including the issue of military exemptions and transfer payments. Moreover, as seen earlier in this chapter, the demographic trends among the Haredi and Israeli Arab communities, and especially their low rates of participation in the labor market, pose grave challenges for Israel's future. Some of these domestic divides are as deep, or deeper, than those over national security issues.

[‡] The question posed to respondents referred to a Palestinian state on "93% of the West Bank and the entire Gaza Strip, including the Arab neighborhoods in Jerusalem . . . where Israel would be recognized as the nation-state of the Jewish people and would retain the settlement blocs, including the Jewish neighborhoods in Jerusalem and the Old City, and maintain a military presence along the Jordan River."

The Counterargument: The National Consensus Remains Strong

A Shared Threat Perception. The intifada in 2000 created a shared sense that every bus, cafe, and home in Israel was a potential target, further reinforced by the low-level terrorism ever since and especially the wave of knife attacks that began in 2015. The result has been broad public support for a tough counterterrorism policy against the Palestinians that persists to this day.

The four major operations in Lebanon and Gaza between 2006 and 2014 also enjoyed broad public support, based on a shared threat perception. Hezbollah and Hamas, as well as Syria and Iran, may have concluded that the home front is Israel's weak spot, but by making it the primary battlefield, they unintentionally produced a strong shared sense that the fight truly is over people's homes. The ongoing rocket fire from Lebanon and Gaza, despite Israel's full withdrawals from both, further strengthened the collective sense that the conflict is over Israel's very existence, not the 1967 borders. Rather than demonstrating that Israeli society is a "cobweb," waiting to be swept away, as Hezbollah leader Hassan Nasrallah once infamously declared, the public has reacted with unity, strong support for government policy, and impressive societal resilience. Much, if not most, of the public today believes that the unilateral withdrawals from Lebanon and Gaza were failures that should not be repeated in the future in the West Bank or any other front.[103]

The danger that a nuclear Iran would pose to Israel is arguably the most consensual issue of all today, even leading to strong support for Prime Minister Netanyahu's attempt to defeat the American-led nuclear deal with Iran by addressing Congress in 2015. In a poll conducted right after the agreement was concluded, 77% viewed it as a threat to Israel's security and 73% even as an existential threat.[104] A large majority of Israelis thus opposed the agreement, just 10% had a positive view, and 21% were undecided; 74% also thought that the deal would not prevent Iran from obtaining a nuclear weapon.[105]

The dangers of growing Iranian influence in the region generally, and especially in Syria, are also broadly shared. A large majority opposes a withdrawal from the Golan Heights, even in exchange for peace with Syria and security guarantees. In 2012 66% opposed any withdrawal from the Golan, 16% favored a partial withdrawal, and 10% would only retain Israeli settlements there. Just 3% said they would agree to return the Golan in its entirety and 5% that they would agree on the condition that the border was moved away from the Sea of Galilee.[106]

There has, of course, been disagreement, often deep and heated, about the appropriate means of dealing with the preceding threats. This, however, is about tactics; on the need to minimize and if possible prevent them, there is broad consensus.

Broad Agreement on the Peace Process. The above divisions on the future of the West Bank notwithstanding, a broad majority of Israelis today wish to reach a negotiated solution to the conflict. In 2015 62%–75% of the public supported negotiations with the Palestinians, and 60% believed that the ongoing impasse was bad for Israel.[107]

Ever since 2000, 50%–60% of the public has favored the establishment of a Palestinian state (compared to only 21% in 1987).[108] Between 2003 and 2013 a stable majority of approximately 70% were in favor of a two-state solution, though terrorism in 2015 led to a significant drop that year (still 50%–60% in favor). In 2015 only 10%–30% favored annexation of the West Bank and a one-state solution under Israeli control.[109]

Even the settlements issue is more consensual than appears at first brush. In 2014, in a situation in which the prospects for peace were bleak at best, 54% favored dismantlement of the small and isolated settlements and 12% all settlements; in other words, two-thirds supported partial or full dismantlement. In 2015 68% of the Jewish population favored ongoing Israeli control over the three settlement blocs as part of a final agreement, and a majority believed that the settlements contribute to Israeli security. There is an overwhelming consensus against a return of Palestinian refugees: only 14% supported this in 2012.[110]

There is also broad consensus in Israel today that significant progress with the Palestinians is not feasible for the foreseeable future. In 2015 fully 70% believed that negotiations with the Palestinians would not lead to peace; only 20% believed that they would. This finding complements the results of polls taken between 2001 and 2014, in which only about a third usually believed that peace was possible (a high of 44% in 2001 and a low of 29% in 2014). The public also remains deeply suspicious of long-term Arab intentions; 67% believed in 2012 that the Arabs' "ultimate aspirations" are to "conquer Israel" or to "conquer Israel and to destroy a large portion of the Jewish population."[111]

In practice, a major shift has taken place over the decades in the Israeli body politic, with many on the right today favoring policies that would have been perceived as dovish not long ago, including support for a two-state solution, significant territorial compromise, and at least some settlement dismantlement. Palestinian rejection of the dramatic Israeli peace proposals in 2000 and 2008, the violence of the second intifada, ongoing rocket fire from Gaza despite the withdrawal in 2005, and other factors have forced the Left to question some of its assumptions as well. The result, it has been argued, has been the emergence of a "new consensus" in Israel, in which most of the public has given up both on the dream of Jewish control of the historic borders of the Land of Israel and on the dream of a permanent peace with the Palestinians, in exchange for Israeli territorial withdrawals.[112] In recent years there has been a partial move back to the Right, though still within the overall shift in public discourse to the Left.

The IDF: The Ultimate Consensus. Public trust in the IDF remains remarkably high, indeed, has been called Israel's "civil religion." In 2014 88% of Israeli Jews expressed strong trust in the IDF, even more than the 84% who felt this way in 2003.[113] Public trust in the IDF is far greater than in any other public institution.

The IDF's ongoing prestige is not self-evident. The Yom Kippur War, Lebanon war in 1982, and the two intifadas did have a significant effect on the IDF's public image. Trust gave way to anxiety and doubt, while heroism, self-sacrifice, and the glamour of military service diminished.[114] IDF affairs and operations had been considered almost sacrosanct in the past, providing it with considerable autonomy of action and even immunity from public scrutiny. Today, the Israeli public demands far greater transparency from the IDF, as it does from all state institutions. Cases of financial impropriety and waste, sexual harassment, and professional incompetence have been given great media attention in recent years, even leading to legal prosecution. Training and operational accidents have become the subject of open criticism, with judicial investigations repeatedly initiated by soldiers' families.[115]

Moreover, maintaining control of the West Bank has entailed ongoing operations in which many IDF soldiers, both conscript and reserve, do not wish to be engaged. The IDF's response at the outbreak of the first intifada, for example, engendered public debate over the adequacy of its preparations and professionalism, as well as the proportionality and moral legitimacy of certain measures adopted. Similarly, the IDF's initial response to the second intifada was criticized by some for having been overly harsh and disproportional, and for possibly having further fanned the flames. The repeated operations against Hezbollah and Hamas, which entailed extensive urban warfare, led to a widespread public sense that the IDF had failed to achieve its objectives and that they had ended inconclusively.[116]

In recent years, the IDF has also become the focus of Israel's domestic "cultural wars," with the contending forces in Israeli society, Right, Left, religious, and secular, seeking to make use of the IDF's unique role and prestige to advance their respective agendas. The Left has criticized the IDF's rules of engagement, conduct in the recent operations in Gaza, and rising religious influence in the IDF. It has also demanded equal rights for women and LGBT conscripts. The Right is concerned about what it perceives to be a lack of moral compass, overwillingness to expose IDF soldiers to risks and even death in order to appease international opinion and law, the corrupting influences of IDF educational programs, and more. The current CoS, Eisenkot, is reportedly so worried about IDF relations with Israeli society that it has become a primary focus of his attention.[117]

The IDF's once pristine reputation and image have thus been dented but remain very strong nonetheless. Indeed the IDF continues to be the ultimate "collective we," in which sons, daughters, parents, family members, and friends have all served. To criticize the IDF is not like criticizing "the military" in any other country; it is to criticize a beloved family member. Greater public demand for transparency and accountability, along with far greater media coverage, a more activist judiciary, and the previously described culture wars have greatly increased scrutiny and criticism of the IDF,[118] but it nevertheless remains a source of unique public identification and support.

Israel's Purported Nuclear Capabilities. The public is strongly supportive of Israel's policy of nuclear ambiguity. Indeed, this has been the one subject in Israel on which there has been a virtually no public dissent for decades. We return to this issue in chapter 8.

The above areas of consensus notwithstanding, Israeli society is deeply concerned by its divisions. In 2012 76% expressed concern regarding the Jewish population's social and religious divisions, and just 79% believed that Israel would prove capable of dealing with them (10% fewer than three years earlier, admittedly still a high number).[119] In the end, it is the issue of the West Bank, on which agreement is actually far broader than generally realized, and especially Israel's domestic divisions, that are the primary reasons for the weakening of the national consensus, despite broad ongoing agreement on most national security affairs.

Emigration

Emigration from Israel (*yerida*) is low, especially for an immigrant society, lower than the OECD average,[120] and decreasing steadily over time, as seen in Figure 5.1.

If the number of emigrants is low, the quality of the human capital lost is not, and Israel is experiencing an ongoing "brain drain." In 2015 5.6% of all Israelis who had received an academic degree between 1980 and 2009 (undergraduate and graduate) had lived abroad for three or more years. The problem is particularly acute among PhDs, of whom 11% in 2015 had lived abroad for three or more years and especially among those with PhDs in mathematics (25%) or in computer science, aeronautic engineering, biology, chemistry, physics, or genetics (16%–18%).[121] Obviously, the three-year cutoff point is arbitrary, and many will ultimately return, but it is a good indication of a worrisome trend.

There is some good news. Among the highly skilled, emigration from Israel was just slightly above the OECD average in 2010/2011 (4.3% compared to 4.1%, not including former immigrants to Israel, which increases the number significantly). The number of those with degrees in the exact sciences and engineering (at all levels) who had lived abroad for three or more years in 2015 was at its lowest levels since the mid-1980s. The overall "academic deficit," that is, the total number of those with academic degrees who have spent three or more

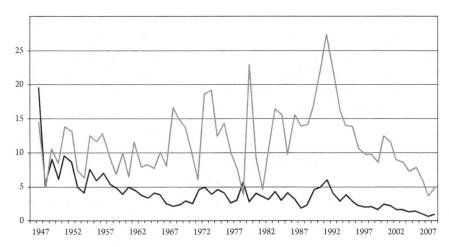

Figure 5.1 Number of Emigrants and Emigration Rates per 1,000 Population, 1947–2010
Source: Israel Central Bureau of Statistics. Adapted from DellaPergola 2015, p. 29.
Note: According to CBS figures the net emigration rate for 2011–2013 was similar to the previous years. The upper line is in absolute numbers, the lower in percentage.

years abroad, compared to those who have returned to Israel, has been steady at a relatively low level of around 1,000 per year, at least since 2013. Moreover, immigration reached a 10-year high in 2015, despite the successive conflicts in Gaza, with 30,000 new arrivals.[122]

Societal Resilience

The term "societal resilience" (often referred to as "staying power") has been the focus of much study in recent years and has a variety of definitions. For our purposes, it will be understood as a society's ability to cope with the demands of a military crisis, such as wars, terrorism, and guerrilla operations, and to "bounce back" to normal life once the crisis-induced disruptions have passed. Resilience in the face of military crises is not just a matter of "resistance," that is, of preventing or minimizing the threat, but of a society's ability to modulate its responses in a manner that is flexible and proportional to the magnitude of the physical damage, casualties, and psychological stress experienced.[123] The frequency and in some cases the severity of such disruptions in Israel make the challenge for its society that much greater.

Societal resilience is essential to the conduct of both effective national security strategy and decision-making. A demoralized population, for example, may constrain a government's freedom to manage a crisis by exerting pressures to end a conflict prematurely and at a heavy price. Conversely, strong societal resilience provides a government with more time to make decisions and greater freedom of maneuver.

The changing nature of the military threats Israel faces has made home front resilience a critical factor today.[124] In the decades after the War of Independence, Israeli military thinking was focused on the IDF's ability to defeat the Arab armies on the battlefield, while the civilian home front was isolated from the fighting and secure. Today, the threat of prolonged asymmetric wars of attrition against the home front, not the military front, has come to pose the greatest military threat Israel faces and thus a severe challenge to its societal resilience. Massive rocket and missile attacks, along with more "standard" forms of terrorism are all designed to cause Israel's civilian population maximal psychological trauma, including those who live far from the actual fighting, and to erode Israel's societal and economic vitality. In an era of instant communications, the effects of these threats are immediate and amplified.[125] The following section assesses the nature of Israel's societal resilience in the face of these new challenges.

Psycho-Societal Resilience

Both Israel's leaders and the public share a self-image of Israel as being deficient in the societal resilience necessary to sustain the casualties and economic costs involved in wars of attrition.[126] In reality, Israel's demonstrated ability to repeatedly absorb shocks and continue living a normal life makes it a model of societal resilience. With the exception of those living in areas under direct rocket attack, the vast majority of Israel's public has learned to continue living during recent conflicts with the alerts and need to take shelter, while continuing the rhythm of daily life, such as going to work, shopping, and participating in leisure activities. Indeed, pictures of Israelis vacating public beaches during rocket attacks became commonplace. Once the fighting ended, the bounceback to the preexisting status quo has been almost immediate.

Nearly 1,200 Israelis were killed during the second intifada, probably the most severe wave of terrorism ever faced by a democracy.[127] Despite the terrorist onslaught, the overall resilience of Israeli society was not shaken. Attendance at schools and the demand for psychological support were affected only slightly and remained stable over time. Cinema attendance—an indication of the public's ability to conduct normal life—also remained relatively stable. Some peaks in the number of attacks and casualties did cause a decrease in cinema attendance, but surprisingly, the opposite was also frequently the case.[128]

Nearly 4,200 rockets were fired at Israel during the conflict with Hamas in 2014.[129] The main threat was concentrated in the areas immediately adjacent to Gaza, where most of the casualties were incurred, while the rest of the country was kept relatively secure by the Iron Dome rocket shield and Israel's offensive operations. Different communities in the Gaza area reacted differently in the face of a mortar barrage, with which Iron Dome was not equipped to deal. Some fled for the duration of the conflict, while others stayed put. Once the fighting ended, routine activities and attendance in schools, even in the most severely affected areas, returned to normal levels almost immediately. Since then, the area has surprisingly seen an increase in population and rising housing prices, as more people decided to move there, both for quality of life reasons and as an act of solidarity.[130]

A strong sense of optimism and confidence seem to be deeply in-bred traits in Israel. At the end of the second intifada, polls showed that more than 80% of the public held an optimistic view of the future, and the number has risen since then. A survey of Israelis' perceptions of their well-being conducted between 1995 and 2003 was striking: not only was the sense of well-being strong and stable over the entire period, but Israelis were particularly optimistic.[131] A poll conducted one week after the outbreak of the Lebanon war in 2006 showed that 85% of the public believed that Israel was demonstrating "high staying power," and 65% reported feeling safe. The figures for the population in the north, the people directly subject to rocket fire, were similar. More Israelis express satisfaction with their lives than the OECD average, making it one of the happier countries in the world.[132]

Socioeconomic Resilience

Military hostilities cause physical damage to private homes, businesses, public buildings, and infrastructure; foreign investment and tourism dry up; consumption decreases, and civilians cease working as they are called-up for reserve duty or stay at home with their families. These disruptions are often invoked to explain Israel's supposed lack of staying power, especially in protracted conflicts.

In practice, Israel's economy has repeatedly withstood conflicts lasting weeks without major damage, including those during 2006–2014. Temporary downward economic trends did occur at the outbreak of hostilities, as consumers and businesses adapted to the changing circumstances, but they did not have long-term effects, and the economy rebounded quickly in all cases. The second intifada was the sole exception, the one case in which the security disruptions did have a severe impact on Israel's economy.[133]

Israeli society's impressive resilience and ability to maintain a sense of well-being and optimism are a function of three primary factors. First is its ability to overcome internal divisions during periods of crisis and to generate a renewed sense of a cohesive and supporting national collective. Second is the public's perception of the nature of the threat; when it is judged critical, and especially existential, the public has manifested a particularly strong ability to mobilize the emotional resources necessary for a resilient response. Terrorism and rocket fire are perceived today to be almost inevitable parts of the conflict with the Arabs and thus to belong to the realm of wars of no choice. Having long experience with terrorism, Israelis have learned to cope with it, to get through it, and "bounce back."[134] Third is the probability of success; as noted above, the greater the public perceives the prospects of success, the greater the societal resilience.

One of the ways Israel helps strengthen its societal resilience is through a (deficient) network of seven "resilience centers," as of 2016, of which five were in the Gaza area. These centers offer area residents 12–18 free counseling sessions to help them cope with the stresses of border life. In 2011, for example, 1,800 people made use of the centers in the Gaza area, and 25% of all Gaza area residents have used them at least once since their establishment in 2007. Additionally, the centers provide training for emergency response teams, doctors, social workers, psychologists, and others and help train local authorities in emergency preparedness.[135]

Ramifications of Societal Change for Israel's National Security Strategy

As seen in the previous chapters, Israel's changing strategic environment, along with the emergence of new types of military threats, have had a major effect on many of the assumptions that lay behind its national security strategy. This chapter argues that some of the socioeconomic and political changes that have taken place in Israel in recent decades, as set out in this chapter, have similarly significant ramifications for the IDF's identity and structure, and operations and for Israel's national security decision-making processes.

Ramifications for the IDF's Identity and Structure

Challenges to the "Nation in Arms" and "People's Army" Model

Already today about one-third of Israel's population, Arabs and Haredim, are exempt from compulsory military service and only a minority now serve in the reserves, which have become, in practice, a semivoluntary force. The "nation in arms" and "people's army" model is thus true today only for the secular and national-religious Jewish populations. In terms of reserve duty, it is true just for a part thereof. In reality, this has long been the case, and Israeli society has learned to live with it in a state of uneasy truce, punctuated by periods of heightened tension, in some cases with significant electoral consequences. The reforms enacted in the early 2000s and 2010s eased the mounting tensions and sense of injustice surrounding both compulsory and reserve service at the time, and there is thus no danger to the existence of the model in the near term.

The rapidly growing number of Haredi exemptions, however, and of those who do not serve in the reserves, make the existing trends untenable in the mid term. As the percentage of Haredim increases, from about 16% of the Jewish population at the time of this writing, to approximately 20% in 2025 and a third in 2050, and conversely, as the number of those who serve in the reserves decreases, tensions will undoubtedly sharpen once again. Indeed, it may only be a matter of time before the "nation in arms" and "people's army" model, which has been at the heart of Israel's defense strategy ever since its establishment, reaches a crisis point.

Some have suggested that Israel adopt an all-volunteer professional military, akin to the American model. Whether this would be suitable to Israel's circumstances is open to debate; there are many reasons to believe not. An alternative solution, or at least means of ameliorating the problem and gaining more time, would be to find means of substantially increasing the already growing numbers of Haredim who do voluntarily elect to serve in the IDF.

In any event, most of the easy fixes have already been made. A more fundamental resolution of the issue is inextricably linked to the broader battle for political power, between the diminishing secular and national-religious majority, and the growing Haredi minority, that is essentially unavoidable in coming years. Current trends do not lend themselves to an optimistic assumption that the issue will be resolved before the crisis point is reached.

Downsizing: "A Smaller and Smarter IDF"

The concept of a smaller and smarter IDF was first invoked by the CoS in the 1980s. Since then virtually all of his successors have sought to downsize and modernize the IDF in order to adapt to evolving social, economic, and defense realities. The basic idea is to have a smaller, but far better trained and equipped, ground force, along with greater reliance on the IAF, Intelligence Corps, and other technologically advanced units, in which Israel's qualitative advantage can be brought to bear.[136]

Numerous attempts have been made over the years to carry out these plans, with limited success. In recent years, however, the impetus for change does appear to have grown, especially since 2014, with the announcement that various ground, air, and naval units would be shuttered, career personnel cut, and a significant percentage of the reserve force discharged. The IDF's current downsizing plans were scheduled for completion in 2017.[137]

Decreasing Importance of the Reserves, Increasing Professionalization

The IDF traditionally viewed its soldiers as "multipurpose" combatants, capable of carrying out a wide range of tasks in various environments. In an era of scarce resources, this approach had the clear advantage of flexibility, including the ability to rapidly redeploy troops between fronts and missions. Budgetary exigencies further forced the IDF to base the ground forces primarily on conscripts and reservists, with a far smaller professional component than the IAF, Intelligence Corps, and other specialized units, whose missions necessitated the highly advanced skills that only professional personnel could provide.[138] Highly successful during the early decades, this model became not just a necessity, but part of the IDF ethos and national lore.

The need for a larger, more disciplined, and highly skilled force, rather than partially trained reservists who serve for just a few weeks each year, essentially a militia, was already recognized following the Six Day War and led to a growing reliance on conscripts and professional personnel during the ensuing decades. The growing complexity of the weapons systems employed by the ground forces, however, and especially the changing nature of the threats Israel now faces, require levels of know-how and proficiency that even conscripts have difficulty achieving today.[139]

Reliance on the reserves has, therefore, diminished greatly over the years, and the role that both they and the regular (i.e. conscript and professional) forces play has been reversed. Heretofore the backbone and fighting spearhead of the IDF, the reserves have become a partially trained secondary element, to be used primarily for purposes of "current security" and as a backup for the regular forces.[140] In so doing, the reserves are intended to free the regular forces for the more difficult missions that they are better trained and equipped to carry out.

The following numbers say it all. During the 1973 Yom Kippur War the IDF mobilized approximately 250,000 reservists, at a time when Israel's total Jewish population numbered only 2.8 million. During the 2006 war in Lebanon it mobilized 80,000 reservists and 90,000 during the 2014 Gaza operation, by which time the Jewish population had reached 6.2 million.[141] The IDF simply needs fewer reservists today, both because of the far larger population base, which has led to an increase in the size of the regular forces, and because of the change in the nature of warfare.

A smaller and especially smarter IDF thus requires greater reliance on better-trained, full-time career personnel. An increasingly professional IDF, however, flies in the face of the long-standing concept of a three-tiered "people's army," in which a small number of professionals provide the core of a primarily conscript and reservist military.

Ramifications for IDF Operations

Preference for Firepower over Maneuver

Casualty aversion and the political costs thereof, especially among the reserves, along with the changing nature of both the military threats and the strategic environment Israel faces, have led the IDF to rely far more on stand-off precision firepower (primarily airpower, some artillery) than on ground maneuver, and on the conscript and regular forces rather than the reserves. In other words, casualty aversion has affected the IDF's operational approach and how it fights both limited military operations and major conflicts.

The change was first manifested in the confrontations with Hezbollah during the 1990s, and to a limited extent even in the war against the PLO in 1982, but came into full relief during the 2006 Lebanon war, in which the IDF fired twice as many artillery shells during the first four days as it had in the entire Yom Kippur War.[142] Stand-off precision firepower has become the preferred method in all IDF operations since then, including the three major operations in Gaza between 2008 and 2014, in which the IDF changed its operational approach, from the tactical level to the strategic, to avoid casualties. In 2008, for example, soldiers made widespread use of heavy mallets to break through walls between Gaza's rabbit-warren type buildings, which minimized their exposure, rather than frontal assault on each building, but also slowed the operational tempo. At the strategic level, casualty aversion was one of the primary reasons Israel did not seek to conquer Gaza in any of these operations, or Lebanon in 2006. The problem is that while stand-off precision firepower does reduce both IDF and enemy casualties, it has proven insufficient to achieve military decision.

Casualty aversion and the consequent preference for firepower are not unique to Israel, but are characteristic of many advanced militaries today.[143] The benefits are clear, but since the IDF has proven unable to achieve military decision without ground maneuver, casualty aversion has had a major effect on the outcomes achieved. The result has been a series of operations that have alleviated the immediate threats but not addressed the root causes, and thereby led to the continuation of the conflict, as happened repeatedly with Hamas rocket fire into Israel. Nevertheless, many of the trends described in this chapter lead to the conclusion that decision-makers will increasingly be forced to opt for firepower over ground maneuver, despite the drawbacks. The 2015 IDF Strategy implicitly recognizes this reality.[144]

The Willingness to Serve Is More Conditional

Soldiers' willingness to carry out missions and to sacrifice today is more conditional than in the past. During the first intifada the CoS feared that political differences among soldiers would lead to the dissolution of the IDF, especially the reserves. Prime Minister Rabin was concerned that a fear of reservists refusing to carry out their missions would make the government hesitant to mobilize them in a nonconsensual war. The IDF has taken the composition of units into account when assigning certain missions, for example, the number of soldiers from settlements and religious soldiers in units ordered to dismantle a settlement or a structure therein. In 2011 the IDF was forced to replace a reservist battalion along the border with Egypt with a regular one, when it refused to hand Sudanese refugees over to Egyptian authorities out of fear of what would happen to them.[145] Many commanders have preferred to ignore refusals to serve by transferring objectors to other duties, rather than resorting to disciplinary means, and the IDF has also chosen to assign some sensitive missions to the regular forces, rather than the reserves, to minimize objections and public criticism.

In practice, the unilateral withdrawal from Gaza in 2005 remains the primary case to date in which possible limitations on soldiers' willingness to serve influenced IDF decisions and operations. A conscious decision was made at the time to only use certain elite units in the withdrawal and to rely to the extent possible on regular army personnel, that is, professionals whose livelihood and careers were at stake. Although the withdrawal went far more smoothly than expected, it nonetheless served as a warning that there are limits to what the IDF can demand of its forces, certainly in highly controversial cases, such as a possible future withdrawal from the West Bank. General casualty aversion serves as a further constraint on what can be demanded today from IDF forces and on how it operates. In the 2006 war in Lebanon and the operations in Gaza ever since, the IDF was hesitant to send soldiers on high-risk operations, preferring stand-off firepower or the massive use of force.

Budgetary Ramifications

In a society that attaches far greater weight to economic considerations than in the past, pressures to cut the defense budget, or at least streamline it, have grown. The defense budget is now at a historic low of 5.2% of the national budget, but pressures for further cuts continue to build, as evinced, inter alia, by the public flap over preferential IDF compensation. Budgetary considerations contributed heavily to the decision to downsize the IDF force structure and drove the shift in IDF operations, from reliance on the reserves as the primary combat force, to the conscript and professional forces.[146]

The increase in efficiency has certainly been beneficial, saving badly needed resources and easing the burden on reservists. The flip side, however, has been that reserve training and combat readiness have deteriorated greatly. In a situation in which most of the IDF budget consists of fixed costs, reserve training has been one of the few areas in which significant cuts could be made easily. The 2006 Lebanon war clearly demonstrated the severe deterioration in reserve capabilities and caused a national shock. This led to a renewed budgetary and training emphasis on the reserves for a few years, until budgetary constraints intervened once again and forced renewed cuts. Budgetary considerations further exacerbate the inequality of the reserve burden, since the IDF still needs reservists for combat roles, but has found alternatives to those in support positions.[147] Following the huge and apparently wasteful use of munitions during the 2014 Gaza operation, the IDF also began speaking of the need for more economical use of weapons and munitions in wartime in the future.

Budgetary cuts and streamlining efforts are not new, and the IDF has long been considered a comparatively lean military. What is new is that the government can no longer take public support for defense spending for granted; indeed, there is growing pressure to cut it in favor of socioeconomic needs. Budgetary considerations have gained a degree of importance in all facets of IDF planning, life, and operations that they did not have in the past.

Ramifications for National Security Decision-Making

Long-Term Political Gridlock: Inability to Resolve Foremost Issue

The ongoing political divide on the peace process and future of the West Bank has led to a decades-long swing of the political pendulum back and forth between left-leaning and right-leaning governments. The former have repeatedly launched, or supported, major diplomatic initiatives aimed at reaching peace agreements on the basis of territorial compromise (Rabin and Peres—Oslo and talks with Syria; Barak—Camp David, the Clinton Parameters, and the Geneva Summit; Olmert—the 2008 proposal). The latter, the right-wing governments, have sought to ensure Israel's control over the West Bank through expanded settlement activity and other measures and have thus sought to block, or slow down, diplomatic processes. They, too, however, have refrained from annexing the West Bank, express at least formal support for a two-state solution, and have not set out an alternative vision of a final settlement. Israeli politics have been partially stalemated by this ongoing divide, and Israel has been unable to chart a clear and stable national course as a result. Long-term demographic trends favor the Right.

Doing Something Right: Consensus, Motivation, and Societal Resilience

Ever since its establishment Israel has lived in a state of perpetual national security tension, often crisis, and as a nation of widely diverse immigrants has also experienced ongoing societal tensions. In these circumstances, Israeli political life has long been unusually fractious, intense, and tension-fraught, and Israelis consistently bemoan their overstated differences and underestimated staying power.

The monolithic consensus of the early decades is certainly a thing of the past. Indeed, it would be unrealistic to expect the former unity of opinion in a complex society increasingly sure of its security and thus far more focused on domestic issues, and in a world of constant change and instant global communications. At the same time, Israeli society is far more consensual than it realizes. The discord over the future of the West Bank truly is an exception, but even here differences have narrowed appreciably over the years. Moreover, this one momentous issue has overshadowed the broad common threat perception Israelis continue to share and consequent consensus on most other national security issues.

It is this overall ongoing national security consensus, despite the endless internal spats and deep domestic divisions, that has enabled decision-makers to build strong support for all of the military operations in recent years, defense policy generally, and much of their foreign policy as well. Motivation to serve remains high, and Israeli society has proven to be remarkably resilient, bouncing back crisis after crisis. After a nearly century-long conflict, Israel is doing something right and the broad national consensus that still exists, Israelis' deep ongoing sense of commitment, and strong societal resilience are strategic assets to be preserved and further nourished.

Two National Liabilities: Cleavages over the West Bank and Domestic Issues

The future of the West Bank remains the one overwhelming wedge issue in national security affairs. It may also lead to a future moment of reckoning that will stretch Israel's national unity to the utmost and involve at least some degree of internecine violence.

The future of the West Bank threatens an early end to the careers of politicians on both sides of the debate, even well short of attempts to reach a final resolution of the issue. Many voters, whether from the Left or Right, view any divergence from their preferred orthodoxies as unacceptable. It is unclear if the Right will accept a decision by a future left-wing government to withdraw from the West Bank. Right-leaning soldiers may refuse to carry out orders to conduct a withdrawal, partial or complete, and to dismantle settlements. Left-leaning soldiers may refuse to carry out annexation and settlement policies of which they disapprove. Initial signs of both have already been manifested. So far they have been highly limited, a testament to the fundamental strength of Israeli democracy, but may grow as the situation evolves and even reach a breaking point.

Fundamental domestic divides, first and foremost, over relations between the secular and religious Jewish populations, and between Israeli Jews and Arabs, exist as well. Demography, both external (the Palestinians in the West Bank) and internal (Haredi and Israeli Arabs), also poses great challenges for Israel. These problems may prove to be as intractable as the external threats, and in some ways of even greater danger to Israel's future. Together, the national security and domestic divides pose a major challenge to Israeli society, and thus to its national security, in the medium and long terms.

Growing Domestic Constraints on National Security Decision-Making

Israel's increasingly activist civil society, competitive market economy, and interventionist judiciary, greatly amplified by a febrile media, constitute an even greater constraint on national security decision-making today than in the past, over and above the impact of the changing nature of warfare and strategic environment described in the preceding chapters. These heightened constraints affect both decisions to initiate military operations and how they are conducted.

In some cases, civil society and market pressures may force the government to respond rapidly to external provocations, if only to minimize the impact on Israel's economy and home front, but with clear ramifications for the nature of the military operation and Israel's international standing. In others, Israel may have to withstand prolonged periods of attack before responding, in order to build domestic legitimacy for military action. The resulting delay can deprive Israel of the benefits of surprise and provide the enemy with time to better prepare and inflict casualties on its rear. The resulting atmosphere of attrition is detrimental to public trust in the political and military leaderships and to Israel's societal resilience.

The far greater role of civil society, the judiciary, and media in national security affairs has made the IDF increasingly accountable to them, not just to the statutorily mandated decision-makers. In many ways, public opinion and the media now serve as the final arbiter of a military operation's perceived success. Civil society's active ongoing engagement in a variety of domestic issues related to the IDF (e.g., Haredi, female, and LGBT military service, human rights) has a constant effect on it and requires continual attention to sustain the IDF's unique role in Israeli society. These societal constraints are likely to be an increasingly prevalent feature of Israeli policy in the future.

Experience shows that when the Israeli public perceives a clear threat, such as that from Hezbollah and Hamas in recent years, it provides the government with a broad, nearly consensual base of support to draw upon and is thus a source of decision-making strength. Nevertheless, decision-makers have to work harder today to make their case to an increasingly skeptical public, and public support can be fickle.

Institutionalization of Casualty Aversion in Decision-Making

Casualty aversion has become institutionalized within the decision-making processes of both the political and the IDF leaderships and has become a core war objective. Today, the military option with the lowest risk of casualties is very likely to be the one chosen, even when it may not provide the optimal solution. Indeed, avoiding casualties has often become more important than achieving the military objectives, and the perceived success or failure of an operation has largely come to depend on the number of casualties, not the achievement of the political and military goals.[148] Israel has always been highly sensitive to casualties, and decision-makers have always taken this into account. The difference, however, is in degree. If casualty aversion was *an important* factor in decision-making in the past, today it is often *the* primary factor, determining the objectives, nature, and scope of military operations.

The 2006 Lebanon war illustrates the problem. The decisions to begin the fighting with an air offensive, without resort to significant ground forces, and later to delay mobilization of the reserves were the consensus approach among both the political and the military leaders. It was adopted not because it was necessarily thought to provide the most effective response to the threat Israel faced, but because it posed the least unacceptable option once the IDF estimated that a major ground offensive might cost the lives of as many as 400 soldiers.[149] The operations in Gaza ever since have all been characterized by similar considerations of minimizing Israeli losses, even at the expense of operational efficiency.

A Demographic and Political Time Bomb

The dramatic demographic growth of the ultra-orthodox population, with a concomitant increase in their political clout, has turned the Haredi exemption from military service and the preferential budgetary transfer payments they have achieved into major national issues. Long simmering, they have become the source of mounting societal and political tensions in recent years and have been primary issues in a number of electoral campaigns. Secular and national-religious Israelis, who bear the defense burden, have become increasingly disturbed by this gross inequality.

The IDF finds itself caught in the middle. Aware that the issue of Haredi service is of concern to secular and national-religious recruits and reservists alike, the backbone of the IDF, it continues to support the principle of universal conscription. It has, however, been reluctant to deal with the problems associated with drafting a population that is strongly opposed to military service, lacks the practical and educational skills necessary, and is often psychologically unprepared for the demands and rigors thereof.[150] This is particularly true at a time when the IDF is downsizing and would prefer to focus on those most suited to its needs.

At the same time, low Haredi participation in the workforce and preferential transfer payments to them have become far more than an issue of social justice. Together with the problem of Arab employment rates, they now pose a major threat to the very future of Israel's economy and thus to its national security.

Primary Observations

- Israel has become two societies, one at the forefront of international technology, the other, largely the Haredi and Arab populations, lagging behind and becoming an untenable burden. If current trends are not altered, Israel will face a severe economic crisis and its Jewish, Zionist, and democratic character will be endangered. The Arab population, still a primarily socioeconomic challenge, may become a separatist and security threat.

- After a century of conflict, Israel is doing something right. Vital sources of its national security, including the motivation to serve, national consensus, public willingness to bear the defense burden and societal resilience, all remain strong, emigration low.

- Conversely, deep divisions over the future of the West Bank, the one major exception to the strong national security consensus, and possibly even more importantly, fundamental cleavages over domestic issues, such as secular-religious and Jewish-Arab relations, threaten Israel's societal strength.

- An increasingly skeptical and demanding public, activist civil society, febrile media, interventionist judiciary, and competitive market economy constrain national security decision-making far more than in the past. When an effective case is made, Israeli society remains committed and supports military operations and spending, but pressures to divert resources to domestic needs will continue growing.

- The "nation in arms" and "people's army" model holds true today only for secular and national-religious conscripts and parts of the reserves. There is no short-term threat to the model, but unless major changes are made to Haredi military exemptions and reservist participation rates, a crisis is likely in the middle term.

- Casualty aversion has been institutionalized in governmental and IDF decision-making, changing the nature of IDF operations. Repeated inconclusive operations, which have only gained short periods of time, demonstrate the difficult in achieving military decision without ground maneuver. Decision-makers will probably have to continue opting for firepower, nevertheless.

- The ongoing political divide on the peace process has led to a decades-long swing of the political pendulum between left- and right-leaning governments. The latter, too, have refrained from annexing the West Bank but have not presented a viable alternative final settlement. Israeli politics have been partially stalemated as a result, and Israel has been unable to chart a clear and stable national course.

PART THREE

ISRAEL'S STRATEGIC RESPONSE

6

The Classic Military Response
in Perspective

We may reach a situation which I do not want to describe in strong
terms, but in which there will be a serious danger to the existence of
Israel and the war will be hard, fierce and with many casualties.
—Chief of Staff Yitzhak Rabin, cabinet meeting on the eve of
the Six Day War, June 2, 1967

The military response to the threats Israel faced, as envisaged by the classic defense doctrine in chapter 1, was based on the following primary elements:

- The "three pillars": deterrence, early warning, and military decision
- The concepts of "the few against the many" and of "a nation in arms," to maximize Israel's qualitative advantages and offset Arab quantitative superiority
- A defensive strategy executed offensively, by transferring the battle to the enemy, pre-emption, short wars, and inflexible defense
- The quest for defensible borders
- Great power alliances, but strategic autonomy and self-reliance

This chapter assesses the degree of success Israel has met in applying these basic concepts of the classic defense doctrine to the threats it has faced, the changes that have already taken place in them over the years, and their relevance to the challenges confronting Israel today. As will be seen, numerous changes have taken place, not the least of them the addition of a new "fourth pillar" to the defense doctrine: defense.

The "Three Pillars"

Deterrence: Mixed Results, Ongoing Importance

Given the Arab states' implacable hostility toward Israel and the fundamental strategic asymmetries with them (territory, population, economic resources, diplomatic support, and more), the classic defense doctrine held that Israel would never be able to achieve military decision in the ultimate sense of the word, as in World War II, and that Israel's deterrence was doomed to periodic failure. Deterrence in Israeli strategic thinking was, therefore, never designed to completely prevent the outbreak of hostilities, but merely to prolong the respites between the rounds for as long as possible. The need for renewed military decision to recharge deterrence was thus not considered a failure, but an essential component and prerequisite thereof: deterrence was a byproduct of military decision. Furthermore, deterrence in Israeli thinking was not a binary concept of either war or no war, but a continuum, and while one type of deterrence might fail, for example, current or specific, general deterrence might be preserved. Finally, Israel's traditional concept of deterrence was based on the assumption of military superiority, of deterring without being deterred.[1]

Bar-Joseph offers a typology of Israeli deterrence praxis based on four components: current, specific, strategic, and cumulative deterrence.[2] In order to assess the degree of success Israel's deterrence policy has met over the years, it is necessary to analyze each of these different types of deterrence separately and to discuss the challenges Israel now faces to its deterrence at different threat levels.

Current Deterrence. Current deterrence was traditionally designed for low-intensity conflict, primarily terrorism. Israel sought to deter both the terrorist organizations themselves and their host-states, in the latter case by trying to force them to assume responsibility for the actions of the former and end their operations against Israel.[3]

From the early 1990s until the end of the second intifada in 2004, Palestinian terrorism became what Prime Minister Rabin termed a "strategic threat" to Israel. Suicide terrorism, essentially a new phenomenon, presented the greatest challenge, since it is extraordinarily difficult to deter someone who is not only willing to sacrifice his life, should this prove unavoidable, but who actually seeks death as the preferred outcome. The sheer magnitude of the terrorist threat during the second intifada, with both suicide and "regular" terrorist attacks occurring with great frequency, presented a severe challenge to the IDF militarily and to Israeli society.

Israel ultimately succeeded in suppressing the intifada and, in so doing, in disproving the common wisdom that conventional armies cannot defeat insurgencies or large-scale terrorism. The process, however, was long, the price in lives and the nation's psyche high, and success was primarily the result of overwhelming force, that is, military decision, rather than deterrence. With the perspective of more than a decade, however, it appears that Israel did succeed in achieving considerable deterrence vis-à-vis the PA and residents of the West Bank, in which terrorism has decreased drastically. The fear of a renewed confrontation with the IDF, severe decrease in economic output and mass arrests, as well as the diplomatic price the Palestinians paid for the massive use of terrorism, all had significant deterrent effects and have so far prevented a resurgence of large-scale terrorism.

At the time of this writing, however, late 2016, there has been a significant uptick in Palestinian terrorism in the West Bank, with a series of knifing and other incidents, mostly by young people acting alone and of their own volition. The IDF has made a major effort to suppress the violence, but it has already claimed over 30 Israeli lives in less than a year. The PA has not been involved and has issued some calls for an end to the violence, the general Palestinian public has not joined in, and there is no central driving force behind the attacks, making Israel's preventative efforts that much harder. A "third intifada" does not yet seem likely, and Israel still appears to have deterrence vis-à-vis the PA and much of the general public. At the same time, it is clear that broad Palestinian opposition continues to boil under the surface. How this will play out, whether we have entered a new stage of heightened ongoing violence, face a major eruption of violence, or, conversely, will see the violence diminish is still unknown.

Israel's attempts to force host-states to stop providing sanctuary to terrorist organizations, or at least to curb these organization's operations against it—known as third-party, or triadic deterrence—have met with mixed results. They worked successfully against Palestinian terrorism operating out of Jordan in the 1950s and early 1960s, but failed in the late 1960s, and succeeded for decades against Syrian-based terrorism.[4] Conversely, in the absence of an effective government, Israel was unable to force Lebanon into curbing PLO terrorism during the 1970s and early 1980s and Hezbollah terrorism ever since. Lacking better options, Israel still tries to hold the Lebanese government accountable for Hezbollah's actions, and its deterrent posture, since the 2006 war, has been based on the threat that Lebanon will again be made to pay the price for any future conflict with Hezbollah, only more so. Israel has been unable to deter third parties, such as Syria and Iran, from providing weapons, financial assistance, and other types of support to Hezbollah, Hamas, and other terrorist organizations.

The concept of mutually reinforcing deterrence and decision served Israel well during the era of primarily conventional wars with the Arab armies. The appearance of hybrid nonstate actors, however, such as Hezbollah and Hamas, and the consequent change in the nature and magnitude of the terrorist threat Israel faces, have brought the current deterrence problem into sharp relief, and arguably to the collapse of the traditional deterrence-decision model.[5] Indeed, actors such as these should probably no longer even be conceived of in current deterrence terms.

Hezbollah's and Hamas's approach to military conflict is diametrically opposed to Israel's, or that of Israel's earlier state adversaries, and they define their military objectives, indeed, the very concept of victory, differently. Fully cognizant of Israel's overwhelming military superiority, they have adopted a strategy of attrition and do not seek military decision, but merely to cause Israel maximal physical pain and damage, and to live to fight again. For Hezbollah and Hamas, nondefeat is victory.[6]

Hezbollah has a truly mammoth rocket arsenal today, estimated to be around 130,000 rockets.[7] Hamas's arsenal is far smaller, but still potent, with a range that also covers most of Israel. Deeply embedded in the local populations, impossible to root out without causing heavy civilian casualties, these arsenals present a uniquely problematic challenge, and Israel's experience trying to deter Hezbollah and Hamas has been mixed. Moreover, the old presumption of clear Israeli superiority and of one-sided deterrence no longer prevails. Today, Hezbollah and Hamas have achieved considerable deterrence toward Israel, too.

The classic defense doctrine emphasized the need for short and decisive wars, to avoid protracted hostilities that would sap Israel's social and economic vitality and undermine its international standing. In practice, Israel has found itself in a decades-long war of attrition with Hezbollah and Hamas, and most of the operations it has conducted since the war in Lebanon in 1982 have been limited ones designed to achieve no more than temporary respites and to restore deterrence, not military decision.[8] The sole exceptions were the operation in the West Bank in 2002, which ultimately led to the suppression of the second intifada, and the initial intent behind the Second Lebanon War in 2006, but the objectives changed as it unfolded.

The three major rounds with Hamas between 2008–2014 ended, in practice, in an asymmetric strategic tie. Hamas survived the Israeli onslaught in all three cases, continued low-level hostilities against Israel thereafter, at least after the first two, and its stature in the Palestinian and Arab arenas grew.[9]

Israel's operations against Hezbollah in Lebanon, from the 1990s through the war in 2006, ended similarly, or even less satisfactorily from its perspective. The operations during the 1990s, including the two primary ones, Grapes of Wrath and Accountability, did not achieve either their immediate objectives or the long-term one of curbing Hezbollah's military buildup. Moreover, Israel's unilateral withdrawal from Lebanon in 2000 was viewed by Hezbollah as a major victory, the first time that an Arab player had ever forced Israel to withdraw from territory without gaining anything in return, and as a major blow to Israel's deterrence. The withdrawal also had a significant impact on the Palestinians, who came to see Hezbollah as a model to be emulated, and severely undermined

Israeli deterrence during the early stages of the second intifada. Israeli threats of severe retaliation were reasonably successful in deterring Hezbollah from striking civilian targets from the late 1990s until early 2006, but not from on-going strikes against military targets.[10]

From 2000 to 2006 Hezbollah's threat to strike Israel's home front deterred Israel from attacking Lebanese civilian and infrastructure targets and created a balance of terror between the two sides. Israel failed to live up to its own deterrent policy, for example, when it did not respond to Hezbollah provocations following the unilateral withdrawal in 2000, despite a declaratory policy of massive retaliation.[11] The six-year period of comparative calm, following the withdrawal of 2000, was punctuated by occasional incidents, but both sides maintained a degree of mutual deterrence until a major Hezbollah attack in July 2006 finally led to an Israeli decision to escalate. The outcome of the 2006 war was initially viewed as a military success for Hezbollah, the first time that Israel had been fought to a military standstill, and the common wisdom held that Israel's deterrence had been hurt badly. Indeed, all of the major rounds between Israel and Hezbollah, from 1983 to 2006, ended unsatisfactorily for Israel and undermined its deterrence.

On the other hand, there have now been over 10 years of virtually uninterrupted quiet on the Lebanese border, the longest such interregnum since the 1960s. In 2013, when another organization fired rockets at Israel, Hezbollah even distanced itself from the act, and the Lebanese government, for the first time, publicly condemned it and even put those responsible on trial.[12] Moreover, Hezbollah has now stayed on the sidelines during three major Israeli operations against Hamas.

Two factors appear to account for this seeming success of Israeli deterrence. The heavy price Lebanon paid for Hezbollah's actions in 2006 appears to have had a significant impact on the public's willingness to continue paying the price of further attacks against Israel, at least for the first few years after the war,[13] and Hezbollah, which is sensitive to domestic Lebanese opinion, refrained from doing so. Paradoxically, an ill-led and ill-fought war actually achieved considerable deterrence. The second factor is Hezbollah's deep involvement in the Syrian civil war, which has absorbed most of its energies and diverted them from Israel. It is thus unclear at this time to what extent the ongoing calm reflects continued Israeli deterrence or the fact that Hezbollah is overextended. Israel's deterrence was the primary factor until sometime around 2013, that is, it achieved a seven-year lull, but this deterrent effect has increasingly dissipated, and the second factor may have been the primary one ever since.

Hamas rocket fire against Israel's civilian population, which began in 2000, has proven to be a particularly intractable threat. Israel was unable to prevent rocket fire even prior to the withdrawal from Gaza in 2005, when it was still in full military control of the area, and has been unable to fully do so ever since, despite repeated attempts. Operations Cast Lead in 2008–2009 and Defensive Pillar in 2012 achieved only temporary deterrent effects, inducing Hamas to greatly curtail rocket fire for a while, but renewed warfare soon broke out. It is as yet unclear whether the fragile ceasefire in place ever since Operation Protective Edge in 2014, marked by periodic rocket fire mostly from organizations other than Hamas, portends a long-term change. Whatever degree of deterrence was achieved in this operation was based on heavy destruction of civilian infrastructure and residential neighborhoods and on protracted warfare, which elicited broad international condemnation. Rockets rained on Israel throughout the operation, the longest in Israel's history, mitigated by the success of the Iron Dome rocket shield. Given the differences in the magnitude of the threat, Iron Dome is likely to prove far less effective in a future round with Hezbollah.

In the absence of an effective Israeli offensive response, or the willingness to pay the human, military, and diplomatic costs required to achieve one, both Hezbollah and Hamas have in effect succeeded in turning Israel's home front into a hostage population, whose security is largely contingent on their interest in maintaining the ceasefire,. Both have repeatedly initiated hostilities designed to challenge and undermine Israel's deterrence, at times even intentionally provoking a response in order to complicate Israel's relations with the international community. Moreover, Israel's desire to avoid confrontations has deterred it from attacking certain targets and from taking actions that might have provided Hezbollah and Hamas with a pretext for escalation.[14]

Israel has not succeeded in deterring Syria from arming Hezbollah and using the organization as an indirect means of exerting ongoing pressure on it. Similarly, Israel has not succeeded in deterring Iran from providing large-scale military assistance to Hezbollah, Hamas, and Syria.[15] Hezbollah's and Hamas's enormous rocket arsenals have ended Israel's monopoly over the ability to strike deep into enemy territory and cause heavy damage to its home front, have offset Israel's supremacy in the air,[16] and have created a degree of mutual deterrence. During the repeated rounds with Hezbollah and Hamas, much of Israel has been shut down, with significant economic and psychological damage, and the threat continues to grow. Indeed, Israel has been forced to display far greater caution regarding its military objectives, and the IDF is instructed not to go beyond certain territorial limits or to undertake certain kinds of operations, which might lead to heightened retaliation against the home front.[17]

Specific Deterrence. Specific deterrence is designed to prevent major military operations, especially surprise attacks, by establishing various "red lines," or casus belli, whose violation would elicit an Israeli response. Specific deterrence was also designed to provide Israel with international legitimacy for the use of force, primarily from the United States, once an established red line had been crossed.[18]

Israel's specific deterrence has been successful in a number of ways. To cite just a few examples, even when the Arabs have taken the military initiative, as in the Yom Kippur War, the scope of the operations and the objectives they set were limited, Syria generally observed Israel's "red lines" regarding its involvement in Lebanon, and no Arab state has ever used chemical or biological weapons against Israel. Even Iran never crossed the red line Prime Minister Netanyahu enunciated in 2012 regarding its enrichment of uranium, though other factors may also account for much of this.[19]

Conversely, Israel's specific deterrence has not been sufficient to prevent the outbreak of wars or major rocket attacks and does not always succeed in lengthening the intervals between such events. For example, Egypt launched the War of Attrition less than two years after its historic defeat in 1967 and the Yom Kippur War six years later, and Saddam Hussein was deterred from firing chemical missiles at Israel, but not conventional ones.[20] Perhaps fearing a failure of specific deterrence, Israel has not enunciated clear red lines regarding Hezbollah or Hamas actions that would lead to Israeli retaliation, making do instead with general deterrent statements. Israel has also not succeeded in deterring Iran from nuclear weapons development, despite the repeated red lines it has drawn over the years, such as production and stockpiling of low- and medium-enriched uranium.[21]

Strategic Deterrence. Strategic deterrence is designed to prevent a general or large-scale war by convincing the adversary that the costs and risks would outweigh the benefits.[22] After repeated failures during the early decades, Israel's strategic deterrence proved extremely successful. Indeed, no Arab state has initiated a military confrontation since 1973, and the Arab states as a whole have come to realize that they simply no longer have a conventional military option against Israel.[23] Moreover, no Arab state has come to the aid of Hezbollah and Hamas during the various rounds, nor of Syria when the IDF clashed with its forces in Lebanon in 1982 and, reportedly, attacked its nuclear reactor in 2007. Conversely, Israel's overwhelming strategic deterrence has led its adversaries to pursue asymmetric responses in the form of terrorism, rocket and missile arsenals, and WMD, all of which are particularly difficult to deter and constitute the primary threats Israel faces today.

The "special relationship" with the United States provides Israel with de facto "extended deterrence"—an Arab assumption that the United States would come to its aid in an hour of crisis—and is thus a further source of Israeli strategic deterrence. Indeed, it has been argued that extended American deterrence, whether through a formal or merely explicit security guarantee, could enable Israel to live with an Iranian nuclear capability with relative equanimity.[24] Conversely, the overarching need to take US interests into account reduces Israel's freedom of maneuver, with adverse effects on its deterrence,[25] especially given Israel's growing international isolation. Israel's purported nuclear capability is a further, possibly crucial, element in the success of its strategic deterrence.

Cumulative Deterrence. Cumulative deterrence was traditionally designed to create an understanding on the part of the Arab states, through repeated Israeli military victories, that it would prevail in every conflict and thus that their military efforts against it were futile. Only then, through a cumulative process, would they ultimately despair of destroying Israel and come to accept its existence. Arab defeats would also provide Israel with a more favorable bargaining position in postwar negotiations.[26]

Israel's cumulative deterrence has been highly successful, achieving the classic defense doctrine's foremost objectives—ensuring Israel's existence over time, convincing the Arab states of the futility of their efforts to destroy it, and consequently leading at least some to seek a diplomatic resolution to the conflict.[27] It took three decades and four wars to achieve this (five with the War of Attrition), but Egypt, the most powerful Arab state and leader of the Arab world, made peace with Israel in 1979, followed 15 years later by Jordan. Intensive, if ultimately unsuccessful negotiations, were also conducted with Syria and the Palestinians. During the 1990s, when the peace process was at its height, a number of Arab countries established low-level relations with Israel, and both they and others apparently wish to renew and further expand them if and when progress is made with the Palestinians. Ever since 2002 the Arab League has repeatedly put forward a peace initiative that is certainly an important change for the better, even if some of its particulars are problematic for Israel.

Conversely, Israel's cumulative deterrence has not convinced all of the regional actors, certainly not Hezbollah, Hamas, and Iran, of the need to accept its existence and make peace, nor has it freed Israel from the need to negotiate over the future of the West Bank and Golan Heights.[28] Arab perceptions, true or not, of Israel's diminishing resolve and ability to wage war, and of the decreasing political utility of war for Israel, have also weakened its cumulative deterrence. Most importantly, all of the rounds with Hezbollah and Hamas in recent decades have ended inconclusively, from Israel's perspective, in contravention of the classic defense doctrine's fundamental injunction that Israel must defeat its adversaries in every confrontation in order to convince them of the futility of their efforts to destroy it. While it might, arguably, have been possible to write off one or two minor setbacks, a series of inconclusive outcomes raises more fundamental questions about Israeli deterrence and strategy generally.

Consequently, Israel increasingly came to be viewed by some on the Arab side as a weak and decadent society, what Hezbollah leader Nasrallah once called a "cobweb," that is, a society that is no longer willing to sacrifice. Israel's sensitivity to casualties is perceived as an especially important weakness, creating deep internal divisions and growing societal reluctance to stay the course. Examples include the widespread public opposition to Israel's ongoing involvement in the "Lebanese morass," which ultimately led to the unilateral withdrawal in 2000, public support for the unilateral withdrawal from Gaza in 2005, and Israel's increasing reliance on defensive measures, such as rocket shields, or the distribution of gas masks, which can be construed as an indication that it no longer considers attacks on its civilians to be unthinkable.[29]

Israel's willingness to make dramatic concessions to the Palestinians under Premiers Barak and Olmert further weakened its deterrent posture. The peace process also complicated Israel's deterrence by imposing constraints on its freedom of maneuver, due to the need to take Arab concerns into account, for example, exercising restraint in the face of terrorist attacks from Sinai in order to maintain the peace with Egypt.[30] These perceptions contributed to the Palestinian decision to wage the second intifada, Nasrallah's decision to provoke the 2006 war,[31] and Hamas's repeated willingness to risk major rounds with Israel. Israel's harsh responses against Hezbollah in 2006 and repeated operations in Gaza ever since, including punishing attacks on (vacated) residential neighborhoods and civilian infrastructure, presumably led to a modification of this perception of societal weakness, but not to its abandonment.

Throughout most of its history, Israel has pursued a policy of deterrence based primarily on prevention, or denial, not retaliation, or punishment. There have, however, been exceptions, such as the retaliation raids against Palestinian terrorism in the 1950s, the War of Attrition with Egypt,[32] the deep penetration strikes in Syria during the Yom Kippur War and especially in recent years, as the threat of prevention has failed to deter the Hezbollah and Hamas rocket threats. During the 2006 war in Lebanon the policy of deterrence through punishment came to be known as the "Dahia doctrine," after Israel severely attacked the Beirut neighborhood of the same name, in which Hezbollah's headquarters and much of its leadership were located. Repeated Israeli deterrent statements since then have warned Hezbollah and Lebanon of the even greater destruction awaiting them in a future round. In the operation against Hamas in 2014, Israel adopted a similar approach, whereas the operations in 2009 and 2012 were far more pinpointed and focused on denial, not punishment.

To summarize this section, Israel's experience with deterrence, the first of the "three pillars," has been a mixture of success and failure. Its current deterrence failed to prevent terrorism from becoming a strategic threat, to dissuade some states from providing sanctuary, arms, and other forms of assistance to terrorist organizations, or to prevent the huge buildup of Hezbollah's and Hamas's rocket arsenals and repeated rocket attacks on Israel. It did, however, succeed in achieving deterrence vis-à-vis the Palestinians following the second intifada and has contributed to Hezbollah's decision to refrain, so far, from further attacks. Israel's specific deterrence successfully moderated Arab behavior, including observance of red lines, but did not prevent the outbreak of wars, major operations, or firing of rockets and missiles at Israel. Israel's strategic deterrence has successfully prevented any Arab state from attacking Israel since 1973, but has led both its state and nonstate adversaries to develop uniquely problematic asymmetric responses. Israel's cumulative deterrence convinced the Arabs of the futility of their efforts to destroy it and led some to seek a diplomatic resolution of the conflict, but not all, and has not freed Israel of the need to negotiate over the territories. In the face of irregular threats from Hezbollah and Hamas, Israel appears to be increasingly moving from denial to punishment-based deterrence.

Early Warning: At Least as Important, Harder to Achieve

In conventional military-to-military warfare, large-scale preparations were necessary before an attack could be mounted, giving Israeli intelligence ample opportunity to provide early warning, even if did not always succeed in doing so.[33] The low-intensity conflicts of the early decades, for example, Syrian shelling of the north, also required preparations by a large and hierarchical military force, and Palestinian terrorism, whether cross-border or even just suicide attacks, often entailed preparations that afforded Israel some opportunity for early warning and interdiction.

Today, Hezbollah, Hamas and Syria can launch rockets and missiles with virtually no preparation,[34] and flight time is literally measured in seconds to minutes (residents of bordering communities had 15 seconds to enter shelters during the recent confrontations with Hamas). Detection and early warning are thus much harder. Further adding to the problem, recent operations have broken out over isolated incidents, without a clearly discernable escalatory process, or even a specific moment at which the sides have decided to go to war.[35] In both the Lebanon war in 2006 and operation in Gaza in 2014, for example, none of the sides were thought to have had an interest in an escalation at the time, but they nevertheless ended up being Israel's two longest military operations since 1948. Future conflicts with Hezbollah and Hamas, as well as on the Golan, are also likely to begin with little if any warning.

Detecting missile launches from distant and large countries, such as Iraq and Iran, requires sophisticated satellite capabilities, some purely Israeli, some subject to US willingness to share them. Flight time is longer, minutes, but preparations are also extremely difficult to detect. Terrorism from transnational actors, such as ISIS, al-Qaeda, and their various offshoots around the globe present further challenges to early warning.

Early warning remains a fundamental component of Israel's defense doctrine, though one that is increasingly difficult to achieve. Some believe that it is less important in today's irregular conflicts against nonstate actors than it was in the wars with the Arab states in the past, because the IDF's regular forces are capable of conducting them on their own, at least in the initial stages, until the reserves are mobilized.[36] Be that as it may, early warning remains critical for the home front.

Military Decision: Much Harder to Achieve

The classic defense doctrine viewed fundamental military decision as an unattainable objective, and consequently Israel has never sought to achieve it.[37] Instead, military decision for Israel has traditionally meant the ability to end the fighting on enemy territory, following significant destruction of its forces, and under favorable strategic circumstances. In practice, Israel only truly achieved this in the first three conventional wars (1948, 1956, and 1967), arguably in the war in Lebanon in 1982, and in the second intifada. It was unable to achieve military decision, or was only partially successful, in the War of Attrition, the Yom Kippur War, war in Lebanon in 2006, and the repeated smaller-scale operations against both Hezbollah and Hamas.[38] The painful reality is that Israel's last decisive and unequivocal military victory was in 1967, some five decades ago.

Even in the three ostensibly decisive wars, Israel only succeeded in destroying a comparatively small percentage of enemy capabilities, sufficient to cause disarray, incoherence, and a short-term loss of will to continue fighting, but not enough to deliver a knockout blow or to turn the military achievements into concrete diplomatic ones. Following the dramatic victory in 1967 Israel was soon involved once again in low-level hostilities on the Egyptian and Jordanian borders, just two years later in medium-intensity hostilities with Egypt (the War of Attrition), and in high-intensity hostilities with Egypt and Syria in the Yom Kippur War. Moreover, the Arab armies were rapidly resupplied and grew greatly in size and quality after each of the wars.

The first and especially the second intifadas had a fundamental effect on Israeli thinking regarding the concept of military decision, further reinforced by the subsequent rounds with Hezbollah and Hamas. Strategic military decision was found to be irrelevant to confrontations of this nature. Instead, the IDF would seek to achieve "tactical decision," in other words, to gain the upper hand in every specific confrontation, but not overall military decision in one conclusive campaign. In effect, Israel was returning to the thinking that had guided its approach to "current security" during the 1950s.[39] Even hardliners such as Prime Minister Sharon and Chief of Staff Yaalon concluded that the intifada could only be won through a gradual, cumulative, and long-term process of physical and economic exhaustion, rather than Israel's previous preference for blitzkrieg, and that victory would be "won by points, not by a knockout blow." In the meantime, Israel would seek to reduce the threat to a level that the public could live with and that would allow it to retain its diplomatic freedom of maneuver.[40]

Hezbollah's and Hamas's irregular concept of "victory by nondefeat," the repeated unsatisfactory rounds with them and the second intifada, led to an IDF conclusion that there was no longer a clear causal relationship between military decision on the battlefield and the deterrent effect achieved, that is, that deterrence was no longer a byproduct of decision, as the classic doctrine had postulated, and that military decision was not an attainable objective against nonstate actors of this sort. Instead of operations designed to achieve decision, the IDF thus now began conducting "deterrence-based operations."

The new approach reflected the recognition that Israel is enmeshed in an ongoing conflict with extremist nonstate actors that cannot be resolved. The use of force is thus designed neither to achieve political ends nor to affect their basic resolve to continue the battle, but merely to decrease their ability to harm Israel and to achieve temporary deterrence, thereby prolonging the intervals between the rounds.[41] Despite Israel's clear preference for quick and decisive wars, it has in effect adopted a strategy of attrition of its own, alternating between ongoing low-intensity operations and occasional escalations, designed to counter that of its nonstate adversaries.

Following what many considered the debacle of the 2006 Lebanon war, the IDF has given considerable thought to the concept of military decision and the means of achieving it in the current strategic circumstances. Based on the experience in the three rounds with Hamas in Gaza since then, it does not yet appear to have found the means of doing so, at least at an acceptable price, and Hezbollah is a much more potent adversary. Nevertheless, the offensive emphasis and desire to achieve rapid military decision, as evinced by the IDF Strategy published in 2015, remain fundamental pillars of Israel's defense doctrine.[42]

Israel's diminishing ability to achieve military decision stems from a number of factors, as explained below. Many of these factors are not unique to irregular threats and have long been manifested in conventional warfare; it is their extent and severity in irregular conflicts that makes them particularly difficult.

A Unique Inability to Dictate the Terms of Peace. In most conflicts in history, the militarily successful side has been able to shape the terms of the postwar settlement. This has not been true in the case of the Arab-Israeli conflict, in which the Arab states long refused not only to acknowledge defeat and accept Israel's conditions for peace, but to negotiate with it and even recognize Israel's very right to exist. Since their grievance was fundamental, Israel's existence, and they were willing to endure harsh long-term consequences in pursuit of their objectives, there were no measures that Israel could have adopted that would have resolved the conflict.

Some of the Arab states have since changed their approach, but this fundamental refusal still holds true of others, as well as of Iran, Hezbollah, and Hamas. When an enemy adopts an extreme position such as this, regardless of the outcome on the battlefield, and views every confrontation as part of a battle to the bitter end, military decision becomes uniquely difficult to achieve.

An Elusive Concept of Victory. In conventional warfare, victory is typically defined as the physical defeat of an enemy's armed forces, in terms of destruction of military formations and equipment, and/or its will to fight. Even here, however, it is not clear cut. Following the Six Day War, the Arab countries knew that they had been severely defeated, but that the fundamental strategic asymmetries were such that Israel could never achieve true military decision and dictate terms. They could thus allow themselves to refuse to recognize Israel and negotiate with it, let alone surrender, and in the case of Egypt, even renew hostilities shortly thereafter.[43]

In irregular conflicts against terrorism and guerrilla warfare, the very concept of military decision and victory is elusive. Israel dealt severe blows to Hezbollah in the 2006 war and the various operations before then, and to Hamas in the major operations in 2008, 2012, and 2014, all to limited avail. Hezbollah and Hamas actors do not have strategic "centers of gravity" (e.g., capitals, vital strategic targets, major military formations) whose destruction has a significant effect on their war-fighting capabilities and forces their surrender. To the contrary, they have an almost endless number of targets whose destruction is of little consequence,[44] and their military capabilities are deeply embedded in civilian populations, making it very difficult to find and destroy them. Moreover, their objective is not to defeat Israel in the near term, which they recognize is unattainable, but to weaken it through a long-term process of attrition and to merely survive each round in the meantime, the aforementioned concept of "victory by not losing." Severely degrading their capabilities thus does not have a fundamental impact either on their willingness to continue the fighting or on their domestic standing.[45] Furthermore, Hezbollah and Hamas are not just terrorist organizations, but mass political, ideological, and socioeconomic movements, and one cannot destroy the ideas they represent nor eliminate the need for the services they provide. The difficulties Israel has encountered in dealing with them have been shared by many conventional armies facing irregular confrontations in the past.

The Solution Is Just Not Worth the Cost. Israel's conventional wars against the Arab countries were viewed both by its leaders and by the public as existential "wars of no choice," leading to a broad national consensus regarding the need to win at virtually all costs. This is not the case with the threats posed by nonstate actors such as Hezbollah and Hamas, which can be significant, even severe, but certainly not existential. It is not that Israel cannot achieve military decision against them; it probably can, but the price in lives and property, on both sides, and in Israel's international standing has been perceived to exceed the magnitude of the threats they pose, painful as they may be.[46]

In the operations against Hezbollah in 2006 and Hamas ever since, Israel could have achieved decisive outcomes had it occupied virtually all of Lebanon and Gaza, respectively. A number of considerations, however, militated against doing this. It would have each entailed large-scale Israeli casualties, Lebanese and Gazan civilian casualties would have been much higher, and the blow to Israel's international standing would have been severe. The various governments in office at the time, Left and Right, clearly did not believe that the threats warranted this cost. The number of casualties, damage to property, and disruption of daily life that Israel had suffered prior to these operations were sufficient to justify significant responses, with overwhelming public support, but not the costs that an attempt to truly "resolve" the problem would have entailed.

Perhaps most critically, Israel would probably not have been able to achieve more than a short-term amelioration of the problem even if it had pursued a strategy of military decision. Iran replenished Hezbollah's and Hamas's rocket arsenals in a relatively short time following all of the operations (at least until 2014) and will presumably do so in the future. This was true of the conventional wars of the past as well, in which the Soviet Union rapidly replenished Arab arsenals, but the intervals gained between the wars were considerably longer, at least than those with Hamas.

Moreover, the consequences of military decision in the operations in Gaza in 2008–2104 might have been even worse from Israel's perspective than the antecedent situations. Israel probably could have toppled Hamas in these operations but knowingly refrained from doing so, because the end result might have been either a completely lawless area, from which various terrorist organizations would have vied to fire more rockets at Israel, or the takeover of Gaza by an even more heinous organization, such as the PIJ, al-Qaeda, or ISIS. Similarly, toppling Hezbollah in Lebanon might have paved the way for a subsequent ISIS takeover.

Had an effective and long-term solution been deemed feasible, Israel might have been willing to pay the price in casualties and international standing required to achieve military decision, but in its absence, Israel concluded that it simply was not worth it. Crucially, the differences in the magnitude of the threats posed by conventional and asymmetric conflicts are such that in the former, there is usually no choice but to seek decisive military outcomes, whereas the latter often do not justify the cost. The question then becomes whether or not the country in question has the societal staying power and resilience to withstand the debilitating long-term effects of irregular conflicts of attrition. To date, as seen in chapter 5, Israel has.

Absence of International Legitimacy. Changing international norms make any military action, let alone military decision, difficult today, especially in populated areas in which the likelihood of civilian casualties is high. Even a country perceived to have been under attack and to be acting in pursuit of its legitimate right of self-defense, is expected to show restraint and to minimize enemy civilian casualties, even if this means less effective warfare and greater losses to its own civilian and military personnel. As civilian casualties mount, international differentiation between the side responsible for the onset of hostilities and the side responding blurs, and the victim often comes to be seen as the aggressor, especially when there is also a fundamental asymmetry in the sides' military capabilities.

Russia could afford to ignore changing international norms in Chechnya and Crimea; Syria ignored them in its civil war. Most countries today, however, certainly democracies, are deeply affected by them, none more so than Israel, whose difficulties in achieving military decision are further magnified by the deterioration that has taken place in its international standing. In the absence of international legitimacy for the use of force, even when Israel has been the victim of clear provocations, it has found it increasingly difficult to take the escalatory measures needed to achieve military decision, in some cases even to respond at all.[47] International opinion turns hostile rapidly, and when Israel has been perceived, rightly or usually wrongly, to have used disproportionate force, it has quickly lost whatever legitimacy it enjoyed at the onset of hostilities.

In most cases Israel has chosen to take action despite international opprobrium, but its freedom of maneuver has been circumscribed considerably, in some cases even by the United States. In 2008, for example, concern over the response of the incoming American administration led Israel to circumscribe the scope of the operation in Gaza and end it rapidly. The mixed American support Israel enjoyed in the 2012 and 2014 operations in Gaza was also a constraint on its freedom of action.

Ineffective Mechanisms for Conflict Resolution. Nonstate actors such as Hezbollah, Hamas, and ISIS, which reject the norms of the international community, and to a lesser extent even radical states like Iran and Syria, are less susceptible to international pressures to end the fighting than most state actors. Moreover, prolongation of the fighting is a fundamental part of Hezbollah's and Hamas's strategy, the price paid notwithstanding, and a sign of success to be trumpeted before their respective domestic and international audiences. The efficacy of the Security Council, always limited when it came to the Middle East, has been further undermined by divisions in recent years among the permanent members.

During the Cold War, a shared interest in preventing the prolongation and es-calation of regional conflicts enabled the superpowers to work together at times, if only under duress. In recent years, with the deterioration in both US-Russian relations and US stature in the region, the ability of either the Security Council or the United States, independently, to intervene to end conflicts has diminished. In the conflicts in Lebanon in 2006 and in Gaza in 2008, 2012, and 2014, the United States had virtually no influence over Hezbollah or Hamas, with whom, as terrorist organizations, it had no direct channels of communication. In 2012 and 2014 Egypt thus served as the primary mediator, even though it lacked the clout to truly influence either side and its relations with Israel, in the former case, and with Hamas in the latter, were poor. In both cases, Israel ultimately sought to end the fighting unilaterally, for lack of a better mechanism of conflict resolution, but in 2014 Hamas repeatedly rejected ceasefire proposals and the fighting continued.

Both Hezbollah and Hamas have also learned through experience that the use of terrorism and violence does not necessarily lead to the imposition of pu-nitive measures by the international community. To the contrary, their use of vi-olence has often been rewarded with generous international reconstruction and development aid, which directly or indirectly abetted the buildup of their stature and military capabilities for future rounds. This was true both of the intentional Hezbollah provocation that led to the war in Lebanon in 2006 and of the 51 days of rocket fire by Hamas during the confrontation in 2014.[48]

Avoidance of Territorial Acquisition and the Demise of Ground Maneuver. With large and hostile populations on virtually all possible fronts today, ground maneuver and the conquest of territory have become both more difficult for Israel and less desirable, often something to be avoided if at all pos-sible. Indeed, Israel has become very reluctant to take even temporary control of additional territory, as evinced by its behavior in the 2006 Lebanon war and the various operations in Gaza since then.[49] Moreover, for a variety of political, demographic, and military reasons, Israel has withdrawn from some territories already under its control (Sinai, southern Lebanon, and Gaza) and has found maintaining control of others to be difficult and costly (West Bank). Without ground maneuver to conquer territory, even temporarily, it is very difficult to achieve military decision. Firepower alone has not proven sufficient.

The apparent end of the era of conventional military conflicts in the Middle East and rise of irregular warfare, has further undermined Israel's ability to de-stroy enemy forces,[50] especially when deeply embedded in civilian populations. Ground maneuver may be effective against short-range rockets near the border, but it is of limited utility against those with ranges of tens or even hundreds of kilometers. Effective ground maneuver against rocket threats at these distances would require massive and prolonged occupations of a magnitude that no gov-ernment in Israel in recent decades has wished to conduct.[51]

Moreover, in an era in which ground maneuver is increasingly circumscribed, the levels of attrition required in order to achieve military decision are unclear. During the Yom Kippur War, for example, Israel neared military decision—but did not quite achieve it—after reaching an attrition rate of some 40% of enemy armor, while the United States achieved military decision in the first Gulf War with an attrition rate of about 50% (the precise figures are the subject of debate). Even so, in both cases it was the threat to continue advancing, destroy the respective militaries, and conquer their capitals that was the truly decisive factor, not the levels of attrition.[52] With respect to wars without significant ground maneuver, such as those Israel has waged in recent decades and is likely to face in the future, one informed scholar speaks of the need to achieve a whopping attrition rate of 70%, 80%, or even 90%.[53]

In conventional warfare territorial conquest is a prelude to the end of the war. In wars against irregular forces, as the United States has learned in Iraq and Afghanistan, and Israel in the confrontations with Hezbollah and Hamas, territorial conquest is merely one stage in a prolonged war, possibly just an early one. The occupying force provides numerous targets for guerrilla operations against it and its "logistical tail," and the irregular actor may actually seek to draw it in, as part of a long-term attrition strategy.[54]

Inability to Bring Power to Bear. In contemporary irregular warfare, whether due to political or operational constraints, or both, the stronger side can bring only a small portion of its capabilities to bear. During the operations against Hamas in recent years and the 2006 war against Hezbollah, the geographic constraints were such that the IDF was actually able to deploy only a small part of its ground forces, and the international reaction to a large-scale invasion would have been severe had this not been the case. Air power was constrained by Hezbollah's and Hamas's practice of embedding their forces among the civilian populations,[55] and of "disappearing from the battlefield," and the IAF was never able to completely suppress rocket fire despite the vast numbers of sorties flown.[56] In practice, Hezbollah and Hamas have developed means of partially neutralizing Israel's technological and operational superiority.[57] The United States, a global superpower with incomparable military might, has encountered similar problems in both Iraq and Afghanistan.

Israel succeeded in achieving military decision in the past in those cases where ground maneuver enabled it to conquer territory, especially when the overall force-space ratio was favorable. Destruction of Arab air capabilities proved sufficient to approach decision, though not fully achieve it, and actual decision was only reached on the ground. In 1973 the problem of a saturated battlefield arose for the first time, as the fighting was conducted by far larger forces and in narrow areas both on the Egyptian and on the Syrian fronts, creating great force-space density and constraining Israel's ability to conduct maneuver. In the operations in Lebanon from 1982 through 2006, and against Hamas ever since, the force-space ratio truly manifested itself, resulting in a dense battlefield and limiting Israel's ability to maneuver, break through, and bring its superiority to bear.[58]

Inability to Achieve Escalation Dominance. Israel has been largely unable to achieve escalation dominance in the confrontations with Hezbollah and Hamas, that is, escalation of the conflict to a level where the adversary no longer can, or wishes not to, continue the fighting. Indeed, in the confrontations to date, Hezbollah and Hamas have manifested a determination and ability to fire the last shot, as a matter of strategic doctrine, even when Israel has conducted lengthy and painful campaigns designed to suppress rocket fire. In practice, it was Israel that was forced to exercise the restraint necessary to bring about a ceasefire.[59] As with the difficulties in achieving military decision generally, it is not that Israel cannot achieve escalation dominance in prolonged irregular conflicts, but that its home front is exposed to continuous rocket fire, international pressure to end the fighting grows, the costs exceed the benefits, and it is simply not worth it. Israel prefers to get it over with, at the expense of its deterrence posture.

A Tenuous Balance of Terror. In past wars Israel had sufficient conventional power to threaten the stability and even the existence of Arab regimes. The Yom Kippur War, for example, ended with IDF forces within striking distance of both Cairo and Damascus, and in 1982 Israel actually conquered Beirut and temporarily succeeded in forcing Lebanon to establish a government friendly to it. Given Israel's air superiority, both the Arab civilian and military rears were vulnerable.

Today, a tenuous "ballistic balance of terror" has evolved both with Hezbollah and with Hamas, and with state actors such as Syria (until the civil war).[60] Given their vast rocket and missile arsenals, on the one hand, and Israel's great deep penetration capabilities, on the other, the wars have become ones of mutual deterrence, or punishment, against the civilian infrastructure and military rear. In Hamas's and Hezbollah's case, the war is against civilians themselves, and both sides now have the ability to cause grave damage to the other even after absorbing a severe first strike.[61] Moreover, long-range and precise rockets, with large warheads, now provide these actors with the ability to significantly disrupt the mobilization of Israel's reserve forces, offensive operations, and national infrastructure.[62]

Distant and Nuclear Adversaries Cannot Be Defeated. The missile and WMD capabilities of countries in the second and third tiers also pose great difficulties in terms of achieving military decision. At these distances, military decision is simply unrealistic for a country like Israel, whose long-distance capabilities are limited. Instead, Israel has to focus on deterrence, whether for punishment purposes, by attacking high-value targets, or denial, by attacking critical military nodes.[63] At the nuclear level, the very concept of military decision is largely meaningless for a country Israel's size,[64] arguably for all others as well.

To summarize this section, Israel was able to achieve military decision in the first three conventional wars, the second intifada, and debatably the 1982 Lebanon war. It neared decision during the Yom Kippur War but has been unable to achieve it in any of the operations against Hezbollah and Hamas. Many reasons have been found to explain Israel's growing difficulty in achieving military decision, inter alia, its inability to dictate the terms of peace, the radical nature of its adversaries, absence of international legitimacy, demise of ground maneuver, inability to bring IDF power fully to bear, and, arguably most importantly, the fact that the solution to the threats posed by nonstate actors is often more costly than the threats themselves.

The ongoing inability to achieve military decision has led the IDF to fundamentally rethink the nature of the concept when facing irregular threats. This includes a new focus on "tactical decision," but not conclusive military decision in one major campaign, and on "deterrence-based operations," as opposed to the former "decision-based operations."

The "Defensive Pillar": An Unwanted Stepchild

A growing debate has been underway in Israel in recent years regarding the relative emphasis to be given to offensive and defensive operations. The outcome of this debate has crucial ramifications both for Israel's strategic posture and for IDF force buildup plans. Given Israel's overwhelmingly offensive approach in the past, first enshrined in the classic defense doctrine, the very existence of the debate is a reflection of the nation's changing strategic circumstances.[65]

The classic defense strategy downplayed the role of defense for a variety of reasons. Israel's strategic circumstances, primarily the absence of strategic and even tactical depth, were assumed to preclude a significant role for defensive operations to begin with. A defensive approach might also have led to prolonged and costly wars of attrition, rather than the swift military victories Israel sought as a means of offsetting the fundamental asymmetries with the Arab states. Moreover, defensive operations would have forced Israel to disperse its limited forces along the various fronts, whereas its adversaries could concentrate forces at select points. Finally, there is a deep-seated belief among Israeli military leaders that wars can only be won, and issues in contention resolved, by offense, not defense, and that defense is simply contrary to the IDF's ethos of rapid maneuver and improvisation. The repeated inconclusive rounds with Hezbollah and Hamas notwithstanding, the fundamental adherence to an offensive strategy remains unshaken, as expressed, inter alia, in the IDF Strategy published in 2015.[66]

In recent decades, however, a number of factors have begun to force a partial rethinking of the role of defense in Israel's defense doctrine. Changes in the nature of warfare provided new opportunities for defensive operations, particularly suited to Israel's advanced technological capabilities and strategic needs. These technological changes also coincided with an era in which Israel's ability to wage offensive operations and to transfer the ground battle to enemy territory, the heart of the classic defense doctrine, became increasingly constrained. Pressures for restraint by the United States and other friendly countries, growing diplomatic isolation, changing international norms, and the presence of large and hostile populations on virtually all fronts, as a result of which territorial conquest was no longer a viable or desirable strategy, all made the need for a more defensive approach palpable, as did the limitations of Israeli deterrence vis-à-vis Hezbollah and Hamas.[67]

Beginning with the massive artillery attacks on Israel's civilian population in the north, prior to the 1982 Lebanon war, and especially the 1991 Gulf War, when Israel was unable to stop Saddam Hussein's missile fire, it became clear that its adversaries had identified the home front as Israel's primary weak point and were turning it into the primary theater of battle. This new reality was further crystallized by the devastating Palestinian terrorism of the second intifada, in which Israel's cities were repeatedly attacked by bombings and suicide bombers, by Hamas's ongoing rocket fire, and Hezbollah's massive use of rockets in the 2006 Lebanon war.[68] The WMD programs in Iraq, Syria, Libya, and, above all, Iran further focused attention on the vulnerability of the home front and the need for improved defensive capabilities.

Today's more prolonged irregular conflicts also increased the need to protect the home front and to strengthen its societal resilience. Improved defenses not only reduce the number of potential Israeli casualties, the primary reason for Israel's responses and escalations to date, as well as the potential damage to strategic targets, such as power plants, but also provide leaders with greater time and flexibility for decision-making. In so doing, they can eliminate the need to respond at all or reduce the scope and magnitude of the response and help preserve Israel's international image and legitimacy.[69] The apparent absence, at the time of this writing, of an effective offensive response to the Hamas and Hezbollah rocket threats, has made the need for heightened defensive capabilities essential.

The convulsions of the Arab Spring further increased the importance of defensive capabilities. Syria and Egypt lost control over their territory, thereby creating a situation that has long prevailed on both the Lebanese and Gazan borders—the absence of a government capable of taking responsibility for the threats emanating from its territory and thus serving as a target for retaliation.

Today, it is not always clear who fired a rocket from these areas or conducted some other form of attack, thereby complicating Israel's deterrent and retaliatory posture. The problem of the absence of a "return address" also exists in regard to cyber-warfare and possible WMD terrorism.[70]

The debate regarding the relative importance of defense and consequent military expenditures is ongoing, despite decades of growing interest in this area.[71] In 2006 the highly respected Meridor Report, a comprehensive and in-depth strategic reassessment of Israel's defense doctrine, recommended that defense be added to the three traditional pillars of the classic doctrine—deterrence, early warning, and military decision.[72] Although the report was never formally adopted, Defense Minister Peretz announced the following year that defense would now be the fourth pillar.[73] The IDF's new operational concept, adopted in 2006, also provided for a greater role for defense,[74] but the IDF still accords overwhelming priority to offense to this day, and has resisted virtually all efforts to fund defensive capabilities out of its own budget. Thus, by way of example, both the Arrow missile and Iron Dome rocket defense programs only really got underway, and overcame IDF budgetary opposition, when the United States agreed to cover half of their cost.[75] The IDF has also insisted that other defensive programs, such as the construction of fences on the various borders, or distribution of gas masks in the past, be funded by special non-IDF budgets.

Nevertheless, a heightened emphasis on defense has begun to be manifested in recent decades in a variety of ways. The terrorist threat led to the construction of the West Bank security fence and later to a similar fence along the entire Egyptian border, in addition to the long-standing ones on the Lebanese, Syrian, and Gaza borders. The border with Jordan remains the only one that has not yet been sealed off by such highly costly barriers, although construction has been approved for an initial segment.

The WMD threat led to the passage of legislation following the first Gulf War requiring that every new home and apartment in Israel have a hardened and gas-resistant room to provide protection against both kinetic and chemical weapons. Israel distributed gas masks to the entire population prior to both Gulf Wars and decided to do so once again in the late 2000s. The program was only suspended in 2013 following the internationally mandated dismantlement of the Syrian chemical arsenal, by which time some 60% of the population was again in possession of masks.[76]

Millions of tablets of an anthrax antidote have reportedly been stored and 15,000 members of the security and rescue forces vaccinated in the early 2000s, both to protect them and to make antidotes from their blood sufficient to vaccinate the entire population.[77] In 2001 fears of an Iraqi response to an American attack were so great that the defense establishment considered vaccinating the entire population against smallpox.[78] Later in the decade research was conducted to develop medicines against chemical weapons.[79] In the early 2000s Israel became the first country in the world to distribute medicine to the public in order to minimize the effects of radiation poisoning following an attack or accident at a nuclear reactor—and, according to press speculation, the use of a "dirty bomb." The medicine was only distributed to those living in the vicinity of the Dimona reactor, but a supply sufficient for the entire population has reportedly been stored and the Home Front Command has conducted exercises to practice mass distribution of the pills.[80]

The most significant manifestation of the new emphasis on defense has been the development of the Arrow missile defense system starting in the late 1980s and the Iron Dome and Magic Wand rocket defense systems starting in the mid-2000s. Israel has also built a national command center reportedly designed to withstand nuclear attacks.[81] Despite the IDF's initial reluctance, rocket and missile defense have become a key component in Israel's strategic thinking today. An analysis of Israel's rocket and missile defense appears in chapter 7.

No Longer Quite "the Few against the Many"

The classic defense strategy posited that Israel would have to focus on qualitative excellence in order to overcome its immutable quantitative inferiority. In recent decades, however, Israel's own economic clout and generous US assistance have enabled it to compete with its adversaries not just qualitatively, but quantitatively as well. In fact, when compared with likely state-participants in a future war, as opposed to Arab states generally, Israel enjoys approximate quantitative parity and, depending on which states one defines as likely, even a clear advantage. When compared to nonstate actors, Israel's quantitative advantage is overwhelming, but this is of only partial importance in irregular warfare. In any event, maintaining a qualitative edge remains a primary tenet and focus of Israel's defense doctrine.

Israel's qualitative advantage, the result of its access to advanced American weaponry, augmented by indigenous development of unique military capabilities of its own, has been partly offset by American sales of essentially equivalent weapons to Egypt, Jordan, Saudi Arabia, and other Arab states and by the sales of advanced weapons by other countries, primarily Russia, to Syria, Iran, and others. The United States is committed to maintaining Israel's "qualitative military edge," but turning this commitment into concrete terms has proven difficult in the face of political and economic pressures to provide virtually unlimited advanced weapons to the Arab states.

Both the state and nonstate actors in the region have increasingly advanced in recent decades, and their populations are better educated and more technologically sophisticated. There is certainly no comparison with the undeveloped Arab societies and poorly trained and led Arab militaries of a few decades ago, or between Fatah and the PLO in the past and Hezbollah today. Iran, in particular, has brought an entirely new level of sophistication to the conflict. All of these changes have made maintaining a qualitative edge increasingly difficult. Israel, too, however, has progressed rapidly, economically and scientifically, turning its technological savvy into military capabilities and in the process becoming a world leader in advanced forms of warfare.

Israel's adversaries have fully recognized their inability to compete with its qualitative superiority and some have consequently resorted to low-tech, irregular responses, designed to neutralize its technological advantages. This is true first and foremost of the nonstate actors, but even Syria took a cue from their past successes against Israel and began adapting its military (prior to the civil war) to employ similar capabilities. Israel has had some success in developing high-tech responses to the threats it faces, especially through new defensive capabilities, such as rocket shields, but quantity (rockets) still poses a difficult challenge.

Still Mostly a "Nation in Arms"

Israel remains a "nation in arms," for most, but not all, of the public. Indeed, better mobilization of Israel's human resources continues to allow it to draft a far greater proportion of the population than its adversaries, and motivation to serve among the secular and "national religious" populations remains high. Nevertheless, growing parts of Israeli society do not participate in the national effort today, there are increasing demands to ease the burden, and budgetary demands have forced a major change in the IDF's reserve system. These and other domestic challenges to Israel's ability to remain a "nation in arms" and consequently to maintain its qualitative advantage were explored in depth in chapter 5.

Increasing Difficulty in Executing a Defensive Strategy Offensively

Transferring the Battle to the Enemy Is Now Rarely Possible. Given its small size and the advantages of offensive warfare, Israel still seeks to transfer the battle to enemy territory to the extent possible. A number of strategic and operational changes, however, have made this increasingly difficult, at least on the ground, whether in regard to bordering enemies, such as Hezbollah and Hamas, and largely irrelevant in the case of bordering friendly countries, such as Egypt and Jordan, or distant ones, such as Iran, Iraq, and Libya.

Hezbollah in Lebanon and Hamas in Gaza are located in heavily populated areas. Transferring the battle to them and conquering territory thus means taking control of large hostile populations, something Israel very much does not wish to do. Moreover, conquering territory from them does not necessarily hold out great military promise. Conquering southern Lebanon, as Israel has done in the past, may push Hezbollah's short-range rockets out of range, but not its medium- and long-range ones, which can hit Israel today from the very northern reaches of the country. As already noted, the only truly effective way to deal with the rocket threat is thus to occupy virtually all of Lebanon for a prolonged period, in order to root out the rockets, an operation that is likely to be far more costly in lives than the threat it was designed to counter. Moreover, it is likely that Iran will rapidly resupply Hezbollah after Israel withdraws and ultimately render the effort futile.

In the case of Hamas, conquest of the Gaza Strip would push its entire arsenal out of range, but Israel would again have to maintain a lengthy and painful occupation to find and destroy all of the rockets, the cost in lives and physical destruction would be great, and Hamas might be able to rebuild much of its arsenal once Israel had withdrawn. In these circumstances, and in an era of both domestic and international norms that mandate minimal Israeli and enemy civilian casualties, Israel has limited all of the rounds against Hezbollah and Hamas since the 1990s to precision stand-off firepower, that is, to "transferring the battle to the enemy by air," not on the ground. It is likely to have to continue doing so for the foreseeable future. The problem, as we have seen, is that this is not as effective as ground invasion and has not enabled Israel to achieve military decision.

The advanced antiarmor weapons in the hands of Hezbollah and Hamas further inhibit Israel's ability to conduct mobile ground warfare in these areas. As to Syria, the extremely dense defensive system it had on the Golan Heights and approaches to Damascus, until the civil war, greatly constrained Israel's ability to conduct mobile maneuver warfare, in any event, and the area is heavily populated.[82]

The strategic imperative of maintaining the peace treaties with Egypt and Jordan means that Israel cannot respond offensively to terrorist attacks emanating from their territory and cannot transfer the fighting to them, certainly when they are attempting to deal with the problem, and must rely either on defensive measures on its side of the border, or refrain from responding at all. Even Sinai is no longer the vast and unpopulated desert buffer of the past, but an increasingly populated one. Finally, ground maneuver is the most costly means of addressing the threats Israel faces, at least in the short term, in both Israeli and enemy lives, and the one assured to generate the strongest international opposition. In short, Israel's ability to transfer the battle to the enemy through ground maneuver has become far more limited.

Pre-emption Has Rarely Been Feasible

Contrary to the popular image, Israel has actually only taken major pre-emptive action on one occasion, the Six Day War, and even then only after a three-week period designed to enable the United States to reach a diplomatic resolution to the crisis. Conversely, it has taken preventative action on numerous occasions.

It is important to understand the difference. Whereas pre-emption refers to an attempt to thwart an imminent attack or one already in the making, prevention refers to an attempt to forestall the emergence of a future threat. In 1948 Israel merely responded to an Arab attack, and the Sinai Campaign in 1956 was a preventative war, to counter both a long-term Egyptian military buildup, not an imminent attack, and to end ongoing terrorist ("fedayeen") attacks. In the Yom Kippur War Israel consciously rejected the option of last-minute pre-emption out of concern over the American response. The operations in Lebanon from 1982 on were the result of developments that were years in the making, not pre-emption, and in 2006 Israel was responding to an immediate attack, not pre-empting. The same was true of the operations in Gaza in 2008, 2012, and 2014. The attacks on the Iraqi and Syrian reactors were also preventative, before they went critical, not pre-emptions of an imminent nuclear attack.[83]

The primary reason for the essentially preventative, rather than pre-emptive, nature of Israeli defense praxis has been the heavy diplomatic costs associated with pre-emption, that is, the difficulty of convincing the international community, first and foremost the United States, that it was the other side that actually intended to strike first or harbored aggressive intentions, and the need to co-ordinate with the United States to ensure a strategic and diplomatic umbrella. Following the acquisition of the 1967 territories, which were thought to provide Israel with "defensible borders," Israel largely abandoned the concept of pre-emption, as manifested most strikingly in 1973.[84] In today's international environment, Israel is hard-pressed to respond even to clear provocations, as happened to varying degrees in the various rounds with Hamas and Hezbollah, let alone conduct a significant pre-emptive strike.

Inflexible Defense Remains the Guiding Concept

The fundamental assumption, that the enemy cannot be allowed to take any Israeli territory whatsoever, even temporarily, and that Israel must therefore maintain an inflexible defense, remains unchanged.[85] It may, however, be put to a greater test in coming years, as Hezbollah has repeatedly warned that, in the next round, it intends to grab a bit of Israeli territory or capture an Israeli town, even if briefly. The logical conclusion from this fundamental assumption, however, that Israel must transfer the fighting to enemy territory, is increasingly challenged by the strategic changes noted above and presents one of the foremost operational problems facing Israel's defense doctrine today.

Longer Wars

Israel still aspires to keep wars as short as possible, to minimize casualties and the expenditure of resources, as well as the risks of broader regional escalation, international intervention, oil price shocks, and disruption to Israel's home front and economy. The nature of the new threats, however—irregular adversaries deeply embedded in civilian populations—has drastically diminished Israel's ability to conduct rapid mobile warfare and has led to more prolonged warfare. Whereas Israel was able to defeat three Arab armies in six days in 1967, the inconclusive wars against smaller adversaries in Lebanon in 2006 and Gaza in 2014 lasted 34 and 51 days respectively, the two longest military operations in Israel's history since the War of Independence.

Defensible Borders

Needless to say, Israel still seeks defensible borders, especially as part of future peace agreements, but the concept and Israel's requirements have changed considerably over the decades.[86] In the past, the concept of defensible borders referred mostly to the ability to create buffers between Israel and its adversaries, such as the Sinai with Egypt and to a lesser extent the Golan Heights with Syria, to territorial width, or strategic depth, and to some extent topography. All were designed to provide Israel with the ability to withstand a surprise attack or initial military setbacks.

Today, the Sinai is far more populated, and hostile groups, some affiliated with ISIS, have attacked Israel from it in recent years. Sinai's ongoing demilitarization, under the terms of the peace treaty, and its comparatively great width, however, enable it to remain an essentially effective buffer vis-à-vis Egypt. Moreover, the government of Egypt, especially under General Sissi, is committed to suppressing terrorism from Sinai. The Golan Heights, in contrast, were never wide enough to be a truly effective buffer; what made it so was both sides' desire to keep the calm. Today, with the weakening of the Syrian regime, and its residual arsenal of precise long-range weapons, the Golan's effectiveness as a buffer has decreased somewhat. It does, however, continue to provide space between Syria's convolutions and Israel's northern population.

From Israel's perspective, the West Bank has two defensive functions.[87] One is against Palestinian terrorism, the other, together with Jordan, against threats from the east, such as a resurgent Iraq, possibly under Iranian domination, a Syrian armored thrust, a hostile new actor such as the Islamic State, or some other currently unforeseen threat. As Israel has increasingly settled the West Bank, however, with settlements scattered throughout its hostile population and the entire area a scene of ongoing confrontation, it has greatly undermined the first defensive function. Rather than being a buffer against Palestinian terrorism, the de facto annexation of the West Bank has become the primary source of terrorism in Israel itself and turned Palestinian terrorism, in effect, into a domestic problem. As to the second function, Jordan is Israel's primary buffer against threats from the east, but its future course as a country, and the stability of the monarchy, are unclear and thus the West Bank remains of importance as a buffer in its own right. Some in Israel believe that the Jordan Valley, the eastern part of the West Bank, must remain under long-term Israeli military control, if not sovereignty, as part of the security arrangements in any future peace agreement with the Palestinians,[88] while others believe Israel can make do with a more limited military presence along the river. This topic has already been addressed in detail in chapter 3.

Modern long-range weapons partly diminish the importance of territorial width, or strategic depth, for purposes of defensible borders. Furthermore, it is clear that if peace agreements with Syria and the Palestinians are ever to be reached, they will require Israeli withdrawals from most of the territory, further diminishing its ability to achieve defensible borders. Assuming that these withdrawals include the Golan Heights ridgeline, the Jordan Valley, or West Bank mountain range, topography will also be of importance. How to ensure defensible borders in these circumstances, that is, the security arrangements that will be needed, will have to be assessed on the basis of the military technology and strategic circumstances at the time.

Great Power Alliance, but Strategic Autonomy: Israel Can No Longer Go It Alone

The need for a close alliance with at least one major power and preferably more, while retaining strategic autonomy, remains a deeply held precept of Israel's defense doctrine. Its practical meaning has changed significantly, however, given Israel's great dependence on the United States and an increasingly interconnected global community. Indeed, the price of a truly extraordinary relationship with the United States has been a loss of much of Israel's independence.

In reality, there have been very few cases of major decisions that Israel has made in recent decades, military or diplomatic, without first consulting with the United States and seeking its approval, or at least acquiescence. Although Israel has developed an impressive indigenous weapons production capability, it remains overwhelmingly dependent on the United States for arms; indeed, it is questionable whether Israel could successfully cope with the military threats it faces today, possibly even survive, without American military assistance. Diplomatically, Israel's dependence on the United States is extreme. Israel has developed unique strategic relationships with countries such as Germany, India, and, in the past, Turkey, but these ties never constituted an even partial alternative to the United States. For many years, Israel was also deeply dependent on the United States for economic aid, though this was phased out in the late 1990s. Chapter 10 returns to the issue of Israel's deep dependence on the United States in far greater detail.

The changing nature and magnitude of the threats Israel faces have further undermined its ability to pursue strategic autonomy and self-reliance. Israel chose not to retaliate against Saddam's use of ballistic missiles in 1991, not just due to its dependence on the United States, which opposed an Israeli response, but because its independent capabilities would probably not have been more effective than the limited effort the United States undertook against the missiles and would have posed a severe risk of failure. Only the United States, if anyone, had the leverage to try to dissuade Russia and North Korea from selling nuclear and missile technology to actors in the region. Similarly, many in Israel believe that the challenge posed by the Iranian nuclear program exceeds its independent military capabilities and that only the United States can deal with it effectively. In 2012 a senior Israeli official, thought to be then-defense minister Barak, stated that "given the differences in capabilities, it is in Israel's interest that the United States act [against Iran] rather than Israel." The very expression of the preference for American action, even if the official hastened to add that Israel would only rely on itself for its security,[89] was a dramatic departure from all previous Israeli thinking. Even unique Israeli military capabilities, such as the Arrow and Iron Dome missile and rocket defense systems, could only be developed with American financing and some technology. Today, even a nation that prides itself on its independence and self-reliance cannot be totally independent.

In recent years Israel has also manifested a limited, but growing, willingness to countenance international involvement in the resolution of its disputes, in contrast with its traditional aversion to this. For example, UN confirmation that Israel had fully withdrawn from Lebanon in 2000 was a central component of the strategy behind the unilateral withdrawal conducted at the time. The expansion and strengthening of UNIFIL, the UN force deployed in southern Lebanon, long derisively dismissed in Israel as ineffectual, became a key component in its efforts to end the fighting in 2006. Israel was a driving force behind the adoption of the international sanctions that played a key role in the effort to stymie the

Iranian nuclear program, the foremost threat Israel has faced in recent decades. In 2014 Israel sought a Security Council resolution as part of the efforts to put an end to the protracted round of fighting with Hamas. These and other examples reflect a growing awareness of the limits to Israel's ability to address the threats it faces today on its own.[90]

In these circumstances, strategic autonomy and self-reliance now mean, at their core, that Israel still insists on fighting its own battles and, unlike virtually all other American allies, that it has generally not been interested either in the deployment of American forces in its territory or in an American security guarantee. Israel's overwhelming dependence on the United States notwithstanding, it does reserve the right to act independently in unusual cases and has also developed a variety of military capabilities of its own. Finally, Israel's purported nuclear capability is the ultimate expression of self-reliance, a reflection of the belief that Israel alone bears ultimate responsibility for its existence and, in the end, that it can only rely on itself.

In conclusion, Israel's experience with deterrence, the first of the "three pillars," has been mixed. Whereas its current and specific deterrence have been a combination of both failures and successes, its strategic and cumulative deterrence has been highly successful. Early warning, the second pillar, remains a fundamental feature of Israel's defense doctrine, but has become more difficult to achieve in an era in which state and nonstate actors can launch rockets and missiles with virtually no warning. Israel has only achieved military decision, the third pillar, in a few cases in the past, and it is much harder to achieve today. The reasons are myriad, but include, inter alia, the radical nature of its adversaries, lack of international legitimacy, demise of territorial conquest as an effective option, and, most importantly, the fact that the price of resolving the threats Israel faces today often exceeds their severity.

Over the decades Israel has gained not just qualitative superiority, but in some areas quantitative, too, and the principle of "the few against the many" is no longer fully appropriate to the new reality. Arab societies and militaries have progressed markedly, but Israel's access to American weapons and indigenous manufacturing capabilities ensure its qualitative advantage, somewhat mitigated by the rise of Iran in the region and asymmetric warfare.

One of the greatest challenges facing Israel's defense doctrine today is the decreasing utility of ground maneuver as a means of transferring the battle to the enemy and of achieving military decision. Stand-off precision firepower, primarily from the air, has not proven to be a fully effective replacement. Contrary to the popular image, Israel has rarely pre-empted and is even less likely to be able to do so in the future. Inflexible defense remains a fundamental guiding concept, but it is harder to achieve in an era in which Israel is increasingly hard-pressed to transfer the battle to the enemy. Short wars remain a basic objective, but the nature of the new threats makes this increasingly difficult. Israel still seeks defensible borders, but the requirements for this have changed, along with the strategic situation and nature of the military threats.

Finally, Israel still attaches overarching importance to the principles of maintaining a great power alliance, along with strategic autonomy and self-reliance. Maintaining the balance between them has become increasingly difficult, however, as Israel's dependence on the United States has grown enormously over the years.

Updating the Defense Doctrine: Past Attempts at Reform

The need for major reform of the defense doctrine, to adapt it to Israel's changed strategic circumstances, has long been recognized by the IDF, senior defense officials, political leaders, and scholars, and numerous attempts to do so have been made. The following section surveys some of the primary reforms proposed over the years, including those changes that were actually implemented. It is a somewhat technical and detailed history and some readers, especially those interested in Israel's contemporary military response, may prefer to skip directly to the next chapter.

The history of defense reform in Israel in recent decades reflects an ongoing attempt to adapt the massive force structure built following the 1973 Yom Kippur War to the dramatic changes that have taken place ever since in the Middle Eastern strategic environment, military technology, and Israeli society.[91] The IDF is a relatively adaptive organization, and much change has, of course, taken place. Nevertheless, it has encountered considerable difficulty, budgetary, bureaucratic, doctrinal, and more, in transforming the "legacy force" to the needs of a new era. Reductions in the size of the IDF force structure, modernization thereof, and the critical balance between firepower and maneuver and between offense and defense have been recurrent themes throughout this period. The resulting changes have been neither consistent nor linear, coming instead in fits and starts, with a variety of plans for reform scrapped or only partly implemented.

The near catastrophe of the Yom Kippur War and the massive Arab arms buildup in its aftermath led to a dramatic and unprecedented Israeli counterbuildup, designed to rebuild the shattered IDF and restore national confidence. In the eight years following the war, Israel acquired more than 100 F-15s and F-16s and doubled both its helicopter fleet and number of divisions. Between 1973 and 1982 the tank force increased from 1,900 to 3,600 and the number of APCs from 2,000 to 8,000.[92] In 2012 the IDF had 16 divisions (12 armored and mechanized) and an estimated 2,442–3,670 tanks, 1,258–2,518 artillery pieces and 459–517 advanced combat aircraft. This force was designed to enable Israel to absorb and defeat simultaneous Arab offensives on two fronts.[93]

The first significant review of Israel's security doctrine during the post–Yom Kippur War era was conducted in the early 1980s by General Avraham Tamir, then the head of the Ministry of Defense's National Security Unit. The review focused primarily on the danger of a massive Arab conventional attack, but also included unconventional threats.[94] Of greater consequence was an internal IDF study in the mid-1980s, later given partial public exposure as the "Wald Report," which questioned the effectiveness of the entire post-1973 approach. Highly controversial at the time, the report charged that the IDF's force structure and offensive concept of operations, based on armor and air power, were anachronistic.[95] In effect, the Wald Report was an early attempt to address the differences between two schools of thought that continue to divide Israeli military thinking to this day.

One school, the traditionalists, viewed large armored formations, designed to counter Arab armies equipped with vast quantities of modern weapons, as the backbone of the IDF. Highly critical of defensive warfare, they believed that preventative offense was preferable to even the briefest defense and that armor, in conjunction with air power and other capabilities, was the optimal means of conducting ground maneuver, acquiring control of territory, and achieving rapid battlefield decision. The reformers, conversely, believed that Israel could no longer afford to wage "breakthrough battles" against the quantitatively superior and nearly impenetrable Arab defenses. Instead, they argued, Israel should use its superiority in the newly emerging technologies of precision munitions and advanced command-and-control systems to inflict heavy losses on the enemy. Israel's qualitative edge, they maintained, along with a more defensive concept of operations, would provide significant strategic advantages.[96]

Initial signs of the IDF's shifting conceptual emphasis, from maneuver to firepower, and from offense to active defense, first appeared at this time,[97] but were only truly manifested years later, in the two major campaigns in Lebanon during the 1990s, Operations Accountability and Grapes of Wrath. During these operations, the IDF began using firepower as a means of transferring the fighting to enemy territory, instead of the previous emphasis on ground maneuver.[98]

In 1987, Dan Meridor, then a member of the Knesset Foreign and Defense Affairs Committee, chaired a review of Israel's defense doctrine that concluded that Israel could no longer afford to conquer additional territory. In so doing, the review overturned a fundamental pillar of the classic defense doctrine, which had long been based on the concept of transferring the ground battle to the enemy as rapidly as possible. The review further found that Israel's comparative advantage was in technology and recommended that it thus seek to achieve military decision deep inside enemy territory, not on its borders, that the traditional role of armor in Israeli military thinking should be downplayed in favor of stand-off precision-guided munitions, and that greater emphasis should be placed on defense. Defense Minister Rabin was reluctant to abandon the long-standing offensive military doctrine and approved a compromise, procuring the new weaponry recommended, but incorporating it within the existing force structure and concept of operations.[99]

The director-general of the Ministry of Defense under Rabin, David Ivry, also attempted to update the defense doctrine in 1987, forming five different working groups comprising leading military and civilian figures. The groups continued to work under two of Rabin's successors, Yitzhak Mordechai and Moshe Arens.[100] By 1991 the need for change was so apparent that Chief of Staff Dan Shomron began speaking publicly of the need to transform the IDF into a "small and smart" military, an objective reiterated, in one form or another, by all of his successors ever since.[101]

The so-called Revolution in Military Affairs (RMA), which integrated long-range precision-guided munitions, advanced command-and-control systems, and sophisticated surveillance and targeting capabilities, had a deep effect on IDF thinking, further magnified by the dramatic American success applying it during the 1991 Iraq war. The United States was the first to produce RMA-type munitions and to use them to great effect in the Gulf War, but the IDF was actually the first to employ them in combat, albeit on a limited basis, as early as the 1982 invasion of Lebanon. The IDF, however, did not integrate the new RMA concepts into a coherent military doctrine, instead incorporating the technological advances into existing organizations and routines. It would take another 10 years before the IDF began adapting its concept of operations, force structure, and broader strategic doctrine to the requirements of the RMA.[102]

Change in the IDF, however, was beginning to take form. A variety of changes in Israel's strategic circumstances during the late 1990s and early 2000s created a growing sense that the traditional strategic concepts of victory, military decision, and defeat were no longer fully appropriate and that IDF doctrinal, structural, and operational reforms were necessary. The strategic changes driving this included, inter alia, the new reality with the Palestinians following the Oslo Accords and second intifada, the changing nature of the military threats Israel faced, which now stemmed primarily from terrorist and nonstate actors and from the rising Iranian nuclear threat, the ramifications of the 2003 war in Iraq, and the growing role of international law and "lawfare."[103] In response, the IDF changed its list of priorities, designating WMD and long-range delivery systems as the primary threats Israel faced, with terrorism and guerrilla warfare demoted to second place and conventional wars, the foremost priority in the traditional defense doctrine, now relegated to third.[104]

Decisions adopted between 2004 and 2006 called for a decrease in the size of the reserve force, especially armored units, larger budgets for technology-intensive units such as the air force and Intelligence Corps, and a cut of no less than 25% in the budget of the ground forces. Events interceded, however, and these changes were not instituted in practice.[105] Conversely, a new "reservists law" was adopted in 2008, reducing the length of annual reserve duty and changing its nature (see chapter 5 for more details). Consideration was also given to a variety of changes in the compulsory service model, including the possibility of differential service, whereby the period of time a soldier served and the remuneration provided would be tied to his position, a dramatic break with the past.

Intensive staff work to formulate a new IDF operational concept began in 2002 or 2003 and continued under three chiefs of staff. The new concept, formally approved in April 2006 under the title of "The General Staff's Operational Art for the IDF and Effects-Based Operations,"[106] was an attempt to adapt IDF doctrine to the changing nature of the military threats and technology Israel faced, from symmetric wars between states to asymmetric conflicts with non-state actors,[107] although one critic charged that it failed to do so and was really more of an outdated attempt to apply the RMA to the threat posed by conventional Arab armies.[108] Be that as it may, the new concept reportedly reflected the IDF's growing concerns regarding the political and operational ramifications of guerrilla warfare and the occupation of additional hostile populations. Two of the new concept's central findings were that the legitimacy of territorial conquest and of the use of territory as a negotiating card had greatly diminished, and that large-scale ground maneuver by the IDF might actually serve enemy needs, by providing legitimate targets. As a result, the classic defense doctrine's emphasis on the need to transfer the battle to enemy territory, through ground maneuver and territorial conquest, was significantly downgraded and now became a last resort.[109]

Rather than ground maneuver to transfer the battle to enemy territory, the new concept sought to do so by means of firepower. To this end, the IDF would wage an integrated campaign of stand-off precision firepower (air and artillery), real-time intelligence, and advanced command-and-control systems, designed to create "systemic effects," such as a disruption of enemy communications and battlefield awareness, undermining its capability and motivation to continue the fighting. Israel's long-standing emphasis on air power and intelligence increased even further under the new concept, and firepower, heretofore a supporting element for ground maneuver, now became the primary means of achieving military decision. The new IDF would have fewer but more advanced tanks, artillery, and aircraft and improved long-range capabilities. The new concept also provided for a somewhat greater role for defense.[110]

The 2006 war in Lebanon broke out just three months after the new operational concept was formally adopted, and the IDF, which was still in an initial state of transition, did not apply it during the war. Indeed, the very week that the war broke out, the IDF was supposed to have made a dramatic decision to cut its tank arsenal by tens of percent, mothball tens of aircraft, and fire 6,000 regular military personnel, all of which was now postponed.[111] The State Comptroller found that the IDF had been hesitant to commit to the drastic changes embodied in the new concept to begin with and consequently ended up with the worst of both worlds, caught somewhere between the outgoing and new concepts.[112] Following the war the new operational concept was formally abandoned, even though several subsequent studies reaffirmed its findings.[113]

The IDF responded to the lessons learned from the 2006 war by launching a new five-year plan in September 2007 ("Tefen"), which was designed to address the four primary challenges the IDF believed it would face in the coming decade; ongoing conventional threats from state adversaries, such as Syria; irregular threats from nonstate actors such as Hezbollah and Hamas; a nuclear Iran; and regional destabilization due to the rise of Islamic fundamentalism. The plan focused on nine essential capabilities that the IDF would have to maintain and upgrade—decisive ground maneuver, air dominance, precise attack, enhanced long-distance reach, active defense against rockets and missiles, intelligence dominance, effective command and control, naval supremacy, and adequate stocks of munitions.[114]

In many ways Tefen, the first IDF five-year plan ever fully implemented was almost a reversal of the previous five-year plan ("Kela"), with the IDF reverting to its former operational concept. Not only was the cut in the tank force canceled, but it was now decided to upgrade it, continue production of the advanced Merkava 4 tank, and scrap many of the organizational changes proposed. Consideration was even given at one point to the establishment of two new armored divisions.[115]

Probably the most ambitious attempt ever undertaken to formulate an Israeli defense doctrine was once again headed by Dan Meridor, in 2006, and resulted in a confidential 250-page report. The product of a number of interagency working groups (terrorism, unconventional weapons, politico-military issues, defense, economics, and technology) and outside experts, the report focused on Israel's strategic environment during the coming decade and the consequent changes needed to the defense doctrine. The report stressed that the primary threats Israel faced no longer stemmed from the conventional battlefield, but from "unconventional" and "supraconventional" dangers and that the civilian rear would become the primary arena of warfare.[116] It thus recommended a decrease in budgets devoted to the conventional threats of the past, such as the size of Israel's tank fleet, but conversely an increase in UFVs and precision weapons.[117]

The report devoted particular attention both to the consequences of a nuclear Iran and to Israel's potential responses. A nuclear Iran was viewed as an existential threat to Israel that was also likely to spur other Middle Eastern nations to pursue nuclear capabilities of their own, and the report recommended that Israel continue to adhere to the policy of nuclear ambiguity. The report further emphasized the difficulties involved in the attempt to deter terrorism, especially from territories lacking in effective government, and stressed Jordan's strategic importance to Israel. It also recommended a greater emphasis on firepower, rather than ground maneuver, and on information warfare.[118] A further recommendation was in regard to the percentage of the GDP to be devoted in the coming decade to defense.[119]

One of the report's primary recommendations was that a new fourth pillar, defense, be added to Israel's military doctrine, in addition to the traditional trio—deterrence, early warning, and military decision. The report stressed that in the absence of adequate defenses, rocket attacks could seriously disrupt efforts to mobilize the reserves and make it impossible for the IDF to respond to an attack rapidly.[120] It also sought to update the traditional pillars of deterrence, early warning, and military decision and to adapt them to contemporary needs. Deterrence, for example, was analyzed in terms of the battle against terrorism, rather than conventional military attack, early warning was broadened from preparations for a conventional military attack to virtually all threats, whether from a lone terrorist to a nuclear weapons development program, and particular discussion was focused on the meaning of military decision in an era of asymmetric warfare.[121] Although widely praised for its comprehensiveness and depth, the report was never formally discussed by the IDF or cabinet, let alone adopted.

In 2012 the National Security Staff (Israel's equivalent of the American National Security Council) completed a draft of a new defense strategy, which was circulated for comments throughout the various agencies of the defense establishment. However, the CoS at the time, Ganz, refused to allow the IDF to respond to the draft, and it has been in limbo ever since. It may have had some impact, nevertheless; various officials, including Ganz's reform-minded successor, Eisenkot, read the draft and were presumably affected by at least some of its findings and recommendations.[122]

In 2013 the IDF's inability to implement the previous five-year plan ("Oz"), for budgetary and strategic reasons, led to its replacement by "Teuza," a further five-year attempt at reform.[123] The new plan was based on the assumption that Israel would continue to face low-intensity conflicts for the foreseeable future, not large-scale ones, and that the IDF therefore had a window of opportunity of a few years to reform its force structure and operational concepts. It further assumed that the IDF would no longer have virtually unlimited time to conduct warfare, as it had in Lebanon in 2006, and that it would have to end future conflicts as rapidly as possible, in order to minimize damage to the home front and achieve military decision.[124]

Under Teuza the planned structural changes were significant, if not dramatic. Six reserve armored brigades (some 600 old-model tanks) were to be cut,[125] along with two outdated air wings, a logistics regiment, two older ships, and some 4,500 professionals, including six out of 90 brigadier generals, 26 out of more than 400 colonels, and an overall cut of 21% in various headquarters staffs.[126] The new IDF would employ an operational concept designed to capitalize on those areas in which it already enjoyed an advantage (e.g., air power, intelligence, and cyber-warfare), rather than seeking to strengthen its weak points, such as ground maneuver. Particular emphasis was given to the ability to strike targets that are vulnerable for no more than a few seconds (such as Hezbollah rockets), by combining state-of-the-art intelligence capabilities with improved precision fire, and to the IDF's abilities to operate at lengthy distances, inter alia, through commando units. Whereas the brigade had been the fundamental IDF formation up to that time, strengthened battalions were to now gain far more independence, in some cases even companies, as part of a decentralization process.[127] The new plan was also to save about $2 billion, which the IDF would reinvest in its areas of advantage, long-range capabilities, and rocket and missile defenses. The IAF and Intelligence Corps were to enjoy clear budgetary precedence.[128]

A major new five-year plan, "Gideon," for 2016–2020, capitalized on much of the changes started under Teuza and is, at the time of this writing, apparently well on its way to fruition. The overall objective is a smaller but far better trained and equipped IDF, with a higher level of readiness. Under "Gideon," the number of professional IDF soldiers was to be cut to 40,000 by 2017, from a 2012 high of 45,000,[129] headquarters staffs by 6%, and rear units by 20%–25%. One to two more brigades, possibly even three, were also to be cut, along with artillery forces, one of six planned submarines, and a number of missile ships.[130] A whopping 100,000 nonessential reservists were discharged.[131] Changes both in military command structures and in pension schemes, a primary source of contention between the IDF and Treasury, with far reaching ramifications for the defense budget, were also adopted.[132] Conversely, the plan included the establishment of new cyber and commando commands, and battalions for border security missions.[133]

The Gideon plan was part of a broader review of IDF strategic thinking embodied in the 2015 "IDF Strategy,"[134] the first time in Israel's history that an official strategic statement, setting out the nature of the threats it faces, its strategic objectives, and military response, had ever been made public. In and of itself, the document was not a novel departure; similar documents had been written on various occasions for internal IDF and governmental use. Moreover, it was a military document, not an overall statement of national strategy. Nevertheless, public dissemination of the IDF Strategy, a clearly intentional—and ultimately successful—IDF effort to spark and enrich public debate on defense affairs,[135] was a landmark development. Its primary findings are presented in the next chapter.

In conclusion, much attention has been devoted during the last 20 years to the need for far-reaching reform of the defense doctrine, IDF force structure, and operational concept. As the preceding discussion demonstrates, however, change has been evolutionary, not revolutionary. The reforms instituted by the current CoS, under the Gideon five-year plan, are the most far-reaching to date and, unlike most of the previous attempts at reform, may be fully implemented.

Primary Observations

- Iran, Hezbollah, and Hamas are waging a decades-long war of attrition against Israel, designed to lead to its destruction. Hezbollah's mammoth rocket arsenal has created mutual deterrence. Hamas's arsenal is potent, but far smaller.
- Israel's strategic and cumulative deterrence were highly successful, its current and specific deterrence somewhat. Israel only succeeded in achieving military decision in a few cases and even then insufficiently to dictate terms. Military decision and deterrence, in Israeli thinking, are not designed to prevent hostilities, merely to prolong the lulls between rounds.
- None of the operations against Hezbollah and Hamas since the 1980s have ended satisfactorily; most did not achieve significant deterrence and a prolonged lull. The deterrence achieved in 2006 and 2014 was based on punishment, not denial, which Israel will be increasingly hard-pressed to repeat. Israel cannot usually conduct major ground maneuver today, without which military decision is very hard to achieve.
- Israel enjoys not just qualitative superiority over its adversaries today, state and nonstate, but in most realistic scenarios, clear quantitative superiority, too.
- Military decision against Hezbollah and Hamas may be more costly than the threats they pose and likely short lived. Military decision is beyond Israel's capabilities against distant states, such as Iran, and is meaningless at the nuclear level. There is no longer a clear relationship between military decision and deterrence, gravely undermining Israel's traditional deterrence-decision model.
- Israel did achieve military decision in the second intifada, demonstrating that conventional armies can defeat insurgencies and large-scale terrorism. Nevertheless, Palestinian opposition continues to boil under the surface, with frequent outbursts, and a return of large-scale terrorism is a constant danger.

- Israel has been increasingly forced to rely on defense, now defined as a "pillar" of the defense doctrine, including rocket and missile shields, hardened rooms and structures, security fences, gas masks, and more. The old offensive approach is no longer sufficient.
- Israel's de facto absorption of the West Bank neutralized its role as a buffer against Palestinian terrorism. Jordan remains Israel's primary buffer against threats from the east, but its future is unclear, and the West Bank thus retains its importance as an external buffer. Syria's domestic upheaval reduces the effectiveness of the Golan as a buffer.
- Israel is increasingly encountering limits to its ability to address the threats it faces on its own, including militarily. Consequently, it has manifested a limited, but growing, willingness to countenance international involvement in the resolution of its disputes.

The Military Response Today

I am not worried about Israel's security situation. We are the strongest
country in the Middle East; we know how to take care of ourselves.
—Chief of Staff Benny Gantz, 2015

In a world of constant change, it is essential that Israel continually examine and
adapt its strategic assumptions. The previous chapter looked at how the strategic
principles underlying Israel's classic defense doctrine have weathered the test of
time, some of the changes that have taken place in them, and their applicability
to the threats Israel faces today. We now turn to the concrete military responses
Israel has developed to each of the primary threats it faces today.

The chapter begins with an overview of Israel's conventional military response. At its heart, the conventional response continues to be based on the four
Ds approach—deterrence, detection, decision, and, in recent years, defense—to
which we have repeatedly alluded throughout this book and which will not be
rehashed here. Instead, we will address a few particularly salient points regarding
the conventional response, taking the 2015 IDF Strategy as a point of departure.
Israel's responses to the other threats it faces today, especially the asymmetric
threats presented by Iran, Hezbollah and Hamas rockets, terrorism and cyber-
warfare, will be addressed in far greater depth.

Israel's nonconventional response is presented in chapter 8 and its diplomatic
response in chapter 9. The 2014 operation in Gaza exposed a new "subterranean
threat," Hamas's use of "attack tunnels" to penetrate Israeli territory, a model
presumably adopted by Hezbollah as well. Countering this new threat will undoubtedly be difficult, but it is a tactical challenge, not a strategic one. Israel is
reportedly well on its way to addressing it and it is not discussed in this book.

Obviously, much of the information regarding Israel's military responses is
classified, as it should be, and appropriate caution has been exercised even in
presentation of the publicly available picture. There will undoubtedly be surprises
in many of the details and the tactics applied by the IDF in the future; indeed,
the IDF Strategy itself stresses the importance of ruse as a basic component of

Israel's military strategy. Nevertheless, the publicly available information seems to present a good impression of the overall nature of Israel's military response and a sufficient basis for a critical analysis thereof.

The Conventional Military Response

Publication of the 2015 IDF Strategy, as stated in the previous chapter, was a landmark event. For the first time, Israel now has a formal military doctrine, if not a national security strategy. Much like the classic defense doctrine of the 1950s, the IDF Strategy remains fundamentally defensive in its objectives and reactive in character, even while offensive in execution. In emphasizing this defensive and reactive character, the Strategy does not address, and seemingly minimizes the possibility of, major pre-emptive action designed to bring about a fundamental change in the nature of the threats Israel faces.[1] As noted, the Strategy also reaffirmed the IDF's ongoing adherence to the four Ds approach.

The IDF Strategy explicitly differentiates between limited operations, such as those in Lebanon and Gaza since 2006, and situations of full-scale war. In the former case, the Strategy states that Israel will seek to rapidly eliminate the immediate causes of the hostilities and return to the status quo ante, without trying to achieve a strategic change in the situation. It will also try to demonstrate to the adversary the futility of further hostilities and the risk that Israel will be forced to pursue military decision, should the adversary refuse to bring the conflict to a rapid conclusion. In cases of war, conversely, Israel will seek to achieve military decision and a strategic change in the situation, either by imposing a ceasefire and diplomatic resolution, or militarily, by denying the enemy the ability or will to continue the fighting.

The Strategy states that Israel will seek to postpone and prevent hostilities, deter adversaries from initiating them, and maintain periods of calm for as long as possible. The Strategy places particular emphasis on deterrence and states that the IDF will continue to pursue both general and cumulative deterrence. This is to be achieved on the basis of IDF force buildup, ongoing interdiction and disruption efforts, and offensive operations, as needed, to demonstrate Israel's determination to respond when the "rules of the game" have been violated.

The Strategy emphasizes the IDF's renewed focus on offense, through both ground maneuver and firepower. In future operations, it will conduct focused ground operations against enemy centers of gravity, to rapidly reach the lines that it intends to hold at the end of the fighting and achieve military decision. In some cases, this will be done during the early stages of the fighting and at long distances. This approach stands in contrast to the attrition-based approach adopted in the last rounds in Lebanon and Gaza, in which prolonged and massive firepower campaigns were followed by only limited ground operations. It may also require large-scale use of the reserves and the willingness to hold enemy territory for periods of weeks to months.[2]

The Strategy's seemingly renewed emphasis on ground maneuver does not resolve the long-standing feud in the IDF regarding the appropriate balance between maneuver and firepower, nor does it explain how the IDF will overcome the difficulties it has encountered in this type of warfare to date. One respected observer believes that the Strategy remains wedded to outdated concepts of ground maneuver as a means of achieving military decision.[3] In any event, a "grab all" approach, emphasizing both ground maneuver and firepower, is not highly enlightening, even if it appears that the IDF does intend to conduct somewhat greater ground maneuver in the future than in recent conflicts. This may be the important message.

During the periods between major operations, the IDF will conduct the "Campaign between the Campaigns" ((*haMaaracha Bein haMaarachot*, "MABAM"), further elucidated later in this chapter. MABAM includes a variety of operations designed to reduce the buildup of enemy forces, deter future rounds, and increase the prospects of success when they happen.

The emphasis on the offensive notwithstanding, the Strategy also recognizes the importance of increased investment in defensive capabilities. Defense is to be conducted on all fronts and dimensions (air, ground, and sea) and against all forms of attack. In recognition of Israel's as yet limited rocket defenses, the Strategy indicates that priority may have to be accorded in some future conflicts to its military rear, rather than to population centers, that is, that Iron Dome and other rocket defenses will be deployed primarily to defend airbases and other IDF installations. The Strategy further states that the IDF will seek to prevent any enemy territorial gains at the *end* of a conflict, implicitly recognizing the danger of Hezbollah land-grabs.

The Strategy stresses, without elucidation, a number of nonmilitary factors that it considers vital to the war effort, from the planning stages of IDF operations through final implementation, for example, the need for international legitimacy and effective, diplomatic, legal, and public diplomacy campaigns. In recognition that Israel can no longer fully resolve its challenges on its own, the Strategy further emphasizes the importance of cooperation with the United States and other partners, as well of pursing new prospects for cooperation with Arab states.

In an interesting and entirely different area, the Strategy also addresses some of the decision-making ills Israel has encountered in recent conflicts. To this end, it emphasizes that it is the political leadership's responsibility to determine the objectives and end states of military operations, how the IDF is to pursue them, including the constraints on military action, and how IDF operations are to be integrated together with additional efforts undertaken in pursuit thereof (diplomatic, economic, media, social, and more).

Over the years Israel has built a very large military capability designed to cope with the conventional military threats it faces, primarily from neighboring Arab armies. In 2014 Israel was thought to have had 16 divisions, with a total of 79 brigades. Beyond that there are significant differences in the publicly available information. To be safe, two sets of data will be cited, by the prestigious International Institute for Strategic Studies (IISS), which refer to 2016, and figures in parentheses by Israel's foremost think tank, the Institute for National Security Studies (INSS), which refer to 2014. According to these sources Israel had 1,260 (2,840) tanks, of which 500 (1,140) were high quality; 530 (756) self-propelled artillery and 430 towed; 5,300 (7,850) armored personnel carriers (APCs), of which 5,000 were in storage; and 440 (446) combat aircraft.[4] In the absence of a significant threat from the neighboring Arab armies, at least for the foreseeable future, many have questioned the need for such a large conventional force and its suitability to the threats Israel faces today,[5] and the IDF itself has at least partially recognized the validity of this argument. In 2016 CoS Eisenkot stated that "the IDF is still a very large army compared to any other in the region" and the five-year force plan he adopted continued the significant cut in the conventional force begun by his predecessors.[6]

The primary focus of IDF modernization programs in recent years has been on the capabilities it will need to counter the new and especially challenging threats posed by Iran, primarily its missile and potential nuclear capabilities, and, of course, Hezbollah's and Hamas's rocket arsenals. The following are some of the major developments in recent years.

- Israel procured 50 F-35s, the most advanced US combat aircraft, which will provide it both with long-range (2,200 km) and stealth capabilities, at a total cost of $7–9 billion, and is planning to procure 25 more in the future.[7]
- Israel has also devoted great resources to the procurement or development of bunker busters, early-warning and command-and-control aircraft, aerial tankers,[8] and satellites designed for intelligence purposes.[9] As of 2016 Israel had launched seven satellites capable of photographing Iranian sites.[10]
- Israel is reportedly developing advanced models of Jericho missiles, with a range of thousands of kilometers, to supplement its existing shorter-range missile arsenal. Some attribute its missile arsenal to a second-strike nuclear capability.[11]
- Israel now has five Dolphin submarines,[12] at a cost of approximately $450 million each. Some sources claim that they are nuclear armed and are also part of a second-strike capability.[13] The naval arena has led to rise of the

concept of "artificial strategic depth," gained by greater use of the sea, including submarines and ships equipped with missiles.[14]

- The IDF established a new "Depth Command," charged with planning and coordinating multiservice operations against terrorist and guerrilla organizations at distances greater than a few tens of kilometers from Israel's borders, which are the responsibility of the long-existing regional commands. Sometimes inaccurately referred to as the "Iran Command," the Depth Command will reportedly be able to assist with special forces operations at great distances, such as Iran, but this is not its primary function.[15]

A deep debate reportedly existed within the national security establishment regarding the best means of addressing the Iranian threat. One school of thought was said to believe that an Israeli attack on the Iranian nuclear program would have achieved a delay of at least two to four years, not insignificant in and of itself, but which might also have destabilized the Iranian regime. Moreover, they believed that an Israeli strike would have forced the international community to become actively engaged, militarily if necessary, to prevent the program's renewal. Those who favored this approach believed that Israel's already existing retaliatory capabilities were sufficient to deter Iran and that what was needed was greater investment in offensive capabilities.[16]

A second school of thought was more skeptical and reportedly believed that Israel was incapable of destroying the Iranian program by military means, or that the delay achieved would not justify the costs, and that the attempt to develop an offensive capability was thus a waste of precious resources. Those who favored this approach supported a greater emphasis on deterrence and consequently investment in Israel's retaliatory capabilities and in the hardening of its critical strategic sites against possible nuclear attack.[17] Some in this camp, who apparently believed that the threat posed by Iran simply exceeds the capabilities of a country Israel's size, harbored a hope, not always discreetly, that the United States would resolve the problem, diplomatically if possible, militarily, if necessary.[18]

Prime Minister Netanyahu and Defense Minister Barak reportedly sought cabinet approval for an attack on Iran's nuclear program on at least three occasions, in 2010, 2011, and especially 2012. They apparently failed to muster the necessary majority when faced with the united opposition of virtually the entire national security establishment, including the CoS and heads of Mossad and ISA, to an attack that did not enjoy at least implicit US approval. Toward the end Barak, too, seems to have backed away from his earlier support for an attack,[19] and it is not inconceivable that Netanyahu, who has forced other difficult positions through the cabinet, but is known for military caution, may have done so as well, his strident public posture notwithstanding.

Be that as it may, Israel expended vast resources on capabilities needed primarily for the Iranian threat. In monetary terms alone, the above F-35 deals alone cost over $5.5 billion, the Dolphin submarines over $2 billion, the missiles, bunker busters, early-warning and command-and-control aircraft, aerial tankers, satellites, and many other capabilities, many billions more. According to one estimate, Israel spent 11 billion shekels on preparations for a conflict with Iran in 2011–2012 alone (approximately $3 billion).[20] The good news for the IDF is that many of these capabilities can be used against a variety of threats and would have been acquired regardless. In any event, in the absence of any peer competitors in the region today, Israel enjoys overwhelming conventional superiority.

Counterterrorism and Irregular Warfare

Surprisingly, perhaps, Israel does not have a formal counterterrorism doctrine.[21] The absence thereof should not be misconstrued, however, to indicate the absence of any conceptual framework or of basic operational guidelines. Indeed, from the earliest days, Israeli counterterrorism policy has been predicated on the assumption that terrorism could never be fully suppressed, just minimized and reduced to a level that Israeli society could tolerate.[22] In these circumstances, deterrence, prevention, and retaliation have long been at the heart of Israel's counterterrorism operations, along with attrition warfare designed to grind down terrorist organizations and the occasional spectacular counterterrorist operation.[23]

Counterterrorism, both "traditional"[24] and the newer rocket threat, the subject of the next section of this chapter, has been the primary focus of Israel's military policy in recent years and is addressed in detail. In some cases, the responses overlap.

Israel's counterterrorism measures have spanned the gamut of operations, as follows.

Offensive Measures

Ongoing Counterterrorism Operations. These are often round-the-clock, ranging from small covert operations to major offensives, such as the 2006 war in Lebanon and Operation Defensive Edge in 2014. Today these counterterrorism operations are also part of the concept of the "Campaign between the Campaigns" presented later in this chapter.

The "Intelligence-Operations Circle." This is a highly honed coordinating mechanism developed during the second intifada, whereby intelligence regarding an impending terrorist attack is transferred to the operational units (air and/or ground forces) and turned into actionable interdiction measures within minutes.[25]

Interdiction of Arms Transfers to Terrorist Organizations. Examples are the multiple air strikes Israel reportedly conducted in Sudan in 2009 and 2011 to prevent the transfer of Iranian weapons to Hamas, the interdiction in 2011 of a ship sailing from Syria to Egypt carrying Iranian missiles for Hamas,[26] and the repeated air-strikes in Syria in recent years to prevent the transfer of missiles and possibly even chemical weapons to Hezbollah.[27]

Blockade and Embargo. The blockade and embargo of Gaza are designed to prevent the transfer of weapons and materials needed for the construction of storehouses, bunkers, command posts, and more. Initially, this was also a form of economic warfare, designed to apply pressure on the population to end the second intifada.

Third-Party Pressure. Israel has exerted pressure on the civilian populations in which terrorist organizations are embedded and on the host governments, for example, Jordan and Lebanon, in order to force them to cease attacks against Israel. Measures of this sort have included attacks on civilian infrastructure and (vacated) residential neighborhoods, designed to erode public willingness to collaborate with terrorists.[28]

Targeted Killings. Political and military heads of the various terrorist organizations, terrorists with special skills, such as explosive-device makers, those involved in particularly heinous attacks, and other key figures, have been targeted. Primary examples include the failed attempts to kill PLO leader Arafat,[29] Hezbollah leader Nasrallah, and Hamas military leader Mohammed Def, the successful targeting of PLO military leader Abu Jihad, Hezbollah leader Mussawi, Hamas leader Rantisi, and the infamous Hamas bomb maker Ayyash.[30]

Defensive Measures

Security Fences. There are fences along the West Bank, Lebanese, Syrian, Gazan, and Egyptian borders, which have virtually eliminated cross-border ground terrorism. Funding has now been approved for the first part of a fence on the border with Jordan as well.

Security Zones. Israel has sought to establish special security zones on a few occasions, especially in southern Lebanon from the early 1980s until 2000, or more recently, a narrow strip (tens to hundreds of meters) inside Gazan territory, in which no potentially hostile activity is tolerated.

Roadblocks and Checkpoints. These impede terrorists' freedom of movement and provide Israel with more time for interdiction efforts.[31]

Border Patrols. These operate in addition to security guards at public institutions, sky marshals, passenger and baggage screening, and "hardening" of Israeli embassies.

Arrests and Administrative Detentions. In the West Bank (and Gaza, prior to the withdrawal in 2005), travel restrictions, deportations, curfews, closures of public institutions, and denials of work permits in Israel are all designed to keep terrorists, or possible terrorist recruits, off the streets. Pressure has also been applied on the civilian populations to cease violence by suspending electricity and telephone service, various kinds of agricultural and economic activity, delaying monetary transfers to the PA, and more.[32]

Diplomatic Measures

Counterterrorism Alliances. Israel has alliances and de facto cooperation with third parties, for example, Egypt against Hamas during the 2014 operation in Gaza, the Maronites in Lebanon in the 1980s, the decades-long behind-the-scenes cooperation with Jordan, and Israel's acquiescence to the Syrian occupation of Lebanon in 1976 in the hope that it would suppress the PLO.

Counterterrorism Cooperation with the PA. This includes intelligence sharing, operational coordination, acquiescence to the transfer of weapons to PA security forces by third countries, and training of these forces by Jordan and the United States.[33]

Strong Cooperation with the United States. Israel cooperates with the United States and other countries around the world in many areas of counterterrorism.[34]

Promotion of Economic Development. Israel promotes development in the West Bank (and in the past in Gaza) to create a Palestinian stake in maintaining calm, in the hope that economic prosperity will lead to a reduction in terrorist activity.[35]

Negotiations with the Palestinians. This should hopefully be the most effective means of counterterrorism in the long term.

These counterterrorism measures have produced a variety of outcomes, some highly successful, others failed and even counterproductive. Given the complexities and exigencies of realpolitik over decades, they have also led to unintended consequences, entailed numerous inconsistencies, and certainly raised difficult quandaries.

The crowning achievement of Israel's counterterrorism policy has been that it has enabled the country to live in relative security and thrive, almost without regard to the ongoing terrorist threat. Arguably its main failure is that terrorism has had a major impact on public opinion, electoral outcomes, and Israel's positions toward the peace process with the Palestinians. Moreover, in the absence of a coherent long-term national security strategy, counterterrorism operations have been conducted largely on an ad hoc basis, without clear long-term objectives. Consequently, day-to-day operations have at times failed to reflect broader national security objectives and even conflicted with them.[36] The following illustrates some of the difficulties and contradictions encountered.

Effective deterrence of terrorism commonly requires a harsh and even disproportionate response, to dissuade terrorists from further attacks. Some have argued that Israel's harsh initial response during the second intifada may have led to an increase in the overall level of ensuing violence, although it did have a significant long-term deterrent impact on the West Bank population. The war in Lebanon in 2006 also had a strong deterrent impact, despite its failings, whereas the operations in Gaza in 2008 and 2012 did not (it is premature, at the time of this writing, to pass judgement on the 2014 operation). Israel, however, often suffers from an asymmetry of deterrence. Its enemies are less sensitive to casualties than it is, have a threshold for pain that often exceeds Israel's willingness, as a democracy, to mete it out, and view both restraint and proportionate responses as signs of Israeli weakness and proof that violence works.[37]

The battle against terrorism often leads to no-win situations. An Israeli failure to respond to attacks may embolden its enemies and dishearten its own people, but retaliation can exacerbate the situation, lead to even more casualties, and elicit heightened international opprobrium.[38] Israel's default preference for maintaining the status quo and exercising restraint can undermine its own deterrence, as it did in the confrontation with Hezbollah between 2000 and 2006 and Hamas since 2008. Prime Minister Barak's failure to implement his declared policy of massive retaliation and respond to a Hezbollah attack in October 2000, following the unilateral withdrawal from Lebanon earlier that year, was a particularly problematic case. While Israel has been successful at times in deterring terrorism, it has clearly not been able to deter the buildup of terrorist capabilities.[39]

Israel's attempts to apply third-party leverage, as a means of countering terrorist organizations, have met with mixed success. Israel has long sought to hold the Lebanese government accountable for terrorists operating from its territory and to force it to evict the PLO, and later Hezbollah, from southern Lebanon. Israel's attempts to do so, however, by bringing pressure to bear on the population in southern Lebanon, failed, since the Lebanese government simply did not have the wherewithal to fulfill its demands. Instead, they ended up increasing the population's hatred for Israel and willingness to take up arms against it. Conversely, earlier efforts of this nature, directed at the Jordanian government, which was in effective control of its territory, proved quite successful. The expulsion of the PLO from Lebanon, a major success in its own right, ended up creating a power vacuum that paved the way for the rise of a far more

intractable and lethal enemy, Hezbollah. Israel's highly successful efforts to prevent cross-border terrorism by Hezbollah and Hamas led them to seek an alternative response, resulting in the far more difficult-to-counter rocket threat.[40]

On a number of occasions Israel's responses to terrorism have risked, or
actually caused, a broader confrontation with Arab states. Israel's attempts to
counter PLO and Hezbollah terrorism from Lebanon, for example, repeatedly
risked an escalation with Syria and even caused a significant clash in 1982. The
operation against Hamas in 2008 strained Israel's relations with Egypt, and
the operation in 2012, when the Muslim Brotherhood was in power, actually
threatened a significant diplomatic rift and even concerns about the future of
the peace treaty.

Arrests and targeted killings of terrorist leaders and fighters have disrupted,
postponed, and limited the ability of terrorist organizations to launch attacks and
forced them both to devote greater resources to self-preservation, rather than
attacking Israel, and to use less well-trained replacements. This had a significant
and at times even decisive impact on their overall effectiveness.[41] Conversely,
some statistical evidence indicates that targeted killings during the second intifada actually resulted in an increase in suicide bombings[42] and that the deterrent
effect of home demolitions and deportations of terrorists not only decreased
as the intifada continued, but stimulated further resistance.[43] Israel has tried to
stake out a harsh and uncompromising policy on terrorism, but has repeatedly
exchanged terrorists for hostages on hijacked airplanes, abducted Israeli soldiers,
and even the bodies of Israeli soldiers.

Israel made every effort to conduct successful peace talks with the Palestinians
during the early months of the second intifada, and the well-meaning attempts
of premiers such as Rabin, Peres, and Barak to separate the talks from terrorism,
that is, to pursue both negotiations and counterterrorism concomitantly, largely
failed. Moreover, they were counterproductive at times, leading Israel to acquiesce to a level of violence that was politically untenable. It also reduced the
Palestinians' incentive to clamp down, in the knowledge that Israel would negotiate anyway, indeed, that heightened terrorism might produce further Israeli
concessions.[44]

The unilateral nature of the withdrawal from Gaza in 2005 ended up
strengthening Hamas. By denying Palestinian moderates the ability to take
credit for the withdrawal, it strengthened the claim made by Hamas and other
radicals that it was terrorism, not the PA's attempts at negotiations, that had
forced Israel out. When one adds Israel's weakening of the PA's security forces
to the picture, as part of its response to the intifada, and the power vacuum in
Gaza following the withdrawal, the highly unintended consequence was that
Israeli policy greatly abetted Hamas's takeover of Gaza in 2007. Israel's counterterrorism measures at times also forced Jordan to show solidarity with Hamas,

which it opposes, and had a highly deleterious effect on relations with Turkey in the 2010s.[45]

The unilateral withdrawal from Lebanon in 2000 enabled Hezbollah to claim that it was the first Arab force to have ever successfully coerced Israel into withdrawing from territory, without gaining anything in return. It also greatly strengthened Hezbollah's stature in Lebanon and throughout the region, and was explicitly cited by the Palestinians as a model to be emulated and as a reason for the outbreak of the second intifada. Israel's failure to achieve decisive outcomes in the operations against Hezbollah in 2006 and Hamas in 2008, 2012, and 2014 allowed them to claim victory, regardless of the military reality, and further strengthened their standing in their respective communities and beyond.

Israel tried to apply pressure on Hamas to end rocket fire, by imposing an economic embargo and blockade, but backed off under international pressure and removed most of the restrictions. In so doing, Israel undermined the deterrent logic of its own policy, but not before paying a heavy price in international condemnation. Following the operation in 2014 Israel even found itself in the awkward position of having to champion the reconstruction of Gaza, which it had just bombed heavily. Israel has done its utmost to minimize civilian losses during counterterrorism operations, but has lost the "PR war," nevertheless, with severe consequences for its international standing.[46] The list of failed or counterproductive counterterrorism efforts goes on.

Israel's heavy focus on counterterrorism operations, that is military measures, has led some to propose that it adopt a comprehensive counterinsurgency strategy, in other words, one that takes into account the political and societal factors that give rise to terrorism, rather than merely trying to suppress it. To an extent, Israel has done so, for example, in the repeated efforts to reach a negotiated settlement with the Palestinians (the Oslo process during the 1990s, Camp David and the Clinton Parameters in 2000, the Olmert proposals in 2008). One can argue, of course, that Israel could have done more, and there is no doubt that some Israeli policies, especially on the settlements, have further exacerbated the situation, but the Palestinians have proven averse to even the most far-reaching peace proposals. Moreover, trying to win over the hearts and minds of the Palestinians, or the Shiites in Lebanon, the essence of a counterinsurgency strategy, in the absence of a final peace agreement and likely for a long time thereafter, is simply unrealistic in the Middle Eastern context. After decades of conflict, the enmity and fundamental differences are too deep.[47]

Finally, domestic politics have played a major role in determining Israel's counterterrorism responses from the earliest years, in terms of leaders' need both to avoid appearing weak and to satisfy public demands for resolute action and retribution. This was true of the responses to the Fedayeen attacks in the 1950s,[48] of the second intifada, including the decision to launch Operation Defensive Shield at its height in 2002, and of all the major operations in Lebanon and Gaza ever since. Political considerations are a legitimate part of national security decision-making, but they certainly affect, and at times skew, the decisions made.

Morag (2005) has suggested the following criteria for assessing the effectiveness of Israel's counterterrorism policy: the number of Israeli and innocent enemy casualties, socioeconomic impact of terrorism on Israel, and its impact on domestic and international support for both Israel and the Palestinians.[49] Drawing on this approach, a number of conclusions can be drawn.

- *Israeli Casualties.* Throughout most of its history, Israel's intensive counterterrorism efforts have succeeded in keeping the number of casualties low. With the exception of a few periods, primarily the second intifada, the effect of "traditional" terrorism in recent decades has been limited mostly to quality-of-life issues and the public's sense of security, not inconsequential in their own right, but with relatively few casualties and minimal disruption of daily life. The impact of Hezbollah's and Hamas's rocket arsenals has been far greater, with lengthy periods in which daily life has been disrupted in entire parts of the country and considerable physical damage caused, but again the number of casualties has been small. This may very well not be the case in a future round with Hezbollah, whose rocket arsenal is now estimated at more than 10 times its already substantial size in 2006.
- *Enemy Casualties.* Israel has gone to great lengths over the decades to prevent innocent enemy casualties, limiting its military objectives and operations, devising special tactics, at times risking IDF personnel and its own civilian population. Its record is certainly favorable compared to other countries that have confronted terrorist threats.[50] These efforts notwithstanding, the cost in innocent victims in counterterrorism operations in the West Bank, Gaza, and Lebanon has been significant. This has been especially true in recent years, as Hamas and Hezbollah have embedded their forces among their civilian populations, using them as human shields and intentionally making Israel cause civilian casualties when it responds. There have also been cases in which the IDF may have used excessive force, resulting in civilian casualties.
- *Socioeconomic Impact.* As already elaborated in chapter 5, the societal impact of terrorism on Israel has been limited. Indeed, Israeli society, for all its tensions, manifests impressive societal resilience. With the exception of the second intifada, the impact of terrorism on Israel's national economy has also been limited, typically localized and fleeting.
- *Domestic and International Support for Israel and the Palestinians.* The domestic and international impact of terrorism and counterterrorism operations, for both Israel and the Palestinians, has been mixed. Domestically, positions have been hardened on both sides and led to a "rallying around the flag"

phenomenon, providing legitimization to hardline policies. Terrorism has had a major impact on Israeli electoral outcomes and public attitudes toward the peace process. The second intifada decimated the moderate and pro-peace camp in Israel, while Hezbollah and Hamas rocket fire has convinced much of the public that the unilateral withdrawals from Lebanon and Gaza were mistakes never to be repeated, especially in the West Bank.

Conversely, the significant public support in Israel for territorial compromise in the West Bank stems, at least in part, from a sense of despair and revulsion engendered by Palestinian terrorism and violence, and a consequent desire to simply separate from them. Similarly, the unilateral withdrawals from Lebanon and Gaza reflected frustration with the ongoing casualties and Israel's inability to end the violence. In all of these cases, terrorism did have a significant effect on Israeli policy. Attitudes toward the Golan Heights, in contrast, in which there has been virtually no terrorism, have remained stable over the years, though additional reasons also account for this.

Israel's counterterrorism measures have contributed significantly to the deterioration in its international standing, particularly when viewed as disproportionate, for example, the crackdowns during the two intifadas, or the 2014 Gaza operation, and have contributed significantly to the campaign of defamation and delegitimization underway against it.[51] The international community's long-standing opposition to Israel's occupation of the West Bank, which it considers to be illegitimate, and in the past Gaza and southern Lebanon, has had a considerable impact on its attitude both toward terrorism against Israel and Israel's responses. Although much of the international community, especially the Western countries, formally denounces terrorism and emphasizes its recognition of Israel's legitimate right to self-defense, it has demonstrated greater understanding of terrorism perpetrated against it than others and has only rarely acknowledged that Israel was, indeed, acting in pursuit thereof.

Palestinian terrorism has had a mixed impact on their international standing. On the one hand, spectacular terrorism succeeded in putting the Palestinian cause on the international agenda in the 1960s and 1970s and led to a dramatic change in their international stature.[52] Ongoing terrorism since then has kept the Palestinian cause in the limelight and convinced many in the world of the need to redress their grievances. Conversely, the bloody excesses of the second intifada turned parts of the international community away from the Palestinians, leading to their temporary isolation and to greater understanding for Israel's security concerns. Palestinian terrorism has also had a particularly negative impact on their relations with the United States. Hezbollah and Hamas have not succeeded in eliciting much international support, and ongoing rocket fire has further contributed to international understanding of Israel's security needs.

Israel's harsh response to the second intifada turned Palestinian public opinion at least partially against violence, at least for a while, not as a matter of principle, but because of the heavy costs incurred. It remains to be seen if the same will prove true of the response in Gaza to the massive destruction caused by the operation in 2014. What Israel and many in the international community consider to be totally unjustified terrorism is viewed by much of the Palestinian population as a legitimate form of warfare and resistance. Facing a strong public consensus, virtually no Palestinian leader has ever condemned terrorism on the normative level, although President Abbas has repeatedly called it counterproductive to Palestinian interests. Despite decades of strenuous efforts, the bottom line is that terrorism very much remains an accepted policy tool for Hezbollah, Hamas, and many Palestinians.

Not surprisingly, Israel has been most successful in combating terrorism when it has been in firm control of the territory the terrorists operate from and, therefore, able to prevent them from gaining refuge and state sanctuary, including a base from which to recruit and train personnel, build up their military capabilities, and launch operations. "Intelligence control" of the territory, that is, the freedom to conduct intelligence operations, for both collection and prevention purposes, has proven essential, as has development of the real-time link between the intelligence and operational units mentioned above (the "intelligence-operations circle"). Following the Oslo Accords, the IDF withdrew from the populated areas of the West Bank and lost control over the territory. It was only when it reoccupied these areas at the height of the intifada, during the spring of 2002, that the conditions for effective intelligence control were reestablished. Since the withdrawals from Lebanon in 2000 and Gaza in 2005, Israel has not enjoyed nearly the same level of intelligence penetration of these areas as in the past.

Israel's counterterrorism policy has thus been an ongoing mix of achievements and failures. It has had a highly deleterious impact on Israel's international standing, there have been many inconsistencies, and Palestinian terrorism has had a deep effect on public opinion and electoral outcomes. Overall, however, Israel's counterterrorism policy has been a great success, enabling Israel to live in relative security and normalcy and to prosper, despite the myriad array of terrorist threats it has faced.[53] Israel's borders have been effectively blocked to cross-border ground terrorism, and the second intifada, the greatest terrorist threat Israel that has ever confronted, indeed, one of the greatest that any democratic country has ever faced, was effectively suppressed. In so doing, Israel succeeded in disproving the common wisdom that conventional armies cannot defeat terrorism and insurgencies.[54] Indeed, Israel has been so successful in preventing cross-border terrorism that Hezbollah and Hamas have been forced to seek indirect means of attacking it, primarily by means of rockets, which have come to constitute the primary terrorist threat Israel faces today.

Countering the Rocket and Missile Threats

Israel has built a multitiered offensive and defensive response to the rocket and missile threats posed by Hezbollah and Hamas, as well as Syria (prior to the civil war) and Iran. On the offensive level, Israel has developed a partial capability to destroy launchers, including mobile ones, albeit often only after they have fired for the first time. This capability was already apparent during the 2006 war in Lebanon, when the IAF succeeded in destroying virtually all of Hezbollah's long-range rocket arsenal during the first night and when, after the first few days, almost no launcher succeeded in firing a second time. Most were destroyed within minutes of the first launch.[55]

At present, this capability appears to be limited primarily to Hezbollah's and Hamas's long-range rockets, which are relatively large and mounted on easily identifiable launchers, and thus comparatively easy to find and attack. As demonstrated in the recent rounds against Hamas, however, Israel does not yet appear to have an effective capability to prevent and suppress either its or Hezbollah's vast number of short-range rockets, which are far smaller and easily hidden in residential and other buildings.

The IDF has apparently concluded that trying to find and destroy every rocket launcher is simply not feasible and that Hezbollah and Hamas will be able to continue rocket fire until the very end of future conflicts, despite all IDF suppression efforts, as happened in the four major rounds since 2006. Instead, the IDF will seek to apply massive and persistent air power in order to progressively diminish their capability and motivation to continue the fighting, and expedite the diplomatic endgame. To this end, the IDF has built a capability to hit targets with precision that is now many times greater than it was during the 2006 operation. During the eight-day operation against Hamas in November 2012, for example, the IDF attacked 1,500 targets, double the number in the 34-day war against Hezbollah in 2006. It struck a similar number during the first week of the operation against Hamas in 2014.[56]

In practice, the short-range rockets continue to pose enormous operational challenges, greatly exacerbated by the fact that they are deeply embedded among the civilian population, well hidden, and protected in underground tunnels, all of which makes finding and destroying them extremely difficult. Addressing the rocket threats, as demonstrated in both the 2006 and 2014 operations, can require weeks of offensive action, during which Israel's civilian population is under continual attack, and is only partly effective in any event, as a significant portion of Hezbollah's and Hamas's rocket arsenals survived. In the latter operation, some 40% of Hamas's short-range rockets were destroyed by Israeli strikes, 40% were fired, and 20% survived the attacks.[57] Intensive air-strikes over the course of 51 days proved insufficient to end Hamas rocket fire, which continued unabated and in large numbers to the very end. Hamas rejected numerous calls for a ceasefire and continued fighting despite the severe damage caused to Gaza. Moreover, in the absence of a clear and crushing defeat, Hamas was able to claim that it had withstood Israel's superior might and thus emerged victorious, much as both it and Hezbollah had done in earlier rounds.

The IDF's difficulties confronting Hamas reflect a fundamental quandary. As painful as Hamas rocket fire and other forms of terrorism have been, Israel clearly does not want to reoccupy Gaza and pay the price (human, diplomatic, and economic) required to root out Hamas's military capabilities and topple it, the solution advocated by some as the only effective means of terminating the threat it poses. The reluctance to do so does not stem from an inability to achieve the goal, but from the belief that Hamas or other organizations will re-build their rocket arsenals once Israel withdraws and that it will have achieved no more than a brief respite. Moreover, a power vacuum may evolve, which will ultimately be filled by organizations even more dangerous than Hamas. The number of casualties involved in reconquering Gaza, with its maze of under-ground tunnels and fortifications, will also be very high for both sides, and the international ramifications severe. Indeed, the IDF estimated that 10–14 days would have been needed to conquer Gaza during the 2014 operation, at a cost of hundreds of IDF soldiers, and that it would have taken another year to fully root out Hamas's rockets and destroy the organization.[58] As a result, Israel refrained from trying to topple Hamas, and from the major grounds operations this would have entailed, in the conflicts in 2008, 2012, and 2014. A similar situation exists regarding the much greater rocket threat posed by Hezbollah. The bottom line is that Israel does not yet appear to have an effective offensive response to the rocket threats posed by Hamas and even more so Hezbollah, and is not likely to have one for the foreseeable future.[59]

In the absence thereof, Israel has developed a variety of passive and active defenses. Passive defenses include shelters, "hardening" of various buildings and installations, reinforced concrete rooms in apartments and homes, and more. A decision was even adopted to "harden" all homes within seven kilometers of the border, and in the future maybe 15, but full implementation of this ex-tremely costly move is contingent on funding and[60] is unlikely to be carried out, at least for the foreseeable future. Israel has also developed a highly targeted early warning system, whereby citizens residing in areas under rocket attack are pro-vided with the necessary warning, for example, via cell phones, while those in other areas, even immediately adjacent ones, are able to move about freely.[61]

An additional form of passive defense is the planned evacuation of entire communities from areas under threat of severe rocket attacks, or from border communities that Hezbollah may seek to overrun and temporarily occupy. The primary focus is on some 50 towns and villages with a combined population of nearly 80,000 people, located within a range of four kilometers from the Lebanese border. A similar plan exists for communities in the Gaza area as well. The planned evacuation is designed to deny Hezbollah or Hamas the ability to achieve what would certainly be a severe shock for the Israeli public, if an entire community was overrun or heavily targeted.[62]

Israel's active defenses include five separate mortar, rocket, and missile defense systems: Iron Dome for short-range rockets, Magic Wand (also referred to as David's Sling) for intermediate-range rockets, Arrow 2 for shorter-range ballistic missiles, such as those in the Syrian arsenal, and Arrow 3 for long-range ones, primarily from Iran. A fifth defensive system, Iron Beam, against mortar fire, is now under development.[63] The different systems are designed to partly overlap and be mutually reinforcing. Additional protection is provided by Israel's links to the American global missile-warning systems and potentially American defenses,[64] should the United States decide, for example, to deploy Aegis ships in the region.

The rocket and missile defense systems have four primary objectives: enabling the public to continue living a comparatively normal daily life, which requires that they be able to provide a 24×7 shield against a very large number of rockets; reducing the economic disruption to the home front caused by even relatively small numbers of rockets; allowing the IDF to continue relatively unrestricted wartime operations, despite large-scale and protracted attacks on major bases, mobilization centers, and force concentrations; and protecting critical infrastructure installations, such as power stations and communications and transportation nodes,[65] whose destruction, or even just disruption, could shut down large parts of the country for prolonged periods.

Iron Dome. Iron Dome has been operational since 2011 and is designed to intercept rockets, with a reported range of up to 70 kilometers, and some mortars and artillery shells.[66] The area defended by each battery is not known, varying by source, from over 60 square kilometers (about twice the size of a city such as Haifa) to an area of over 100 square kilometers.[67] Some sources claim that current plans call for a total of 10–13 batteries, 10 of which were already operational in 2014, the minimum number the IDF believes necessary to provide basic defense for the entire country.[68] Some analysts estimate that a total of 20 or more batteries will be required to provide truly effective country-wide defense.[69]

During the 2006 Lebanon war, which took place before Iron Dome was operational, Hezbollah fired 4,228 rockets at Israel. Some 80% of the rockets fired were short-range, though a small number reached as far south as Hadera (a Tel Aviv exurb).[70] Between 100,000 and 250,000 people fled from the north, and an estimated million were forced to stay in shelters, with northern communities turning into virtual ghost towns and public services barely functioning. Two thousand homes and apartments were destroyed or severely damaged, and numerous civilian structures, including public utilities, hospitals, and tens of factories, were damaged. The port, oil refinery, and chemical industries in Haifa were forced to suspend operations, the latter two out of fear of an environmental disaster, and the naval base was forced to move operations to the south.[71] Fifty-three Israelis were killed in the rocket attacks, of whom 41 were civilians. Approximately 250 were severely wounded and 2,400 lightly or moderately so. An average of 79 rockets were fired for each fatality.[72]

During the far briefer operation in Gaza in December 2008, also before Iron Dome became operational, Hamas fired 813 rockets and mortars at Israel. Thirteen soldiers and civilians were killed, with 62 rockets fired for every casualty.[73]

During a brief round of rocket fire in March 2012, Hamas fired over 160 rockets, but due to the newly operational Iron Dome, the number of casualties was minimal, one person severely wounded, two lightly so, and the material damage was significantly less than expected.[74] During the operation in Gaza in November 2012 Hamas fired 1,506 rockets at Israel (1,600 according to other sources), but Iron Dome achieved an interception rate of 88%.[75] A total of five Israelis were killed and 240 wounded by rocket fire. For every fatality, 300 incoming rockets (320 assuming 1,600 rockets) were now required.[76]

During the operation in Gaza in 2014 Hamas fired approximately 4,600 rockets and mortars at Israel,[77] including vital infrastructure sites, such as Ben-Gurion Airport, the seaports in Ashdod and Haifa, an offshore gas rig, and the Dimona nuclear reactor. Only two people were killed by rocket fire and a further 15 by mortars; 836 were wounded, of whom just 69 were directly caused by the rockets, while the rest were trauma victims and various accidents. Crucially, 1,500 rockets were now required for each fatality, and Iron Dome proved so successful that it led to problems of overconfidence among the civilian population, including a failure to take appropriate precautions. With the exception of those in the immediate vicinity of Gaza, where the distance was too short to enable effective interception, the rest of Israel was able to continue daily life with only limited disruption.[78] In effect, Iron Dome largely neutralized the military threat posed by Hamas rockets.

Table 7.1 shows the effects of rocket fire in the conflicts in 2006 and 2008, before Iron Dome was operational, and in 2012 and 2014, after it became operational. The change was dramatic, leading to an increase in the number of rockets required for each fatality, from 79 to 1,500.

The extraordinary success of the rocket shield constituted a severe blow for Hamas, and indirectly Hezbollah and Iran, which have built their military strategies on the assumption that the Israeli home front would be vulnerable and desperate for an end to the fighting.[79] The Hezbollah rocket threat, however, is infinitely larger than Hamas's and increasingly precise, so only limited inferences

Table 7.1 **Rocket Casualties, 2006–2014**

Operation	Iron Dome Batteries	Rockets fired	Fatalities from rockets	Ratio
2006 Lebanon	0	4,200	53	1/79
2008 Gaza	0	813	13	1/62
2012 Gaza	5	1,600	5	1/300
2014 Gaza	10	3,000[a]	2	1/1,500

Source: Table adapted from Rubin 2015 and other sources. Figures for 2006, 2012, and 2014 were adapted from Rubin 2015, pp. 7, 15–16, 19, 22, 27. Figures for 2008 are from Shafir in Brom 2012, p. 34; Rapaport 2010, pp. 31–32; and www.mako.co.il/pzm-israel-wars/operation-cast-lead/Article-4082602e2847431006.html.

[a] Not including mortars.

can be drawn from Israel's success in 2014. Nevertheless, the operation clearly marked a turning point, and Israel's adversaries will presumably have to at least partially reconsider their capabilities and strategies.

Magic Wand. Magic Wand is designed to intercept short-range missiles at a distance of 40–240 kilometers,[80] long-range and precise rockets, and cruise missiles.[81] Operational as of 2016,[82] current plans call for the deployment of four batteries to cover all of Israel, possibly by 2017, though budgetary constraints may cause a delay.[83] At least one source estimates that as many as 12 batteries may ultimately be needed.[84]

Arrow. Arrow is designed to intercept ballistic missiles. Development began in the late 1980s and the Arrow first became operational in 2000,[85] with a total of three batteries deployed.[86] Procurement of the Arrow 2 was completed some years ago, and Israel is now focusing on development of the Arrow 3 and 4.[87] Arrow 3 is designed to intercept long-range missiles from Syria and Iran, in space, including ones with multiple re-entry vehicles.[88] According to some reports, it was to have been operational in 2016, although another source states that it will only become operational if and when Iran goes nuclear.[89] If Arrow 3 fails to intercept incoming targets, Arrow 2 will be launched as a backup and if it too fails, Magic Wand will provide the final opportunity for interception.[90]

Israel's Rocket and Missile Defense: Advantages and Disadvantages

Financial Limitations. One of the major problems Israel faces is the severe disparity between the comparatively inexpensive cost of the incoming rockets and its very expensive defensive systems. The precise cost of each Iron Dome interceptor is not known, but most sources estimate it between $35,000 and $50,000 (the latter figure is used by most sources) and usually $60–$80 million for each battery, with a low of $50 million.[91] By 2016 Israel and the United States, which funds nearly half of the Iron Dome program, had committed approximately $4.5 billion to it.[92] In contrast, the per unit cost of Hamas's and Hezbollah's Katyusha and Grad rockets is only a few thousand dollars.[93]

Each Magic Wand interceptor is estimated at $700,000–$1.25 million, not including the launcher and R&D costs, and Israel will presumably need hundreds of interceptors to deal with the Hezbollah threat, if not far more. Each battery is estimated at $100 million.[94] The number of Arrow interceptors Israel has is not known, but as early as 2000 foreign sources estimated that it would procure a total of about 240, at a cost of approximately $2 million each (others estimate up to $3 million), though this number may very well have increased significantly ever since.[95] As of 2014 approximately $2.36 billion were to have been invested in the Arrow, with the United States again covering nearly half.[96]

One study of the rocket and missile defense systems contemplated by the IDF concluded that the total cost would exceed $10 billion, a walloping figure for Israel, and that Israel would continue to incur major expenses in the future, as it expended its store of interceptors during each round. The study thus concluded that defense does not provide an effective overall response to the missile and rocket threats Israel faces. Another study concluded that the cost of an overall rocket and missile shield would be simply ruinous.[97]

Others argue that these sums, when broken down on a multiyear basis, do not exceed Israel's capabilities, especially since the United States will continue to bear much of the burden.[98] Indeed, the 10-year US assistance package for Israel, for 2018–2027, includes $500 million annually for rocket and missile defense.[99] Moreover, the otherwise exorbitant prices of the defensive systems become far more palatable when the overall costs of the confrontations with Hamas and Hezbollah are taken into account, rather than just comparing the cost of the incoming rockets to the defensive systems. The precise figures are a source of dispute, but the following is at least highly indicative: the direct military cost of the 2006 war in Lebanon was 8.2 billion shekels[100] (not including replenishing spent stores and over 3 billion shekels in damage to the infrastructure, investment-capital flight, lost productivity, and tourist revenue);[101] 3.8 billion shekels for the 2008 Gaza operation; 3 billion shekels for the 2012 Gaza operation (the cost of Iron Dome during the operation was just 90–160 million shekels);[102] and 6.2–8.6 billion shekels for the 2014 Gaza operation (not including an IDF request for a few billion shekels more to further improve its capabilities). An informed source estimates the combined direct costs of these operations at over 25 billion shekels.[103]

For purposes of limited confrontation such as these, the defensive systems thus provide a relatively good and cost-effective response, as they are likely to do against Iran's limited conventional missile arsenal. The true question is in regard to a future confrontation with Hezbollah's already mammoth and growing rocket arsenal. The problem will be further exacerbated by the increasing number of precise rockets and missiles in Hezbollah and other enemy arsenals, which must be intercepted, thereby creating a need for a greater number of interceptors. Today, most are highly imprecise and fall in open spaces, and Israel's defensive systems do not bother to intercept them, to save costs.

Operational Limitations. The minimum range required for an Iron Dome interception is not known, but has been estimated to be five to seven kilometers. Communities falling within this distance of the border, for example, Sderot, which has been hit repeatedly by Hamas rocket fire, are thus not protected, as was painfully evident during the operation in 2014. The same may hold true for Kiryat Shmona, for example, on the Lebanese border, which has been struck repeatedly by Hezbollah rocket attacks. Moreover, there is no assurance that Iron Dome and the other defensive systems will achieve such high success rates in the future, given the danger of saturation, that is, the number of incoming targets they can engage at one time should large-scale salvos be fired, the broader areas requiring defense, and various improvements Hezbollah and Hamas will undoubtedly make to their penetration capabilities.[104] Magic Wand and the Arrow have yet to be tried in combat and their interception rates remain a matter of speculation.

Strategic Limitations. Although Iron Dome has proven to be remarkably effective, bringing the number of casualties down to minimal levels, civilian life in areas under attack is greatly disrupted nevertheless. The public still has to seek shelter, schools and places of employment are closed, and overall socio-economic activity is largely paralyzed.[105] The primary danger posed by Hamas's rocket arsenal and Iran's (conventional) missile arsenal is thus not in the relatively small number of casualties they can cause, but the disruptive effect on the economy and the public's ability to continue normal life, despite Israel's defensive systems. Hezbollah's rocket arsenal, on the other hand, poses a threat of an entirely different order of magnitude, with a far greater number of casualties and possibly large-scale physical destruction.

Moreover, unless a full nationwide Iron Dome shield is deployed, painful choices will have to be made between those areas and sites that will be defended, and those that will not. Airbases, for example, and various other military installations, are essential to winning the war. Damaged power stations, or water, communications, and transportation systems, could leave much of Israel with diminished public services for months. The tendency, at least in large-scale confrontations, will thus be to deploy Iron Dome batteries to defend them rather than population centers.

Paradoxically, Iron Dome's very success can further exacerbate the threat. Iron Dome allows Israel's enemies to fire rockets on its cities, disrupt the lives of its people and economy, and, in so doing, create deterrence, in the knowledge that the number of casualties and physical destruction actually caused will be limited. In the absence of significant casualties and physical destruction, however, Israel will have less domestic and international legitimacy to launch major offensive operations and pursue military decision, and may be forced to respond in a more limited and less effective manner, as may have already been the case in Gaza in 2014.[106] In some circumstances, Iron Dome can thus actually encourage an adversary to fire even more rockets at Israel.

Finally, a problem relevant to the Arrow alone is that it is of limited efficacy against nuclear missiles; if just one got through, this would constitute a catastrophic failure that would negate Arrow's potentially great success in shooting down all of the rest.[107] Arrow may actually spur deployment of nonconventional warheads, so that even if only a few missiles were able to penetrate Israel's defenses, it would still suffer devastating damage.[108] At least for the meantime, these fears have yet to be materialized.

Advantages. Iron Dome has not eliminated Israel's rocket threats, but it has proven to be a resounding success, at least in limited conflicts, such as in 2014. The number of casualties and physical damage were brought down to minimal levels, and most of the country, though not the border communities in the immediate vicinity of Gaza, was able to continue functioning relatively normally. In so doing, Iron Dome has also prevented a situation whereby virtually any Palestinian or other faction could inflict casualties on Israeli population centers at will and, in effect, hold them hostage.

Moreover, Iron Dome has largely freed Israel's leaders of the pressures to preempt, or counterattack immediately, generated by a population under severe attack, and thus provided them with far greater decision-making latitude. During the operation in Gaza in 2012, for example, the government did not deem it necessary to launch a ground attack, since Iron Dome provided sufficient protection, and in 2014 the limited ground operation that was launched was directed against the new tunnel threat, not the rockets. The sense of at least partial protection also greatly reduced the public's sense of helplessness and contributed to its resilience and ability to withstand the prolonged rocket onslaught. At a minimum, Iron Dome provides decision-makers with more time to prepare for offensive action, especially when taken by surprise by events, as in 2014.[109]

Finally, an assumed, but as yet untested, advantage of Israel's rocket and missile shields is that they would guarantee a second-strike capability, by ensuring that most of the IAF would survive a first strike and be able to continue functioning.[110] This would be true of both conventional and nonconventional attacks.

The Campaigns and the "Campaign between the Campaigns" ("MABAM")

The three confrontations in Gaza between 2008 and 2014 were all "deterrence-based operations." and their formal objectives, as defined by the government, were similar: to end the Hamas rocket attacks then underway and restore calm, weaken Hamas significantly, and deter it from renewing hostilities for as long as possible, that is, to force a return to the status quo, without specifying how long these affects were designed to last. In the long term, Israel hoped that repeated deterrence-based operations such as these would achieve a level of cumulative deterrence that would result in a cessation of the attacks, but had no pretensions to fully resolving the problem in the short term.[111]

In effect, Israel was seeking to counter Hamas's, as well as Iran's and Hezbollah's, long-term strategy of defeating Israel through attrition, with a new attrition strategy of its own. Part of this new strategy is MABAM, the "Campaign between the Campaigns," known colloquially as "mowing the grass."[112] MABAM is an ongoing effort designed to maintain and strengthen Israel's deterrence between the major campaigns, dissuade Hezbollah and Hamas from beginning further rounds for as long as possible, or at least reduce the magnitude of the confrontations once they break out, and best position Israel, militarily, diplomatically, and otherwise, when this does happen. On the military level, MABAM entails the use of various types of force to affect Hezbollah's and Hamas's "consciousness," that is, their sense of vulnerability and self-confidence, and disrupt the buildup of their capabilities. Over the years there have been numerous reports and analyses indicating that MABAM includes the interdiction of advanced weapons transfers to them from Syria or Iran. It also includes a variety of diplomatic, economic, legal, and media operations. Since these organizations cannot, in practice, be defeated in one major operation, it is necessary to repeatedly "mow the grass."[113] Some argue that the nature of the threat Israel faces today is such that conflicts have become nearly continuous and, therefore, that the "campaign between the campaigns" *is* the campaign, not a distinct concept.[114]

In Lebanon in 2006 and the operations in Gaza in 2008 and 2012, Israel launched massive air strikes at the outset of the fighting, both to significantly downgrade Hezbollah and Hamas rocket arsenals and to try to convince them to return to the status quo ante. Recognizing that this was unlikely to occur, however, Israel also took the steps necessary to prepare for large-scale ground operations, but never actually carried them out. The very act of mobilizing the reserves and concentrating forces in preparation was considered a threat to Hezbollah and Hamas and a means of applying pressure on them to end the fighting. In practice, Hezbollah and Hamas may have viewed Israel's actions very differently, as an opportunity to draw IDF forces into areas that had been prepared precisely for this purpose.[115]

In the Gaza operation in 2014 a different approach was attempted. Instead of a massive air attack at the outset, Israel started operations at a much lower level and expressed its willingness to end the fighting quickly and return to the status quo. Once Hamas rejected this, however, a new concept of a "map of pain" was applied, that is, a process of gradual and controlled escalation designed to demonstrate to Hamas the growing costs and futility of continued hostilities. As in other "deterrence-based operations," the objective was to affect Hamas's "consciousness," not achieve military decision, and to do so in a manner that would gain international legitimacy. To this end, Israel repeatedly agreed to ceasefire proposals to demonstrate to the international community that it was willing to end the fighting, unlike Hamas, which rejected them, and worked with the UN and various NGOs to address humanitarian concerns. It also sought, unsuccessfully, to find targets of importance to Hamas, such as military infrastructure, rocket stores, government buildings, and more, whose loss would hasten its willingness to end the fighting.[116] Many of the air strikes were directed at the homes of Hamas commanders, in the hope that they would see the destruction wrought and be more amenable to ending the fighting. These hopes proved illusory.[117]

Ground operations in the launch areas, during the various operations since 2006, have not achieved an appreciable decrease in rocket fire, and changes in the level thereof were largely a result of Hezbollah and Hamas decisions, not Israel's actions. The launch areas were dispersed throughout the built-up parts of Lebanon and Gaza, with the civilian population serving as a human shield, and the launching systems were decentralized and well hidden, enabling them to continue functioning effectively even during Israeli ground operations. Given the huge investments made in intelligence and operational capabilities in the years prior to these conflicts, the number of Hezbollah and Hamas fighters killed was limited.[118]

The 2014 operation demonstrated the limits of Israel's offensive capabilities against hybrid nonstate actors, such as Hamas in Gaza, even more than its predecessors. Much as 34 days of air strikes and limited ground maneuver did not prove sufficient to force Hezbollah to agree to a ceasefire in 2006, 51 days of the new "map of pain," including 5,200 air strikes, over a third of which were designed to suppress rocket fire, failed to do so in 2014 against a much weaker adversary.[119] Of the four "strategic pillars," only defense proved successful in 2014, whereas the IDF failed to provide early warning of the imminent confrontation, did not succeed in deterring Hamas, and never sought to achieve military decision in the fighting to begin with.[120]

Moreover, what Israel views as attrition may not really weaken nonstate actors like Hezbollah and Hamas. They have very few physical assets whose destruction causes real damage and are capable of sustaining relatively high levels of losses among their fighters. Given the nature of the fighting, it is hard to cause them large numbers of casualties in any event. They are not impervious to civilian losses, but use them to their advantage for PR purposes. Prolongation of the fighting strengthens their ethos of standing up to Israel and sacrifice, and increases their prestige both within their constituent publics and beyond.[121]

Hezbollah and Hamas were hit badly in the rounds between 2006 and 2014 despite the limited ground operations conducted. Nevertheless, all of these operations ended with a feeling on their part that they had survived the Israeli response and that the outcomes achieved were acceptable, in many ways even a success. Moreover, Israel's international standing took a severe hit. In effect, all of the operations ended with what former IDF intelligence chief Amos Yadlin has called an "asymmetric strategic tie," hardly a resounding success.[122] Moreover, the heavy cost of the last four rounds, more than 25 billion shekels in direct costs alone, led one of Israel's foremost military analysts to warn that all Hezbollah and Hamas have to do is to renew hostilities every two years or so and Israel's economy will be ruined.[123]

A more optimistic analysis holds that the operation in 2014 led Hamas to conclude that rocket fire had failed to extract Israeli concessions of significance, that hiding behind civilians forced it to blink first, and that it cannot afford another round with Israel, beyond scattered skirmishes, at least for the next few years.[124] Time will tell. If the ceasefire holds for a prolonged period, the 2014 operation, unlike its predecessors, will have succeeded in achieving deterrence against Hamas.

The 2006 war with Hezbollah also gained a few years of deterrence, possibly lasting until 2012. Since then it is unclear how much of the ongoing calm on the Lebanese border is a function of Israel's deterrence or of Hezbollah's overextension in the Syrian civil war, but even six years is a considerable achievement. If a similar period of calm is achieved with Hamas, Israel may be able to conclude that it has achieved the kind of limited deterrence it has set as its objective in conflicts such as these, albeit at the expense of a heavy blow to its international standing.

Further major rounds with Hezbollah and Hamas appear virtually inevitable, just a matter of time. In preparation, and as part of its deterrent strategy, Israel has repeatedly warned that it will hit Hezbollah and Hamas far harder than in the past. Indeed, senior IDF officers have warned that the destruction caused in the next round will set Lebanon back by tens to hundreds of years and that it will become a country of refugees.[125] Senior former officers have stated that the next round may even result in a weakening of Hezbollah and consequent rise in Lebanon of radical Sunni elements, a grave threat for the Shiite population, from which Hezbollah draws its strength. The problem it would then face would not be just the destruction of their villages in the fighting with Israel, but how to survive with their radicalized Sunni compatriots now ascendant.[126]

Israel's response, in the next major round with Hezbollah, will reportedly include three primary elements, designed to deter the following war for 10 years.[127] One, a large-scale ground operation, is to be launched this time without delay, at the onset of hostilities, in order to rapidly push Hezbollah's short-range rockets, some 95% of its arsenal,[128] out of range of northern Israel. In so doing, the ground operation would reduce what appears to be an absolutely daunting arsenal of some 130,000 rockets to a still a very large, but far more manageable, 10,000 or so.[129] The second element, a massive and precise air campaign against Hezbollah's rockets and other military capabilities is to be tens of times more powerful than the campaign in 2006, with thousands of targets hit each day. Hezbollah's strategic rear, including command-and-control facilities, logistical supply lines, and external sources of support, will also be struck, as will "dual use" Lebanese infrastructure sites, that is, those that abet its war effort.[130] The third element, rocket defense, is to protect Israel's home front and military rear from Hezbollah rocket attacks. These elements appear fully consistent with the more general contours of the Israeli response set out in the 2015 IDF Strategy[131] and would also appear to constitute a general model for Israel's future response to the Hamas threat as well.

The problem, however, is that this response does not provide a truly satisfactory solution to the threats it is designed to address. As already noted, to effectively root out the rockets would require that Israel occupy virtually all of Lebanon or Gaza for a lengthy and bloody period, something no one in Israel wishes to do today, and Hezbollah and Hamas would likely be able to replenish their arsenals within a few years.[132] In the case of Hezbollah, the Israeli home front would also sustain severe damage, for what may be a comparatively short-lived benefit. Moreover, in the power vacuum that may follow a major Israeli operation, Hezbollah and Hamas may be replaced by even more extreme actors, such as ISIS. Both have proven at least somewhat deterrable and, paradoxically, Israel has thus far preferred their ongoing rule, at least in the case of Hamas, over the alternatives.[133] Conversely, should Israel achieve a 10-year lull between rounds, the above-stated objective, this would constitute an effective offensive response.

Israel has created a truly impressive offensive capability against Hezbollah and Hamas, which will undoubtedly cause them unprecedented harm, and which is the basis for the at least limited and tentative deterrence Israel may have gained. The bottom line, however, is that the costs associated with this capability have thus far been deemed to exceed the magnitude of the threat, and the likelihood of Israel actually carrying out major ground operations appears low.[134] As a result, Israel has been forced into an increasingly defensive posture, the IDF's clear preference for the offense notwithstanding, and into temporary stopgaps, designed to "mow the grass."

The Cyber-Response

The cyber-threat has come to occupy an important place in contemporary Israeli defense thinking and has forced Israel to rapidly develop capabilities that have made it a global front-runner in the field.[135] Nevertheless, there is growing concern that Israel's adversaries, especially state actors, will be able to catch up, or at least narrow the technological and doctrinal gaps sufficiently, to undermine its current superiority.[136]

Israel has responded to the cyber-threat on both the offensive and defensive levels and by building up its national educational and technological bases in the cyber-realm. On the offensive level, the IDF has expressed its ability and readiness to use cyber-weapons,[137] if necessary, but has not elaborated on the nature of these weapons and the conditions under which they might be used. The 2015 IDF Strategy states that cyber-defense is vital in both emergency and war situations, in order to ensure the ongoing operation of state institutions and effective IDF operations, and that the IDF would conduct cyber-operations for defensive, offensive, and intelligence collection purposes.[138] As in other spheres, Israel neither confirms nor denies cyber-attacks.

Little is known publicly about Israel's offensive cyber-capabilities, but the following examples are at least illustrative. The (suspected) Israeli cyber-attack that has received the most attention was the Stuxnet virus, reportedly launched in 2010 in collaboration with the United States, which was designed to sabotage Iran's nuclear program by targeting the supervisory control and data acquisition systems used by its uranium enrichment centrifuges.[139] Stuxnet was particularly useful because, unlike kinetic strikes, which can only destroy known facilities, the virus could expand on its own to secret facilities whose existence Israel and the United States suspected, but may not have had firm information about.[140] Moreover, a military strike would have posed a number of major challenges, both operational and diplomatic, whereas Stuxnet provided a unique opportunity to accomplish a vital military objective with minimal risk.[141] In the end, Stuxnet apparently succeeded in causing only a short-lived delay in the Iranian nuclear program, not in derailing it, the ultimate goal. Nevertheless, Stuxnet was likely the first cyber-attack ever to inflict physical damage and thus a milestone in the history of warfare.[142]

Israel has reportedly also worked with the United States to deploy the Flame virus, again to sabotage Iran's nuclear program. Flame enabled Israel to remotely take screenshots, record audio conversations, view network traffic, and likely retrieve information from infected computers.[143] Israel has also been reported to be developing malware for other offensive purposes, including attacks on potential enemies' critical infrastructure.[144] There have also been reports that Israel has penetrated Lebanon's cellular telephone infrastructure for intelligence purposes.[145]

Israel is further reported to have used cyber-tools in support of combat operations, such as the air strike on the Syrian nuclear reactor in 2007 that it is alleged to have carried out.[146] In this incident, the IAF is said to have entered Syria's airspace and bombed the reactor, without alerting its air defenses. Additional reports stated that to accomplish this, it took control of Syrian radar systems and temporarily reprogrammed them into thinking that all was okay even while the attack was underway.[147]

On the defensive level, the IDF has been working to defend its communications and weapons systems and to gather intelligence on parties that might have the ability to infiltrate them.[148] The General Staff's C4I Branch currently bears primary responsibility for defending IDF communications and computer-based systems, but the IDF ultimately plans on establishing an independent "cyber-command,"[149] similar to the existing air, ground, naval, and intelligence services, which would presumably have responsibility for offensive operations, as well. The Ministry of Defense has a cyber-defense body to help protect Israel's defense industry, and the Mossad has, reportedly, also built broad cyber-defense capabilities.[150]

Responsibility for cyber-defense of the civil ministries and agencies lies with the National Cyber Bureau (NCB), which reports directly to the prime minister. The NCB is further charged with securing critical infrastructure against cyber-attacks and recommending policy regarding cyber-space, including development of a national cyber-space security doctrine.[151] Israel has also established a Computer Emergency Response Team (CERT), which focuses on cyber-attacks on the aviation, transportation, health, finance, and energy sectors. The CERT develops cyber-defense guidelines and provides recommendations to government agencies and companies on means of improving their cyber-defenses.[152]

Israel's cyber-defense policy aims to protect not only government networks, but all critical infrastructure, public and private. To this end, criteria have been formulated to determine which infrastructure facilities should be considered "critical" and thus protected, for example, the likely number of people injured in a successful attack, the severity of the economic damage caused, and the impact on Israeli morale. To date, over 80 bodies have been defined as "critical infrastructure," including hospitals, heavy industrial plants, and energy, communications, and transportation systems.[153] The ISA contains a unit responsible for defending against cyber-attacks on critical cyber-infrastructure, as they occur, and for running simulations of attacks so that Israel is prepared.[154] In 2014 it was decided to create a new agency responsible for defending critical networks, major companies, and the public more generally.[155]

Israeli cyber-defense policy further seeks to prevent attacks from happening in the first place, not just to respond to them after networks have been breached.[156] To this end, ISA reportedly has a unit dedicated to tracking potential cyber-threats in order to pre-empt attacks, and Israel has created units that employ hackers to try to breach its defenses, in both the public and private realms, in order to expose potential vulnerabilities and fix them in advance.[157] Israel has also developed systems that identify which Internet service providers (ISPs) and countries are most likely to be used to host attacks (including Turkey, Saudi Arabia, and Iran), and cyber-defenders are given wide latitude in blocking them, even before their responsibility has been fully determined.[158]

Israel conducts drills to help ensure cyber-readiness, to test the effectiveness of its defenses and various contingency plans for cyber-attacks.[159] Given the nature of the threat, Israel conducts extensive international cyber-cooperation, especially with the United States,[160] but was also to conduct joint exercises with the UK.[161]

The IDF offers computer-savvy students the chance to attend one of its technical high schools, which then channel them to cyber-units.[162] In 2012 the IDF graduated its first "cyber-defenders" from a year long program[163] in which they were trained to examine IDF computers and networks in an effort to prevent and detect attacks.[164] Graduates are placed in the air force, navy, intelligence, and communications branches.[165] The IDF C4I Branch has been working with defense industries to create cyber-simulators that train military personnel to protect critical military assets and networks.[166]

An important part of the cyber-response is at the national educational and technological levels. To this end, Israel is attempting to improve enrollment in high school cyber-science classes and has a special program designed to identify and train students with exceptional computer skills. Colleges and universities have also created or expanded cyber-security programs, and private companies offer training to their employees.[167]

As cyber-defense impacts both the civilian and military sectors, Israel seeks to promote close cooperation between the cyber-defense industry and the government,[168] as exemplified by the Advanced Technology Park (ATP) on the campus of Ben-Gurion University. Opened in 2013, ATP created a space in which government officials, academics, corporations, and the IDF can collaborate on cyber-projects, share data and assist each other with personnel, resources, and ideas.[169] Major technology companies have taken notice of Israel's accomplishments in the cyber-realm and established offices in Israel.[170] As of 2014 there were 200–250 startup companies in Israel dealing with the cyber-realm and 20 R&D centers run by multilateral corporations, a number equal to all of the companies in this field worldwide, outside of the United States.[171]

Israel has sought to emphasize its advanced cyber-defense capabilities in the hope that exposure to them will be sufficient to deter potential attackers, both state and nonstate, by demonstrating their limited chances of success and the futility of their efforts.[172] It is not clear, however, how successful this effort has been. To date, Israel has yet to suffer a critical cyber-attack, but the sheer number and persistence of the ongoing attacks suggests that it faces an uphill battle.

Chapter 7 has set out Israel's military responses to the primary threats it faces today. Israel has undertaken a major modernization of its military forces, designed primarily for the threat posed by Iran, but may not have been able to develop a sufficient military option, and, in any event, the possibility of military action has been postponed indefinitely, as long as the 2015 nuclear deal holds. Israel's counterterrorism policy has been a mixture of achievements and failures, successfully enabling it to live in relative security and normalcy and to prosper, but causing a severe deterioration in its international standing. Israel has achieved an effective defensive response to the rocket threat posed by Hamas, but not Hezbollah, which remains the primary threat Israel faces, and does not yet appear to have an effective offensive response against it either. Israel has been at the international forefront of cyber-warfare, both for defensive and for apparently offensive purposes, but like other technologically advanced states, is still struggling to develop an effective response.

Primary Observations

- In the absence of any peer competitors, at least for the foreseeable future, Israel enjoys overwhelming conventional superiority and has significantly cut its conventional forces. The real challenge today stems from asymmetric threats, such as terrorism, rocket fire, cyber-warfare, and, above all, Iran's ongoing nuclear program.
- Iran's nuclear program was the primary focus of IDF modernization programs. Many of the capabilities built can be used against other adversaries; some were specific. Israel's defense leaders strongly opposed an attack on Iran without US approval. It is unclear whether Israel truly intended to attack and what the outcomes would have been.
- The crowning achievement of Israel's counterterrorism policy is that it has reduced the threat to a level its society can tolerate, and enabled it to live in relative security and thrive. Conversely, terrorism has had a major effect on

Israeli public opinion, electoral outcomes, and positions on the peace process, and thus remains a strategic threat nevertheless.

- In future rounds Israel will hit Hezbollah and Hamas massively from the air and will likely also conduct broader ground operations. Nevertheless, it does not yet appear to have an effective offensive response to the threats they pose, at a price acceptable to it, and is not likely to for the foreseeable future. Greater emphasis is thus being placed on defense.

- Conversely, Israel has now enjoyed over 10 years of quiet with Hezbollah, some of which is attributable to the deterrent impact of the 2006 war. If it is able to gain a similar period of calm with Hamas, following the 2014 operation, and again after a future conflict with Hezbollah, Israel will have achieved the limited deterrence it seeks in conflicts such as these and an effective offensive response.

- Israel's rocket defenses largely neutralized the Hamas threat, providing its leaders with greater decision-making latitude and strengthening its societal resilience. For limited threats such as this, they provide a good and cost-effective response. The real challenge is Hezbollah's huge rocket arsenal. Without a nationwide shield, priority will have to be given to the military rear and national infrastructure, not population centers.

- Israel clearly does not want to reoccupy Lebanon or Gaza and topple Hezbollah or Hamas, not because this cannot be done, but because the rocket arsenals will likely be rebuilt once it withdraws, even more dangerous organizations may emerge, casualties will be heavy, the international ramifications significant, and, above all, the benefits transient. Nevertheless, further rounds with both are likely.

- The cyber-threat has forced Israel to rapidly develop capabilities that have made it a global leader in the field. Nevertheless, there is growing concern that Israel's adversaries will be able to catch up, or at least narrow the technological and doctrinal gaps.

Nuclear and Regional Arms Control Policy

Israel does not intend to introduce nuclear weapons, but if people are afraid that we have them, why not? It's a deterrent.
—Shimon Peres, early architect of Israel's nuclear program

I begin this chapter with a special remark. Israel has long maintained a policy that has commonly come to be known as one of "nuclear ambiguity," or "opacity," a policy that the author fully believes was, and remains, the correct approach for Israel. None of the following should thus be misconstrued as in any way confirming or denying reports of Israel's nuclear capabilities. The book would not be complete, however, without at least some reference to Israel's reported nuclear strategy, regional arms control policy, related issues, and some consequent policy questions. The chapter is based in its entirety on open sources, whether factually correct or not, and should be understood as one that is conducted for analytical purposes only.

Under the policy of nuclear ambiguity, Israel neither confirms nor denies having nuclear capabilities and merely reiterates a by-now well-known refrain, according to which "Israel will not be the first country to introduce nuclear weapons into the Middle East." In some cases, it adds that Israel will also "not be the second one to do so." Others argue that Israel's nuclear posture is not truly ambiguous, opaque, or designed to fool anyone, but merely undeclared, what might be better termed a policy of nuclear restraint and hedging.[1]

Nearly five decades after the international community concluded that Israel had become a nuclear power, its assiduous adherence to the policy of ambiguity appears unnecessary, almost childish, to those unfamiliar with the intricacies of international nonproliferation policy. As one observer has written, "Everyone already knows that Israel has the bomb. What then would be the purpose of further belaboring the obvious"?[2] Or as another has stated, "By now Israel's possession of nuclear weapons is well known to friends and foes alike."[3] In practice, the policy of nuclear ambiguity, as developed over the years, if not as originally conceived, is probably one of the best-thought-out and most successful policies Israel has ever adopted.

The policy of nuclear ambiguity and consequent secrecy notwithstanding, much has been written about it over the years, by scholars, practitioners, and journalists, both Israeli and foreign. The following chapter presents a brief overview of some of the salient issues raised in these materials, all of which are readily available in any university library and the media. We do not know, of course, how accurate this information is, but a seemingly coherent picture does emerge.

The chapter begins with a presentation of Israel's purported unconventional capabilities and the reasons it might wish to possess them, as well as the rationale behind the ongoing policy of nuclear ambiguity and potential circumstances under which Israel might consider changing it. It then turns to Israel's policies toward regional arms control agreements and nonproliferation regimes, efforts to prevent the proliferation of WMD through diplomacy, military action, and covert operations, including the so-called Begin Doctrine, and a brief mention of some of the defensive measures Israel has taken. The chapter concludes with some of the major conundrums Israeli policy in this area may face in the future.

Nuclear Policy

Israel's Unconventional Capabilities. Assessments of Israel's capabilities over the years have ranged as high as 400 nuclear weapons,[4] some of which may be of the more powerful hydrogen bomb variety.[5] US intelligence reportedly assessed Israel's arsenal at a stable 80–90 warheads during the 1990s and early 2000s.[6] In 2015 the Institute for Science and International Security, a prestigious American think tank specializing in nuclear issues, estimated Israel's capabilities at 115 warheads.[7] Israel is further believed to have built a second-strike capability based on a "triad" of nuclear weapons deliverable by aircraft and land- and submarine-based missiles.[8] Various reports have named sites in Israel in which different parts of the nuclear program are thought to be located.[9] In addition to the weapons systems themselves, the reports also refer to a national crisis management center for the cabinet, and a similar bunker for the military leadership, which are supposedly safe even from nuclear attack.[10]

There are conflicting reports regarding Israeli capabilities in the areas of chemical and biological weapons. In the chemical area, Israel is believed to have the capability, but not actual weapons. In the biological area, the Arms Control Organization states that no conclusive evidence exists of an Israeli offensive weapons program.[11]

Motivations for the Nuclear Program. Israel's nuclear capabilities, according to Avner Cohen, one of the foremost students of the issue today, are the strategic embodiment of its determination to prevent a second Holocaust, of the vow of "never again." They thus have their origins in Israel's primal existential fears and fundamental sense of insecurity, as a tiny Jewish enclave in the midst of a hostile Muslim world, and were designed as the ultimate guarantor of its survival. Israel's nuclear capabilities were also to be the "great equalizer," which would compensate for its quantitative inferiority in manpower, territory, resources, and more, and were the very embodiment of the classic defense doctrine's emphasis on self-reliance.[12]

Over the years it has been claimed that Israel's purported nuclear capabilities were designed to deter and offset the existential threats posed by the Arab states' far larger conventional forces, the danger that Israel would prove unable to compete with the Arabs in a conventional arms race, and the possibility that it would find itself alone, following a conventional defeat, without support from the outside world. Observers also claimed that they were designed as a deterrent, in the event that Arab states acquired nuclear weapons in the future, and to persuade Arab leaders that they could not destroy Israel without facing assured destruction themselves. Today, with the dissipation of Arab conventional capabilities, the Iranian nuclear program, and other nuclear threats in the future, are presumably the primary focus of Israel's unconventional strategy.[13]

Most observers consider Israel's nuclear capabilities a "doomsday option," to be used only as a last resort if its very survival was at stake. It has thus come to be known as the "Samson Option," the idea that Israel would be willing to do everything possible to ensure its survival, including the threat of devastating retaliation, making an enemy attempt to destroy it the equivalent of national suicide.[14]

The Policy of Ambiguity. Nuclear deterrence can only be achieved if Israel's adversaries believe that it actually has a nuclear capability. The strategic objective of the ambiguity policy, Cohen argues, was thus never total secrecy, but partial and unconfirmed knowledge, sufficiently credible to achieve deterrence, but ambiguous enough to avoid the costs attendant to an explicit nuclear posture.[15] With only a few partial and limited exceptions over the decades, including a possible slip or two of the tongue,[16] Israeli leaders and officials have assiduously adhered to the policy of ambiguity. Some observers, however, maintain that Israel has also made veiled statements and intentional leaks that essentially confirmed its nuclear status, spread information (some deliberately incorrect) to bolster its nuclear deterrence or deter Saddam Hussein from attacking Israel with nuclear weapons in 1991, and indicated that it has a second-strike capability.[17]

The policy of ambiguity initially began as an improvisation but rapidly developed into an elaborate national concept written in doctrinal form in the 1970s.[18] Numerous reviews of the policy have reportedly been conducted ever since, including one after the Indian and Pakistani nuclear tests in 1998, all of which concluded that ambiguity still best serves Israel's strategic interests. The highly regarded Meridor Report, mentioned in chapter 6, probably the most comprehensive governmental review ever conducted of Israel's overall national security strategy, also recommended that Israel continue to adhere to the ambiguity policy for as long as possible.[19]

The Rationale for Ambiguity. The ongoing policy of nuclear ambiguity is an outgrowth, first and foremost, of Israel's relations with the United States and specifically of two historic meetings between Israeli and American leaders. During the first meeting, in 1963, between President Kennedy and Shimon Peres, then the deputy minister of defense, Peres was caught off guard by an unexpected question regarding Israel's nuclear capabilities. Peres temporized and used the by now familiar formulation, which he had first overheard Ben-Gurion use the year before, according to which "Israel will not be the first to introduce nuclear weapons into the Middle East."[20]

The second meeting, in 1969, between President Nixon and Prime Minister Golda Meir, followed a decade of American efforts to halt Israel's nuclear program. It also came just one year after the signing of the landmark Nonproliferation Treaty (NPT) and a year before it was to come into force. Meir reportedly rebuffed Nixon's repeated demands that Israel sign the NPT, but they reportedly reached a secret and unwritten compromise, confirmed by neither government to this day. Under the terms of the agreement, the United States would no longer press Israel to sign the NPT and divulge and dismantle its nuclear capabilities, and would end the repeated inspections of Israel's nuclear facilities it had conducted throughout the 1960s. In exchange, Israel undertook to refrain from declaring and testing its capabilities, that is, to maintain the policy of ambiguity already extant at the time, and from providing nuclear weapons to third parties, or threatening any other state with them.[21] As Henry Kissinger wrote to Nixon in 1969, in a then classified memo, "The international implications of an Israeli (nuclear) program are not triggered until it becomes public knowledge."[22] A related agreement reportedly defined "non-introduction" as an Israeli commitment to keep the nuclear weapons cores unassembled and under the custodianship of the prime minister.[23]

In effect, the 1969 agreement heralded American acquiescence to Israel's nuclear program and exempted it from US nonproliferation policy, including the universality of the NPT.[24] Given Israel's unique history and strategic circumstances, the United States concluded that the nuclear program was an existential matter for Israel and that it could not deny it the ultimate means of ensuring its survival. It thus adopted a policy of "Do not ask, do not tell" and has kept the nuclear issue separate from all other bilateral matters ever since. Some view US policy in this area as a component of the "special relationship."[25]

A further possible reason for ambiguity, related to American policy, has to do with military aid. One of the reasons the United States supplied Israel with conventional weapons, at least in the past, may have been to reduce its reliance on what the United States perceived to be Israel's nuclear capabilities and thereby increase regional stability.[26] Evron maintains that there was even a tacit bargain, whereby the United States provided Israel with conventional arms in exchange for its ongoing adherence to ambiguity.[27]

Over time, the United States has come to provide political cover and a de facto political shield for Israel's nuclear capabilities in international forums, such as the International Atomic Energy Agency (IAEA) and NPT Review Conferences.[28] Reaffirmation of the bilateral understandings in this area has reportedly become a tradition in the first meeting between a prime minister and each new president. In 1998 Prime Minister Netanyahu reportedly reached an agreement with President Clinton providing for the preservation of Israel's strategic deterrence, in effect, renewed American acceptance of its nuclear program, as long as the state of war with the Arab countries continued and peace agreements had not yet been concluded. Prime Minister Barak received a similar assurance a year later, when Clinton committed the United States to the preservation of Israel's "strategic deterrence capabilities," its "ability to defend itself by itself against any threat," and to consult with Israel in advance of global arms control initiatives. President Obama renewed these assurances in 2009.[29]

Israel's purported nuclear capabilities may actually have important advantages for the United States.[30] Unlike most other US allies today, Israel's strategic circumstances are such that the need for an actual American military intervention on its behalf is not unimaginable. Were the United States to force Israel to forgo what it perceives as Israel's nuclear capabilities, it would have to assume a highly problematic and unwanted strategic and moral burden. Conversely, an independent Israeli nuclear option would relieve the United States of the need to implement this highly costly security commitment, at least in most scenarios, and to serve as the ultimate guarantor of Israel's security. Moreover, Israel, as a democracy, could be trusted to use its potential nuclear capability responsibly. The United States has thus basically accepted Israel's position that changes in its nuclear posture are only feasible after peace is achieved in the region.[31]

Advantages of Ambiguity. Numerous observers have speculated over the years about Israel's reasons for maintaining the policy of ambiguity or, conversely, the consequences of modifying or ending it, should it, indeed, be found to possess the capabilities attributed to it. One obvious consequence is that a significant change in ambiguity would violate the understandings reportedly reached with the United States. Under American law, the nearly immediate consequence, as with any other country thought by the United States to be pursuing a military nuclear program, would be the mandatory imposition of sweeping restrictions on the bilateral relationship and punishing sanctions,[32] including a cessation of military aid and the diplomatic cover the United States had provided Israel in a variety of international organizations, including on the nuclear issue. Economic sanctions would have to be imposed and diplomatic ties would be reduced to little more than the minimum necessary to convey US fury and opposition to the change in policy. Israel, which is so heavily dependent on the United States, could hardly afford this. Ambiguity has thus provided both sides with plausible deniability and enabled them to avoid a head-on collision.[33]

Ambiguity, it has been further argued, has insulated the program from the outside world. No one could intervene because no one knew exactly what was happening. The widespread conviction that Israel is a nuclear power notwithstanding, the international community has no hard proof, and thus Israel could not be fully regarded as a nuclear state.[34]

The policy of ambiguity, when combined both with US diplomatic cover and Israel's careful and responsible stewardship of its nuclear capabilities, has enabled many Western and even non-Western countries to treat it as an exceptional case.[35] Some of the same considerations that animated US policy in this regard, such as a recognition of Israel's uniquely precarious strategic circumstances and a moral commitment to its security following the Holocaust, appear to have also contributed to the broader international acceptance of Israel's status, at least in the case of countries such as Germany and France.

The likely Arab response to a change in ambiguity is a further primary reason for Israel's ongoing adherence to the policy. Syrian President Assad once declared that "if Israel gets nuclear weapons, we shall get them as well." In 2008 the Arab League declared that the Arab states would withdraw from the NPT if Israel admitted to having nuclear weapons but did not commit to destroying them. A former senior Saudi official indicated that Riyad might seek nuclear weapons in response to Iran's and Israel's capabilities.[36] Indeed, an explicit Israeli posture might have united the Arab world against it as almost no other step could and would have exposed Arab leaders to strong domestic pressures to pursue nuclear capabilities of their own. Some did anyway, partially in response to Israel's purported capabilities, but ambiguity made it easier for others to live with them, however grudgingly.[37]

It is not, of course, that these Arab leaders, or their publics, are ignorant of the widely accepted international assessment that Israel is a nuclear power. There is, however, a significant difference between "knowing" something in a general sense, something that no one has ever seen and Israel refuses even to acknowledge, and having it stuck in one's face. The fact that Israel has gone to great lengths to maintain its policy of nuclear ambiguity has helped moderate and contain both the Arab response and nuclear ambitions, even if it has not fully prevented them. Accordingly, ambiguity is believed in Israel to have prevented, or at least significantly postponed, a regional nuclear arms race and to have also reduced the Arab countries' incentive to attack Israel's nuclear facilities.[38]

Ambiguity further enabled Israel to base its strategic posture on its conventional capabilities, rather than nuclear deterrence. Were it hypothetically to adopt an explicit posture, Israel would be accused of violating important international nonproliferation norms and regimes, including the NPT. An end to ambiguity would certainly have made it much harder for the United States to pursue its efforts to stem the proliferation of WMD in the region, and European states, China, and others would presumably have also felt freer to transfer knowhow and materials for nuclear and other WMD to states in the region. An explicit posture would thus have made it easier for the Arabs to pursue nuclear weapons and more difficult for Israel to justify efforts to prevent or delay this through diplomatic and military means.[39]

Some believe that Egypt and other Arab countries have accepted the reality of Israel's nuclear status, at least until a full peace is reached, on the condition that Israel agrees to discuss the possibility of future disarmament and refrains from declaring its status.[40] In the past, ambiguity may have also helped avoid a conflict with the Soviet Union over the issue, provision of Soviet assistance for an Arab nuclear capability, or a Soviet security guarantee for their Arab clients.[41]

The international community and the Arab states believe that Israel's purported nuclear capabilities are intended solely for deterrence and as a doomsday option, not for offensive or aggressive purposes. In effect, Israel is today the only non-NPT state that the world's most influential countries believe to have nuclear capabilities, but which has not been subject to severe pressures to expose its nuclear secrets.[42]

Finally, and most importantly, ambiguity is viewed in Israel as a policy that has allowed it to enjoy the best of all worlds. It enjoys essentially all of the deterrent benefits of an overt nuclear posture, regardless of the true nature of its capabilities, without having to pay the attendant costs.[43]

Not surprisingly, ambiguity is perceived in Israel as a great success, and there exists a virtually wall-to-wall consensus within the defense establishment, political leadership, and public at large in favor of its continuation.[44] Zeev Schiff, a highly respected Israeli military analyst, once stated that if Israel had a national award for strategy, it should have been given to those who invented the policy of ambiguity.[45] A number of observers have noted that the Israeli public attaches such importance to the nuclear issue, for existential reasons, and has been so successfully socialized to the policy of ambiguity, that it prefers not even to discuss the issue, which is considered to be outside the sphere of legitimate public discourse.[46] In practice, this is only partially true. Some public and especially academic discussion of the issue does take place.

A Possible End to Ambiguity. Israeli proponents of an end to ambiguity are few, and virtually all have voiced only conditional support. Shai Feldman, an early proponent, believed that Israel should have combined an explicit nuclear deterrence posture with a willingness to withdraw from the territories acquired in the 1967 war. Had Israel done so, Feldman argued, the balance of deterrence would have swung in its favor. Any major Arab attack would have threatened Israel's survival, making it clear to them that they could only contemplate its destruction at an enormous risk to themselves and rendering the Israeli nuclear deterrent credible.[47]

Feldman further maintained that an overt posture would minimize the dangers of war through misunderstanding, would lend greater credibility to Israel's capabilities, in contrast with ambiguity, which left too much room for uncertainty, and would facilitate development of a coherent Israeli doctrine for the use of nuclear weapons, thereby reducing the danger of misuse during crises, when leaders do not have time for deep deliberation. An overt posture, he further argued, would facilitate the communication of intentions, costs and thresholds, which is key to a mutually shared code of nuclear conduct, but which is impossible if the parties' capabilities are undisclosed. It would also enable socialization of Mideast elites to the realities of life in a nuclear region, thereby increasing Arab awareness of the costs of a conflict with Israel and moderating policies calling for its destruction. Similarly, an overt posture would reduce pressures in Israel to take frequent preventive action and increase the willingness to withdraw from most of the 1967 territories. Thus, the socialization process would also lead to greater strategic stability.[48]

In the decades following the publication of his highly regarded book, Feldman has somewhat modified his views, which were appropriate to the conditions existing at the time. Today, he believes that Israel's nuclear posture is no longer "ambiguous," but rather "undeclared," and consequently that the marginal advantages associated with an overt posture are questionable.[49]

Reuven Pedazur argued that Israel should change its posture gradually, in coordination with the United States, but that this would only be feasible in the context of a comprehensive peace agreement and if Israel agreed to end production of fissile materials. Yair Evron averred that Israel would have no choice but to adopt an explicit doctrine of nuclear deterrence, if an enemy state acquired a nuclear capability. Shlomo Brom and Gerald Steinberg have also raised the possible need to reconsider ambiguity in these circumstances.[50]

Cohen, in contrast, has argued that Israel would gain little if it ended ambiguity in response to Iran's crossing of the nuclear threshold and would actually risk much, including even more widespread nuclear proliferation in the region and an unraveling of the global nonproliferation regime. Conversely, he has noted that ambiguity makes it hard to conduct meaningful regional arms control talks and for Israel to become a fuller and more responsible partner in the international nonproliferation regime. Cohen therefore advocates a gradual loosening and even end to ambiguity, in the mid to long term, as part of a regional peace process.[51]

Arguably the most outspoken advocate of an end to ambiguity—outside of the international arms control community—is an American academic, Louis-Rene Beres, who has written extensively about Israel's nuclear strategy. He, too, maintains that the timing for change should be linked to Iran's possible crossing of the nuclear threshold. The objective, according to Beres, would not be to reveal what he believes to be the obvious, that Israel has the bomb, but to strengthen its nuclear deterrence in two ways: first, by removing any lingering doubts that Iran, or any other nuclear enemy in the future, might still harbor about Israel's nuclear resolve and, second, by convincing it that Israel's nuclear capabilities are both invulnerable to a first strike and capable of penetrating its defenses. To this end, Beres advocates a selective and gradual release of information regarding Israel's nuclear capabilities and strategy. He also advocates adoption of a countervalue strategy, rather than a counterforce one (targeting population centers and other high-value targets, for deterrence, as opposed to enemy nuclear forces, for nuclear war-fighting purposes), along with the dispersion, multiplication, and hardening of its arsenal. He believes that a selective end to ambiguity is also needed in order to make the "Samson Option" credible.[52]

Some consider India and Pakistan to be precedents for Israel. Like Israel, these observers claim, India and Pakistan have not signed the NPT, but unlike Israel, they have chosen to openly declare their status as nuclear weapons states and even conduct nuclear tests in 1998. The result was the imposition of sweeping American and international sanctions on both countries, which were lifted in the end after just over two years. India, approximately a fifth of humanity, simply proved too big and important to sanction for long, and once the decision had been made to lift sanctions from India, there was no justification for keeping them on Pakistan.

In fact, the alleged precedent for Israel is limited. Israel's dependence on the United States bears no comparison to India's or Pakistan's, and "just" two years of American and international sanctions would impose a burden on Israel that it could afford, if at all, only in truly extreme circumstances. Feldman has argued, however, that the likely US punishment of Israel, such as a termination of military aid, would be ineffective in a case such as this, in which Israel would clearly have been acting out of desperation and taken the American response into account. The United States would thus stand to lose whatever remaining influence it had over a crisis situation, and termination of conventional military aid might force Israel to adopt a primarily nuclear strategic posture, thereby lowering the threshold for use of nuclear weapons, a clearly counterproductive outcome from the US perspective.[53]

For these reasons, especially given the long-standing American commitment to Israel's security, Feldman concludes that the United States would rapidly come to focus on how to cut its losses and that its response to an Israeli declaration might be less severe than otherwise thought. Moreover, it could be argued that the circumstances of the Israeli declaration could have a significant impact on the nature of the American response. If, for example, it was coupled with Israeli willingness to make major concessions on the peace process, was a response to a declaration by one of Israel's adversaries that it had acquired nuclear capabilities, or was made on the eve of an Arab attack that threatened Israel's destruction, the American response would be more muted.[54]

Finally, a number of Israeli proponents of an end to ambiguity have linked this to issues having to do with the quality of Israeli democracy and questions of regulation and safety. They argue that ambiguity has resulted in deficient parliamentary oversight of a matter of vital importance and in the absence of free and open public debate on the issue, also important in a democracy. Moreover, they argue that regulatory and safety problems may arise in organizations long used to working behind a veil of secrecy.[55]

The Utility of Nukes for Israel. A nuclear capability would provide Israel with the ability to threaten its adversaries with unacceptable punishment in retaliation for a threat to its survival. The sheer magnitude of the expected punishment, it has been argued, would make it nearly certain that Arab states, or Iran, would correctly assess the damage they would suffer and thereby remove challenges to Israel's survival from the range of acceptable options open to them. It might also be useful to deter a chemical or biological threat and to offset Arab conventional military superiority.[56]

Although Israel would presumably always prefer to refrain from the use of nuclear weapons, some scholars have noted that this possibility cannot be entirely discounted and that Israel might be forced to do so in a variety of scenarios: for example, in response to a nuclear first strike against it, an accidental or unintentional nuclear attack, a case of nuclear terrorism, or as a weapon of last resort following a defeat of its conventional forces. These scholars claim that Israel might even be forced to make pre-emptive use of nuclear weapons to prevent an enemy from acquiring nuclear or other WMD, from launching chemical and biological attacks against it, from escalating from conventional to unconventional warfare, or from one form of unconventional warfare to another (e.g., chemical warfare to biological, or biological to nuclear), and to support conventional preemptions against enemy nuclear and even nonnuclear assets.[57]

One potentially powerful argument in support of a nuclear option is that Israel's purported nuclear capabilities convinced the Arab states that its destruction was no longer a viable option and thus led to the Egyptian and Syrian decision to pursue only limited military objectives during the Yom Kippur War. Moreover, it has been argued that it was the recognition that Israel could not be destroyed that forced Arab states to come to terms with its existence, conduct the negotiations that ultimately led to peace with Egypt and Jordan, and refrain from using WMD against Israel, for example, during the 1991 Gulf War. For these and other reasons, some believe that Israel's purported nuclear capabilities have contributed significantly to a reduction in the intensity of the Arab-Israeli conflict and to greater regional stability and security.[58]

Others have a less charitable view and believe that Israel's nuclear capabilities may have had the opposite effect of that intended, increasing the motivation of some enemy states to acquire nuclear and other WMD capabilities of their own and lending their efforts greater legitimacy. Both Iraq's and Iran's nuclear programs, they argue, were at least partially motivated by what these countries perceived to be Israel's capabilities, and presumably Syria's, as well. Indeed, they believe that Israel's nuclear capabilities may have accelerated the unconventional arms race in the region, encouraging some states to pursue nuclear weapons, while others made do with a "poor man's" deterrent in the form of biological and chemical weapons and ballistic missiles. The contention that Israel's nuclear capabilities limited Egypt's and Syria's military objectives during the 1973 war is also disputed by some, who believe that this can be explained by their perceptions of Israel's conventional military might, or that their objectives were limited to begin with.[59]

To be truly effective, nuclear deterrence would have to convince Israel's adversaries that a first strike would always be irrational, that is, that the costs would greatly exceed the benefits. To this end, enemy states would have to be convinced that Israel not only possessed the capacity to retaliate with nuclear weapons, but the willingness to do so, and that its capabilities are both invulnerable to a first strike and have an assured capability of penetrating their defenses.[60]

A number of scholars have considered whether Israel should prefer a countervalue or counterforce nuclear strategy. A countervalue strategy would be designed to cause the enemy massive destruction by targeting cities and other major civilian sites and would require only a small and not necessarily accurate missile arsenal. A counterforce strategy, conversely, designed for nuclear war-fighting purposes, would require a larger number of accurate weapons, capable of penetrating hardened sites. Since the threshold for use in a countervalue strategy would presumably be far higher, it might be perceived by an enemy as less credible than one designed for counterforce purposes. It has thus been suggested that Israel might wish a mixed force.[61]

If, hypothetically, Israel ever actually used nuclear weapons, there would undoubtedly be massive international pressure on it to dismantle its capabilities ("use them and lose them"). This then raises the question of the credibility of an all-out nuclear response in the face of anything but an existential attack and whether Israeli might therefore wish to have the capacity to respond at lower levels, with a proportional nuclear response, or other types of weapons systems.

Given Iran's obvious awareness of Israel's presumed nuclear capabilities, and of the devastating price it would pay for a nuclear attack against it, many Israeli strategists today attribute greater plausibility to a nuclear attack stemming from miscalculations during crises, accidental or unauthorized launches, and nuclear terrorism than to unprovoked "out of the blue" ones. Moreover, some fear that MAD (mutually assured destruction), the basis for US-Soviet nuclear stability, could prove destabilizing in the Middle Eastern context. The differences in territorial and population sizes and the absence of channels of communication among the parties make this especially worrisome in the case of Israel and Iran.[62]

There are a number of other fundamental differences between the US-Soviet nuclear rivalry and a potential one in the Middle East, which further fan Israeli fears of an Iranian nuclear capability. Neither the United States nor the Soviet Union had territorial claims against the other, and the conflict was over influence and control in distant regions. Both the United States and the Soviet Union were characterized by high levels of social and political stability, which ensured that transfers of power were relatively smooth and that control over nuclear weapons would not be jeopardized by political turmoil. Both sides also had highly developed command, control, and communication systems, as well as assured second-strike capabilities, in the absence of which they might have been motivated to pre-empt.[63] None of these conditions necessarily exist in the Middle East.

Furthermore, neither the United States and the Soviet Union, nor India and Pakistan, sought the other's destruction. Indeed, the superpowers went to great lengths to prevent a nuclear showdown, including the establishment of a direct hotline between the leaders, when they grew concerned that the existing channels of communication (ambassadors, military attaches, and more) might not prove sufficient in a crisis. India and Pakistan have diplomatic relations and multiple channels of communication. Iran and other potential nuclear powers in the region seek Israel's destruction and do not maintain any channels of communication with it, or often with each other. Neither the United States nor the Soviet Union was a theocracy, whose rationality may be somewhat different than that of secular states. Moreover, the US-Soviet balance was bipolar, whereas in the Middle East a number of nuclear powers may emerge, thereby severely complicating the difficulties of crisis management. The greater the number of nuclear actors, the greater the dangers of devastating miscalculation.

Further complicating the picture, the short distances involved in the Middle East provide for only very short response times. In a multinuclear Middle East, it might not even be possible to determine which state had launched an attack, and

the short response times before the first wave of incoming missiles hit would increase the motivation to ensure a second-strike capability, but also to pre-empt
and launch a first strike. In an asymmetric nuclear balance, the stronger side
might wish to use its superiority while it lasts, while the weaker side might view
a first strike as the only means of overcoming its disadvantage. Iran and other
potential nuclear powers in the region might also be tempted to extend nuclear
deterrence to others,[64] or to further proliferate to them.

Nonproliferation and Regional Arms Control Policy

Israel is threatened by WMD more than any other state in the region and thus
has a great interest in international agreements and regimes designed to prevent their proliferation. Indeed, Israel views regional WMD disarmament as a
"coveted end-state" and is formally committed to an ultimate Middle Eastern
WMD-free zone in a variety of policy statements.[65] On the other hand, arms
control agreements have repeatedly failed to prevent states in the Middle East
from developing WMD programs, even though they were signatories to them,
and Israel believes that they have simply proven irrelevant to regional realities to
date and for the foreseeable future. Israel's attitudes toward nonproliferation and
regional arms control agreements have, therefore, been mixed.[66]

Israel has not signed the NPT, even while expressing strong support for it
and global efforts to prevent the proliferation of WMD generally.[67] Israel has
also not signed the Biological Weapons Convention (BWC). It has signed, but
not ratified, the Comprehensive Test Ban Treaty (CTBT) and the Chemical
Weapons Convention (CWC). Israel observes the terms of the Missile
Technology Control Regime (MTCR), which bans the export and import of
certain types of ballistic missiles, but has not been accepted as a member state
due to its refusal to sign the NPT.[68]

Israel seeks to counterbalance this problematic stance and to demonstrate
its support for international nonproliferation norms and regimes in those cases
where it believes that it can do so without undermining its national security. To
this end, it has long taken an active role in the IAEA and the Comprehensive
Nuclear Test Ban Treaty Organization, including the establishment of three
seismic monitoring stations in its territory, as part of the treaty's global
monitoring system. Israel has harmonized its nuclear export control legislation
and regulations with the guidelines adopted by the Nuclear Suppliers Group
(NSG), a voluntary grouping now numbering 48 states, which refrains from
sales of civilian nuclear materials and technologies to countries that pose proliferation risks. It also adheres to the Convention on the Physical Protection of

Nuclear Materials and to the IAEA's safety standards. Israel signed the CWC even though Egypt and Syria rebuffed its demand that they do so as a precondition for Israel's signature. In 2013–2014 Israel played an active role in the informal talks designed to prepare an international conference on a Middle East nuclear weapons-free zone, despite deep reservations regarding the wisdom of the initiative.[69]

Israel has sought to further bolster its nonproliferation credentials by pursuing an agreement with the NSG, under which it would be recognized as "a responsible state with advanced nuclear technology." The Israeli proposal draws on the exemption granted to India, which agreed to place its civil nuclear facilities (but not military ones) under international supervision and which was allowed to procure nuclear materials and technologies in exchange. If agreement is reached, Israel would become eligible for sales of civilian nuclear materials and technologies from NSG members and, for all practical purposes, nearly a recognized nuclear power, even though it is not an NPT signatory. To date, the United States and other members have rebuffed Israel's entreaties, claiming that the timing is not right.[70]

Israel's hesitance to sign the various global nonproliferation regimes stems from a number of considerations. Israel argues that it is simply unrealistic to expect that it, or any other state, would join the various regimes at a time when many other regional states are still in a state of war with it and refuse to even negotiate, or to consider measures needed to ensure ongoing stability and coexistence. One could also view the Arab position as an attempt to strip Israel of any capabilities it may possess, without commensurate reciprocation. Moreover, Israel argues that what is needed is not just agreement on nuclear disarmament, an area in which the Arabs believe that it holds the advantage, but comprehensive WMD and ballistic missile disarmament, which would bring Arab and Iranian WMD programs into play as well.[71]

Israel further stresses that a number of states in the region have intentionally deceived the international community and undermined arms control agreements by systematically cheating, for example, signing the NPT and then developing nuclear weapons programs. Indeed, four of the five violations of the NPT to date have occurred in the Middle East (Iraq, Iran, Syria, and Libya). Some states in the region have also used chemical weapons, including Iraq (a signatory to the CWC), Syria, and Egypt. For reasons of verifiability, Israel is therefore deeply concerned about the feasibility and effectiveness of global nonproliferation regimes in the Middle East and believes that they have not proven an adequate response to the threats it faces.[72]

Instead, Israel supports the adoption of special regional disarmament arrangements that, it hopes, would include more robust verification regimes. These regimes would be negotiated by the states in the region themselves and be based on a step-by-step process, designed to build confidence between them, reduce tensions, and achieve comprehensive regional peace. Arms control, under this approach, would be the final result of an incremental process designed to transform the security situation in the region and lead to peace and normalization, rather than being the first step and a precondition, as the Arab side has demanded.[73]

The CWC, the most far-reaching arms control agreement yet adopted, which provides for the complete elimination of this type of weaponry and for highly intrusive inspections, poses a particular set of concerns for Israel. For example, Arab states or Iran might request inspections at the nuclear reactor in Dimona on the false pretext that Israel had hidden chemical weapons there, but really as a backdoor means of trying to understand its nuclear capabilities. Israel has thus maintained that it cannot afford to ratify the treaty as long as Arab states have chemical weapons and do not join the CWC. Israel, officials noted, would have to observe the convention once ratified, whereas Iran and Syria, among others, feel no such compunction.[74]

In the past, Israel strongly opposed the Fissile Missile Cutoff Treaty (FMCT), which provides for an end to the production of all fissile materials by member states. Some have speculated that Israel might be able to accept the treaty if limited to future production, as originally formulated, rather than existing arsenals.[75] Prime Minister Netanyahu, however, reportedly reacted unambiguously when the issue was raised in 1998, informing President Clinton that Israel "will never sign the convention and do not delude yourselves, no pressure will help. This convention touches on things that are at the basis of our existence and we will not commit suicide."[76]

Israel apparently feared a slippery slope if it agreed to discuss the FMCT before fundamental political change had taken place in the region. The Arab states would likely argue that the FMCT was not a sufficient substitute for a nuclear weapons-free zone (NWFZ) and that it would legitimize what they perceive to be an Israeli nuclear monopoly. Rather than considering Israeli adherence to the treaty a major step forward, they would view it as an opportunity to present further demands designed to erode what they suspect as Israel's nuclear capabilities and achieve a NWFZ. One informed source maintains that Israel's policy toward the treaty has become one of "reluctant tacit support."[77]

Prevention and Counterproliferation

Prevention and counterproliferation have long been a primary component of Israel's nuclear strategy. The heart of this has been an intensive, decades-long diplomatic and PR effort designed to inform leading international actors and their publics of Arab and Iranian WMD programs and to convince them of the threat they posed not only to Israel, but to international security. Facing an international community that has often been deeply unattuned to issues of WMD proliferation, an important part of the effort has simply been the provision of intelligence regarding the status of the various programs and analyses of the intentions behind them. Israel had much to share, and its intelligence agencies enjoyed significant credibility.

In meetings with foreign officials and in public statements, all of the premiers in recent decades, and most other senior officials, have given high priority to the dangers of WMD proliferation in the region. Indeed, efforts by Israel and its supporters in the United States contributed to the decision to impose unilateral American sanctions on Iran as early as 1996. Israel later waged a broad international campaign against the Iranian nuclear program that contributed significantly to the imposition of severe international sanctions on Iran in 2012. The efficacy of the 2015 Iran nuclear deal is a subject of debate, but it was in many ways the culmination of over two decades of Israeli diplomacy and set the Iranian program back by several years at least.

Israel's role in regard to the Iraqi nuclear program was similar, if less significant. Here, too, however, its diplomatic efforts, supported by intelligence sharing and public diplomacy, contributed to the prolongation of sanctions on Iraq. In both cases, Iran and Iraq, diplomacy may have had a more lasting impact on their WMD programs than military action would have.

Numerous press reports have referred to covert Israeli operations designed to sabotage, delay, and derail enemy WMD programs. Some have also referred to targeted killings of Iranian nuclear scientists, others to explosions at Iranian nuclear and missile sites. The Stuxnet virus, reportedly a joint US-Israeli covert cyber-attack, which led to the destruction of Iranian nuclear centrifuges and to the postponement of Iran's program by an unknown period,[78] is the most famous of these efforts.

Perhaps the ultimate manifestation of Israel's counterproliferation policy is the so-called Begin Doctrine.[79] Named for the prime minister who ordered the air strike that destroyed Iraq's nuclear reactor in 1981, the term has come to refer to a general Israeli commitment to prevent any hostile state in the region from acquiring a military nuclear capability. Referring to the Iraqi nuclear program, Begin stated that "another Holocaust would have happened . . . we shall defend our people with all the means at our disposal. We shall not allow any enemy to develop weapons of mass destruction turned against us."[80] Then-defense minister Sharon stated that "Israel cannot afford the introduction of nuclear weapons (into the Middle East). For us, it is not a question of a balance of terror, but a question of survival. We shall, therefore, have to prevent such a threat at its inception."[81]

In addition to the acknowledged destruction of the Iraqi reactor in 1981, Israel is widely thought to have conducted the air strike that destroyed the Syrian reactor at al-Kibar in 2007,[82] a second case in which the Begin Doctrine appears to have been implemented. Much press speculation surrounded the question of whether Israel would take military action against the Iranian nuclear program. This further potential manifestation of the Begin Doctrine has yet to happen, and the nuclear deal of 2015 makes it increasingly unlikely, at least as long as Iran refrains from a major violation thereof. Nevertheless, Prime Minister Netanyahu has continued to warn that Israel will not allow Iran to go nuclear.[83]

Defensive Measures

A final component of Israel's unconventional response is defense, both active and passive. These measures have been discussed at length in chapter 7, but let it suffice to recount here that Israel has developed a multilayered antimissile and antirocket shield, based on the Iron Dome, Magic Wand and the Arrow system. In addition to such active defenses, many homes in Israel today have shelters and sealed rooms that provide at least partial protection against chemical attacks. Israel has also distributed gas masks to the entire population in the past.

Needless to say, missile defenses could mitigate the effects of a nuclear attack on Israel, but not eliminate them. If even one nuclear missile penetrated an otherwise completely effective defensive system, the outcome would be catastrophic. Defensive measures against chemical and biological weapons, on the other hand, would be far more effective.

Conclusions and Conundrums

The policy of ambiguity means that Israel does not behave like a nuclear power. Unlike India and Pakistan, which have adopted explicit nuclear postures and tested, Israel would probably also prefer not to be one. Indeed, it ultimately even aspires to a Middle East which is free of WMD. This is certainly a far-off eventuality at this time, and the strategic exigencies of the Middle East leave it with little choice but to take measures to defend itself, while adopting a healthy skepticism toward the very disarmament agreements that it supports in principle.

Israel continues to face a uniquely harsh external environment, including the possible emergence of Iran and other regional actors as nuclear powers. Even assuming that the 2015 nuclear agreement holds, Iran will be better positioned to renew its military nuclear program in 2025–2030 and "break out" in a relatively brief period, should it be willing to incur the international costs of doing so at that time. In some ways, it is already better positioned to do so. The sanctions regime has been lifted, renewing international efforts to prevent Iran from going nuclear will be difficult and time-consuming, and the likely efficacy of the inspections regime provided for by the agreement is also the subject of debate. Furthermore, the de facto international recognition of Iran as a nuclear threshold state may encourage other actors in the region to begin military nuclear programs of their own.

Israel must therefore prepare both for the day after the agreement expires and for its potential violation by Iran long before then, as well as the possible emergence of additional nuclear actors, declared or undeclared, and various possible ambiguous or partial stances. Indeed, when it comes to its nuclear posture, Israel must seek to make decisions today that will still be appropriate decades hence, in what will almost assuredly be very different strategic circumstances. As in all cases of strategic planning, the question is how Israel aspires to position itself at that time and how to best achieve this. Even before this, the foremost question Israel faces at this point is how to try to make sure that Iran never crosses the nuclear threshold and that it never reaches these critical decision points.

In addition to preventative diplomacy, Israel faces the following primary options. Some may be pursued in tandem.

Option 1: Preserve Nuclear Ambiguity, Seek Gradual Legitimization

Decades after Israel is thought by the international community to have become a nuclear power, the policy of ambiguity has proven a resounding success. Some regional actors may have pursued WMD programs in the past at least partly in response to what they perceived as Israel's capabilities, but for various reasons they have largely been dismantled, and Iran's nuclear program was motivated primarily by fear of Iraq, later the United States, and today a drive for regional hegemony, not Israel's alleged capabilities. Possible Saudi and other nuclear programs, should they emerge in years to come, will similarly reflect a fear of Iran, not Israel. Moreover, limited diplomatic pressure aside, the international community, even the Arab world, has learned to live with Israel's exceptional status and is convinced that it is a nuclear power, irrespective of its actual capabilities.

Ambiguity thus truly appears to have enabled Israel to enjoy all of the deterrent benefits that would have accrued from an overt posture, without the attendant costs. If, hypothetically, Israel's possesses the capabilities attributed to it, any further deterrence to be gained from an end to ambiguity would appear to be marginal at best, at least for the foreseeable strategic circumstances.

It is also hard to envision what additional deterrent advantages of significance Israel would gain were it to end the policy of ambiguity because Iran crossed the nuclear threshold or a multinuclear Middle East emerged. Regional actors already consider Israel a nuclear power. Moreover, the regional and international ramifications of revealing its nuclear secrets would still be significant even in these mitigating circumstances and might be perceived as reckless and even aggressive. There may, however, as explained subsequently, be some benefit to a limited and selective easing of ambiguity in these circumstances.

Israel may face growing pressures in coming years to join the NPT, but no insurmountable problems are likely to arise as long as it maintains US backing. As the years go by, Israel's purported nuclear capabilities have gained a form of de facto legitimization, and it can take various measures to further strengthen this, such as signing or ratifying those arms control agreements that it does not deem a danger to its interests. This option is in accord with Israel's long-established policies and appears feasible.

Option 2: End Ambiguity

A second option, which might be likely only in the event that all other diplomatic and military measures fail to prevent Iran from going nuclear, is to acquiesce to the new reality, end ambiguity, and base Israel's policy on what its enemies would perceive as mutually assured destruction (MAD).[84] Adoption of an approach such as this would be contingent on the assumption that Iran is a rational actor, a likely assessment based on its behavior over the years, but one that is compromised by the radical and theocratic nature of its regime and which thus introduces an element of doubt regarding the presumed stability of MAD-based deterrence.

Moreover, under the cover of what Iran would perceive to be a MAD balance, it would be able to pose a variety of severe, if less than existential, threats to Israel, and even limited confrontations would risk the danger of escalation and possible Iranian use of nuclear weapons. Conversely, the overarching need to avoid such confrontations would serve as a constraint on the actors' freedom of maneuver, including Iran's ability to threaten Israel with ballistic missiles.

A decision to end ambiguity need not necessarily be a binary, black or white one. Even a partial and indirect indication of some of Israel's capabilities and of select dimensions of its nuclear doctrine might suffice to achieve the goal of heightened deterrence. For example, Israel could hint at or leak partial information regarding the invulnerability of its capabilities to a first strike, or their ability to penetrate enemy defenses.[85]

If the stability of MAD in the Middle Eastern context is questionable in a bilateral nuclear balance with Iran, it would be highly doubtful in a multilateral one. A multinuclear Middle East, in which the regimes involved are either radical theocracies or unstable authoritarian ones, with poor or nonexistent channels of communication, is a potentially unmanageable nightmare scenario and recipe for nuclear disaster. MAD, which is based on an assumption of rationality and the ability to convey intent and capabilities, is thus not an attractive option, as necessary as it might prove in certain circumstances.

Even if one assumes rationality and the possible effectiveness of a MAD balance, the need to end ambiguity, or even just ease it, would reflect a significant change for the worse in Israel's strategic circumstances and also fly in the face of fundamental strategic beliefs in Israel. The prospects of this happening, even in the event that Iran or some other state crosses the nuclear threshold, are unclear. The anticipated international response, primarily the American one, and the Arab response, would presumably be critical factors.

Option 3: Covert Operations, Military Action, or Both

Such efforts would be designed to destroy, or at least postpone, the Iranian nuclear program or others in the future. The fact that Israel has not, at the time of this writing, taken military action against the Iranian nuclear program has already raised doubts regarding the applicability of the Begin Doctrine in this critical case and whether Israel actually had any alternative but to accept the less than fully satisfactory diplomatic agreement reached with Iran in 2015. Similarly, the apparent inability of covert operations attributed to the United States and Israel, to date, to set Iran's nuclear program back by more than a few years, despite the considerable efforts invested, is at least some indication of the difficulties that might be encountered in the future as well.

The possible development or acquisition of nuclear weapons by additional regional actors might present an even more difficult set of considerations should Israel seek to uphold the Begin Doctrine in the future. The primary candidates are Saudi Arabia, Egypt, and Turkey. Given their proximity to Israel, the primary problems are not operational.[86]

Saudi Arabia, which possesses some 25% of the world's oil reserves and is the Keeper of the Holy Places (Mecca and Medina), sacred to the entire Muslim world, is a US ally that has enjoyed a de facto American security guarantee for decades. To attack a Saudi nuclear facility would thus be very different from doing so in the case of a rogue state such an Iran, Iraq, or Syria. Moreover, were Saudi Arabia to pursue a military nuclear program, even covertly, this would indicate a calculated willingness to risk the consequences of a rupture with the United States.

Turkey, even under President Erdogan, is far from being an enemy state, despite the ugly tenor of relations. Moreover, Turkey is a member of NATO, with its second largest military (after the United States), and as such enjoys a collective security guarantee from all members of the alliance. In the absence of a dramatic further downturn in Turkey's attitude toward Israel and in its international standing generally, Israel would be hard pressed to even object to a Turkish nuclear program, let alone launch an attack against it.

Egypt has been at peace with Israel for four decades and remains a US ally, despite the tensions in the bilateral relationship in recent years. Israeli diplomatic objections to an Egyptian nuclear program, in the absence of demonstrable proof at a level approaching a "smoking gun," would have severe repercussions and would be highly problematic even then. An attack would cause not just a rupture with Egypt, but possibly a confrontation with the broader Arab world, as well. Moreover, as in the case of Saudi Arabia, an Egyptian military nuclear program would indicate a calculated willingness to risk the consequences of a rupture with the United States.

Military action against Iran may still be required. Doing so without US approval, however, which was clearly lacking during the Obama era, and in the face of serious operational challenges, would make this option highly problematic. This may change under President Trump. A strike might also achieve the opposite of that intended and actually lead to a decision by Iran to accelerate its efforts and rapidly cross the nuclear threshold. Even the militarily more effective possibility of an American attack would gain a hiatus of no more than a few years, unless repeated as necessary. In any event, a military strike against Iran appears to be unlikely as long as the nuclear deal is deemed to be holding.

Option 4: A US Security Guarantee

This option might be a means of further bolstering Israel's own deterrent capabilities ("extended deterrence") and of eliminating any residual doubts that Iran, or any other nuclear power in the region in the future, may still harbor regarding the assured destruction they would face in a nuclear crisis with Israel. The pros and cons of an American security guarantee are analyzed in detail in chapter 10 and will not be repeated here. As an addition to Israel's own purported strategic capabilities, not a substitute, a US security guarantee might prove to be a necessary and even effective means of deterring a nuclear Iran.

Option 5: Regional Alliance and Security Guarantee

The United States might form an alliance with the Saudis, small Gulf states, and possibly Egypt and Jordan, formal or even just declared, designed to dissuade Iran from crossing the nuclear threshold by presenting it with a united regional front and demonstrating the strategic isolation and military threat it would face if it did so. The alliance would also include a US security guarantee in the event that Iran did succeed in crossing the threshold, but the primary aim would be to prevent this from happening, and thus might include a joint commitment to act militarily if need be. European and other states, for example, Turkey, might be asked to join in a coalition of the willing as well. In all likelihood Israel would not be a part of such an alliance, at least not formally or publicly, but obviously has a part to play in American strategic planning in this regard and possibly in encouraging the emergence of such an option. Israel would presumably prefer not to be constrained by the exigencies of a regional alliance and to have a bilateral American security guarantee, but there might be benefits to this as a further strengthening factor.

Option 6: Regional Disarmament, WMD-Free Zone

One of the gravest decisions that Israel may ever have to make is whether to maintain its purported nuclear capabilities if and when Iran (or some other regional actor) goes nuclear, or to seek an agreement on regional arms control and ultimately disarmament.[87] In other words, would Israel prefer that both it and Iran have nuclear weapons, or that neither has them? Despite the grave consequences, some believe that Israel would prefer the former option, at least as long as the nuclear balance remained bilateral.[88] Israel's distrust of Iran, based on its well-founded experience that regional actors cannot be counted on to observe the arms control regimes they have signed, might outweigh all other considerations. Israel would face an even greater dilemma in the event that a multinuclear Middle East emerges, in which case the prospects for stable MAD would truly be dim.

In the long term, Israel truly prefers a Middle East free of weapons of mass destruction. Unlike India and Pakistan, it does not wish to be a nuclear power or view this as a source of national stature, and its approach is solely utilitarian, not an objective in its own right. Given the existential enmity that Iran and some Arab countries continue to manifest toward Israel, however, their WMD programs and aspirations, past and present, as well as the turmoil in the region today, the very idea of nuclear disarmament (or of all types of WMD, as Israel prefers) appears out of context, almost fanciful. Nevertheless, the potential change in the nature of the nuclear threat, from rogue states to US allies and even countries friendly to Israel, the need to minimize the extreme dangers of nuclear instability, and the limitations of the options presented above, such as the Begin Doctrine, indicate that heretofore unimaginable options may have to be considered in the future, including both a regional declaration of capabilities and an American security guarantee.

Primary Observations

- Israel's nuclear potential is the ultimate embodiment of the principle of self-reliance. If Israel has the nuclear capabilities attributed to it, an enemy seeking its destruction would have to be willing to risk a devastating response, presumably eliminating this as a viable option.
- Ambiguity has been highly successful. Israel appears to enjoy the benefits of an overt nuclear posture without the costs, and the United States and much of the world have apparently come to terms with the reports of its capabilities. Ambiguity has also enabled Israel to base its strategic posture on its conventional capabilities rather than nuclear deterrence.
- Israel's relations with the United States and the likely international and regional responses have greatly shaped the policy of ambiguity. An end to ambiguity would trigger US law, requiring sweeping sanctions, as well as international sanctions, and would make it easier for Arab states and Iran to pursue nuclear programs of their own.
- Should Israel possess nuclear capabilities, this may actually be advantageous for the United States, relieving it of the practical need to serve as the ultimate guarantor of Israel's security. The United States appears to believe that changes to Israel's nuclear posture are only feasible after peace is achieved in the region and shields Israel from hostile initiatives in international forums.
- Fundamental asymmetries in territorial and population size, the nature of the regional regimes, and absence of channels of communication, may make MAD inappropriate to the Middle East. In a multinuclear Middle East, it might not even be possible to determine who had launched an attack, and short response times would increase the motivation to ensure a second-strike capability, but also to strike first.
- International nonproliferation regimes have repeatedly failed to prevent regional states from developing WMD. Israel supports comprehensive regional WMD agreements with robust verification measures. Regional arms control would be the outcome of an incremental confidence-building process, not a precondition thereof.
- Israel has conducted an intensive, decades-long diplomatic and PR effort to prevent regional WMD proliferation. Its efforts contributed significantly to the imposition of American and later international sanctions on Iran, and the 2015 nuclear deal was, in many ways, the culmination thereof. Diplomacy may have delayed the Iranian nuclear program longer than military action could have.
- The Begin Doctrine, under which Israel destroyed the Iraqi and, reportedly, Syrian reactors, is the ultimate manifestation of its counterproliferation

policy. Barring a major Iranian violation of the 2015 deal, it is increasingly unlikely it will be able to uphold the doctrine in the future.

- Even assuming that the nuclear deal holds, Iran will be better positioned to "break out" in 2025–2030 than it was prior to the agreement, indeed, already is. Israel must prepare both for its expiration and possible violation long before then, as well as the possible emergence of additional nuclear actors. A multinuclear Middle East is a nightmare scenario.
- One of the gravest dilemmas Israel may ever face, if Iran or other regional actors go nuclear, is whether to prefer that all sides retain their existing capabilities or that none do and to pursue regional arms control. Israel would face an even greater dilemma if a multinuclear Middle East emerges.
- Seemingly unnecessary and even fanciful options today, such as an end to ambiguity, a defense treaty with the United States, or regional disarmament, may have to be considered in the future.

The Foreign Policy Response

Small states do not have a foreign policy, only a security policy.
—Moshe Dayan

Israel has no foreign policy, just domestic policy.
—Henry Kissinger

Kissinger's famous quip is an exaggeration, of course, as is Dayan's, but both contain more than a kernel of truth. In Israel, as in other democracies, maybe more so, domestic politics certainly have an important impact on foreign policy. Given the primacy of defense affairs in Israel's national security thinking, however, many observers have traditionally held that its defense policy essentially is its foreign policy.

The chapter begins with an attempt to identify the primary characteristics of Israel's foreign policy, as distinct from its defense policy, and to show how they have evolved over time. It then presents a brief overview of Israel's primary foreign relations with countries around the world today. Together, they comprise the equivalent of a "foreign policy response," similar in intent, if not substance, to the many military responses Israel has developed to cope with the threats and opportunities it faces. Given the vast importance for Israel of its relations with the United States, they are addressed separately in chapter 10.

Israel's Foreign Policy: Primary Characteristics

A Historic Legacy and Primal Sense of Insecurity

To understand Israel's foreign policy is to comprehend a historic mindset. For its people and supporters around the world, Israel is more than just another state among many, but the culmination of a long, rich, and often bitter history, and of a 2,000-year-old dream of national redemption. Not surprisingly, "The nineteen centuries from Masada to Maidanek,"[1] as Israeli political scientist Aharon Klieman has so eloquently put it, weigh heavily on Israel's leaders, the public, and foreign policy.[2] In truth, Israel's historical memory goes back much further, to the destruction of the First Temple and earlier, and it is being written to this very day, with the searing contemporary experiences of the bitter dispute with the Arab countries and Iran, terrorism, and international opprobrium.

The long history of persecution, culminating in the Holocaust, has imbued Israel's national psyche with a fundamental sense of insecurity. For two millennia, life in the diaspora was an ongoing struggle for survival, and the fear of extermination, as demonstrated by the Holocaust, was not just some abstract notion, but very real. Israel's encirclement by enemies openly avowed to its destruction, with greater populations, resources, and, at least in the early decades, military power, magnified the deep-seated sense of insecurity and led to the basic Israeli assumption that the nation faced a constant existential threat. The resulting "siege mentality," "Masada complex," and "Holocaust syndrome," various characterizations attached to Israel, all reflect this primal fear and consequent national preoccupation with survival and security, the foremost driving factors behind Israeli national security policy to this day.[3]

When foreign leaders visit Israel, they do so not only as the heads of their respective governments, but also as the representatives of collective histories, as ambassadors of memory. Leaders of countries such as Poland, Russia, Ukraine, Hungary, Romania, and above all, of course, Germany, cannot visit Israel as they do any other country, but carry with them the burden of a long history—in the case of Spain, from the 15th century.[4] Israeli leaders, similarly, carry with them the Jewish memory of the relations with these countries when on visits abroad. Even if most day-to-day relations are conducted on a pragmatic basis, the historical baggage is always there.

The historical memory of persecution, helplessness, and extermination and consequent preoccupation with security have led to the preeminent role played by the IDF in Israeli society. The IDF is not just another national military, whose sacrifices accord it the reverence common to militaries in many countries, but a unique embodiment of national rebirth and the guarantor of the nation's existence. Following the Nazi extermination, the Jewish people desperately needed to demonstrate that they were more than just defenseless victims and could ensure their own security. For Jews everywhere, not just in Israel, the IDF's successes were evocative proof that centuries of Jewish victimhood were finally over.[5]

A corollary of the sense of national isolation is the exaggerated reaction to any sign of friendship or estrangement from other countries. With the memory of the French "betrayal" in 1967 still imprinted in Israelis' minds, they are especially obsessed with the constant need to be recognized by the United States as an unalterable strategic asset. As Abba Eban once observed, Israel suffers from an ongoing "hypochondriac fear of an imminent collapse in American-Israeli relations."[6] The exaggerated need for friendship was manifest in Israel's all-out embrace of Turkey in the 1990s, the first Muslim country to have a strong diplomatic, economic, and even military relationship with Israel, and conversely, in the severe sense of rejection after the relations suffered a significant downturn in the 2000s. All countries experience ups and downs in their foreign relations; for Israel they are personal and visceral.

Even today, some seven decades after Israeli independence, at a time when Israel has become a regional power and arguably more secure than ever before, the importance of this primal sense of insecurity cannot be overstated, and Israel cannot be understood in its absence. It is a perceptual prism through which all issues of importance are viewed. Prime Minister Netanyahu, for example, repeatedly alluded to 1938 and the eve of the Holocaust when speaking of the Iranian nuclear program, Eban spoke of Israel's "Auschwitz borders" to describe its tenuous pre-1967 security situation, and during the First Lebanon War Prime Minister Begin famously compared PLO leader Arafat to Hitler cowering in his bunker in Berlin.[7] The fundamental sense of insecurity is so deeply imbued that all of Israel's military victories, probably no level of military might, could ever alleviate it, or the fears of "dwelling alone" and of imminent annihilation.

Promoting Zionism and the Interests of the Jewish People

Israel is the only Jewish and Zionist state among the numerous Christian, Muslim, and other nations of the world. Although it pursues a primarily statist foreign policy, similar to other nations, in which the raison d'état is preeminent, Israel's unique character has a significant effect on its foreign policy. The following section addresses those elements of Israel's foreign policy that can be considered uniquely Jewish and Zionist and some of the changes that have taken place in them over the years.

A Nation with a Mission. Israel was established with the express purpose of being a Jewish state; indeed, this remains its raison d'être, and maintaining and securing its existence as such is the overriding objective of Israeli national security policy. As a Jewish and Zionist state, Israel's national mission includes constituting a refuge for Jews the world over, gathering in the exiles from all far-flung parts of the Jewish diaspora and thus encouraging immigration, assisting Jewish communities in distress, and comprising the spiritual and cultural center of contemporary Jewish life.[8] As Israeli political scientist Yehezkel Dror has so aptly put it, Israelis and many diaspora Jews share a sense that Israel is "special" in ways that cannot be fully expressed by words, that they are participants in a great historic enterprise of the rebuilding a unique new-old state and assuring the future of the Jewish people, and that their efforts are part of a "sacred" mission, with and without the religious connotations.[9]

Over the decades, as Israel's existence has become an established reality and the controversy regarding some of its policies has increased, the lure of Zionism has faded somewhat for many Jews in Israel and the diaspora. Following the mass emigrations of Russian and Ethiopian Jewry, few Jews now live in countries in which they are oppressed, and while Israel plays an important emotional role for Jews the world over, it only partially constitutes a spiritual and cultural center for most.

Promoting Immigration. The ingathering of the Jewish exiles remains one of Israel's fundamental objectives as a nation, the very embodiment of Zionism. Israel is thus one of the few countries in the world today that not only encourages immigration (*aliyah*), but does so for ideological reasons, without regard to immigrants' socioeconomic background. Moreover, it is the only country in the world for whom the promotion of immigration is a primary foreign and defense policy objective.

Israel has gone to great lengths and expended substantial resources over the years to promote immigration. Doing so from undeveloped countries, such as Ethiopia in the 1980s and 1990s, or from Yemen in the past, which required large-scale covert operations to smuggle immigrants out, including emergency air- and sealifts, made little socioeconomic sense. The absorption of a million Russian immigrants during the 1990s imposed a huge burden on an already overtaxed national economy and infrastructure. None of these cases, however, or others, were the subject of domestic economic controversy, since the consideration was ideological, not utilitarian. Israel worked for long years to achieve the right of Syrian Jews to leave the country[10] and supplied arms to Morocco, Argentina, and Romania to secure the right of Jewish emigration.[11] Romania also received hundreds of millions of dollars in "compensation for investments in education" in exchange for the freeing of its Jewish community.[12] A thousand Jews were smuggled out of Sarajevo in 1994.[13]

Israel's efforts to promote immigration have had a significant impact on its relations with the countries directly involved, other countries, and Jewish communities. Until the early 1990s Israel was forced to provide military and later economic aid to Ethiopia in order to secure the right of Ethiopian Jews to emigrate to Israel.[14] The United States was also involved in the contacts with the Ethiopian government and in the airlift that ultimately led to their arrival in Israel. Israeli policy toward the Soviet Union and later the Russian Federation has certainly been affected by considerations of its possible consequences for the Jewish population. In the 1980s, after the Islamic Revolution, Israel managed to smuggle thousands of Jews out of Iran, partly by supporting its war effort against Iraq. In the 1970s difficulties arose both with Austria (the transit country) and with the American Jewish community over the question whether Russian Jewish émigrés, who had been granted exit permits on the assumption that they were immigrating to Israel, should be allowed to settle elsewhere, at the expense of those truly waiting to depart for Israel.[15]

Promotion of immigration is an active policy conducted by state institutions. Israel sends emissaries abroad to encourage immigration, including from prosperous and secure diaspora communities, such as the US, UK, and Australia, and provides immigrants with generous financial incentives to facilitate their acclimatization and absorption. Immigration promotion is not just an ideological commitment, but a practical tool of national security strategy—the larger Israel's population, the stronger the state and its military capabilities.[16] In recent years, however, following the mass immigrations from the former Soviet Union and Ethiopia, and as the Jewish communities with the greatest potential for immigration have dwindled, the issue has lost much of its salience.

A Unique Relationship with Diaspora Jewry. A small majority of the world's Jews still live in the diaspora, although Israel has overtaken the United States as the single largest Jewish community. Of all of the countries in the world with large diaspora communities (Greece, China, and India to name a few), none have ever gone to the lengths Israel has to promote a return to the homeland, protect them, or forge such close ties. The Zionist presumption, however, has always been that Israel's well-being is the foremost interest of the Jewish people. Thus, when conflicts have arisen between Israeli interests and those of diaspora communities, the former have usually been accorded precedence. Moreover, diaspora interests do not have a significant constituency in the Israeli decision-making process.[17]

The political and economic support provided by the diaspora extends Israel's national security far beyond its own resources and is a vital strategic asset. The American Jewish community is, of course, the primary case in which diaspora influence has become an extension of Israel's power. The massive support that Israel has received from the United States over the years, military, economic and diplomatic, is a result of numerous factors, but there is no doubt that the political influence of the Jewish community, so carefully cultivated, accounts for much of it. Jewish political influence is far less prevalent in other countries, but has also played a role at times. Diaspora financial support has been significant over the decades, but has declined in more recent times both in absolute terms and especially as a percentage of Israel's growing economy.

For existentially angst-ridden Israel, living in a world of changing strategic interests and alliances, diaspora Jews have always been considered Israel's one truly dependable ally. In recent years, however, changes have begun to manifest themselves in the relationship. Most diaspora Jews today live in the West and many are deeply affected by the currents of opinion regarding Israel typical of their home communities. As the older generation of the Holocaust and the heroic period of Israel's early decades has passed away, and as criticism of Israel has grown, a growing number of diaspora Jews have begun to share some of the criticisms themselves and feel uncomfortable with what was previously largely unquestioning support for Israel. Most young diaspora Jews, in particular, are less interested and committed to Jewish organizations and pro-Israel activity.[18] Nevertheless, the overall Israel-diaspora bond remains an important factor in Israel's strategic calculus, especially in times of crisis.

The Israeli-diaspora relationship has always been reciprocal, but this too has begun to change. During Israel's early decades its survival was the primary preoccupation of the Jewish people throughout the world. Today, Israel is increasingly secure, but also increasingly concerned about the survival of the diaspora.[19] Assimilation and intermarriage are major challenges to the future of the diaspora and, as such, to its vitally important contribution to Israel's national security. Nowhere is the problem more apparent than the American Jewish community.

Protecting Jewish Communities and Interests Abroad. In terms of the diaspora communities, Israel's primary security function is as a haven, but it has also assumed limited responsibility for the safety of imperiled Jewish communities around the world, in some cases providing basic security guidance and training.[20] Extreme care is exercised lest Israel be accused of intervening in the domestic affairs of foreign countries, and there is also a danger that well-meaning security assistance can be misconstrued as a matter of dual loyalties and end up harming the Jewish community it is designed to assist.[21] In recent years, the number of diaspora communities requiring security assistance in order to cope with anti-Semitism has diminished, while those requiring counterterrorism assistance has grown. In 2016, for example, Israel provided warnings to the Turkish Jewish community about possible terrorist attacks.[22]

Israel also acts, at times, as a moral voice in regard to anti-Semitism and other issues of interest to the Jewish people. In 2000 Israel brought its ambassador to Austria home for consultations and announced a reassessment of bilateral relations after a radical right-wing politician joined the governing coalition. The cabinet also expressed concern and issued a strong condemnation. In 2002 Prime Minister Sharon, concerned by the rise of anti-Semitic incidents around the world, especially in Europe, directed the Foreign Ministry to turn to the relevant governments and demand action. In 2014 Israel expressed concern over rising anti-Semitism in Hungary and in 2015 succeeded in initiating a General Assembly session devoted to the rise of anti-Semitism around the world.[23] Acts such as these, however, tend to be isolated events, not part of an ongoing involvement in the issue of anti-Semitism, which Israel leaves primarily to the Jewish organizations abroad.

The West Bank, or Judea and Samaria. In no area has the Jewish and Zionist impact on Israeli foreign policy been more pronounced in recent decades than on the future of the West Bank, or Judea and Samaria, including the settlements. Indeed, these issues cannot be understood otherwise. The debate about the future of the West Bank is not just about security, but fundamental beliefs regarding Israel's mission as a state and the nature and aims of Judaism and Zionism.

One school of thought, a territorial one, believes that Israel should try to gain control over as much of the historic Land of Israel as possible, and that the more Israel succeeds in doing so, the more Jewish and Zionist it will be. For this school of thought, settlements are an expression of the fundamental Jewish claim to the Land of Israel, with Palestinian concerns to be accommodated primarily through domestic autonomy or self-rule. Many in this camp have, however, come to recognize that Israel will not be able to maintain control over all of the West Bank.[24]

A second, societal school, does not ignore the historic Jewish link to Judea and Samaria, but stresses the composition of Israeli society, rather than territory, as the decisive factor. For demographic reasons, the societal school argues, an Israel that encompasses more territory in the West Bank would not be more Jewish and Zionist, but the opposite: it would become a binational state and force Israel to choose between its Jewish and democratic characters. Settlements are thus viewed as counterproductive and a threat to Israel's future,[25] though most people in this camp have come to accept that the three primary settlement blocs will remain a part of Israel, in exchange for territorial swaps with the Palestinians. Ongoing divisions over the future of the West Bank have partially paralyzed Israel's foreign policy and certainly had a highly deleterious impact on its international standing.

The divide on the future of the West Bank is indicative of the broader division in Israeli strategic thinking, between the truly pragmatic and the ideologically driven. Jerusalem, the spiritual center of all Jewish identity since antiquity, is an issue of particular ideological and religious importance for all.

No Overarching Strategy

Israel does not have a formal foreign policy doctrine, much as it does not have a defense doctrine. Unlike the defense area, however, few attempts have even been made to develop a foreign policy doctrine. Israel's foreign policy, indeed, its national security generally, is thus conducted in the absence of an overall strategic formulation or construct. As noted, Israel does not formulate major policy statements, such as the American National Security Strategy, Presidential Policy Directives, Quadrennial Defense Reviews, or British White Papers, which set out broad policy objectives and strategies. As a result, the national security decision-making process is focused on the here and now and on responses to specific challenges, rather than attempts to realize a coherent strategy. Israel enjoys the benefits of pragmatic, ad hoc, and flexible decision-making, along with the disadvantages associated with a comparatively uninstitutionalized policymaking system.[26]

Diplomacy as an Instrument of Defense Policy

Israel gained rapid diplomatic recognition during its early years, but diplomatic successes have become few and far between ever since. The importance of diplomacy soared in the 1990s, as the peace process with the Palestinians and Syria got underway, but the talks failed and Israel's international delegitimization has grown in recent years. The seemingly immutable hostility Israel faces in the UN and other international organizations, and ongoing criticism from Western countries, which are often unrelated or disproportional to the actions it has taken, contributes to the diminution of the foreign policy component of Israel's national security policy.

As a result, Israeli diplomacy retreated over the years into a defensive siege mentality, with minimalist goals. Much of the focus came to be on holding the line and arresting a further erosion in Israel's international standing, legitimacy, and positions, rather than promoting Israel's interests. Small decreases in the number of countries supporting any one of the myriad array of anti-Israeli resolutions in the UN and elsewhere, or minor changes in the text thereof, came to be seen as significant victories. In these circumstances, most Israeli officials have largely given up on diplomacy, and it has become, at best, an instrument designed to support the defense effort and minimize disruptions to it, rather than the reverse,[27] the normal state of affairs.

Making matters worse, diplomatic options in Israel's uniquely harsh strategic environment are few, rarely appealing, and often not politically feasible. This unfortunate reality has further contributed to the development of a national mindset that favors the use of military force, believes that even complex political problems can be resolved through military means, and is biased against the efficacy of noncoercive measures as a means of accommodation with Israel's adversaries.[28]

Further adding to the subordination of diplomacy to defense considerations is the chronically weak stature of the Ministry of Foreign Affairs (MFA) in the Israeli decision-making process. Most foreign ministers have been appointed in recent decades for reasons of coalition politics, not personal expertise or even interest in the area. Moreover, the defense establishment and Prime Minister's Office have gradually encroached on the MFA's areas of responsibility, leading to its growing marginalization. The premier, for example, has largely taken over issues of importance pertaining to relations with the United States, Russia, Egypt, and Jordan, the peace process, and Iran. The IDF, too, plays a major role in these issues and, given the importance of Israel's defense ties, has spearheaded relations with strategically important countries, such as the United States, Russia, China, India, and Turkey. The MoD is the primary player in relations with Egypt. According to press reports, the Mossad was given responsibility for coordinating policy regarding the Iranian nuclear program, including the extensive diplomatic activity this required, and the Atomic Energy Commission has also been deeply involved.[29] The list goes on. The MFA has been further weakened by the establishment of largely artificial ministries for reasons of coalition politics, such as the ministries of Regional Cooperation and of Strategic Affairs.

In these circumstances, the MFA typically finds itself left with responsibility for those issues and countries that other players are not interested in, or for explaining Israeli policy abroad, a mere mouthpiece, with limited involvement in policy formulation. Although the Winograd Commission of Inquiry recommended in 2008 that the MFA be strengthened both organizationally and in terms of its role in the national decision-making process, little has changed; if anything, its stature has further deteriorated.[30]

The defense establishment, especially the IDF, remains the most influential bureaucratic player, with the most highly developed policymaking capabilities by far. No other power center can compete, certainly not the MFA. The defense establishment's capabilities are a vital asset; it is the weakness of the civilian agencies, including the MFA and National Security Staff, that is the problem.[31]

The MFA has a total of approximately 1,000 employees, of whom 600 work at the headquarters in Jerusalem (professional diplomats, clerical and support staff) and 400 are diplomats posted in over 100 missions abroad. The MFA's budget in 2012 says it all; the total budget was approximately $137 million, of which the overwhelming majority was for fixed costs, leaving just $37 million dollars for everything else, including public diplomacy (*hasbara*), media outreach, economic affairs, diaspora relations, and foreign aid, which had a paltry budget of just over $10 million.[32]

Pragmatism with Strong Ideological Elements

Israel's foreign policy has been overwhelmingly pragmatic, but at times also displays strong elements of ideology and faith, far beyond that typical of Western democracies. In some historical situations, it has been argued, careful and rational planning can actually be counterproductive, leading to self-defeating prophesies and paralysis, whereas unwavering adherence to national dreams, to an "unattainable future," can help make them possible. At times, especially during the early decades, when considerations of pragmatism would have counseled caution and even immobility, Israel's leaders had to make leaps of faith based on the force of will, a historic sense of destiny, and a willingness to take the risks necessary to overcome objective assessments of Israel's capabilities.[33] It has long been said, wryly, that anyone in Israel who does not believe in miracles is simply not a realist.

A precarious balance between hardheaded realism and ideology is thus a basic feature of Israeli national security policy. The entire Zionist project, Israel's very establishment, against all odds, was based on will, ideological romanticism, and a sense of destiny, not pragmatic considerations of relative power.[34] In more recent decades, no one could have predicted that the 2003 war in Iraq would have saved Israel from a presumed Iraqi WMD threat, which could potentially have been coordinated with the Iranian, Libyan, and Syrian WMD programs, or that the Arab Spring would then lead to the demise of the latter two countries and programs. Similarly, no one could have predicted that the collapse of the Soviet Union would result in a nearly 25% increase in Israel's Jewish population and in the realization of Ben-Gurion's dream of a population of five million Jews (now some 6.5 million), which he believed would be sufficient to ensure the nation's existence. Many religiously inspired supporters of Israel settlement policies are clearly imbued with this ideological romanticism.

With the exception of a few isolated decisions, however, such as the establishment of the state, and a very small number of select issues, usually limited to matters having to do with the future of the West Bank, Israeli decision-making has been characterized by an overwhelmingly pragmatic approach. Israel assisted Soviet Jewry covertly in order to avoid antagonizing an already hostile superpower and did not, in fact, do everything it could have done to help secure Jewish emigration, leaving it to diaspora Jewry to spearhead the effort. Israel refused for many years to recognize the Armenian genocide and discouraged American Jewish organizations from doing so, in order to promote relations with Turkey in the 1990s.[35] Although defined as an existential threat, Israel has not attacked the Iranian nuclear program. Day-to-day management of the conflict with the Palestinians, Hezbollah, and Hamas has been free of ideology and driven by essentially pragmatic considerations, as well. Even the highly charged issues of the future of the West Bank and the settlements, the preeminent examples of ideological decision-making, have been handled with relative pragmatism; Israel has never officially annexed the West Bank, an act that even right-wing governments understood would not be tolerated by the international community, and has pursued the settlement policy in a gradualist and at times covert manner, in order to minimize international opposition.

Promoting Legitimacy and Acceptance

On one level, Israel's foreign policy has actually been quite successful. In the early years Israel enjoyed a great deal of international favor, based on sympathy for the historical circumstances of its birth, especially the Holocaust, as well as the unremittent Arab hostility; indeed, Israel was commonly viewed as a David to the Arab Goliath. Consequently, Israel rapidly achieved the recognition and support of the world powers and became a member of the UN shortly after its establishment.

In 2016 Israel had diplomatic relations with 158 countries, including extensive economic and military ties. Egypt and Jordan made peace with Israel and bilateral security cooperation has reached new levels. Syria and the Palestinians have conducted intensive and advanced, if ultimately unsuccessful, negotiations with Israel, and a number of Arab countries would clearly like to establish ties if and when sufficient progress is achieved with the Palestinians to provide the necessary political cover. A partial thaw is already underway with some. Israel has a special relationship with the United States and strategic relationships with a few more. Given a long-term perspective, Israel has thus made important strides toward fulfilling its objective of becoming an accepted part of both the international arena and the region.

Conversely, seven decades after its establishment, Israel faces a severe problem of diplomatic warfare and delegitimization around the world. The campaigns underway against Israel were addressed at length in chapter 4 and will not be repeated here.

Wielding "Soft Power"

Eminent American political scientist Joseph Nye defines "soft power" as a country's ability to achieve its goals through the attractiveness of its culture (e.g., literature, art, education, mass media, scientific and economic prowess), the justness and moral authority of its political ideals (such as human rights, equality, and democracy), and the quality of its policies, both domestic and foreign, rather than by the imposition of costs and fear of consequences, that is, coercion. The more universal the values the country represents, the greater their appeal, and consequently its soft power.[36]

Israel enjoyed great soft power in its early decades and still possesses some today, much for certain groups. The horrors of the Holocaust created an international wave of sympathy and support for the Jewish people, and Israel, indeed, has become an international symbol of the ultimate evil. It is not by chance that Israel succeeded in gaining independence just three years and one week to the day after the end of the war in Europe. Seven decades later, the Holocaust still remains a source of sympathy and legitimacy for Israel, and many cite it as a reason for a Jewish state.

The heroic struggle of Israel's early years, of the Zionist pioneers who reclaimed the ancient land and made the barren desert bloom, gathered in the exiles, both the remnants of European Jewry and those from the Arab countries, all the while fighting to defend themselves against Arab marauders, was the subject of many a book, story, movie, song, and art. The saga of the "Exodus," made into a novel, movie, and music, was a highly idealized symbol of Israel's struggle. The dramatic stories of the ingathering of the exiles, whether those smuggled out of Europe during and after World War II, the "Magic Carpet" airlift from Yemen in the early years, or in more recent times, the daring sea and airlift of Ethiopian Jewry, Operations Moses and Solomon, are all the story of legend.

Israel's early decades were also characterized by the attempt to build a new, just, and almost revolutionary society, based on utopian values of equality, social justice, humanism, and socialism. The kibbutz (collective commune), never truly more than a small part of Israeli society, came to symbolize the young, pioneering, and morally just new state and the Zionist enterprise as a whole. Israeli democracy and egalitarian values were widely respected, and Israel viewed itself, and was seen by many around the world, as a "light unto the nations." Its moral authority was considerable for decades.

Israeli development projects, especially in the areas of agriculture and water, were emulated in many Third World countries, either through bilateral cooperation programs, or when thousands of students from these countries returned home from training programs in Israel in the 1950s. Israel's military victories, up to and including the Six Day War, were a source of international admiration. They were also a balm for the souls of Jews worldwide, who saw in them the ultimate revenge against the Nazis, proof that Jews were not destined to be helpless victims and a symbol of the new "fighting Jew." Jews around the world cheered, cried, and rejoiced all at once upon Israel's rebirth and continue to celebrate its annual independence day, with the warm support of many Gentiles.

The decades of occupation following the Six Day War, however, and especially the settlement movement, have fundamentally transformed Israel's image. Whereas Israel was once viewed as the underdog and enjoyed international sympathy as a result, it now appears to be the Goliath to the Palestinian David. Today Israel is viewed by much of the international community as an aggressive occupying power, bent on possessing Palestinian lands and denying their rights, and has completely failed to convince the international community of its claim to Judea and Samaria, the West Bank.[37] The Palestinians, who have repeatedly rejected dramatic peace proposals, never presented a peace proposal of their own, and are governed by a dictatorship in the West Bank and a radical theocracy in Gaza, are winning most of the soft power battles today.

Israel's image has also been tarnished by questions relating to the quality of its domestic policies and democracy, such as the power and excessive prerogatives of the ultra-orthodox community, the status of Israeli Arabs, and rise of a radical right wing in Israel. As Israel has evolved into a competitive market economy, its economic gaps have become among the widest in the developed world.

Some of the international criticism, but certainly not all, stems from an unfair double standard; people expect more of Israel. When it acts in ways that appear harsh and unjust, but are often little different from other countries' behavior, it violates their expectations. Israel was deeply criticized in the past for conducting "targeted killings" of Palestinian terrorists. Yet this became the standard modus operandi of the Obama administration against al-Qaeda and ISIS, and to a lesser extent the Bush administration before it.

Nevertheless, as Israel approaches the beginning of its eighth decade, it still enjoys many sources of soft power. The tragic and epic story of Israel's rebirth and early decades has faded, but still remains vivid for many around the world, certainly of older generations. Jews around the world still harbor a deep sense of identification and caring for Israel's travails and support it in numerous ways, monetary, political, emotional. Christians around the world view Israel as the Holy Land, a continuation of the biblical story and realization of divine scripture. Israel's vibrant, chaotic, cacophonous democracy, for all of its faults, stands out in a sea of Middle Eastern autocracy and theocracy. Israel's military victories are still a source of admiration for many, who often attribute to Israel capabilities far beyond its true power.

In an era in which Israel has become far better known internationally for its scientific and technological prowess, as the "start-up nation,"[38] many people still buy Jaffa oranges, an outdated symbol of Israeli agriculture in the early decades, or fly El Al, long a fully privatized company, out of a sense of identification and commitment. Today, businesspeople and scientists from around the world come to Israel seeking the technological creativity and solutions they cannot find elsewhere, and numerous multi-national corporations have established research centers in Israel. Israeli academics are among the most widely published in the world, and five Israeli scientists were awarded Nobel prizes in the last decade alone. Israeli medicine, agriculture, water, and cyber-technology, among other areas, are among the most advanced in the world. Israeli literature, music, and art enjoy an international reputation.

Arguably nowhere is Israel's soft power better expressed than in the vast support it has received over the decades from the United States. US support is certainly the result of hardball politics in Congress, in which the pro-Israel lobby has gained great influence, but it draws its fundamental strength from the broad support Israel enjoys among the American public as a whole, without which it could not have continued for decades. We address this issue in detail in chapter 10, but let it suffice to say here that 62% of Americans in 2015 said that their sympathies lie with Israel, only 16% with the Palestinians.[39] The Jewish community numbers less than 2% of the total population. Tens of millions of evangelical Christians are passionate supporters of Israel, as are many other groups. In recent years some 16,000 people have attended the annual conference held by AIPAC, "the Israel lobby," in an outpouring of support. The very fact that Prime Minister Netanyahu could have challenged the Iran nuclear deal in Congress in 2015, in unprecedented opposition to a presidential foreign policy initiative, an act that many found deeply misguided, reflected his (over)confidence in the soft power Israel enjoys in the United States.

Soft power is typically of limited efficacy as a direct instrument of policy. It is hard to influence other countries and sway their policy just because they feel a sense of warmth and identification toward another.[40] Nevertheless, no country should be better attuned to the advantages of soft power than Israel, which at least partially owes both its independence and vast American support to it to this day. Moreover, Israel has succeeded in closing many a deal with foreign leaders and officials over the years, not as a direct result of its soft power, but because in situations in which they could have chosen more than one option, their sense of identification with Israel was the final consideration that swayed them in its favor. In recent decades Israel has generally ceded the battle for "soft power" to its adversaries.

Promoting Superpower Alliances, with Strategic Autonomy

As already noted in chapter 1, Israel has always sought to secure at least one patron from among the major international powers, in order to ensure diplomatic, economic, and strategic support and, above all, ongoing access to weapons. Conversely, Israel has also sought to maintain strategic autonomy, that is, the will and capacity for independent action, even in the face of opposition from outside powers. One of the greatest successes of Israeli foreign policy to date has been the strategic relationship with the United States,[41] which has certainly provided it with generous support in all of the above areas while allowing Israel to maintain a modicum of strategic autonomy.

Superpower support for major military operations has also been deemed vital. In 1956 Israel went to war after reaching agreement with France and Britain on what was essentially a coordinated operation. Ever since 1967 Israel has only launched major military operations following close consultation with the United States. Chapter 10 provides a detailed account of the lengths Israel has gone to ensure American support for its military actions, along with an analysis of the ramifications of Israel's dependence on the United States.

Pursuing Peace, but Security above All

Israel's strategic exigencies, ever since its establishment, have led to a situation in which defense considerations have eclipsed almost all others. During the early decades, the overarching objective of Israeli foreign policy was the struggle to obtain and ensure the ongoing supply of weapons. This objective was largely achieved in the 1980s with the establishment of a stable military procurement relationship with the United States, thereby creating new space for diplomacy. Many countries remained hesitant to establish formal relations with Israel, however, and most of the Arab countries, which had refused to have any contact whatsoever for decades, continue to do so. Peace has always been the fundamental goal of Israeli foreign policy, but has appeared ephemeral and elusive, leaving defense considerations at the forefront.

In recent years there has been considerable criticism of Israel's policies regarding the peace process with the Palestinians, not only from the international community, but from within Israel itself. While some of the criticism is certainly warranted, it is only part of the picture and does not do justice to the highly proactive role some of Israel's leaders have taken in recent decades in the attempt to promote peace.

Former Egyptian president Sadat is rightly remembered for his dramatic visit to Israel, but it was repeated overtures by Prime Minister Begin that paved the way for the Sadat initiative. Rabin, as premier in the early 1990s, initiated talks with the Syrians and Palestinians that led to a decade of highly intensive, if ultimately unsuccessful, negotiations. In the talks with Syria the outlines of an agreed peace agreement were negotiated, based on an Israeli withdrawal from the Golan Heights, in exchange for security arrangements, diplomatic relations, and "normalization." Rabin also negotiated the dramatic Oslo Agreement with the Palestinians, ending decades of a mutual refusal to recognize the other's right to exist, and setting out a framework agreement designed to lead to a final peace agreement. As prime minister, Peres continued and accelerated the talks.

The height of Israeli peacemaking efforts came with Barak's brief tenure as premier, during which he sought to achieve dramatic breakthroughs both with the Palestinians and Syrians. At the Camp David Summit in 2000 Barak submitted far-reaching proposals and under the Clinton Parameters, later that year, was willing to withdraw from some 97% of the West Bank, plus a 2% land swap, establish a Palestinian state, divide Jerusalem along its ethnic lines, and divide sovereignty over the Temple Mount. In the negotiations with the Syrians, culminating in the Geneva Summit in 2000, Barak was willing to withdraw from the Golan Heights.[42]

Barak's successor, Sharon, long known to be a hardliner, withdrew unilaterally from all of Gaza and dismantled four settlements in the West Bank, despite withering domestic opposition. Had he not fallen ill, Sharon apparently intended to continue with a further withdrawal in the West Bank.[43] Prime Minister Olmert was elected on a campaign platform that explicitly called for "consolidation" in the West Bank and for a withdrawal to the security fence, equivalent at the time to a withdrawal from some 90% of the West Bank. In 2008 he submitted a proposal to Palestinian president Abbas based on a withdrawal from 93.5% of the West Bank, with a full 6.5% land swap, a division of Jerusalem along its ethnic lines, and establishment of a multilateral mechanism to govern the holy sites. In short, most Israeli prime ministers in recent decades have undertaken major and even dramatic peace initiatives. The two exceptions were Shamir and Netanyahu.

This is not the place to discuss why these dramatic initiatives failed to elicit commensurate Arab responses and pave the way to final peace agreements, and Israel shares the responsibility. It is, however, certainly fair to say that Israel went to great lengths to achieve peace. More importantly, it demonstrates that the pursuit of peace has been an active and central part of Israeli foreign policy in much, though not all, of recent decades. This policy has been based on major territorial withdrawal, accompanied by security guarantees, including demilitarized zones and early warning stations, international monitoring, the establishment of diplomatic relations, and full "normalization." Unfortunately, as the peace process floundered, Israel's goals have narrowed from conflict resolution and peace, to conflict management, military deterrence, and war avoidance, with a focus on stability.[44]

Limited Multilateral Involvement

In an era in which multilateral institutions and multilateralism as a norm have gained growing international currency, Israel stands out not just for its limited involvement in multilateral diplomacy, but the mixed love-hate relationship it has long had with the UN and a variety of multilateral institutions. Israel achieved independence and international recognition with the UN's blessing and saw itself, in the early years, as an enthusiastic player in the UN and multilateral forums, especially in Third World development projects. Over the decades, however, as the UN and other multilateral forums became a primary locus of the Arab effort to delegitimize and isolate Israel, it developed an adversarial and even derisive attitude toward the UN and many of its agencies.

The nadir in Israel's relations with the UN came with the infamous resolution in 1975 equating Zionism with racism, subsequently revoked in 1991. As the decades went by and the endless flow of virulently anti-Israeli rhetoric and resolutions in the UN multiplied, Israel largely gave up on it as an arena of diplomatic discourse and became a relatively passive participant in the various UN forums. Moreover, it has generally refrained from even proposing resolutions in the UN in the knowledge, based on bitter experience, that the Arab, Muslim, and Third World majority would reject them regardless of the merits, or attach amendments that totally changed their intent and even turned them into anti-Israeli resolutions. In effect, Israel was forced to adopt a defensive approach designed to minimize dangers and came to downplay the importance of multi-lateral forums generally.

By the late 1990s Israel's attitude toward the UN had begun to evolve. A limited turning point came in 2000, when Congress made payment of US dues to the UN contingent on Israel's acceptance in the "Western European and Others Group," the first time Israel was ever accepted as a member of any of the UN's regional groupings (Arab opposition kept it out of its natural membership in the Asian or Middle Eastern groups).[45] More importantly, the UN proved too influential an arena to be ignored, and Israel, which found itself increasingly running up against the limits to military force, concluded that it could at times play a limited positive role after all.

In 2000 Prime Minister Barak asked the UN to send a special cartographic team to confirm that Israel had, indeed, completely withdrawn from Lebanon, thereby providing his unilateral initiative with the international legitimacy needed for success. In the years between the withdrawal and the war with Hezbollah in 2006, Israel sought to base its Lebanon policy on the relevant UN resolutions, UN legitimization, and UN forces,[46] as part of an effort to prolong the period of calm with Hezbollah. Under Prime Minister Olmert Israel supported, indeed sought, the adoption of Security Council Resolution 1701, which put an end to the fighting in 2006 on terms favorable to it. In 2014 some contingents of UNDOF, the UN force stationed in the Golan Heights since the Yom Kippur War, were forced to withdraw under pressure by various ISIS-affiliated groups, heightening Israeli fears of an escalation along the Syrian front and clarifying the importance of this heretofore almost invisible and seemingly anachronous UN force. The International Atomic Energy Agency (IAEA), always one of the less politicized of the UN agencies, has played a vital role in the effort to curb Iran's nuclear program, emphasizing the positive, at times even critical, importance of UN agencies for Israel.

Nevertheless, the overall relationship with the UN and its affiliated bodies remains adversarial and problem-fraught. As noted in the section on the delegitimization campaign (see chapter 4), the anti-Israeli onslaught in the UN and such highly politicized bodies as the High Commissioner for Refugees continues, while the Palestinian attempt to use the Security Council and General Assembly to reach statehood by fiat undermines Israel's already limited faith in the UN's ability to play a positive role in the resolution of the conflict.

Israel has never been a member of a multilateral economic, diplomatic, or military alliance, such as the EU and NATO. The lack of involvement in multilateral forums and, consequently, in many of the "soft issues" that engage much global attention today (e.g., food, water, environment, global warming, human rights) means that Israel in increasingly out of sync with much of the international community.

Playing to the Periphery and Arab Divisions

Observers have long noted two ostensible components of Israel's foreign policy, the so-called periphery doctrine and attempts to exploit divisions among the Arab countries. In reality, both were ad hoc attempts to take advantage of developments, rather than fundamental strategies, even if couched in conceptual frameworks.

The periphery doctrine, which had its heyday in the 1950s and largely dissipated thereafter, certainly by the 1980s, was an attempt to make common cause with the primary non-Arab players bordering the region, Iran under the shah, Turkey, and Ethiopia, hence the name "periphery." Isolated in the region, Israel looked for friends wherever it could find them. By promoting defense and other forms of cooperation with these countries, whose relations with the Arab countries were tense for reasons of their own, Israel hoped to tie down Arab forces, deflect attention from itself, project an image of greater regional power, and strengthen its deterrence. A similar logic guided Israel's attempts to develop relations with various non-Arab minorities in the region, primarily the Christians in Lebanon and Sudan and the Kurds.[47]

The relationship with Iran ended with the overthrow of the shah, and Iran has come to be seen as the greatest threat to Israel's national security ever since the early 1980s. Relations with Turkey have deteriorated dramatically since the rise of the Islamist AK Party in 2002, and it is today viewed more as an adversary than a friend. Relations with Ethiopia are limited. Israel's ties with the Lebanese Christians, which reached their height during the 1982 Lebanon war, are indelibly imprinted on its national psyche as a severe betrayal and strategic failure. Ties with the Kurds, who never acted on Israel's requests that they take measures to dissuade Iraq from dispatching forces to Jordan and Syria during the 1967 and 1973 crises, respectively, never amounted to much. The Sudanese Christians have been too weak to be of any real benefit, though a positive relationship does exist today with South Sudan.[48]

In recent years, some have spoken of a new periphery doctrine that, like its predecessor, is more an amalgamation of separate relationships than a coherent strategy. With the collapse of relations with Turkey, Israel has greatly strengthened ties with other countries in the eastern Mediterranean, primarily Greece, Cyprus, and Italy, as well as Bulgaria and Romania. Greece has expressed considerable interest in developing a long-term strategic partnership with Israel and has even participated in a number of joint military exercises. A bilateral military relationship between Israel and Cyprus has also developed, although most of the focus has been on the prospects of trilateral cooperation, together with Greece, regarding the gas fields in the eastern Mediterranean.[49]

Israel's military relationship with Italy, long an important trading partner, has grown greatly since the early 2000s, including a defense cooperation agreement, joint aerial exercises, and multi-billion-dollar arms deals. Bulgaria, too, has participated in joint aerial exercises, allowing Israel to practice tactics against aircraft and antimissile systems similar to Iran's.[50] Some today add Azerbaijan, with whom Israel has a considerable military relationship, to the updated periphery strategy, as well as Kenya, Uganda, and again Ethiopia.[51] Israel clearly has an interest today in closer relations with the Kurds. In 2017 it was the sole country to express explicit support for the Iraqi Kurds' failed bid for independence.

Political and military divisions in the Arab world have traditionally been viewed as advantageous to Israel. A divided Arab world could not act in concert against Israel, certainly not militarily, and could not bring its collective economic and political clout to bear against it. Israel thus sought at times to exploit and further deepen already existing cleavages within the Arab world, especially on the battlefield and at the negotiating table.

In the former, Israel has always sought to avoid multifront wars and to confront the Arab armies sequentially. Its ability to do so was at the heart of its military successes in 1948 and 1967. In 1973, when Israel was forced to fight on two fronts simultaneously, it was hard pressed to achieve victory, especially after suffering a surprise attack. In terms of peace negotiations, Israel has always been loath to participate in multilateral forums, in which it feared that the dynamics of inter-Arab politics would lead to the adoption of maximalist positions, and has preferred bilateral negotiations instead. A high point in such efforts was the attempt to remove Egypt from the circle of confrontation states[52] and reach an essentially separate peace in 1979. A low point was the failure of Israel's intervention in Lebanese domestic affairs in 1982.

In fact, Arab divisions have been so deep that most of Israel's efforts to take advantage of them have been minor in comparison and, in any event, they rarely worked.[53] Ever since the traumatic failure of its ties with the Lebanese Christians in the early 1980s, Israel has largely given up on attempts to intervene in intra-Arab affairs. The events of the Arab Spring further indicated the wisdom of greater restraint. Israel's hands-off approach toward events in Syria ever since the outbreak of the civil war is an example of this far more cautious approach.

Israel's Foreign Relations:
A Contemporary Overview

The fundamental objective of Israel's foreign policy is, if course, to promote better relations with the countries of the world, in support of its overall national security objectives. The following section provides an overview of Israel's primary foreign relations today. As noted, Israel's relations with the United States are addressed separately in the following chapter.

Diplomacy in Support of Israel's Primary Relations

Israel has a long and complex relationship with each of the European countries and, in recent decades, the EU. Approximately half of Israel's population is of European descent, and Israeli society, culture, and politics derive much of their character from Europe. The EU as a bloc is Israel's largest trading partner (the United States is the largest individual partner), and given geographic proximity, the claustrophobic nature of Israel's tiny dimensions, and the inability to visit neighboring countries, Israeli tourists flock to Europe in droves.

Israel enjoys an advanced Association Agreement with the EU, which provides it with preferential relations in terms of diplomatic dialogue, trade, agriculture, R&D, academic ties, and more. The Association Agreement was upgraded in 2008, despite calls from some member states to make it contingent on the settlements issue and progress on the peace process. In 2009 the EU foreign ministers decided that the upgrade would be frozen unless Israel accepted the principle of two states for two peoples. In 2012, these disagreements notwithstanding, a further major strengthening of the Association Agreement took place in 60 different areas. Although the move fell short of the full upgrade Israel sought, overall ties between the EU and Israel are more extensive than ever before.[54]

On various occasions the EU has offered Israel significant inducements as a means of encouraging it to go forward on the peace process and has "rewarded" it when it has done so.[55] The ultimate inducement, mooted in the early 2000s, is possible EU membership, or more likely, and largely for reasons of Israeli reservations, a status just short of full membership. Membership in NATO has also been mooted as part of an overall package of upgraded relations following a peace agreement.[56] Israel already enjoys the broadest cooperation agreement with NATO of any nonmember country, in the areas of intelligence, joint exercises, nuclear nonproliferation, and more.[57]

Over the years, Europe has grown increasingly critical of Israel's policies regarding the Palestinians and other aspects of the Arab-Israeli conflict generally. The criticism, often acerbic and strident, has clouded the considerable convergence of views that actually exists on the terms of a final peace agreement, Iran, and other issues. Nevertheless, an unwritten "division of labor" has evolved between Europe and the United States. Whereas the United States is viewed as Israel's staunch supporter and the only outside power with the clout to influence its policies, Europe has come to be seen as the champion of the Palestinian cause and almost irreparably critical of Israel.

Israel has responded to Europe's perceived one-sidedness by turning almost entirely to the United States for its defense and diplomatic needs. It has also done its best to minimize European participation in the peace process, refusing to provide it with any role in the bilateral talks with Syria and the Palestinians, though not in the multilateral forums. In the latter, Israel (and usually the United States too) held that Europe could "pay but not play," that is, provide the necessary financial and other inducements to the Palestinians and other Arab actors, but not influence the talks themselves.[58]

In recent years, as European frustration with Israel's policies has grown, and limited diplomatic pressure has repeatedly failed to elicit the desired changes, there have been growing demands for a harder line. The pressure for further action, from countries that are especially critical of Israel, such as Spain, Ireland, and France, has been partially counterbalanced by the newer central European members, especially Poland and the Czech Republic, and eastern European countries, such as Greece, Romania and Bulgaria.[59]

Various European countries have imposed partial or complete arms embargoes on Israel at times, including Britain, France, and Germany, even without formal EU decisions to this effect. Israel is often presented with highly critical diplomatic demarches by the EU and individual European states.[60] Popular pressure in Europe for steps against Israel has also been increasing rapidly, as discussed in chapter 4 on the delegitimization and sanctions campaign.

These tensions notwithstanding, Israel now conducts joint training exercises with a variety of European militaries nearly every year. In 2012 Britain and Germany joined the biannual US-Israeli exercise Juniper Cobra, making it the largest ever.[61] In 2013 Israel hosted an exercise that involved hundreds of aircraft from Germany, Italy, Poland, and the United States, simulating both asymmetric operations and traditional air-to-air combat. Other recent exercises have included special forces training with the Czech Republic and long-distance bombing runs with the Greek, Italian, Dutch, and German air forces. Arms sales to European countries in 2015 totaled $1.16 billion.[62]

British-Israeli trade has boomed in recent years. Indeed, Britain has become Israel's second-largest export market, after the United States, and Israel is Britain's second-largest trading partner in the Middle East, after Saudi Arabia. Israel and France signed agreements to upgrade the bilateral relationship in the areas of political dialogue, trade, culture, and science, and France has also resumed limited weapons purchases from Israel. Both countries conduct broad strategic dialogues with Israel,[63] providing top officials with an opportunity for regularly scheduled consultations on a variety of matters. In the 2010s, as Britain and France became deeply involved in the Iranian nuclear issue, and as their concerns grew over

Islamic extremism and terrorism, Syria, and developments in the Middle East generally, the areas of joint strategic convergence have broadened considerably.

Poland, formerly considered "the cemetery of the Jewish people," has become one of Israel's closest friends. Seeking to do away with its anti-Semitic image and improve relations with the United States, Poland defines Israel as a vital ally and strategic asset, repeatedly acting to defend Israel in international forums. There is also a rapidly growing military and economic relationship.[64]

Israel has particularly close relations with Canada and to a lesser extent Australia. In recent years, Canada has actually emerged as the most outspokenly pro-Israel country in the world, often exceeding the United States. The relationships with both Canada and Australia are primarily diplomatic and economic in nature, though some limited military cooperation has taken place as well.

Russian-Israeli relations have a long and tortuous history. More than two-thirds of all Jews lived in Russia in the 19th century, in which an enormously rich Jewish culture had developed over the course of a thousand years. Modern Zionism largely took hold in Russia, and the Soviet Union supported Israeli independence in 1948, even providing arms in the early years. The exigencies of Soviet strategic needs during the Cold War and Israel's early gravitation toward the American sphere led to a rapid deterioration in relations and to a formal rupture in 1967. For decades the Soviet Union became, for all practical purposes, an enemy state, providing the Arab countries with vast quantities of weaponry and economic assistance, virtually unconditional diplomatic support, and strategic backing.

Formal relations were restored in 1991, with the collapse of the Soviet Union, and the two countries enjoy a close bilateral relationship today, greatly buttressed by the influx of approximately one million Russian Jewish immigrants in the 1990s. Bilateral trade nearly tripled in the 2000s and, at least in some years, Russia has become Israel's second-largest source of tourism.[65] Diplomatic consultations are extensive, including at the most senior levels, the two National Security Councils have conducted a strategic dialogue over the years, and there are even initial signs of an emerging military relationship.[66] At Israel's (and the United States') request, Russia refrained from providing advanced SA300 anti-aircraft systems to Iran for years,[67] and Israel, too, has shown restraint in arms sales to Russia's neighbors. In 2015, following the Russian military intervention in Syria, a close coordinating mechanism was established for purposes of deconfliction between the two air forces[68] and in 2016 bilateral strategic consultation reached unprecedented heights. The two countries also share a broad range of strategic concerns, such as the rise of Islamic fundamentalism in the Middle East and Central Asia, terrorism, and the transformational changes in the region. Russia's policies vis-à-vis the Palestinian issue have not been significantly different from that of the European countries.

At the same time, the two countries find themselves on the opposite sides of a number of issues of major importance, such as Russian support for the Assad regime and Iranian involvement in Syria ever since the civil war, and the Iranian nuclear issue. Russia played a mixed role in the negotiations leading to the 2015 nuclear deal with Iran, built Iran's Busher nuclear plant, and was involved in the past in various illicit forms of nuclear and missile assistance to Iran. In 2016 Russia finally provided the SA300 to Iran, and Israel is deeply concerned over some of its other arms sales to Iran, Syria (some of which have reached Hezbollah),[69] and of late Egypt.

In reality, these areas of disagreement reflect a fundamental divide between the two countries. Israel, as Russia recognizes, is firmly and unalterably located in the American sphere of influence, whereas Russia, in recent years, has pursued a policy of growing confrontation with the United States, as part of its strategic effort to regain a more prominent international role. The Middle East is particularly important to the Russian strategy, and since Moscow has little to offer countries in the region other than weapons and nuclear assistance, they play a major role in its efforts. These highly problematic Russian policies do not reflect malevolence toward Israel, but are at the heart of some of the most important strategic threats it faces today, nonetheless. Israel is also concerned about the rise in Russian influence in the region generally, particularly at a time of decreasing American involvement and stature.

China has long been supportive of the Arab positions in the conflict with Israel, especially on the Palestinian issue, and has adopted a critical approach in the UN and other international forums. China usually opposes sanctions against rogue regimes and proliferators, such as Iran, Iraq, and Syria, and has long been on the opposite side of the United States and Israel on these issues. Ever since the establishment of formal diplomatic relations in 1992, however, this has not prevented China from developing a strong bilateral relationship with Israel. Indeed, bilateral trade has increased almost 200-fold, from a paltry $50 million in 1992 to over $10 billion ever since 2013, and talks are underway for a free trade agreement.[70]

Israel has established a special task force to promote economic ties with China, which it has identified as a "primary strategic objective." In 2013–2014 Chinese corporations purchased Israeli companies worth over $5 billion, in areas as diverse as dairy, agriculture, health, a port, and high tech. Israel's advanced scientific and high-tech capabilities lend it an importance for China that exceeds its otherwise objective weight as a potential trading partner.[71]

In the late 1990s and early 2000s, China actually sought to develop a broad strategic relationship with Israel, viewing it as a major potential source of sophisticated weapons and technologies. The first major breakthrough came in 1997 with a deal for the sale of advanced Israeli early warning aircraft (Phalcons), which was really just a harbinger of the major military supply relationship China apparently envisaged. By 2000, however, the Phalcon deal had caused a severe crisis in Israel's relations with the United States, which viewed the aircraft as a threat to American forces in a future conflict with China. Under extreme US pressure, Israel was forced to cancel the deal, leading to a near rupture in its relations with China, which concluded that Israel was unduly subject to American influence and not a reliable potential strategic ally. China ultimately decided to adopt a mixed response; it continued to promote growing economic ties with Israel, but also terminated the planned strategic relationship and ceased procurement of weapons from Israel. The bilateral military and strategic relationship has not recovered to this day.[72] We return to this issue in detail in the following chapter.

China has yet to significantly assert its strategic influence in the Middle East and has focused to date primarily on its economic interests, especially oil. The possibility of greatly heightened Chinese involvement in the region, however, especially at a time of diminished American influence, may have significant ramifications for Israel's strategic interests in a variety of areas, such as the Iranian nuclear program. The "One Belt One Road" initiative, designed to link China to Western Europe through Central Asia, Turkey, India, and Iran, and to Africa, via land and sea routes, may have a major effect on its standing in the region in the coming years. The dramatic changes underway in the Middle East, which threaten China's fundamental interest in regional stability, may create broader shared interests with Israel.

In recent years Israeli-Japanese relations have expanded considerably, primarily in the economic field. Relations with South Korea have also expanded, on all levels, including the military, and a variety of shared interests portend a deeper relationship in the future.

Diplomacy in Support of Peace

Israel's peace treaties with Egypt and Jordan were transformational events, psychologically and strategically. After decades of warfare, peace with Egypt not only terminated the bilateral conflict, but also had the practical effect of ending the broader Arab conventional military option against Israel, thereby enabling Israel to cut its defense budget and divert resources to other threats and domestic needs. Peace with Jordan ended the direct threat of an "eastern front" and showed that Egypt was not an isolated case, but a harbinger of what Israel's future in the region could be. For decades now, virtually no Israelis have been killed on either border.

The bilateral relationships with both Egypt and Jordan, however, are cold and laden with mutual recrimination, little more than the minimum possible on the diplomatic and economic levels. For Egypt, peace with Israel has really meant confrontation by nonmilitary means and has been part of a strategy aimed at keeping Israel to its "natural size," as defined by Cairo, that is, its 1967 borders, devoid of a nuclear capability, and with little or no regional integration and normalization. For decades, Egypt has thus kept the bilateral relationship cold and even acted, at times, to prevent normalization between Israel and other countries in the region. It has also championed efforts, in every possible international forum, to force Israel to expose and dismantle its nuclear capabilities. In 30 years in power, President Mubarak refused to visit Israel, except briefly, under US pressure, for Rabin's funeral.

Israel remains concerned about Egypt's ongoing American-supplied arms buildup. It is also concerned about the resumption of Egypt's military ties with Russia, including reports of the possible procurement of advanced weapons systems, and by a deal the two signed in 2015 for the supply of Russia nuclear power reactors to Egypt.[73] Although not significant proliferation dangers in and of themselves, the deal, if actually carried out, will constitute the basis for an Egyptian nuclear infrastructure that could be used for proliferation purposes,[74] particularly if the Iran nuclear deal fails to rein in its nuclear program.

Paradoxically, military cooperation is today the one significant bright spot in the bilateral relationship. Israel and Egypt share important strategic interests regarding the rise of Iran and its allies in the region; radical Sunni forces, such as ISIS; jihadi elements operating in Sinai; and, maybe above all, Hamas. Israel has thus repeatedly acceded to Egyptian requests, during the Mubarak era and to this day, to deploy forces in Sinai in excess of those permitted by the peace treaty, in order to help Egypt restore its control over the area. Military cooperation in these areas continued even during the brief rule of the Muslim Brotherhood and has reached new heights ever since President Sissi took power.[75] Israel has also come to Egypt's aid in the United States, for example, helping to convince the Obama administration to refrain from defining the 2013 coup as such. Had it done so, American law would have triggered a mandatory cutoff of military aid to Egypt. It has also sought to impress upon Congress the importance Israel attaches to continued American military aid to Egypt.

Jordan, at least initially, sought a warmer and more cooperative relationship with Israel on the economic level, and continues to maintain strong defense ties. In the 1990s and early 2000s Jordan clearly saw Israel as a strategic ally and bulwark against threats to the regime's future, primarily from Iraq, and it still views Israel as such today, against ISIS and other threats, even as the overall relationship has cooled. Jordan has typically played a moderating and positive role vis-à-vis the Palestinians and will presumably play an important role part in any future resolution of the Jerusalem and refugee issues, in which Israel has long recognized that Jordan has a special stature and interest.

For Israel, Jordan ensures a stable and terrorism-free eastern border and is a buffer against threats from a disintegrating Syria, Iraq, and broader Arab world. Signs of an ISIS presence in Jordan, as well as long-standing threats to the viability of the regime, have been sources of great concern to Israel, which has a deep interest in the longevity of the Hashemite monarchy and which has long provided it with various forms of support over the years. According to media reports Israel has supplied attack helicopters to Jordan, in conjunction with the United States, as well as drones. Israeli drones have reportedly also used Jordanian airspace to monitor events in Syria and the two countries have participated in multilateral military exercises.[76]

For decades, virtually no one in Israel has spoken of the "Jordanian option," in which Jordan, whose population has a significant Palestinian majority, would serve as the Palestinian state. New opportunities might arise, however, were the Hashemite Kingdom to fall in the future, despite all efforts to prevent this from happening.

Diplomacy in Support of Strategic Partnerships

Israel's relations with Germany will always bear the heavy burden of historical memory, but Germany has probably become Israel's closest ally after the United States. The relationship has developed in particular under Chancellor Merkel, who initiated periodic intergovernmental summits, designed to strengthen and institutionalize the bilateral relationship in such a way that it will no longer be subject to political developments or changes in leadership. In the years since this high-level exchange began in 2008, it has proven to be an important forum for strategic dialogue, discussing, inter alia, the Iranian nuclear issue, peace process, settlements, Israel's international standing, science and innovation, and regional developments.[77]

As part of its commitment to Israel's security, Germany has undertaken to supply it with six Dolphin submarines by 2018, completely funding the cost of the first two and a third of the rest, for a total of $1.5 billion. Five have already been delivered, and negotiations are apparently underway for the supply of additional submarines, starting in the second half of the 2020s. According to press reports, the submarines can carry Israeli-made cruise missiles, with a range of 1,500 kilometers, and are even armed with nuclear warheads, designed to provide Israel with a second-strike capability.[78] Germany also agreed to sell Israel four missile boats and to cover a third of the $450 million cost.[79] The two militaries have also begun conducting joint military exercises, still on a small scale, including urban warfare.[80]

Germany has long taken a more pro-Israel policy than most of its European partners, both in EU institutions and in a variety of international forums, moderating anti-Israeli initiatives and resolutions. In recent years, however, disagreement over the Palestinian issue has overshadowed the relationship; German criticism has grown, and in some cases it has provided less diplomatic cover than in the past. The intimacy of the intergovernmental summits, for example, has not prevented Merkel from using them as a forum for expressing strong criticism of Israeli policy.[81]

India, a founder and leader of the Non-Aligned Movement, long pursued a highly pro-Arab and especially pro-Palestinian policy, and formal diplomatic relations with Israel were only established in 1992. In the years since then, the development of a highly robust economic and defense relationship has made India a country of strategic importance for Israel, despite its ongoing support for the array of anti-Israel resolutions in the UN and other international forums.

Indeed, by 2015 India had become Israel's largest or second-largest market for weapons exports, with sales of over a billion dollars annually in each of the two previous years[82] and approximately $10 billion during the previous decade, including early-warning aircraft, satellites, missiles, and a variety of other advanced systems. The relationship, however, is more than just weapons sales: India has helped co-fund weapons development programs, thereby enabling Israel to develop and deploy weapons it would not have had the financial wherewithal to do otherwise. Furthermore, the two countries engage in a broad-ranging strategic dialogue and exchange of intelligence, cooperate in the area of counterterrorism, and share a broad interest in the issue of Islamic radicalism.[83] On the economic level, trade has increased from just $200 million in 1992 to $4.5 billion in 2014, and discussions are underway regarding a free trade agreement. India has become Israel's tenth-largest trading partner overall and the third largest in Asia, after China and Hong Kong.[84]

Israel's relations with Turkey took off dramatically in the 1990s and early 2000s, on all levels, diplomatic, economic, and military. Turkey became a primary export market for Israeli arms sales; the two countries engaged in co-production programs, joint exercises, intelligence exchanges, a strategic dialogue, and a variety of forms of strategic cooperation. The idea of such a deep and overt relationship between a Muslim country, the heirs to the Ottoman Empire, and Jewish Israel caught the imagination of many in Israel and beyond, affirmed Israel's long-standing belief that religious differences do not have to stand in the way of a warm relationship with a Muslim country, and heralded the possibility of future integration in the region. With partial justification, but considerable hype, some came to oversell the relationship as a "strategic alliance." Be that as it may, the relationship has undergone a deep crisis ever since the AKP came to power in 2002. Economic ties continued to expand, but diplomatic relations are dismal, and the military relationship has come to an end. The prospects of a significantly improved relationship appear bleak as long as the AKP, or at least President Erdogan, remains in power.

Beginning in 2015, a shared threat perception regarding Iran, ISIS, and other extremist groups in the region led to numerous reports of growing contacts and cooperation between Israel and the Sunni states, not just Egypt and Jordan, but Saudi Arabia and other Gulf countries. Little is known of the substance of these contacts, and doubts regarding the potential for concrete cooperation are warranted. Nevertheless, the very existence of such contacts would be a significant change from the past, and Israel will undoubtedly pursue all avenues of possible cooperation.

Diplomacy in Support of Economic Growth

The MFA, together with the Ministry of Trade and Commerce, is responsible for promoting Israel's economic ties with countries around the world and opening new markets to trade.[85] Israel has also sought in recent years to increase its participation in multilateral economic forums, such as the OECD (Organization for Economic Cooperation and Development), which it joined in 2010.

The great growth in Israel's economy over the decades notwithstanding, the defense burden has created an enormous dependence on foreign aid, especially from the United States and, to a far lesser extent, Germany. Socioeconomic needs have also created ongoing dependence on diaspora Jewry for support, though the sums raised, important as they are for beneficiary institutions, pale in comparison to US aid and to Israel's own resources today. Israeli diplomacy has been very successful in gaining such support, at the price of heightened dependence.[86]

Covert Diplomacy and Arms Sales in Support of Israel's Foreign Relations

Israel has conducted covert ties with a broad array of countries through intelligence channels. Covert ties reflect a pragmatic attempt to reduce Israel's diplomatic isolation and to promote its interests by working outside of formal diplomatic channels.[87] In some cases, the initially covert contacts ultimately evolved into formal low-level ties (e.g., Morocco, Oman, and Tunisia in the past), into close relationships (India),[88] and even into peace agreements (Egypt, Jordan). In other cases, covert ties continued for lengthy periods and included extensive cooperation in a variety of fields; in others they remained limited to periodic exchanges.[89] In recent years, as noted, there has been a flurry of media speculation regarding possible covert Israeli relations with Saudi Arabia and other Gulf countries.

Arms sales are an important source of foreign income for Israel, as for many other countries, exceeding $6 billion annually in recent years, with a peak of $7.5 billion in 2012.[90] Arms sales and military cooperation are not, in and of themselves, a fundamental attribute of Israel's foreign policy and would not ordinarily be included in this chapter. Given the reluctance of many countries to maintain diplomatic relationships with Israel, however, they have gained a level of importance in Israel's foreign relations that does warrant special mention.

The list of countries that have bought Israeli weapons is impressive and at times surprising. In some cases, military ties were the primary motivator and substance of the relationship; in others they spurred the subsequent development of diplomatic and economic relations, for example, with Turkey and India. The United States is the number one export market for Israeli arms, followed in recent years by India. Azerbaijan purchased nearly $4 billion in Israeli arms between 2011 and 2014. A variety of European countries have also bought Israeli arms, including Italy, France, Germany, Spain, Poland, Portugal, and Belgium, as have Japan, South Korea, Vietnam, Australia, New Zealand, and South American and African countries. A number of Arab countries have reportedly also bought Israeli weapons, but in most cases this was probably as subcomponents of weapons bought from third parties, such as the United States or Europe.[91]

To conclude this chapter: Israel does not have a formal foreign policy doctrine, but one can see in the above the emerging contours of a coherent one. Founded in a historical legacy and primal sense of security that overshadow all Israeli national security thinking, Israel has devoted extensive efforts to the pursuit of peace, at least much of the time, but has placed security above all. Indeed, Israel's foreign policy has largely been subordinate to and designed to serve its defense policy.

Promoting better relations with the countries of the world and, especially, establishing and maintaining a strong alliance with at least one superpower are at the heart of Israel's foreign policy. Israel's relations with the United States, to which we turn in the next chapter, are thus the preeminent focus of its foreign policy. With some hyperbole, one could almost argue that Israeli foreign policy today is its relationship with the United States. At the same time, Israel seeks to maintain positive relations with numerous countries, starting with Europe, Russia, China, and more; to build strategic relations with countries such as Germany, India, and in the past Turkey; and to promote better economic and military ties with all. Seven decades after Israel's establishment, international legitimacy and acceptance remain a central pursuit of its foreign policy.

Israel pursues a fundamentally pragmatic foreign policy based on its raison d'état, or national interests, in which its unique character as a Jewish and Zionist state plays only a limited role. In a few select areas, however, one cannot understand Israeli foreign policy in the absence of this unique character, including the fundamental sense of insecurity that has driven its security demands in the peace negotiations and its approach toward the Iranian nuclear program. The area in which Israel's Jewish and Zionist character has had the greatest impact in recent years, is on its policies on the West Bank issues.

Primary Observations

- Israel's primal sense of insecurity is a product of Jewish history, culminating in the Holocaust. It is so deeply imbued that probably no level of security could eliminate its fears of living on the edge of an existential abyss.
- Israel is a nation with a mission, to rebuild and be the Jewish state, gather in the exiles, provide a refuge, and more. Its foreign policy is overwhelmingly pragmatic, but with elements of ideology beyond that of most democracies. Nowhere is this more pronounced than on the West Bank issues.
- Seemingly immutable Arab hostility and international isolation forced Israel's foreign policy to retreat into a defensive posture, with minimalist goals, designed to hold the line. Israel's foreign policy has become an instrument of defense policy, not the opposite, and a means of minimizing disruptions to it. Israel's diplomatic options are often quite limited, though greater than in the past.
- Israel's foreign policy response includes strategic relationships with a number of countries, above all the United States; unique ties with the diaspora, which constitutes an extension of Israel's own capabilities and a vital strategic asset; and the pursuit of peace. A number of Israeli governments have been highly proactive and made dramatic proposals for peace.
- Israel enjoyed great "soft power" in the past, which was vital to its "hard power," especially in the United States, and still retains significant soft power for some. Israel's West Bank policies have eroded its international image, and it has come to be viewed as a pariah state. Israel has ceded the battle for "soft power."
- The greatest challenge to Israel's foreign policy today is in Europe and other Western countries, its national reference group. Nevertheless, Israel has extensive and deep ties with them which may partially mitigate and postpone the mounting crisis.
- Israel prefers bilateral peace negotiations over multilateral ones, in which intra-Arab politics would lead to maximalist positions. Its attempts to intervene in Arab politics were never very successful, and it has largely ceased trying to do so.

- A shared threat perception of Iran, ISIS, and other extremist actors is creating a new potential for cooperation with the Sunni states, although the Palestinian and other issues will probably continue to constrain it in practice.
- Israel has strong strategic interests in the longevity of the Jordanian monarchy. Should it fall, despite all efforts to the contrary, new possibilities for progress with the Palestinians may emerge, along with new dangers from the east.

10

The "Special Relationship"

Israel's fundamental strategic quandary is that it is too close to God, too
far from the United States.
—Walter Russell Meade, American strategist

The importance of the relationship with the United States for Israel's national security cannot be overstated. It is the be-all and end-all of most policy
deliberations in Israeli national security decision-making forums. Washington
is usually the first and often even sole port of call for strategic consultations on
emerging events, almost always the foremost one, and inevitably the primary
means of addressing them. Indeed, Israel's dependence on the United States is so
great today that its very survival is at least partly dependent on it, and Israel has
lost much, though not all, of its freedom of maneuver to it.

From the vantage point of contemporary readers, it may be surprising to
learn that the US-Israeli relationship was actually quite limited and even cool
until the late 1960s, then evolved into a more classic patron-client relationship
in the 1970s, and only started becoming the institutionalized and strategic one
we know today in the 1980s. President Truman was the father of the historic
American recognition of Israel, but also imposed an arms embargo on Israel at a
time when the Arab states had access to other sources of arms.

Under the Eisenhower administration the relationship continued to be tenuous, with the United States generally endorsing Arab positions and maintaining
the arms embargo. Following the 1956 war, the United States even forced Israel
to withdraw from the Sinai under the threat of crippling sanctions. A thaw in relations began toward the end of the Eisenhower administration, but really began
under the Kennedy and Johnson administrations, which approved the first arms
sales, and even more so under President Nixon, especially following the Yom
Kippur War. It was only under President Reagan, however, that the United States
began to view Israel as a strategic asset and partner and that the foundations
were laid for what later became a nearly all-encompassing strategic relationship.[1]

American support for Israel today is deep and broad based, going far beyond any one segment of American society or religious or political belief. Despite decades of conflict and endless criticism of Israeli policies in the media, 62% of Americans in 2015 said that their sympathies lie with Israel, only 16% with the Palestinians. Deep-seated public antipathy for foreign assistance notwithstanding, 48% believed in 2015 that the level of US aid for Israel was about right, 29% that the United States is not supportive enough, and just 18% that it is too supportive. By some measures, American popular support for Israel has never been higher.[2]

One would hardly expect a complete confluence of interests between a global superpower and a small regional player, and no bilateral relationship is free of tensions, certainly not the US-Israeli one. Despite the intimacy of the relationship and vast American aid for Israel, the history of the relationship is replete with cases of disagreement and even ongoing discord in a number of areas. It is a mark of the fundamental strength of the relationship that it has always bounced back from these disagreements and continued on a long-term path to ever deeper ties.[3]

The following chapter has two primary parts. The first presents an overview of the strategic relationship between the United States and Israel today, beginning with a brief mention of the economic dimension, but then focusing on the military and diplomatic ties. Accordingly, it knowingly presents only a part of the overall relationship between the two countries, whose extraordinarily rich and varied fabric cannot be captured in one chapter, or even an entire book. The second part addresses three critical questions for the future of Israeli national security; the extent to which Israel has lost its independence and freedom of maneuver to the United States, whether it can even survive today without the United States, and the future of the bilateral relationship.

The Strategic Relationship: An Overview

The Economic Dimension

The United States is Israel's single largest trading partner (the EU as a bloc is larger); Israel, perhaps surprisingly, is the United States' twenty-fourth largest. In 2016 bilateral trade was approximately $35.5 billion.[4] The two countries signed a free trade agreement in 1986, the first such bilateral deal ever concluded by the United States.

Total American assistance to Israel, from 1949 to 2016, amounts to a whopping $124 billion, making Israel the largest beneficiary of American military aid in the post–World War II era.[5] In 2007 the United States and Israel concluded a 10-year $30 billion military aid package, thereby providing the IDF with the fixed financial basis it so badly needs for purposes of force structure planning. A further 10-year $38 billion military aid package was signed in 2016.

The importance of US aid is not just in the absolute dollar amount, but in the way it is disbursed. Ever since 1981 all assistance to Israel has been in the form of grants, not loans. Israel is the only US aid recipient that receives all of its aid at the beginning of the year, rather than in installments, thereby enabling it to invest part of the sum during the year and earn interest on it, in the past worth tens of millions of dollars annually. It is also the only recipient that was allowed for decades to spend part of the assistance for domestic procurement in Israel, rather than in the United States, a preferential arrangement that will be phased out as part of the 2016 package. Moreover, the annual aid package, which ranged in the area of $3 billion annually during the 2000s, did not include a variety of special programs, such as the Iron Dome and Magic Wand rocket defense systems, the Arrow missile defense system, and a variety of others in the past that have significantly added to the total level of US aid. As of 2015, total US assistance for Israeli rocket and missile defense amounted to $4.6 billion.[6]

Over the years the United States has also provided Israel with emergency economic assistance and loan guarantees. In 1985 the United States provided a special $1.5 billion economic bailout package in order to help stabilize the Israeli economy, which was reeling at the time from hyperinflation and economic stagnation. In 1991 the United States provided $650 million to cover damages and other costs after the first Gulf War. That year it also provided $10 billion in loan guarantees to help Israel absorb immigrants from the former Soviet Union and a further $10 billion in loan guarantees during the second intifada. In effect, the loan guarantees are a form of indirect economic assistance, since they enable Israel to borrow from commercial lenders at lower rates.[7]

The Military Dimension

Military Assistance

American military support for Israel has had many motivations over the years. In some cases, primarily in the earlier years, during the 1970s and into the 1980s, there was a degree of linkage between military aid and Israel's positions on the peace process. Only a militarily secure Israel, the United States believed, would feel confident enough to make the diplomatic concessions it wanted, and weapons served as an inducement.[8] During the 1980s the supply relationship gained an institutionalized character, and the impact of the assistance package as a source of leverage has decreased significantly. More recently, the aid program has come to be based on agreed 10-year programs, further decreasing its potential use as a source of leverage, a reflection both of the need for certainty in long-term force planning and of the fact that both sides have come to consider it a long-term American commitment. Special assistance programs, however, have been used both by members of Congress to demonstrate their commitment to Israel and by administrations as a limited source of leverage.

Preserving the regional balance of power and consequent stability was a further major motivation for the military assistance program. Whereas US aid to Israel was designed in the past to counterbalance Soviet arms deliveries to the Arab countries, especially after the 1967 and 1973 wars, in recent decades, paradoxically, it has mostly been to counter American arms sales to them. In both cases, a less secure Israel could have led the Arabs to believe that military victory was possible and thus to initiate hostilities. Conversely, a less secure Israel, fearing the growing military capabilities of one or more of its neighbors, might have been tempted to pre-empt, or launch a preventive war, whether during the tense Cold War years or more recently against Iran's nuclear program. The assistance program was thus also a means of influencing Israel's decision-making process and shaping its outcomes.[9]

At its core, the military assistance program simply reflects the fundamental American commitment to Israel's security and survival. The United States, however, never wanted to be placed in a situation in which it would have been called upon to actually live up to this commitment in its ultimate form; direct American military intervention. Providing Israel with the weapons necessary to defend itself, by itself, obviated this danger. Finally, an unstated American motivation for the military aid program was the fear that a conventionally weak Israel might place greater emphasis on a nuclear posture and even contribute to a decision to end Israel's long-standing policy of nuclear ambiguity.[10]

The above notwithstanding, on various occasions US administrations have used weapons sales as a means of indicating American displeasure with Israeli actions. The Reagan administration, considered the most pro-Israeli administration up to its time, imposed sanctions on the supply of weapons on three occasions, following the application of Israeli law to the Golan Heights in 1981, the attack on the Iraqi reactor, also in 1981, and the First Lebanon War in 1982. In 2008 the highly pro-Israel Bush administration rejected Israeli requests for weapons that it believed might constitute an indication of imminent Israeli plans to attack Iran's nuclear program, as did the Obama administration. During the operation in Gaza in 2014 the Obama administration also briefly held up the supply of Hellfire missiles.[11] For the most part, however, the institutionalization of the strategic relationship has made the use of weapons sales for purposes of leverage an increasingly rare instrument of US policy.

Many in Israel, nevertheless, came to an important conclusion as a result of the limitations the United States placed at times on arms sales: when Israel responded by developing similar weapons of its own, the United States would ultimately agree to sell them,[12] both to preserve some influence over their use and for commercial reasons. Paradoxically, US limitations have thus become an important impetus for indigenous Israeli weapons development programs. According to media sources, when the United States imposed limitations on sales of bunker busters, for example, Israel reportedly succeeded in developing its own.[13] Similarly, media sources report that Israel may have developed cruise missiles after the United States refused to sell it Tomahawks.[14]

The downside to the assistance program, from the American perspective, was twofold: the anger it engendered on the Arab side and the possibility that a well-armed Israel might gain greater freedom of action, diplomatically and militarily, not necessarily in concert with American positions, and consequently be less amenable to American pressures.[15] In practice, the aid program to Israel, accompanied as it was with increasing aid to Arab countries, as well, never truly became an obstacle to American relations with them, and Arab countries' anger waned in any event after the first years, as they became used to what has become a long-term US policy. The second American concern is ongoing, though in practice, as this chapter will argue, Israel has adapted its policies to US preferences on most issues.

The importance of American military aid for Israel can only be understood in the context of the size of Israel's defense budget. The defense budget has ranged in recent years between approximately $15 billion and $17 billion (reflecting both fluctuating budgets and dollar conversion rates), and American aid has thus constituted some 17%–20% of the total budget, a large share in itself, but almost the entire procurement budget.[16]

Most, but not all, of the political and technological constraints that existed on US arms sales to Israel have been lifted over the years, and Israel generally has access to the latest American technologies. In 2005, for example, the United States supplied Israel with GBU bunker busters that had never before been sold to any other country and then accelerated delivery of additional such bombs during the Lebanon war in 2006.[17] Israel was the first foreign country to purchase F-35s, the most advanced American fighter today. Some weapons systems are codeveloped and coproduced in Israel.[18] In practice, the United States has almost become Israel's sole foreign source of sophisticated weapons. The only exception of significance is Germany, which has provided Israel with partial funding to buy six conventionally powered submarines, which the United States no longer produces.

The arms relationship creates a form of mutual dependence. For members of Congress, voting for military aid has become the lowest bar for demonstrating their support for Israel, and any wavering on this issue would immediately be construed as abandonment. The multiyear nature of military assistance programs—sales are implemented over periods of years, and are followed by the supply of munitions, parts, and maintenance—further contributes to the creation of a US commitment to continue the relationship, as do the weapons manufacturers, who in effect become a prosales lobby. In Israel's case, the unusual magnitude of the package and its long-term nature have become self-perpetuating factors. As one wag once put it, "If you receive $30 million a year you are a welfare case, if you receive $3 billion you are a line item."[19]

Israel's Qualitative Military Edge

Since the 1980s the United States has been committed to preserving an Israeli qualitative military edge (QME) over any possible combination of hostile Arab armies. How to define and maintain the QME in practice, however, has been a source of ongoing concern and even disagreement between the two countries. The United States, for which arms sales are a means of promoting closer relations with the Arab countries and has a commercial interest in them, and whose threat assessment, as a superpower, is different from Israel's, has naturally taken a narrower view of those sales that constitute a threat to Israel. Israel, conversely, has sought a more expansive definition. Defining a qualitative military edge is highly complex to begin with.

Disagreements have arisen primarily over sales to Egypt and Saudi Arabia. In regard to Egypt, as long as the peace treaty holds, the United States refuses to even take its military capabilities into account when calculating the QME, but has tacitly agreed to restrict aircraft sales to F-16s, not F-15s.[20] With the Saudis, US considerations have been colored by oil and the Saudis' ability to pay cash for vast quantities of arms. According to media sources, certain limitations have been imposed on Saudi deployments of weapons, but basically the US spigots have been open.[21]

In 2002 Congress mandated that future arms sales to states in the region would require a presidential determination that they do not adversely affect Israel's QME. It also sought to resolve the conceptual issue by defining the QME as "the ability to counter and defeat any credible conventional military threat from any individual state, or possible coalition of states, or from non-state actors, while sustaining minimal damage and casualties . . . including weapons . . . superior in capability to those of such other individual or possible coalitions of states and non-state actors."[22]

In the mid-2010s President Obama approved a new improved approach to evaluating and maintaining the QME, including heightened efforts to reach agreement with Israel on the ramifications of arms sales to Arab countries and the appropriate compensation. In 2014 Congress further provided for more frequent QME assessments and directed that they include evaluations of US arms sales' potential impact on the regional balance of power and Israeli capabilities.[23] Maintaining the QME will undoubtedly remain a focus of ongoing dialogue and often disagreement.

Strategic Dialogue and Planning

It is hard to imagine two countries engaged in closer and more intensive bilateral dialogue than Israel and the United States, at all levels, from the president and premier down.[24] Israeli premiers meet with the president, senior officials, and congressional leaders on a regular basis, more than almost any other foreign leader, and there is an ongoing exchange between meetings. The national security establishments of the two countries are also engaged in intensive and ongoing contact, including an endless array of delegations and professional teams that visit each country and various working groups that convene on a regular basis. Indeed, it has been argued elsewhere that exchanges with the United States are so extensive that American policymaking capabilities almost become a de facto extension of Israel's. Despite this nearly unprecedented wealth of bilateral consultation, the depth of actual dialogue has varied over time, and misunderstandings and disagreements have been frequent.[25]

Over the years the United States has consistently demanded that Israel not "surprise" it, that is, refrain from taking controversial measures without at least first consulting.[26] For the most part, Israel has done so, but both sides have acted at times without consulting, on the basis of their national interest. Israel gave the United States an essentially welcome surprise with the Oslo Accords in 1993, but has repeatedly angered it with settlement expansion and other matters related to the West Bank. The United States demanded that Israel not surprise it with an attack on Iran's nuclear program, but surprised Israel under Bush by adding an American diplomat to secret EU talks with Iran and more consequentially, under Obama, by holding the secret negotiations with Iran that ultimately led to the nuclear deal in 2015.[27]

Consultations prior to the 2003 Gulf War were extensive. The United States opposed Israeli involvement in the war, out of concern that it might disrupt its efforts to build an Arab coalition, and made this clear repeatedly during the months prior to the war's outbreak. During a meeting with Prime Minister Sharon in October 2002, President Bush and senior officials presented US war plans, including how it would respond to Iraqi missile and WMD attacks against Israel, in the attempt to convince Sharon to exercise restraint even in the face of such attacks. Sharon made it clear that Israel reserved the right of self-defense, would have to respond if attacked by WMD, and would not be bound by predetermined limitations, but that it would confer with the United States first.[28]

Some months earlier a team of US officers had arrived in Israel to conduct joint operational planning and coordination with the IDF, including a joint missile defense exercise. Once the war broke out, a US liaison officer was sent to Israel, as part of the early warning, communications, and coordination mechanisms put in place. Patriot air defense systems were deployed around Israeli population centers, and the United States provided Israel with special military assistance and compensation for expenses incurred in preparation for the war.[29] Iraq, in the end, did not attack, and Israel did not have to respond, but the strategic coordination was unprecedented.

The strike that Israel reportedly conducted against the Syrian nuclear facility in 2007, according to multiple foreign sources, including former secretary of defense Robert Gates and former secretary of state Condoleezza Rice,[30] is also a possible example of the nature of the bilateral dialogue. According to Gates, Israel first grew suspicious that Syria had renewed its nuclear program in late 2006, when North Korean technicians were found working at what turned out to be a nearly complete plutonium reactor at al-Kibar. Israel had to act quickly; an attack against an operational reactor would have released radiation and no longer been feasible.[31] Intelligence was reportedly transferred to the United States for the first time in April 2007, and extensive contacts took place over the following months between President Bush and Prime Minister Olmert, along with senior intelligence and other officials.[32] According to Gates and Rice, American intelligence confirmed the Israeli information but did not have definitive proof of an overall nuclear weapons program, and Bush informed Olmert that without such proof, the United States could not attack. Olmert responded that if the United States did not do so, Israel would. He did not ask for a green light, and Bush, who apparently accepted Olmert's contention that the reactor posed an existential threat to Israel, did not present a red one, despite strong opposition to an Israeli strike from some senior administration officials.[33] In practice, according to Gates, Bush did give Olmert a green light.[34] The Bush administration subsequently gave full backing to Israel's actions.

The Iranian nuclear program was the focus of extraordinarily close strategic coordination for some two decades, beginning under Prime Minister Rabin and President Clinton. It was apparently Israel that first convinced the US of the severity of the threat posed by the Iranian program. For the next 20 years the United States and Israel shared a close assessment of the Iranian program's progress and generally of the means of addressing the threat. Disagreement ultimately emerged with the Bush and Obama administrations over the possibility of military action, and the previously close dialogue even turned acrimonious over the nuclear deal the latter signed with Iran in 2015.

The broad strategic consensus that existed with the Bush administration notwithstanding, media sources report that it repeatedly rejected Israel's requests for weapons that it believed might indicate an imminent intention to attack the Iranian program and warned Israel not to do so, stating that such an attack would endanger American interests and that the United States would not permit Israel to fly over Iraq. US opposition to an Israeli attack was reportedly conveyed both publicly and privately and was further accompanied by a number of leaks from the Pentagon regarding a long distance IAF exercise over the Mediterranean, which were interpreted in Israel as direct attempts to undercut the possibility of Israeli action.[35]

In exchange for Israel's refraining from an attack, the Bush administration agreed to station an advanced radar system in Israel, in order to connect it directly to the American global satellite early warning system, further assist Israel in funding missile and rocket defense systems, and provide other weapons. Israel, for its part, informed the United States that it reserved the right to act in the event that the efforts to block the Iranian nuclear program by other means failed.[36]

Intensive US-Israeli contacts on the Iranian nuclear program continued throughout the early years of the Obama administration as well. The administration, which essentially took a US military option off the table, in practice if not in word, also made plain its opposition to an Israeli operation, even though the two countries reportedly cooperated intensively on a cyber-attack known as the "Stuxnet" virus.[37] Cooperation remained extensive at all levels until sometime around 2012, when the two sides adopted essentially divergent approaches. Whereas the United States began the secret negotiations that ultimately led to the agreement with Iran in 2015, Netanyahu conducted a public campaign pressing for ever harsher measures.[38]

Consultations continued at senior working levels, but Netanyahu and Obama simply talked past each other, and Netanyahu's ongoing opposition to the interim deal in 2013 led to his marginalization by the administration, an unprecedented event given that the United States shared Israel's view that an Iranian nuclear capability might pose an existential threat to it. The United States repeatedly spied on what it thought were Israeli preparations for an attack; Israel used its own intelligence means to keep indirectly informed of US negotiations with Iran. Neither side fully trusted the other, nor shared diplomatic and military plans, and the United States even feared that Israel would use information about the talks to sabotage them.[39]

Netanyahu's decision to fight the deal to the end in Congress ultimately led to one of the deepest crises in the history of the bilateral relationship, certainly since the "special relationship" truly got underway in the 1970s. Both sides subsequently did their best to put the crisis behind them, and Obama promised an expanded aid package designed to at least partially offset the dangers to Israel stemming from the nuclear deal.[40] Nevertheless, it will be years before the fallout from this controversy fully dissipates.

The peace process has been one of the biggest issues on the bilateral agenda for decades, probably the biggest, involving both very close coordination and considerable contention. Israeli governments firmly committed to the concept of a two-state solution have found broad common ground with the United States and been able to achieve very close, if not complete, or friction-free, co-ordination with the various administrations. Those governments that were less committed to a two-state solution have had greater difficulty in maintaining and promoting bilateral dialogue. Some issues have been a focus of discord for years, primarily the settlements, but on many of the fundamentals there has been broad agreement. We will return to the peace process later in this chapter.

Strategic Military Cooperation

As with strategic dialogue, the examples of bilateral strategic military cooperation are numerous and no more than an overview thereof can be offered.

Missile Defense. The United States has provided Israel with generous aid to help develop and deploy its own missile and rocket defenses (Arrow, Iron Dome, and Magic Wand) and may even deploy American missile defense systems to Israel in times of crisis (Aegis ships and THAAD systems), thereby fully linking Israel to its global early warning system and defenses.[41] In 2008, as noted, the United States deployed a special radar in Israel, linked to this system, that will provide it with significantly earlier warning time in the event of missile attacks from Iran, thereby enabling it to launch Arrow interceptors earlier, considerably improve the chances of a successful intercept, and better prepare the home front. The radar is operated by American troops and defense contractors and constitutes the first indefinite US military presence in Israel ever.[42]

Joint Military Exercises. Such exercises are an area in which Israel is not just a beneficiary of American assistance and know-how, but makes a contribution of its own. American soldiers and marines came to Israel prior to the 2003 war in Iraq to study urban warfare techniques and train in Israeli facilities, including special models of Arab villages that the IDF had built.[43] In 2007 the US Army completed construction of a large-scale mock Arab city in the Negev that both militaries use for urban combat training.[44] Following the operation in Gaza in 2014 the United States sent a special team to Israel to further study urban war-fare and counterterrorism techniques.[45]

Since the early 2000s IAF aircraft have been deployed at times in the United States, saving it the need to fly them back and forth, and allowing aircrews to arrive on a rotating basis for training purposes and to conduct joint exercises with their American counterparts.[46] Given Israel's tiny dimensions, it simply does not have the airspace necessary to conduct all of the aerial exercises its large and advanced air force requires, nor the topographic diversity needed to train for operations in unfamiliar environments. The exercises in the United States are thus of great importance for Israel and have included aerial refueling, air-to-ground attacks, dogfights, and paratroop drops.[47] In 2017 the US, Israeli, French, German, Polish, Greek, Italian and Indian air forces held the largest joint aerial exercise Israel had ever participated in, simulating dogfights, defenses against surface-to-air missiles, and more.[48] There have also been reports of joint exercises with Jordanian participation.[49]

In the past the United States and Israel conducted trilateral naval exercises with Turkey as well.[50] In recent years, following the deterioration in Israeli-Turkish relations, trilateral naval exercises have been held with Greece, including antisubmarine warfare, naval maneuver, command and control, interoperability, and port security.[51] Nearly a dozen surface ships and submarines participated in the 2015 exercise, the fifth and largest at the time.[52]

An exercise of particular importance, Juniper Cobra, is designed to test joint preparations for various scenarios of missile attacks on Israel. A total of 6,000 soldiers from the US European Command (EUCOM) took part in the 2014 exercise, along with two Aegis antimissile ships.[53] Another regularly held exercise, Austere Challenge, brought 1,000 US soldiers to Israel in 2012, out of a combined total of some 4,500, for missile defense and other scenarios.[54]

Bilateral naval exercises have included explosive ordnance disposal, diving and salvage operations, and more.[55] Thousands of marines have participated in joint exercises in Israel, including long-range helicopter raids and mobile and amphibious assault.[56]

Prepositioning. In 1983 an agreement was first reached providing for the prepositioning of American weapons and munitions in Israel. Initially very limited in scope, a mere $100 million, the US stockpile in Israel now stands at $1.8 billion and includes, inter alia, missiles and other aerial munitions, artillery shells, vehicles, spares for armored vehicles, and a 500-bed military hospital. Israel is allowed to make use of some of these items on a regular basis, such as munitions with a limited shelf-life, and others with special permission, as it did during the 2006 Lebanon war and 2014 Gaza operation.

The importance of this prepositioned American stockpile for Israel is three-fold. Given the limited shelf-lives of many highly expensive munitions, Israeli use of the US stockpile enables more cost-effective management of both countries' inventories. Second, prepositioning in Israel saves on transportation time during periods of conflicts and eases the American approval process. Finally, prepositioning is a further element of strategic cooperation that demonstrates Israel's importance for the United States and the strength of the bilateral relationship.[57]

Homeland Security. Cooperation has increased greatly since 9/11, in this case with Israel often providing the experience and know-how, at least in the beginning. The two sides formed a joint working group on homeland security, in addition to a variety of counterterrorism forums and agreements.[58] In 2010 an MoU was signed with the Transportation Security Administration (TSA) on airport security, including behavioral screening. The US Customs and Border Protection (CBP) operates Israeli-designed UAVs, and the United States has used Israeli know-how in mall security.[59] Israel has benefited from US assistance to screen against smuggling of nuclear materials through ports.[60] At one point, the United States provided an additional $200 million in aid, over and above the regular annual assistance, to improve Israeli border crossings, including special means for X-raying shipping containers.[61]

Unconventional and Cyber-cooperation. The area in which there has been the most sensitive strategic coordination between the two countries has, arguably, been in regard to Israel's purported nuclear capabilities. We have already addressed this in detail in the chapter 8, but suffice it to recall that the diplomatic cover the United States has provided for what it perceives as Israel's nuclear capabilities is considered, at least by one informed observer, to be a vital component of the "special relationship."[62]

The two countries signed a bilateral agreement on defense against unconventional terrorism, including cooperation in the operational, scientific, legal, medical, and intelligence areas.[63] The United States has provided Israel with funding for research to develop medicines and vaccinations against chemical weapons agents[64] and supplied it with advanced detection and identification systems against chemical and biological attacks.[65]

As already noted, the two countries have reportedly also cooperated extensively in the field of cyber-warfare, both for defensive and for offensive purposes. The Stuxnet virus, a joint effort according to press reports, is the first known case of offensive cyber-action of this kind.[66]

Multilateral Strategic Cooperation

This has taken many forms over and above the trilateral military exercises noted above. As part of a policy designed both to build a supporting regional framework for the peace process and to promote Israel's regional and international standing,[67] the United States has worked to help Israel improve relations with Jordan and Egypt, as well as the Gulf and North African countries. One effort worthy of particular note was the establishment of Qualifying Industrial Zones (QIZs) in Jordan and Egypt, which had a dramatic effect on Israeli trade relations with them. The QIZs enabled exports of Jordanian and Egyptian products to the United States under the preferential terms of the US-Israeli free trade agreement, on the condition that they contained a certain Israeli component. The success of these zones led to a situation in which both countries were actually enjoying the long-sought "fruits of peace," with large numbers of workers employed in QIZ industries, although this was unfortunately largely kept from their respective publics.

The United States exerted considerable efforts to further strengthen the Israeli-Turkish relationship in its heyday and tried to help revive it in recent years. Going further afield, the United States has supported Israel's successful efforts to maintain good relations with Azerbaijan, as well as its acceptance in international and regional forums, such as the Organization for Economic Cooperation and Development (OECD) and the Western and Others Working Group (WEOG) in the UN.[68] It is in the UN and its various agencies, especially the IAEA, in which multilateral cooperation has been most salient and in which the United States has worked closely with Israel to try to prevent various anti-Israeli resolutions.

Strategic Agreements and Upgrades

A long-standing common assumption holds that the United States would come to Israel's assistance in the event that its existence was threatened; indeed, that Israel even enjoys a de facto US security guarantee. There is, however, no formal assurance that this is the case, and it has never been fully explicated in a binding statement of American policy.[69]

Over the years, numerous measures have been adopted to upgrade the bilateral strategic relationship, and consideration has even been given to a formal defense treaty. The United States was reportedly first willing to consider providing Israel with a security guarantee as early as 1967, although this was contingent on a virtually complete withdrawal from the occupied territories.[70] In 1979, in a last-ditch effort to save the peace talks between Israel and Egypt from collapse, President Carter reluctantly acceded to an Israeli request for a US commitment to act in the event of an Egyptian violation of the peace treaty. In a narrowly drafted MoU, the United States stipulated that "if a violation of the treaty of peace is deemed to threaten the security of Israel . . . [it] will be prepared to consider, on an urgent basis, such measures as the strengthening of the United States presence in the area, the providing of emergency supplies to Israel and the exercise of maritime rights in order to put an end to the violations."[71]

Bilateral strategic cooperation truly developed under President Reagan, who defined Israel for the first time as a "major strategic asset" and viewed it as the only reliable US ally in the region.[72] In 1981 a bilateral MoU was signed, establishing a framework for strategic consultation and cooperation. Essentially a Cold War document, it contained a US commitment to assist Israel if it was threatened by the Soviet Union or Soviet controlled forces from outside the region. It further provided for joint exercises and R&D and expanded defense trade, but not for cooperation regarding states from the region, or joint measures in the event of an Arab attack against Israel.[73] The MoU was suspended due to US anger over the 1981 Golan Law and was never formally resumed, but served as a conceptual basis for some of the later measures adopted.

Ever since then Israel has consistently sought to further upgrade the strategic relationship. A first opportunity came as early as 1983, when Reagan signed National Security Decision 111, which provided for a more formalized structure of strategic cooperation, including joint military exercises, prepositioning of US equipment and munitions in Israel, sharing of intelligence, naval visits, and, of particular importance, joint contingency planning, leading to the establishment of the Joint Political-Military Group (JPMG). The JPMG has generally met ever since under the leadership of the assistant US secretary of state and the director general of the Israeli MoD, though at times the levels of representation have been higher. Meetings of the JPMG have covered such topics as the Iranian nuclear program, Iraq, Israeli-Egyptian relations, the peace process, Syria, and terrorist threats such as Hezbollah. In addition to the JPMG, a Joint Security Assistance Planning Group (JSAP) was established to discuss Israel's annual military assistance requests, prior to their submission to Congress.[74]

Although an important step forward, the Reagan directive, like the 1981 MoU, was still focused on the Soviet Union, not Israel's Arab adversaries. Later that year, however, a new MoU provided for joint planning regarding the Mediterranean part of the Middle East, though not the Persian Gulf, and further expanded on joint exercises and US prepositioning in Israel.[75]

In 1986 a new MoU was signed, providing for Israeli participation in the US ballistic missile defense program, the Strategic Defense Initiative ("Star Wars"), the first bilateral agreement in the area of missile defense. Two years later a further milestone was reached when the United States agreed to joint development and production of Israel's Arrow missile defense system.[76] This agreement followed a period of deep contention over the Lavi fighter aircraft, in whose funding and development the United States had reluctantly participated and whose termination it ultimately forced.[77]

In 1987 Israel was designated a Major Non-NATO Ally (MNNA), at the time a coveted status, the highest level of strategic partnership with the United States short of NATO membership. The new strategic upgrade was part of a 10-year MoU that established rules for military commerce between the two countries and provided Israel with greater access to US military tenders. As an MNNA, Israel was now also able to conclude an MoU with the United States that provided for heightened cooperation in defense R&D and eased Israeli military exports to the United States.[78]

The 1991 Gulf War led to a further major deepening in strategic relations, including the establishment of a direct communications link between the two defense ministers and defense establishments. Real-time warnings of Iraqi rocket launches were transferred to the IDF headquarters, and US Patriot antimissile systems were deployed in Israel, the first time that American forces had ever participated in its defense.[79] The United States did so, admittedly, primarily as a means of forestalling a possible Israeli operation in western Iraq, which might have disrupted the American-led coalition, but it marked a turning point nonetheless.

The Rabin government weighed the idea of asking the United States to station forces on the Golan Heights, as part of the security arrangements needed for a peace treaty with Syria, along with some form of American military presence in Israel itself.[80] Another idea that was mooted for a while in Congress was for Haifa to become a home port for the US Sixth Fleet, which operates in the Mediterranean,[81] thereby demonstrating the depth of the US commitment to Israel's security and, in effect, comprising a "tripwire."

In 1998 an MoU was concluded dealing with the ballistic missile threat to Israel. In language evocative of NATO's Chapter 5 guarantees, it stated:

> The United States Government would view with particular gravity direct threats to Israel's security arising from the regional deployment of ballistic missiles of intermediate range or greater. In the event of such a threat, the United States Government would consult promptly with the Government of Israel with respect to what support, diplomatic or otherwise, or assistance, it can lend to Israel.[82]

In this MoU the United States further undertook to maintain Israel's qualitative military edge, enhance its defensive and deterrent capabilities, and upgrade the overall strategic and military relationship.[83]

President Bush reportedly raised the possibility of an American defensive umbrella for Israel in the face of the Iranian nuclear threat. He also made sure to reaffirm the US commitment to Israel by stating that "Israel is a close friend and ally of the United States, and in the event of any attack on Israel [by Iran], the United States will come to Israel's aid."[84] President Obama took a similar stance, averring in public, "I'm willing to make the kinds of commitments that would give everybody in the neighborhood, including Iran, a clarity that if Israel were to be attacked by any state, that we would stand by them."[85] Secretary of State Clinton raised the idea of a regional defense umbrella as a means of assuaging both Israel's and the Arab states' fears of a nuclear Iran.[86]

In 2014 Congress adopted the US-Israel Strategic Partnership Act, which designated Israel as a "major strategic partner." This ostensibly upgraded status—which has yet to be granted to any other country or defined by statute or policy—still remains to be translated into concrete policy.[87]

Over the years, various Israeli premiers have sought to further upgrade the level of bilateral dialogue, leading to the establishment of additional strategic forums, such as the short-lived Special Policy Planning Group (SPPG), and in 2001 to the ongoing "strategic dialogue" between the two countries' diplomatic, defense, and intelligence establishments. These forums have discussed such issues as Palestinian terrorism and the state of the Palestinian Authority, Iraq, the Iranian nuclear program, the situation in Syria and Lebanon, including arms transfers to Hezbollah, arms control conventions, and the QME.[88]

Defense Treaty

For Ben-Gurion a defense treaty with the United States was a foremost strategic objective in the early years, but his overtures were rebuffed.[89] In 1954 Israel sought membership in NATO and then a defense treaty to counterbalance the Baghdad Pact (an alliance between Western and Arab countries). In 1977 Foreign Minister Dayan expressed doubt that the United States was ready for a defense treaty, but stated that he "would regard [this] as an achievement of the utmost importance for the State of Israel."

Since then the idea of a defense treaty has been mooted at various times and in various forms by leaders on both sides.[90] The Carter administration repeatedly tried to tempt Israel into making concessions in the peace process, by proposing a formal security guarantee, on the condition, which Israel rejected, that it withdraw from almost all of the territories.[91] Clinton first raised the idea of a defense treaty with Israel in early 1998, during Netanyahu's first term, in the context of an Israeli withdrawal from the Golan Heights and peace agreement with Syria.[92] As prime minister, Peres tried to reach agreement with Clinton on a defense treaty but received a cold response. As foreign minister he raised the idea once again.[93] Prime Ministers Rabin and Barak preferred a less binding strategic upgrade.[94]

The dramatic breakthroughs to peace Barak sought to achieve, during his brief tenure as premier, both with the Palestinians and Syrians, were the basis for the most intensive and advanced talks ever held on a US security guarantee for Israel, bordering on a defense treaty. Knowing that both peace deals would be highly controversial in Israel and that they would probably require unprecedented national referendums whose passage was not assured, Barak and the Clinton administration sought a means of convincing the Israeli public of their merits and of downplaying the fears they would engender. A dramatic strategic upgrade, it was hoped, might be the answer and was thus at least as much a matter of Israeli domestic politics as of strategic necessity. Few on either side were eager: the Israeli national security establishment adamantly opposed a formal defense treaty, although it welcomed a major upgrade, and Clinton approached the idea as a price to be paid for peace. When the peace talks collapsed, both sides favored a more limited agreement.[95]

The Israeli national security establishment's opposition to a formal defense treaty stemmed from a number of reasons. One was that the formal requirement to consult with the United States prior to taking action, the very essence of a bilateral defense treaty, would tie Israel's hands and restrict its independence and freedom of maneuver.[96] Whereas the far more stable strategic circumstances of the NATO allies and bilateral US treaty partners, such as Japan, South Korea, and Australia, enabled them to accept this limitation as the price of a defense treaty, the endlessly volatile and uniquely hostile Middle East did not permit Israel to do so. The United States, it was argued, would hardly be willing, or capable, of coming to Israel's aid in every low- to medium-scale conflict with Arab actors.[97]

A second major concern was in regard to Israel's strategic capabilities. If Israel were to enjoy an American defense guarantee, it was feared, the United States might question Israel's continuing need for an independent nuclear deterrent and possibly demand that it sign the NPT and disclose, even dismantle, "Dimona."[98]

A further concern was in regard to which Israeli borders the United States would be committing to defend. It would certainly not commit to the West Bank borders and probably not the Golan Heights,[99] the likely scenes of future wars, thereby making it unclear what the US security guarantee would cover, as well as the circumstances in which it might be invoked.

Moreover, a defense treaty might undermine the implicit bargain that had been the basis for the US-Israeli security relationship from the beginning, that the United States provides Israel with weapons, but Israel does its own fighting. A change in this understanding, it was feared, might weaken American public support for Israel.[100] Moreover, it was argued, Israel has to defend itself by itself, not just as a strategic imperative, but as a moral one and a matter of its national ethos. Generations of Israelis had been brought up believing in the concept of self-reliance, and a defense treaty might weaken their resolve to fight, as had happened to other American treaty partners in the past.

Finally, and crucially, many in the defense establishment believed that Israel already enjoyed most of the benefits of a formal treaty, without the above disadvantages.[101] The United States, by way of example, had conducted a large-scale airlift of arms to Israel during the Yom Kippur War and deterred the Soviets from intervening, deployed Patriot antimissile batteries to Israel during the first

Gulf War and undertook to do its best to protect Israel from missile attacks in the second one, cofinanced and developed Israel's multitiered rocket and missile defense systems, and much more. What Israel needed, they believed, was a series of increasingly comprehensive and binding strategic upgrades in the form of MoUs, but not an actual treaty.

Given these concerns, Barak sought the maximum upgrade possible just short of a formal defense treaty, a new status as a "strategic ally," capable of defending itself by itself, something approaching the intimacy of US relations with Britain and Canada. No other country in the world was so defined, and the administration was reluctant to use this term, preferring one that was less committal.[102]

The draft agreement, which underwent a number of iterations during the course of the talks, provided for long-term US military assistance to Israel at a significantly higher level, along with a special military aid package to enable Israel to confront the new threats it faced, and access to sensitive American weapons and weapons technologies. Specifically, the draft provided for the strengthening of Israeli missile defenses, the IAF's long-distance capabilities, and IDF force mobility. It contained assurances that the United States would maintain the IDF's qualitative advantage, provide special aid to Israel during emergencies, increase intelligence and terrorism cooperation, and ensure supplies of oil to Israel during crises. Moreover, the draft agreement included wording designed to allay Israel's concerns regarding its future freedom of maneuver and its deterrent capabilities (an implicit reference to Israel's supposed nuclear capabilities), and a US commitment to coordinate policy regarding regional arms control initiatives in the Middle East.[103]

Having rejected the idea of a formal defense treaty, but also seeking the most binding upgrade possible, Israel contemplated various legal options at the time. One was simply to conclude a new MoU, but it might not have been fully binding on future administrations and seemed, in any event, like a case of "been there, done that." Various forms of congressional sanction of the agreement were thus considered, including submission of the MoU for approval by a two-thirds majority of the Senate, or a decision of both houses of Congress by a regular majority. Both options were close to congressional approval of a formal bilateral treaty, the highest possible US commitment, but intentionally fell just short of that. The lesser commitment was also designed to prevent the humiliating and strategically adverse, but not unrealistic, possibility that Congress might not be willing to go quite as far as a formal defense treaty.[104]

The Diplomatic Dimension

In addition to providing Israel with the military wherewithal to ensure its security, the United States has also used its diplomatic leverage, in a variety of international forums, to protect Israel from an endless array of injurious resolutions in regard to the peace process, various Israeli military and diplomatic initiatives, and, of particular note, its alleged nuclear capabilities. To cite just a few examples, between 1954 and 2011 the United States vetoed a total of 38 one-sided or clearly anti-Israeli resolutions in the Security Council (41 depending on how one classifies them), 10 alone in the decade between 2001 and 2011.[105] Congress made payment of US debts to the UN contingent on acceptance of Israel in the Western and Others (regional) Group.[106] Unequivocal American support for Israel during the 2006 war in Lebanon made it the first military confrontation in the history of the Arab-Israeli conflict in which Israel did not face limitations of "diplomatic time."[107]

Although the United States has long been committed to an Israeli withdrawal from most of the 1967 territories, it has historically backed Israel's view that Security Council Resolution 242, the bedrock resolution on which all peace negotiations between Israel and its Arab interlocutors have been based, does not necessarily require a complete withdrawal. Instead, American leaders have variously spoken of Israel's need to have "defensible borders," of "minor adjustments," Israel incorporating the "settlement blocs," and other formulations. Moreover, the United States shares Israel's view that a final agreement must address its security concerns and has tried on more than one occasion to ascertain how this might be done in practice, most notably by General Allen during the 2014 "Kerry initiative." The United States supports Israel's opposition to a large-scale return of Palestinian refugees, which would undermine its character as the nation state of the Jewish people, and has supported its demand that the Palestinians recognize it as such. This is not to say that there are not significant differences even in these areas of overall agreement, and Jerusalem and the settlements remain major issues on which the gaps are substantial. Nevertheless, on the fundamental principles of a two-state solution the two countries share much agreement.

In 2004, in a letter to Prime Minister Sharon, President Bush provided two vitally important assurances to Israel. The first was that "the United States is strongly committed to Israel's security and well-being as a Jewish state. It seems clear that an agreed, just, fair and realistic framework for a solution to the Palestinian refugee issue, as part of any final status agreement, will need to be found through the establishment of a Palestinian state, and the settling of Palestinian refugees there, rather than in Israel." The second was that "in light of new realities on the ground, including already existing Israeli population centers, it is unrealistic to expect that the outcome of final status negotiations will be a full and complete return to the armistice lines of 1949."[108] President Obama, who initially walked away from the Bush letter, a problematic act with ramifications for Israeli trust in future American commitments,[109] ultimately adopted a largely similar formulation, at least in regard to the latter issue.

Ever since the Six Day War, every US administration has been involved in the effort to promote the peace process, some intensively. Two presidents, Carter and Clinton, went so far as to put their personal reputations on the line by convening summits at Camp David (with Egypt in 1978 and the Palestinians in 2000), the highest possible level of presidential involvement. Both even went the last mile and presented US position papers, successfully in the Egyptian case. Others have undertaken significant diplomatic initiatives, such as Bush's 2002 "Vision for Peace in the Middle East" and 2003 "Roadmap for Peace in the Middle East," or Obama's (and Secretary of State Kerry's) mediation efforts in 2014, even if they did not go quite as far.

The United States has also provided strong support for Israeli diplomatic initiatives, even if in some cases this required that Israel first devote considerable efforts to convincing it of the benefits of the proposed approach. Rabin surprised Clinton with the Oslo talks, but once he had been brought into the picture, Clinton became an avid promoter of the process. Barak went to great lengths to gain Clinton's support for the dramatic initiatives he envisaged both with the Palestinians and with Syria, and once he had succeeded in doing so, could not have had a more committed partner. Bush was initially hesitant to support Sharon's surprise decision to withdraw unilaterally from Gaza and demanded a number of important changes as a condition for American backing, but was ultimately fully supportive. Other presidents, such as Bush senior and Obama, took a more confrontational approach, with notably less success, although the former's secretary of state, James Baker, did succeed in convening the Madrid Conference in 1991.

Over the years Israel has worked with the United States to impose sanctions on a variety of regional actors, not just Iran and Iraq, but Syria, Hezbollah, and Hamas, or to add them to the State Department terrorist list. The United States and Israel have discussed ways of both making the PA a more effective governing body in its own right and increasing its military capabilities to prevent terrorism against Israel.[110]

Three Critical Questions

Question 1: Has Israel Lost Its Independence to the United States?

Critics have long maintained that Israel repeatedly allows itself to go its own way and thumbs its nose at the United States, or that this is even a case of the tail wagging the dog.[111] Israel does act independently at times, possibly more often than one might expect in a totally asymmetric relationship of this sort. This section will argue, however, that with the exception of a few cases of existential consequence and the highly politically charged issues of the future of the West

Bank, US policy has been the primary determining factor in virtually all major national security decisions Israel has made ever since the "special relationship" evolved in the 1970s and 1980s, and in many cases long before.

These are important exceptions. Unless, however, one expects nearly complete Israeli pliability and subservience—which would not be an entirely unwarranted US expectation, given Israel's great dependence on it—the reality is that Israel's acts of independence, or "defiance," have been few and confined to the above issues of preeminent national concern. On matters pertaining to major military operations and on most diplomatic issues as well, Israel virtually always accords primacy to the US position. As a consequence, Israel has lost much of its independence to the United States. This conclusion is strongly contested by some Israelis and Americans alike and thus requires substantiation. The following section seeks to do so.

In 1967, at a time when US-Israeli relations were still quite limited, Israel only went to war after a protracted waiting period, when President Johnson informed it that he would not be able to fulfill an earlier US commitment to open the Straits of Tiran, which Egypt had closed to Israeli shipping, and arguably provided a "yellow light" for Israeli action. In 1973 the primary reason Israel refrained from launching a pre-emptive strike, even once it had become clear that an Egyptian and Syrian attack was imminent, was the fear of the American reaction. Israel's behavior in both of these wars preceded the emergence of the "special relationship."

Israel only launched the First Lebanon War, in 1982, after at least partially convincing the United States of the need for a large-scale military operation, a process that took the better part of a year. In 1991 Israel refrained from responding to Iraqi missile attacks largely due to American pressure. The American demand that Israel refrain from attacking Lebanon's civil infrastructure, during the 2006 Lebanon war, left the IDF without a viable military strategy and was one of the primary reasons for the difficulties Israel encountered. Concern over a potential lack of support by the incoming Obama administration led Israel to terminate the 2008 operation in Gaza earlier than intended.

Israel's decision to refrain from a strike on the Iranian nuclear program, even though it considered it an existential threat, is a particularly important example of the primacy it attaches to the US position, and especially of the need for American support for military action. American opposition was not the only Israeli consideration; some doubted the efficacy and even feasibility of an Israel strike, but it was certainly a primary consideration, quite possibly the decisive one.[112] Israel's reported strike against the Syrian reactor in 2008, conversely, was conducted with American understanding, if not outright support, and only after intensive consultations and the United States had made it clear that it would not attack on its own.[113]

On the peace process, too, the American position has had an enormous impact on Israel's positions, if not quite as decisive as on military matters. Israel
had strong reasons of its own for seeking peace with Egypt, but some of the
concessions it made, especially at the Camp David Summit in 1978, were
largely because of American pressure. Indeed, Carter reportedly threatened
Begin that if he did not agree to sign the agreement, Israel would lose its nuclear
capabilities: "Don't rely on Dimona, I will see to it that you don't have Dimona
either."[114]

With the important exception of the initial Oslo Agreement itself, Rabin
and Peres closely coordinated Israel's positions in the negotiations with the
Palestinians and Syrians in the early 1990s with the United States. Barak met
with Clinton just days after assuming office to gain American support for his
highly ambitious plan to achieve peace with both the Palestinians and Syrians
within a year. He then spent the following year in extraordinarily close consultation with Clinton, meeting with him on a number of occasions and often
speaking with him and other top American officials a number of times a day.
Indeed, Barak's strategy and bargaining posture at the Camp David Summit in
2000, and again prior to the Clinton Parameters later that year, was intentionally
aligned with the US position.

Sharon, initially dismayed by Bush's "Roadmap for Peace," rapidly adopted
it and closely coordinated the unilateral withdrawal from Gaza with the United
States. In fact, it was the American position that led to his decision to withdraw
from all of Gaza, dismantle all of the settlements there, and remove four in the
West Bank as well. The American administration knew the details of the dis-
engagement plan long before senior Israeli officials, including the defense minister. Prime Minister Olmert similarly sought to coordinate his positions with
the United States, both at the Annapolis Conference and in regard to his far-
reaching proposal to Palestinian president Abbas in 2008.

One of the worst crises in US-Israeli relations unfolded over the sale of advanced Israeli weapons to China. Probably on no other issue have the administration and Congress joined hands to exert such heavy, even brutal, pressure
on Israel. The case demonstrates Israel's overwhelming dependence on the
United States as do few others and is thus worthy of the somewhat lengthy
treatment given.

In 2000 a newly emerging relationship with China led to a major breakthrough, with a $2 billion deal for the sale of Israeli early warning aircraft (the
Phalcon).[115] A significant sum in and of itself, especially for a country Israel's
size, the true importance of the deal was that it was a harbinger of the broad strategic relationship that China sought with it, including arms sales of a far greater
magnitude. The aircraft had no American technology or components and there
was thus no formal legal barrier to the deal. Nevertheless, the United States

demanded that Israel cancel it, out of concern that the aircraft might contribute to Chinese air capabilities in some future conflict.[116] Israel, which had unwittingly come up against the global considerations of a superpower, and which sought to preserve the emerging relationship with China, tried to stonewall. The American response was unambiguous.

Some in Congress threatened a partial cutoff of military assistance, while the Pentagon postponed action on Israeli requests for new weapons and the US Air Force canceled a joint exercise with the IAF. High-level talks on a strategic upgrade of the bilateral relationship were suspended, and the administration even linked US willingness to assist Israel in promoting the peace process and to grant it access to advanced defense technologies. In the end, Israel was forced to accede to the establishment of a bilateral mechanism to monitor all future Israeli arms sales to countries of concern, cancel the deal, and pay China $300 million in compensation. The Sino-Israeli military relationship has yet to recover to this day.[117]

Five years later, the issue erupted anew, this time over follow-on support for a sale of Israeli UAVs to China that actually predated the Phalcon affair. The United States again imposed sanctions on arms sales, joint projects, and exchanges of information and technology, and Israel was barred from participating in the planning of the new F-35 fighter. Relations between the two defense ministries were disrupted, and a planned meeting of the JPMG was postponed.

Under American pressure, Israel was forced to provide details of more than 60 arms sales to China and allow the United States to examine its arms exports procedures, in order to understand the supervisory process, why it had failed and why the Israeli civilian leadership had not been involved, and the punitive measures that Israel planned on taking against those involved in the deal. Moreover, the United States insisted that the Knesset pass a new law regulating arms exports, the MoD establish an arms exports branch, and the cabinet set up an interministerial coordinating committee to supervise exports of dual-use items. Finally, the MoD director general, whom the United States held personally responsible for having misled it over the issue, was forced to resign.[118] Cases of such blatant intervention in the sovereignty of another country are very rare, certainly among friendly democracies.

The development of Israel's purported nuclear capabilities is held to be a primary example of Israeli defiance of the United States in the early decades. The United States actively sought to block the Israeli nuclear program in its formative years during the 1950s and 1960s, and has ostensibly tried to bring it under the NPT ever since. In reality, however, the United States never did everything it could to stop the program,[119] certainly never exerted the kind of effort it has made to prevent other countries from pursuing nuclear capabilities. Moreover, as elaborated in chapter 8, the United States has come to accept the Israeli program over the years and to provide diplomatic cover for it, and the case can be made that it believes an independent Israeli nuclear capability actually serves US interests. Indeed, on the assumption that the capability is intended solely for defensive purposes, in the face of a concrete threat to Israel's existence, it should be sufficient to deter all such dangers on its own, thereby relieving the United States of the need to come to Israel's assistance. Israel's "independent behavior" in this regard looks less so when viewed in this light.

In the decades since the "special relationship" began emerging, there have been virtually no cases in which Israel has taken major military action without first consulting with the United States. The one major exception, which is therefore almost always cited, is the bombing of the Iraqi nuclear reactor in 1981. The United States did not know about the plan to attack the reactor, but a lengthy period of intensive consultations did precede it.

Prime Minister Netanyahu's sharp opposition to the 2015 Iran nuclear deal stands out as a case of uniquely defiant behavior. Even supporters of the deal, however, recognized the potentially existential threat and severe dilemmas it posed for Israel. Had Netanyahu ultimately resorted to force, it would have been hard to argue that this was not a legitimate exercise of Israeli independence in the face of an existential threat. Conversely, history would have judged him harshly had he refrained both from attacking the Iranian program and from expressing strong opposition to the deal—and Iran ultimately went nuclear. In any event, the way in which Netanyahu chose to oppose the deal was clearly an aberration. Other Israeli leaders expressed strong opposition at the time, but none advocated open defiance of the United States, and they would probably have handled matters in a far more restrained, much less public, and, therefore, far more legitimate and palatable manner from a US perspective

The one area in which some Israeli governments truly have taken independent positions in recent decades, in defiance of the United States, is in regard to the peace process, primarily the issues of Jerusalem and the settlements and, in the past, the Golan Heights. It is these issues that are the primary basis for the argument that Israel goes its own way, despite its dependence on the United States.

The first two of these issues, Jerusalem and the settlements, are not existential, but are of supreme ideological importance for their supporters. A large majority of the Israeli electorate is deeply attached to Jerusalem, which it considers the very heart of Judaism and Israeli statehood. A large, highly motivated, and well-organized minority, about one-third of the electorate, opposes any concessions on the settlements. The future of the West Bank, as a whole, is existential for Israel, possibly in the physical sense, more likely in terms of its future character as a nation. As for the Golan Heights, an overwhelming majority attaches existential importance to Israel's control of them. It is appropriate for Israel to set its own course in matters of such importance to its future. Moreover, no leader in any democracy could afford to take issues of such deep public sentiment lightly.

Nevertheless, even the most right-wing premiers have refrained from annexing the West Bank, generally sought to minimize differences with the United States over it, and instituted some restraints. Netanyahu, for example, who was embattled with the United States as no other premier, agreed to a 10-month settlement freeze at the beginning of his premiership and again reined in settlement activity in 2015 because of American opposition.[120] Other premiers pursued policies that were far more closely aligned with those of the United States (Rabin, Peres, Barak, Olmert, even Sharon) and, in at least one case, Barak, greatly exceeded American expectations.

There is a common thread to the above cases of Israeli independence—they were all matters of either existential consequence or great ideological importance for the Israeli electorate. One can certainly question the wisdom of Israel's policies in some of these cases, but an appropriate regard for its democratically elected institutions should, and has, moderated the American response.

Having said that, there have also been cases of seemingly gratuitously provocative Israeli behavior, which have fanned the perceptions of its ongoing defiance, such as announcements of new settlement activity immediately following visits of senior American leaders. Nevertheless, and without belittling the impact of acts such as these for the United States, they are a petty reflection of domestic Israeli politics, not decisions of strategic importance.

One of the unique characteristics of the totally asymmetrical American-Israeli relationship is that the United States itself neither expects nor desires complete Israeli subservience and, therefore, accords Israel a modicum of independence that it might not ordinarily consider appropriate for a client-state so overwhelmingly dependent on it. Part of this may reflect that intangible "something" that does make the American-Israeli relationship "special," part may be the influence of the pro-Israel lobby, but mostly it appears to reflect a calculation of American strategic interests. The United States has long recognized that Israel faces uniquely difficult and harsh external circumstances and that preservation of Israel's security does require that it take unusual measures at times, even if there has been disagreement regarding the nature of the appropriate response. Were the United States to demand complete Israeli pliability, it would have to assume responsibility for addressing the threats Israel faces on its own, a burden the United States does not seek. By allowing Israel a measure of freedom, especially at the low and high ends of the threat scale, the United States frees itself of the responsibility for them.

The security ramifications of a potential peace agreement with Syria are a case in point. The United States has long recognized the gravity of the threats Israel faces on the Golan Heights and has consequently been hesitant to assume both the strategic and the moral responsibility involved in making untoward demands of it. A similar, if less pronounced reticence, has also informed American thinking regarding the security aspects of a deal on the West Bank. A possible invasion of Israel through the West Bank, along its vulnerable narrow waist, or massive rocket attacks against Israel's main population centers, constitute severe threats, of which the United States is fully cognizant.

At least to some extent, cases of Israeli independence today should be viewed not as defiance of the United States, but as a success of American policy and indication of the maturity of the relationship. US military and diplomatic support has built a strong and prosperous Israel, increasingly confident of its security and existence, the true long-term objective of the "special relationship," and therefore able to take independent positions on issues of vital importance to it. It is never easy for a patron to see a ward spread its wings, but it is a healthy sign, some cases of inappropriate or egregious Israeli behavior aside. The United States has differences with other allies as well.

For the most part, however, as a small actor facing numerous and often severe threats, but with limited influence of its own, Israel has become reliant on the United States as the panacea for virtually all of its problems. Israel can and does appeal to other countries, but this is usually of marginal utility, and what the United States cannot achieve, Israel almost certainly cannot, so there has often been limited interest in even trying. Whether on the peace process, in which there has been competition with the Arab side for American favor, the Iranian nuclear program, other issues of regional WMD proliferation, terrorism, efforts to delegitimize and impose sanctions on Israel, and just about everything else, turning to Washington has been Israel's preferred and often sole recourse.

For Israelis, brought up on the ethos of self-reliance, the reality of dependence is difficult to accept and rubs against their every national instinct, as well as concrete strategic needs. The United States is a generally reliable patron that does try to live up to its commitments, but it has failed Israel on a number of occasions of importance: to cite just a few, Johnson's aforementioned failure to open the Straits in 1967, Nixon's intentional delay of the military airlift in 1973,[121] Bush's inability to deal with the Syrian nuclear reactor, Obama's disavowal of the 2004 Bush letter to Sharon, and, more debatably, the nuclear deal with Iran. In some of these cases Israel has been forced to take action on its own, thereby demonstrating the strategic imperative of maintaining its independent capabilities and of not putting all of its eggs in one basket, the overall reality of dependence notwithstanding. They also help explain the Israeli defense establishment's strong opposition to a bilateral defense treaty. They are, however, the exceptions.

Israel's great fortune, if it must rely on another country, is that it is dependent on the United States, usually a well-intentioned benefactor, and the relationship has become so close that for many Israelis the national borders separating the two countries have blurred, psychologically and emotionally. Almost as many

Jews live in the United States as in Israel, and numerous Israelis live in the United States, have family there, and travel to the United States for work or pleasure. Officials in the national security establishment, in particular, are in constant contact with their American counterparts and operate in the setting of a strategic relationship that is often close to being familial.

As a result, Israelis find it hard at times to truly internalize the fact that the United States is not just a senior partner, a big brother, but a global superpower with multiple and at times conflicting interests in any given issue, that these interests may be different from Israel's and even conflict with them, and that the United States has become reasonably adept at managing conflicting situations such as these, if not quite in the ways Israel always wishes. The Phalcon affair, West Bank and settlements issues, Israel's QME, and the Iran nuclear deal offer disparate examples of how the United States handles multiple conflicting interests in any given issue.

Nearly four decades into the "special relationship," the price of a remarkable bilateral relationship has been a significant loss of Israeli independence and freedom of maneuver. In effect, the United States and Israel long ago reached an unwritten understanding. The United States provides Israel with a de facto security guarantee, massive military assistance, broad but not complete diplomatic support, and, in the past, economic assistance. In exchange, Israel is expected to consult with Washington on issues of importance prior to taking action, demonstrate military restraint and diplomatic moderation, even make concessions,[122] and accord the American position overriding importance.

Israel can still respond to limited events on its borders, but most military and strategic issues beyond that, and almost all important diplomatic ones, require prior consultation and, in practice, adherence to the American line. There are exceptions, but they are essentially matters of an existential nature or of overwhelming domestic political importance. Disagreements on the settlements, an outlier, and to a lesser extent Jerusalem, have obscured the broader reality, that in most cases Israel does accord clear primacy to American policy. The ultimate manifestation of Israel's overwhelming dependence on the United States is the very need to raise the question posed in the next section, whether Israel could even survive today without the United States.

Question 2: Can Israel Survive Today without the United States?

Given Israel's great dependence on the United States, a second critical question is whether it could even survive today without it. This is, of course, a speculative question that is hard to answer in any definitive manner. Necessity and desperation can produce creative solutions that are not apparent at this time.

Israel clearly could survive if the United States stopped the military assistance program. In the mid-2010s US aid constituted approximately 3% of Israel's state budget and 1% of its GDP, a painful but not insurmountable cut. Conversely, an end to US aid would certainly be a severe blow to the defense budget. US aid has constituted some 17%–20% of the defense budget in recent years, a very large sum, and almost the entire procurement budget. Moreover, the IDF budget in recent years has actually comprised less than half of the total defense budget (the difference consists of highly expensive rehabilitation and compensation programs for the injured and widows, pensions, and more), approximately 30 billion shekels out of a total of over 60 billion. American aid thus constitutes approximately 40% of the IDF's budget, a whopping amount,[123] and its end would be devastating unless a major reordering of national priorities took place, with profound ramifications for Israel's economy and society.

The consequences might be even more severe in regard to the supply of the weapons themselves, where Israel's dependence on the United States is critical. Unlike the Arabs, who can procure weapons from numerous sources, with few constraints, the United States may be the sole source for Israel. If one looks at the other major arms producers today—Britain, France, Russia, China—it is very hard to imagine any of them stepping in to fill the United States' place. Even were we to assume the political willingness to do so—a highly questionable assumption—none would be willing to provide the funding, and there is no qualitative substitute for American arms.[124]

Furthermore, the US-Israeli military relationship is far more than just the supply of weapons. As seen above, it has numerous vitally important strategic components, such as the link to the American global missile launch system, bilateral and trilateral exercises, prepositioning, and even a de facto security guarantee. No other country can or would provide Israel with such capabilities and assurances or could deal with Iran's nuclear program, an existential threat for Israel, as the United States did, even if there were differences in the end. No other country would have helped Israel build a rocket and missile shield, the only one of its kind in the world, or, reportedly, engaged in joint offensive cyber-operations.[125]

On the diplomatic level, too, there is no alternative today to the United States and probably not in the future. No other permanent member of the Security Council would repeatedly use its veto to protect Israel from sanctions, even when it itself often disagrees with Israeli policy. No other major power would provide Israel with diplomatic cover in virtually all international forums, including for its purported nuclear capabilities, or even try to take a balanced position on the peace process. As Israel's international isolation has grown, its dependence on US diplomatic cover has become almost complete.

So could Israel survive without the United States? Maybe. Maybe it could somehow "tough it out" virtually alone in a globalized world, but it would certainly be very difficult economically, requiring a drastic change in the nature of Israel's economy and society, and in truth it would be almost impossible militarily and diplomatically. This should give great pause to those in Israel who have advocated taking a more independent approach to its superpower patron, as happened during the 2015 brawl over the Iran nuclear deal. No one likes to be dependent on a foreign power, even one as friendly and well-meaning toward Israel as the United States. This, however, is the reality, and there are clear policy ramifications for a country whose dependence on the United States is as great as Israel's, as outlined in the recommendations in chapter 12.

Question 3: Where Is the US-Israeli Relationship Heading?

A third question is where the bilateral relationship is headed in the medium and long term, that is, whether it will remain as robust as ever or has peaked and is bound to decline. The political and cultural foundations of the relationship are sufficiently strong so that a 1967-style French abandonment of Israel by the United States is virtually unthinkable. Moreover, the United States is too invested in Israel's existence and security, and the strategic relationship has become too institutionalized, for it to simply walk away. The question is thus not a black-or-white one. Israel can count on medium to long-term American support for its security, but the degree of support may change. Even a marginal change would have profound ramifications for Israeli national security.

Overall support for Israel in the US public remains high, but there are political and demographic trends in both countries that are likely to have a deleterious impact on the relationship in the future. One of the secrets of American support for Israel has been its historically bipartisan nature. In recent years, however, even before the dramatic confrontation over the Iran nuclear deal in 2015 greatly accentuated the problem, Republicans and conservatives had become far more supportive of Israel than liberals and Democrats.[126] There is nothing wrong with rising support for Israel on the Right; it is the loss of support on the Left, and identification of Israel as a partisan issue, that should be of deep concern.

There is also a significant decline in support for Israel among young Americans, who are less likely today to sympathize with it than the American public as a whole, primarily due to the Palestinian issue. Having come of age in recent decades, in an era in which Israel has been consistently portrayed as a brutal and even racist occupier, with little memory of the Holocaust and of Israel's heroic early years, this is hardly surprising, and the anti-Israel campaign on college campuses is widespread. Indeed, one devastating 2011 survey found that 25% of American students thought Israel was an apartheid state, with a further 50% unsure.[127] These young people are hardly likely to be supporters of Israel in the future, whether as voters or holders of positions of influence. The medium- to long-term consequences may be severe.

A similarly problematic process is underway among young Jewish Americans, only about a third of whom now view Israel as a very important component of their Jewish identity, compared to 53% of those 65 and older. Whereas more than 80% of young Jewish Americans felt that Israel's destruction would be a personal tragedy for them in 1981, less than half did so in 2007. One-quarter of young Jewish Americans believe the United States supports Israel too much, compared to 5% of those 65 and older. Low birth rates, intermarriage, and assimilation continue to undermine the strength and support of the Jewish community, the irreplaceable bedrock of support for Israel in the United States. Among the Jewish community as a whole, nearly 60% intermarried between 2005 and 2103, 71% if one excludes the Orthodox. Over 80% of the children of intermarried couples intermarry. Survey data demonstrate clearly that support for Israel is far weaker among children of intermarriages.[128]

The religious composition of the Jewish population is also changing, with a growing percentage of the Orthodox and the unaffiliated and a decrease among the Conservatives and Reform, traditionally the groups at the forefront of pro-Israel support. Already today, 35% of all American Jewish children under the age of five are Orthodox, and by 2050 the Orthodox community as a whole may increase from 10% of the total Jewish population today to 25%. Among Orthodox Jews support for Israel is firm, though of a more Republican and right-wing approach than among the majority of the contemporary Jewish community.[129]

The centrally directed approach toward Israel that had long characterized the Jewish community began eroding during the 1980s, if not earlier, leading to the institutionalization of growing ideological divisions in the form of such organizations as Americans for Peace Now and J Street on the Left, and American Friends of Likud and the Zionist Organization of America on the Right. This has had a negative impact on the leverage of the pro-Israel lobby as a whole, with the different organizations working at times at cross-purposes, and weakening AIPAC's heretofore unchallenged role as the sole representative of the pro-Israel community. This trend is likely to increase further as time goes by[130] and weaken the American Jewish community's role as Israel's "strategic hinterland."

The Hispanic population and the religiously unaffiliated, the two groups in the United States among whom support for Israel is the lowest, are growing rapidly. Hispanics, who numbered about 15% of the population in 2010, are the largest minority group in the United States today. Almost six million Hispanics voted in 2000, 12.5 million in 2012, and the number is expected to double by 2050. The religiously unaffiliated, only 8% of Americans in 1990, already constituted about 20% in 2012. Religiosity has always been an important determinant of support for Israel.[131]

To these tectonic shifts in the US population one has to add a sense that support in Congress, never stronger based on voting records, appears to have become "a mile wide and an inch deep." Given the controversies surrounding Israel in recent decades and, conversely, the strength of AIPAC, much of the ongoing support may have become merely smart politics, superficially mouthed "political boilerplate" that elected officials have learned to repeat without much conviction. Staunch support for Israel plays well in a number of highly committed and influential constituencies, with little downside, whereas failing to express strong support can have a high cost.

Tectonic demographic changes are taking place within Israeli society, as well. The rapid increase in the size of the ultra-orthodox Jewish population and growing number of Israeli Arabs, as presented in chapters 4 and 5, is also likely to put pressure on the bilateral relationship. Neither community is committed to the values associated with the US-Israeli relationship, nor to the relationship itself, and will continue to pursue policies that are not conducive to it. Moreover, to the extent that Israel looks like a tension-fraught religious or binational society, Americans are less likely to identify with it.

Some American Jewish and Israeli critics believed President Obama to have been less friendly toward Israel than his predecessors. The real question, however, if that assessment is true, is whether Obama was an exception, or heralded an emerging trend. Obama was a product of an American generation that has come of age with a very different conception of Israel than its predecessors and with greater sympathy for the Palestinian cause. President Trump may or may not be more friendly to Israel. The crucial question is how Israel should position itself for an era, not of hostile presidents, but of ones who may lack the instinctive warmth and support of many of their predecessors. This in itself may have profound ramifications. Strategic interests are a primary determinant of international relations; so, too, more often than many believe, are human emotions.

In conclusion, the above political and demographic trends in the United States and Israel and in US-Israeli relations are certainly a cause for concern. This is not to suggest a significant downturn in relations anytime in the foreseeable future. Two countries that could weather the crisis they experienced over the Iran deal, in addition to long existing differences over the future of the West Bank, are likely to continue enjoying a strong relationship. There are, however, highly worrisome medium -term trends, and the relationship can no longer be taken for granted in ways that it could in recent decades. Some of the sources of concern are already apparent today, and, crucially, the relationship has likely passed its peak. Even a small modulation in American support is of great consequence for Israel. Given current trends, the change may become more than marginal.

Primary Observations

- The US-Israeli relationship is truly "special," possibly unprecedented. Israel has received more US assistance than any country since World War II and enjoys broad, though not complete, diplomatic and strategic backing, as well as a de facto security guarantee. Turning to the United States has become the panacea for most of Israel's problems.
- The price of a remarkable relationship has been a significant loss of Israel's independence. Israel is expected to consult prior to acting, exercise military and diplomatic restraint, even make concessions, and adapt to US policies. There have been very few cases in which Israel has taken major military action without according primacy to US positions. This is true of most diplomatic issues, too.
- It is questionable whether Israel could survive today without the United States. Maybe Israel could somehow "tough it out," but this would require major socioeconomic change and pose essentially insurmountable military and diplomatic obstacles. Dependence is undesirable, but is the reality and has clear policy ramifications.
- Israel does act independently at times, but with few exceptions on issues only of potentially existential consequence, such as Iran's nuclear program, or of supreme ideological importance for much of Israel's electorate, for example, the future of the West Bank. It is appropriate for Israel to set its own course in matters such as these, although there have been cases of gratuitously provocative behavior.
- The United States has long recognized Israel's uniquely harsh external circumstances. By allowing it a modicum of independence, especially at the low and high ends of the threat scale, the United States frees itself of the moral and strategic need to address them itself.
- US support has built a secure and prosperous Israel, the ultimate objective of the "special relationship." At least some cases of Israeli independence today should be viewed as a success of American policy and indication of the maturity of the relationship.
- The United States is a generally reliable patron, which tries to live up to its commitments. Nevertheless, it has failed Israel on a number of important occasions, thereby demonstrating the importance of Israel's ongoing independent capabilities.

- Support for Israel in the United States remains high, but Israel is increasingly a partisan issue, and young people, including Jews, are significantly less supportive. Large population groups in both countries who are not committed to the relationship are growing rapidly. A new generation of leaders and officials, who lack the instinctive support of many of their predecessors, is coming to power. The ramifications for Israel will be profound.

- Low birth rates and high intermarriage have greatly undermined the size and strength of the non-Orthodox Jewish community, the bedrock of US support for Israel. Moreover, growing internal divisions are weakening AIPAC's heretofore unchallenged role and the influence of the pro-Israel lobby as a whole. The Jewish community's ability to serve as Israel's "strategic hinterland" is diminishing.

- The relationship has likely passed its peak, and there are highly worrisome medium-term trends. The foundations of the relationship are sufficiently strong that Israel can count on medium to long-term American support, but it may change in extent and character. Even a marginal change would be severe for Israel.

PART FOUR

A NATIONAL SECURITY STRATEGY FOR AN ERA OF CHANGE

11

Primary Conclusions

In Israel, in order to be a realist, you must believe in miracles.
—David Ben-Gurion

The fundamental thesis of this book, as stated in the introduction, is that far-reaching changes have taken place in Israel's strategic environment, the nature of the threats it faces, and its society, and that a commensurate change in its national security strategy is thus warranted. The previous chapters presented the extensive changes that have taken place in all three areas, as well as in Israel's defense and foreign policy responses. The following chapter sets out the primary conclusions derived from the information and analyses presented above, as a basis for the comprehensive national security strategy proposed in the final chapter.

As comprehensive as this book aspires to be, no one scholar's work can truly encompass the breadth and richness of a topic of such great complexity. In the absence, however, of any official statement of Israel's national security strategy, this book will now constitute, at a bare minimum, a common basis for discussion and hopefully facilitate systematic debate, public, academic, and governmental. Should it do so, the book will have achieved its fundamental purpose.

The proposed strategy is a broad set of principles designed to serve as guidelines for future national security planning and decision-making. It is not, and does not purport to be, a detailed policy prescription regarding all of the major issues Israel faces today, each of which warrants a separate strategic statement, though it does touch on them.

In a proposal for an overall national security strategy, a number of potential pitfalls of consequence present themselves. First, the conclusions and recommendations are likely, at least at some level, to reflect the author's normative preferences and may thus not constitute an "objective" assessment of Israel's needs. This is particularly true of highly charged issues such as the future of the West Bank or some of the diplomatic and demographic challenges Israel faces today.

Every effort has been made throughout the background chapters to maintain maximal academic distance and neutrality. In the concluding chapters, the conclusions and recommendations, a particular effort has been made to demonstrate that they stem directly from the information and analyses presented in the background chapters, that is, from Israel's strategic needs, rather than personal preferences, and that the proposed policies are preferable to the primary alternatives. Readers will judge the author's success. At a minimum, the conclusions and recommendations should be acceptable to those who share a commitment to an Israel that remains a predominantly Jewish, Zionist, and liberal democratic state.

A second pitfall is that some of the conclusions and recommendations may appear unoriginal, having long been proposed by others. It is, however, once again, the fact that they are based on a systematic analysis of Israel's strategic circumstances and needs, not subjective political observation, that justifies their inclusion. The challenges Israel faces are well known, numerous experts and political figures have addressed them, and this book is greatly enriched by their work. No strategy can be entirely original, nor should it aspire to be; much of the common wisdom is just that, the result of the work of many wise people. It is the integration of the common wisdom, together with some original contributions, that makes the recommendations below the first public attempt to formulate a coherent and comprehensive Israel national security strategy.

A third potential pitfall is whether the proposed strategy is both implementable in practice and politically viable. A strategy that fails to meet either of these criteria may be of theoretical interest, but is not the basis for practical policy, as this book presumes to be. All of the recommendations in the next chapter meet the first criterion: they are implementable should the government so wish, and many will be acceptable to all Israeli governments regardless of their political orientation. Others, however, will clearly not be acceptable to the government in office at the time of this writing, or some future ones. In these cases the recommendations thus address the measures required in the interim, pending adoption of those elements of the proposed strategy that are not currently politically viable or await the emergence of the prerequisite strategic circumstances.

Fourth, the devil, as is well known, is often in the details, in the actual nitty-gritty of policy implementation and in the politics of the issue. In the recommendations below the attempt has thus been made, where appropriate and feasible, to present, not just broad prescriptive statements regarding what should be done, but concrete means of actually doing so in practice, including how to address the politics of the issues.

Fifth, not all of the necessary information is available, whether because it is classified or for other reasons. This constraint is particularly true of the military recommendations and is a fact of life all researchers face.

Finally, all strategies are relevant to a given time frame and set of assumptions. In a dramatically changing Middle East, it would be difficult to aspire with any degree of confidence to a strategy relevant to much more than 10 years, and even that may prove ambitious. Conversely, a proposal appropriate to a significantly shorter period could hardly be considered a strategic blueprint for national action. The national security strategy presented below thus strives to relevancy for some 10 years, longer for some issues, but recommends a mid-course assessment and recalibration every five years.

A nation's vital national security objectives are a core set of fundamental, essentially immutable interests, that are independent of and transcend specific opportunities or threats and the government in office at any given time.[1] In this context, Israel's vital national security objectives, as set out in the introduction, are the following:

- Preserving Israel's character as the democratic nation state of the Jewish people and constituting a national home and spiritual center for them
- Ensuring Israel's existence, territorial integrity (including the West Bank and Golan Heights, pending resolution of their final status), the security of Israel's citizens, and the effective functioning of its core governmental system and critical infrastructure, both civilian and military
- Achieving peace with Israel's neighbors, or at least coexistence
- Promoting the socioeconomic well-being of Israeli society

In addition, Israel has a variety of lesser, though still highly important national security objectives, some relatively permanent, others that change with circumstance. Current examples, at the time of this writing, include preventing Iran from acquiring nuclear weapons and spreading its influence in the region, especially in Syria and Lebanon, preventing Hezbollah and Hamas rocket attacks and other forms of terrorism, maintaining close strategic cooperation with the United States, defeating international delegitimization efforts, expanding new opportunities for dialogue and cooperation with Sunni states, and more.

The following are the primary means by which Israel can pursue these vital national objectives. Although mere "instruments" of policy, they are of such importance that they can be considered vital objectives in their own right and are part of the overall basis for the recommendations in chapter 12:

- Preserving Israeli society's fundamental consensus, motivation to serve, willingness to bear the burden, and resilience
- Maintaining a strong military force, including strategic capabilities, and qualitative superiority over any reasonable combination of enemies

- Preserving the "special relationship" and de facto alliance with the United States
- Preserving the peace with Egypt and Jordan, achieving a resolution of the Palestinian issue that ensures Israel's character as a predominantly Jewish and democratic state, at a minimum separating from the Palestinians, and broadening peace to additional neighbors
- Strengthening Israel's international standing
- Promoting economic growth and Israel's qualitative edge (human capital, educational, and scientific achievements)

For the reader's ease, the conclusions have been grouped into the following categories: general, politico-military (i.e., those that are at least largely diplomatic in nature), military, and domestic. The differences between the categories are not always entirely straightforward, and the categorization under the different headings is a judgment call. Some of the conclusions are mutually conflicting, a reflection of Israel's complex strategic circumstances.

General Conclusions

Israel's Classic National Security Doctrine Was a Dramatic Success. It achieved its primary objectives: Israel won its existence, most of the Arab countries have given up on any practical aspiration to destroy it, Egypt and Jordan made peace, and Israel has become an established, secure, and prosperous state. Ben-Gurion's belief that Israel's existence would be assured if and when it had a population of five million Jews, an almost miraculous aspiration at the time, has long been achieved—Israel now has a Jewish population of 6.5 million.

Israel Has Never Been Stronger and More Secure Militarily. Israel no longer faces existential threats, the Arab armies are in disarray or at peace with Israel, and there is virtually no danger of conventional military-to-military warfare. Syria's chemical arsenal has been largely dismantled, Hamas poses a painful but limited threat, Hezbollah a major but not existential one. Iran's nuclear aspirations, the only potentially existential threat, have been checked, at least for the interim. If the nuclear deal holds, Israel will not have faced an existential threat for 50 years, a dramatic transformation in its strategic circumstances.

Israel's Diplomatic Vulnerability Is Growing, Brewing Crisis. Ongoing diplomatic warfare and delegitimization have severely undermined Israel's international standing. Its isolation in international forums is extreme and its bilateral relationships are increasingly affected, too. Much of the opprobrium reflects fundamental enmity, but the settlements policy has played into Israel's adversaries' hands and harmed its international standing as no other. To the international community, it is gratuitously provocative, rendered inexplicable because it appears incompatible with Israel's character as a Jewish and democratic state. Conversely, Israel has ties today with more countries than ever before. What is different is the collapse in its standing among traditionally friendly states and growing international delegitimization. A crisis point may be nearing with European and other Western countries. If Israel could, arguably, afford to lose the support of European states and publics, even a modulation in American support would be dire. No state, certainly not one as tied into international affairs as Israel, can long afford such isolation and delegitimization.

Major Threats Remain; Military Power Is Still the Basis of Israel's National Security. Israel cannot base its national security on a static snapshot of its strategic circumstances, favorable as they are today. Iran has probably not abandoned its long-term nuclear aspirations, others in the region may go nuclear in response, and a Middle East with multiple nuclear actors would be a nightmare scenario. Hezbollah is a major threat, backed by Iran, a regional power that is rapidly expanding its influence. A major regional arms buildup is underway, and cyber-warfare presents a new and potentially severe threat. In a dramatically changing Middle East, in which enmity toward Israel unites a broad spectrum of opinion, military power remains the fundamental basis of Israel's national security.

Israel Faces a Critical Decade. The ongoing stalemate over the West Bank issue is likely to reach a critical turning point in the coming decade; either a two-state solution will be achieved or the de facto annexation will truly become irreversible. Israel likely faces a 5- to 15-year hiatus in the Iranian nuclear issue,[2] at the end of which it will be clear whether Iran intends to cross the nuclear threshold, additional actors in the region also go nuclear, and Israel has to make critical decisions in response. The regional turmoil inspired by the "Arab Spring" is likely to continue undermining the stability of states in the region, with major ramifications for Israel. Domestic challenges, such as low Haredi and Arab participation rates in the labor force, will either be addressed or become an untenable economic burden.

No National Vision: Reactive and Military Decision-Making. The dissipation of the existential threats, lack of consensus on the Palestinian issue, and domestic divides have left Israel without the clearly defined strategic objectives of the early decades. Israel's national security thinking has thus lost much of the sharp focus it had in the past, and Israel too often finds itself reacting to events, muddling through rather than seeking to chart a preferred course, and typically left solely with military responses. This has been especially true of those governments that have refused to set out a blueprint for resolving the Palestinian issue. The absence of clearly defined strategic objectives also makes it harder for the IDF to decide which military threats to prepare for, how to structure itself and even which weapons systems to acquire.[3] In the absence of clear objectives, Israel's leaders cannot assess the success of their policies, a politically expedient, but strategically destructive, state of affairs.

A Fundamental Insecurity Syndrome Continues to Color Israel's Thinking. Some 70 years after the Holocaust and Israel's rebirth, Israeli national security policy still cannot be understood in the absence of the primal fear of annihilation instilled by this cataclysmic event and preceding centuries of Jewish persecution and insecurity. Indeed, Israel can probably never acquire enough weapons to feel truly secure, and it does live in a uniquely harsh region. As a result, Israel responds to events, at times, in a manner more appropriate to the weak state of the early decades, whose existence was on the line, than to an established and secure nation, a regional power, whose existence is now assured.

The Bottom Line: Israel Has Never Been Better Able to Chart Its National Course. Israel's strategic environment has been transformed, much of it for the better, its adversaries are in disarray, and its existence is no longer in doubt. Major challenges remain, and Israel's freedom of maneuver remains circumscribed. A peace agreement with the Palestinians is probably unattainable, at least for the foreseeable future, regardless of Israel's positions, and there is nothing Israel can do to change the enmity of Iran, Hezbollah, Hamas, and others toward it. Nevertheless, Israel's positions have greater influence over its affairs than ever before,[4] and Israel could fundamentally change its international standing, turn the diplomatic tables on the Palestinians, cement the alliance with the United States, ensure its future character as a Jewish and democratic state, and greatly strengthen its prospects for socioeconomic and scientific growth were it to change its West Bank policies. The change in its standing would also provide Israel with greater international legitimacy in the battle with Iran and other extremists. For all of the daunting constraints it faces, Israel is at the height of its national power,[5] and Israel has never been better positioned to chart its national course. The open question is whether it will take advantage of the window of opportunity it has, before history charts a new course for it.

Politico-Military Conclusions

Resolving the Palestinian Issue, at Least Separating from the Palestinians, Is Israel's Foremost National Interest, but Not a Panacea. A resolution of the conflict with the Palestinians, and if that proves unachievable, at least separation from them, is vital for Israel's future character as a state and the pre-eminent challenge it faces as a nation. It is also key to many of Israel's other national security challenges, such as a fundamental change in its regional and international standing and the long-term strength of its relationship with the United States.

Nothing is more important. A Palestinian state, however, is unlikely to be more stable, moderate, and socioeconomically successful than other Arab countries, indeed, is more likely to be a poor, unstable, and even failed and irredentist one, with whom tensions will be ongoing. Peace with the Palestinians will not end Iran's, Hezbollah's, and Hamas's enmity toward Israel, which is a function of its existence, not policies.

There Is No Military Solution; There May Not Be a Diplomatic One. The Arab-Israeli conflict has raged for a century. Israel has repeatedly won the wars, secured its existence, and forced two of its neighbors to make peace. Nevertheless, Israel has been unable to end the conflict militarily, truly absorb the West Bank after half a century of occupation, or suppress Palestinian nationalism, and the West Bank has become a threat to its character as a state. The Palestinians have rejected or ignored dramatic proposals for peace, face a difficult succession process that may further diminish the prospects for peace and, in any event, cannot conclude a final peace agreement with Israel until the West Bank and Gaza reunite. The gaps between the sides may simply be unbridgeable. It is an open question whether the conflict with the Palestinians is about Israel's existence or the 1967 issues. Israel has also been unable to defeat Hezbollah and Hamas, and Iran is probably too big for Israel to take on alone. There may well not be a diplomatic solution to the threats Israel faces, but there is no long-term military one, either.

Demography Poses a Grave, Possibly Existential Threat. The demographic ramifications of Israel's de facto annexation of the West Bank for its future as a Jewish and democratic state are inexorable and existential. Already today only some 60% of the combined population of Israel and the West Bank is Jewish. Neither declining Palestinian fertility rates nor increased Jewish population growth (whether from natural growth or immigration) can reverse the demographic reality. There is no known solution other than separation, presumably based on the "two-state" paradigm.

The Status Quo Is an Illusion; the Window for a Two-State Solution Is Closing. The number of settlers is growing, even if most of the growth in recent years has been limited to the "settlement blocs," which will presumably be part of a land swap, and the land available for the swaps is increasingly being used for other purposes. Moreover, the Palestinian split between the West Bank and Gaza continues and may be long term, the rise of Islamism makes the conflict even harder to solve, and positions on both sides are hardening. Palestinian rejectionism may be the primary obstacle, postpone wrenching decisions is human nature and there is no immediate deadline, but the current impasse is untenable in the long term and we are rapidly approaching a point of "no return" for a two-state solution. Some believe we may have already crossed it.[6] Either way, Israel is running out of time and cannot postpone the day of reckoning much longer. Should the election of President Trump portend a further period of prolonged diplomatic impasse, a two-state solution may not survive another eight years. The prospects of large-scale Palestinian violence, even a "third intifada," will also grow.

Maintaining the Peace with Egypt and Jordan Is a Supreme Interest. Peace with Egypt and Jordan has transformed Israel's national security circumstances, eliminating the existential conventional threat to its security, allowing it to greatly cut defense expenditures and divert defense resources to other threats and, more importantly, to domestic needs. Israel thus has strong strategic interests in the longevity of the Egyptian regime and Jordanian monarchy. Should the latter fall, however, despite all efforts to the contrary, new possibilities for progress with the Palestinians may emerge, along with new dangers from the east.

Israel Is Not Yet Accepted in the Region; the Fundamental Asymmetries Remain. Arab countries have accepted the reality of Israel's existence, not its legitimacy, and those who seek cooperation do so for lack of choice, not out of reconciliation. Even Egypt and Jordan only terminated belligerency, rather than truly making peace. Israel has overcome some of the fundamental asymmetries with the Arab states, even achieving quantitative superiority against any likely Arab coalition today, but others, such as population and territorial size, potential economic and military resources, and war objectives continue to pose major challenges.

Israel Depends on the United States for Its Survival and Has Lost Much of Its Independence. Israel has become so militarily and diplomatically dependent on the United States that it is questionable whether it could even survive today without it. The price of an extraordinary relationship and de facto security guarantee, however, has been a loss of much of Israel's independence. Israel does act independently at times, but, with very few exceptions, only on issues of existential consequence or supreme ideological importance for much of its electorate. US support has built a secure and prosperous Israel, the ultimate objective of the "special relationship," and at least some cases of Israeli independence should thus be viewed today as a success of American policy. The United States itself has long accorded Israel a modicum of independence, especially at the low and high ends of the threat scale, thereby freeing itself of the moral and strategic need to address them. The United States is a generally reliable patron but has failed Israel on a number of important occasions, thereby demonstrating the importance of its ongoing independent capabilities.

Diminished US Stature Weakens Israel's National Security. The United States' overall international standing has diminished, and its stature in the region is at a decades-long nadir. As a consequence, its ability to effectively address an array of major regional issues, such as the peace process, Iran's ongoing nuclear program and generally problematic regional behavior, the possibility of further regional nuclear proliferation, and the situations in Syria, Lebanon, and Iraq, to name just a few, has been undermined. For Israel, which is so closely identified with the United States and whose national security is so dependent on it, the deleterious ramifications are numerous and significant. The concomitant rise of Russian influence in the region has already posed grave challenges for Israel, even if not directed against it and though Russia is a friendly country today.

American Support for Israel Is Strong, Yet with Worrisome Trends. Overall support for Israel in the United States remains high, but political and demographic trends in both countries have already had a negative impact on the relationship, and cracks have emerged. Low birth rates and high intermarriage, along with growing internal divisions, have greatly undermined the strength of the Jewish community, the bedrock of US support for Israel, and its ability to serve as Israel's "strategic hinterland." A significant deterioration in the relationship is unlikely for the foreseeable future and the foundations are sufficiently strong that Israel can count on medium- to long-term American support. The relationship has, however, probably passed its peak, and even a small change in American support will have great consequences for Israel.

Israel Is No Longer a "Nation Dwelling Alone." It has a remarkable relationship with the United States, close ties with Germany, Poland, Canada, Australia, India, and more, and extensive commercial and military ties with numerous countries around the world, even many that do not maintain diplomatic relations with it. The West Bank issue poisons all of Israel's relations and has contributed greatly to its isolation and even delegitimization, but when perceived to act justifiably, Israel still enjoys much understanding in the West, at least among leaders, less so the public. Israel does not formally belong to any bloc, alliance, or association but is in practice very much part of the American camp and to a lesser extent the Western one as a whole.

Israel Is Affected by Changing International Norms Far More Than Others. In a world in which the use of military power has become increasingly rare and unacceptable, Israel is unusual in that it is frequently forced to resort to it. Add to this the diplomatic and delegitimization campaigns long waged against Israel, together with the criticism of Israel's West Bank policies, and Israel is subject to totally disproportionate and often biased attention by the international media and institutions, almost entirely to its detriment. Israel has repeatedly used military force, despite the new international norms, but has suffered severe opprobrium as a result and has been forced to change the nature and length of its operations.

Crisis Management and Resolution Mechanisms Are Weaker Than in the Past. The ability of the Security Council and the superpowers, as well as certain Arab states, to play a moderating role and intervene to end regional conflicts has diminished. Crisis management and resolution mechanisms are thus weaker than in the past, making efforts to end a confrontation, or to plan an exit strategy, more complex.

Israel Still Enjoys Considerable "Soft Power." Even after decades of conflict and delegitimization efforts, Israel still enjoys considerable soft power. The sources of its soft power are diverse, including the support of Jews the world over, Christian identification with Israel as the Holy Land, its democratic values, reputation as a "start-up nation," Holocaust remembrance, and more. Israel's soft power is also the basis for much of its "hard" political power, especially in the United States. Israel, however, has largely forgotten, or downplayed, the soft power that was the primary basis for the broad international support it enjoyed during the early decades, or undermined it through some of the policies it has adopted. The Palestinians have used "soft power" very effectively and are winning the war for international opinion and support.

The Jewish Diaspora Is a Vital National Security Asset. This is especially the case in the United States. Direct financial assistance from the diaspora is important but pales in comparison with US military aid and diplomatic support, which are vital today to Israel's national security and even existence. American support for Israel is largely a result of the Jewish community's efforts, however, and thus, sentiment aside, the diaspora constitutes a vital national security asset, which greatly expands Israel's capabilities beyond its indigenous ones.

Military Conclusions

Iran and Hezbollah Are the Foremost Threats Today. Iran is the most sophisticated adversary Israel has ever faced and its ongoing nuclear program the greatest threat. The danger is not primarily of use, but the risk that almost every regional conflict could become an existential one, the influence Iran would gain and the possible emergence of a multinuclear Middle East. The 2015 nuclear deal diverted international diplomatic and intelligence attention to other issues, Iran's economic and diplomatic standing are improving, and the prospects for surprise have grown as a result. Iran is already establishing one long strategic arc from its own territory through Iraq and Syria to Lebanon and turning Lebanon and Syria into one united front under its leadership. Accordingly, Iran will remain Israel's overriding concern for the foreseeable future. Hezbollah, a substate actor with unprecedented capabilities, and an Iranian proxy, poses a major threat and will be Israel's immediate focus in the coming years. Hamas poses a much smaller, yet still highly disruptive, threat. Various jihadi organizations may present important threats in the years to come, but probably of a much more limited magnitude.

The Primary Threat Posed by the Arab States Today Is Their Weakness. The Arab states are either in a state of crisis, at peace with Israel, or long uninterested in a direct military clash. Most today are weak or failed states, and the vacuum in central authority provides fertile ground for radical nonstate actors. The future stability of Egypt, Jordan, and the PA is far from assured, with important ramifications for the future of peace with them. The future stability of Iran, Syria, Iraq, Lebanon, Saudi Arabia, Libya, and Yemen will have major ramifications for the prospects of military hostilities. The regional turmoil is likely to continue for many years, possibly decades. The primary threat the Arab states pose to Israel no longer stems from their strength, but their weakness.

The Military Conflict Is Now Limited Primarily to Nonstate Actors and Iran. The Arab states are either at peace with Israel or no longer capable of, or interested in, waging war. With the important exception of Iran, the interstate stage of the Arab-Israeli conflict has ended, at least for the foreseeable future, and the military conflict today is limited to substate actors, primarily Hezbollah and Hamas. Whereas the Arab states are focused today on the 1967 territories, Iran and the substate actors still seek Israel's destruction.

Israel's Home Front and Military Rear Are Now the Primary Battlefield. Iran, Hezbollah, and Hamas know they cannot defeat Israel militarily today, but view its home front and military rear as an Achilles heel, a strategic vulnerability that provides them with the basis for an effective, decades-long strategy of "attrition until destruction," designed to neutralize Israel's superiority, undermine its society, and ultimately lead to its collapse. The home front is now the primary battlefield and the wars a matter of mutual deterrence and destruction. The advent of precise rockets and missiles is a potential game changer, allowing Israel's adversaries to target its military rear extensively in future conflicts and disrupt both offensive and defensive operations. Repeated operations every few years have taken a heavy toll on Israel's economy and standing. Attrition is particularly hard for Israel, whose national culture is focused on the short-term and quick responses.

The Classic Strategic Pillars and Deterrence-Decision Model No Longer Fully Apply. All of the rounds with Hezbollah and Hamas to date have ended in asymmetric ties, undermining Israel's deterrence. Their ability to cause severe damage to Israel's home front has created a balance of terror, and they have proven deterrable for only limited periods. Israel's growing reliance on deterrence by punishment, rather than denial, results in severe international opprobrium and is likely to be increasingly constrained. Rockets and missiles can be launched virtually without preparation, making early warning almost impossible. Military decision is usually no longer a viable option today either, because of Israel's reluctance to occupy further territory, diplomatic constraints, warfare's changing nature, and the possibility that Hezbollah and Hamas will rearm rapidly or be replaced by even more heinous enemies if toppled. Maybe most important is that the price in casualties, physical damage, and international condemnation has been deemed to exceed the threat itself. Israel thus does not yet appear have an effective offensive response to the Hezbollah and Hamas threat, at an acceptable price, and has thus preferred to "mow the grass" to lengthen the lulls, and rely increasingly on defense.

In reality, Israel was never able to achieve full deterrence and military decision against the Arab states. The magnitude of the threats they posed, however, led to a broad consensus that decision was essential and worth the price. Should the Hezbollah and Hamas threats be deemed to warrant the price in the future, Israel will presumably once again seek military decision, defined as a prolonged lull, significant reduction in their capabilities and ability to rearm, and improved diplomatic standing.

Israel Has Not Unequivocally Won a War since 1967. Even then it did not achieve military decision: the War of Attrition broke out just two years later and the Yom Kippur War four years after that. Israel ultimately prevailed militarily in 1973, but lost the war strategically, as its overall postwar position was weakened, the Arab countries were able to negotiate from a position of strength, and Israel's economy was devastated. The 1982 war in Lebanon ultimately ended in failure. Israel has been unable to defeat Hezbollah and Hamas, or even gain a decisive advantage over them, in repeated operations spanning four decades. It has caused them significant losses and pain and gained deterrence that has led, in some cases, to periods of calm, but no more.

Israel Is Reaching the Limits to Military Force. Israel can continue to suppress the Palestinians, at least for the meantime, but a resolution of the issue is possible only through negotiations, and Israel faces growing constraints on the use of force against Hezbollah and Hamas. None of the operations against them since the 1980s have ended satisfactorily or achieved prolonged deterrence, and the price of military decision has outweighed the benefits. The deterrence achieved in 2006 and 2014 was based on punishment, not denial, which leads to severe international opprobrium and which Israel will be increasingly hard pressed to repeat. Israel no longer seeks to transfer the fighting on the ground to the enemy and to conquer territory, making military decision very hard to achieve. Military decision is beyond Israel's capabilities against distant states, such as Iran, and is meaningless at the nuclear level. Israel's increasing inability to resolve the threats it faces on its own has required growing reliance on diplomacy, for example, the international sanctions imposed on Iran, the Egyptian and US roles in ending the recent rounds in Gaza, and the UN's role in the unilateral withdrawal from Lebanon and in ending the 2006 Lebanon war. For much of the international community today, force is simply not an option, those who wield it are perceived to be wrong by definition, and there is an expectation that matters will be resolved through nonviolent means. This may be somewhat naive and even hypocritical, but Israel has little choice but to play by the new rules of the game. In the coming years, Israel is likely to find diplomatic tools to be both increasingly necessary and often more effective than military means.

Israel Has Been Forced into a More Defensive Posture. An effective offensive response will presumably be achieved at some point, but in the meantime Israel has been forced to increasingly rely on defense, which has come to be defined as a fourth strategic pillar. Israel has achieved an effective defensive capability against a limited rocket threat, such as Hamas demonstrated in 2014, but presumably only a partial one against Hezbollah's massive arsenal. In future rounds, Hamas and especially Hezbollah may conduct massive rocket fire against IDF airbases, mobilization centers, and other targets to disrupt its offensive operations, as well as on national infrastructure sites, and Iran's missile arsenal is also growing. Israel has responded by investing large sums in rocket and missile defense. Both internal terrorism from the West Bank and external terrorist threats on Israel's borders have led to increasing resort to physical barriers and hardening of homes and public buildings.

Israel's Adversaries Will Continue to Seek Asymmetric Responses. Israel's conventional military superiority led its adversaries to seek asymmetric responses in the form of heightened terrorism and WMD programs. Unable to penetrate Israel's borders on the ground, they sought to go over it by deploying rocket arsenals, now increasingly precise. Partially blocked by Israel's rocket shield, they are also attempting to tunnel under the border. In the future, they will undoubtedly pursue new asymmetric means of overcoming Israel's defenses, including attempts to penetrate virtual borders through cyber-attacks, possibly renewed interest in chemical weapons or other WMD, and surprise attacks of a nature we cannot yet foresee.

Israeli Counterterrorism Has Been Very Successful, but Terrorism Remains a Strategic Threat. Israel's counterterrorism efforts have kept terrorism to a level its society can tolerate and provided decision-makers with the latitude necessary to pursue preferred policies. Israel achieved military decision in the second intifada, demonstrating that conventional armies can defeat insurgencies and large-scale terrorism. Terrorism, however, has hardened public opinion toward the peace process, affected Israel's negotiating positions, and determined electoral outcomes. It thus remains a strategic threat. The de facto annexation of the West Bank has incorporated terrorism into Israel, undermining its potential role as a buffer, while the emergence of a radical terrorist entity in Gaza is the living embodiment of Israel's fears of a future Palestinian state in the West Bank. The efficacy of potential security arrangements is a subject of debate. Future rounds with Hezbollah and Hamas are probably just a matter of time.

Nuclear Ambiguity and the "Begin Doctrine" Have Succeeded but Face New Challenges. Israel's policy of nuclear ambiguity has been a resounding success. The international community and even the Arab world have become accustomed to Israel's exceptional status, it appears to enjoy the benefits of an overt nuclear posture, without the costs, the United States provides political cover for it, and Israel's destruction is no longer a viable enemy option, the equivalent of national suicide. Israel has successfully applied the Begin Doctrine (prevention of enemy acquisition of nuclear weapons, if need be by force) in the Iraqi case and, reportedly, in Syria, though it has yet been put to the test regarding Iran. If, hypothetically, Israel possesses the capabilities attributed to it, one of the gravest dilemmas it would ever face, if some other regional actor(s) were to go nuclear, would be whether to prefer that all sides retain their existing capabilities or that none do, and therefore to pursue regional arms control. International nonproliferation regimes, however, have repeatedly failed to prevent regional states from developing WMD, and Israel's ability to rely on them is thus limited. The possible proliferation of nuclear weapons to other states in the region, largely in response to the inconclusive nature of the Iran nuclear deal in 2015, will present Israel's long-standing nuclear posture with growing difficulty.

Domestic Policy

A Growing Crisis of Governability, Political Deadlock, and Legitimacy. Israel has been mired in a decades-long crisis of governability and state of political deadlock, as a result of which the political system has proven increasingly incapable of making essential decisions, both in domestic and in national security affairs, and of implementing those decisions that have been made. Right-wing governments have refrained from formally annexing the West Bank and from unbridled settlement activity, and their policies have suffered from internal contradictions. Left-leaning governments have pursued far-reaching proposals for peace, but Palestinian terrorism and rejectionism undermined their efforts and swayed electoral outcomes, and they have been unable to sustain their agendas. The ongoing impasse, and crisis of governability, have undermined governmental legitimacy and popular faith in democracy and prevented Israel both from charting a clear national course and from effectively addressing the major challenges it faces. Accordingly, they have become a threat to Israel's national security.

Israeli Society's Strength Is a Vital Strategic Asset, but Growing Casualty Aversion. The discord over the future of the West Bank hides the broad agreement that unites most Israelis today on almost all other national security issues and which, the popular impression to the contrary, notwithstanding, is the basis for a strong ongoing national consensus. The motivation to serve and societal resilience remain high, and Israelis manifest high levels of identification with their state, happiness with their lives, and support for military operations. The strength and resilience of Israel's society and its ongoing national consensus are strategic assets that provide its leaders with broad decision-making leeway. Israel is doing something right. In a society increasingly sure of its security, but unconvinced that the irregular conflicts Israel faces today justify the supreme sacrifice, casualty aversion has grown and been institutionalized in governmental and IDF decision-making, deeply affecting the national decision-making process and changing the nature of IDF operations.

Multiple Societies in One: Domestic Cleavages Are Strategic Liabilities. Israel has become a number of different societies rolled into one, living together in a tenuous balance. The secular and national-religious populations are at the forefront of international technology; the Haredi and Arab populations lag far behind and are becoming an untenable burden on the whole. If current trends continue, Israel will face an economic crisis, its Jewish, Zionist, and democratic character will be further challenged, the "people's army" model will come under severe stress, and its Arab population, still primarily a socioeconomic issue, may become a security threat. A public that has become increasingly cynical and demanding, with an activist civil society, frenetic media, interventionist judiciary, and competitive market economy, constrains national security decision-making far more than in the past, with growing pressures to divert resources to domestic needs. The fundamental cleavage over the future of the West Bank saps Israel's national unity, and future attempts to resolve the issue, one way or the other, are likely to stretch Israeli society to a crisis point and even lead to bloodshed. None of these challenges are new and Israel has successfully managed them for decades, but all are nearing critical turning points.

Home Front Preparation Is Still Deficient. Israel still does not have a national strategy for defense and management of the home front during hostilities, or a work plan setting out what the different agencies involved are to do in the coming years. Long-standing bureaucratic disputes over home front management have yet to be resolved, and the gap between the threat and the response is still too wide.[7] IDF thinking has made important strides, but has still not fully internalized the need for heightened emphasis on defense of the home front and military rear, in terms of budgets, manpower and training, doctrine, and more.

On the basis of these conclusions, we now turn to the final chapter, policy proposals.

Policy Recommendations

Where there is no vision, the people perish.

—Proverbs 29: 18

The following chapter presents recommendations in the areas of politico-military and military policy and some relevant issues of domestic policy, drawing on the conclusions in chapter 11. Taken together, the recommendations are designed to comprise a proposal for a coherent and comprehensive new Israeli national security strategy.

The overall thrust of the proposed strategy is that Israel has never been more secure and better positioned to chart its future course as a nation, and can thus adopt a more long-term approach, based on greater strategic patience and a heightened emphasis on diplomacy and defense. At the same time, the strategy fully recognizes the significant threats that Israel still faces and the vital need to maintain robust conventional and strategic capabilities, both offensive and defensive. The strategy further emphasizes the need to preserve and strengthen Israel's domestic sources of power and thus the need for socioeconomic and electoral reforms as high-priority national security objectives.

To facilitate the reader's understanding of the overall nature of the proposed strategy, a brief list of the policy recommendations appears below. The detailed recommendations follow.

Politico-Military Policy Recommendations:
- Separate from the Palestinians as foremost national objective
- Aspire to more diplomatic response; pursue comprehensive new foreign policy
- Define relations with United States as fundamental national security pillar
- Seek independence where possible; adapt to reality of dependence
- Seek defense treaty with United States at appropriate timing

Military Policy Recommendations:

> ➤ Adopt an approach of strategic patience, that is, restraint and defense
> ➤ Maintain robust offensive capabilities but pursue smart offense as part of "long game"
> ➤ Develop a national mortar, rocket, and missile defense shield
> ➤ Review the defense budgetary process
> ➤ Ensure Iran never crosses nuclear threshold, ensure capability to strike
> ➤ Maintain nuclear ambiguity
> ➤ Prepare for era in which "Begin Doctrine" may no longer be feasible

Domestic Policy Recommendations:

> ➤ Treat home front as priority and accord greater resources
> ➤ Nourish qualitative edge and societal cohesion and resilience
> ➤ Amend electoral system

We now turn to a detailed discussion of the policy recommendations.

Politico-Military Policy Recommendations

Separate from Palestinians as Israel's foremost national objective, if possible through two-state solution; preserve viability of two-state solution pending agreement, including settlement freeze outside the blocs; act unilaterally, if necessary, to determine Israel's borders on the basis of demography and security; prevent West Bank from becoming Gaza-like launching pad for attacks.

Peace with the Palestinians, at a minimum separation from them, is a supreme Israeli interest. This is neither a political statement nor a normative assertion, but a strategic imperative that derives directly from an analysis of Israel's strategic interests. Even though a resolution of the Palestinian issue may not be achievable for the foreseeable future, quite possibly far beyond, this does not, by any means, detract from its vital importance for Israel and the consequent need to conduct its policy in the meantime in a manner that does not preclude the possibilities for reaching an agreement.

Israel's ongoing control of the West Bank, especially the settlements issue, has had a ruinous effect on its international standing, further fueled the delegitimization campaign, and undermined Israel's otherwise strong national security consensus. The reality is that Israel simply cannot effectively address these grave challenges without resolving the Palestinian issue, or at least achieving significant progress. Decades-long efforts to convince the international community of the legitimacy of the settlement policy have failed and cost Israel the support of Europe and much of the rest of the world. Indeed, much of the Israeli public opposes them. Rather than staunching the flood of opprobrium, Israel today is losing the support of parts of the American public as well. This is a danger it simply cannot afford.

Peace with the Palestinians will have a highly beneficial impact on Israel's international standing and economy. Even the limited progress achieved in the Madrid Conference and Oslo Agreement in 1991 and 1993, respectively, led to the establishment of diplomatic relations with many countries and to a flood of foreign investment and business. A peace agreement, or just a change in Israeli policy, that alters the international perception that it is Israel, not the Palestinians, that is the primary obstacle to progress today would have a significant impact. A number of Arab states, primarily in North Africa and the Gulf, have long been interested in a closer relationship with Israel, if and when progress with the Palestinians is achieved, as are a variety of Muslim and Third World countries. A revitalized relationship with Europe and other Western countries, avoidance of growing isolation and even sanctions, and most importantly, a guarantee of the long-term vitality of the relationship with the United States are all contingent on this.

As demonstrated in chapter 4, the demographic threat to Israel's future as a Jewish and democratic state, stemming from the de facto annexation of the West Bank, is inexorable. Various attempts to downplay the magnitude of the problem, whether through misrepresentation of demographic trends, or schemes designed to mitigate it, such as providing for Palestinian representation by allowing them to vote for their own parliament, while Israeli settlers vote for the Knesset, will be rejected by the Palestinians, the international community, or both, and are doomed to failure. There is only one known solution that both preserves Israel's fundamental character as a state and addresses Palestinian aspirations. Difficult to achieve as this solution will likely continue to be, it remains the "two states for two peoples" paradigm.

The issue has been with us for five decades, and just a few more years will not make a critical difference, at least if the increase in the settler population is limited to the "settlement blocs," as most has in recent years, and which the Palestinians, too, recognize will be part of a future land swap. The issue is pressing, nevertheless, and cannot be put off for long. The number of settlers outside the blocs is slowly increasing, open territory available for land swaps is being used for other purposes, positions are hardening on both sides, the split between the West Bank and Gaza may become long term, the PA's legitimacy and viability are eroding, and popular faith in the prospects for a solution has collapsed. The actual political ability of an Israeli government, of any political stripe, to relocate close to 100,000 settlers, the approximate number required today assuming a withdrawal from all of the West Bank, less the settlement blocs, is already questionable, and every additional settler makes a future agreement that much harder.

Moreover, the Palestinians' seemingly never-ending rejection of any and all compromise proposals, from the earliest days of the conflict to this very day, which is the only realistic basis for an agreement, makes the prospects of a two-state solution minimal, at least for the foreseeable future, regardless of who is in office in Israel. In the meantime, the hard Right has also become increasingly entrenched in power in Israel. Should the Trump administration herald another eight years of diplomatic failure or inactivity, a two-state solution may not survive.

Israel's deep-seated, historic sense of insecurity, together with its justified concerns regarding the security ramifications of territorial withdrawal, have produced a tendency to be overcautious in the pursuit of peace and overexpecting in terms of security guarantees. There is no such thing as complete security, nor permanent peace. All countries have experienced strife at one point or another, and the pursuit of absolute security guarantees insecurity for the other side. Vigilance and security measures are essential, but overcautiousness can be self-defeating.

The politics of peacemaking are difficult on both sides. Decades of Palestinian terrorism and repeated rejections of dramatic peace proposals have devastated the peace camp in Israel. Nevertheless, polls consistently show that a clear majority of Israelis are opposed to a binational solution and thus to unbridled settlement, thereby creating a political basis for an Israeli leader to work with, difficult though it will be. To convince the Israeli electorate that an agreement will truly produce a Palestinian state willing to live in peace and security next to a Jewish Israel, and overcome the concrete gaps in positions, substantive changes will have to occur in both sides' positions. It is, however, also partly a matter of political leadership, wherewithal, and positioning, all of which can be at least partly manufactured by a determined leader. Measures will obviously have to be taken to restore Palestinian faith in Israel's intentions, as well, which has been severely undermined by its settlement policy.

Policy Recommendations:

➢ Do everything Israel can, at all times, to pursue peace, preferably through a two-state solution, and at a bare minimum to position itself as the side actively seeking a solution.

➢ Seek an agreement based on an updated version of the Clinton Parameters, that is, withdrawal from the West Bank, minus a few percent land swap for the settlement blocs, and a division of Jerusalem, in exchange for stringent security arrangements and an end to the demand for a "right of return" to Israel. A broad international consensus exists in support of an agreement along these lines.

➤ Maintain the future viability of a two-state solution, pending emergence of the necessary conditions. To this end:

- End settlement activity outside of the blocs (and parts of East Jerusalem), unilaterally if necessary, preferably in exchange for US recognition of Israel's right to settle in these limited areas, in effect, reaffirmation of President Bush' s 2004 letter to Prime Minister Sharon. A proposal to this effect was raised, surprisingly perhaps, by erstwhile ultra-hard-line defense minister Lieberman, in November 2016.[1]

- Take measures to ensure the viability of the PA, whose ongoing rule is an Israeli interest, and improve the economy and quality of life in the West Bank generally, as part of a peace-building—or at least violence-reducing—approach.

- Take measures designed to strengthen moderate elements within the PA and facilitate the emergence of a viable Palestinian partner.

➤ Act unilaterally, if agreement continues to prove elusive, to determine Israel's borders, on the basis of demographic and security considerations, and create de facto separation from the Palestinians, as recommended by the Israeli National Security Council as early as 2002.[2] This might take the form of providing inducements to settlers to voluntarily move back into Israel proper, and some limited withdrawals, while maintaining IDF military control over the entire West Bank, to ensure Israeli security.

➤ Restore close strategic dialogue and cooperation with the United States on the Palestinian issue. Little is more important to the prospects of an agreement or the quality of the US-Israeli relationship. Where agreement is not achievable, proactively act to minimize friction, inter alia, through the above limitations on settlement activity. The Trump administration is as yet an unknown quantity, which may prove congenial to Israel's current hard-line government, but may also prove to be willing to exert a degree of pressure on Israel that its predecessors were not.

➤ Manage the conflict, rather than seek to resolve it, until there are leaders in Jerusalem, Ramallah, and Washington who have both the determination and political wherewithal to reach an agreement. The above proposal for a proactive peace policy notwithstanding, further failed peace processes will simply undermine whatever residual good faith and belief in peace exists on both sides.

➤ Change public discourse from a near complete focus on the threats, stemming from terrorism, to the dangers to Israel's international standing and especially the demographic realities, as Sharon did prior to the unilateral withdrawal from Gaza, or Rabin prior to Oslo. A change of this sort would help address the difficult domestic politics of the proposed change in policy. They are undoubtedly hard, but not impossible. Right-wing premier Netanyahu started his second term with a 10-month settlement freeze (not including the three blocs and Jerusalem), and a similar freeze in the future is not unthinkable.

➤ Prevent the West Bank, which has a commanding presence overlooking much of Israel's territory and population, from becoming a second Gaza, that is, a launching pad for rocket and other attacks.[3] The threat is unacceptable and must guide Israel's demands for stringent security arrangements in future peace negotiations.

If a realistic solution to the conflict with the Palestinians could be found that achieves Israel's foremost national objective, as set out here—being a predominantly Jewish and democratic state—without requiring a withdrawal from the overwhelming majority of the West Bank and a division of Jerusalem, so be it. This, however, has not been the case for five decades and remains an illusory hope.

The only true alternative to the "two states for two peoples" paradigm is a binational "one-state solution" in which Israel rapidly loses its Jewish or democratic character or both. In reality, there is nothing new or novel about the one-state solution, despite the false impression generated by the renewed attention devoted to it in recent years; it has been the preferred Arab option from the earliest days of the conflict. A one-state solution would have a Palestinian majority and result in Israel's demise as a Jewish state; Israel cannot win the demographic race. Furthermore, we unfortunately know today what a one-state solution looks like; it is called Syria, Iraq, or Yemen. The bitter strife between Israel and the Palestinians, in the first and second intifadas, and more recently, the ongoing series of stabbings and other terrorist attacks that began in mid-2015, were early indications of what a future binational reality looks like. History does not often provide us with a preview.

The unstated solution favored by supporters of Israel's long-term retention of the West Bank appears to be an inchoate hope that "something" will happen that will enable Israel to absorb it without having to pay the price of a binational reality. A "something" of this sort might take the form of a fundamental change in Jordan that enables resolution of the Palestinian issue there, or possibly a future conflict that leads to a large Palestinian exodus from the West Bank. Given Israel's dramatic history, as well as the upheaval in the region in recent years, belief in the unusual, even the semimiraculous, is not entirely beyond reason. National policy must, however, be founded in reality, both current and our best forecasts of the future. Hope and belief are not a sound basis for policymaking.

Aspire to more diplomatic response and pursue comprehensive new foreign policy: proactive posture on peace, international support for military operations, focused diplomacy with target states, emphasis on PR and war of narratives, revived "Jewish foreign policy," use of Israeli soft power, ties with Sunnis, greater multilateralism; United States at the center.

Israel's traditional modus operandi has been heavily military, not as a matter of preference, but because the nature of the conflict with the Arab countries, including their decades-long refusal to make peace or even negotiate, left it with little choice. Moreover, force, when applied to conventional Arab armies, ultimately worked; Israel won its survival, Egypt and Jordan made peace, and even Syria and the Palestinians conducted advanced negotiations. In recent decades, the predisposition to resort to force was further reinforced by the unremitting hostility of actors such as Hezbollah and Hamas, as well as Israel's own dearth of diplomatic objectives.

Advocating a more diplomatic response is easy, of course, and many of the issues Israel faces will continue to require a military response in the future. Moreover, Israel's adversaries not only do not play by the accepted norms of international conflict, but abuse them for their own advantage. This further complicates the difficulties of selling a more diplomatic approach to a public clamoring for a strong response to terrorism and rocket attacks or to Iran's nuclear program. Above all, Israel will not be able to fundamentally alter its international standing without resolving the West Bank issue, or at least significant progress to that end, and even then its circumstances are such that the problem will be significantly mitigated, but not fully resolved.

For a variety of reasons explicated in the background chapters and summarized in chapter 11, Israel appears to be reaching the limits to the efficacy of military force, as manifested by the never-ending strife with the Palestinians, repeated inconclusive rounds with Hezbollah and Hamas, the magnitude of the Iranian threat, and growing international opprobrium. This phenomenon is true of other countries, as well, including a global superpower such as the United States.

Some of the policy recommendations below are not significantly different from current practice and do not require major changes to Israeli policy but are more a matter of emphasis and effort; others are more far reaching. Together, however, they form the outlines of a comprehensive Israeli foreign policy and generally more diplomatic response. The most important element of Israeli foreign policy, relations with the United States, is addressed separately.

Policy Recommendations:
➤ Adopt a proactive and dynamic peace policy, as outlined above, designed to shape Israel's future, rather than seeking to preserve the status quo, or just

reacting to events. Nothing has hurt Israel's international standing more than the image that it, not the Palestinians, has become the obstacle to peace. When Israel was viewed as actively pursuing peace (Oslo talks in 1993; Camp David Summit and Clinton Parameters in 2000; withdrawal from Lebanon in 2000 and Gaza 2005; Olmert initiative in 2008), it has enjoyed considerable international support, certainly from the United States, and it transpired that policy differences with Western and other nations on many of the primary issues were not as great as previously thought.

➤ Place the onus for the stalemate on the other side:

- Implement the settlement freeze, as described above, thereby forcing the international community to confront the reality that the Palestinian demand for a "right of return," refusal to recognize Israel as the nation state of the Jewish people, and rejection of past proposals for a division of Jerusalem are the primary obstacles to peace. On these issues, Israel enjoys considerable international support.

- Adopt a positive orientation toward signs of Arab moderation, even deficient ones, or various proposals to hold international forums, by taking a conditional "yes, but" approach, welcoming them but establishing conditions for Israel's participation. Among other measures, recognize the Arab Peace Initiative as a basis for negotiations, while stressing that some of its components are unacceptable.

- Take interim measures to achieve some limited progress and restore good faith. Many such measures have been proposed over the years, for example, lifting restrictions on construction in the West Bank.

➤ Make the use of force subject to clear diplomatic objectives, including the war of the narratives and Israel's international standing. These objectives must be formulated prior to the onset of military operations, not once they have begun, as has repeatedly been the case in the past.

➤ Do the utmost to gain maximal international support and legitimacy for future military operations, at least from the United States. In an era of asymmetric confrontations with nonstate actors, deeply embedded in civilian populations, and of instant global communications, international support and legitimization have a direct bearing on Israel's ability to wield its military power effectively and on the postconflict diplomatic arrangements achieved, that is, on its fundamental ability to achieve its objectives.[4] To this end:

- Adopt the aforementioned policy of restraint and defense to the extent possible, before acting militarily. Prior to the operations in 2006 and 2014, for example, Israel exercised restraint in the face of ongoing attacks from Hezbollah and Hamas, respectively, before responding. In 2014 it also agreed to repeated ceasefires in the attempt to demonstrate that Hamas was responsible for the prolongation of the fighting. In both cases, Israel was initially thought by much of the international community to be in the right, and consequently gained greater support from Western countries than in the past, or at least less criticism, and surprisingly even from some Arab countries. It is not by chance that these operations were the first in Israel's history in which it was not constrained by "political time" and had far greater latitude to conduct operations.

- Seek agreement with the United States, and other actors relevant to a particular case, regarding the terms and mechanisms for ending an operation, prior to its onset, if possible, or during the opening stages.[5] To this end, Israel can establish predetermined criteria for ending the fighting, such as the number of rockets destroyed, or distance enemy forces are to be pushed from the border, and coordinate with the United States regarding the ceasefire, Security Council resolution, or whatever mechanism is appropriate for ending the hostilities in the specific case. Prior consultation has the advantage of making the United States a partner to the problem and its solution, thereby increasing the prospects of support, but may also lead to the need to limit the scope of an operation, or even refrain from acting completely. As we have seen, however, Israel almost always closely coordinates with the United States in any event; this is the price of an extraordinary relationship, and Israel can afford it, certainly in the face of limited threats. In the event of major and even existential threats, Israel always retains the ability to act independently.

➤ Pursue a sustained diplomatic campaign toward a number of countries, tailored to the needs of each relationship, inter alia:

- The UK, Germany, France, Italy, Poland, the Czech Republic, EU generally, as well as Canada and Australia:
  - Leverage the many interests they share with Israel today (Islamic radicalism and terrorism, regional turmoil and consequent migration problem, Iran's regional and nuclear ambitions, Mediterranean environmental issues, promotion of democracy, and more) to build on the deep diplomatic, economic, and in some cases military relations that already exist today. A situation in which the Middle East has become the primary threat to European and much of international security is a unique opportunity to further strengthen ties.
  - Solidify and formalize the already extant strategic relationship with Germany, which is increasingly emerging as a world leader, already is Israel's second largest source of weapons and financing, and with which ties could be greatly deepened. The "intergovernmental summits" begun under Chancellor Merkel remain a unique avenue to this end, undermined by the discord over the Palestinian issue.

- ○ Accord Europe and other Western countries a greater role in the peace process, building on the importance of the fundamental issues on which they share Israel's positions (effective security arrangements, Israel's Jewish character, some border changes, peaceful coexistence), rather than areas of disagreement. This is obviously largely contingent on a change in Israeli policy, but also requires a greater appreciation of the positive role they can play, such as providing resources essential for establishing a viable Palestinian state, or important economic inducements for Israel.

- ○ Seek a unique "association agreement" that provides Israel with essentially all of the benefits of full membership, without some potentially unacceptable downsides. The idea, even the possibility of full Israeli EU membership, were broached in the early 2000s and may become feasible again in the context of peace with the Palestinians. Moreover, following "Brexit" and other developments, the idea of a "tiered" EU membership is gaining currency.

- Deepen already existing strategic ties with Russia and India and seek to expand economic relationships with China. Continue the close strategic dialogue with Russia, which has already paid dividends, for example, on Russian arms sales to Iran and deconfliction in Syria. India is already a strategic partner, and the prospects for further cooperation are significant. Explore means of participating in China's new "Silk Road" strategy, for example by building the Ashdod-Eilat railway, possibly with an extension to the Jordanian port of Aqaba.[6]

- Deepen ties with Greece and Cyprus, both for diplomatic and for military reasons, and to further exploit the major gas finds in the eastern Mediterranean. Heightened relations with these countries are both a counterweight to the deterioration in relations with Turkey and an incentive to it to at least partially restore ties.

- Strengthen ties with Ethiopia, Kenya, South Sudan, and Uganda, Christian-majority countries in East Africa threatened by radical Islam.

- Reach out to the Iraqi and Syrian Kurds, both as actors who may comprise independent, or nearly independent, Kurdish states, with which Israel may enjoy good relations, and because of the major role they will have in shaping the overall futures of Iraq, Syria, Iran, and Turkey.

- Significant progress with the Palestinians would likely enable improved relations with Muslim countries such as Indonesia, Malaysia, and even Pakistan.

- ➤ Strengthen ties with Egypt and Jordan, to preserve the peace treaties, which are both a supreme Israeli strategic interest and the only realistic basis for either an expanded regional peace process or cooperation with the other

Sunni countries (see below). Should the relationship with either country change significantly for the worse, Israel would have to devote far greater resources to defense than it does today, and a severe deterioration in its entire national security posture would be in the offing. A situation in which Egypt has been taking a harder line toward Hamas than Israel, and in which the Jordanian monarchy has been in some danger from ISIS and other sources, lends itself to expanded cooperation. To this end, Israel should:

- Accord greater importance and sensitivity to Egypt's and Jordan's concerns and at least modulate Israeli policies, where substantive change is not feasible, in ways designed to reduce friction and help them overcome domestic opposition to bilateral ties.

- Conduct a concerted effort, together with the United States, to strengthen ties, for example by expanding the highly successful Qualifying Industrial Zone (QIZ) program, or other means of promoting greater commercial ties.

- Champion increased aid for Egypt and Jordan in Congress, or at least prevention of possible cuts. To this end, Israel could also try to leverage a celebration of 25 years of Israeli-Jordanian peace and 40 years of Israeli-Egyptian peace, both of which occur in 2019, to gain greater US and international economic assistance for them. For Egypt, whose image in the United States has been severely tarnished by its internal convolutions, some positive coverage would be beneficial.

- Continue and seek to expand military cooperation with Egypt and Jordan against Hamas, ISIS and other extremist forces.

- Prepare for a situation in which the Jordanian monarchy is in danger, including the measures Israel could take to help ensure its longevity. A Jordan in which radical elements have taken control, would have severe repercussions for Israel.[7] Conversely, should the monarchy collapse, despite all efforts to keep it in power, consider new possibilities for a resolution of the Palestinian issue.

▷ Leverage Israel's growing shared interests with Sunni countries, such as Saudi Arabia and the other Gulf states, to address common threats. Healthy skepticism regarding the likely extent of concrete cooperation aside, Israel should pursue the possibilities, whether covertly or, as appropriate, overtly.

- Focus on Iran's nuclear program and regional role. Even if joint action is beyond the realm of the feasible, greater common understanding could lead to parallel measures aimed at achieving shared objectives. Coordinate much of this with the United States, in some cases with Israel playing a role in the background only, for example, by encouraging the United States to build and lead a Sunni regional coalition against Iran, including a military component, and even to provide security assurances (see below).

- Should contacts lead to the conclusion that greater direct cooperation is possible than indicated here, Israel should be willing to extend important inducements,[8] such as a freeze on settlements beyond the three recognized settlement blocs, expansion of Palestinian control in Area C, greater acceptance of the Saudi-led Arab Peace Initiative, or help in restoring the standing of these countries in the United States. Israel could also demand some normalization steps in return.

➤ Minimize involvement in intra- and inter-Arab affairs. Israel has a fundamental and legitimate interest in events in neighboring states and the broader region and has thus intervened at times in their affairs, especially in Lebanon, among the Palestinians, and in inter-Arab politics. Experience indicates, however, that Israel's ability to shape events in desired directions is minimal. Moreover, the Middle East is in a state of historic flux today, and many of the dangers it poses exceed the restorative capabilities even of superpowers. In many cases, a policy of noninvolvement, even in the face of potentially significant consequences, or near noninvolvement, such as Israel has pursued regarding the Syrian civil war, is the wiser course of action. When circumstances do require that Israel take a more active part in intra- and inter-Arab affairs, it should be modest and cautious in the role and goals it adopts.

➤ Pursue a revived "Jewish foreign policy," designed to leverage the Israel-diaspora relationship and based on the understanding that the diaspora—especially the highly influential American Jewish community—is a fundamental pillar of Israel's national security and must be accorded commensurate importance. Intermarriage and assimilation, however, are severely undermining the "Jewish base," at a time when diaspora interest in Israel is already decreasing for other reasons and some alienation has even set in.

  - Devote greater resources to preservation of the diaspora's long-term vitality and to Israel-diaspora ties, even at the expense of financial transfers to Israel. This is especially true of Jewish education and of programs designed to promote identification with Israel, such as "Birthright," probably the most successful Israel-diaspora program ever, which brings young Jews from around the world to Israel for free study tours. Develop new such programs, including with Israeli budgets, and devote even more time to Jewish communities when Israeli leaders visit abroad. Work with diaspora communities to revitalize, or replace, long-existing organizational frameworks.

  - Take diaspora concerns into account far more than Israel has to date. This would entail difficult (and at this time unrealistic) changes in domestic Israeli politics, such as an end to orthodox domination of the rabbinate and consequent derogation of the status of Reform and Conservative Judaism in Israel, effectively addressing the "who is a Jew" controversy, and more.

Pending the necessary changes in Israel's political circumstances, a variety of partial measures are feasible to mitigate existing sources of tension, such as recognition of the non-orthodox communities' right to pray near the Wailing Wall.

▷ Emphasize public diplomacy, PR, or *hasbara*—whichever term is used, the message is almost as important today as the substance of the policy, in some cases more so. International standing, narratives, images, and delegitimization campaigns have a significant and even decisive impact on the outcome of policy initiatives, especially those that involve military action. In recent decades, Israel has typically won the military battles but lost the war of narratives. It simply must invest more in this area, in terms of budgets, manpower, and other resources.[9] Most importantly, considerations of public diplomacy must be part of the policy-planning process, whether for military operations or in peacetime. The MFA's total budget for public diplomacy in 2015, 40 million shekels (just over $10 million), was a joke.[10] Once again, a fundamental change in Israel's international standing is unrealistic pending a breakthrough with the Palestinians, but much more can be done.

▷ Make greater use of Israeli "soft power." Soft power does not usually have a direct or immediate effect on concrete policy but is certainly a source of long-term standing and influence. In some cases, such as the pro-Israel lobby in the United States, soft power is an indispensable basis for "hard" political power; indeed, its success is largely contingent on it. Israel has lost much of its soft power over the years, but still retains some important sources thereof, as explained in chapter 9. Israel's ability to make effective use of its soft power is directly linked to its broader domestic and foreign policy.

▷ Support international coalitions, participate where possible. Multilateral diplomacy, for example, in the case of the Iranian nuclear program, proved crucial to thwarting, or at least postponing, a strategic threat that Israel may not have been able to deal with effectively on its own. The long-term results of a strike on the Iranian nuclear program would have been determined by the American and international responses, no less than the concrete outcome of the attack itself. A Security Council resolution proved critical to ending the fighting in Lebanon in 2006. To counter Hamas, Israel must cooperate with Egypt, Jordan, the PA, and other foreign governments. Al-Qaeda and other jihadi organizations, as well as cyber-warfare, are global threats and can only be countered by a multilateral response. Whereas Israel has traditionally preferred to operate on its own ("blue and white" operations), the challenges and threats it now faces are such that cooperation with various international players, and where possible participation in international coalitions, has become an effective and essential instrument of policy. Even the United States can no longer go it alone.[11]

➤ Fight the good fight in the UN, other international organizations, and NGOs, deeply biased though they are. The Palestinians miss virtually no opportunity to present their case in every possible international forum, insignificant as it may be, with a long-term cumulative effect. Israel can and should do more, including:

- Firmly facing the false accusations brought against it and making its case. A simple refusal to cooperate with biased international organizations appears to be arrogant disregard for international law and opinion, whereas a reasoned argument regarding the composition and terms of reference of the bodies involved cannot be completely ignored and will receive a much more welcome response from Western and other moderate countries. Israel, for example, successfully fought to modify the composition and terms of reference of the Palmer Report (on the Turkish flotilla incident in 2010). Leaving the diplomatic and NGO battleground to the Palestinians and their supporters, out of an often-justified sense of futility and even repugnance, is understandable, but does not alleviate the problem.

- Targeting, together with the United States and others, a few select and less politicized international organizations in which a sustained effort can be made. The IAEA stands out as an example of an international organization, that deals with matters of critical importance for Israel, in which it has adopted an active role, based its approach on carefully constructed professional arguments, to which other professionals have proven receptive, and taken a constructive role in broader issues that go beyond its own concerns.

- Making more systematic use of friendly NGOs.

➤ Pursue greater involvement in the international agenda and multilateralism. Much of the international community is focused today on issues such as food security, agriculture generally, water, the environment and global warming, migration, poverty, and entrepreneurship. Israel has much to contribute in many of these areas, indeed, is even a world leader in some, and can use this as an important source of "soft power." As with other international forums, Israel partly abandoned the scene out of sheer frustration following decades of successful Arab efforts to thwart, mispresent, or derail even the best-intentioned efforts. Frustration, however, is not an effective policy prescription, and Israel's aid programs still stand out for many in beneficiary countries, decades after they ended. For comparatively small sums, Israel stands to gain significant benefits, even if they are not always immediate or quantifiable.

- Significantly increase Israeli aid programs (*Mashav*), which are currently a pittance. At a time when Israel's defense budget is under great pressure, this is not easy; however, some of the programs do not entail great costs and are primarily a matter of providing expertise and experience.

- Establish a joint Israel-diaspora "Jewish Peace Corps," both as a means of expanding Israeli involvement in these areas and of deepening Israeli-diaspora ties at the same time, especially among the young. It could be linked to "Birthright," as a possible route for follow-on activity.
- Continue to provide emergency assistance in times of crisis,[12] as Israel has so successfully done to date in a variety of countries, notably Haiti and Turkey. The assistance has been both of great value substantively and has generated much favorable coverage.

Define the "special relationship" with the United States as a fundamental pillar of Israel's national security strategy; align Israeli policies with the United States'; minimize differences and friction; build new bilateral agenda.

The vital need to ensure long-term American support, as a fundamental pillar of Israel's national security, is self-evident to most Israeli strategists,[13] certainly within the national security establishment. Differences on some issues are par for the course in any long-term bilateral relationship, even with close allies, and a global superpower, such as the United States, is experienced in managing them.

In recent years, however, some Israeli leaders have either failed to grasp the corrosive effects of some of their actions on the relationship with the United States or have knowingly ignored this for reasons of cynical political expedience. The result, along with the long-standing differences on the West Bank issue and, more recently, the crisis over the Iran nuclear deal, has been the emergence of growing elements of dissatisfaction in the bilateral relationship. Needless to say, Israel is not to blame for all of the tensions in recent years—the Obama administration made a number of egregious errors in its handling of the relationship—but there is nothing symmetric about it. Moreover, long-term demographic trends in both countries do not bode well for the future vitality of the bilateral relationship.

Policy Recommendations:
- Formally define the preservation of the "special relationship" as a fundamental pillar of Israel's national security strategy[14] and do everything possible to maintain the close strategic dialogue and cooperation that has long guided its relationship with the United States. The American consideration must usually prevail, and few issues should be allowed to mar the relationship. Where fundamental differences do exist, Israel must do everything it can to minimize friction.
- Seek to reach an agreed strategic agenda with the United States, or at least understanding, inter alia, on the following:
  - How to go forward on the peace process with the Palestinians or to manage the conflict in the absence of realistic prospects thereof. At a minimum,

disagreement over the settlements issue should be minimized, on the basis of the above proposal (US recognition of Israel's right to settle in the settlements blocs, in exchange for a halt to all other settlement activity).

- Addressing Iran's regional role and above all the nuclear issue, including agreed definitions of what violations of the 2015 agreement constitute, measures to bring Iran back into compliance in the event of a violation, possible responses should it fail to do so, and how best to ensure that Iran never crosses the nuclear threshold following the agreement's expiration. A possible follow-on international agreement after the current one expires, the conditions for military action, and means of deterring Iran, whether through bilateral and/or regional measures, are issues worthy of particular attention.

- The terms of a future resolution of the Syrian crisis. Whereas the United States has been focused on ISIS, which Israel, too, recognized as the immediate issue, the true danger for Israel lies in an Iranian-dominated Syria. American influence must be brought to bear with Russia, the true power broker today in Syria, to reduce the Iranian role there.

- Preserving the long-term viability of the Hashemite Kingdom in Jordan and the government in Egypt,[15] as well as how to address broader trends in regional change, including dangers to the stability of Saudi Arabia and other important actors.

- Future rounds between Israel and Hezbollah and Hamas, and counterterrorism generally.

- The US role in the region.

In the end, Israel is a sovereign nation, and only it can and should decide its ultimate national course. There is, however, no realistic alternative today to Israel's special relationship with the United States. Maybe Israel could survive without the United States (see chapter 10), but it would certainly be a very different existence, one that no one of any political significance in Israel today wishes to even contemplate. This recognition should guide Israeli thinking.

Seek independence from United States where possible, adjust to reality of dependence and align policies; resolve Palestinian issue as greatest means of reducing dependence; improve ties with other powers, but not at expense of US interests; consider phaseout of US aid after 10-year package or if strategic circumstances improve; preserve independent capabilities.

The price of the extraordinary bilateral relationship with the United States, including a de facto security guarantee, has been a significant loss of Israel's independence and freedom of maneuver. In reality, it serves neither side's interests for Israel to be so heavily dependent on the United States. No country wishes to place all its eggs in one basket, even if it is a uniquely friendly one, and Israel's dependence is a burden for the United States, too, at times. Israel has no alternative today but to acquire weapons from the United States and to rely on it for diplomatic cover and strategic backing. Some, however, have advocated that it at least begin weaning itself off American military aid, over a period of time, much as it did from economic aid in the late 1990s. At some point, this will undoubtedly have to happen; the question is one of political and strategic timing and whether Israel should proactively initiate the change.

As seen in chapter 10, a multiyear phaseout of US military assistance would not constitute an insurmountable blow to Israel's overall economy. It would certainly be a severe blow to the defense budget, impose a heavy strain on an already overstretched national budget and lead to a lowered standing of living, presumably resulting in heightened social tensions, but if forced to do so, Israel could absorb the burden. It is, however, very hard to forgo billions of dollars in annual aid, especially at a time when Israel continues to face major threats, the United States attaches importance to Israel's economic and social vitality, and there is no pressure in Congress to end military aid. Indeed, military aid has become a symbol of the bilateral relationship, vivid proof to foreign countries, including the Arab states, of its strength, and a litmus test that members of Congress cite to demonstrate their pro-Israel credentials. Moreover, an end to aid would not materially decrease Israel's dependence on the United States; it would still depend on it for weapons (to be paid for in full in this scenario), as well as diplomatic and strategic support, and little, in practice, would actually change other than the cost. For Israel, there thus do not appear to be any tangible benefits to a reduction in American military assistance, other than some symbolism and possibly preempting a future downturn in congressional sentiment. This too is of importance.

Policy Recommendations:
- ➤ Seek maximal independence in the long term, but make peace with the reality of dependence, for the meantime. To this end, adopt the above emphasis on maximal alignment with US policies and pursue the closest strategic relationship possible. Concomitantly, maintain the elements of self-reliance that are fundamental parts of Israel's classic defense doctrine, including robust military and strategic capabilities, for those cases where Israel does not need the United States or the United States cannot, or does not wish to, address the threats it faces.
- ➤ Continue to build closer ties with other powers, both as an objective in its own right and for those cases where Israel's interests differ from those of the United States, as long as they do not materially harm them. For example, Israel did not fully embrace the American position regarding Russian involvement

in the Ukraine in 2014, which strengthened its relationship with Moscow, without ill effect to the United States.

➢ Initiate, subject to the strategic circumstances at the time, a multiyear phaseout of US military aid beginning in 2027, at the end of the next 10-year aid package, by which time approximately 50 years will have passed since the massive aid program began. In the unlikely event that Israel's strategic circumstances take an unexpected turn for the better, for example, a clear end to Iran's nuclear aspirations, or significant political pressure for a cut builds in the United States, Israel should proactively initiate an earlier phaseout, rather than being swept along by a possible change in future sentiment.

Finally, a resolution of the Palestinian issue would be one of the most effective means possible of reducing Israel's dependence on the United States. It would greatly reduce Israel's international isolation, ease the conflict with the Arabs, make it harder for Iran, Hezbollah, Hamas, and others to pursue their anti-Israeli agendas, and lead to dramatic economic growth, thereby reducing Israel's need for US backing.

Seek a defense treaty with the United States to cement the "special relationship" for the long term, if a multinuclear Mideast emerges, or to provide the "political packaging" for a peace deal.

The idea of a formal defense treaty has been favored by some Israeli political leaders, but strongly opposed by the national security establishment. In Washington, the idea has met with tepid support in the past, primarily as a price the United States might be willing to pay as an inducement for Israel to make the concessions necessary for peace with the Palestinians or Syria. There are important arguments on all sides of the issue, as presented in detail in chapter 10 and briefly recounted below, and yet the advantages, at least in the specific circumstances set forth in the following, predominate.

On the positive side, a defense treaty would symbolize and cement the "special relationship" as a permanent feature of Israel's national security posture, at a time when there are signs that it may not be quite as deep in the future as in recent decades; constitute a binding commitment to Israel's security that would ensure the ongoing supply of weapons; remove any residual limitations on the supply of arms and technologies; and ensure its long-term QME. Crucially, a defense treaty might prove to be the only partially effective response to a multinuclear Middle East and even just a nuclear Iran. It would ease Israel's existential fears and, whether actually militarily necessary or not, might provide the psychological assurance and "political packaging" needed to tip public opinion in favor of the difficult concessions required for a peace deal. Over time, it might also enable a cut in Israeli defense expenditures.

On the negative side, Israel already enjoys a very close strategic relationship with the United States, including a probable de facto security guarantee, and does not have a military need for a defense treaty, at least as long as no regional power acquires a nuclear capability. Moreover, Israel has long feared that a defense treaty would result in a loss of its military and diplomatic freedom of maneuver and that the United States might demand that it divulge its secrets in exchange. Secondarily, there has also been concern that a defense treaty would erode Israel's national ethos of self-reliance and diminish support for Israel in the United States, which has long been predicated on the assumption that Israel, unlike other allies, defends itself, and that the United States might ultimately demur, with the very attempt to conclude a treaty exposing the limits of the relationship it was designed to enshrine.

None of these concerns appear fully warranted in practice, but are of sufficient weight to warrant consideration. First, it is unlikely that either side would wish the treaty to apply to cases of low- to medium-level threats and hostilities: the United States because it would not want to be involved in every such case and would presumably prefer to continue providing Israel with the means to address them on its own, and Israel because of its preference for self-reliance and operational autonomy. Second, Israel already coordinates with the United States very closely on virtually all issues, rarely acts independently, even in extreme circumstances (as Dennis Ross has put it, "Israel already behaves as if it has a defense treaty"),[16] and it is hard to see how a formal treaty would materially change things. Moreover, the commitment to consult is reciprocal and might, for example, have made it harder for the United States to refrain from informing Israel of the substance of its talks with Iran and the breakthrough that ultimately led to the nuclear deal in 2015. Third, the United States would know that a demand that Israel divulge its nuclear secrets would be a nonstarter and negate Israeli interest in the treaty to begin with. Fourth, an independent Israeli nuclear capability probably relieves the United States of the possible need to live up to its de facto commitment to its security and thus serves US interests. Finally, both sides would presumably insist on a "supreme national interest" clause, as is customary in agreements such as this, that is, one that enables them to act independently in cases of extremis.[17]

Policy Recommendations:

➤ Pursue a defense treaty to cement the long-term future of the "special relationship." Seek to time negotiations to propitious or pressing circumstances, such as advanced peace talks, an emerging nuclear threat, or willingness to cut military aid, but do so at an opportune time in the coming years. Israel's standing in the United States has probably passed its peak, and if the United

States was reluctant to provide a commitment of this sort in the past, it will likely be even more hesitant to do so in the future.

➤ Limit the treaty to major, or even potentially existential threats and ensure that it includes a "supreme national interest" clause, thereby addressing Israel's concerns regarding limitations on its freedom of maneuver and strategic capabilities. Make Israel's interest in the treaty clearly contingent on the absence of untoward limitations.

➤ Should a formal defense treaty prove unattainable, seek a further upgrade of the strategic relationship through a less formal instrument, such as a memorandum of understanding, possibly approved by both houses of Congress for added weight. In the shorter term, give concrete meaning to Israel's already heightened strategic status under the US-Israel Strategic Partnership Act of 2014, which has yet to be translated into practical policy. In the final analysis, in most scenarios, but not all, the most important US security assurance is the commitment to provide Israel with the weapons it needs to defend itself by itself, against any enemy or coalition thereof.

Military Policy Recommendations

Adopt approach based on "strategic patience" and the "long game"[18] to best position Israel for the war of attrition underway against it; more judicious use of offense, greater emphasis on restraint, resolve, and defense; revert to offensive approach when military decision, or at least 5–10 years of calm, can be achieved.

Israel is no longer a young state fighting for its survival, but a mature, prosperous, and, most importantly, essentially secure state, whose long-term survival has been ensured. This is a highly controversial statement for many Israelis and is certainly relative, particularly at a time when Israel continues to face a variety of major threats. Nevertheless, Israel has never been so secure, and its strength provides it with the luxury of adopting an approach based on a longer-term perspective and greater strategic patience, which its narrow security margins precluded in the early years.[19]

There is thus a psychological gap between how Israelis perceive themselves and Israel's strategic reality. After decades of warfare and hostilities, Israelis have become used to thinking in terms of "dire" and even "existential" threats, and Israel still tends to respond to events, such as terror or rocket attacks, as if it was the young, embattled, and weak state of the early years, whose very existence hung in the balance. The public understandably clamors for security and retribution, and political leaders pander to public opinion and adopt short-term solutions. The attacks are undoubtedly a tragedy for those involved and their loved ones, but are not tragedies of national magnitude, and the media and political arena amplify them beyond the importance they warrant. In a nation of over eight million people today, the actual impact of these events, if not the psychological one, is limited.

Israel does not have to respond to every terrorist and rocket attack and, in practice, does not. As a senior IDF officer stated in 2015, "We don't have to turn every rocket into a national event."[20] The responses typically achieve little in practical terms anyway; indeed, the targets are often of little military value and are chosen primarily to demonstrate resolve and assuage public opinion. As such, they end up being perceived by both sides primarily as symbolic, tit-for-tat responses, largely devoid of substance. The IDF's constant refrain that these responses are necessary to "sustain deterrence," an important justification if correct, requires empirical substantiation; the very frequency of the attacks suggests that the deterrent effect has not succeeded, even though Israel has been pursuing deterrence of this sort for decades.

Over a decade after the IDF added defense as the fourth strategic pillar of its military doctrine (in addition to early warning, deterrence, and military decision), it still goes against Israel's military instincts. An offensive approach won Israel its existence and continues to inspire both the IDF ethos and the 2015 IDF Strategy. Wars, as IDF officers are wont to note, are only won through offense. It is, however, important to recognize the reality of irregular warfare, as painful as it may be; despite massive efforts at times, Israel has been unable to defeat Hezbollah and Hamas or even gain a decisive advantage over them in any of the conflicts since the 1980s. Repeated attempts to do more of the same, including the "mowing the grass" approach adopted against Hamas in Gaza, are unlikely to produce substantially better outcomes, at least for the foreseeable future.

In chapter 6 we addressed in detail the reasons for Israel's inability to achieve military decision against irregular substate opponents, inter alia, the desire to avoid further territorial conquest and inability to achieve decision solely from the air. The respites gained from the 2009 and 2012 operations in Gaza were far too brief (it is too early, at the time of this writing, to assess the outcome of the 2014 operation), deterrence was not truly restored, and the end result was that the IDF's capabilities were partly squandered and Israel's international standing severely harmed, at a heavy cost to the national budget. The 2006 war in Lebanon appears to have achieved a more lasting effect, although it is unclear at what precise point Hezbollah's heavy involvement in the Syrian civil war replaced Israeli deterrence as the primary reason for the ongoing calm.

For reasons of professional training, bureaucratic responsibilities, and a resultant "mindset," Israeli defense planners, both IDF and civilian alike, have proven overly focused on offense and have consequently consistently failed to appreciate—and continue to underestimate—the impact of damage and disruption to the home front on Israel's overall national security posture and societal resilience. As a result, they have consistently resisted expenditures for home front defense for decades, ever since the missile attacks of 1991 and even the artillery barrages of 1981, reluctantly being drawn into them and often at the minimum levels deemed feasible.

Iran, Hezbollah, and Hamas, as Islamist fundamentalists, take a long-term approach to their efforts to weaken and ultimately destroy Israel. They fully understand that they do not have the capability to do so for the foreseeable future and have adopted a long-term attrition strategy in response. Israel is a frenetic democracy whose national culture, reinforced by frequent electoral cycles, is focused on the here and now.

Policy Recommendations:
- ➤ Adopt an approach of greater strategic patience, appropriate to an established state engaged in long-term challenges, not a battle for its survival. Offensive capabilities remain an essential part of Israel's response, but heightened perseverance, resolve, and restraint, which Israel already practices to a significant extent, are more appropriate to many of the threats it faces today. The recommendation is thus not for a black-and-white change in policy, but in emphasis. Israel's focus must go beyond the immediate effects of each incident, round, or threat, to how it can best position itself for the long-term war of attrition its adversaries are waging against it.
- ➤ Attach greater importance and resources to defense. If the IDF does not yet, at this time, have the offensive capability to prevent massive rocket fire on the home front, it must do so defensively, despite the costs, and build an effective national shield (as defined below). The growing danger of Hezbollah trying to conquer border towns or bases means that more must also be invested in defensive fortifications and forces, though the primary response in this regard is offensive. The impact of these threats on Israel's overall national security posture and societal resilience is unacceptable.
- ➤ Revert to a primarily offensive response to the threats posed by Hezbollah and Hamas, and to other such threats in the future, if and when Israel succeeds in developing an "effective offensive response," that is, one that essentially leads to 5- to 10-year periods of calm, and when the strategic circumstances are appropriate. Also act offensively, in select cases, where there are immediate and concrete benefits to be gained, such as disruptions of enemy arms transfers and operational planning, destruction of significant enemy capabilities, or demonstrable deterrent effects.
- ➤ Modify leadership style and political messaging to encourage public perseverance and resilience. The severity of a situation is often a function of how

the national leadership chooses to define it: as something that is tolerable and which a determined and united public can "tough out," or as a crisis requiring an immediate and more aggressive response.

➤ The Iranian nuclear program remains a potentially existential threat but is not immediate and may be manageable through a long-term diplomatic approach. See separate section below.

The politics of the proposed change are hard. It is very difficult, in any country, to counsel forbearance and restraint when rockets are raining on one's cities or terrorism threatens. Americans, half a world away from the Middle East, have come to fear a direct threat from ISIS because of isolated incidents in the United States. Israelis live with this daily. Nevertheless, the national leadership in the early years encouraged Israelis' sense of strength; in recent years it has fed its primal fears. A change in degree is not unfeasible, and politicians who fail to adopt a more constrained style, whether from the coalition or opposition, could be called to task by a determined premier. The alternative is ongoing inconclusive confrontations that sap Israel's international standing, societal resilience, and, ultimately, its military might and deterrent image.

Maintain robust offensive capabilities but pursue "smart offense": manage nonexistential conflicts; conduct short and sharp operations, not wars of attrition; act forcefully to achieve objectives or refrain from acting; make military operations part of a clear diplomatic strategy, with defined criteria and mechanisms for ending the conflict.

The three pillars of Israel's classic defense doctrine (early warning, deterrence, and military decision) are particularly hard to achieve when facing hybrid combinations of terrorist, guerrilla, and substate actors waging a long-term war of attrition against it. Military history is replete with such examples of changing military paradigms and technologies. As one side has gained superiority, the other has always sought a counterresponse to offset it, and it then takes time before the pendulum swing backs in the first side's favor, but with persistence, it does. Much as it took Israel decades to achieve military decision over the Arab states, in the sense that they gave up on the concrete aspiration to destroy it and either made peace or largely ceased offensive operations against it, it will take a similarly lengthy period with Hezbollah and Hamas. The grave danger posed today by rockets has been largely neutralized at the Hamas level, and in time answers to Hezbollah's infinitely larger arsenal will be found as well.

Some have concluded that Israel cannot defeat substate actors such as Hezbollah and Hamas, as ostensibly evinced by the repeated inconclusive operations it has waged against them over the years. This book, in contrast, has argued that Hezbollah and Hamas can be defeated, but that the cost of doing so—to date—has exceeded the magnitude of the threat and so Israel has made do with limited operations. If and when Israel's cost calculus changes, so will its response, and it will act decisively against Hezbollah or Hamas, even if the gain is temporary. When Palestinian terrorism became intolerable in 2002, for example, Israel took decisive action and suppressed the second intifada. Israel was never able to achieve more than a temporary respite against the Arab armies either, but the threat was deemed sufficiently severe to justify the repeated rounds.

In 2006 Premier Olmert proudly stressed that his government had succeeded in providing the IDF with unlimited time to conduct military operations (34 days). The operation in 2014 lasted even longer (51 days), as Israel attempted a new, graduated form of attrition warfare of its own, whereby the level of military force applied was increased incrementally over time, in order to affect the adversary's "consciousness." Protracted confrontations, however, do not play in Israel's favor. To the contrary, they are a central element in Iran's, Hezbollah's, and Hamas's attrition strategy. Time enables them to cause growing casualties and physical damage to Israel's home front and military rear, undermines Israel's international standing, regardless of the reasons for the hostilities' outbreak, imposes heavy economic costs on Israel, and demonstrates its inability to achieve military decision, thereby strengthening its adversaries' standing within their respective constituencies. Moreover, it is not clear that what Israel defines as attrition is viewed as such by Hezbollah and Hamas; they have a high tolerance for losses, seek damage and casualties, at least up to a significant point, as a means of advancing their PR campaigns, and do not present targets of significant military value to begin with.[21]

In a future round with Hezbollah, in which it may fire thousands of rockets at Israel's home front each day and damage vital infrastructure sites, for example, leaving parts of Israel without electricity, water, or communications, Israel will presumably enjoy greater international legitimacy to respond heavily, at least at the beginning, and as long as large-scale civilian casualties are not caused. The international community, however, possibly including the United States, is likely to react harshly to the kind of massive destruction the IDF apparently considers essential for its war plans, and will seek to end the fighting as rapidly as possible. Moreover, the list of effective targets, that is, those whose destruction has some significant impact on Hezbollah's and Hamas's ability to continue fighting, is usually exhausted within the first days and the IAF ends up attacking targets of limited military utility, mostly in the attempt to keep up the pressure on them. In fact, the result is often the opposite: the actual intensity and effectiveness (if not tempo) of operations dissipates rapidly, the enemy and its supporters conclude that they have once again survived the onslaught by the vastly more powerful IDF, and their narrative of resistance and victory is reinforced.[22]

A further complication is that Hezbollah and Hamas may not want an early end to hostilities or a limit to them—on the contrary.[23] It is unlikely, for example, that a more limited Israeli response to the Hezbollah attack that precipitated the 2006 war, or even a decision to refrain from responding at all, would have led to a commensurate response by Hezbollah, which explicitly sought a confrontation, though not on the scale that emerged. In 2014, similarly, Hamas repeatedly rejected calls for ceasefires, intentionally prolonging the conflict and increasing the destruction wrought on Gaza. Indeed, up to a point, the longer the fighting continues and the greater the loss of life and damage, the more they believe they have won. Israel comes under increasing international criticism, the legitimacy of its military operations and right to self-defense is progressively curtailed from operation to operation, and even its legitimacy as a state is undermined.

Some have advocated an attempt to hold Lebanon, the state, responsible for attacks emanating from its territory, an eminently reasonable position in and of itself, as well as under international law, and to do so by attacking Lebanon's civilian infrastructure and military. The Lebanese government, in which Hezbollah is a major player and has predominant influence, has long claimed, partly disingenuously, that it is simply too weak to be able to assert its sovereignty and take responsibility. Israel, too, has long maintained that it is ineffectual, nonexistent for all practical purposes, making it somewhat difficult to now demand that it assume responsibility. In any event, the international community, including the United States, which is invested in Lebanon's stability, is highly unlikely to accede to major attacks either on Lebanon's civilian infrastructure or military, much as it did not in 2006, even though it was strongly supportive of Israel's overall war effort at the time.

Colin Powell, former chairman of the US Joint Chiefs of Staff, proposed a number of conditions that he believed American policymakers should consider prior to resorting to military force. The "Powell Doctrine" was predicated on the assumption that a vital national security interest was at stake and that nonviolent means of achieving the desired policy objectives (diplomatic, economic, covert) had been exhausted. It further presumed that policymakers had formulated clearly defined objectives, realistically achievable through military force, at acceptable costs and with a plausible exit strategy, and that the proposed operation was likely to enjoy both domestic and international support. If the proposed operation met these criteria, Powell advocated bringing preponderant force to bear to achieve the objectives adopted.[24]

Policy Recommendations:
➢ Adopt a modified "Israeli Powell Doctrine":
  ▪ Resort to military force when important, though not necessarily vital, national security interests are at stake and other (diplomatic, economic, or covert) means of addressing them have been exhausted.

- Formulate clearly defined military objectives, realistically achievable through force, at acceptable costs and embedded in a broader diplomatic strategy. In too many cases, Israel's objectives have been primarily military, such as degradation of enemy capabilities and an "improved situation on the ground," important in their own right, but without a clearly defined strategy beyond a gain of time.

- From the outset, even before operations begin, embed military planning in a multifaceted diplomatic approach, along with information campaigns, humanitarian measures, considerations of international law, and more.

- Prepare a clearly defined exit strategy or mechanism for ending the confrontation, preferably worked out in advance with the United States and/or additional actors (see recommendations on US relations).

- Ensure maximal domestic and international (at least American) support for military operations.

➤ Maintain robust offensive capabilities as a sine qua non for all other Israeli national security policy. The greater emphasis this strategy places on restraint, diplomacy, and defense notwithstanding, Israel will have to conduct major offensive operations in the future, in some cases preventatively.

➤ In limited confrontations:

  - Manage and mitigate the threat, avoiding simplistic temptations to resolve them. The severity of the Hezbollah and Hamas threats, and consequently Israel's cost-benefit calculus, may reach a point that warrants occupying Lebanon or Gaza, rooting out the rockets, and even toppling them. The very factors that have militated against doing so to date, however, will most likely continue to do so in the future—above all, the belief that the costs of the solutions outweigh the magnitude of the threats and that only a temporary change can be effected, in any event. Those who believe that Israel should adopt the more extreme approach must demonstrate either why the price has now become justified or why significantly better outcomes are likely to be achieved.

  - Adopt narrow definitions of deterrence and military decision: a rapid return to a ceasefire followed by protracted periods of calm, on an order of 5–10 years, not a fundamental change in the situation; a significant degradation of enemy capabilities, but not the elimination thereof; and postconflict arrangements that make it harder for the enemy to rearm and redeploy near the border and better position Israel diplomatically, in preparation for the next round.

➤ In major confrontations and wars, act with force and determination to achieve the predetermined objectives and to win, inter alia, by threatening the future of the adversary's regime and territorial control, with the requisite willingness, on the part of both the public and leadership, to stay the course and pay the price. In the absence thereof, pursue limited objectives, as above. One lesson is abundantly clear from Israel's and others' experience in recent decades: partial measures in the pursuit of major objectives, or "full solutions," invariably fail and end up leading to the worst of all worlds. They should be attempted, if at all, only when the objectives are similarly limited.

➢ Pursue long-term strategic and cumulative deterrence against Hezbollah and Hamas, not military decision. Israel was never able to achieve full military decision against the Arab states either, but succeeded in forcing them to either make peace or forgo any practical aspiration to defeat it militarily, through repeated limited victories, each of which gained time and strengthened its cumulative deterrence. The battle against Hezbollah and Hamas is similarly long term, and, with patience, eventually Israel will force a fundamental change in their cost-benefit calculus, leading to strategic and cumulative deterrence. In the end, if managed properly, Israel's resources and capabilities, staying power, and societal resilience are greater than theirs.

➢ Dictate the terms of the battle by conducting short, sharp, and focused campaigns, designed to achieve maximal impact at the outset, not lengthy wars of attrition, which play to Hezbollah's and Hamas's strengths. To this end, utilize the IAF's extraordinary capability to strike thousands of targets a day[25] and maintain the capability to mobilize the reserves and launch a major ground operation within days, not weeks, as in recent confrontations.[26]

➢ End the fighting upon achievement of the predetermined objectives, through a diplomatic mechanism if readily available, unilaterally if not. The combined impact of short and sharp campaigns, with a rapid end to the fighting, will maximize the blow to Hezbollah or Hamas and strengthen Israeli deterrence; they will not have time to recover or cause severe damage to Israel's home front and will be unable to claim success. This approach may require a willingness to absorb fire for a time and a recognition that Israel may ultimately be forced to renew the fighting, if they prove unwilling to end the conflict. At a minimum, Israel will have gained legitimacy for further operations.

➢ Focus on prevention and destruction of Hezbollah and Hamas capabilities, minimizing the impact on their civilian populations, but retain the capacity to cause severe punishment, both for deterrent purposes and, if necessary, as a means of forcing them to return to a ceasefire should they demur. To this end, invest heavily in real-time intelligence and operational capabilities to conduct precision warfare, primarily from the air. This is essential both to destroy as many of Hezbollah's and Hamas's rockets and other targets as possible and to enable Israel to conduct targeted attacks against a limited number of critical military nodes and political and military functionaries, without whom they may not be able to operate effectively,[27] the essence of "network-centric" or "effects-based" operations. This is a problematic recommendation. The IDF cannot effectively address Hezbollah's and Hamas's rocket arsenals without a massive attack on the homes and public buildings they are hidden in, thereby causing extensive civilian casualties and damage to the civil infrastructure. A recommendation that focuses solely on prevention and destruction of enemy capabilities would thus leave Israel without an offensive response to the threat they pose. Attempts to identify the critical nodes and leaders are obviously difficult, and past attempts at such targeted warfare have produced mixed results.

It has been argued, however, that Israel does not yet have an effective offensive capability (as defined above), in any event, at least at a price it finds acceptable, and if it does, that the international community and even the United States are unlikely to be willing to countenance the degree of destruction necessary to achieve the desired outcome. This complex reality reinforces the need for the approach outlined above, which places greater emphasis on restraint and defense, along with a limited degrading of enemy capabilities, until such a time as the IDF is able to achieve the desired outcome, without the concomitant casualties and damage. At the same time, it is the concrete threat of massive destruction that has achieved at least some measure of deterrence against Hezbollah and Hamas in recent years and must be preserved.

➤ Consider a coercive modular approach. In some cases, Israel may be able to pursue coercive diplomacy and a modular military approach, by conveying to the adversary, whether discreetly or publicly, the intended levels of force and destruction to be applied, should certain demands not be met, or it refuse to return to a ceasefire.[28] If successful, an approach such as this may ease the process of building international legitimacy and limit the magnitude of hostilities. The danger is that it may fail to dissuade Hezbollah and Hamas and play into their strategy of attrition, as indeed happened when applied against Hamas in 2014, and may be more appropriate to conflicts with state actors. It should thus be considered carefully in future confrontations.
➤ Conduct ongoing efforts to interdict, disrupt, and prevent the buildup of enemy capabilities through overt operations, such as strikes against transfers of advanced weapons, and covert means, including cyber-attacks, when truly necessary.

Build a national mortar, rocket, and missile defense shield; the true basis of comparison is the overall cost of damage and disruption to Israel's home front, international standing, strategic posture, and societal resilience; Israel can afford it.

It is easy, of course, to make recommendations involving major budgetary outlays; the question is where the money should come from and at the expense of which other programs, military or civilian. The argument is frequently made that the cost of rocket defense is ruinous, that Israel cannot afford it, and, in any event, that offense must remain at the heart of IDF doctrine. The latter contention is certainly true; the first two not necessarily so. The following section seeks to demonstrate that the budgetary sources for a nationwide mortar, rocket, and missile shield can and must be found.

Hezbollah is thought to have over 100,000 rockets today, maybe 130,000, Hamas many thousands. We do not know how many rockets the IDF will be able to destroy in offensive operations, likely a significant number; how many will fall in open areas and thus cause little if any damage, also a significant number; or how many interceptors the IDF already has. What is publicly known is that the IDF had 10 Iron Dome batteries in 2015, that press reports spoke of 13 as the minimum number the IDF considers necessary for a limited national rocket shield, and that some experts estimate that as many as 20 will ultimately be required. It is further known that each Iron Dome battery is estimated to cost $60–$80 million and each interceptor $35,000–$50,000, that the IDF plans to procure four Magic Wand batteries, at an unknown cost, and that each interceptor is estimated to cost $700,000–$1.25 million.[29]

Should Israel wish to procure a further 10 Iron Dome batteries and increments of 50,000 interceptors, the costs would be approximately as follows.

➤ Ten batteries would cost between $600 and $800 million, for simplicity, say $700 million.
➤ The cost of 50,000 interceptors, at $35,000 each, would be $1.75 billion; or $2.5 billion at $50,000. Most reports believe the lower figure to be correct. For simplicity let us estimate the cost at $2 billion.

The cost of a national rocket shield, with 50,000 additional interceptors, would thus be on an order of magnitude of $2.7 billion, or $4.7 billion for 100,000 interceptors. Iran could, of course, continue providing Hezbollah with more and more rockets, and the above does not include the costs of Magic Wand, mortar defense systems, or Arrow missile defense costs. It also does not include the need for greater investment in passive defenses, such as hardening public institutions in border areas (e.g., schools and hospitals), and strategic infrastructure sites, as well as ensuring that the entire population has ready access to shelters. At present, only about one-third of the public has shelters in their homes, another third has access to public shelters, and the remainder no shelter at all.[30]

The cost calculation above is, therefore, a simplistic one, the figures used are mere estimations, based on the incomplete information publicly available, and the overall cost of a national defensive shield is far higher. Nevertheless, the correct basis for assessing the cost of a national shield should not be just the highly expensive price of active and passive defenses, especially when compared to the cheap incoming rockets, but the overall cost and disruption to Israel's economy, society, strategic posture, and international standing. When considered on this basis, the costs become far more manageable, especially when broken down on a multiyear basis.[31]

The benefits of added defenses should also be compared to the incremental costs of additional offensive weapons. To illustrate, Israel has already ordered 50 F-35 aircraft, at a cost of $7-8.5 billion,[32] clearly designed to augment Israel's long-distance strike capabilities, not just to replace outdated platforms. Given the large sums Israel has already spent on the ability to attack the Iranian program, the 2015 nuclear deal, and likelihood that the threat has been postponed by a period of years, possibly a decade or more, these heretofore high-priority procurement plans may no longer be quite as essential or may be deferrable by some years, in favor of defensive systems. This is not to argue that this is necessarily the case; these weapons may very well remain essential and urgent. The analysis is, however, one indication of how the budgetary resources could be found should a change in Israel's strategic order of priorities and a more defensive approach be adopted. In any event, the new US military assistance package starting in 2017 includes $5 billion for rocket and missile defense over 10 years.

Policy Recommendations:

➤ Build an active and passive national mortar, rocket, and missile shield. The objective is not truly a 100% effective shield, protecting every last civilian and potential target, but one that reduces destruction to the home front and military rear to the extent that they can continue functioning without severe disruption and that eliminates the current need to choose between defense of population centers, strategic infrastructure sites (e.g., power plants, communications nodes, and fuel depots), and IDF bases and capabilities, thereby ensuring Israel's freedom of military and diplomatic maneuver.[33]

➤ Make the defensive shield a foremost national priority and complete it within a few years at most, thereby neutralizing the Hezbollah threat, much as the Hamas rocket threat has now been essentially neutralized, and in so doing upend Hezbollah's and Hamas's strategy of attrition. Base the cost-benefit calculus on the overall cost to Israel's national economy, society, strategic posture, and international standing. To cover the costs, either reorder budgetary priorities or engage the public in a national effort based on a special "Iron Dome tax."

➤ At a bare minimum, and as an immediate priority, complete active and passive defenses of military targets, essential to Israel's ability to wage effective offensive operations, and vital infrastructure sites, whose destruction or disruption would have severe nationwide effects, possibly shutting down large parts of the country for prolonged periods.

➢ Invest in new technologies designed to enable Israel to cope with increasingly vast arsenals at acceptable prices, such as laser-based systems. The technological cost-benefit calculus is changing, and previously unviable technologies will become increasingly so in coming years.

Conduct fundamental review of defense budget and set fixed multiyear budget; accord the NSS and Finance Ministry a far greater role in the budgetary process; adjust budgetary priorities to more defensive approach.

IDF force planning is based on sophisticated processes in which extant and expected threats are assessed and prioritized and then matched by an allocation of available military capabilities or those to be developed. In the end, it comes down to a determination of priorities, budgets, manpower, and weapons systems.

Today, the IDF basically makes these determinations on its own. Given the IDF's great prestige and near monopoly on the necessary information, it is very hard for any minister or governmental body to challenge its assertions. The cabinet itself is incapable of assessing whether procurement plans presented by the IDF are truly essential and is subject to political considerations that largely mandate approval of whatever the IDF requests. The NSS and Ministry of Finance have statutorily mandated roles in the budgetary process, but their actual impact is limited, partly as a result of their own deficient organizational capabilities and partly the defense establishment's reluctance to be transparent and cooperate. As a result, the cabinet is almost a rubber stamp.

In recent years the IDF budget has grown considerably in absolute terms, though not as a percentage of the GDP. The IDF acknowledges that the overall threat has diminished, but justifies the increase on the grounds that it is now engaged in a new and nearly perpetual type of warfare, requiring uniquely expensive capabilities, such as finding and destroying tens of thousands of Hezbollah rockets, and in preparations for strategic threats, such as a possible strike on Iran's nuclear program. This is undoubtedly true, and in many ways the challenge is daunting. Important questions have also been raised regarding the prevalent assumption that conflicts with substate actors can be waged successfully with smaller armies, based on firepower, sophisticated weaponry, and effective intelligence.[34] Mass has a role, too. Nevertheless, in an era in which the overall threat has diminished and societal needs have grown increasingly pressing, the need for such a large force structure and budget can be legitimately questioned, and Israel must achieve its military objectives with less.

The IDF itself is cognizant of the need for significant reform of its force structure and doctrine, as expressed in the 2015 IDF Strategy, 2016 "Gideon Five Year Work Plan," and its predecessors, presented in detail in chapters 6–7.

Assuming that the publicly available estimates of the IDF force structure are reasonably accurate, the cuts already made are significant.[35] It is, however, the very rare organization that is capable of making truly far-ranging changes on its own, especially in the absence of a determination by the political leadership of its national security objectives and the capabilities it wishes the IDF to have in order to achieve them.

The IDF no longer faces significant ground threats from Arab armies but certainly requires a robust armored capability against Hezbollah and Hamas, along with a reserve in the event of unforeseen developments in the Arab countries in the future. It no longer confronts enemy air forces of significance, and IAF capabilities are now needed primarily for purposes of massive ground attack against Hezbollah and Hamas targets, not air supremacy, as well as deep penetration raids at great distances. For purposes of long-term strategic planning, it must also take the Saudi and Egyptian air forces into account, as well as Iran's growing capabilities in the air.

A former head of the IDF Planning Branch has proposed that Israel adopt a new threat-based budgeting process. Under the proposal, a new Minimal Defense Standard would be determined, based on IDF overhead costs and the budgets needed for a given set of threats, such as defending Israel's airspace, addressing the Hezbollah and Hamas rocket threats, and deterring war. To the Minimal Defense Standard he would add additional missions that the government deems important, such as the ability to attack the Iranian nuclear program, prepare for a renewed "eastern front," or deploy a national rocket defense system. He estimated the total savings to be gained through this approach at approximately six billion shekels a year, a savings of a full 10% at the time. The problem with the proposal, he maintained, was that it posed a threat to the political and bureaucratic interests of the players involved in the budgetary process and was thus unlikely to ever be adopted.[36] Even if some of the proposal's specific cost estimates and assumed savings can be challenged, it does demonstrate a responsible means by which significant cuts could be made.

Policy Recommendations:
➤ Fundamentally revise the defense budgetary process:
  • Build the capabilities that the Ministry of Finance and especially the NSS need in order to effectively fulfill their statutorily mandated roles in the defense budget process and end the IDF's de facto near monopoly thereof.
  • Require the IDF to conduct fundamental, "bottom-up," budgetary reviews on a periodic (five- to seven-year) basis. Consider supporting the review process by appointing independent "blue ribbon" commissions.

- Guarantee the IDF and other defense agencies a fixed multiyear budget so that they can plan effectively, along with the ability to funnel some savings back into modernization programs. A revised process will only gain their support and be successful if they have "buy-in," that is, an interest in the proposed changes, in terms of both process and substance; otherwise unwanted reforms will be derailed, as they have been in the past.

➤ In the absence of essential classified information, in the intelligence, operational, and budgetary realms, informed recommendations regarding the specific changes needed to the defense budget and force structure are not feasible. Some procurement programs are needed simply to replace aging weapons platforms; others are vital to maintain Israel's future qualitative edge. IDF force cuts and changes already underway appear significant.

➤ Amend budgetary priorities in accordance with the more defensive approach outlined above, including the necessary funding for the mortar, rocket, and missile shield described and home front defense. As already stressed, this is a call for a change in emphasis, taking advantage of a strategic window of opportunity, not in Israel's fundamental reliance on its offensive capabilities.

➤ Consider proposals for a two-tiered ground force: a relatively small number of advanced tanks and APCs with sophisticated active defense systems, along with older models for lower-level threat operations; a highly trained and equipped reserve force, along with a secondary one, trained for just a few days a year, as a hedge in the event of a severe downturn in the situation, and a discharge of all other reservists.[37]

Part of the difficulties Israel faces in defense budget planning are typical of all countries, while others are immanent in the quirks of Israel's chaotic decision-making process and will not be fully resolved pending electoral reform. Nevertheless, small improvements can be made over time, as outlined above.

Ensure Iran never crosses nuclear threshold; maintain military capability to strike nuclear program at any point during lifetime of 2015 agreement and thereafter; intensively monitor Iranian compliance and work with allies to reverse violations; wage international campaign against Iran's malign role in region; restore intimate dialogue with United States on Iran.

Assuming that Iran observes the 2015 nuclear deal or, maybe more correctly, does not violate it to an extent that Israel finds intolerable, it will have gained a decade or more, considerably longer than could have been achieved through military action, during which it can divert at least some resources to other threats. In the meantime, however, Israel must prepare for the day after the agreement expires, its possible violation by Iran, and the possibility that the Trump administration will wish to reopen the issue. A nuclear Iran remains the only potentially existential threat to Israel for the foreseeable future.

Having seemingly "resolved" the Iranian file, it would be only natural for the international community to lower its vigilance. Moreover, there will be strong political and psychological pressures on most of the leaders of the P-6 (the five permanent members of the Security Council and Germany, which concluded the deal with Iran), but not the new US administration, to discount the importance of possible violations and affirm that the agreement is being upheld, even in the face of significant information to the contrary. Already today, the international sanctions regime has been dismantled, and restoring it and other international efforts to prevent Iran from going nuclear, in a world that has moved on to other issues, will be difficult and time-consuming.

Once the agreement expires, in 2025–2030, Iran will be better positioned to renew its military nuclear program and to "break out" in a relatively brief time, should it be willing to incur the international costs of doing so at that time. Israel's security margins are such that it cannot tolerate the emergence of a nuclear Iran.

Policy Recommendations:

➤ Maintain a credible Israeli capability to strike the Iranian program at any point during the lifetime of the agreement and thereafter, as a deterrent. Act militarily to prevent Iran from crossing the threshold, if and when all other measures have been exhausted, even if the time gained is relatively limited and the ramifications severe. Make it clear that Israel views the Iranian nuclear issue as the responsibility of the United States and other members of the P-6, but will act independently should they fail to satisfactorily address violations or an Iranian attempt to cross the nuclear threshold. Since an attack may strengthen Iran's motivation to rapidly cross the threshold, Israel must be capable of striking once again, if necessary.

➤ Maintain the capability, as a further deterrent, to destroy additional targets of high value, including missile and regime sites. Ensure that Israel has an effective response to the Hezbollah threat, Iran's primary means of retaliating for an attack on its nuclear program, at least on the defensive level. Continue building defensive and strategic deterrent capabilities at the same time.

➤ Intensively monitor Iranian compliance with the 2015 agreement, employing Israel's advanced intelligence capabilities to bring possible violations to the attention of the United States, P-6, and other relevant actors, and make the necessary operational and budgetary investments to this end.

➤ Restore close strategic dialogue and cooperation with the United States on Iran, inter alia, by aligning Israel's policies with the United States', seeking mutual agreement on what significant violations of the 2015 deal constitute and how they are to be addressed, measures to ensure that Iran does not cross the nuclear threshold the "day after" the agreement expires, and the circumstances in which military action might have to be undertaken, either by the United States or by Israel.[38] If the Trump administration seeks to reopen the issue, Israel should make it clear that, in the present circumstances, following the dismantlement of the international coalition and sanctions regime against Iran, it prefers the existing agreement to none all. Unless the United States is determined to take extreme measures, including military action, if needed, changes to the agreement should thus be designed to address a few critical weaknesses, first and foremost the "sunset" clause, which allows for the agreement's expiration, but not to endanger its very existence.

➤ Concomitantly conduct a campaign designed to focus international attention on Iran's regional role, such as its support for the Assad regime, massive supply of weapons to Hezbollah, and de facto domination of Iraq. Seek to convince the United States and others that Iran remains the primary long-term threat in the region, and that an Iranian-dominated Syria is the most dangerous possible outcome.

➤ Promote a new international suppliers' norm making the sale of nuclear reactors contingent on the buyer's legal commitment to refrain from building an independent nuclear fuel cycle and to purchase all fuel from the reactor's supplier, for the lifetime of its operation. In other words, reactor sales would include supply of fresh fuel, and spent fuel removal, and any country that insisted on having a fuel cycle (such as Iran today) would not be eligible to buy them. A norm of this sort would only require agreement among the five existing suppliers today (United States, France, Russia, South Korea, and Japan) and China in the not-distant future. All share some commitment to nonproliferation, and the proposed norm reflects economic realities—Iran's enrichment program is unnecessary and uneconomical. Moreover, Iran's Russian supplier actually prefers a build-own-operate contract today that imposes even greater restrictions than the suggested norm. As such, it should be acceptable, in principle, to all, and the primary obstacle would appear to be a potential fear on the part of the commercial manufacturers that they would lose out if they impose the norm but others do not.[39] These concerns are not insignificant, but do not appear insurmountable. Convincing the United States to pursue the proposal could be key to its success.

➤ Pursue all avenues for cooperation with those international and regional players who share Israel's concerns regarding Iran, including Saudi Arabia and the small Gulf States, as noted above. The primary avenue of activity will likely be indirect, through the United States.

➤ Consider bilateral security assurances from the United States, whether in the form of a defense treaty or other means, as already discussed, and encourage the United States to build a regional alliance designed to contain Iran. Make clear to Iran that the costs of crossing the threshold are unacceptable and allay the fears of other regional actors regarding its nuclear program,[40] thereby eliminating, or at least minimizing, their motivation to develop military nuclear programs of their own. The alliance, under US leadership, and combining diplomatic, economic, and military components, would have to find a delicate balance between a level of pressure sufficient to deter Iran from crossing the nuclear threshold, but not so great that Iran would fear a threat to the regime, the factor most likely to lead it to do so.

Maintain nuclear ambiguity; consider other options if Iran and/or other states cross nuclear threshold.

Irrespective of its actual capabilities, the international community is convinced that Israel is a nuclear power, and its adversaries must surely presume this to be the case for planning purposes. Israel thus enjoys the deterrent benefits of an overt nuclear posture, without the costs. Any further deterrence to be gained from an explicit nuclear posture would be marginal at best and would lead to an unavoidable crisis with the international community, including the United States, as well as Iran and the Arab world.

There certainly are benefits in a democracy to open and forthright public debate in national security areas, as in others, both as an intrinsic value and for reasons of legislative and public oversight. Nevertheless, all democracies live with national security secrets, and Israel's public justifiably views the nuclear realm as an area of such crucial importance to the nation's defense that it has knowingly waived its right to fully informed discussion. The number and stature of those who find the current policy truly troublesome is negligible.

Policy Recommendations:
➤ Maintain the international perception of Israel's existing strategic posture, including the belief that it has a nuclear triad, designed as a "doomsday option," that is, a deterrent in the event of an imminent threat of national demise.
➤ Maintain the policy of nuclear ambiguity for the long term, barring fundamental changes in Israel's strategic circumstances. Much like the 2002 National Security Assessment compiled by the NSS and the 2006 Meridor Report,[41] this study, too, concludes that the policy of nuclear ambiguity has been highly successful and should be continued.

> Consider a limited easing of ambiguity in a situation in which Iran or other actors in the region are about to cross the nuclear threshold (a concept that requires definition in its own right) or have done so. This would depend on the broader strategic circumstances prevailing at the time and might take the form of a partial and possibly indirect indication of some of Israel's doctrine. Barring a fundamental change in US policy, however, or in Israel's relations with the Sunni states, the basic elements of the ambiguity policy, or its entirety, should be preserved even then.

> Strengthen and revitalize legislative and public oversight mechanisms to eliminate any possibility of wrongdoing in this critical area. In so doing, preserve and strengthen Israel's nuclear posture, not change it.

Prepare for era in which the Begin Doctrine may no longer be feasible and previously unacceptable options may become necessary: end to ambiguity; US security guarantee; regional arms control talks.

As explained in chapter 8, Israel may be increasingly hard-pressed to uphold the Begin Doctrine in the future, whether in regard to Iran, or especially a decision by some other regional state, which may be a US ally or country friendly to Israel, to pursue a nuclear capability of its own. If and when Israel has truly exhausted all feasible diplomatic and military means of preventing them from acquiring nuclear weapons, it would hypothetically be left with just three primary options; a termination of ambiguity, US security guarantee, or regional arms control.

The above options have been analyzed in chapter 8 and this chapter will thus suffice just with the following. The stability of a hypothetical nuclear balance in the Middle Eastern context is questionable. The prospects for regional arms control agreements in the Middle East are fanciful for the foreseeable future, probably the long term. Moreover, Israel cannot rely on regional arms control agreements as long as its adversaries continue to be ruled by authoritarian or theocratic regimes. The likelihood of cheating, as demonstrated in a number of cases in the region in the past, is simply too great. In these circumstances, a US security guarantee might prove a necessary means of balancing a nuclear Iran and the only—partially—effective means of stabilizing and balancing a multinuclear Middle East.

Iran's nuclear aspirations have been postponed for the meantime, and it is unlikely that any of the other primary nuclear candidates, Saudi Arabia, Egypt, and Turkey, will cross the threshold during the coming decade (although the Saudis' financial clout could enable them to procure a turnkey capability). They may, however, begin development, and an actual capability might be feasible sometime during the next decade or thereafter. No immediate change in Israeli policy is thus required, but given the long time frames involved in strategic choices such as these, the time to begin preparing is now. The argument that even weighing these options constitutes an indirect admission of the ultimate failure of Israel's counterproliferation efforts and is therefore self-defeating, and that Israel should focus solely on preventing the emergence of the threats, is facile. Contingency planning is an essential part of all strategic planning.

Policy Recommendations:

➤ Do everything possible, in terms of diplomatic, covert, and military efforts, to prevent Iran and other regional states from achieving a nuclear capability, thereby avoiding the need to choose between military action and the above measures designed to enable Israel to live with an Iranian nuclear capability (end to ambiguity, regional arms control agreements, or a security guarantee).

➤ Begin positioning Israel for an era in which another actor or multiple actors in the region have acquired nuclear capabilities, despite all efforts to the contrary. If Israel wishes to shape future developments in directions commensurate with its strategic interests, it must be engaged proactively in the process.

- Explore the possibilities for a US security guarantee, as an addition to Israel's own deterrent capabilities, not in their stead. For reasons explained in the recommendations regarding Israel's relations with the United States, the time to begin discussions is not far off.

- Play an active role in regional arms control talks and, subject to certain conditions, even encourage them, as a long-term Israeli interest. To this end, Israel could initiate a Regional Security Dialogue Forum, open to all states in the region, that would address all WMD and ballistic missile capabilities, along with the broader regional issues of peace and normalization.[42] A number of important issues could be discussed even in the current regional circumstances, for example, the components of a putative Middle Eastern WMD-Free Zone (MEWMDFZ), how it might be brought into creation, and the means of establishing a truly effective inspections and verification regime, appropriate to regional needs.[43] A continued policy of prevention (diplomatic, covert, and especially military) would be more effective if coupled with a willingness to explore prospects for regional arms control.

- Demonstrate Israel's nonproliferation bona fides and strengthen its international standing generally by continuing the constructive position it took in the preparatory talks for the Helsinki Conference on a MEWMDFZ, or by signing and/or ratifying arms control regimes that do not pose unacceptable dangers to its national security interests, such as the CWC,

CTBT, and BWC. This could be done all at once, for maximal effect, as a new arms control initiative, or over time, as an indication of a sustained change.

- Link these changes in Israel's regional arms control policies to other issues, to derive maximal diplomatic benefit, for example, relations with leading Sunni states, such as Egypt or Saudi Arabia, or an NSG waiver for Israel from its nuclear export regulations, similar to that granted to India.

Israel will presumably be reluctant to make such changes, which are important both for substantive reasons and as negotiating cards, without commensurate responses on the part of Iran and the Arab states, of the United States, and international community. There is no immediate urgency, and waiting for the appropriate circumstances is warranted, while Israel continues to adopt a more proactive approach in this area.

Domestic Policy Recommendations

Recognize the home front as a primary front and allocate commensurate resources; invest in programs to better prepare and manage the home front for wartime and to strengthen societal resilience; resolve the issue of division of authority between governmental agencies.

With the likely postponement of the Iranian nuclear threat, the IDF has defined Hezbollah, and the threat it poses to the home front, as its primary focus. To date, the Israeli home front has demonstrated remarkable resilience in the face of recurring challenges, but the magnitude of destruction it may suffer in a large-scale conflict with Hezbollah is something it has never experienced before and will put it to a severe test.

The MoD has won the bureaucratic battle, for the meantime, and the former Ministry of Home Front Defense, never consequential at its height, is now defunct, but this is a victory the MoD and IDF are not fully equipped to handle. No other organization can provide emergency services as efficiently as the IDF Home Front Command (from the rescue of civilians in buildings hit by rockets, to the distribution of food and medicine to communities under siege), but the IDF's ability to manage the home front is limited. The very term "home front" is misleading; it is not a "front" in the military sense, but a loose agglomeration of hundreds of local authorities and political figures, government ministries, the health, educational, and other social welfare systems, emergency services (police, firefighters, ambulance corps), national infrastructure (communications, energy, transportation, finance), local businesses, NGOs, and more. Unlike the military front, no one is in "command," and thus preparation of the home front for wartime management is uniquely difficult.

Policy Recommendations:

➢ First and foremost, a change in IDF mindset: offense is vital and the decisive factor, but is no longer enough, and far more emphasis must be placed on defense of the home front and military rear. The IDF has long lagged behind in appreciating the need for defensive measures and continues to do so.

➢ Far better preparation and management of the home front for wartime, including:

- Formulation of a national home front strategy, along with a final division of responsibilities between the different bodies involved in home front management, such as the IDF Home Front Command, MoD's National Emergency Authority ("RAHEL"), the Ministries of the Interior and Internal Security (police and emergence services), and more.

- A national mortar, rocket, and missile shield, as elaborated above, construction of shelters and hardening of vital infrastructure. Little is more conducive of societal resilience.

- Programs to strengthen the local authorities, who bear primary responsibility for wartime services, and societal resilience, such as preparatory exercises, designed to train public and emergency service providers in wartime conduct, establishment of emergency crisis management centers in those local authorities that do not yet have them, provision of teams of experts to assist local authorities during crises, and establishment of additional "resilience centers" (see chapter 5).[44]

- Greater involvement of civil society organizations in wartime services.

➢ Resources, financial and otherwise, must be allocated in a manner commensurate with the magnitude of the threat, just as to any other vital "front."

Nourish Israel's qualitative edge, societal cohesion, and fundamental consensus: formulate a national strategy to reduce poverty and social gaps; increase Haredi and Arab employment; implement vital educational, socioeconomic, and quality-of-life reforms.

This book has focused primarily on the defense and foreign policy dimensions of Israel's national security strategy, only addressing some of the major societal and economic dimensions in chapter 5. The key to Israel's success to date, however, both militarily and as a nation generally, has been its qualitative edge, societal strength and resilience, and basic national consensus in the face of the many challenges it has confronted. The fundamental principle enunciated in Ben-Gurion's classic defense doctrine, of a qualitative response, the "few against the many," remains the basis for Israel's national security today. This is true even in an era, probably almost unimaginable to Ben-Gurion, in which Israel has gained not only qualitative superiority over its adversaries, but in many important areas, quantitative superiority, too.

Nevertheless, a number of domestic issues pose serious challenges today to Israel's societal strength and cohesion, and to its overall qualitative edge. The rapidly growing, but significantly less productive, Haredi and Arab populations have become untenable burdens on the economy and threaten a severe economic crisis in the coming years. The issue of Haredi military exemptions and preferential budgetary transfers cannot remain a political football forever; the nature of policies based on inequality and prevarication is that they ultimately fail all sides, including those they are designed to benefit. Israel's large Arab minority, 20% of the population, may not fully accord with Zionist dreams, but is a human and political reality, and Israel will only enjoy long-term domestic security if the Arab population is integrated into its society, enjoys the benefits thereof, and identifies with it.

Moreover, the challenges Israel faces today are not limited to these problematic population groups. The educational system is in a state of protracted crisis, and there are indications that Israel's high-tech sector, the engine driving its economic growth in recent decades, may be losing some of its cutting-edge innovative status. The cleavages over the future of the West Bank, between secular and religious Jews, and between Jews and Arabs, as well as Israel's deep social gaps, are of similarly great importance today, with a deleterious effect on its fundamental national consensus. Political exigencies in recent decades have produced a style of political discourse and actual policies that have further exacerbated some of these challenges and have increasingly generated a sense of unease, even disaffection, among significant parts of the very public that contributes the most to Israel's national security, especially young people considering their futures following military service.

The substance of the socioeconomic reforms required to preserve and nourish Israel's long-term qualitative edge, national consensus, and societal resilience is the subject of another book, but a few general points can be made. The deterioration in the educational system has taken place despite the investment of major budgetary resources and reform is thus at least largely a matter of substance and political will, not finances.[45] Targeted efforts are also necessary to improve quality-of-life issues, such as the cost of housing and preschool care, which are a primary source of discontent among young adults. Current efforts to promote Haredi and Arab employment must be increased greatly, as a matter of vital necessity, to avert the impending economic crisis. This will also have the added benefit of promoting their integration into Israeli society and sense of identification with the state.

To address the above issues, and in so doing strengthen Israel's fundamental social cohesion and national consensus, the government should formulate and implement a comprehensive national strategy designed to greatly alleviate poverty and reduce social gaps within a given period,[46] say a generation, an Israeli version of what the United States once dubbed a "War on Poverty." This is certainly an ambitious aspiration, one that is probably never fully achievable, but also not entirely unrealistic. Israel has achieved no less ambitious objectives in the past, such as successfully absorbing the huge influx of Russian immigrants in the mid-1990s, an increase of approximately 25% in Israel's Jewish population in just a few years.

Part of the solution depends, of course, on budgetary resources, but it is also a matter of adopting a national vision, setting long-term goals, and making a commitment on the part of successive leaders to formulate, implement, and update the policies needed to achieve them. A national vision such as this could serve as the basis for a new definition of the Zionist mission and provide a galvanizing and unifying focus for Israeli society, which has long been inspired by grand national projects. A "war on poverty" could be part of a new definition of Israel's national security strategy, in which socioeconomic development is once again accorded an importance similar to that of defense and foreign policy, much as was the case in Ben-Gurion's classic defense doctrine.

Finally, and it is admittedly easy to say, but Israel's leaders must accord greater importance to the effects of their statements and policies on the nation's fundamental long-term national consensus and sense of cohesion. Some policies in recent years have been intentionally divisive and exacerbated societal tensions; others have been gratuitously, even if unintentionally, so.

Mobilizing the political will for these changes will obviously not be easy in Israel's fractious political system, and any realistic policy recommendation must acknowledge that the politics involved are daunting. Sometimes a "good crisis" is required to engender the necessary political will, but national campaigns, causes célèbres, can also be a means to this end. Either way, major reform will be necessitated by some of the existing trends, whether Israel's leaders address them proactively or not. The alternative is not more of the same, or long-term muddling through, but domestic crises that have been brewing for years and are likely to reach turning points in the foreseeable future.

Amend the electoral system so that most governments serve full four-year terms and can conduct more policy-based decision-making processes, Knesset becomes accountable to voters and cabinet and MCoD become accountable to the premier and effective decision-making forums; strengthen role of the NSS and MFA.

Little is more important to Israel's national security today than a reform of the electoral system, designed to enable most premiers and coalitions to govern for a full four-year term and to do so far more effectively. Only a stable, effective government will be able to make the difficult and even historic decisions that Israel may face in the coming years, especially vis-à-vis the Palestinian issue, adopt and implement a new national security strategy suited to Israel's changing circumstances, and make the kind of domestic reforms noted above. It is precisely because electoral reform is of such crucial importance for Israel's national security and domestic well-being alike, that it was decided to make it the concluding recommendation of this book.

A detailed analysis of the strengths and weaknesses of the Israeli electoral and decision-making systems, and of the needed reforms, has been presented elsewhere,[47] and the following is merely a brief recapitulation thereof. One of the plagues of Israel's electoral system has been the fragility of the cabinet coalitions it produces and consequently the short tenures they serve, typically no more than two to three years, at times less. This has had many negative ramifications for Israeli policymaking in all areas, including an inability to develop coherent long-term policies, as premiers and ministers are forced to focus inordinately on coalition maintenance and re-election rather than governance.

National security decision-making in today's world is extraordinarily complex, requiring a medium- to long-term perspective and hence an expectation of at least some continuity in office on the part of elected officials. The likelihood of a full four-year term would greatly reduce the pressures on premiers and ministers to focus so overwhelmingly on short-term considerations and enable a more policy-based, rather than politics-based, decision-making process. For this reason, national leaders in some countries, France for example, are elected to term of even longer than four years, as are American senators.

The cabinet and even the Ministerial Committee on Defense (MCoD), the statutory forums for national security policymaking in Israel, are far too large and politicized for expeditious and discreet decision-making and are simply dysfunctional. In the absence of an effective statutory national security decision-making forum, the true loci thereof are the informal forums convened by the premier, whether the various "kitchen cabinets" or the frequent consultations premiers hold with the defense minister, CoS, and other defense chiefs, with or without the participation of the foreign minister and other seemingly relevant actors. These informal forums lack statutory decision-making authority, but their recommendations to the MCoD or cabinet plenum do carry considerable weight.

Israel's system of proportional representation (PR), in which voters elect parties, rather than individual members of Knesset, and in which the entire country comprises one national constituency, is designed to provide maximal representation to virtually all currents of thought within the body politic. In practice, this laudable goal ends up magnifying what are often small differences, creating artificial fragmentation and polarization. Moreover, voters do not truly have any representatives who are accountable to them. The result is greatly impaired governability, an unnecessary erosion of the national consensus, and loss of faith in the efficacy of the democratic system.

The issues of electoral and decision-making reform have received considerable attention in Israel over the years. Indeed, Israel enacted a significant reform in the late 1990s, which was in effect for two electoral cycles, before the Knesset concluded that the disadvantages outweighed the benefits and decided to return to the previous system. Numerous reforms have been proposed, each of which has a variety of benefits and weaknesses. This chapter will make do with a few specific recommendations regarding some of the essential changes needed.

Policy Recommendations:

➤ Reform the system so that premiers and cabinets can usually expect to serve a full four-year term. Most democracies have opted for the advantages of a parliamentary system, in which premiers and cabinets can be ousted midterm, as opposed to American- or French-style presidential systems, in which this is feasible only in exceptional cases. Israel's circumstances are such that it should preserve the option while greatly reducing the frequency of its possible occurrence.

➤ Restructure the cabinet and MCoD in a manner designed to make them far less politicized and far more effective decision-making bodies, truly accountable to the premier. Membership in the MCoD should be limited to the premier, defense and foreign ministers, vice or deputy premiers, and, on an as-needed basis, additional ministers, such as internal security, justice, and finance. The total number of permanent members should not exceed five to seven ministers.

➤ Elect at least a large part of the Knesset on a constituency basis, so that voters have representatives clearly beholden and accountable to them. There are numerous options for this, whether winner-takes-all constituencies or weighted systems. Most past proposals have suggested electing between 60 and 90 members of the Knesset in constituencies, with the rest to be elected on the basis of the current PR system.

➤ At the institutional level, the NSS must finally be given the influential role it was accorded by statute, as the premier's and cabinet's policymaking arm. The stature of the MFA must also be greatly strengthened, possibly by enacting a "Foreign Ministry Law."[48] Better-formulated policy, with clear and actionable policy objectives and priorities, is essential to the success of the new, broader national security strategy set out herein.

In practice, the prospects for major electoral reform, or a significant change in the status of the NSS and MFA, are not encouraging. In the meantime, small steps can be taken, designed to achieve incremental progress toward the overall changes outlined above, much like the recent raising of the electoral threshold. Although a fundamental change in the stature of the NSS and MFA would entail a significant political battle, which premiers to date have been loath to undertake, some improvement, consequential in its own right, would require little more than a decision by the premier to do so.

Conclusion

Israel was reborn in order to end the historic condition of Jewish insecurity and helplessness and has achieved great progress to that end. A hopeful and positive vision, in which peace is ultimately possible, even if still not for the foreseeable future, must replace the apocalyptical visions of continual conflict and even a renewed Holocaust that some Israeli leaders have espoused in recent years. Just days before President Sadat announced his dramatic visit to Israel in November 1977 the very idea seemed fanciful, as did the thought of peace with Egypt just two years later, Jordan 15 years after that, and advanced, if ultimately unsuccessful, talks with Syria and the Palestinians in the 1990s and 2000s.

Despite the daunting threats it still faces, Israel has become a stable and prosperous country, more secure than ever before and, most importantly, here to stay. At 70, Israel can be proud of its achievements, take a deep breath, and adapt itself to the reality of what will unfortunately remain a long-term conflict, but one in which its existence is no longer in doubt and its ability to shape its future is greater than ever before.

Being a "light unto the nations" was never quite achievable. As a fundamental national aspiration, however, something to constantly strive for, it remains a shining vision. Israel must continually strive to ensure its future as a predominantly Jewish and liberal democracy, a secure home for the Jewish people and all of its citizens, a nation that pursues socioeconomic growth with social equality, and constantly strives to reach peace with its neighbors.

Appendix

UN RESOLUTIONS ON ISRAEL
AND SELECT COUNTRIES

UN Security Council

Table A.1 **Security Council Resolutions Addressing or Condemning Israel**

	2000	2001	2002	2003	2004	2005	2006	2007	2008	2009	2010	2011	2012	2013	2014
Israel	1288	1337	1391	1461	1525	1583	1697	1759	1821	1860	1934	1994	2052	2108	2172
	1300	1351	1397	1488	1544	1605	1685	1773	1832	1875	1937	2004	2084	2115	
	1328	1365	1402	1496	1550	1614	1701	1788	1848	1884	1965	2028	2064	2131	
	1322	1381	1403	1515	1553	1648	1729		1850	1899					
			1405	1520	1578										
			1415												
			1428												
			1435												
			1451												
Total: 59	4	4	9	5	5	4	4	3	4	4	3	3	3	3	1

Table A.2 **Security Council Resolutions Condemning Selection Countries (or recalling previous resolutions)**

	2000	2001	2002	2003	2004	2005	2006	2007	2008	2009	2010	2011	2012	2013	2014
Syria						1636	1680						2042	2118	2139
						1644							2043		2163
															2165
Total: 9						2	1						2	1	3
Iraq	1293	1360	1409	1483				1762	1830	1883	1936	2001	2061	2107	2169
	1302	1382	1441	1511				1770		1905	1956	2016		2110	
	1330		1443								1957	2017			
			1447								1958				
			1454												
Total: 28	3	2	5	2				2	1	2	4	3	1	2	1
Iran							1696	1747	1803		1929	1984	2049	2105	2159
							1737		1835						
Total: 10							2	1	2		1	1	1	1	1
Lebanon	1310					1595	1697							2004	2172
							1701								
							1680								
Total: 7	1					1	3							1	1

(continued)

Table A.2 Continued

	2000	2001	2002	2003	2004	2005	2006	2007	2008	2009	2010	2011	2012	2013	2014
Yemen													2051		2140
Total: 2													1		1
Libya												1973	2040	2095	2144
												2016			2146
												2017			
Total: 7												3	1	1	2
North Korea							1718			1874	1928	1985	2050	2087	2141
														2094	
Total: 8							1			1	1	1	1	2	1
Myanmar															
Total: 0															
Uzbekistan															
Total: 0															
Turkmenistan															
Total: 0															
Belarus															
Total: 0															
Eritrea															
Total: 0															

UN General Assembly

Table A.3 **General Assembly Resolutions Addressing or Condemning Israel (or recalling previous resolutions)**

	2000	2001	2002	2003	2004	2005	2006	2007	2008	2009	2010	2011	2012	2013
Israel	55/50	56/31	57/110	58/21	59/31	60/39	61/25	62/83	63/29	64/10	65/16	66/73	67/19	68/15
	55/51	56/32	57/111	58/22	59/32	60/40	61/27	62/84	63/30	64/19	65/17	66/74	67/20	68/16
	55/55	56/52	57/112	58/23	59/33	60/41	61/112	62/85	63/31	64/20	65/18	66/75	67/23	68/17
	55/57	56/54	57/117	58/91	59/117	60/100	61/113	62/93	63/91	64/21	65/98	66/76	67/25	68/77
	55/87	56/56	57/119	58/92	59/118	60/101	61/114	62/102	63/93	64/88	65/99	66/77	67/115	68/78
	55/125	56/57	57/121	58/93	59/120	60/102	61/115	62/103	63/92	64/89	65/100	66/78	67/116	68/79
	55/128	56/58	57/122	58/94	58/292	60/103	61/116	62/105	63/94	64/90	65/101	66/79	67/118	68/80
	55/129	56/59	57/123	58/95	59/121	60/104	61/117	62/106	63/95	64/91	65/102	66/80	67/119	68/81
	55/130	56/60	57/124	58/96	59/122	60/105	61/118	62/107	63/96	64/92	65/103	66/118	67/120	68/82
	55/131	56/61	57/125	58/97	59/123	60/106	61/119	62/108	63/97	64/93	65/104	66/146	67/121	68/83
	55/132	56/62	57/126	58/98	59/124	60/107	61/120	62/109	63/98	64/94	65/105	66/225	67/24	68/84
	55/133	56/63	57/127	58/99	59/125	60/108	61/152	62/110	63/99	64/95	65/106	66/19		68/15
	55/134	56/142	57/128	58/100	59/173	60/146	61/154	62/146	63/140	64/125	65/134	66/17		68/235
	55/209	56/204	57/188	58/155	59/179			62/181	63/165	64/150	65/179	66/18		
			57/198	58/163						64/185	65/202			
				58/229										
Total: 195	14	14	15	16	14	13	13	14	14	15	15	14	11	13

Table A.4 General Assembly Resolutions Addressing or Condemning Select Countries (or recalling previous resolutions)

	2000	2001	2002	2003	2004	2005	2006	2007	2008	2009	2010	2011	2012	2013
Syria												66/176	67/183	68/182
													66/253	67/262
Total: 6												1	2	3
Iraq	55/115	56/174	57/232											
Total: 3	1	1	1											
Iran	55/114	56/171		58/195	59/205	60/171	61/176	62/168	63/191	64/176	65/226	66/175	67/182	68/184
Total: 13	1	1		1	1	1	1	1	1	1	1	1	1	1
Libya												65/265		
Total: 1												1		
North Korea						60/173	61/174	62/167	63/190	64/175	65/225	66/174	67/181	68/182
Total: 9						1	1	1	1	1	1	1	1	1
Myanmar	55/112	56/231	57/231	58/247	59/26	60/233	61/232	62/222	63/245	64/238	65/241	66/230	67/233	68/242
Total: 14	1	1	1	1	1	1	1	1	1	1	1	1	1	1
Uzbekistan						60/174								
Total: 1						1								

Turkmenistan	58/194	59/206	60/172
Total: 3	1	1	1
Belarus: 0			
Eritrea: 0			
Lebanon: 0			
Yemen: 0			

UN Human Rights Council

Table A.5 **UN Human Rights Council Resolutions Addressing or Condemning Israel (or recalling previous resolutions), Regular and Special Sessions**

	2006	2007	2008	2009	2010	2011	2012	2013	2014
Israel	A/HCR/RES/S-3/1	A/HRC/RES/6/19	A/HRC/RES/9/18	A/HRC/RES/S-12/1	A/HRC/RES/14/1	A/HRC/RES/16/31	A/HRC/19/14	A/HRC/RES/22/29	A/HRC/RES/25/31
	A/HRC/RES/2/4	A/HRC/RES/6/18	A/HRC/RES/7/18	A/HRC/RES/10/19	A/HRC/RES/13/8	A/HRC/RES/16/30	A/HRC/19/15	A/HRC/RES/22/28	A/HRC/RES/25/29
	A/HRC/RES/2/3	A/HRC/RES/OM/1/2	A/HRC/RES/7/17	A/HRC/RES/10/18	A/HRC/RES/13/7	A/HRC/RES/16/29	A/HRC/19/16	A/HRC/RES/22/27	A/HRC/RES/25/28
	A/HRC/DEC/1/106	A/HRC/RES/4/2	A/HRC/RES/7/30	A/HRC/RES/10/20	A/HRC/RES/13/6	A/HRC/RES/16/17	A/HRC/19/17	A/HRC/RES/22/26	A/HRC/RES/S-21/1
	A/HRC/S-1/1		A/HRC/RES/7/1	A/HRC/RES/10/17	A/HRC/RES/15/1			A/HRC/RES/22/17	A/HRC/RES/25/27
	A/HRC/S-2/1		A/HRC/RES/S-6/1	A/HRC/RES/S-9/1	A/HRC/RES/13/5				
Total: 46	6	4	6	6	6	4	4	5	5

Table A.6 **UN Human Rights Council Resolutions Addressing or Condemning Select Countries (or recalling previous resolutions)**

	2006	2007	2008	2009	2010	2011	2012	2013	2014
Syria						A/HRC/RES/ S-16/1	A/HRC/21/26	A/HRC/RES/ 24/22	A/HRC/ RES/27/16
						A/HRC/RES/ S-18/1	A/HRC/20/22	A/HRC/RES/ 23/26	A/HRC/ RES/26/23
						A/HRC/S-19/1	A/HRC/19/1	A/HRC/RES/ 23/1	A/HRC/ RES/25/23
							A/HRC/RES/ 19/22	A/HRC/RES/ 22/24	
Total: 14						3	4	4	3
Iran						A/HRC/RES/ 16/9	A/HRC/19/12	A/HRC/RES/ 22/23	A/HRC/ RES/25/24
Total: 4						1		1	1
Libya						A/HRC/RES/ 6/33			
						A/HRC/RES/ S-15/1			
Total: 2						2			
North Korea			A/HRC/ RES/7/15		A/HRC/ RES/13/14	A/HRC/RES/ 16/8	A/HRC/RES/ 19/13	A/HRC/RES/ 22/13	A/HRC/ RES/25/25
Total: 6			1		1	1	1	1	1

(continued)

Table A.6 Continued

	2006	2007	2008	2009	2010	2011	2012	2013	2014
Myanmar		A/HRC/RES/6/33	A/HRC/RES/8/14	A/HRC/RES/10/27	A/HRC/RES/13/25	A/HRC/RES/16/24	A/HRC/RES/19/21	A/HRC/RES/22/14	A/HRC/RES/25/26
		A/HRC/RES/S-5/1	A/HRC/RES/7/31						
			A/HRC/RES/7/32						
Total: 11		2	3	1	1	1	1	1	1
Belarus						A/HRC/RES/17/24	A/HRC/RES/20/13	A/HRC/RES/23/15	A/HRC/RES/26/25
Total: 4						1	1	1	1
Eritrea							A/HRC/RES/20/20	A/HRC/RES/23/21	A/HRC/RES/26/24
							A/HRC/RES/21/1		
Total: 4							2	1	1
Turkmenistan: 0									
Uzbekistan: 0									

LIST OF INTERVIEWS

Professor Dima Adamsky, Herzlia Interdisciplinary Center, January 15, 2012

Major General Yaakov Amidror, former national security adviser, December 30, 2015

Major General Orna Barbivai, former head of IDF Personnel Branch, January 10, 2016

Dr. Yehuda Ben-Meir, former deputy foreign minister (interview conducted by Saskia Becaud), October 21, 2015

Brigadier General Shlomo Brom, former deputy national security adviser, January 6, 2016 and July 10, 2016

Professor Stuart Cohen, Bar Ilan University, January 3, 2015

Major General Uzi Dayan, former national security adviser, August 17, 2016

Ron Eldadi, former director general, Ministry of Intelligence Affairs, January 14, 2013

Brigadier General Meir Elran, senior research fellow, INSS, July 20, 2016, and October 20, 2015 (interview conducted by Saskia Becaud)

Eran Etzion, former deputy national security adviser, November 3, 2014

Gideon Frank, former director general, Atomic Energy Committee, October 19, 2016

Lt. General Dan Halutz, former chief of staff, December 16, 2012

Amos Harel, journalist, Haaretz, January 20, 2015

Brigadier General Yoram Hemo, former head of Dado Center for Interdisciplinary Military Research, January 10, 2016

Brigadier General Yossi Kuperwasser, former head of Research Division, Military Intelligence, December 18, 2012

Gur Laish, National Security Staff, January 3 and January 10, 2013, December 30, 2015

Dr. Emily Landau, senior research fellow, INSS, July 10, 2016

Dr. Eli Levite, former deputy director general, Atomic Energy Committee, April 6, 2016

Dr. Martin Malin, executive director, Project on Managing the Atom, Harvard Belfer Center, February 16, 2016

Dan Meridor, former cabinet minister, December 24, 2012, January 1, June 12, and June 23, 2013, June 21, 2016

Major General Yair Naveh, former deputy chief of staff, January 14, 2016

Major General Ido Nechustan, former air force commander and head of IDF Planning Directorate, December 30, 2015

Brigadier General Assaf Orian, former head of IDF Strategic Planning Division, December 29, 2015

Tamir Pardo, former head of Mossad, July 26, 2016

Lt. General David Petraeus, former director of CIA, April 22, 2016

Ambassador Dennis Ross, special assistant to the president, Mideast peace envoy, April 14, 2016

Lt. General Moshe Yaalon, former minister of defense, July 24, 2016

Major General Amos Yadlin, former head of Military Intelligence, January 13, 2013

NOTES

Introduction

1. Head of military intelligence Major General Herzi Halevy, Herzlia Conference, June 16, 2016.
2. See for example, Major General Herzi Halevy, Herzliya Conference, June 16, 2016; interview, senior defense official, July 27, 2016.
3. fortune.com/2015/09/01/why-israel-dominates-in-cyber-security/; David Sanger, *New York Times*, June 1, 2012; David Sanger and Mark Mazzetti, *New York Times*, February 16, 2016.
4. www.jpost.com/Middle-East/US-sent-lessons-learned-team-to-model-Israel-tactics-in-Gaza-operation-381078; www.high-level-military-group.org/pdf/hlmg-assessment-2014-gaza-conflict.pdf.
5. INSS, the Institute for National Security Studies, Israel's premier think tank, and the Institute for Policy and Strategy both have programs focusing on Israel's defense strategy, though neither has yet published a major study of the issue. A high-level working group, headed by practitioner turned scholar Uzi Arad, published a "grand strategy"; see Arad et al. 2017.
6. Posen 1984, pp. 13, 25; Art 2003, pp. 1–2.
7. Amidror in Efrati 2002, p. 9.
8. Shabtai 2010, pp. 7–16.
9. Kimchi, July 2007, p. 11.
10. Teran in Efrati 2002, pp. 24–26; Tal 1996, p. 53.
11. Amidror in Efrati 2002, p. 9.
12. Quoted in Tamari 2014, p. 2.

Chapter 1

1. Yaniv 1987, pp. 18–19.
2. Ben-Israel 2013, pp. 59–60.
3. Freilich 2012, p. 138.
4. Zisser 2001, pp. 3–10.
5. Pedatzur in Bar-Tal 1998, pp. 144; Ben-Horin and Posen 1981, p. 13.
6. Freilich 2012, p. 12; Dror 2011, pp. 13, 16; David in Freedman 2009, pp. 299–300; Ben-Meir 2009, p. 37; Brun 2008, pp. 4–15.
7. http://www.pitgam.net/data/%5B%D7%9E%D7%A0%D7%97%D7%9D+%D7%91%D7%92%D7%99%D7%9F%5D/1/1/0/.
8. Peter Hirschberg, *Haaretz*, November 14, 2006.
9. For a moving presentation of the Israeli existential fear, see Shavit 2013, chapter 1; Freilich 2012, p. 12.
10. Freilich 2012, p. 12.

11. Freilich 2012, p. 12; Maoz 2006, p. 8; Horowitz in Yaniv 1993, p. 32; Heller 2000, p. 10; Amidror in Efrati 2002, p. 148; Tal 1996, pp. 49, 73; Allon 1976, pp. 38–53; Adamsky 2010, pp. 112.
12. Luft 2004, p. 2.
13. Tal 1996, p. 68; Bar-Joseph 2000, pp. 99–114, p. 100; Shabtai 2010, pp. 7–16, p. 8; Cohen 2008, p. 41.
14. Maoz 2006, p. 8.
15. Handel 1973, p. 1.
16. Ben-Horin and Posen 1981, p. 26; Allon 1976, pp. 38–53, pp. 42–43; Maoz 2006, p. 9; Yariv 1980, pp. 3–12, p. 6; Levite 1989, p. 35; Newman in Bar-Tal 1998, p. 75.
17. Ben-Horin and Posen 1981, p. 5; Dayan 1955, pp. 250–268.
18. Dayan 2012, pp. 23–31.
19. Handel 1973, pp. 4–5; Yanai 2005, p. 9.
20. Ben-Horin and Posen 1981, p. 6; Gelber 2014, p. 1.
21. www.mefacts.com/outgoing.asp?x_id=10191.
22. Allon 1976, pp. 38–53; Ben-Israel 2013, pp. 28–29, 35; Tal 1996, p. 50; Maoz 2006, p. 8; Levite 1989, pp. 31, 33; Amidror in Efrati 2002, p. 48; Kober 1955, pp. 147–154.
23. Shelah 2003, p. 30; Yariv 1980, pp. 3–12; Tal 1996, p. 69; Handel in Murray 1994, p. 538; Gelber 2014, p. 1.
24. Kober 2009, pp. 1, 3, 36; Feldman and Toukan 1997, p. 10.
25. Kober 2009, pp. 1, 3, 36; Kober 1995, p. 152; Handel in Murray 1994, p. 545.
26. Bar-Joseph 2004–5, pp. 137–156; Bar-Joseph 2005, pp. 10–19; Feldman and Toukan 1997, p. 9; Heller 2000, pp. 11–12; Levite 1989, p. 39; Kober 1995, pp. 156–158; Ben-Dor in Yehezkeli 2001, p. 31; Kober in Karsh 1996, p. 189; Adamsky 2010, p. 112; Horowitz in Yaniv 1993, p. 12; Inbar and Sandler 1993–94, p. 331.
27. Tal 1996, pp. 49, 119; Ben-Israel 2013, pp. 30, 35, 39; Bar-Joseph 2004–5, pp. 141; Bar-Joseph 2005, p. 13; Feldman and Toukan 1997, p. 9; Heller 2000, pp. 11–12; Levite 1989, p. 39; Kober 1995, pp. 156–158; Ben-Dor in Yehezkeli 2001, p. 31; Kober in Yehezkeli 2001, p. 189; Adamsky 2010, p. 112; Horowitz in Yaniv 1993, p. 12; Inbar and Sandler 1993–94, p. 331.
28. Kober 1995, p. 150.
29. Tal 1996, pp. 62–63.
30. Cohen 1998, pp. 19–20; Kober 1995, p. 155; Ben-Horin and Posen 1981, pp. 7–9; Levite 1989, pp. 37–40; Rabin in Klieman and Levite 1993, p. 11.
31. Adamsky 2010, p. 112; Bar-Joseph 2004–5, pp. 137–141; Bar-Joseph 2000, p. 100; Levite 1989, p. 47.
32. Yaniv 1987, p. 1.
33. Dror 2011, p. 20; Ben-Horin and Posen 1981, pp. 14, 18–19; Maoz 2006, p. 15; Feldman and Toukan 1997, p. 12; Yaniv 1987, pp. 18–19; Inbar and Sandler 1993–94, p. 331; Rabin in Klieman and Levite 1993, p. 10; Ben-Dor in Yehezkeli 2001, p. 33; Tal 1996, p. 62; Ben-Dor in Bar-Tal 1998, p. 121.
34. Cohen 1992, p. 342; Feldman in Klieman and Levite 1993, pp. 124–125; Levite 1989, p. 125. Yaniv (1987, p. 22) attributes a somewhat greater, yet still limited, role to punishment in Israeli deterrence policy.
35. Heller 2000, p. 13; Ben-Dor in Bar-Tal 1998, pp. 114–115; Feldman and Toukan 1997, pp. 9–10.
36. Ben-Horin and Posen 1981, p. 16; Cohen 1998, pp. 24–25; Inbar 1983, p. 51; Inbar 2008, pp. 18–19; Horowitz in Yaniv 1993, pp. 21–22; Bar 1990, p. 156.
37. Bar-Joseph 2004–5, pp. 137–156, p. 141; Bar-Joseph 2005, pp. 10–19, p. 13; Feldman and Toukan 1997, p. 9; Heller 2000, p. 11; Levite 1989, p. 39; Kober 1995, pp. 156–158; Ben-Dor in Yehezkeli 2001, p. 31; Kober in Karsh 1996, p. 189; Adamsky 2010, p. 112; Kober in Yehezkeli 2001, pp. 13–14.
38. Horowitz in Yaniv 1993, pp. 16–18.
39. Horowitz in Yaniv 1993, p. 15; Tal 1996, pp. 70, 73; Maoz 2006, pp. 12–13; Rodman 2005, p. 11; Adamsky 2010, pp. 113–114; Feldman and Toukan 1997, pp. 9, 13; Heller 2000, p. 11; Ben-Israel 2013, pp. 52–54; Yaron in Efrati 2002, p. 59.
40. Pedatzur in Bar-Tal 1998, pp. 147–148.

41. Ben-Israel 2013, p. 40; Ben-Horin and Posen 1981, p. 10; Maoz 2006, p. 13; Pedatzur in Bar-Tal 1998, p. 141; Bar-Joseph 2004–5, pp. 137–156; Amidror in Efrati 2002, p. 152; Ben-Dor in Bar-Tal 1998, pp. 120.

42. Rodman 2005, pp. 8–9; Cohen 1998, p. 21: Levite 1989, p. 34; Tal 1996, pp. 68, 74, 125; Feldman and Toukan 1997, p. 18.

43. Tal 1996, pp. 74–75; Heller 2000, p. 12.

44. Tal 1996, pp. 74–75; Heller 2000, p. 12; Rodman 2005, pp. 8–9.

45. Tal 1996, p. 77; Ben-Horin and Posen 1981, p. 5.

46. Inbar 2008, p. 5; Ben-Dor in Yehezkeli 2001, p. 30; Newman in Bar-Tal 1998, p. 78; Tamari 2014, p. 6.

47. Maoz 2006, p. 13; Levite 1989, pp. 7, 28; Inbar 1983, p. 38; Bar-Joseph 2000, p. 100; Inbar 2008, p. 5; Tal 1996, pp. 55–56; Levite 1989, p. 48; Gelber 2014, p. 1.

48. Bitzur 2009, pp. 12–19, p. 14; Levite 1989, p. 3; Kober 1995, pp. 162–163; Kober in Karsh 1996, p. 195; Ben-Israel 2013, pp. 73–74; Ben-Horin and Posen 1981, p. 29; Cohen et al. 1998, pp. 18–19; Tal 1996, pp. 70, 80–81; Yaniv 1987, p. 11; Levite 1989, pp. 7, 35, 49; Feldman and Toukan 1997, p. 18; Rodman 2005, pp. 12–13; Even and Michael in Elran et al. 2016b, p. 46.

49. Rodman 2005, p. 5; Kober 1995, p. 149; Ben-Israel 2013, pp. 73–74; Ben-Horin and Posen 1981, p. 29; Cohen 1998, 18; Tal 1996, p. 81; Yariv 1980, p. 11; Levite 1989, pp. 7, 35, 49, 84–85; Feldman and Toukan 1997, p. 18; Shelah 2003, p. 30.

50. Ben-Horin and Posen 1981, p. 5; Cohen 1998, p. 18; Levite 1989, pp. 7, 99; Tal 1996, p. 69; Handel in Murray 1994, p. 538.

51. Maoz 2006, p. 16; Tal 1996, pp. 69–70; Handel 1973, p. 5; Newman in Bar-Tal 1998, pp. 84–85.

52. Kober 2009, p. 3; Cohen 1998, pp. 19–20; Levite 1989, p. 34; Tal 1996, p. 80; Rodman 2005, pp. 12–13; Inbar 2008, p. 87; Maoz 2006, pp. 13–14; Kober 1995, p. 161; Ben-Horin and Posen 1981, pp. 38–39; Kober in Karsh 1996, p. 194; Handel in Murray 1994 pp. 538–539.

53. Horowitz in Yaniv 1993; Ben-Horin and Posen 1981, p. 26; Tal 1996, pp. 69, 202; Catignani 2008, p. 55; Rodman 2013, p. 3; Inbar 1983, pp. 36–55, p. 38.

54. Inbar 2008, p. 86; Ben-Israel 2013, p. 82; Maoz 2006, p. 15; Rodman 2005, p. 20; Heller 2000, p. 15.

55. Ben-Horin and Posen 1981, p. 23; Cohen 1998, p. 27.

56. Tal 1996, pp. 62–63; Levite 1989, p. 35.

57. Rodman 2005, p. 18; Feldman and Toukan 1997, p. 8.

58. Tal 1996, p. 72; Cohen 1998, p. 44; Inbar 2008, p. 88.

Chapter 2

1. For a related argument, see Laish 2010, p. 5.

2. SIPRI, "Military Expenditure Data by Country," 2000–2014.

3. Amos Gilad, ICT Conference on Terrorism, Herzliya, September 10, 2013.

4. Luft 2004, pp. 2–3; Peri 2006, p. 33.

5. Sima Kadmon, *Yediot Aharonoth Weekend Magazine*, November 18, 2006.

6. http://www.timesofisrael.com/text-of-netanyahus-holocaust-remembrance-day-speech/; Aluf Benn, *Haaretz*, May 10, 2009; Ari Shavit, *Haaretz*, April 19, 2012.

7. Ewen MacAskill and Chris McGreal, *Guardian*, October 26, 2005, www.theguardian.com/world/2005/oct/27/israel.iran; Nazila Fathi, *New York Times*, October 27, 2005.

8. Ariel Ben Solomon, *Jerusalem Post*, November 20, 2013, www.jpost.com/Iranian-Threat/News/Khamenei-Israeli-regime-is-doomed-to-failure-annihilation-332403; *Telegraph*, February 13, 2012, www.telegraph.co.uk/news/worldnews/middleeast/iran/9059179/Iran-We-will-help-cut-out-the-cancer-of-Israel.html; Antonia Molloy, *Independent*, November 10, 2014, www.independent.co.uk/news/world/middle-east/irans-supreme-leader-ayatollah-khamenei-outlines-plan-to-eliminate-israel-9850472.html.

9. David in Bar-Tal 1998, p. 301.

10. Bar-Tal 1998, pp. 120, 132; Feldman in Feldman and Toukan 1997, p. 13; Eiland 2007, p. 17.

11. Heller 2000, pp. 37–38.

12. Robert Satloff, *New Republic*, December 4, 2012.
13. Dan Halutz, interview, December 12, 2012; Amos Gilad, ICT Conference on Terrorism, Herzlia, September 10, 2013.
14. Dror 2011, pp. 13, 16.
15. Rodman 2013, pp. 4–5; Inbar 2008, p. 5; Tal 1996, pp. 202.
16. Handel 1973, p. 5.
17. Maoz 2006, pp. 546–547; Rodman 2013, pp. 4–5.
18. Yaniv 1987, p. 162.
19. Rodman 2013, pp. 4–5; Peri 2006, pp. 36–37; Brun 2008, pp. 11–12.
20. Bystrov and Sofer 2008, p. 23.
21. State of Israel, State Comptroller 2008, p. 180.
22. Bar-Tal 1998, p. 73.
23. Bar-Tal 1998, p. 124; Kober 1995, p. 149.
24. Tal 1996, pp. 203–204.
25. Rubinstein 2001.
26. Amidror 2010, p. 8; Dayan 2012, pp. 25–26.
27. www.cia.gov/library/publications/the-world-factbook/geos/is.html; State of Israel, Ministry of Finance, The Israeli Economy Fundamentals, Characteristics and Historic Overview, Fall 2012.
28. www.wipo.int/ipstats/en.
29. The World Bank, "Research and Development Expenditure (% of GDP)." www.data. worldbank.org/indicator/GB.XPD.RSDV.GD.ZS; UNESCO, "Science, Technology and Innovation: Gross Domestic Expenditure on R&D (GERD), GERD as a Percentage of GDP, GERD per Capita and GERD per Researcher"; http://data.uis.unesco.org/Index. aspx?queryid=74.
30. Ben-Israel 2013, p. 37.
31. Cordesman 2008, p. 52; Maoz 2006, p. 566.
32. Kober in Bar-Joseph 2001, pp. 183, 185.
33. Kober 1995, pp. 444–445; Kober in Bar-Joseph 2001, p. 177.
34. Ben-Israel 2013, p. 53; Ben-Horin and Posen 1981, p. 10; Kober 1995, p. 444.
35. Feldman and Toukan 1997, p. 14.
36. Maoz 2006, p. 546.
37. Yaniv 1987, p. 30; IISS, The Military Balance 2016, www-tandfonline-com.ezp-prod1.hul. harvard.edu/toc/tmib20/116/1.
38. Kober 2009, p. 191; Kober 1995, pp. 445–446.
39. Cohen 1998, pp. 61–62.
40. The following section draws on Freilich 2012, pp. 14–15.
41. Inbar 1996 (no page); Kam in Brom 2012, p. 16.
42. Dan Meridor, interview, December 24, 2012.
43. http://foreignpolicy.com/2016/08/17/how-the-islamic-state-seized-a-chemical-weapons-stockpile/; Amos Harel, *Haaretz*, April 29, 2014.
44. Amos Harel, *Haaretz*, October 21, 2016.
45. AFP and TOI Staff, *Times of Israel*, April 20, 2016, http://www.timesofisrael.com/top-idf-general-israel-egypt-have-unprecedented-intel-cooperation/; Amos Harel, *Haaretz*, July 12, 2016.
46. Ayesha Daya and Dana El Baltaji, *Bloomberg*, September 4, 2012, www.bloomberg.com/news/2012-09-04/saudi-arabia-may-become-oil-importer-by-2030-citigroup-says-1-.html; Matt Clinch and Hadley Gambel, CNBC, April 26, 2015, www.cnbc.com/2016/04/25/saudi-arabias-government-officially-unveils-long-term-economic-plan.html.
47. Barak Ravid, *Haaretz*, July 22, 2016, www.haaretz.com/israel-news/.premium-1.732776.
48. Gozansky and Kulik 2010, pp. 41–42.
49. Dan Meridor, interview, December 24, 2012; Amos Harel, *Haaretz*, December 27, 2013, p. 6.
50. Head of Military Intelligence Herzi Halevi, Herzliya Conference, June 16, 2016; Amos Harel, *Haaretz*, December 12, 2013, pp. 1, 5, 22, and December 27, 2013.
51. http://www.foreignaffairs.com/articles/62085/zeev-schiff/israels-war-with-iran.
52. Head of Military Intelligence Hertzi Halevi, Herzliya Conference, June 16, 2016.

53. Itai Brun, IDC conference "The Arab Spring in Search of a Tomorrow," Herzliya, January 18, 2015.
54. Robert Satloff, *New Republic*, December 4, 2012.
55. Robert Satloff, *New Republic*, December 4, 2012.
56. Head of Military Intelligence Hertzi Halevi, Herzliya Conference, June 16, 2016.
57. Dan Meridor, interviews, January 14, 2013, and February 24, 2013.
58. Dan Halutz interview, December 12, 2012.
59. Dan Meridor interview, January 14, 2013; Dan Meridor, class at Tel Aviv University, November 25, 2013.
60. Dan Meridor, class at Tel Aviv University, November 25, 2013.
61. Israel Central Bureau of Statistics, //www.cbs.gov.il/hodaot2015n/11_15_355matzeget.pdf.

Chapter 3

1. State of Israel 2015, pp. 3, 11; Laish 2010, p. 5; Rubenstein 2001; Amos Harel, *Haaretz*, January 12, 2013; Dan Halutz speaks of conventional wars as being less likely, interview, December 12, 2012; Cordesman 2008, p. 11.
2. Amos Harel, *Haaretz*, October 11, 2013.
3. Dayan 2012, p. 28.
4. Interviews with Dan Meridor, February 24, 2013, June 11, 2013, June 25, 2013; Dan Meridor, lecture at Tel Aviv University, November 25, 2013; Dan Meridor, INSS Conference on Intelligence, Tel Aviv, May 26, 2013.
5. Bar-Joseph 2004–5, p. 146; interview with Dan Halutz, December 12, 2012; Amos Gilad, ICT Conference on Terrorism, Herzlia, September 10, 2012.
6. Cohen 1998, pp. 83–84; Marcus 1999, pp. 35–36; Rubenstein 2001Eisenkot 2010, p. 23; Zeev Schiff, *Haaretz*, April 21, 2006.
7. Cordesman 2008, p. 11; Eiland 2009, p. 12.
8. Joby Warrick and Loveday Morris, *Washington Post*, September 10, 2013; Eisenkot 2010, p. 24.
9. Eiland 2009, pp. 12–13; Zeev Schiff, *Haaretz*, August 9, 2002; Yoav Zitun, Ynet, August 24, 2003; Aviashai Apergon, Israel Defense, December 28, 2012; *Defense Industry Daily*, August 15, 2015; Scott Neuman, NPR, May 31, 2013.
10. Reuven Pedhazur, *Haaretz*, October 23, 2007; Zeev Schiff, *Haaretz*, August 9, 2002, April 21, 2006; Siboni 2008, p. 12.
11. Amos Harel, *Haaretz*, May 23, 2010, September 25, 2013, December 27, 2013, and February 7, 2014.
12. Amos Gilad, ICT, Conference on Terrorism, Herzlia, September 10, 2013.
13. Cordesman 2008, pp. 11, 12, 22–23, 50.
14. Brun 2010, p. 547; Siboni 2010, p. 4; Ben-Israel 2013, p. 89; Ronen Bergman, Bloomberg.com, June 25, 2013; Shelah 2003, p. 58.
15. Cohen 1992, pp. 335–338; Cohen 2008, p. 40.
16. Byman 2011, p. 60.
17. Kober 2009, p. 40; Rodman 2005, p. 15; Cohen 2008, pp. 40–41.
18. Gray 2015, p. 241.
19. Baidatz and Adamsky 2014, p. 19; Chorev 2015, p. 11; Shamir and Hecht 2014–15, p. 85; Kober 2009, p. 36; Brun and Valensi in Adamsky and Bjerga 2012, pp. 116–117; Siboni 2009, p. 26; Gilad Erdan, Minister of the Homefront, INSS Conference on the Home Front, Tel Aviv, July 25, 2013; Laish 2010, pp. 5–6.
20. Chorev 2015, p. 11; Shamir and Hecht 2014–15, p. 85; Kober 2009, p. 36; Brun 2010, pp. 547–551; Brun and Valensi in Adamsky and Bjerga 2012, pp. 116–117; Siboni 2009, p. 26; Paz 2015, pp. 5–6.
21. Chorev 2015, p. 11; Shamir and Hecht 2014–15, p. 85; Kober 2009, p. 36; Brun 2010, pp. 547–551; Brun and Valensi in Adamsky and Bjerga 2012, pp. 116–117; Siboni 2009, p. 26; Paz 2015, pp. 5–6.
22. Eiland 2007, p. 14.

23. Chorev 2015, p. 11; Shamir and Hecht 2014–15, p. 85; Kober 2009, p. 36; Brun 2010, pp. 547–551; Brun and Valensi in Adamsky and Bjerga 2012, pp. 116–117; Siboni 2009, p. 26; Paz 2015, pp. 5–6.

24. Chorev 2015, p. 17.

25. Eisenkot 2016, p. 7.

26. Amos Harel, *Haaretz*, November 17, 2013; Amos Yadlin, interview, January 13, 2013.

27. Moshe Yaalon, interview by Ari Shavit, *Haaretz*, June 16, 2012; Yadlin and Golob 2013, p. 8; Yaakov Lapin, quoting Uzi Rubin, *Jerusalem Post*, January 15, 2014.

28. Meridor in Yehezkeli 2001, pp. 50–51.

29. Uzi Rubin, INSS Conference on Aerial Threats, Tel Aviv, June 3, 2013; Moshe Yaalon, interview by Ari Shavit, *Haaretz*, June 16, 2012; Gili Cohen and Noa Speigel, *Haaretz*, October 22, 2017.

30. Kam 2016, p. 33.

31. Amos Harel, *Haaretz*, November 17, 2013.

32. Rubin 2015, p. 19.

33. Dan Meridor, interview, February 24, 2013; Amos Harel, *Haaretz*, April 16, 2010, April 23, 2010; Steinitz 2005, pp. 5–6.

34. Eiland 2010, p. 60; Elran and Altschuler 2012, p. 23.

35. Dan Meridor, interview, December 24, 2012.

36. Dan Meridor, interview, January 14, 2013 and June 23, 2013.

37. Yoav Zitun, Ynet, August 24, 2013; Amos Harel, *Haaretz*, February 7, 2014, December 24, 2014.

38. Yaakov Lapin, quoting Uzi Rubin, *Jerusalem Post*, January 15, 2014.

39. Moshe Yaalon, interview by Ari Shavit, *Haaretz*, June 16, 2012; Yadlin and Golob 2013, p. 8; Yaakov Lapin, quoting Uzi Rubin, *Jerusalem Post*, January 15, 2014.

40. Rubin 2007, pp. 5, 26.

41. Itai Brun, Herzlia Conference, Herzlia, June 10, 2014; Amos Harel, *Haaretz*, May 29, 2015; Amidror 2015b, p. 4.

42. Eisenkot 2016, p. 9; General Moskowitz gives the figure of 150–170 villages in southern Lebanon, with 40–50 sites that would have to be attacked in each one. Amos Harel, *Haaretz*, April 28, 2016. The difference in figures is unclear, though Eisenkot speaks of villages, towns, and cities, whereas Moskowitz refers only to villages.

43. Steven Erlander and Isabel Kushner, *New York Times*, July 8, 2014; Itai Brun, Herzlia Conference, Herzlia, June 10, 2014; Avi Isacharoff, *Times of Israel*, March 4, 2016.

44. Amidror 2015b, p. 4; Avi Isacharoff, *Times of Israel*, March 4, 2016.

45. http://www.idfblog.com/facts-figures/rocket-attacks-toward-israel/; Byman 2011, p. 183; Rubin 2015, p. 15.

46. Gili Cohen, *Haaretz*, March 31, 2015, April 2, 2015, September 16, 2016; Yossi Yehoshua, *Yediot Aharonoth*, September 16, 2016.

47. Erez and Perel 2013, pp. 76–78; Meir Elran, quoted by Amos Harel, *Haaretz*, July 24, 2013; Former minister of the home front Matan Vilani in Elran and Altschuler 2012, p. 41.

48. Gili Cohen, *Haaretz*, September 16, 2016.

49. Amos Harel, *Haaretz*, May 20, 2010.

50. Gili Cohen, *Haaretz*, September 16, 2016; Yossi Yehoshua, *Yediot Aharonoth*, September 16, 2016.

51. Shaham and Elran 2016, p. 45; Yossi Yehoshua, *Yediot Aharonoth*, September 16, 2016; Yoav Zitun, Ynet, September 15, 2016; Gili Cohen, *Haaretz*, March 31, 2015; Amos Harel, *Haaretz* August 2, 2012, March 29, 2013.

52. Ron Ben Yishai, Ynet, September 11, 2014; Amos Harel, *Haaretz*, June 5, 2014; Rotem Shtarkman, *Haaretz*, September 16, 2014.

53. Dekel, Siboni, and Einav 2016 (no pages).

54. Pollak 2016, p. 4.

55. Amos Harel, *Haaretz*, November 17, 2013, June 5, 2014; Dan Meridor also foresees a massive Hezbollah rocket barrage at the beginning of a future conflict, interview, December 24, 2012.

56. Itai Brun, quoted by Amos Harel, *Haaretz*, June 13, 2014.

57. Dayan 2012, pp. 23–31, p. 26.

58. Gray 2015, pp. 218, 222, 224; Edo Hecht, communication to author, January 7, 2016.
59. Kober in Yehezkeli 2001, p. 20; Catignani 2008, p. 3.
60. Brun 2010, pp. 552–553; Tamari 2011, pp. 9–10; Kulik 2009, p. 21; Eisenkot 2010, p. 23; Siperco 2010, p. 127.
61. Dan Meridor, interview, January 14, 2013; Eisenkot 2010, p. 23.
62. Gur Laish, interview, January 3, 2013.
63. Eiland 2010, p. 57; Byman 2011, p. 7.
64. Eiland 2010, p. 58.
65. Eiland 2007, p. 16; Shalom and Handel 2011, pp. 18–19.
66. Shweitzer in Kurtz and Brom 2014, p. 22.
67. Eiland 2007, pp. 14–15; Zeev Schiff, *Haaretz*, April 21, 2006; Dan Meridor, INSS Conference on Intelligence, Tel Aviv, May 26, 2013.
68. Eiland 2007, pp. 15–16.
69. Eiland 2007, pp. 15–16.
70. Eiland 2007, p. 14.
71. Eiland 2007, pp. 16–17.
72. Eiland 2010, p. 57.
73. Dan Meridor, lecture, Tel Aviv University, December 2, 2015.
74. Eiland 2007, p. 17.
75. The following section on terrorism draws heavily on Freilich 2015.
76. Laish 2010, pp. 5–6.
77. Shweizer 2010, p. 20.
78. Amos Yadlin, ICT Conference on Terrorism, Herzlia, September 10, 2012.
79. Ben-Israel 2013, p. 20. Another source speaks of 19 killed by Arab guerrillas and terrorists in 1950 (Byman 2011, pp. 19, 32); Catignani 2008, p. 47; Yehezkeli in Efrati 2002, p. 96; Gilbert 2008, p. 291.
80. Byman 2011, pp. 38, 40; Catignani 2008, p. 82.
81. www.shabak.gov.il/English/EnTerrorData/decade/Fatalities/Pages/default.aspx; www.shabak.gov.il/SiteCollectionImages/Hebrew/TerrorInfo/decade/DecadeSummary_he.pdf; www.shabak.gov.il/publications/study/Pages/summary2012.aspx; www.idfblog.com/facts-figures/rocket-attacks-toward-israel/; Byman 2011, pp. 115, 142, 183; Kober 2009, p. 87; Ben-Israel 2013, pp. 88–89.
82. Cohen 2008, p. 41.
83. Byman 2011, pp. 228–240, 256.
84. Cohen 2008, p. 41; Byman 2011, pp. 228–240, 256; http://he.wikipedia.org/wiki/%D7%AA%D7%95%D7%A6%D7%90%D7%95%D7%AA_%D7%9E%D7%9C%D7%97%D7%9E%D7%AA_%D7%9C%D7%91%D7%A0%D7%95%D7%9F_%D7%94%D7%A9%D7%A0%D7%99%D7%99%D7%94.
85. Kober 2009, p. 43; Lavie 2010, p. 87; Catignani 2008, pp. 107, 138; Byman 2011, p. 140; Inbar 1991, p. 33; Kaplinsky 2009, p. 19.
86. Byman 2011, p. 372.
87. Byman 2011, p. 87; Shalom and Handel 2011, p. 17; Catignani 2008, pp. 107–108.
88. Uzi Dayan, ICT Conference on Terrorism, Herzlia, September 8, 2013.
89. www.boi.org.il/he/NewsAndPublications/RegularPublications/Pages/heb_inf0602h.aspx; Motti Basuk, *The Marker*, January 13, 2015.
90. Catignani 2008, p. 142; www.mof.gov.il/research_e/trends 2004e.pdf.
91. www.idfblog.com/facts-figures/rocket-attacks-toward-israel/; Byman 2011, p. 183.
92. Edo Hecht, communication with author, January 8, 2016.
93. "Akbar Hashemi Rafsanjani," *Wikiquote*, http://en.wikiquote.org/wiki/Hashemi_Rafsanjani.
94. Moshe Yaalon, interview by Ari Shavit, *Haaretz*, June 6, 2012; Giora Eiland, interview by Ari Shavit, *Haaretz*, July 13, 2012.
95. "The Decision Maker," interview by Ari Shavit, *Haaretz*, June 16, 2012.
96. Freilich 2007, p. 3.
97. Moshe Yaalon, interview by Ari Shavit, *Haaretz*, June 6, 2012; Giora Eiland, interview by Ari Shavit, *Haaretz*, July 13, 2012; Amos Yadlin, interview by Ari Shavit, *Haaretz*, September 12, 2012; "The Decision Maker," interview by Ari Shavit, *Haaretz*, June 16, 2012.

98. Amos Yadlin, interview by Ari Shavit, *Haaretz*, September 12, 2012; Moshe Yaalon, interview by Ari Shavit, *Haaretz*, June 6, 2012; "The Decision Maker," interview by Ari Shavit, *Haaretz*, June 16, 2012; Ephraim Halevy, interview by Ari Shavit, *Haaretz*, August 13, 2012; Ephraim Sneh, interview by Ari Shavit, *Haaretz*, August 22, 2012; Yossi Beilin, interview by Ari Shavit, *Haaretz*, August 18, 2012.

99. Moshe Yaalon, interview by Ari Shavit, *Haaretz*, June 6, 2012; Giora Eiland, interview by Ari Shavit, *Haaretz*, July 13, 2012.

100. www.nti.org/country-profiles/egypt/.

101. Cordesman 2008, p. 8.

102. Ely Karmon, *Haaretz*, September 18, 2013; *Wall Street Journal*, July 23, 2015; AFP, *Telegraph*, January 29, 2014; Russel Goldman, *New York Times*, July 11, 2016; Spencer Ackerman, *Guardian*, September 22, 2016.

103. http://www.nti.org/country-profiles/saudi-arabia/nuclear/; Alexander Sehmer, *Independent*, May 18, 2015; *Newsweek*, April 2, 2015; Jason Burke, *Guardian*, June 29, 2011.

104. See Freilich 2010; Gat in Adamsky and Bjerga 2012, pp. 16–17.

105. The section on the cyber-threat is adopted from Freilich et al. 2015.

106. Alon Ben-David, *Aviation Week and Space Technology*, June 27, 2011, p. 57; Clarke and Knake 2012, pp. 155; Elizabeth Nigro, "Cyber security: The Vexed Question of Global Rules. An Independent Report of Cyber-preparedness around the World," https://gssd.mit.edu/search-gssd/site/cyber-security-vexed-question-global-59906-mon-02-11-2013-1116; Eisenstadt and Pollock 2012, p. 35; David Shamah, *Times of Israel*, July 9, 2014.

107. Jonathan Silber, Ynet, January 26, 2012; Anshel Pfeffer, *Haaretz*, June 15, 2009; Mohammed Herzallah, *Newsweek*, July 27, 2009.

108. James Vincent, *Independent*, July 29, 2014; Or Hirshoga and Nati Toker, *The Marker*, November 22, 2012; Olga Khazan, *Washington Post*, November 17, 2012; Siboni et al. 2013, p. 7; Michal Zippori, CNN, January 26, 2012; Nati Toker, *Tech Nation*, November 22, 2012; Stuart Winer, *Times of Israel*, August 17, 2014; Jack Moore, *Newsweek*, April 7, 2015.

109. Mohammed Herzallah, *Newsweek*, July 27, 2009; Reuters, June 9, 2013; Siboni and Kronenfeld 2014c.

110. Yakov Katz, *Jerusalem Post*, May 6, 2012, May 31, 2012; Yakov Lappin, *Jerusalem Post*, May 11, 2013, August 17, 2014.

111. Even and Siman-Tov 2011, pp. 36–37; Alon Ben-David, *Aviation Week and Space Technology*, June 27, 2011, p. 57.

112. Carr 2012, pp. 21–22.

113. Barak Ravid, *Haaretz*, June 21, 2014; Yaakov Katz, *Jerusalem Post*, June 6, 2012.

114. Dayan 2014, pp. 27–29.

115. Dayan in Jerusalem Center 2014, p. 38.

116. Dayan 2014, pp. 27–29.

117. Dayan 2014, pp. 27–29.

118. Eiland 2009, pp. 3–4; Bar-Joseph 1998a, p. 48.

Chapter 4

1. The following section draws heavily on Freilich and Cohen 2015.

2. Siboni 2010b, p. 3.

3. Ministry of Foreign Affairs website; Klieman 1990, p. 8; Yaron in Efrati 2002, p. 63.

4. http://globalizatihttp://globalization.kof.ethz.ch/on.kof.ethz.ch/

5. Curtis 2012, p. 351; Inbar 2013a, p. 18; Gilboa 2006, pp. 724–725; Neuer 2007, p. 45; http://blog.unwatch.org/index.php/2013/11/25/this-years-22-unga-resolutions-against-israel-4-on-rest-of-world.

6. The issues that constituted the basis for the figure include

   • Respect of humanitarian law
   • Rights to self-determination for Palestinians
   • Need to open borders and gates in Gaza
   • Illegality of settlements

- Israeli excavation undertaken in the Old City
- Israeli demolition of Palestinian homes
- Respect of the Geneva convention
- Withdrawal from Syrian Golan
- Threats to the well-being and safety of Palestinians under occupation
- Repatriation/compensation for refugees
- Right of return for those displaced in June 1967
- Killing of refugee children in UNWRA schools by Israel
- Refugees entitled to their property and to the income derived therefrom
- Breach of international law during military operations
- Destruction of infrastructures such as water pipelines and sewage networks in Occupied Territories
- Wall impeding the Palestinian right to self-determination
- Inadmissibility of the acquisition of territory by war
- Excessive use of force toward Palestinians
- Restrictions on the freedom of movement of the agency's staff
- Israeli violence against Lebanese civilians
- Investigation on Israeli practices
- Harm to Palestinian children
- Exploitation of natural resources by Israel

7. Curtis 2012, p. 351; Gilboa 2006, p. 724.
8. Gilboa 2006, p. 25; Timon Dias, *Jerusalem Post*, August 5, 2013; Spyer 2008, pp. 1–2.
9. Tovah Lazaroff, *Jerusalem Post*, July 7, 2013; Curtis 2012, p. 351; Gilboa 2006, pp. 724–725.
10. Lous Charbonneau, Reuters, June 13, 2016.
11. Barak Ravid, *Haaretz*, September 5, 2012, December 3, 2012.
12. Israel Hayom Staff, Israel Hayom, July 16, 2013; Herb Keinon, JPost.com, July 17, 2013; Eli Brandnstein, NRG, October 17, 2013; Barak Ravid, *Haaretz*, October 24, 2013.
13. Barak Ravid, *Haaretz*, December 3, 2012: Herzlia Conference Task Force, Herzlia Interdisciplinary Center, 2011, p. 5.
14. Kuperwasser in BESA 2016, p. 9.
15. Steinberg 2006, pp. 748, 755–757; Steinberg 2012, p. 373; Inbar 2013a, p. 20–22; Nisan 2013, p. 263.
16. Steinberg 2006, pp. 756, 757.
17. Bakan and Abu-Laban 2009, pp. 39, 42; Fishman 2012, p. 416.
18. Inbar 2013a, p. 9; Kuperwasser in BESA 2016, p. 10.
19. Joel Bainerman, *The Middle East*, Issue 382, October 2007, pp. 17–18; Farsakh 2011, p. 56; Karmi 2011, pp. 64–65, 72; Karsh 2012, pp. 322–323; Stein 2004, p. 330; Alexander Yakobson, *Dissent*, Fall 2010, p. 14.
20. E. Redden, InsideHigherEd.com, December 17, 2013; S. Jaschik, InsideHigherEd.com, January 10, 2014; Lidar Gravé-Lazi, *Jerusalem Post*, November 21, 2015.
21. Hallward and Shaver 2012, p. 403; Bakan and Abu-Laban 2012, pp. 42, 45; Gerstenfeld 2012, p. 394.
22. Inbar 2013a, p. 21.
23. "Anti-Israel Activity on Campus, 2014–2015: Trends and Projections," ADL, November 18, 2015, www.adl.org/israel-international/anti-israel-activity/c/anti-israel-activity-on-campus-2014-15.html#.V81oZpgrLIU.
24. T. Peterson and N. G. A. Pour, *Jerusalem Post*, October 1, 2013.
25. United Church of Canada, BDSMovement.net, May 23, 2013.
26. Algemeiner.com, May 3, 2012.
27. Jaweed Kaleem, *Huffington Post*, June 23, 2014; "Divestment: Frequently Asked Questions," www.pcusa.org/site_media/media/uploads/oga/pdf/ga221-middle-east-faq.pdf.
28. Jeremy Rabkin, *Wall Street Journal*, July 13, 2004; Pressman 2006, p. 363.
29. Jeremy Rabkin, *Wall Street Journal*, July 13, 2004; Pressman 2006, p. 363; Lynk 2005, p. 6.
30. Lynk 2005, p. 15.
31. Shimon Shamir, www.news.walla.co.il/?w=/9/262836.

32. Steinberg 2012, p. 376.
33. Vennesson 2012, pp. 414–416.
34. Israel Ministry of Foreign Affairs, "The UN General Assembly Ignores Terrorism," November 19, 2006.
35. Steinberg 2012, pp. 379–380.
36. Vennesson 2012, pp. 419–420; Weizman 2010, p. 11.
37. Berkowitz 2011, pp. 23–24.
38. Vennesson 2012, p. 421.
39. Vennesson 2012, p. 421; Sterio 2010, p. 252.
40. Steinberg 2012, p. 382.
41. Sterio 2102, p. 253; Berkowitz 2011, pp. 18, 24, 28.
42. Martin Peretz, *New Republic*, April 28, 2011, p. 6; Vennesson 2012, p. 422; Steinberg 2006, p. 372; Yakov Katz, *Jerusalem Post*, April 4, 2011; Berkowitz 2011, p. 14.
43. Sterio 2010, p. 253; Yonah Jeremy Bob, *Jerusalem Post*, October 25, 2012; Blank 2010, p. 79; Steinberg 2012, pp. 372, 384; Yakov Katz, *Jerusalem Post*, April 14, 2011.
44. Schabas 2010, p. 307.
45. Blank 2010, p. 282.
46. Inbar 2013a, p. 21.
47. Blank 2010, pp. 283, 303.
48. The Palestinians were killed by Christian Maronites, Israel's allies at the time, but Sharon, who was the defense minister at the time, was found by an Israeli investigative committee to bear indirect responsibility and was forced to resign.
49. Seener 2009, p. 44, 47; Curtis 2012, p. 353.
50. Aceves 2010, pp. 314–315; Seener 2009, pp. 47, 49.
51. Seener 2009, pp. 47, 52; Cohen and Cohen 2011, p. 16.
52. Yonah Jeremy Bob, *Jerusalem Post*, September 13, 2012.
53. Bolgiano 2010, p. 396; Curtis 2012, p. 351; Barak Ravid, *Haaretz*, June 10, 2011; Seener 2009, p. 50; https://unitedwithisrael.org/uk-officials-apologize-for-detaining-idf-officer-charged-with-war-crimes/.
54. Curtis 2012, p. 351.
55. Seener 2009 p. 54; Curtis 2012, p. 351.
56. Berkowitz 2011, p. 10; Buchan 2012, p. 266.
57. N. Feldman 2016, pp. 33–34.
58. N. Feldman 2016, pp. 33, 46.
59. http://www.jewishvirtuallibrary.org/jsource/anti-semitism/bdsstates.html.
60. Eiland 2007, pp. 16–18.
61. Siboni 2010b, p. 4.
62. Catignani 2008, pp. 4–5; Meridor in Yehezkeli 2001, pp. 52–55; Brun and Valensi in Adamsky and Bjerga 2012, p. 117; Siboni 2010b, p. 4; interviews with Dan Meridor, February 24, 2013, and June 25, 2013.
63. Gilboa 2006, pp. 726–728; Shamir, *Walla*, August 1, 2002.
64. Curtis 2012, pp. 344–345.
65. Gilboa 2006, pp. 731, 735–736.
66. Director general of the Ministry of Strategic Affairs, quoted by Barak Ravid, *Haaretz*, August 7, 2016.
67. BBC World Service, May 22, 2013.
68. "Views of China and India Slide in Global Poll, While UK's Ratings Climb," Globescan, May 22, 2013, www.globescan.com/news-and-analysis/press-releases/press-releases-2013/277-views-of-china-and-india-slide-while-uks-ratings-climb.html.
69. Aluf Benn, *Haaretz*, December 17, 2004.
70. Aluf Benn, *Haaretz*, September 12, 2008.
71. Barak Ravid, *Haaretz*, June 21, 2011, June 27, 2013, September 26, 2015.
72. World Population Prospects 2017, Key Findings and Advance Tables, United Nations, Department of Economic and Social Affairs Population Division, p. 3. https://esa.un.org/unpd/wpp/Publications/Files/WPP2017_KeyFindings.pdf.
73. DellaPergola 2011, pp. 122, 242–243.

74. Zimmerman 2006.
75. DellaPergola 2011, pp. 118, 242; Nir Hasson, *Haaretz*, June 30, 2013; *Jerusalem Post*, May 29, 2014.
76. Brom and Kurz 2016, p. 39; Tamir Pardo, interview, July 26, 2016.
77. Shaul Arielli, *Haaretz*, June 17, 2016.

Chapter 5

1. Inbar 2009, p. 158.
2. State of Israel 2015, p. 11.
3. https://he.wikipedia.org/wiki/%D7%A8%D7%9E%D7%AA_%D7%94%D7%97%D7%99%D7%99%D7%9D_%D7%91%D7%99%D7%A9%D7%A8%D7%90%D7%9C#/media/File:Gdppercapita.png; CIA World Factbook.
4. http://atlas.media.mit.edu/en/profile/country/isr/#Trade_Balance.
5. www.mfa.gov.il/MFA/AboutIsrael/Economy/Pages/ECONOMY-%20Sectors%20of%20the%20Economy.aspx.
6. Andres et al. 2012, pp. 96–97.
7. Israel Democracy Index, Israel Democracy Institute, Jerusalem 2014; Arian et al. 2005.
8. Y. Levy 2008, pp. 54, 254.
9. Y. Levy 2011, p. 68.
10. Y. Levy 2011, p. 64.
11. S. Cohen 2011, p. 200; Judah Ari Gross, *Times of Israel*, May 30, 2016, www.timesofisrael.com/just-a-quarter-of-all-eligible-reservists-serve-in-the-idf/.
12. Y. Levy 2011, pp. 53–54, 70.
13. Gili Cohen, *Haaretz*, January 10, 2015; Amos Harel, *Haaretz*, July 24, 2015; Yoav Zitun, Ynet, February 1, 2015; Cohen in Rubin and Keany 2002, p. 166.
14. Orna Barbivai, interview, January 10, 2016; Gili Cohen and Amos Harel, *Haaretz*, July 22, 2015; Sami Peretz, *The Marker*, July 22, 2015; M. Levy 2004, p. 30.
15. Chuck Freilich, "A Big Bang in Israeli Politics," *American Interest*, January 22, 2015; Z. Israeli in Brom and Kurz 2016, p. 101; Lora Moftah, International Business Times, March 11, 2015.
16. Ram 2008, p. 154; Andres et al. 2012, p. 97; Lebel 2007, p. 76.
17. Ariane et al. 2007, p. 58; Arian 2009, p. 52.
18. Andres et al. 2012, p. 96; Y. Levy 2012a, p. 49.
19. Eiland 2007, p. 17; Lebel 2007, p. 70.
20. http://fas.org/irp/world/israel/iraq_intel.pdf; S. A. Cohen 2008, pp. 61, 68.
21. S. A. Cohen 2008, pp. 61, 77; Cohen and Cohen 2011, pp. 1, 15–16.
22. Ben-Dor in BESA 2016, p. 37.
23. Kane 2005, no pages; Jon Henley, *Guardian*, November 19, 2015.
24. Faris 2013, p. 214; Leon 2015, p. 6; Bagno-Moldavsky and Ben-Meir in Kurz and Brom 2015, p. 44; Ben-Meir and Bagno-Moldavsky 2013, p. 39.
25. Israel Central Bureau of Statistics, "Long-Range Population Projections for Israel: 2009–2059," 2012; Elran and Ben-Meir 2012, pp. 9–10.
26. *Economist*, June 27, 2015.
27. Zicherman 2014, no pages; Amos Harel, *Haaretz*, July 11, 2012; Elran and Ben-Meir 2012, p. 34.
28. Lahav Larkov, *Jerusalem Post*, March 13, 2014; Jeremy Sharon, *Jerusalem Post*, April 29, 2015.
29. Gili Cohen, *Haaretz*, February 15, 2016, October 10, 2016; Gal 2015, p. 15; Jeremy Sharon, *Jerusalem Post*, July 15, 2015; Aron Heller and Isaac Sharf, *Huffington Post*, May 3, 2014; Haim Bior, *Haaretz*, April 18, 2015; Amos Harel, *Haaretz*, January 2, 2014.
30. Yair Etinger, *Haaretz*, August 17, 2006.
31. Radai 2015, pp. 94–98; http://news.walla.co.il/item/2920606.
32. Yashiv and Kasir 2014, p. 19.
33. Israel Central Bureau of Statistics 2009 and 2015, from PowerPoint presentation, Government of Israel, Minority Economic Development Authority, 2016.
34. National Security Administration 2014, from PowerPoint presentation, Government of Israel, Minority Economic Development Authority, 2016.

35. http://brookdaleheb.jdc.org.il/_Uploads/dbsAttachedFiles/MJB-Facts-and-Figures-on-Arab-population-December-2015-Hebrew-final.pdf.

36. Higher Education Council, from PowerPoint presentation, Government of Israel, Minority Economic Development Authority, 2016; Ministry of Industry, Research and Economics Administration, from PowerPoint presentation, Government of Israel, Minority Economic Development Authority, 2016.

37. Edmund Sanders, *Los Angeles Times*, May 10, 2010; Seth Frantzman, *Jerusalem Post*, December 31, 2013, Ben-David 2015, p. 56; Lidar Gravé-Lazi, *Jerusalem Post*, December 9, 2015; David Horovitz, *Jerusalem Post*, April 9, 2010; Ben-David 2015, p. 19.

38. Ben-David 2015, pp. 4, 34, 37–38, 40–42, 79; David Horovitz, *Jerusalem Post*, April 9, 2010.

39. S. A. Cohen 2008, p. 30.

40. Yaakov Katz, *Jerusalem Post*, November 18, 2011; S. A. Cohen 2007, p. 2.

41. Amos Harel, *Haaretz*, September 7, 2012; State of Israel, Ministry of Defense 2011, p. 1629; Gili Cohen, *Haaretz*, February 24, 2015; see Libel and Gal 2015.

42. Amos Harel, *Haaretz*, December 31, 2012 and November 10, 2013.

43. *Jerusalem Post*, July 30, 2007; Amos Harel provides similar data; 13% of those who do not serve are Haredi, with the remaining 12% divided between the 3% who live abroad, 3% who do not meet minimum IDF recruitment standards, and 6% with physical and psychological problems. Between a third and 40% of the psychologically unfit were Haredi, *Haaretz*, July 11, 2012; Gili Cohen, *Haaretz*, February 24, 2015; S. A. Cohen 2007.

44. Orna Barbivai, interview, January 20, 2016; Ben Hartman, *Jerusalem Post*, March 8, 2015; Amos Harel, *Haaretz*, November 10, 2013; Yoav Zitun, Ynet, November 7, 2013, and November 17, 2011; Ben Hartman, *Jerusalem Post*, March 8, 2015.

45. Orna Barbivai, interview, January 20, 2016.

46. Amos Harel, *Haaretz*, July 11, 2012; Rodman 2013, p. 6; Bar-Joseph 2004–5, p. 144.

47. Gili Cohen, *Haaretz*, February 24, 2015.

48. Gal in Elran and Sheffer 2015, p. 56; Andres et al. 2012, p. 94.

49. Amos Harel, *Haaretz*, November 30, 2013.

50. Amos Harel, *Haaretz*, December 18, 2013, October 23, 2016.

51. Yair Ettinger, *Haaretz*, September 23, 2015, November 25, 2015; "Women in the Israel Defense Forces," www.jewishvirtuallibrary.org/jsource/Society_&_Culture/idfwomentoc.html.

52. Y. Levy 2012a, p. 54; Y., Levy 2009b, p. 136; Andres et al. 2012, pp. 100, 104, 106.

53. Interview with Major General Orna Barbivai, former head of IDF Personnel Branch, January 10, 2016; interview with Meir Elran, October 20, 2015 (conducted by Saskia Becaud); interview with Yehuda Ben-Meir, October 21, 2015 (conducted by Saskia Becaud); Stuart Cohen, in an interview January 3, 2016, estimated the potential downturn in motivation to serve among the secular population at 5% at most, though his estimate was a general one, not necessarily in combat units, especially some of the less "glamorous" traditional units, such as the armored corps; Yoav Zitun, Ynet, November 12, 2014, and November 7, 2013; Amir Buchbut, *Walla News*, November 7, 2013, and November 12, 2014; Yoav Itiel, *Magazine Hamoshavot*, vol. 309, April 2, 2012.

54. Stuart Cohen, interview, January 3, 2016.

55. jppi.org.il/news/114/58/The-People-s-Army/; Libel and Gal 2015, p. 223.

56. Gal in Elran and Sheffer 2015, p. 54; Gal 1999, pp. 12–13; Perliger 2011, p. 221.

57. Ben-Dor and Pedahzur 2006, p. 433; Gal in Elran and Sheffer 2015, pp. 54–57; Gal 1999, pp. 13–14; Andres et al. 2012, p. 96; S. A. Cohen 2000, p. 132.

58. Kober 2013, p. 10.

59. Ben-Dor and Pedahzur in Lebel 2008, p. 67.

60. www.idf.il/1133-22449-he/Dover.aspx; Amos Harel, *Haaretz*, January 30, 2014.

61. Orna Barbivai, interview, January 20, 2016; Ben-Dor and Pedahzur in Lebel 2008, p. 68.

62. Amos Harel, *Haaretz*, January 23, 2005 and January 30, 2014; Amnon Barzilai, *Haaretz*, December 24, 2004; Ilan Schkori et al., *Haaretz*, April 3, 2008; Y. Levy 2011, pp. 70–71.

63. Ben-Dor et al. 2008, p. 572.

64. Ben-Dor et al. 2008, p. 572.

65. Y. Levy 2011, p. 69.

66. Amos Harel, *Haaretz*, February 13, 2015.
67. S. A. Cohen 2010, p. 200.
68. Orna Barbivai, interview, January 10, 2016; Amos Harel, *Haaretz*, September 10, 2003 and June 13, 2014; Yossi Yehoshua, *Yediot Aharonoth*, June 30, 2016.
69. Inbar 2008, p. 21.
70. Malka 2008, p. 6.
71. Orna Barbivai, interview, January 10, 2016; Uzi Dayan, interview, August 17, 2016; Tamir Pardo, interview, July 26, 2016; Zipi Livni, INSS Conference on the Home Front, August 1, 2012; Y. Levy 2012a, pp. 2, 127.
72. Y. Levy 2012a, pp. 129–130; Kober 2009, p. 74.
73. S. A. Cohen 2008, pp. 57–58.
74. Bohrer and Osiel 2013, p. 16.
75. Lebel 2008, p. 83.
76. *Jerusalem Post*, January 23, 2008; Amos Harel, *Haaretz*, August 28, 2015.
77. Yehuda Ben-Meir, interview (conducted by Saskia Becaud), October 21, 2015; Filson and Werner 2007, p. 711; see also Feaver 2005, for the American experience in Iraq.
78. Arian 2000, p. 25.
79. Levy 2012a, p. 72; Michael Omer-Man, *Jerusalem Post*, May 20, 2012.
80. Ben-Meir in Brom and Elran 2007, p. 93; Ben-Meir in Kurz and Brom 2014a, p. 129; John Ward Anderson, *Washington Post*, July 26, 2006; "Northern Israelis Flee Hezbollah Rockets," August 4, 2006, http://www.abc.net.au/news/2006-08-04/northern-israelis-flee-hez-bollah-rockets/1231030; Freilich 2012, p. 56.
81. Ben-Meir in Kurz and Brom 2014a, p. 132; Yossi Verter, *Haaretz*, August 1, 2014; Eva Illouz, *Haaretz*, December 19, 2014; Ben-Meir 2009, p. 30.
82. Lebel 2011, p. 74; Levy 2012a, p. 41.
83. Kober 2013, p. 10; Y. Levy 2009a, p. 79; Y. Levy 2009b, p. 160; Y. Levy 2009b, pp. 140, 201; Kober 2013, p. 110; Y. Levy 2009a, p. 79; Y. Levy 2009b, p. 140; Y. Levy 2012a, p. 160; S. A. Cohen 2000, p. 123.
84. Y. Levy 2012a, p. 105; Eiland 2007, p. 20; Kober 2013, p. 97.
85. State of Israel, State Comptroller 2008, p. 395.
86. Y. Levy 2012b, p. 13.
87. Cornfeld and Danieli 2015, p. 51.
88. "Military Expenditure (% of GDP)," http://data.worldbank.org/indicator/MS.MIL.XPND.GD.ZS.
89. Y. Levy 2009b, p. 140.
90. Even in Kurz and Brom 2013, p. 251.
91. Orna Barbivai, interview, January 1, 2016; State of Israel 2015, p. 11.
92. Kobi Nachshoni, Ynet, March 25, 2014.
93. Ben-Meir and Sher in Kurz and Brom 2014, p. 159, Avineri 1986, p. 5.
94. Jeremy Sharon, *Jerusalem Post*, January 28, 2015. See also Hermann 2014.
95. Hermann 2014 p. 26.
96. Dan Illouz, *Jerusalem Post*, April 22, 2015.
97. Heller 2000, p. 36.
98. S. A. Cohen 2008, p. 61.
99. http://www.archives.gov.il/ArchiveGov_Eng/Publications/ElectronicPirsum/SixDayWar/; http://www.jewishvirtuallibrary.org/jsource/isdf/text/golan.html.
100. When asked to rank by order of importance the principles of "Jewish majority", "democracy", "state of peace", and "greater Israel", the latter ranks as the lowest priority for the Israeli public. Nevertheless, 29% still rank the aspiration to a "greater Israel" as a first or second priority. Ben-Meir and Sher in Kurz and Brom 2014b, p. 163.
101. Bagno-Moldavski and Ben-Meir 2014, p. 43; Ben Meir and Sher in Brom and Kurz 2014, p. 135; Bagno-Moldavsky and Ben-Meir in Kurz and Brom 2015, pp. 43–44.
102. Bagno-Moldavski and Ben-Meir 2014, p. 43; Ben Meir and Bagno-Moldavsky 2012, p. 84; Ben Meir and Sher in Brom and Kurz 2014, pp. 135, 165.
103. Shlomi Eldar, Al Monitor, July 15, 2015; Herb Keinon, *Jerusalem Post*, July 20, 2015.
104. Israeli in Brom and Kurz 2016, p. 106.

105. Judy Maltz, *Haaretz*, August 12, 2012.
106. Ben Meir and Bagno-Moldavsky 2012, p. 28.
107. Israeli in Brom and Kurz 2016, p. 104.
108. Bagno-Moldavsky and Ben-Meir in Kurz and Brom 2015, p. 42.
109. Israeli in Brom and Kurz 2016, p. 105.
110. Bagno-Moldavsky and Ben-Meir in Kurz and Brom 2015, p. 43; Israeli in Brom and Kurz 2016, p. 105; Ben Meir and Bagno-Moldavsky 2012, p. 76.
111. Israeli in Brom and Kurz 2016, p. 104; Ben Meir and Bagno-Moldavsky 2012, p. 74; Bagno-Moldavsky and Ben-Meir in Kurz and Brom 2015, p. 41; see also Inbar 2013b, who agrees with the overall argument that disagreements over the peace process are overblown and that the national consensus is strong.
112. Sandler and Rynhold 2007, pp. 234–235.
113. Arian et al. 2005, p. 57; S. A. Cohen in Rubin and Keaney 2002, pp. 176–177; Hermann et al. 2014, p. 38.
114. S. A. Cohen 2008, pp. 3, 56; Brun 2008, pp. 7–9.
115. Lebel 2007, p. 79.
116. Israeli in Brom and Kurz 2016, p. 114; Kober 2009, p. 165.
117. Amos Harel and Gili Cohen, *Haaretz*, August 12, 2016.
118. S. A. Cohen 2006, 778–779.
119. Ben Meir and Bagno-Moldavsky 2012, p. 60.
120. Editorial, *Jerusalem Post*, October 16, 2014.
121. Israel Central Bureau of Statistics, media announcement, July 19, 2015.
122. OECD 2015, pp. 178–179, 220; www.cbs.gov.il/reader/newhodaot/hodaa_template.html?hodaa=201606221; Omri Efraim, Ynet, December 29, 2015.
123. Elran 2015, p. 7; Elran and Altshuler in Kurz and Brom 2014, p. 108; Elran 2006, p. 17; Elran, Lecture at Tel Aviv University, October 12, 2012; Gal 2014, p. 453.
124. Elran 2007, p. 5.
125. Kirschenbaum in Friedland et al. 2005, p. 36.
126. Kober 2009, p. 3.
127. Mfa.gov.il, "Victims of Palestinian Violence and Terrorism since September 2000," http://www.mfa.gov.il/mfa/foreignpolicy/terrorism/palestinian/pages/victims%20of%20palestinian%20violence%20and%20terrorism%20sinc.aspx.
128. Gal 2014, p. 11.
129. Jodi Rudoren, *New York Times*, August 28, 2014.
130. Elran et al. 2015, p. 17; Ben Sales, Jewish Telegraphic Agency, August 4, 2015; *Jerusalem Post*, July 29, 2016.
131. Kober 2009, p. 88; Ben-Dor in BESA 2016, p. 34; Gal 2013, p. 14.
132. http://www.oecdbetterlifeindex.org/countries/israel/; Ben-Dor in BESA 2016, p. 34.
133. Bank of Israel, Office of the Spokesperson and Economic Information, Press Release, March 16, 2015; Niv Elis, *Jerusalem Post*, July 28, 2014; "National Accounts in 2014 and the Fourth Quarter," Ministry of Finance, Chief Economist Department; Bank of Israel, "The Bank of Israel Lowers the Interest rAte for March 2007 by 25 Basis Points to 4 %," February 26, 2007; Kober 2009, p. 107.
134. S. A. Cohen 2008, p. 60; Kober 2005, p. 235; Kober 2009, p. 74.
135. www.israeltraumacoalition.org/?CategoryID=196.
136. S. A. Cohen 2008, p. 85.
137. Amos Harel, *Haaretz*, October 24, 2013; http://www.idf.il/1133-22449-he/Dover.aspx; Yehonatan Liss, *Haaretz*, June 26, 2015; Gili Cohen, *Haaretz*, March 25, 2015; https://www.calcalist.co.il/local/articles/0,7340,L-3664856,00.html.
138. S. A. Cohen 2000, p. 125; Kober in S. A. Cohen 2010, p. 83.
139. Yaakov Lappin, *Jerusalem Post*, August 2, 2014.
140. Amnon Barzilai, *Haaretz*, December 24, 2004.
141. Even and Michael in Elran et al. 2016b, pp. 49–50.
142. Brun 2008, pp. 7–13; State of Israel, State Comptroller 2008, p. 322; Smith 2005 p. 491; Stuart Cohen, interview, January 3, 2016; Kober in S. A. Cohen 2010, p. 81; Y. Levy 2011, p. 55; Y. Levy 2009b, p. 146; Handel 2008, p. 32.

143. Kober in Yehezkeli 2001, p. 18.
144. www.idfblog.com/blog/2015/11/23/idf-strategy/.
145. Catignani 2008, p. 55; Y. Levy 2011, p. 56.
146. Gili Cohen, *Haaretz*, March 25, 2015; Y. Levy 2011, pp. 53–54.
147. *Jerusalem Post*, May 19, 2014; Gili Cohen, *Haaretz*, March 25, 2015.
148. Brun 2008, p. 10; Kober 2009, p. 137.
149. Lambeth 2011, pp. xxi–xxii, 295–298; Y. Levy 2011, pp. 56, 58.
150. Amos Harel, *Haaretz*, January 1, 2010.

Chapter 6

1. Baidatz and Adamsky 2014, pp. 11, 14, 15, 38; Sobelman 2016, pp. 163, 165.
2. Bar-Joseph 1998, pp. 145–181.
3. Bar-Joseph 1998, pp. 145–181, pp. 148, 151; Feldman in Klieman and Levite 1993, p. 126.
4. Evron in Klieman and Levite 1993, p. 100.
5. Baidatz and Adamsky 2014, p. 7.
6. Baidatz and Adamsky 2014, p. 19; Chorev 2015, p. 24; Sobelman 2016, p. 168.
7. Amos Harel, *Haaretz*, May 29, 2015.
8. Chorev 2015, pp. 9, 24.
9. Yadlin in Kurtz and Brom 2014, p. 171; Yadlin 2014.
10. Malka 2008, p. 2.
11. Zeev Schiff, *Haaretz*, June 8, 2001; Malka 2008, pp. 1, 2, 5, 11.
12. Jackie Houri, *Haaretz*, September 3, 2013.
13. Siboni 2008, p. 13.
14. Amir Oren, *Haaretz*, September 4, 2001; Zisser 2001, pp. 4–5; Gordon in Golan and Shaul 2004, pp. 189–190; Ben-Israel, *Haaretz*, April 16, 2002; Malka 2008, pp. 4, 5, 9–10.
15. Malka 2008, pp. 2–3.
16. Laish and Amir 2012, p. 5; Levran 2001, p. 15.
17. Meridor in Yehezkeli 2001, p. 50.
18. Bar-Joseph 1998, pp. 148, 153, 155; Evron in Klieman and Levite 1993, p. 103; Rodman 2005, p. 3.
19. Bar-Joseph 2005, p. 11; Rodman 2005, p. 4.
20. Kober 1995, p. 154; Rodman 2005, p. 4.
21. Malka 2008 p. 3; Graham Allison, *Atlantic*, August 1, 2013.
22. Bar-Joseph 1998, pp. 148, 155.
23. Rodman 2005, p. 4; Tal 1996, p. 63; Lieberman in Freedman 2009, p. 325; Siboni 2008, p. 12.
24. See for example Freilich 2007, pp. 15–17.
25. Inbar and Sandler 1993–94, p. 349; Malka 2008, p. 12.
26. Dror 2011, p. 20; Ben-Horin and Posen 1981, pp. 14, 18–19; Maoz 2006, p. 15; Feldman, and Toukan 1997, p. 12; Yaniv 1987, pp. 18–19; Inbar and Sandler 1993–94, p. 331; Rabin in Klieman and Levite 1993, p. 10.
27. Bar-Tal 1998, p. 115; Kober 2009, p. 166; Kober 1995, p. 154; Lieberman in Freedman 2009, p. 325; Gordon in Golan and Shaul 2004, p. 194; Amidror in Efrati 2002, p. 150.
28. Maoz 2006, p. 551.
29. Malka 2008, p. 6; Inbar 1998, p. 73.
30. Ben-Israel, *Haaretz*, April 16, 2002; Inbar and Sandler 1993–94, p. 349; Malka 2008, pp. 11–12.
31. Inbar and Sandler 1993–94, p. 349; Malka 2008, pp. 3, 5, 11–13.
32. Kober 1995, p. 159; Rodman 2005, p. 4.
33. Bar-Joseph 2005, p. 12.
34. Ben-Meir 2009, p. 42.
35. Shelah 2015, p. 154.
36. Even and Michael in Elran et al. 2016b, p. 47.
37. Ido Hecht, communication with the author, August 23, 2014.
38. Bar-Tal 1998, p. 116; Ben-Israel in Yehezkeli 2001, pp. 84–85; Bar-Joseph 2005, p. 13; Bar-Joseph 2004–5, p. 142; Kober 1995, pp. 161, 431; Kober 2009, p. 144.

39. Ido Hecht, communication with the author, August 23, 2014.
40. Kober 2009, pp. 3, 42–43, 45; Siboni 2009, p. 27; Siboni 2000, p. 99l; Cohen in Rubin and Keaney 2002, p. 47; Catignani 2008, p. 159.
41. Inbar and Shamir 2013 pp. 6, 9, 11; Baidatz and Adamsky 2014, pp. 8, 19, 21; Sobelman 2016, p. 168.
42. State of Israel 2015; Kober 2009, p. 40.
43. Ido Hecht, communication with the author, August 23, 2014.
44. Shelah 2015, p. 74.
45. Morag 2005, p. 307.
46. N. Yanai 2015, p. 9; Paz 2015, p. 3.
47. Eiland 2007, p. 14; Shalom and Handle 2011, pp. 18–19.
48. Halevi 2014.
49. Kober 1995, p. 162; State of Israel, State Comptroller 2008, p. 538.
50. Bar-Joseph 2004–5, p. 142.
51. Laish and Amir 2012, p. 6.
52. Ido Hecht, communication with the author, August 23, 2014.
53. Kober in Yehezkeli 2001, pp. 16–17.
54. N. Yanai 2016, p. 6; Chorev 2015, pp. 45–46.
55. Eiland 2007, p. 18.
56. Tamari 2011, pp. 10, 12.
57. Paz 2015, p. 5; Chorev 2015, p. 44.
58. Kober 1995, pp. 162, 432, 450.
59. Kober 2009, pp. 155, 157–158; Laish and Amir 2012, p. 6.
60. Baidatz and Adamsky 2014, p. 38; Meridor in Yehezkeli 2001, pp. 38, 49–50.
61. Dan Meridor, interview, December 24, 2012; Meridor in Yehezkeli 2001, pp. 49–50.
62. Eiland 2010, p. 60.
63. Rubenstein 2001, p. 272.
64. Bar-Joseph 2004–5, p. 143.
65. Advocates of a greater emphasis on defense have included, inter alia, Levite 1989; Bitzur 2009; and Laish 2010. Simchoni and Bar-Joseph 2012 support a limited change in emphasis. Former chief of staff Dan Halutz believes defense should be much more dominant than in the past (interview, December 16, 2012), whereas former head of intelligence and deputy commander of the IAF Amos Yadlin has been an outspoken opponent (INSS Conference on the Home Front, July 25, 2013).
66. Kober 1995, pp. 164–165; Dan Halutz, interview, December 16, 2012; Amos Yadlin, INSS Conference on the Home Front, July 25, 2013; Elran and Altshuler 201, p. 2.
67. Kober 1995, p. 165; Kober in Karsh 1996, p. 195; Brun 2008, p. 9.
68. Dan Meridor, interview, February 24, 2013.
69. Dan Halutz, interview, December 16, 2012.
70. Dan Meridor, interviews, December 24, 2012, and January 14, 2013.
71. Gur Laish, interview, January 3, 2013.
72. Cohen 2008, p. 162.
73. Rubin 2007, p. 30.
74. State of Israel, State Comptroller 2007, p. 49; Zeev Schiff, *Haaretz*, September 7, 2004; Brun 2008, pp. 13–14; Adamsky 2010, pp. 104–105; Rapaport 2010, pp. 7–9.
75. Meir Elran, quoted by Amos Harel, *Haaretz*, July 24, 2013; Gur Laish, interview, January 3, 2013.
76. Gili Cohen, *Haaretz*, May 26, 2013, and August 26, 2013; Amos Harel and Gili Cohen, *Haaretz*, November 11, 2013.
77. Chaim Shedmi, *Haaretz*, April 21, 2002; Chaim Shedmi et al., *Haaretz*, December 23, 2002.
78. Reuven Pedhazur, *Haaretz*, December 5, 2001.
79. Yossi Melman, *Haaretz*, November 1, 2007.
80. Amir Oren, *Haaretz*, August 14, 2002; Amnon Barzilai and Chaim Shedmi, *Haaretz*, August 15, 2002; Nana News, August 8, 2004; Tapuz News, April 2, 2009; Chaim Shedmi et al., *Haaretz*, December 23, 2002; Yossi Melman, *Haaretz*, May 6, 2009.
81. Aluf Benn and Zafir Rinat, *Haaretz*, November 15, 2002.

82. Levite 1989, p. 85.
83. Feldman and Toukan 1997, p. 18; Ben-Horin and Posen 1981, p. 35; Kober in Karsh 1996, p. 199; Heller 2000, p. 32; Kober 1995, p. 170.
84. Kober 1995, p. 169–170.
85. Shelah 2003, p. 30.
86. For Israel's security arrangements, see the works by Schiff 1998; S. Yanai 2005; Jerusalem Center for Public Affairs 2014.
87. S. Yanai 2005, p. 9.
88. Dayan 2014, p. 4 and interview, August 17, 2016.
89. "The Decision Maker," interview with Ari Shavit, *Haaretz*, August 10, 2012.
90. Aluf Benn, *Haaretz*, May 30, 2005.
91. Shelah 2015, pp. 158–159, 162–163.
92. Bar-Joseph 2005, p. 15.
93. www.inss.org.il/index.aspx?id=4513; www.inss.org.il/index.aspx?id=4513; Rodman 2005, pp. 15–16; Inbar 1983, p. 36; Bar-Joseph 2005, p. 16.
94. Zeev Schiff, *Haaretz*, August 2, 2004.
95. Adamsky 2010, pp. 96–97.
96. Adamsky 2010, pp. 96–97.
97. Cohen 1998, pp. 83–86.
98. Levy 2011, p. 56.
99. Adamsky 2010, p. 97; Shelah 2003, p. 37.
100. Zeev Schiff, *Haaretz*, August 2, 2004.
101. Adamsky 2010, p. 98.
102. Adamsky 2010, pp. 2, 4–5, 97–98.
103. State of Israel, State Comptroller 2007, p. 48; State of Israel, State Comptroller 2008, p. 270.
104. Heller 2000, p. 50.
105. Amos Harel, *Haaretz*, March 24, 2013.
106. Brun 2008 p. 13.
107. State of Israel, State Comptroller 2007, p. 48; State of Israel, State Comptroller 2008, p. 270; Tamari and Kalifi 2009, pp. 33–34; Brun 2008, p. 13; Rodman 2005, p. 9.
108. Shelah in Elran et al. 2016b, p. 69.
109. State of Israel, State Comptroller 2007, p. 49; Zeev Schiff, *Haaretz*, September 7, 2004; Brun 2008, pp. 13–14; Adamsky 2010, pp. 104–105; Rapaport 2010, pp. 4–6, 7–9; N. Yanai 2016, p. 9.
110. State of Israel, State Comptroller 2007, p. 49; Zeev Schiff, *Haaretz*, September 7, 2004; Brun 2008, pp. 13–14; Adamsky 2010, pp. 104–105; Rapaport 2010, pp. 4–6, 7–9.
111. Tamari and Kalifi 2009, pp. 34–36; Brun 2008, p. 14; Rapaport 2010, pp. 11, 16; Kaplinsky 2009, pp. 21–22; Zeev Schiff, *Haaretz*, February 27, 2007, March 16, 2007; Amos Harel, *Haaretz*, August 19, 2007.
112. State of Israel, State Comptroller 2008, pp. 183, 270–272; State Comptroller, see Annual Reports 1999, 2000, and 2007: Brun 2008, p. 14.
113. Tamari and Kalifi 2009, pp. 34–36; Brun 2008, p. 14; Rapaport 2010, pp. 11, 16; Kaplinsky 2009, pp. 21–22; Zeev Schiff, *Haaretz*, February 27, 2007, March 16, 2007; Amos Harel, *Haaretz*, August 19, 2007.
114. Lambeth 2011, pp. 15, 229–230; Rapaport 2010, p. 16.
115. Tamari and Kalifi 2009, pp. 34–36; Brun 2008, p. 14; Rapaport 2010, pp. 11, 16; Rapaport in BESA 2014, pp. 22–23; Kaplinsky 2009, pp. 21–22; Zeev Schiff, *Haaretz*, February 27, 2007, March 16, 2007; Amos Harel, *Haaretz*, August 19, 2007.
116. Cohen 2008, p. 39; Sobelman 2016, pp. 169–170
117. Dan Meridor, email to author, April 14, 2016.
118. Zeev Schiff, *Haaretz*, April 24, 2006.
119. Dan Meridor, email to author, April 14, 2016.
120. Cohen 2008, p. 162.
121. Shabtai 2010, pp. 9–10.
122. Gur Laish, interview, December 30, 2015.
123. Amos Harel, *Haaretz*, January 2, 2013, September 13, 2013; Gili Cohen, *Haaretz*, July 11, 2013.

124. Amos Harel, *Haaretz*, January 12, 2013, October 11, 2013; Rapaport 2013; Kober 2013.
125. Amos Harel, *Haaretz*, August 24, 2013.
126. Gili Cohen, *Haaretz*, July 10, 2013, July 11, 2013; Amos Harel, *Haaretz*, January 12, 2013, July 31, 2013, January 3, 2014; Aluf Benn, *Haaretz*, May 28, 2014.
127. Amos Harel, *Haaretz*, January 12, 2013, October 11, 2013; Rapaport 2013; Rapaport in BESA 2014, p. 23; Kober 2013.
128. Gili Cohen, *Haaretz*, July 11, 2013; Rapaport 2013.
129. Moti Basuk and Gili Cohen, *Haaretz*, July 22, 2015.
130. Yoav Zitun, Ynet, July 21, 2015; Gili Cohen, *Haaretz*, November 11, 2015; http://www.idf. il/1133-22449-he/Dover.aspx.
131. Eisenkot 2016, p. 14; Amos Harel, *Haaretz*, June 5, 2015, November 11, 2015; Gili Cohen, *Haaretz*, November 11, 2015; Yonatan Lis, *Haaretz*, June 16, 2015.
132. Amos Harel, *Haaretz*, June 5, 2015, November 11, 2015; Gili Cohen, *Haaretz*, November 11, 2015; Yonatan Lis, *Haaretz*, June 16, 2015.
133. Yoav Zitun, Ynet, July 21, 2015; Gili Cohen, *Haaretz*, November 11, 2015; http://www.idf. il/1133-22449-he/Dover.aspx.
134. www.idfblog.com/blog/2015/11/23/idf-strategy/.
135. See, for example, on the IDF Strategy Elran et al. 2016b.

Chapter 7

1. Dekel in Elran et al. 2016b, p. 63.
2. www.heb.inss.org.il/index.aspx?id=4354&articleid=10446; Doron Meinrath, *Haaretz*, August 25, 2015.
3. Dekel in Elran et al. 2016b, pp. 63, 65.
4. http://www-tandfonline-com.ezp-prod1.hul.harvard.edu/doi/pdf/10.1080/ 04597222.2016.1127573?needAccess=true; http://www.inss.org.il/uploadImages/ systemFiles/Israel106082368.pdf.
5. For example, Dan Meridor, "The Lessons of Defensive Edge," INSS Conference, September 30, 2014.
6. Eisenkot 2016, p. 14.
7. www.mod.gov.il/Defence-and-Security/articles/Pages/22.2.15.aspx; www.news.walla. co.il/item/2831971; Amos Harel, *Haaretz*, December 29, 2012, November 29, 2016; Rapaport 2013; Amnon Barzilai, *Haaretz*, March 21, 2012; Gili Cohen, *Haaretz*, October 29, 2014; Moran Azulay, Ynet, November 27, 2016. The first deal, for 19 F-35s, was signed in 2010 at a cost of $2.75 billion, with delivery scheduled by 2018. A second deal, for 14 F-35s, was signed in 2015 at a cost of $2.82 billion, with delivery by 2021. A third deal for 17 more aircraft was signed in 2016. The average cost of the aircraft in the first two deals was $110 million; the rest of the sum is for the physical and logistical infrastructure needed for the aircraft, training, and other support needs. The cost of each aircraft in the third deal is estimated at $80–$85 million, but the overall cost is as yet unknown. Based on the previous deals, it should be on an order of magnitude of under $3 billion.
8. Aluf Benn, *Haaretz*, August 13, 2008; Adam Entous, *Wall Street Journal*, October 22, 2015.
9. Rapaport 2013; Amnon Barzilai, *Haaretz*, March 21, 2012.
10. Gili Cohen, Haaretz.com, April 10, 2014; Yuval Azulai, *Globes*, September 13, 2016; Amnon Barzilai, *Haaretz*, March 21, 2012.
11. Amnon Barzilai, *Haaretz*, March 21, 2012; Avi Lewis, *Times of Israel*, April 1, 2015; Rapaport 2013; http://globalmilitaryreview.blogspot.com/2011/11/israel-tests-jericho-series-ballistic.html; Alon Ben-David, "Israel Tests Enhanced Ballistic Missile," July 29, 2013, http://aviationweek.com/awin/israel-tests-enhanced-ballistic-missile; "Jericho 3," Missilethreat.com, www.missilethreat.com; Lennox 2009.
12. Judah Ari Gross, *Times of Israel*, December 17, 2015: Amos Harel, *Haaretz*, December 12, 2015.
13. Amos Harel, *Haaretz Weekend Magazine*, September 9, 2016; Amnon Barzilai, *Haaretz*, July 4, 2000; Jones in Hinnebusch and Ehteshami 2002, p. 120; Cordesman 2008, p. 145; Rapaport 2010, p. 26.

14. Reuven Pedhazur, *Haaretz*, January 17, 2001.
15. Amos Harel, *Haaretz*, December 18, 2011.
16. Aluf Benn, *Haaretz*, December 21, 2008.
17. Aluf Benn, *Haaretz*, December 21, 2008.
18. Ari Shavit, interview with "The Decision Maker," *Haaretz*, August 10, 2012.
19. Amos Harel, *Haaretz*, September 3, 2013, October 18, 2013.
20. Amos Harel, *Haaretz*, June 7, 2013; Aluf Benn, *Haaretz*, January 12, 2013; www.nrg.co.il/online/1/ART2/524/169.html; Even 2014, p. 8.
21. The National Security Staff was charged with formulating a counterterrorism doctrine in 2014 and completed a draft version for the review of the various governmental agencies the following year. It is questionable whether the draft will ever be finalized and formally adopted.
22. Ganor 2005, pp. 27–28, 288–290; Catignani 2008, p. 48.
23. Ganor 2005, chapters 4–5; Jones and Catignani 2010, p. 68; Rodman 2013, pp. 3, 11.
24. Bombings, suicide bombings, stabbings, and more, as opposed to the current rocket threats.
25. Eiland 2007, pp. 15–16; Byman 2011, p. 4.
26. Amos Harel and Barak Ravid, *Haaretz*, March 27, 2009; Yossi Melman et al., *Haaretz*, March 26, 2009; Amos Harel and Avi Isacharoff, *Haaretz*, April 7, 2011; Amos Harel, *Haaretz*, January 31, 2013, May 5, 2013 and August 7, 2013.
27. Barak Ravid, *Haaretz*, January 5, 2014; Amos Harel, *Haaretz*, January 31, 2013, May 5, 2013.
28. Catignani 2008, p. 48; Byman 2011, pp. 364; Jones and Catignani 2010, p. 68.
29. Bar-Joseph 2004, p. 141.
30. Ben-Israel 2013, pp. 112–113; Kober 2009, p. 149; Byman 2011, pp. 52, 56, 58–59.
31. Byman 2011, p. 159.
32. Catignani 2008, p. 84; Byman 2011, pp. 84, 160.
33. Aluf Benn, *Haaretz*, August 8, 2008.
34. Byman 2011, pp. 4, 63.
35. Byman 2011, p. 360.
36. Byman 2011, pp. 4–6.
37. Byman 2011, p. 362, 364.
38. Byman 2011, p. 2.
39. Nitzan Nuriel, lecture at Tel Aviv University, December 3, 2012.
40. Amidror 2010, p. 12.
41. Ben-Israel 2013, p. 112.
42. Kober 2009, p. 149.
43. Catignani 2008, p. 83.
44. Byman 2011, pp. 85, 125.
45. Byman 2011, pp. 29, 44, 133, 189, 362, 369, 375; Jones and Catignani 2010, pp. 77–78; Honig 2007.
46. Byman 2011, pp. 364, 368.
47. Inbar and Shamir 2013, p. 10; Byman 2011, p. 378.
48. Byman 2011, pp. 143, 37; Honig 2007.
49. Morag 2005, pp. 307–320.
50. A British expert, Col. Kemp, former commander of British forces in Afghanistan, estimates that no other military in the world exercises as much caution as the IDF does in seeking to avoid civilian casualties and that in the 2014 operation in Gaza, for example, the number of civilians killed was about one-fourth of the international average, Lahay Harkovi, *Jerusalem Post*, September 3, 2014. A multinational group of former chiefs of staff, generals, and senior governmental officials found that the IDF exceeded international standards in its efforts to prevent civilian deaths during the 2014 operation, *Times of Israel*, June 3, 2015.
51. Shalom and Handel 2011, p. 17.
52. Byman 2011, p. 30.
53. Byman 2011, p. 4.
54. Inbar and Shamir 2013, p. 16; Kober 2009, pp. 158, 170; Ben-Israel 2013, p. 115; Amos Harel and Avi Isacharoff, *Haaretz*, September 19, 2007; Shalom and Handel 2011, p. 16; Amidror 2010, p. 12 and 2007, p. 32.
55. Ben-Israel 2013, p. 120; Rubin 2007, p. 18.

56. Barbara Opall-Rome, *Defense News*, October 27, 2013; Dan Williams, Reuters, January 29, 2014; Erez and Perel 2013, p. 77.
57. Defense minister Moshe Yaalon, INSS Conference on the Lessons of Defensive Edge, September 30, 2014; Gili Cohen and Jackie Huri, *Haaretz*, September 30, 2014.
58. Amos Harel, *Haaretz*, August 4, 2014, and August 29, 2014; Even and Michael in Elran et al. 2016b, p. 48.
59. Harel 2016, p. 46; Ofer Shelah, Herzlia Conference, June 16, 2016; Reuven Pedatzur, *Haaretz*, October 30, 2012; Amos Harel and Avi Isacharoff, *Haaretz*, November 24, 2012; Amos Harel, *Haaretz*, August 4, 2014, August 29, 2014; HaCohen in Elran et al. 2016b, p. 101; Meir Elran and Carmit Pedan, *Israel News* (Hebrew) 34, September–October 2016, pp. 22–24.
60. Erez and Perel 2013, p. 88.
61. Amos Harel, *Haaretz*, April 16, 2010.
62. Amos Harel, *Haaretz*, November 18, 2016.
63. Yaakov Lappin, *Jerusalem Post*, April 2, 2014.
64. Aviram in Elran and Altschuler 2012, p. 30.
65. Laish and Amir 2012, pp. 11–12.
66. Amos Harel and Avi Isacharoff, *Haaretz*, March 16, 2012; Shafir 2013, p. 67.
67. Siperco 2010, pp. 127–140, p. 132; Shafir 2013, p. 71.
68. www.themarker.com/news/macro/1.2381540; Amos Harel and Avi Isacharoff, *Haaretz*, March 16, 2012; Shafir 2013, p. 68; Yoav Zitun, Ynet, August 24, 2013; Amos Harel and Gili Cohen, *Haaretz*, March 13, 2014.
69. Amos Harel, *Haaretz*, April 16, 2010; Meir Elran, quoted by Amos Harel, *Haaretz*, July 24, 2013; Yoav Zitun, Ynet, August 24, 2013; Shafir 2013, p. 71.
70. Amos Harel, *Haaretz*, August 2, 2012; Rubin 2007, pp. 9, 10, 13, 18; Lambeth 2011, p. 145.
71. Rubin 2007, pp. 14–15, p. 17; Ophir 2006, p. 15.
72. Kober 2009, p. 91; noted rocket defense expert Uzi Rubin (2012b) estimates an average of just 75 rockets per fatality.
73. Shafir in Brom 2012, p. 34; Rapaport 2010, pp. 31–32; http://www.mako.co.il/pzm-israel-wars/operation-cast-lead/Article-4082602e2847431006.htm.
74. Rubin 2012a, pp. 1, 3; Vilnai in Elran and Altschuler 2012, p. 15.
75. That is, 88% of the rockets it sought to intercept. Iron Dome is programmed not to waste interceptors on rockets that will fall in unpopulated areas.
76. Rubin 2015, pp. 16–19, 27; Rubin 2012b; Shafir 2013, p. 69; Kam in Brom 2012, p. 15; Levite and Shimshoni, *Haaretz*, December 20, 2012.
77. Israeli media sources estimated that 1,300–1,600 were mortars, which Iron Dome is not designed to intercept.
78. Rubin 2015, pp. 16–19, 27; Amos Harel et al., *Haaretz*, July 14, 2014; Amos Harel, *Haaretz*, July 14, 2014; Jody Rudoren, *New York Times*, August 27, 2014; www.haaretz.co.il/news/politics/1.2393220; www.nrg.co.il/online/1/ART2/604/437.html; Shafir in Kurtz and Brom 2014, pp. 42–43.
79. Amos Harel, *Haaretz*, July 15, 2014.
80. Siperco 2010, p. 132.
81. Aviram, in Elran and Altschuler 2012, p. 15; www.israeldefense.co.il/?CategoryID=472&ArticleID=5805.
82. Yoav Zitun, Ynet, March 1, 2016.
83. Gili Cohen, *Haaretz*, December 22, 2005; Anshel Pfeffer, *Haaretz*, October 23, 2012; Amos Harel and Avi Isacharoff, *Haaretz*, March 16, 2012; Amos Harel and Gili Cohen, *Haaretz*, March 13, 2014.
84. Finkel 2015, p. 14.
85. Ben-Israel 2013, p. 92; Rubin and Keaney 2002, p. 171; Shafir in Bar-Joseph 2001, p. 153.
86. Shafir in Bar-Joseph 2001, p. 155.
87. Siperco 2010, p. 133; Moti Basuk and Zvi Zarachia, *The Marker*, October 17, 2012; Shafir 2013, p. 70; Anshel Pfeffer, *Haaretz*, October 23, 2012; Finkel 2015, p. 4.
88. Aviram in Elran and Altschuler 2012, pp. 31–32; Amnon Barzilai, *Haaretz*, August 27, 2004.
89. Zeev Schiff, *Haaretz*, March 17, 2000; Reven Pedatzur, *Haaretz*, August 20, 2000; Aviram in Elran and Altschuler 2012, pp. 31–32; AP, November 20, 2013; Col. Aviram Hasson, INSS

Conference on Aerial Threats, June 3, 2013; Reuters, January 3, 2014; Gili Cohen, *Haaretz*, June 4, 2013.

90. Yoav Zitun, Ynet, August 24, 2013.
91. Siperco 2010, p. 133; Moti Basuk and Zvi Zarachia, *The Marker*, October 17, 2012; Shafir 2013, p. 70; Anshel Pfeffer, *Haaretz*, October 23, 2012; Finkel 2015, p. 4.
92. This approximation includes $225 million in special emergency aid for Iron Dome approved during Operation Defensive Edge in August 2014. Brendan McGarry, "U.S. Rushes Funding for Israel's Iron Dome," August 1, 2014, http://defensetech.org/2014/08/01/u-s-rushes-funding-for-israels-iron-dome/; Eraz and Perel 2013, p. 99; Inbal Orpaz and Amir Taig, Tech Nation, *Haaretz*, October 23, 2012; Moti Basuk, *The Marker*, October 19, 2012; Amos Harel, *Haaretz*, September 15, 2016.
93. Siperco 2010, p. 133; Moti Basuk and Zvi Zarachia, *The Marker*, October 17, 2012; Shafir 2013, p. 70; Anshel Pfeffer, *Haaretz*, October 23, 2012.
94. http://www.globes.co.il/news/article.aspx?did=1000954494; http://www.ishitech.co.il/1212ar2.htm; Yoav Zitun, Ynet, November 27, 2012, http://www.ynetnews.com/articles/0,7340,L-4312556,00.html; Finkel 2015, p. 14.
95. Amnon Barzilai, *Haaretz*, December 5, 2000; Amos Harel, *Haaretz*, April 16, 2010; Arzi in Elran and Altschuler 2012, pp. 41–42; Gili Cohen, *Haaretz*, April 4, 2005.
96. Sharp 2015; Amnon Barzilai, *Haaretz*, March 15, 2000; Zeev Schiff, *Haaretz*, March 17, 2000.
97. Nathan Praver, cited by Reuven Pedatzur, *Haaretz*, October 10, 2013.
98. Yanai 2016, p. 11.
99. Barak Ravid, *Haaretz*, September 15, 2016; Julian Borger, *Guardian*, September 13, 2016.
100. In recent years the shekel has generally fluctuated within a range of 3.5–3.9 to the dollar.
101. Siperco 2010, p. 133.
102. Moti Basuk, *The Marker*, July 9, 2014; Rubin 2012b; Shafir in Brom 2012, p. 36.
103. Amos Harel, *Haaretz*, September 16, 2014, and September 19, 2014; Laish and Amir 2012, p. 14.
104. Shafir 2013, p. 70; Brom in Elran and Altschuler 2012, p. 49; Laish and Amir 2012, p. 13; Shafir in Bar-Joseph 2001, p. 155; Amos Harel and Avi Isacharoff, *Haaretz*, October 21, 2012; Yoav Zitun, Ynet, August 24, 2013.
105. Shafir in Brom 2012, p. 36; Kam in Brom 2012, p. 15.
106. Yakov Amidror, interview, October 30, 2015; Yakov Amidror, conference "Thoughts on the Strategic-Existential Dialogue in Israel," Tami Steinmetz Center, Tel Aviv University, December 29, 2015; Gur Laish, interview, December 30, 2015; Shelah 2015, p. 155.
107. Shapir in Bar-Joseph 2001, p. 156; Cohen et al. 1998, pp. 41–42.
108. Reuven Pedhazur, *Haaretz*, February 4, 2002.
109. Shafir 2013, p. 73; Rubin 2012b, pp. 5–6; Brom in Elran and Altschuler 2012, p. 49; Shafir in Brom 2012, p. 35; Amos Harel, *Haaretz*, July 26, 2011.
110. Amir Oren, *Haaretz*, September 4, 2001.
111. Chorev 2015, pp. 25, 28, 33; Shamir and Hecht 2014, pp. 88–89.
112. Inbar and Shamir 2013 certainly popularized the term, though it is unclear who coined it.
113. Inbar and Shamir 2013, pp. 12–13; Mintz and Shai 2014b, p. 5; Brom and Kurtz 2014, p. 114; Sobelman 2016, p. 168.
114. Ido Nechushtan, interview, December 30, 2015.
115. Chorev 2015, pp. 45–46.
116. Chorev 2015, pp. 35, 39–40.
117. Ofer Shelah, interview by Amos Harel, *Haaretz*, April 2, 2015.
118. Chorev 2015, pp. 43–44, 47.
119. Shelah 2015, pp. 38–39.
120. Ofer Shelah, interview by Amos Harel, *Haaretz*, April 2, 2015; Yadlin in Kurtz and Brom 2014, pp. 171–172.
121. Shelah 2015, pp. 97–99.
122. Yadlin in Kurtz and Brom 2014, pp. 171–172.
123. Amos Harel, *Haaretz*, September 19, 2014; Paz 2015, p. 11.
124. Yaari 2014, p. 3.

125. Gili Cohen and Jackie Houri, *Haaretz*, June 16, 2016; http://news.walla.co.il/item/2844809; http://www.maariv.co.il/news/new.aspx?pn6Vq=E&0r9VQ=GGDDJ.
126. Dekel and Orion in Brom and Kurtz 2016, p. 83; Assaf Orion, interview, December 29, 2015.
127. Amos Harel 2016, p. 46.
128. IBA News, special report, "Ten Years to the War," July 12, 2016; Dekel and Orion in Brom and Kurtz 2016, p. 83; Yossi Yehoshua, *Yediot Aharonoth*, September 16, 2016.
129. Amos Yadlin, INSS Conference on the Home Front, August 1, 2012.
130. Dekel and Orion in Brom and Kurtz 2016, p. 83; Amidror 2016, pp. 1–2.
131. www.idf.il/SIP_STORAGE/FILES/9/16919.pdf.
132. Senior IDF officer, interview, January 14, 2016.
133. Yadlin in Kurtz and Brom 2014, p. 174; Amos Harel, *Haaretz*, July 7, 2014.
134. Yadlin in Elran et al. 2016b, p. 179; Nechushtan in Elran et al. 2016b, p. 112.
135. The section on the cyber-response is adopted from Cohen, Freilich, and Siboni 2015.
136. Grauman 2012, pp. 1–104; Baram 2013, p. 20; Alon Ben-David, *Aviation Week and Space Technology*, June 27, 2011.
137. Ynet, June 4, 2012.
138. www.idf.il/SIP_STORAGE/FILES/9/16919.pdf.
139. David Fulghum, *Aviation Week and Space Technology* 172 (2010), pp. 29–30; Farwell and Rohozinski 2011, p. 25; Parmenter 2013, p. 49; Joint Advanced Warfighting School 2014, pp. 14.
140. Farwell and Rohozinski 2011, p. 25.
141. Parmenter 2013, p. 39.
142. Parmenter 2013, pp. 40, 42–43; Joint Advanced Warfighting School 2014, pp. 14–15; David Sanger, *New York Times*, July 1, 2012.
143. Kim Zetter, *Wired*, May 28, 2012; Yaakov Katz, *Jerusalem Post*, May 31, 2012.
144. Yaakov Katz, *Jerusalem Post*, May 31, 2012; Richard Silverstein, richardsilverstein.com, October 23, 2012.
145. Egozi 2011, p. 6.
146. Parmenter 2013, pp. 35–38; Clarke 2008, p. 310; Carr 2012, p. 51.
147. Fulghum, *Aviation Week and Space Technology* 172 (2010); Egozi 2011, pp. 4–6.
148. Ynet, June 4, 2012.
149. Yaakov Katz, *Jerusalem Post*, May 6, 2012; Gili Cohen, *Haaretz*, December 3, 2015; Amos Harel, *Haaretz*, December 3, 2015.
150. Yonah Jeremy Bob, *Jerusalem Post*, March 22, 2013; Yaakov Katz, *Jerusalem Post*, May 31, 2012.
151. Rami Efrati and Lior Yafe, *Israel Defense*, August 11, 2012; Ben-David 2011, p. 57; Even and Siman-Tov 2012, p. 79.
152. https://il-cert.org.il/; Yaakov Lappin, *Jerusalem Post*, February 5, 2013.
153. Yaakov Lappin, *Jerusalem Post*, February 5, 2013; Ben-David 2011, p. 57.
154. Ronen Bergman, Ynet, December 12, 2012; Tova Dvorin, *Arutz Sheva*, April 25, 2014.
155. Barak Ravid, *Haaretz*, September 14, 2014.
156. Ben-David 2011, p. 57.
157. Tova Dvorin, *Arutz Sheva*, April 25, 2014; Ronen Bergman, Ynet, December 12, 2012.
158. Yaakov Lappin, *Jerusalem Post*, February 5, 2013; Sklerov in Carr 2012, p. 195; Even and Siman-Tov 2012, p. 19.
159. Yoav Zitun, Ynet, January 25, 2012.
160. Eisenstadt and Pollock, 12, p. xiii, 32; Baram 2013, pp. 30–32. http://mfa.gov.il/MFA/PressRoom/2013/Pages/Deputy-FM-Elkin-Israel's-Cyber-Security-16-Oct-2013.aspx.
161. Ami Rojkes Dombe, "UK and Israel Will Hold Joint Cyber Exercises," Israel Defense, September 17, 2015, http://www.israeldefense.co.il/en/content/uk-and-israel-will-hold-joint-cyber-exercises.
162. Richard Silverstein, richardsilverstein.com, October 23, 2012.
163. Yaakov Katz, *Jerusalem Post*, May 31, 2012.
164. Yaakov Katz, *Jerusalem Post*, May 31, 2012.
165. Gili Cohen, *Haaretz*, January 9, 2013.

166. Yaakov Katz, *Jerusalem Post*, May 6, 2012; http://mfa.gov.il/MFA/PressRoom/2013/Pages/Deputy-FM-Elkin-Israel's-Cyber-Security-16-Oct-2013.aspx.

167. Ram Levi, Israel Defense, December 16, 2011; *Jerusalem Post*, January 1, 2013; UPI, June 4, 2012.

168. Even and Siman-Tov 2012, p. 22; Executive Cyber Intelligence Bi-Weekly Report, INSS, June 15, 2014.

169. Jason Hiner, Tech Republic, October 1, 2013.

170. Tal Steinherz, "Israeli Innovation in Cyber-technology," Herzlia Conference, June 9, 2014; Eisenstadt and Pollock 2012, p. xiii, 32.

171. Tal Steinherz, "Israeli Innovation in Cyber-technology," Herzlia Conference, June 9, 2014; Amitai Ziv, *The Marker*, September 14, 2014.

172. Yonah Jeremy, *Jerusalem Post*, March 22, 2013.

Chapter 8

1. Karsh 1996, pp. 96–97; Evron 1994, p. 252, Landau 2013, p. 2, Maoz 2006, p. 342.

2. Beres 2016, p. 50.

3. Cohen 2010, p. 47.

4. Cordesman estimates 200–300 nuclear weapons (2008, p. 145); Reuven Pedazur, *Haaretz*, December 25, 2009.

5. Reuven Pedazur, *Haaretz*, December 25, 2009.

6. Cohen 2010, pp. xxvi, 82.

7. https://isis-online.org/uploads/isis-reports/documents/Israel_Military_Plutonium_Stock_November_19_2015_Final.pdf; also quoted in Amir Oren, *Haaretz*, November 20, 2015.

8. Lilach Shuval, *Yisrael Hayom*, January 12, 2016; Cohen 2010, pp. 83–84; Rodman 2005, p. 16; Cordesman 2008, pp. 8, 142, 145; Rapoport 2010, pp. 26, 34; Amnon Barzilai, *Haaretz*, March 21, 2012; https://isis-online.org/uploads/isis-reports/documents/Israel_Military_Plutonium_Stock_November_19_2015_Final.pdf.

9. Dov Ben Meir 2009, pp. 360–361.

10. Tzafrir Rinat and Aluf Benn, *Haaretz*, November 15, 2002; Rapoport 2010, p. 34.

11. www.nti.org/learn/countries/Israel/; www.nti.org/learn/countries/israel/biological/; Reuven Pedazur, *Haaretz*, May 14, 2002; www.armscontrol.org/factsheets/cbwprolif.

12. Cohen 2010, pp. x, xx, xxii; Levite 2010, p. 162; Bar-Joseph 2004–5, p. 148; Beres 2016, p. 2.

13. Evron 1994, p. 254; Cohen 1998, pp. 38–39; Ben-Israel 2013, p. 78; Brom in Blechman 2011, pp. 37, 43; Inbar 2008, p. 88; Ben-Dor in Bar-Tal 1998, p. 118.

14. Ben-Dor in Bar-Tal 1998, p. 118; Ben-Israel 2013, p. 78; Bar-Joseph 2005, p. 16; Cohen and Miller 2010, p. 35; Evron 1994, p. 256; Brom in Blechman 2011, p. 38; Maoz 2006, pp. 303–304; Maoz 2003, pp. 46–47; Beres 2007, p. 96.

15. Cohen 2010, p. 46.

16. Maoz 2006, p. 305.

17. Maoz 2006, p. 305; Maoz 2003, p. 47; Reuven Pedazur, *Haaretz*, August 25, 2002 and March 14, 2003.

18. Cohen 2010, p. xxxiii.

19. Cohen 2010, p. 81; Zeev Schiff, *Haaretz*, April 24, 2006.

20. Cohen 2010, p. xiii; Avner Cohen, *Haaretz*, July 10, 2016; Yossi Melman, *Haaretz*, December 13, 2006.

21. Cohen 2010, pp. xxxi, 26, 28, 49; Aluf Benn, *Haaretz*, April 24, 2000, February 18, 2001, September 9, 2001, March 13, 2001, April 3, 2006, December 19, 2008; Reuven Pedazur, *Haaretz*, January 14, 2004; Yossi Melman, *Haaretz*, December 13, 2006; Zeev Schiff, *Haaretz*, August 24, 2000; Feldman 1996, p. 18; Cohen and Miller 2010, p. 34.

22. Cohen and Miller 2010, p. 34.

23. Cohen 2010, p. 27.

24. Cohen 2010, p. xxxi, 27; Yossi Melman, *Haaretz*, December 13, 2006; Zeev Schiff, *Haaretz*, August 24, 2000.

25. Cohen 2010, pp. 30–32.
26. Brom in Blechman 2011, p. 45; Feldman 1982, p. 11; Feldman 1996, p. 18.
27. Evron 1994, p. 252.
28. Cohen 2010, p. 32; Cohen and Miller 2010.
29. Cohen 2010, pp. 32, 33, 233, 237; Yossi Melman, *Haaretz*, May 19, 2011; Aluf Benn, *Haaretz*, September 17, 2001 and May 31, 2010; Reuven Pedazur, *Haaretz*, September 30, 2012 (Pedazur says the letter was in 2010).
30. Feldman 1996, p. 18; Karpin 2009, pp. 31–40, p. 37.
31. Feldman 1996, p. 18.
32. Amir Oren, *Haaretz*, January 5, 2014.
33. Reuven Pedazur, *Haaretz*, March 14, 2003; Feldman in Feldman and Toukan 1997, p. 17.
34. Cohen 2010, pp. 48–49; Horowitz in Yaniv 1993, p. 46.
35. Cohen and Miller 2010, p. 39; Cohen 2010, pp. 48–49.
36. Feldman 1982, p. 12; Cohen 2010, p. 234; Associated Press in *New York Times*, December 6, 2011.
37. Dowty in Beres 1986, p. 20; Feldman 1982, p. 13; Feldman in Feldman and Toukan 1997, p. 17; Landau 2013, p. 2.
38. Raz 2016, pp. 29, 31; Bar-Joseph 2005, p. 16.
39. Zeev Schiff, *Haaretz*, August 24, 2000; Emily Landau and Tamar Meltz, *Haaretz*, February 23, 2000; Evron 1994, p. 273; Horowitz in Yaniv 1993, p. 61.
40. Cohen and Miller 2010, p. 31; Zeev Schiff, *Haaretz*, August 24, 2000.
41. Evron 1990, p. 52; Bar-Joseph 2005, pp. 10–19, p. 16; Feldman in Feldman and Toukan 1997, p. 17; Yaniv 1987, p. 220.
42. Karpin 2009, pp. 31–40, pp. 37, 40; Ben-Israel 2013, p. 79.
43. Cohen 2010, pp. xxxiii, 47; Cohen and Miller 2010, p. 31; Bar-Joseph 2005, p. 16; Bar-Joseph 2004–5, pp. 137–156, p. 147.
44. Zeev Schiff, *Haaretz*, August 24, 2000; Ben-Dor in Bar-Tal 1998, p. 117; Yossi Melman, *Haaretz*, December 13, 2006; Steinberg 1999, p. 216; Baram 1992, p. 399; Cohen 2010, pp. 45, 47, 214; Aluf Benn, *Haaretz*, September 9, 2001; Sneh 1996, p. 27; Yaniv 1987, p. 24; Bar-Joseph 2004–5, p. 147; Bar-Joseph 2005, pp. 10–19, p. 16; Raz 2016, pp. 29–41, p. 29; Maoz 2006, p. 553; Maoz 2003, pp. 44, 47, 56, 74–75.
45. Cohen 2010, p. xxxii.
46. Karpin 2009, p. 31; Raz 2016, pp. 30, 34, 36.
47. Feldman 1982, pp. 4, 67, 103, 107, 110–112.
48. Feldman 1982, pp. 4, 9–10, 18–19, 22–23, 67, 103.
49. Feldman, email to author, July 29, 2016.
50. Reuven Pedazur, *Haaretz*, January 14, 2004; Evron 1994, p. 245; Brom in Blechman 2011, p. 47; Steinberg 1999, p. 216.
51. Cohen and Miller 2010; Cohen 2010, pp. xxxiv, 217, 230, 253.
52. Beres 2007, pp. 89–104; Beres 2015, pp. 89–90, 92, 94–98; Beres 2016, pp. 6–7, 34.
53. Feldman 1982, pp. 212–213, 215.
54. Feldman 1982, p. 229.
55. Cohen 2010, p. xxxiv; Cohen and Miller 2010, p. 39; Maoz 2003, pp. 45, 76; Raz 2016, p. 36.
56. Feldman 1982, p. 54.
57. Beres 2015, p. 98; Beres 2016, pp. 3–4; Dowty in Beres 1986, pp. 15–16; Eytan in Beres 1986, p. 93; Cohen and Miller 2010, pp. 54–58.
58. Cohen 2010, p. 49; Zeev Schiff, *Haaretz*, August 24, 2000; Yossi Melman, *Haaretz*, December 13, 2006; Mintz and Shai 2014b, p. 4; Steinberg 1999, p. 216; Ben-Dor in Bar-Tal 1998, p. 118; Evron 1994, pp. 73, 73; Dowty in Beres 1986, p. 18; Handel in Murray 1994, p. 552; Maoz 2003, p. 44, 48; Maoz 2006, pp. 307–308; Karpin 2009, pp. 37, 40.
59. Evron 1994, pp. 68, 72; Evron in Klieman and Levite 1993, p. 111; Bar-Joseph 2005, pp. 16, 18; Maoz 2003, p. 73; Maoz 2006, pp. 301, 337–338, 340, 553–554; Brom in Landau and Kurz 2016, p. 104.
60. Beres 2016, pp. 5, 50, 53.
61. Feldman 1982, p. 1; Beres 2016, pp. 6, 13, 120; Beres in Karsh 1996, pp. 115–117.

62. Cohen 2010, pp. 220–221.
63. Evron 1994, pp. 88–91.
64. Brom in Landau and Kurz 2016, pp. 103, 107–108, 110, 113.
65. Levite 2010, p. 160.
66. Brom in Blechman 2011, p. 47; Levite 2010, pp. 159, 162, 165.
67. Feldman in Feldman and Toukan 1997, p. 17.
68. Aluf Benn, *Haaretz*, November 23, 2000, May 9, 2001; Reuven Pedazur, *Haaretz*, November 26, 2001.
69. Finlay et al. 2015; Haim Levinson, *Haaretz*, February 10, 2016 and April 26, 2016; Landau and Stein 2015b; Cohen and Miller 2010, p. 39; Evron 1994 p. 256; Bar 2010, p. 26.
70. Cohen 2010, p. 252; Yossi Melman, *Haaretz*, May 19, 2011; Levite 2010, p. 165; Martin Malin, email to author, July 12, 2016.
71. Ambassador Jeremy Issacharoff in Landau and Bermant 2014, pp. 196–197; Ambassador Eytan Bentsur, Director General MFA, Statement before the Conference on Disarmament, Geneva, September 4, 1997; Feldman in Feldman and Toukan 1997, p. 26; Bar 2008, p. 150.
72. Finlay et al. 2015; Landau 2013, p. 3; Levite 2010, pp. 159, 161; Ambassador Jeremy Issacharoff in Landau and Bermant 2014, p. 197; Brom in Blechman 2011, p. 50; Feldman in Feldman and Toukan 1997, pp. 17, 26.
73. Ambassador Jeremy Issacharoff in Landau and Bermant 2014, pp. 196–197; Ambassador Eytan Bentsur, Director General, Statement before the Conference on Disarmament, Geneva, September 4, 1997; Levite 2010, p. 160; Landau and Stein in Foradori and Malin 2013, pp. 23–24.
74. Aluf Ben, *Haaretz*, November 29, 2000.
75. Reuven Pedazur, *Haaretz*, January 14, 2004.
76. Aluf Benn, *Haaretz*, February 18, 2001.
77. Cohen 2010, pp. 51, 234; Levite 2010, p. 163.
78. *Jerusalem Post* Staff, August 7, 2015; "Israel's Mossad Trained Assassins of Iran Nuclear Scientists, Report Says," *Haaretz*, February 9, 2012, www.haaretz.com/israel-news/israel-s-mossad-trained-assassins-of-iran-nuclear-scientists-report-says-1.411945; Julian Borger, "New Book Claims Mossad Assassination Unit Killed Iranian Nuclear Scientists," July 11, 2012, www.theguardian.com/world/julian-borger-global-security-blog/2012/jul/11/israel-iran-nuclear-assassinations; Israel Today Staff, "Reports: Iran Nuclear Facility Destroyed," *Israel Today*, January 27, 2013, www.israeltoday.co.il/NewsItem/tabid/178/nid/23644/Default.aspx; David Sanger, "Obama Order Sped Up Wave of Cyberattacks against Iran," *New York Times*, June 1, 2012, www.nytimes.com/2012/06/01/world/middleeast/obama-ordered-wave-of-cyberattacks-against-iran.html?_r=0.
79. www.npolicy.org/books/Nuclear_Armed_Iran/Ch6_Brom.pdf; Vielhaber and Bleek 2012.
80. "The Begin Doctrine?," editorial, *New York Sun*, January 21, 2015, www.nysun.com/editorials/the-begin-doctrine/89027/.
81. Hendel 2012, p. 31.
82. Leonard S. Spector and Avner Cohen, "Israel's Airstrike on Syria's Reactor: Implications for the Nonproliferation Regime," Arms Control Today, www.armscontrol.org/print/3095; David Makovsky, "The Silent Strike," *New Yorker*, September 17, 2012, www.newyorker.com/magazine/2012/09/17/the-silent-strike; David E. Sanger and Mark Mazzetti, "Israel Struck Syrian Nuclear Project, Analysts Say," *New York Times*, October 14, 2007, www.nytimes.com/2007/10/14/washington/14weapons.html.
83. Barak Ravid, *Haaretz*, September 22, 2016.
84. Article by Brom in Blechman 2011, p. 54.
85. Beres 2016, p. 50.
86. The following section, on Saudi Arabia, Turkey and Egypt, is based on a series of conversations with Dr. Martin Malin, director of the Harvard's Managing the Atom Project, during the spring 2016 semester.
87. The following section is based on a series of conversations with Dr. Martin Malin, director of the Harvard's Managing the Atom Project, during the spring 2016 semester.
88. Article by Brom in Blechman 2011, p. 54.

Chapter 9

1. Respectively, the heroic scene of the final collapse of the Jewish rebellion against Rome in A.D. 73 and one of the infamous Nazi concentration camps.
2. Kleiman 1990, p. 53.
3. Adamsky 2010, p. 115; Wald 1992, pp. 23–25; Handel in Murray et. al 1994, p. 543; Klieman 1990, p. 24.
4. Garfinkle 2000, p. 202.
5. Cohen 1991, p. 38.
6. Inbar 1990, p. 165.
7. Adam Levick, "If Palestinians Don't Respect 6 Million Murdered Jews, How Can They Co-exist with 6 Million Living Ones?," *Algemeiner*, June 23, 2014, www.algemeiner.com/2014/06/23/if-palestinians-dont-respect-6-million-murdered-jews-how-can-they-co-exist-with-6-million-living-ones/.
8. Klieman 1990, pp. 32–33; Inbar 1990, p. 165; Jones in Hinnebusch and Ehteshami 2002, pp. 124–125; Cohen 1991, p. 32; Tal 1996, p. 48; Avineri 1986, p. 3; Garfinkle 2000, p. 202.
9. Dror 2011, p. 18.
10. Jones and Murphy 2002, p. 92; Cohen 1991, p. 32; Inbar 1990, p. 169; Garfinkle 2000, p. 199.
11. Rodman 2005, pp. 105, 108; Avineri 1986, p. 12; Mualem 2012, pp. 201–202.
12. Yossi Melman, *Haaretz*, January 1, 2000.
13. Jones and Murphy 2002, p. 92.
14. Rodman 2005, p. 105; Mualem 2012, pp. 201–202.
15. Klieman 1990, p. 8.
16. Rodman 2005, p. 96.
17. Rodman 2005, pp. 98–99; Inbar 1990 pp. 167, 171.
18. Sheffer 2012, pp. 77–82, 84.
19. Sneh 1996, p. 137.
20. Amos Harel, *Haaretz*, January 11, 2015, January 16, 2015.
21. Klieman 1988, p. 71.
22. Yaniv Kubovich, *Haaretz*, July 5, 2016.
23. *Haaretz*, February 3, 2000; Dan Margalit, *Haaretz*, February 3, 2000; Nitzan Horowitz and Aluf Ben, *Haaretz*, February 6, 2000, January 7, 2000, January 4, 2002; Yehonatan Liss, *Haaretz*, February 2, 2014; Somini Sengupta, *New York Times*, January 22, 2015.
24. Avineri 1986, p. 5; Rodman 2005, pp. 95–96.
25. Avineri 1986, pp. 6–7; Rodman 2005, pp. 95–96.
26. See Freilich 2012.
27. Klieman 1990, pp. 10, 29; Klieman 1988, pp. 41–42; Handel in Murray 1994, p. 563; Horowitz 1993, p. 11; Barak Ravid, *Haaretz*, January 19, 2016.
28. Klieman 1990, pp. 89–90.
29. Aluf Benn, *Haaretz*, September 4, 2003, November 24, 2003. and December 31, 2003.
30. The above section is derived from Freilich 2012, pp. 68–70.
31. Freilich 2012, p. 232.
32. Eran Etzion, former head of MFA Planning Division, lecture at Tel Aviv University, December 10, 2014.
33. Dror 2011, pp. 4, 14.
34. Cohen 1991, pp. 28, 30.
35. Rodman 2005, pp. 98–99; Inbar 1990, pp. 169–170.
36. Nye 2004, pp. X, 1–2, 5–6, 10–14.
37. Klieman 1990, pp. 27–28.
38. Senor and Singer 2009.
39. Sharp 2015, p. 1.
40. Gray 2011, pp. VI, IX.
41. Klieman 1990, p. 25.
42. Indyk 2009, pp. 276–277, 366–367; Ross 2004, pp. 752–753.
43. Rice 2011, pp. 383, 414.
44. Klieman 1990, p. 20.

45. Nitzan Horowitz, *Haaretz*, April 16, 2000; Aluf Benn, *Haaretz*, May 4, 2000.
46. Amos Harel, *Haaretz*, June 7, 2000; Aluf Benn, *Haaretz*, April 3, 2001; Shlomo Shamir et. al., *Haaretz*, June 18, 2000.
47. Heller 2000, p. 15; Feldman in Feldman and Toukan 1997, p. 15; Ben-Dor in Yehezkeli 2001, p. 32; Alpher 2015, pp. 8–9, 76, 102.
48. Lindenstrauss and Eran 2014, pp. 79–80; Heller 2000, p. 15; Feldman in Feldman and Toukan 1997, p. 15; Ben-Dor n Yehezkeli 2001, p. 32; Rodman 2005, p. 22; Maoz 2006, pp. 369–371.
49. Gili Cohen, *Haaretz*, June 9, 2017; Gili Cohen, *Haaretz*, July 2, 2013; I24 News, October 9, 2013; Yoav Zitun, "IAF, US Air Force Hold Largest Joint-Military Exercise in Israel's History," Ynet, November 25, 2013, www.ynetnews.com/articles/0,7340,L-4457770,00.html; "Greek Presence in US-Israel Drill Sends Message to Turkey," *Israel Hayom*, April 1, 2012, www.israelhayom.com/site/newsletter_article.php?id=3775.
50. Amnon Barzilai, *Haaretz*, June 17, 2003; Anshel Pfeffer, *Haaretz*, December 10, 2009; Gili Cohen, *Haaretz*, July 2, 2013.
51. Alpher 2015, p. 136.
52. Feldman in Feldman and Toukan 1997, p. 14; Jones and Murphy 2002, p. 97.
53. Maoz 2006, pp. 382–383.
54. Barak Ravid, *Haaretz*, June 17, 2008, April 2, 2009; Henry Jackson Society 2014, p. 3.
55. For example, the 1994 Hessen Declaration, Aluf Benn, *Haaretz*, April 3, 2000.
56. Aluf Benn, *Haaretz*, April 3, 2000; Barak Ravid, *Haaretz*, December 7, 2013; Sharon Sadeh, *Haaretz*, December 10, 2002; Adar Primor, *Haaretz*, July 12, 2003; Asmus and Jackson 2005, pp. 49–50; Arad and Steiner, Herzlia Conference Working Paper, Herzlia Interdisciplinary Center, December 2004; Monin 2003, pp. 151–159, 177, 190–195, 222; Eran, Herzlia Conference Working Paper, Herzlia Interdisciplinary Center December 2004, p. 2.
57. Henry Jackson Society 2014, pp. 8–9; Herzlia Conference Task Force, Herzlia Interdisciplinary Center 2011, p. 5.
58. Adar Primor, *Haaretz*, April 4, 2000.
59. Barak Ravid, *Haaretz*, March 22, 2012: Herzlia Conference Task Force, Herzlia Interdisciplinary Center 2011, p. 5.
60. Barak Ravid, *Haaretz*, September 5, 2012, December 3, 2012.
61. Henry Jackson Society 2014, pp. 8–9.
62. Henry Jackson Society 2014, p. 10; Gili Cohen, *Haaretz*, April 6, 2016.
63. Henry Jackson Society 2014, pp. 11, 15; http://rt.com/uk/194244-uk-israel-trade-inrcease/ ; Eilam 2005, p. 92; Aluf Benn, *Haaretz*, September 17, 2003; Amnon Barzilai, *Haaretz*, June 14, 2004; Barak Ravid, *Haaretz*, December 3, 2001.
64. Amnon Barzilai, *Haaretz*, June 17, 2003, November 17, 2004; Yossi Melman, *Haaretz*, April 4, 2008; Adi Primor, *Haaretz*, February 25, 2011.
65. Magen and Naumkin 2013, pp. 62, 87.
66. Magen and Naumkin 2013, pp. 37, 54.
67. Magen and Naumkin 2013, p. 4.
68. http://www.haaretz.co.il/news/politics/1.2736388.
69. Magen and Naumkin 2013, p. 53.
70. www.jewishvirtuallibrary.org/jsource/Politics/ChinaIsraelRelations.html; Ministry of Economics, Foreign Trade Administration, May 30, 2016, and https://www.themarker.com/news/macro/1.2897942.
71. Lavie et. al. 2015, pp. 74–75.
72. Amnon Barzilai, *Haaretz*, January 4, 2000, March 23, 2001, May 17, 2000, July 2, 2000; Aluf Benn, *Haaretz*, March 24, 2000, April 11, 2000, May 4, 2000, May 23, 2000, July 25, 2000, August 27, 2000, January 31, 2001; Nitzan Horowitz, *Haaretz*, March 1, 2000.
73. "Egypt, Russia Sign Deal to Build a Nuclear Power Plant," Reuters in *Jerusalem Post*, November 19, 2015, www.jpost.com/Breaking-News/Egypt-Russia-sign-deal-to-build-a-nuclear-power-plant-434696.
74. Shay 2015.
75. *Haaretz* Staff, July 12, 2016.
76. JPost.com Staff, "Jordan Opens Skies for IAF Drones Flying to Syria," *Jerusalem Post*, April 22, 2013, www.jpost.com/Defense/Jordan-opens-skies-for-IAF-drones-flying-to-Syria-310654;

"Israel to Supply Jordan with Drones to Help Fight Islamic State: Report," August 17, 2015, i24 News, www.i24news.tv/en/news/international/82398-150817-israel-to-supply-jordan-with-drones-to-help-fight-islamic-state-report.

77. Barak Ravid, *Haaretz*, February 2, 2008, April 5, 2009, January 31, 2011, December 5, 2012.
78. Barak Ravid, *Haaretz*, March 23, 2012; Amos Harel, *Haaretz*, December 11, 2015; Amos Harel, *Haaretz Weekend Magazine*, September 9, 2016; Gili Cohe, *Haaretz*, October 23, 2016.
79. Yoav Zitun and Eldad Beck, Ynet, April 30, 2016.
80. Gili Cohen, *Haaretz*, October 28, 2015.
81. Barak Ravid, *Haaretz*, February 2, 2008, April 5, 2009, January 31, 2011, December 5, 2012.
82. Amos Harel, *Haaretz*, February 18, 2015.
83. Ningthoujam 2014; Amnon Barzilai, *Haaretz*, March 7, 2004; Yossi Melman, *Haaretz*, March 22, 2009; Inbar and Ningthoujam 2012, pp. 2, 4–6, 9 11–13.
84. Embassy of India, "Bilateral Trade Relations," http://www.indembassy.co.il/pages.php?id=14#.VLZtLivF_Z4; Ministry of Economics, Foreign Trade Administration, May 30, 2016.
85. Klieman 1990, p. 26.
86. Dror 2011, p. 5.
87. Klieman 1988, p. 38.
88. Inbar and Ningthoujam 2012, p. 2.
89. Kumaraswamy 2000, p. 10.
90. Motti Basuk and Orah Koren, *The Marker*, July 24, 2013; Gili Cohen, *Haaretz*, October 7, 2014, http://www.haaretz.com/news/diplomacy-defense/.premium-1.619700.
91. Aluf Benn, *Haaretz*, June 11, 2013; Barbara Opall Rome, *Defense News*, September 10, 2014; Amos Harel, *Haaretz*, January 12, 2011; Rojkes Dombe, Israel Defense, April 2013.

Chapter 10

1. Rodman 2005, pp. 61–63.
2. Sharp 2015, p. 1; Rynhold 2015, p. 1.
3. Rynhold 2015, p. 4.
4. Zanotti 2015, p. 54; https://www.census.gov/foreign-trade/balance/c5081.html#2016.
5. Sharp 2015, p. 29; Zanotti 2015, p. 34.
6. Sharp 2015, pp. 5–6, 9–12, 27.
7. Sharp 2015, pp. 20, 27.
8. Inbar 2008, p. 26.
9. Inbar 2008, p. 26.
10. Inbar 2008, p. 26.
11. Eran and Calin 2014; Aluf Benn, *Haaretz*, August 13, 2008; Adam Entous, *Wall Street Journal*, October 22, 2015; p. David Hornik, *Front Page Magazine*, October 21, 2014.
12. Amnon Barzilai, *Haaretz*, March 28, 2000.
13. Thom Shanker, *New York Times*, September 23, 2011.
14. Aaron Klein, WND, June 9, 2004.
15. Inbar 2008, p. 26.
16. www.nrg.co.il/online/1/ART2/455/619.html; Shmuel Even, email exchange with author, October 22, 2015.
17. Aluf Benn, *Haaretz*, April 28, 2005; Amos Harel and Aluf Benn, *Haaretz*, September 11, 2008.
18. Gili Cohen, *Haaretz*, February 22, 2015; Sharp 2015, p. 7.
19. Private communication.
20. Aluf Benn, *Haaretz*, January 1, 2002.
21. "Saudis Move F-15s Near Israel's Border," WND, September 12, 2013, http://www.wnd.com/2003/09/20743/.
22. Sharp 2015, p. 2.
23. Ross 2015, p. 350; Zanotti 2015 p. 32.
24. Ross 2015, p. 350.
25. Freilich 2012, p. 73; Zeev Schiff, *Haaretz*, July 29, 2005.
26. Ross 2015, pp. 400–401.

27. Aluf Benn, *Haaretz*, May 15, 2009, July 22, 2008; Barak Ravid, *Haaretz*, November 24, 2013.

28. Aluf Ben, *Haaretz*, October 4, 2002, October 7, 2002, October 14, 2002, November 12, 2002, December 13, 2002, April 9, 2003; Aluf Ben and Nathan Guttman, *Haaretz*, October 17, 2002; Zeev Schiff, *Haaretz*, October 18, 2002.

29. Aluf Ben, *Haaretz*, October 4, 2002, October 7, 2002, October 14, 2002, November 12, 2002, December 13, 2002, April 9, 2003; Aluf Ben and Nathan Guttman, *Haaretz*, October 17, 2002; Zeev Schiff, *Haaretz*, October 18, 2002.

30. Rice 2011, p. 708; Gates 2014, pp. 171–177.

31. David Makovsky, *New Yorker*, September 17, 2012; Ross 2015, pp. 333–335; Elliott Abrams, *Commentary Magazine*, February 1, 2013.

32. David Makovsky, *New Yorker*, September 17, 2012; Ross 2015, pp. 333–335; Elliott Abrams, *Commentary Magazine*, February 1, 2013.

33. Gates 2014, pp. 171, 174–176; Rice 2011, p. 708; David Makovsky, *New Yorker*, September 17, 2012; Ross 2015, pp. 333–335; Elliott Abrams, *Commentary Magazine*, February 1, 2013.

34. Gates 2014, p. 176.

35. Aluf Benn, *Haaretz*, August 13, 2008; Amos Harel and Aluf Benn, *Haaretz*, September 11, 2008.

36. Aluf Benn, *Haaretz*, August 13, 2008; Amos Harel and Aluf Benn, *Haaretz*, September 11, 2008.

37. David Sanger, *New York Times*, June 1, 2012.

38. Adam Entous, *Wall Street Journal*, October 22, 2015.

39. Adam Entous, *Wall Street Journal*, October 23, 2015.

40. Gili Cohen, *Haaretz*, October 22, 2015.

41. Aluf Benn and Shmuel Rosner, *Haaretz*, January 3, 2007; Yaakov Katz, *Jerusalem Post*, December 20, 2011.

42. Sharp 2015, pp. 12–13; Aluf Benn and Amos Harel, *Haaretz*, September 28, 2008.

43. Nathan Goodman, *Haaretz*, November 5, 2002.

44. "U.S.-Israel Strategic Cooperation: Joint Infantry Training," December 2015, Jewish Virtual Library, www.jewishvirtuallibrary.org/jsource/US-Israel/marines.html.

45. Avaneesh Pandey, *International Business Times*, November 07, 2014.

46. Amos Harel, *Haaretz*, April 29, 2001, June 26, 2001.

47. Amos Harel, *Haaretz*, April 29, 2001; http://www.jewishvirtuallibrary.org/us-israel-joint-air-force-training; www.iaf.org.il/4421-45094-en/IAF.aspx.

48. Yoav Zitun, Ynet, November 25, 2013.

49. Yaniv Kubovich, *Haaretz*, November 9, 2017.

50. Amos Harel, *Haaretz*, December 12, 2002.

51. Israel Defense, March 30, 2014; http://cne-cna-c6f.dodlive.mil/noble-dina-2015-kicks-off-in-souda-bay/.

52. Barbara Opal Rome, *Defense News*, May 12, 2015.

53. Gili Cohen, *Haaretz*, May 18, 2015.

54. AP and Philip Podolsky, *Times of Israel*, October 24, 2012.

55. Commander, U.S. Naval Forces Europe-Africa / U.S. 6th Fleet Public Affairs, "Exercise Nobel Melinda Continues," America's Navy, August 2, 2013, www.navy.mil/submit/display.asp?story_id=75727; *Haaretz* Staff, May 6, 2001.

56. Yoav Zitun, Ynet, June 3, 2014; Austin Hazard, "22nd MEU, IDF Complete Exercise Nobel Shirley 2014," Marines, www.22ndmeu.marines.mil/News/ArticleView/tabid/196/Article/510449/22nd-meu-idf-complete-exercise-noble-shirley-2014.aspx.

57. Sharp 2015, p. 15; Amos Harel, *Haaretz*, January 11, 2010; *Haaretz* staff, May 6, 2001.

58. Nathan Guttman, *Haaretz*, February 6, 2002.

59. Nathan Guttman, *Haaretz*, February 6, 2002; www.aipac.org/~/media/Publications/Policy%20and%20Politics/AIPAC%20Analyses/Issue%20Memos/2015/The%20US%20Israel%20Strategic%20Partnership.pdf.

60. Goodby et al. 2007, p. 13; nnsa.energy.gov/aboutus/ourprograms/nonproliferation/programoffices/internationalmaterialprotectionandcooperation/-5.

61. Yossi Melman, *Haaretz*, September 1, 2000.

62. Cohen 2010, p. 32.

63. Zeev Schiff, *Haaretz*, August 13, 2000.
64. Yossi Melman, *Haaretz*, November 1, 2007.
65. Yossi Melman, *Haaretz*, September 1, 2000.
66. Barbara Opall Rome, *Defense News*, March 24, 2014; David Sanger, *New York Times*, June 1, 2012; www.aipac.org/~/media/Publications/Policy%20and%20Politics/AIPAC%20 Analyses/Issue%20Memos/2015/The%20US%20Israel%20Strategic%20Partnership.pdf.
67. Aluf Benn, *Haaretz*, April 18, 2001.
68. Nitzan Horowitz, *Haaretz*, April 16, 2000.
69. Reich 1994–95, pp. 64–83, pp. 71–72.
70. Yaniv 1987, pp. 152–158.
71. Yaniv 1987, pp. 216–217.
72. Reich 1994–95, p. 69.
73. Yaniv 1987, p. 219; Reich 1995, p. 41.
74. Yossi Melman, *Haaretz*, April 8, 2011; Feldman 1996, p. 13. Zanotti 2015, pp. 29–30.
75. Reich 1995, p. 43; Feldman 1996, p. 13.
76. Reich 1995, p. 44.
77. For a detailed case study of US-Israeli cooperation regarding the Lavi, see Freilich 2012.
78. Feldman 1996, p. 13.
79. Feldman 1996, p. 15.
80. Inbar 2008, p. 105.
81. Mitchell Bard, "It's Time for a U.S.-Israel Defense Treaty," mitchellbard.com, http://www.mitchellbard.com/articles/treaty.html.
82. https://www.state.gov/s/l/treaty/tias/120101.htm.
83. Peacekeeping, Memorandum of Agreement between the United States of America and Israel, www.state.gov/documents/organization/120311.pdf.
84. CNN (No author), May 24, 2006; Aluf Benn, *Haaretz*, February 7, 2006.
85. JTA, *Forward Magazine*, April 6, 2015.
86. Mike Schuster, NPR, August 26, 2009.
87. Zanotti 2015, pp. 29–30.
88. Aluf Benn, *Haaretz*, August 13, 2001, November 27, 2005; Shmuel Rosner, *Haaretz*, June 7, 2007.
89. Zeev Schiff, *Haaretz*, February 14, 2000; Karpin 2009, p. 32.
90. Mitchell Bard, "It's Time for a U.S.-Israel Defense Treaty," mitchellbard.com, http://www.mitchellbard.com/articles/treaty.html.
91. Yaniv 1987, p. 215.
92. Aluf Benn, *Haaretz*, March 14, 2000.
93. Aluf Benn, *Haaretz*, November 6, 2001; Zeev Schiff, *Haaretz*, February 14, 2000; Inbar 2008 p. 101.
94. Aluf Benn, *Haaretz*, November 6, 2001; Zeev Schiff, *Haaretz*, February 14, 2000.
95. Aluf Benn, *Haaretz*, September 20, 2000, March 12, 2000; Akiva Eldar, *Haaretz*, February 14, 2000.
96. Aluf Benn, *Haaretz*, February 23, 2000, March 1, 2000, November 6, 2001, January 5, 2008; Akiva Eldar, *Haaretz*, February 14, 2000; Zeev Schiff, *Haaretz*, February 14, 2000; Maoz 2006, p. 15; Inbar 2008, p. 105.
97. Evron in Shaked and Rabinovich 1980.
98. Aluf Benn, *Haaretz*, February 23, 2000, March 1, 2000, November 6, 2001; Feldman 1996, pp. 19, 51; Inbar 2008, p. 105; Mitchell Bard, "It's Time for a U.S.-Israel Defense Treaty," mitchellbard.com, www.mitchellbard.com/articles/treaty.html.
99. Aluf Benn, *Haaretz*, November 6, 2001; Reich 1995, p. 32; Mitchell Bard, "It's Time for a U.S.-Israel Defense Treaty," mitchellbard.com, www.mitchellbard.com/articles/treaty.html; Feldman 1996, p. 2.
100. "Israelis Urge Netanyahu to Work with Obama," *Defense News*, www.defensenews.com/story/defense/policy-budget/leaders/2015/04/19/israelis-urge-netanyahu-to-work-with-obama/25927271/.

101. Feldman 1996, p. 49.
102. Aluf Benn January 5, 2000, February 23, 2000, August 31, 2000, September 20, 2000; Akiva Eldar, *Haaretz*, February 14, 2000.
103. Aluf Benn, *Haaretz*, January 5, 2000, February 23, 2000, August 31, 2000, September 20, 2000, January 5, 2008; Akiva Elder, *Haaretz*, February 14, 2000.
104. Aluf Benn, *Haaretz*, February 23, 2000; March 1, 2000; Akiva Eldar, February 14, 2000.
105. These numbers are based on a manual count and analysis of all US Security Council vetoes conducted for this book. They are also consistent with numbers presented by Gilboa 2006, p. 724. The 10 vetoes between 2001 and 2011 are the following:

> 2011, February 18 (Draft 24)
>
> 2006, November 11 (Draft 878)
>
> 2006, July 13 (Draft 508)
>
> 2004, October 5 (Draft 783)
>
> 2004, March 25 (Draft 240)
>
> 2003, October 14 (Draft 980)
>
> 2003, September 16 (Draft 891)
>
> 2002, December 20 (Draft 1385)
>
> 2001, December 14-15 (Draft 1199)
>
> 2001, March 27–28 (Draft 270).

106. Nitzan Horowitz, *Haaretz*, April 16, 2000.
107. Dayan 2012, p. 24.
108. "Exchange of Letters between PM Sharon and President Bush," Israel Ministry of Foreign Affairs, April 14, 2004, www.mfa.gov.il/mfa/foreignpolicy/peace/mfadocuments/pages/exchange%20of%20letters%20sharon-bush%2014-apr-2004.aspx.
109. Ross 2015, p. 372.
110. Aluf Benn, *Haaretz*, December 5, 2000, March 16, 2001, April 18, 2001.
111. Ross 2015, pp. 361–363.
112. Barak Ravid, *Haaretz*, August 21, 2015; Amos Harel, *Haaretz*, September 3, 2013, October 18, 2013; Dennis Ross, interview, April 14, 2016.
113. Rice 2011; Ross 2015, pp. 333–335; Elliott Abrams, *Commentary Magazine*, February 1, 2013.
114. Yoel Markus, *Haaretz*, February 21/95.
115. Aluf Benn, *Haaretz*, May 4, 2000.
116. Amnon Barzilai, *Haaretz*, March 23, 2000; Aluf Benn, *Haaretz*, March 24, 2000.
117. Aluf Benn, *Haaretz*, March 24, 2000, April 30, 2000, May 4, 2000, May 23, 2000, August 20, 2000; Akiva Eldar, *Haaretz*, June 12, 2000; Amnon Barzilai, *Haaretz*, July 2, 2000; Zeev Schiff, *Haaretz*, August 11, 2000; Nitzan Horowitz, *Haaretz*, March 1, 2000.
118. Zeev Schiff, *Haaretz*, June 12, 2005, June 26, 2005, August 28, 2005, February 27, 2006; Aluf Benn, *Haaretz*, June 27, 2005; Sharp 2015, p. 18.
119. See Cohen 1999 for a detailed account of the US efforts to stop Israel's nuclear program in the 1960s.
120. Barak Ravid, *Haaretz*, October 8, 2015.
121. Ross and Makovsky 2009, pp. 57–58.
122. Kramer, *Mosaic Magazine*, May 18, 2016.
123. Motti Basuk, *The Marker*, April 16, 2015.
124. Inbar 2008, p. 24.
125. David Sanger, *New York Times*, June 1, 2012.
126. Waxman 2016, pp. 133, 200, 260; Alterman and Brown 2013, p. 8; Rynhold 2015, p. 31.
127. Alterman and Brown 2013, p. 11; Rynhold 2015, p. 59, 87, 89.
128. Rynhold 2015, pp. 146, 150; Waxman 2016, pp. 55, 134, 232; Abrams 2016.
129. Waxman 2016, pp. 50, 134, 199–200, 207–208, 243; Alterman and Brown 2013, p. 16.
130. Rynhold 2015, pp. 170, 178; Waxman 2016, p. 148, 169–173.
131. Alterman and Brown 2013, p. 7; Rynhold 2015, p. 85.

Chapter 11

1. Commission on America's National Interests, July 2000, pp. 16–17.
2. Eisenkot 2016, pp. 6–7; Yakov Amidror, Tami Steinmetz Center, Tel Aviv University, Conference on Israel's National Security Strategy, December 29, 2015.
3. Yoram Hemo, interview, January 11, 2016. Only the opinion expressed in this sentence, not the entire paragraph, may be attributed to General Hemo.
4. Head of Military Intelligence Herzi Halevy, Herzlia Conference, January 16, 2016.
5. Dan Meridor, interview, June 21, 2016.
6. Brom and Kurz 2016, p. 39; former Mossad head Tamir Pardo fears it may already be too late. Interview, July 26, 2016.
7. Elran et al. 2016, p. 2.

Chapter 12

1. Barak Ravid, *Haaretz*, November 17, 2016.
2. Aluf Ben, *Haaretz*, July 22, 2002.
3. Dayan 2012, p. 29.
4. Chorev 2015, p. 31; Yadlin 2013.
5. Eiland 2010a, p. 16.
6. Chaziza 2016.
7. Brom and Kurz 2016, p. 53.
8. Dan Meridor, interview, June 21, 2016.
9. Paz 2015, p. 17.
10. Barak Ravid, *Haaretz*, February 3, 2010. The 10-million-shekel MFA budget does not include a special budget of 140 million shekels for the anti-delegitimization campaign, run by the Ministry of Strategic Affairs.
11. Dan Meridor, interview, January 14, 2013.
12. Dahab 2015, p. 5.
13. Mintz and Shai 2014a.
14. Mintz and Shai 2014b, p. 5; Dekel in Kurz and Brom 2014, p. 2.
15. The above areas of dialogue draw on recommendations presented by Valensi and Dekel 2016, pp. 24–26.
16. Dennis Ross, interview, April 14, 2016. See also Ross 2015.
17. Freilich and Rosecrance, bitterlemons-international.org, edition 25, vol. 4, July 6, 2006.
18. The term "strategic patience" was suggested to the author by Dennis Ross, interview, April 14, 2016, "long game" by Brigadier General Assaf Orion, interview, December 9, 2015.
19. Dennis Ross, interview, April 14, 2016.
20. Amos Harel, *Haaretz*, July 8, 2015.
21. Shelah 2015, pp. 74–75, 97–99.
22. Dan Halutz, interview, December 16, 2012; Amidror 2010, p. 13.
23. Ofer Shelah, interview by Amos Harel, *Haaretz*, April 2, 2015.
24. Stephen M. Walt, "Applying the 8 Questions of the Powell Doctrine to Syria," *Foreign Policy*, September 3, 2013, www.foreignpolicy.com/2013/09/03/applying-the-8-questions-of-the-powell-doctrine-to-syria/; Shelah 2015, pp. 91–93.
25. See chapter 6 for the definitions of the different types of deterrence.
26. Shelah 2015, p. 119.
27. Dan Meridor, interview, June 21, 2016.
28. This recommendation draws on an idea raised by Dan Meridor, interview, June 11, 2013.
29. For sources regarding Iron Dome and Magic Wand cost and numbers, see chapter 7.
30. Sofer in Elran and Altshuler 2012, p. 55.
31. Dan Halutz, interview, December 12, 2012.
32. For sources regarding F-35 costs, see chapter 7. For sources on the Osprey, see TOI Staff, "US Said to Have Approved Sale to Israel of Ospreys, Capable of Reaching Iran," *Times of Israel*, November 2, 2015, http://www.timesofisrael.com/f-35s-f-15s-ospreys-on-israeli-shopping-list-of-desired-us-military-materiel/; "Israel Angles to Extend US Offer for V-22s," *Defense*

News, http://www.defensenews.com/story/defense/policy-budget/industry/2015/01/04/israel-yaalon-v-22-osprey-namer/21184117/.

33. Yoram Hemo, interview, June 11, 2016.
34. See Hecht and Shamir 2016; Kober in S. A. Cohen 2010.
35. For the IDF force structure see Table 3.3 in chapter 3. For the cuts made in recent years see chapter 7.
36. Meirav Arlozorov, *Haaretz*, November 26, 2012.
37. Shelah 2015, pp. 174, 206, 217.
38. Amos Yadlin, INSS Annual Conference, Tel Aviv, January 28, 2016.
39. Gideon Frank, interview, October 19, 2016.
40. Gideon Frank, interview, October 19, 2016.
41. Aluf Benn, *Haaretz*, August 22, 2002; Zeev Schiff, *Haaretz*, April 24, 2006.
42. Landau and Stein in Foradori and Malin 2013, p. 25.
43. Shlomo Brom, interview, July 10, 2016; Martin Malin, interview, February 16, 2016.
44. Meir Elran, Lecture, Tel Aviv University, November 11, 2015 Matan Vilnai, INSS Conference on the Home Front, Tel Aviv, August 1, 2012.
45. Lior Detel, *The Marker*, December 7, 2016.
46. Former head of the IDF Planning Branch and air force commander Major General Ido Nechushtan raised the idea of a national campaign to close social gaps, suggesting that this be done within one to two generations, interview, December 30, 2015. The former head of the IDF Strategic Planning Division, Brigadier General Assaf Orion, similarly stressed the importance of investment in education and social welfare for Israel's national security, interview, December 9, 2015.
47. Freilich 2012. See, in particular, chapter 2 and Part 3: "Conclusions and Recommendations."
48. Freilich 2012, pp. 252–253.

BIBLIOGRAPHY

Abrams, E. 2016. If American Jews and Israel are Drifting Apart, What's the Reason? *Mosaic*, April 4.

Aceves, W. J. 2010. Litigating the Arab-Israeli Conflict in U.S. Courts: Critiquing the Lawfare Critique. *Case Western Reserve Journal of International Law* 43.1, pp. 313–325.

Adamsky, D. 2010. *The Culture of Military Innovation*. Stanford, CA: Stanford University Press.

Adamsky, D. and Bjerga, K. J. 2012. *Contemporary Military Innovation: Between Anticipation and Adaption*. London: Routledge.

Allon, Y. 1976. Israel: The Case for Defensible Borders. *Foreign Affairs* 55.1, October, pp. 38–53.

Alpher, Y. 2015. *Periphery: Israel's Search for Middle East Allies*. Lanham, MD: Rowman and Littlefield.

Alterman, O. and Brown, C. 2013. American Public Support for Israel Changing Direction (Hebrew). *Strategic Assessment* 15.4, January, pp. 7–24.

Amidror, Y. 2002. *Reflections on the Army and Security: Articles, Letter, and Lectures on the Fight with the Palestinians* (Hebrew). Tel Aviv: Misrad Habitachon.

———. 2007. The Necessary Conditions for Victory in the War on Terror. *Maarachot* (Hebrew) 412, May, pp. 32–37.

———. 2010. The Range of Threats Facing the State of Israel. *Military and Strategic Affairs* (Hebrew) 2.1, June, pp. 7–8.

———. 2015b. *The Terrorist Defense Force*. Perspectives Paper No. 281. Ramat Gan: BESA, January 13.

———. 2016. *Lebanon, 2006–2016: Deterrence Is an Elusive Concept*. Perspectives Paper No. 349. Ramat Gan: BESA, July 10.

Andres, E., et al. 2012. The Individual's Level of Globalism and Citizen Commitment to the State: The Tendency to Evade Military Service in Israel. *Armed Forces and Society* 38.1, pp. 92–116.

Anthony, C. R., et al. 2015. *The Costs of the Israeli-Palestinian Conflict*. Santa Monica, CA: Rand.

Arad, U. et al., 2017. Grand Strategy for Israel, Technion, Sameul Neeman Institute, Haifa,

Arad, U. and Steiner, T. 2004. *Israel and the Euro-Atlantic Community: An Israeli Perspective*. Herzlia Conference Working Paper, Herzlia, December.

Arian, A. 2000. *Israeli Public Opinion on National Security 2000*. Tel Aviv: Jaffee Center for Strategic Studies.

———. 2009. *2009 Social Values of Israeli Jews*. Israel Democracy Institute Poll.

Arian, A., et al. 2005. *Auditing Israeli Democracy 2005: A Decade after the Assassination of Prime Minister Yitzhak Rabin*. Jerusalem: Israel Democracy Institute.

———. 2007. *Auditing Israeli Democracy 2007: Cohesion in a Divided Society*. Jerusalem: Israel Democracy Institute.

Art, R. J. 2003. *A Grand Strategy for America*. Ithaca, NY: Cornell University Press.

Asmus, R. D. and Jackson, B. P. 2005. Does Israel Belong in the EU and NATO? *Policy Review* 129, February–March, pp. 47–56.

Avineri, S. 1986. Ideology in Israel's Foreign Policy. *Jerusalem Quarterly* 37, pp. 3–13.

Baidatz, Y. and Adamsky, D. 2014. *The Development of the Israeli Approach towards Deterrence: A Critical Discussion of Its Theoretical and Practical Dimensions* (Hebrew). Tel Aviv: Eshtonot, National Security College, Research Center, October.

Bagno-Moldavski, O. and Ben-Meir, Y. 2009. Who in Israel Is Ready for a Peace Agreement with the Palestinians and under What Conditions? *Strategic Assessment* (Hebrew) 17.1, pp. 39–48.

Bakan, A. B. and Abu-Laban, Y. 2009. Palestinian Resistance. *Race and Class* 51.1, pp. 29–54.

Bar, A. 2010. Israel and the CTBT. *Strategic Assessment* 13.2, August, pp. 25–32.

Bar, M. 1990. *Red Lines in Israel's Deterrence Policy* (Hebrew). Tel Aviv: Maarachot Press.

———. 2008. *Arms Control and National Security* (Hebrew). Tel Aviv: Maarachot Press.

Bar-Joseph, U. 1998a. Israel's Northern Eyes and Shields: The Strategic Value of the Golan Heights Revisited. *Journal of Strategic Studies* 21.3, September, pp. 46–66.

———. 1998b. Variations on a Theme: The Conceptualization of Deterrence in Israeli Strategic Thinking. *Security Studies* 7.3, Spring, pp. 145–181.

———. 2000. Towards a Paradigm Shift in Israel's National Security Conception. *Israel Affairs* 6.3–4, pp. 99–114.

———, ed. 2001. *Israel's National Security towards the 21st Century*. London: Frank Cass.

———. 2004–5. The Paradox of Israeli Power. *Survival* 46.4, Winter, pp. 137–156.

———. 2005. The Crisis in Israel's Security Concept. *Maarachot* (Hebrew) 401, June, pp. 10–19.

Bar-Tal, D., et al., eds. 1998. *Security Concerns: Insights from the Israeli Experience*. Stamford, CT: JAI Press.

Baram, A. 1992. Israeli Deterrence; Iraqi Responses. *Orbis* 36.3, Summer, pp. 397–409.

Baram, G. 2013. Influence of the Development of Cybernetic Warfare Technology on Changes in the Israeli Force Structure. *Military and Strategy* 5.1, May, pp. 19–36.

Barnaby, F. 1989. *The Invisible Bomb: The Nuclear Arms Race in the Middle East*. London: I.B. Tauris.

Barnett, M. N. 1992. *Confronting the Costs of War: Military Power, State and Society in Egypt and Israel*. Princeton, NJ: Princeton University Press.

Ben-Ami, S. 2006. *Scars of War, Wounds of Peace*. Oxford: Oxford University Press.

Ben-Ari, E. 2005. Epilogue: A "Good" Military Death. *Armed Forces & Society* 31.4, pp. 651–664.

Ben-David, D. 2015. *Shoresh Handbook on Israel's Society and Economy*. Shoresh Institution, October.

Ben-Dor, G. and Pedahzur, A. 2006. Under the Threat of Terrorism: A Reassessment of the Factors Influencing the Motivation to Serve in the Israeli Reserves. *Israel Affairs* 12.3, pp. 430–438.

Ben-Dor, G., et al. 2002. Israel's National Security Doctrine under Strain: The Crisis of the Reserve Army. *Armed Forces and Society* 28.2, Winter, pp. 233–255.

———. 2008. Motivation during War and Peace, I versus We: Collective and Individual Factors of Reserve Service. *Armed Forces and Society* 34.4, July, pp. 565–592.

Ben-Horin, Y. and Posen, B. 1981. *Israel's Strategic Doctrine*. Santa Monica, CA: Rand.

Ben-Israel, I. 2013. *Israel Defense Doctrine* (Hebrew). Ben Shemen: Modan.

Ben-Meir, D. 2009. *The Israeli Defense System* (Hebrew). Tel Aviv: Miskal.

Ben-Meir, Y. 1986. *National Security Decision Making: The Israeli Case*. Boulder, CO: Westview.

———. 2009. Operation Cast Lead: Political Dimensions and Public Opinion. *Strategic Assessment* 11.4, February, pp. 29–34.

Ben-Meir, Y. and Bagno-Moldavsky, O. 2013. *The Voice of the People: Israeli Public Opinion on National Security 2012* (Hebrew). Tel Aviv: Institute for National Security Studies, December.

2010. *Vox Populi: Trends in Israeli Public Opinion on National Security 2004-2009*, Tel Aviv: Institute for National Security Studies, November

———. 2014. Who in Israel Is Ready for a Peace Agreement with the Palestinians and under What Circumstances? *Strategic Assessment* (Hebrew) 17.1, April, pp. 39–48.

Ben-Porat, G., et al. 2008. *Israel since 1980*. Cambridge: Cambridge University Press.

Benziman, Y. and Romm, L. 2014. *Key Elements of Israel's Foreign Policy Paradigms*. Ramat Gan: Mitvim Institute, March.

Beres, L. R, ed. 1986. *Security or Armageddon: Israel's Nuclear Strategy*. Lexington, MA: Lexington Books.

———. 2000. *Security Threats and Effective Remedies: Israel's Strategic, Tactical and Legal Options*. Policy Paper No. 102. Shaarei Tikva: Arial Center for Policy Research, April.

———. 2007. Israel's Uncertain Strategic Future. *Parameters*, Spring, pp. 37–54.

———. 2013. Facing Myriad Enemies: Core Elements of Israeli Nuclear Deterrence. *Brown Journal of World Affairs* 20.1, Fall–Winter, pp. 18–30.

———. 2015. Israel's Strategic Doctrine: Updating Intelligence Community Responsibilities. *International Journal of Intelligence and Counter-intelligence* 28, pp. 89–104.

———. 2016. *Surviving amid Chaos: Israel's Nuclear Strategy*. Lanham, MD: Rowman and Littlefield.

Berkowitz, P. 2011. The Gaza Flotilla and International Law. *Policy Review* (Hoover Institution), August 1.

BESA. 2008. *IDF Preparations for Future Challenges* (Hebrew). Conference Proceedings. Discussions in National Security No. 24. Ramat Gan, July.

———. 2014. *The IDF Force Structure* (Hebrew). Conference Proceedings. Discussions in National Security No. 28. Ramat Gan, May.

———. 2016. *IDF Challenges* (Hebrew). National Security Proceedings No. 30, August.

Bitzur, A. 2009. The Status of the Rear in Israel's Defense Concept. *Maarachot* (Hebrew) 426, August, 12–19.

Blank, L. A. 2010. Finding Facts but Missing the Law: The Goldstone Report, Gaza and Lawfare. *Case Western Reserve Journal of International Law* 43.1, pp. 279–305.

Blechman, B. 2011. *Unblocking the Road to Global Zero: Pakistan and Israel*. Washington, DC: Stimson Center.

Bohrer, Z. and Osiel, M. 2013. Proportionality in War: Protecting Soldiers from Enemy Captivity and Israel's Operation Cast Lead—"the Soldiers Are Everyone's Children." *USC Interdisciplinary Law Journal* 637, p. 16.

Bolgiano, D. A. 2010. Nationalist's View of Lawfare. *Orbis* 54.3, pp. 387–399.

Boot, M. 2006. *War Made New: Technology, Warfare and the Course of History 1500 to Today*. New York: Gotham Books.

Brecher, M. 1972. *The Foreign Policy System of Israel: Setting, Images, Process*. New Haven: Yale University Press.

Brom, S., ed. 2012. *Following Operation "Defensive Pillar": Gaza Strip, November 2012* (Hebrew). Memorandum No. 123, INSS, December.

Brom, S. and Elran, M., eds. 2007. *The Second Lebanon War: Strategic Perspectives*. Tel Aviv: INSS.

Brom, S. and Kurz, A., eds. 2016. *Strategic Assessment for Israel 2015–2016* (Hebrew). Tel Aviv: INSS.

———. 2014. *Strategic Assessment for Israel, 2013–2014* (Hebrew). Tel Aviv: INSS.

Brun, I. 2008. Where Did Maneuver Disappear To? *Maarachot* (Hebrew) 420–21, September, pp. 4–15.

———. 2010. "While You're Busy Making Other Plans"—the "Other RMA." *Journal of Strategic Studies* 33.4, August, pp. 535–565.

Buchan, R. 2012. The Palmer Report and the Legality of Israel's Naval Blockade of Gaza. *International and Comparative Law Quarterly* 61.1, pp. 264–273.

Byman, D. 2011. *A High Price: The Triumphs and Failures of Israeli Counterterrorism*. Oxford: Oxford University Press.

Byman, D. and Waxman, M. 2002. *The Dynamics of Coercion: American Foreign Policy and the Limits of Military Might*. Cambridge: Cambridge University Press.

Bystrov, E. and Sofer, A. 2008. *Israel: Demography and Density, 2007–2020*. Chaiken Chair in Geostrategy, University of Haifa, Haifa.

Carr, J. 2012. *Inside Cyber Warfare*. Cambridge: O'Reilly.

Catignani, S. 2008. *Israeli Counterinsurgency and the Intifada: Dilemmas of a Conventional Army*. London: Routledge.

Cavari, A. and Nyer, E. 2016. *Trends in Congressional Support for Israel*. Mideast Security and Policy Studies No. 121. Ramat Gan: BESA, June.

Chen, Y. 2011. China's Relationship with Israel, Opportunities and Challenges: Perspectives from China. *Israel Studies* 17.3, Fall, pp. 1–21.

Chaziza, M. 2016. The Red-Med Railway: New Opportunities for China, Israel and the Middle East. Perspectives Paper No. 385. Ramat Gan: BESA, December 11.

Chorev, M. 2015. *"Deterrence Campaigns": Lessons from IDF Operations in Gaza* (Hebrew). Studies in Middle Eastern Security No. 115. Ramat Gan: BESA.

Clarke, R. A. and Knake, R. K. 2012. *Cyber War: The Next Threat to National Security and What to do About It*. New York: HarperCollins.

Cohen, A. 1999. *Israel and the Bomb*. New York: Columbia University Press. Hebrew edition, Tel Aviv: Shoken, 2000.

———. 2010. *The Worst Kept Secret: Israel's Bargain with the Bomb*. New York: Columbia University Press.

Cohen, A. and Cohen, S. A. 2011. Israel and International Humanitarian Law: Between the Neo-realism of State Security and the "Soft Power" of Legal Acceptability. *Israel Studies* 16.2, Summer, pp. 1–23.

Cohen, A. and Miller, M. 2010. Bringing Israel's Bomb out of the Basement. *Foreign Affairs* 89.5, September–October, pp. 30–44.

Cohen, E. A., et al. 1998. *Knives, Tanks and Missiles: Israel Security Revolution*. Washington, DC: Washington Institute for Near East Policy.

Cohen, R. 1991. Israel's Starry-Eyed Foreign Policy. *Middle East Quarterly* 1.2, pp. 28–41.

Cohen, S. A. 1992. Changing Emphases in Israel's Military Commitments, 1981–1991: Causes and Consequences. *Journal of Strategic Studies* 15.3, September, pp. 330–350.

———. 2000. Changing Societal-Military Relations in Israel: The Operational Implications. *Contemporary Security Policy* 21.3, pp. 116–138.

———. 2006. Changing Civil-Military Relations in Israel: Towards an Over-subordinate IDF? *Israel Affairs* 12.4, October, pp. 769–788.

———. 2007. *The False Crisis in Military Recruitment: An IDF Red Herring*. Perspectives Paper No. 33. Ramat Gan: BESA, July.

———. 2008. *Israel and Its Army: From Cohesion to Confusion*. London: Routledge.

———. 2010. *The New Citizen Armies: Israel's Armed Forces in Comparative Perspective*. London: Routledge.

Cohen, S. M. and Kelman, A. Y. 2007. *Beyond Distancing: Young Adult American Jews and Their Alienation from Israel*. www.bjpa.org/Publications/downloadFile.cfm?FileID=317.

Colby, E., et al. 2013. *The Israeli "Nuclear Alert" of 1973: Deterrence and Signaling in Crisis*. Alexandria, VA: Center for Naval Analyses, April.

Commission on America's National Interests. 2000. *America's National Interests*. July.

Cordesman, A. H. 2008. *Arab-Israeli Military Forces in an Era of Asymmetric Wars*. Stanford, CA: Stanford University Press.

———. 2015. *Military Spending and Arms Sales in the Gulf*. Washington, DC: Center for Strategic and International Studies, April 28.

Cornfeld, O. and Danieli, O. 2015. The Origins of Income Inequality in Israel: Trends and Policy. *Israel Economic Review* 12.2, pp. 51–95.

Curtis, M. 2012. The International Assault against Israel. *Israel Affairs* 18.3, pp. 344–362.

Dahab, M. 2015. *Israeli Foreign Policy and the Modern Diplomacy of the 21st Century*. Ramat Gan: Mitvim Institute, May.

Dayan, M. 1955. Israel's Border and Security Problems. *Foreign Affairs* 33.2, pp. 250–268.

Dayan, U. 2012. Israel's National Security Consideration in Its Approach to the Peace Process. *Jewish Political Studies Review* 24.12, Spring, pp. 23–31.

———. 2014. *The Jordan Valley Is Israel's Only Defensible Border*. Perspectives Paper No. 244. Ramat Gan: BESA, April 14.

Dekel, U. and Einav, O. 2017. An Updated National Security Concept for Israel, INSS, Special Memorandum, February 2017

Dekel, U. and Einav, O. 2015. The Need for an Updated Strategy in the Face of Regional Upheaval: The Northern Front as a Case Study. *Strategic Assessment* (Hebrew) (INSS) 18.1, April, pp. 37–48.

Dekel, U., Siboni, G., and Einav, O., eds. 2016. *The Quiet Decade, 2006–2016* (Hebrew). Special Project, INSS. www.inss.org.il/uploadImages/systemFiles/DekelOrion.pdf.

DellaPergola, S. 2003. Demographic Trends in Israel and Palestine: Prospects and Regional Implications. *American Jewish Yearbook*. Vol. 103. New York: American Jewish Committee.

———. 2011. *Jewish Demographic Policies: Population Trends and Options in Israel and the Diaspora*. Jerusalem: Jewish People Policy Institute.

———. 2015. World Jewish Population. *American Jewish Yearbook*. Vol. 115. New York: American Jewish Committee.

Dror, Y. 1989. *A Grand Strategy for Israel* (Hebrew). Jerusalem: Academon.

———. 2011. *Israeli Statecraft: National Security Challenges and Responses*. London: Routledge.

Efrati, H., ed. 2002. *An Introduction to National Security*. Tel Aviv: Ministry of Defense Press.

Egozi, A. 2011. "The Secret Cyber War." *Military Technology* 35, pp. 5–6.

Eilam, E. 2016. The Struggle against Hezbollah and Hamas: Israel's Next Hybrid War. *Israel Journal of Foreign Affairs* 10.2, pp. 247–255.

Eilam, U. 2005. *A New European Defense Identity* (Hebrew). Memorandum No. 75. Tel Aviv: Jaffee Center for Strategic Studies, March.

Eiland, G. 2007. The Changing Nature of Wars: Six New Challenges. *Strategic Assessment* 10.1, June, pp. 13–18.

———. 2009. *Defensible Borders on the Golan Heights*. Jerusalem: Jerusalem Center for Public Affairs.

———. 2010a. Fundamentals of the Response of the State of Israel. *Military and Strategic Affairs* (Hebrew) 2.1, June, pp. 57–66.

———. 2010b. The IDF and the 2nd Intifada: Conclusions and Lessons. *Strategic Assessment* 13.3, October, pp. 23–31.

Eisenkot, G. 2010. A Changed Threat? The Response on the Northern Arena. *Military and Strategic Affairs* (Hebrew) 2.1, June, pp. 23–32.

———. 2016. IDF Challenges, 2015–2016. *Military and Strategic Affairs* (Hebrew) 8.1, July, pp. 5–16.

Eisenstadt, M. and Pollock, D. 2012. *Asset Test: How the United States Benefits from its Alliance with Israel*. Strategic Reports No. 7. Washington, DC: Washington Institute for Near East Policy.

Elran, M. 2002. "Turning Point 4": National Emergency Exercise, Lessons and Ramifications (Hebrew). *Strategic Assessment* 13.1, June, pp. 55–62.

———. 2006. *Societal Resilience in Israel: Effects of the Second Intifada on Israeli Society* (Hebrew). Memorandum No. 81. Tel Aviv: Jaffee Center for Strategic Studies, January.

———. 2007. Turning Our Back on the Civilian Front. *Strategic Assessment* 10.2, August, pp. 4–10.

Elran, M. and Altschuler, A., eds. 2012. *The Complex Mosaic of the Civilian Front in Israel* (Hebrew). Memorandum No. 120. Tel Aviv: INSS, July.

———. 2015. How (Un)Prepared is Israel for an Emergency? *INSS Insight*, No. 761, November 1.

Elran, M. and Ben Meir, Y., eds. 2012. *Drafting the Ultra-Orthodox to the IDF: Renewing the Tal Law* (Hebrew). Memorandum No. 119. Tel Aviv: INSS, June.

Elran, M. and Sheffer, G., eds. 2015. *Military Service in Israel: Challenges and Ramifications* (Hebrew). Memorandum No. 148. Tel Aviv: INSS, September.

Elran, M., et al. 2015. Societal Resilience in the Gaza Region during Operation Defensive Edge. *Military and Strategic Affairs* 7.2, September, 5–26.

———. 2016a. An Expanded Comprehensive Threat Scenario for the Home Front in Israel. *INSS Insight*, No. 828, June.

———. 2016b. *IDF Strategy in the Perspective of National Security*. Tel Aviv: INSS.

Eran, O. 2004. *Israel and Europe: Options for Future Relations*. Herzlia Conference Working Paper, Herzlia, December.

———. 2015. Active Israeli Policy in the Mediterranean Basin. *INSS Insight*, No. 775, December 6.

Eran, O. and Calin, L. G. 2014. Were, Are, and Will Sanctions Be Effective against Israel? *Strategic Assessment* 16.4, January, pp. 61–73.

Erez, Y. and Perel, G. 2013. Integrating Technologies for Defending the Home Front against Ballistic and Cruise Missile Threats. *Military and Strategy* (Hebrew) 5.3, December, pp. 75–93.

Even S. and Siman-Tov, D. 2012. *Cyber Warfare: Concepts, Trends and Implications for Israel*. Memorandum No. 179 (Hebrew). Tel Aviv: INSS, June.

Evron, Y. 1990. Opaque Proliferation: The Israeli Case. *Journal of Strategic Studies* 13.3, pp. 45–63.

———. 1994. *Israel's Nuclear Dilemma*. Ithaca, NY: Cornell University Press.

———. 2007. Israeli-Chinese Relations after the Crisis: Opportunities and Challenges. *Strategic Assessment* 10.2, August, pp. 54–62.

Faris, H. A., ed. 2013. *The Failure of the Two-State Solution: The Prospects of One State in the Israel-Palestine Conflict*. London: I.B. Tauris.

Farsakh, L. 2011. The One-State Solution and the Israeli-Palestinian Conflict: Palestinian Challenges and Prospects. *Middle East Journal* 65.1, pp. 55–71.

Farwell, J. P. and Rohozinski, R. 2011. Stuxnet and the Future of Cyber War. *Survival* 53.1, pp. 23–40.

———. 2012. The New Reality of Cyber War. *Survival* 54.4, pp. 107–120.

Feaver, P. D., et al. 2005. Success Matters; Casualty Sensitivity and the War in Iraq. *International Security* 30.3, pp. 7–46.

Feldman, N. 2016. In the Shadow of Delegitimization: Israel's Sensitivity to Economic Sanctions. Memorandum 163. Tel Aviv: INSS, June.

Feldman, S. 1982. *Israeli Nuclear Strategy*. New York: Columbia University Press.

———. 1996. *The Future of US-Israeli Strategic Cooperation*. Washington, DC: Washington Institute for Near East Studies.

Feldman, S. and Toukan, A. 1997. *Bridging the Gap: A Future Security Architecture for the Middle East*. Lanham, MD: Rowman and Littlefield.

Filson, D. and Werner, S. 2007. Sensitivity to Costs of Fighting versus Sensitivity to Losing the Conflict: Implications for War Onset, Duration, and Outcomes. *Journal of Conflict Resolution* 51.5, pp. 691–714.

Finkel, M. 2015. Iron Dome: The New Maginot Line? *Maarachot* (Hebrew) 461, June, pp. 11–16.

Finlay, B., et al. 2015. *CTBT: What's New and What's Next?* Transcript, Carnegie International Nuclear Policy Conference 2015. Carnegie Endowment for International Peace, March 23.

Fishman, J. S. 2012. The BDS Message of Anti-Zionism, Anti-Semitism, and Incitement to Discrimination. *Israel Affairs* 18.3, pp. 412–425.

Foradori, P. and Malin, M. B., eds. 2013. *A WMD Free Zone in the Middle East: Regional Perspectives*. Discussion Paper No. 2013-09. Cambridge, MA: Belfer Center, Harvard Kennedy School.

Freedman, R. O. ed. 2009. *Contemporary Israel: Domestic Politics, Foreign Policy and Security Challenges*. Boulder, CO: Westview.

Freilich, C. D. 2007. *Speaking about the Unspeakable: US Israeli Dialogue on Iran's Nuclear Program*. Policy Focus No. 77. Washington, DC: Washington Institute for Near East Policy, December.

———. 2010. *The Armageddon Scenario: Israel and the Threat of Nuclear Terrorism*. Mideast Security and Policy Studies No. 84. Ramat Gan: BESA, April.

———. 2012. *Zion's Dilemmas: How Israel Makes National Security Policy*. Ithaca, NY: Cornell University Press.

———. 2015. Israel's Counter-terrorism Policy: How Effective? *Terrorism and Political Violence* 29.2, pp. 359–376.

Freilich, C. D. and Cohen, M. S. 2015. The Delegitimization of Israel: Diplomatic Warfare, Sanctions, and Lawfare. *Israel Affairs* 9.1, pp. 29–48.

Freilich, C. D., et al. 2015. Israel and Cyberspace: Unique Threat and Response. *International Studies Perspectives* 17.3, pp. 307–321.

Friedland, N., et al. 2005. *The Concept of Societal Resilience*. Haifa: Forum of National Security, Samuel Neaman Institute.

Frisch, H. 2016. *The ISIS Challenge in Syria: Implications for Israeli Security*. Mideast Security and Policy Studies No. 118. Ramat Gan: BESA, May 8.

Gal, R. 1999. The Motivation for Serving in the IDF in the Mirror of Time. *Strategic Assessment* 2.3, December, pp. 11–16.

———. 2014. Social Resilience in Times of Protracted Crises: An Israeli Case Study. *Armed Forces & Society* 40.3, pp. 452–475.

———. 2015. *Haredim in Israeli Society: 2014 Update* (Hebrew). Haifa: Shmuel Neaman Institute, January.

Ganor, B. 2005. *The Counter-terrorism Puzzle: A Guide for Decision Makers*. New Brunswick, NJ: Transaction.

———. 2014. *Security Challenges in Israel in the Area of Coping with Terror in the Present and Future* (Hebrew). Policy Paper No. 4. Herzlia: Herzlia Interdisciplinary Center, Institute for Policy and Strategy, May.

Garfinkle, A. M. 2000. *Politics and Society in Modern Israel: Myths and Realities*. Armonk, NY: M.E. Sharpe.

Gat, A. 2010. *Victorious and Vulnerable: Why Democracy Won in the 20th Century and How It Is Still Imperiled*. Lanham, MD: Rowman and Littlefield.

Gates, R. M. 2014. *Duty: Memoirs of a Secretary at War*. New York: Knopf.

Gazit, S. 1999. *Trapped* (Hebrew). Tel Aviv: Zmora Bita.

Gelber, Y. 2014. *The Defense Doctrine and Place of the Army in Israeli Society*. Policy Paper No. 3. Herzlia: Policy and Strategy Institute, May.

Gerberg, I. 2010. *India-Israel Relations: Strategic Interest, Politics and Diplomatic Pragmatism*. Haifa: Israel National Defense College.

Gerstenfeld, M. 2012. De-legitimization Currents in Europe. *Israel Affairs* 18.3, pp. 389–402.

Gilbert, M. 2008. *Israel: A History*. New York: Harper.

Gilboa, E. 2006. Public Diplomacy: The Missing Component in Israel's Foreign Policy. *Israel Affairs* 12.4, October, pp. 715–747.

Giles, G. F. 2006. *Continuity and Change in Israel's Strategic Culture*. Prepared for Defense Threat Reduction Agency, SAIC.

Golan, H. and Shaul, S., eds. 2004. *Low Intensity Conflict* (Hebrew). Tel Aviv: Maarachot Press.

Goodby, J., Coffey, T., and Loeb, C. 2007. *A Proposed Strategy for Combating Nuclear Terrorism*. Center for Technology and National Security Policy, National Defense University, July.

Goodman, H. and Carus, W. S. 1990. *The Future Battlefield and the Arab-Israeli Conflict*. New Brunswick, NJ: Transaction.

Gordon, S. L. 2002. *Israel against Terror: A National Assessment* (Hebrew). Meltzer.

Gorenberg, G. 2006. *The Accidental Empire*. New York: Holt.

Gozansky, J. and Kulik, A. 2010. State Failure and Its Ramifications for Israel's Strategic Environment. *Strategic Assessment* 13.2, August, pp. 33–46.

Grauman, B. 2012. *Cyber-security: The Vexed Question of Global Rules*. Security and Defense Agenda, Brussels. www.files.ethz.ch/isn/139895/SDA_Cyber_report_FINAL.pdf.

Gray, C. S. 2005. *Another Bloody Century*. London: Weidenfield and Nicolson.

———. 2011. *Hard Power and Soft Power: The Utility of Military Forces and Instruments of Policy in the 21st Century*. Strategic Studies Institute, US Army War College, April.

Hacohen, G. 2014. *What Is National about National Security* (Hebrew). Ben-Shemen: Modan.

Halevi, J. 2014. *Hamas Policy after Operation Protective Edge*. Jerusalem Center for Public Affairs 14.29, September 18.

Hallward, M. C. and Shaver, P. 2012. War by other Means or Nonviolent Resistance? Examining the Discourses Surrounding Berkeley's Divestment Bill. *Peace and Change* 37.3, pp. 389–412.

Handel, M. I. 1973. *Israel's Political-Military Doctrine*. Cambridge, MA: Harvard University Press.

Handel, Y. 2008. The Return of the Reserve Force. *Strategic Assessment* 10.4, February, pp. 31–35.

Harel, A. 2016. Israel's Evolving Military. *Foreign Affairs* 95.4, pp. 43–50.

2013. Let Every Hebrew Mother Know: The Face of the New IDF, Kinneret-Zmora Bitan, Or Yehuda.

Harel, A. and Isacharoff, A. 2004. *The Seventh War*. Tel Aviv: Miskal.

Hareven, A. 2006. *Israel in Space: Strategic Dimensions* (Hebrew). Discussions and National Security No. 20. Ramat Gan: BESA, July.

——. 2009. *Israel's Civil Space Program: Cooperation with Other Countries* (Hebrew). Memorandum No. 2. Ramat Gan: BESA, May.

Hecht, E. and Shamir, E. 2016. *Medium-Intensity Threats: The Case for Beefed-Up IDF Ground Forces*. Mideast Security and Policy Studies No. 125. Ramat Gan: BESA, October.

Heiman, A. 2004. The Reserve Force, the IDF and Israeli Society: Past, Present, and Future. *Maarachot* (Hebrew) 394, May, pp. 4–12.

Heller, M. A. 2000. *Continuity and Change in Israeli Security Policy*. Adelphi Paper No. 335. Oxford: Oxford University Press.

Hendel. Y. 2012. Iran's Nukes and Israel's Dilemma. *Middle East Quarterly* 19.1, Winter, pp. 31–38.

Henry Jackson Society. 2014. *Added Value: Israel's Strategic Worth to the EU and Its Member States*. January.

Hermann, T. 2014. *Religious? National? The National Religious Camp in Israel in 2014*. Jerusalem: Israel Democracy Institute.

Hermann, T., et al. 2014. *The Israeli Democracy Index 2014*. Jerusalem: Israel Democracy Institute.

Herzlia Interdisciplinary Center. 2011. *Israeli Foreign Policy in an Era of Global Change*. Report of Herzlia Conference Task Force, February.

Hinnebusch, R. and Ehteshami, A., eds. 2002. *The Foreign Policy of Middle East States*. Boulder, CO: Lynne Reiner.

Hoffman, R. 2014. *The Absence of an Effective Foreign Policy in Israel's National Security Establishment*. Policy Paper No. 9. Herzlia: Herzlia Forum for Formulating Israel's Defense Strategy, Policy and Strategy Institute, Herzlia Interdisciplinary Center, June.

Honig, O. 2007. The End of Israeli Military Restraint. *Middle East Quarterly* 14.1, Winter, pp. 63–74.

Horowitz, D. 1993. The Israeli Concept of National Security. In *National Security and Democracy in Israel*, ed. A. Yaniv. Boulder, CO: Lynne Reiner

Horowitz, D. and Lissak, M. 1989. *Trouble in Utopia: The Overburdened Polity of Israel*. New York: SUNY Press.

Inbar, E. 1983. Israeli Strategic Thinking after 1973. *Journal of Strategic Studies* 6.1, March, pp. 36–59.

——. 1989. The No Choice War Debate in Israel. *Journal of Strategic Studies* 12.1, March, pp. 22–37.

——. 1990. Jews, Jewishness and Israel's Foreign Policy. *Jewish Political Studies Review* 2.3–4, Fall, pp. 165–183.

——. 1991. Israel's Small War: The Military Response to the Intifada. *Armed Forces and Society* 18.1, Fall, pp. 29–50.

——. 1996. Contours of Israel's New Strategic Thinking. *Political Science Quarterly* 111.1, Spring, pp. 41–64.

——. 1998. Israeli National Security 1973–96. *Annals, AAPSS*, 555, January, pp. 62–81.

——, ed. 2007. *Israel's Strategic Agenda*. London: Routledge.

——. 2008. *Israel's National Security: Issues and Challenges since the Yom Kippur War*. London: Routledge.

——. 2009. *Israel's Strategic Agenda*. New York: Routledge.

——. 2011. Israeli-Turkish Tensions and Their International Ramifications. *Orbis* 55.1, pp. 132–146.

——. 2013a. *Israel Is Not Isolated*. Mideast Security and Policy Studies No. 99. Ramat Gan: BESA, March.

———. 2013b. Time Favors Israel. *Middle East Quarterly* 20.4, Fall, pp. 3–13.

Inbar, E. and Ningthoujam, A. S. 2012. *Indo-Israeli Defense Cooperation in the 21st Century*. Ramat Gan: BESA, January.

Inbar, E, and Rapaport, A. 2014. *The Gaza War: An Initial Assessment*. Memorandum No. 7. Ramat Gan: BESA, December.

Inbar, E. and Sandler, S. 1993–94. Israel's Deterrent Strategy Revisited. *Security Studies* 3.2, Winter, pp. 330–358.

Inbar, E. and Shamir, E. 2013. *"Mowing the Grass": Israel's Strategy for Coping with Ongoing and Unsolvable Crises* (Hebrew). Studies in Middle Eastern Security No. 105. Ramat Gan: BESA, December.

———. 2104. *Mowing the Grass in Gaza*. Perspectives Paper No. 255. Ramat Gan: BESA, July 20.

Indyk, M. 2009. *Innocent Abroad: An Intimate Account of American Peace Diplomacy in the Middle East*. New York: Simon and Schuster.

International Institute for Strategic Studies (IISS). 2012–16. *The Military Balance*. London.

Israel Democracy Institute. 2007. *The Rear as the Front: Economic Dimensions Stemming from the Change in the Nature of Conflict*. Caesarea Forum No. 15, June.

Jerusalem Center for Public Affairs. 2014. *Israel's Critical Requirements for Defensible Borders: The Foundation for a Secure Peace*. Jerusalem.

Johnson, D. E. 2010. *Military Capabilities for Hybrid War: Insights from the Israel Defense Forces in Lebanon and Gaza*. Santa Monica, CA: Rand.

Jones, C. and Catignani, S., eds. 2010. *Israel and Hezbollah: An Asymmetrical Conflict in Historical and Comparative Perspective*. London: Routledge.

Jones, C. and Murphy, E. C. 2002. *Israel: Challenges to Identity, Democracy and the State*. London: Routledge.

Kam, E. 2016. Russia and Iran, Will They Go Together? *Strategic Assessment* 19.2, July, pp. 31–42.

Kane, T. 2005. *The Demographics of Military Enlistment after 9/11*. Washington, DC: Heritage Foundation, November.

Kaplinsky, M. 2009. The IDF in the Years before the War. *Military and Strategic Affairs* (Hebrew) 1.2, October, pp. 21–22.

Karmi, G. 2011. The One-State Solution: An Alternative Vision for Israeli-Palestinian Peace. *Journal of Palestine Studies* 40.2, pp. 62–76.

Karpin, M. 2009. Deep in the Basement: Israel's Harmonious Nuclear Ambiguity. *World Policy Journal*, Fall, pp. 31–40.

Karsh, E., ed. 1996. *Between War and Peace: Dilemmas of Israeli Security*. London: Frank Cass.

———. 2012. The War against the Jews. *Israel Affairs* 18.3, pp. 319–343.

Keridis, D. 2004. *Europe and Israel: What Went Wrong?* Ramat Gan: BESA, February.

Kimchi, Y. 2007. *The Internal Security Concept of the Ministry for Internal Security: Is It Realistic in Israel's Circumstances?* Position Paper No. 1. Tel Aviv: Israel Defense Forces, National Defense College, July.

Klein, D. 2008. Protecting the Rear in the Gaza Area Settlements: An Examination of the National Investment (Hebrew). *Strategic Assessment* 10.1, February, pp. 6–10.

Klieman, A. S. 1990. *Israel and the World after Forty Years*. Washington, DC: Pergamon-Brassey.

———. 1988. *Statecraft in the Dark: Israel's Practice of Quiet Diplomacy*. Boulder, CO: Westview.

———. 2013. The Sorry State of Israeli Statecraft. *Israel Journal of Foreign Affairs* 7.2, pp. 9–18.

Klieman, A. and Levite, A., eds. 1993. *Deterrence in the Middle East: Where Theory and Practice Converge*. Tel Aviv: Jaffee Center for Strategic Studies.

Kober, A. 1995. *Military Decision in the Arab-Israeli Wars, 1948–1982* (Hebrew). Tel Aviv: Maarachot Press.

———. 2005. From Blitzkrieg to Attrition: Israel's Attrition Strategy and Staying Power. *Small Wars & Insurgencies* 16.2, pp. 216–240.

———. 2008. The Israel Defense Forces in the Second Lebanon War: Why the Poor Performance? *Journal of Strategic Studies* 31.1, February, pp. 30–40.

———. 2009. *Israel's Wars of Attrition: Attrition Challenges to Democratic States*. London: Routledge.

———. 2013. *Can the IDF Afford a Small Army?* Perspectives Paper No. 209. Ramat Gan: BESA, July 18.

———. 2015. From Heroic to Post-heroic Warfare: Israel's Way of War in Asymmetrical Conflicts. *Armed Forces & Society* 41.1, January, pp. 96–122.

Kovacs, A. and Miller, M. 2013. *Jewish Studies VII*. Budapest: Central European University.

Kramer, M. 2016. Israel and the Post-American Middle East: Why the Status Quo Is Sustainable. *Foreign Policy*, July–August, pp. 51–56.

Krulitzky, A. 2004. The Reserve Force: Directions and Trends. *Maarachot* (Hebrew) 394, May, pp. 40–43.

Kulik, A. 2009. Intelligence and the Challenge Posed by Indirect Fire. *Military and Strategic Affairs* (Hebrew) 1.3, December, pp. 19–32.

Kumaraswamy, P. R. 2000. *Beyond the Veil: Israel-Pakistan Relations*. Memorandum No. 55. Tel Aviv: Jaffee Center for Strategic Studies, March.

Kurz, A. and Brom, S. 2013. *Strategic Assessment for Israel, 2012–2013* (Hebrew). Tel Aviv: INSS.

———, eds. 2014a. *The Lessons of Operation Protective Age* (Hebrew). Tel Aviv: INSS, November.

———. 2014b. *Strategic Assessment for Israel, 2013–2014* (Hebrew). Tel Aviv: INSS.

———. 2015. *Strategic Assessment for Israel, 2014–2015* (Hebrew). Tel Aviv: INSS.

Laish, G. 2010. Towards a New Defense Concept: Victory without Decision. *Maarachot* (Hebrew) 430, April, pp. 4–11.

Laish, G. and Amir, R. 2012. Surface to Surface Missile Warfare: The Offensive Strategy and the Defense of Response. *Maarachot* (Hebrew) 442, April, pp. 4–15.

Lambeth, B. S. 2011. *Air Operations in Israel's War against Hezbollah: Learning from Lebanon and Getting It Right in Gaza*. Santa Monica, CA: Rand.

Landau, E. B. 2013. Israel's Nuclear Ambiguity, Arms Control Policy and Iran: Is the Time Ripe for Basic Changes? *INSS Insight*, No. 478, October 22.

Landau, E. B. and Bermant, A., eds. 2014. *The Nuclear Nonproliferation Regime at a Crossroads*. Memorandum No. 137. Tel Aviv: INSS, May.

Landau, E. B. and Kurz, A. 2014. *The Interim Deal on the Iranian Nuclear Program: Toward a Comprehensive Solution?* Tel Aviv: INSS, September.

———, eds. 2016. *Arms Control and Strategic Stability in the Middle East and Europe*. Memorandum No. 155. Tel Aviv: INSS, June.

Landau, E. B. and Stein, S. 2015a. NPT RevCon 2015: Considerations for Convening a WMDFZ Conference. *INSS Insight*, No. 691, April 27.

———. 2015b. NPT RevCon 2015: WMDFZ Conference Off the Table, for Now. *INSS Insight*, No. 705, June 3.

Lavie, E. 2010. How Israel Coped with the Intifada: A Critical Examination. *Strategic Assessment* 13.3, October, pp. 87–104.

Lebel, U. 2007. Civil Society versus Military Sovereignty: Cultural, Political, and Operational Aspects. *Armed Forces and Society* 34.1, pp. 67–89.

———. 2008. *Communicating Security: Civil-Military Relations in Israel*. London: Routledge.

———. 2011. Militarism versus Security? The Double-Bind of Israel's Culture of Bereavement and Hierarchy of Sensitivity to Loss. *Mediterranean Politics* 16.3, pp. 365–384.

Lennox, D. 2009. Jericho 1/2/3 (YA-1/YA-3) (Israel), Offensive Weapons. *Jane's Strategic Weapon Systems* 50, January, pp. 84–86.

Leon, N. 2015. *Moshe Kahlon and the Politics of the Mizrahi Middle Class in Israel*. Research Paper No. 14. Institute for Israel Studies, University of Maryland, January.

Levite, A. 1989. *Offense and Defense in Israeli Military Doctrine*. Boulder, CO: Westview.

———. 2010. Global Zero: An Israeli Vision of Realistic Idealism. *Washington Quarterly* 32.2, April, pp. 153–168.

Levran, A. 2001. *The Decline of Israeli Deterrence*. Policy Paper No. 113. Ariel: Ariel Center for Policy Research.

Levy, M. 2004. Has the Time Come to Abandon the Model of the People's Army? *Maarachot* (Hebrew) 397, October, pp. 26–33.

Levy, Y. 2008. Israel's Violated Republican Equation. *Citizenship Studies* 12.3, pp, 249–264.

———. 2009a. An Unbearable Price: War Casualties and Warring Democracies. *International Journal of Political Culture and Society* 22, pp. 69–82.

———. 2009b. Is There a Motivation Crisis in Military Recruitment in Israel? *Israel Affairs* 15.2, April, pp. 135–158.

———. 2010. The Tradeoff between Force and Casualties: Israel's Wars in Gaza, 1987–2009. *Conflict Management and Peace Science* 27.4, pp. 386–405.

———. 2011. The Decline of the Reservist Army. *Military and Strategic Affairs* 3.3, December, pp. 63–74.

———. 2012a. *Israel's Death Hierarchy: Casualty Aversion in a Militarized Democracy.* New York: New York University Press.

———. 2012b. *Who Controls the IDF? Between an "Over-subordinate Army" and "a Military That Has a State".* Working Paper No. 23, Open University.

Libel, T. and Gal, R. 2015. Between Military-Society and Religion-Military Relations: Different Aspects of the Growing Religiosity in the Israel Defense Forces. *Defense and Security Analysis* 31.2, pp. 213–227.

Libicki, M. C. 2009. *Cyber-deterrence and Cyberwar.* Santa Monica, CA: Rand.

Lindenstrauss, G. and Eran, O. 2014. The Kurdish Awakening and Ramifications for Israel. *Strategic Assessment* (Hebrew) 17.1, April, pp. 73–82.

Luft, G. 2004. *All Quiet on the Eastern Front? Israel's National Security Doctrine after the Fall of Saddam.* Analysis Paper No. 2. Washington, DC: Saban Center, Brookings Institution, March.

Luttwak, E. and Horowitz, D. 1975. *The Israeli Army.* London: A. Lane.

Lynk, M. E. 2005. Down by Law: The High Court of Israel, International Law, and the Separation Wall. *Journal of Palestine Studies* 35.1, pp. 6–24.

Magen, Z. and Naumkin, V., eds. 2013. *Russia and Israel in the Changing Middle East.* Memorandum No. 129. Tel Aviv: INSS, July.

Malka, A. 2008. Israel and Asymmetrical Deterrence. *Comparative Strategy* 27.1, February, pp. 1–19.

Maman, D., et al. 2001. *Military, State and Society in Israel: Theoretical and Comparative Perspectives.* New Brunswick, NJ: Transaction.

Maoz, Z. 2003. The Mixed Blessing of Israel's Nuclear Policy. *International Security* 28.2, Fall, pp. 44–77.

———. 2006. *Defending the Holy Land: A Critical Analysis of Israel's Security and Foreign Policy.* Ann Arbor: University of Michigan Press.

Marcus, J. 1999. Israel's Defense Policy at a Strategic Crossroads. *Washington Quarterly* 22.1–2, Winter, pp. 33–48.

Michael, K. 2009. Who Really Dictates What an Existential Threat Is: The Israeli Experience. *Journal of Strategic Studies* 32.5, pp. 687–713.

Milstein, M. 2010. A Decade since the Outbreak of the Al-Aqsa Intifada: An Overview. *Strategic Assessment* 13.3, October, pp. 7–22.

Mintz, A, and Shai, S. 2014a. *Adaptation as an Element in Israel's Defense Strategy.* Policy Paper No. 2. Herzlia: Herzlia Forum for Formulating Israel's Defense Strategy, Policy and Strategy Institute, Herzlia Interdisciplinary Center, May.

———. 2014b. *The Need to Reformulate Israel's Defense Strategy.* Policy Paper No. 1. Herzlia: Herzlia Forum for Formulating Israel's Defense Strategy, Policy and Strategy Institute, Herzlia Interdisciplinary Center, March.

Monin, N. 2003. *The EU and Israel: State of the Play.* Jerusalem: Government of Israel, Ministry of Finance, International Division.

Morag, N. 2005. Measuring Success in Coping with Terrorism: The Israeli Case. *Studies in Conflict and Terrorism* 38, pp. 307–320.

Morris, B. 1997. *Israel's Border Wars, 1949–1956: Arab Infiltration, Israeli Retaliation and the Countdown to the Suez War.* Oxford: Clarendon.

Mualem, Y. 2012. Israel's Foreign Policy: Military-Economic Aid in Assisting Jewish Communities in Distress; Can the Two Coexist? *Israel Affairs* 18.2, pp. 201–218.

Murinson, A. 2014. *The Ties between Israel and Azerbaijan*. Mideast Security and Policy Studies No. 110. Ramat Gan: BESA, October.

Murray, W., et al., eds. 1994. *The Making of This Strategy: Rulers, Status and Wars*. Cambridge: Cambridge University Press.

National Commission on the Future of the US Army. 2016. *Report to the President and Congress of the United States*, January 28.

Neuberger, B., ed. 1984. *Diplomacy and Confrontation: Selected Issues and Israeli Foreign Policy, 1948–1978*. Tel Aviv: Open University.

Neuer, Hillel. "The United Nations and Anti-Semitism 2004-2007 Report Card." *UN Watch*, November 1, 2007.

Ningthoujam, A. S. 2014. *India-Israel Defense Cooperation* (Hebrew). Perspectives Paper No. 236. Ramat Gan: BESA, January 27.

Nisan, M. 2013. In Defense of the Idea of a Jewish State. *Israel Affairs* 19.2, pp. 259–272.

Nye, J. S. 2002. *The Paradox of American Power: Why the World's Only Superpower Can't Go It Alone*. Oxford: Oxford University Press.

———. 2004a. *Power in the Global Information Age: From Realism to Globalization*. New York: Routledge.

———. 2004b. *Soft Power: The Means to Success in World Politics*. New York: Public Affairs.

Oded, A. 2010. Africa in Israeli Foreign Policy, Expectations and Disenchantment: Historical and Diplomatic Aspects. *Israel Studies* 15.3, Fall, pp. 121–142.

OECD. 2015. *Connecting with Emigrants: A Global Profile of Diasporas 2015*. Paris: OECD.

Offer, Z. and Kober, A. 1985. *Quality and Quantity in Military Buildup* (Hebrew). Tel Aviv: Maarachot Press.

Ophir, N. 2006. The Solution Is Not in the Sky: The Air Force's Struggle with Rocket Launchers (Hebrew). *Strategic Assessment* 9.3, October, 15–19.

Orian, A. 2016. UNIFIL II, Ten Years On: Strong Force, Weak Mandate. *INSS Insight*, No. 844, August 14.

Paikowsky, D. 2007. Israel's Space Program as a National Asset. *Space Policy* 23, pp. 90–96.

Parmenter, R. C. 2013. *The Evolution of Preemptive Strikes in Israeli Operational Planning and Future Implications for Cyber Domain*. School of Advanced Military Studies, US Army Command and General Staff College, Fort Leavenworth, May 23.

Paz, A. 2015. *Transforming Israel's Security Establishment*. Policy Focus No. 140. Washington, DC: Washington Institute for Near East Policy.

Pedahzur, A. 2009. *The Israeli Secret Services and the Struggle against Terrorism*. New York: Columbia University Press.

Peleg, I. 1987. *Begin's Foreign Policy, 1977–1983*. New York: Greenwood Press.

Peri, Y. 2006. *Generals in the Cabinet Room: How the Military Shapes Israeli Policy*. Washington, DC: United States Institute of Peace Press.

Perliger, A. 2011. The Changing Nature of the Israeli Reserve Forces: Present Crises and Future Challenges. *Armed Forces & Society* 37, April, pp. 216–238.

Pew Research Center. 2013. *A Portrait of Jewish Americans: Overview*. October 1.

Pollak, N. 2016. *The Transformation of Hezbollah by Its Involvement in Syria*. Research Notes No. 35. Washington, DC: Washington Institute for Near East Policy, August.

Posen, B. R. 1984. *The Sources of Military Doctrine: France, Britain and Germany Between the World Wars*. Ithaca, NY: Cornell University Press.

———. 2014. *Restraint: A New Foundation for US Grand Strategy*. Ithaca, NY: Cornell University Press.

Pressman, J. 2006. Israeli Unilateralism and Israeli-Palestinian Relations, 2001–2006. *International Studies Perspectives* 7.4, pp. 360–376.

Radai, I., et al. 2015. Arab Citizens of Israel: Updated Trends According to the Latest Polls. *Strategic Assessment* (Hebrew) 18.2, July, pp. 93–108.

Ram, U. 2008. *The Globalization of Israel: McWorld in Tel Aviv, Jihad in Jerusalem*. New York: Routledge.

Rapaport, A. 2010. *The IDF and the Lessons of the Second Lebanon War.* Mideast Security and Policy Studies No. 85. Ramat Gan: BESA, December.

———. 2013. *Where Is the Israeli Military Heading?* Perspectives Paper No. 210. Ramat Gan: BESA, August 7.

Raz, A. 2016. The Routinization of Nuclear Ambiguity. *Strategic Assessment* 8.14, January, pp. 29–41.

Reich, B. 1994–95. Reassessing the United States–Israeli Special Relationship. *Israel Affairs* 1.1–2, pp. 64–83.

———. 1995. *Securing the Covenant: United States–Israel relations after the Cold War.* Westport, CT: Greenwood Press.

Rice, C. 2011. *No Higher Honor.* New York: Crown.

Richards, J. 2012. *A Guide to National Security: Threats, Responses and Strategies.* Oxford: Oxford University Press.

Rodman, D. 2002–3. Israel's National Security Doctrine: An Appraisal of the Past and a Vision of the Future. *Israel Affairs* 9.3–4, pp. 115–140.

———. 2005. *Defense and Diplomacy in Israel's National Security Experience.* Brighton: Sussex Academic Press.

———. 2013. *Sword and Shield of Zion: The Israel Air Force and the Arab-Israeli Conflict, 1948–2012.* Brighton: Sussex Academic Press.

Rosenberg, H. 2012. *Missile Warfare: A Realistic Assessment.* Perspectives Paper on Current Affairs No. 161. Ramat Gan: BESA, January 25.

Ross, D. 2004. *The Missing Peace; The Inside Story of the Fight for Middle East Peace.* New York: Farrar, Straus and Giroux.

———. 2015. *Doomed to Succeed: The US-Israel Relationship from Truman to Obama.* New York: Farrar, Straus and Giroux.

Ross, D. and Makovsky, D. 2009. *Myths, Illusions and Peace: Finding a New Direction for America in the Middle East.* New York: Viking.

Rubin, B. and Keaney, T. A., eds. 2002. *Armed Forces in the Middle East: Politics and Strategy.* London: Frank Cass.

Rubin, U. 2007. *The Rocket Campaign against Israel during the 2006 Lebanon War.* Mideast Security and Policy Studies No. 71. Ramat Gan: BESA, June.

———. 2012a. *"Iron Dome" vs. Grad Rockets: A Dress Rehearsal for an All-Out War?* Perspectives Paper No. 173. Ramat Gan: BESA, July 3.

———. 2012b. *Palestinian Rockets versus Israeli Missile in the Second Gaza War.* Policy Watch 2011. Washington, DC: Washington Institute for Near East Policy, December 21.

———. 2015. *Israel's Air and Missile Defense during the 2014 Gaza War.* Mideast Security and Policy Studies No. 111. Ramat Gan: BESA, February 11.

Rubinstein, A. Z. 2001. Israelis Ponder Their Long-Term Security. *Orbis* 45.2, Spring, pp. 259–281.

Rynhold, J. 2015. *The Arab-Israeli Conflict in American Political Culture.* New York: Cambridge University Press.

Sanders, R. 2009. Israel and the Realities of Mutual Deterrence. *Israel Affairs* 15.1, January, pp. 81–97.

Sandler, S. 1987. Is There a Jewish Foreign Policy? *Jewish Journal of Sociology*, December, pp. 115–121.

Sandler, S. and Rynhold, J. 2007. From Centrism to Neo-centrism. *Israel Affairs* 13.2, April, pp. 229–250.

Sanger, D. E. 2012. *Confront and Conceal: Obama's Secret Wars and Surprising Use of American Power.* New York: Crown.

Sasson, T., et al. 2010. *Still Connected: American Jewish Attitudes about Israel.* Waltham, MA: Brandeis University Study.

Schabas, W. A. 2010. Gaza, Goldstone, and Lawfare. *Case Western Reserve Journal of International Law* 43.1–2, pp. 307–312.

Schiff, Z. 1998. *Security for Peace: Israel's Minimal Security Requirements in Negotiations with the Palestinians*. Washington, DC: Washington Institute for Near East Policy.

Seener, B. 2009. Targeting Israelis via International Law. *Middle East Quarterly* 16.4, pp. 43–54.

Segal, O. 2004. The Reserve Force's Ground Training: Present and Future. *Maarachot* (Hebrew) 394, May, pp. 50–57.

Sela, A. 2002. The United States' Influence on the IDF's Qualitative Age. *Maarachot* (Hebrew) 83, May, pp. 42–49.

Seener, B. 2009. Targeting Israelis via International Law. *Middle East Quarterly* 16.4, pp. 43–54.

Senor, S. and Singer, S. 2009. *Start Up Nation*. New York: Council on Foreign Relations.

Shabtai, S. 2010. Israel's Security Concept: Updating Basic Terms (Hebrew). *Strategic Assessment* 13.2, August, pp. 7–16.

Shafir, Y. 2013a. Chemical Assad? On the Chemical Warfare Attack in Syria. *INSS Insight*, No. 458, August 26.

———. 2013b. Lessons from the Operation of "Iron Dome." *Military and Strategy* 5.1, May, pp. 67–78.

Shaham, Y. and Elran, M., Evacuation of Israeli Communities during an Emergency: Dilemmas and Proposed Solutions (Hebrew), INSS, *Strategic Assessment* 19 #3, October 2016

Shai, A. 2009. *Sino-Israeli Relations: Current Reality and Future Prospects*. Memorandum No. 100. Tel Aviv: INSS, September.

Shaked, H. and Rabinovich, I., eds. 1980. *The Middle East and the United States: Perceptions and Policies*. New Brunswick, NJ: Transaction.

Shalom, Z. and Handle, Y. 2011. The Unique Characteristics of the Second Intifada among Israel's Wars. *Military and Strategic Affairs* (Hebrew) 3.1, May, pp. 18–19.

Shamir, E. and Hecht, E. 2013. *Neglect of IDF Ground Forces: A Risk to Israel's Security*. Perspectives Paper No. 225. Ramat Gan: BESA, December 4.

———. 2014–15. Gaza 2014: Israel's Attrition vs. Hamas' Exhaustion. *Parameters* 44.4, Winter, pp. 81–90.

Sharp, J. M. 2015. *US Foreign Aid to Israel*. Washington, DC: Congressional Research Service, June 10.

Shavit. A. 2013. *My Promised Land: The Tragedy and Triumph of Israel*. New York: Random House.

Shay, S. 2015. *The Egypt Russia Nuclear Deal*. Institute for Policy and Strategy, Lauder School of Government, Diplomacy and Strategy, IDC Herzliya. November.

Sheffer, G. 2012. Loyalty and Criticism in the Relations between World Jewry and Israel. *Israel Studies* 17.2, Summer, pp. 77–85.

Shelah, O. 2003. *The Israeli Army: A Radical Proposal* (Hebrew). Or Yehuda: Kinneret.

———. 2015. *Dare to Win: A Security Policy for Israel* (Hebrew). Tel Aviv: Miskal.

Shelah, O. and Limor, Y. 2007. *Captives of Lebanon* (Hebrew). Tel Aviv: Miskal.

Shweizer, Y. 2010. The al-Qaeda and Global Jihad Terror Threat against Israel. *Military and Strategic Affairs* (Hebrew) 2.1, pp. 17–22.

Shimshoni, J. 1988. *Israel and Conventional Deterrence: Border Warfare from 1953 to 1970*. Ithaca, NY: Cornell University Press.

Simchoni, A. and Bar-Joseph, A. 2012. The Security Concept: Preserving and Updating. *Maarachot* (Hebrew) 443, June, pp. 12–17.

Siboni, G. 2008. Indirect Fire, Guerrilla Warfare and the Validity of the Defense Concept. *Strategic Assessment* 10.4, February, pp. 11–16.

———. 2009. From the Second Intifada, through the Second Lebanon War, to Operation Cast Lead: A Puzzle in One Act. *Military and Strategic Affairs* (Hebrew) 1.1, April, pp. 25–32.

———. 2010a. Defeating Suicide Terrorism in Judea and Samaria, 2002–2005. *Military and Strategic Affairs* (Hebrew) 2.2, October, pp. 95–104.

———. 2010b. The Changing Threat: Introduction. *Military and Strategic Affairs* (Hebrew) 2.1, June, pp. 3–6.

———. 2014. Combat Challenges in Densely Populated Territories. *Military and Strategic Affairs* (Hebrew), Special Edition, April, pp. 5–8.

————. 2015. The IDF Strategy: A Focused Operating Approach. *INSS Insight*, No. 739 (Hebrew), August 27.

Siboni, G. and Kronenfeld, S. 2014a. Developments in Iranian Cyber Warfare, 2013–2014. *Military and Strategy* 6.2, pp. 83–104.

————. 2014b. Iranian Cyber Espionage: A Troubling New Escalation. *INSS Insight*, No. 561, June 16.

————. 2014c. The Iranian Cyber Offensive during Operation Protective Edge. *INSS Insight*, No. 598, August 26.

Siboni, G., et al. 2013. The Threat of Terrorist Organizations in Cyberspace. *Military and Strategy* 5.3, pp. 2–29.

Siperco, I. 2010. Shield of David: The Promise of Israeli National Missile Defense. *Middle East Policy* 17.2, Summer, pp. 127–140.

Smith, H. 2005. What Costs Will Democracies Bear? A Review of Popular Theories of Casualty Aversion. *Armed Forces and Society* 31.4, Summer, pp. 487–512.

Sneh, E. 1996. *Responsibility: Israel After Year 2000* (Hebrew). Tel Aviv: Miskal.

Sobelman, D. 2016–17. Learning to Deter: Deterrence Success and Failure in the Israel-Hezbollah Conflict, 2006–16. *International Security* 41.3, pp. 151–196.

Sofer, A. and Bystrov, E. 2013. *Israel: Demography, 2013–2034*. Haifa: University of Haifa, September.

Spyer, J. 2008. *UNRWA: Barrier to Peace*. Perspectives Paper No. 44. Ramat Gan: BESA, May 27.

State of Israel. 2015. *The IDF Strategy*. Tel Aviv: IDF, Office of the Chief of Staff, August.

State of Israel, Ministry of Defense. 2011. *The Civil Front: The Management of the Civil Front in Time of Crisis*. Tel Aviv.

State of Israel, Ministry of Social Equality, Minority Economic Development Authority, 2016. *Disparities among the Minority Population and Government Activity to Promote Its Economic Development*. PowerPoint presentation.

State of Israel, Prime Minister's Office. 2007. *Prime Minister's Comments on the State Comptroller's Draft Report: Preparation of the Homefront for Emergencies and Its Management during the War in the North*. Jerusalem, July.

State of Israel, State Comptroller. 2007. *Winograd Commission: Interim Report*. Jerusalem, April.

————. 2008. *Winograd Commission: Final Report*. Jerusalem, January.

————. 2011. *Annual Report 62 for 2011*. Jerusalem: Government Printing Office.

Stein, D. 2004. Palestine: The Return of the One-State Solution. *Asian Affairs* 35.3, pp. 321–337.

Steinberg, G. M. 1999. Re-examining Israel's Security Doctrine. *RUSI International Security Review* (Royal United Services Institute for Defence Analysis, UK), pp. 215–224.

————. 2006. Soft Powers Play Hardball. *Israel Affairs* 12.4, pp. 748–768.

————. 2012. From Durban to the Goldstone Report: The Centrality of Human Rights NGOs in the Political Dimension of the Arab-Israeli Conflict. *Israel Affairs* 18.3, pp. 372–388.

Steinberg, G. M. and Herzberg, A., eds. 2011. *The Goldstone Report Reconsidered: A Critical Analysis*. Jerusalem: Jerusalem Center for Public Affairs.

Steinitz, Y. 2005. Comments on the Security Concept. *Maarachot* (Hebrew) 398, January, pp. 4–7.

Sterio, M. 2010. The Gaza Strip: Israel, Its Foreign Policy, and the Goldstone Report. *Case Western Reserve Journal of International Law* 43.1–2, pp. 229–254.

Tal, I. 1977. Israel's Doctrine of National Security Background and Dynamics. *Jerusalem Quarterly* 4, Summer, pp. 44–57.

————. 1978. Israel's Defense Doctrine: Background and Dynamics. *Military Review* 58, March, 22–37.

————. 1996. *National Security: The Few Against the Many* (Hebrew). Tel Aviv: Dvir.

Tamari, D. 2011. Air Power to Where? *Maarachot* (Hebrew) 437, June, pp. 4–13.

————. 2012. *The Armed Nation: The Rise and Decline of the Israel Reserve System*. Ben Shemen: Modan.

————. 2014. *Israel's Defense Doctrine: Definitions and Characteristics*. Policy Paper No. 7. Policy and Strategy Institute, June.

Tamari, D. and Kalifi, M. 2009. The IDF's Operational Concept. *Maarachot* (Hebrew) 423, February, pp. 26–41.

Tamir, A. 1988. *Soldier in Search of Peace* (Hebrew). Tel Aviv: Eidanim.

Theohary, C. A. 2015. *Conventional Arms Transfers to Developing Nations, 2007–2014.* Washington, DC: Congressional Research Service, December 21.

Tira, R. 2010a. *The Nature of War: Conflicting Paradigms and Israeli Military Effectiveness.* Brighton: Sussex Academic Press.

———. 2010b. The Search for the "Holy Grail": Can a Military Achievement Be Translated into a Political One? *Military and Strategic Affairs* 2.2, pp. 39–58.

———. 2015. An Israeli Strategy for the Era Following Sykes-Picot. *Strategic Assessment* (Hebrew) 18.1, April, pp. 49–60.

———. 2016. The Second Israeli War Doctrine. *Strategic Assessment* (Hebrew) 19.2, July, pp. 129–140.

Tur, O. 2012. Turkey and Israel in the 2000's: From Cooperation to Conflict. *Israel Studies* 17.3, Fall, pp. 45–66.

United Nations, Department of Economic and Social Affairs Population Division. 2017. *World Population Prospects 2017: The Revision Key Findings and Advance Tables.* New York.

An Updated National Security Concept for Israel (Hebrew). 2017. Special Memorandum, February.

Valensi, C. and Dekel, U. 2016. Need for Joint US-Israeli Strategy Given Middle Eastern Challenges (Hebrew). *Strategic Assessment* 19.1, April, pp. 17–30.

Vardi, G. 2008. Pounding Their Feet: Israeli Military Culture as Reflected in the Early IDF Combat History. *Journal of Strategic Studies* 31.2, April, 295–324.

Vennesson, P. 2012. The Transnational Politics of Warfare Accountability. *International Relations* 26.4, pp. 409–429.

Vielhaber, D. and Bleek, P. C. 2012. Shadow Wars. *Nonproliferation Review* 19.3, pp. 481–491.

Wald, E. 1992. *The Gordian Knot: Myths and Dilemmas of Israeli National Security* (Hebrew). Tel Aviv: Yedioth Aharonoth.

Waxman, D. 2016. *Trouble in the Tribe: The American Jewish Conflict over Israel.* Princeton, NJ: Princeton University Press.

Weinstock, D. and Elran, M. 2016. *Securing the Electrical System in Israel: Proposing a Grand Strategy* (Hebrew). Memorandum No. 152. Tel Aviv: INSS, March.

Weizman, E. 2010. Legislative Attack. *Theory, Culture and Society* 27.6, pp. 11–32.

White, J. 2014. The Combat Performance of Hamas in the Gaza War of 2014. *CTC Sentinel* 7.9, September, pp. 9–12.

Wunderle, W. and Briere, A. 2008. *US Foreign Policy and Israel's Qualitative Military Edge: The Need for a Common Vision.* Policy Focus No. 80. Washington, DC: Washington Institute for Near East Policy, January.

Yaari, E. 2014. *Hamas Searches for a New Strategy.* Policy Notes No. 29. Washington, DC: Washington Institute for Near East Policy, October.

Yadlin, A. 2014. Operation Protective Edge: Six Insights, Six Recommendations. *INSS Insight*, No. 579, July 27.

Yadlin, A. and Golob, A. 2013. If Attacked, How Will Iran Respond? *Strategic Assessment* (Hebrew) 16.3, pp. 7–20.

Yanai, N. A 2015. Defensive Strategy for Israel. *Maarachot* (Hebrew) 463, October, pp. 4–12.

Yanai, S. 2005. *Israel's Core Security Requirements for a Two State Solution.* Analysis Paper No. 3. Washington, DC: Saban Center, Brookings Institution, January.

Yaniv, A. 1987. *Deterrence without the Bomb: The Politics of Israeli Strategy.* Lexington, MA: Lexington Books.

———, ed. 1993. *National Security and Democracy in Israel.* Boulder, CO: Lynne Reiner.

Yariv, A. 1980. Strategic Depth. *Jerusalem Quarterly* 17, Fall, pp. 3–12.

Yashiv, E. and Kasir, N. 2014. *The Labor Market of Israeli Arabs: Key Features and Policy Solutions.* Tel Aviv : Tel Aviv University, January.

Yehezkeli, P., ed. 2001. *Between "Decision" and "Victory"* (Hebrew). Studies in National Security No. 2. National Security College, July.

Zanotti, J. 2015. *Israel: Background and US Relations.* Washington, DC: Congressional Research Service, June 1.

Zicherman, H. 2014. *The IDF and the Ultra-Orthodox: An Overview of the Current Situation.* Israel Democracy Institute, March 12.

Zigdon, Y. 2004. Building the Reserve Force in the Era of the Post-modern Army. *Maarachot* (Hebrew) 394, May, pp. 28–35.

Zimmerman, B., et al. 2006. *The Million Person Gap: A Critical Look at Palestinian Demography.* Perspectives Paper No. 15. Ramat Gan: BESA, May 7.

Zisser, E. 2001. Is Anyone Afraid of Israel? *Middle East Quarterly* 8.3, Spring, pp. 3–10.

INDEX